Contents

Delivering the GUEST EXPERIENCE

SUCCESSFUL HOTEL, LODGING & RESORT MANAGEMENT

MICHAEL D. COLLINS

Florida Gulf Coast University

Kendall Hunt
publishing company

www.kendallhunt.com
Send all inquiries to:
4050 Westmark Drive
Dubuque, IA 52004-1840

Copyright © 2019 by Kendall Hunt Publishing Company

ISBN 978-1-5249-4332-5

Published in the United States of America

DEDICATION

This book is dedicated to the memory of my grandparents,
Mr. and Mrs. L.H. Clune

"Education creates wealth that may never be lost or stolen, yet always pays dividends."
–L.H. Clune

Marcia A. Knopik
Anita L. Rankin

For a lifetime of encouragement, love, and support.

Rita Garcia Collins
And our respective children,
Cameron D. Collins
Claudia N. Ortuño
Connor R. Collins

Thanks for tolerating the endless hours, days, weeks, and months that I spent on my computer these past 2+ years creating *Delivering the Guest Experience*.

Acknowledgements:
Thank you to *Kendall Hunt Publishing Company*, particularly **Paul B. Carty,** Director of Publishing Partnerships, and **Stefani DeMoss**, Senior Regional Project Coordinator, and to my *Florida Gulf Coast University* faculty colleagues that reviewed and suggested content for *Delivering the Guest Experience*, including professors **Lan Jiang**, **Collin Ramdeen**, **Marcia Taylor**, and **Mary Wisnom**.

Brief Contents

Section 3: Delivering the Core Service: The
Rooms Division...177

Section 5: Delivering a Return to Hotel Investors 351

Preface

PURPOSE AND DESIGN OF THIS TEXTBOOK

This textbook is designed to be used in a lodging or hotel management course on the undergraduate or graduate level. It is written from the perspective of a 40-year hospitality management veteran that enjoyed a successful 25-year hospitality industry career in hotel operations, followed by nearly 15 years as a hospitality educator. Simply put, it is the author's intent to explain the effective management principles and best practices that must be implemented to ensure the successful operation of a hotel enterprise, based upon 25 years of personal, hands-on industry experience, coupled with extensive academic preparation and study.

The book is divided into five sections, with each section serving a specific purpose as outlined below:

1. ***Section 1: Hotel Industry Overview*** provides an explanation of the industry's structure in *Chapter 1: Introduction to the Hotel Industry*, by identifying the key players in the hotel industry: hotel parent companies (brands), hotel investors or owners, and professional hotel management firms. *Chapter 2: Successful Hotel Management* examines key management tactics employed by successful hotel managers as well as the organizational structure of a full-service hotel.

2. ***Section 2: Building Guest and Client Relationships*** defines the various guest segments pursued by hotels in *Chapter 3: Defining Guest Segments*. *Chapter 4: Effective Sales and Marketing* then discusses the marketing strategies that are commonly used by hotel marketers to attract the various guest segments, which is followed by *Chapter 5: Optimizing Revenue* that examines how hotel managers appropriately select customers from the demand that is generated through these marketing efforts. *Section 2* concludes with a special supplement, *Sales Team Deployment: A Tale of Two Markets*, which discusses sales team deployment in which two markets—Fort Myers, Florida and San Francisco, California—are com-

pared; this comparison illustrates how specific market characteristics impact sales team deployment and guest segmentation.

3. ***Section 3: Delivering the Core Service: The Rooms Division*** begins with *Chapter 6: Guest Services Operations* in which the role, function, and successful management of the front office or guest services operations is outlined, beginning a more in-depth discussion on day-to-date hotel operations. This is followed by a look at the heart-of-the-house rooms operation in *Chapter 7: Housekeeping and Laundry Operations.*

4. ***Section 4: Delivering Peripheral Services: Food, Beverage, Conference Services and Recreation*** delves first into *Chapter 8: Food and Beverage Operations*, which provides an overview of outlet (restaurant, bar, and in-room dining) operations; banquets, catering, and conference services; as well as culinary arts and food production. *Chapter 9: Resort Operations* is a bonus chapter that discusses various resort structures and how a hotel may tie into that structure; it also addresses the management of resort and recreational amenities, showing how many of the principles used to manage traditional hotel operations apply in a resort setting.

5. ***Section 5: Delivering a Return to Hotel Investors*** examines the support functions provided by the property operations and maintenance (POM) and the administrative and general (A&G) support teams to ensure that the hotel's assets are protected, and financial goals achieved. This section includes *Chapter 10: Maintaining the Hotel Asset and Sustainability* and *Chapter 11: Administration and Control: Human Resources, Accounting, and Loss Prevention.* Finally, the textbook concludes with *Chapter 12: Hotel Investment*—a brief discussion on hotel operations from an ownership perspective.

A NOTE TO INSTRUCTORS

Many chapters within this textbook cover the assigned topic in great depth—greater than an instructor may be able to cover within a lodging or hotel operations course; however, each chapter is broken into sections and includes 'Boxes' that may be assigned as optional or required reading, allowing instructors to assign the topics of relevance within each chapter. One goal throughout the textbook is to help students connect content from other hospitality and business courses—accounting, event management, facilities management, finance, food and beverage management, human resource management, information systems, leadership, marketing, operations management, recreation management, and revenue management—to its application in a hotel setting. The depth and level of detail provided are also intended to provide essential knowledge, skills, and abilities in topic areas that may not be supported by required coursework within a specific hospitality curriculum.

About the Author

© University of San Francisco

Michael D. Collins, Ph.D., is an Associate Professor in the *School of Resort & Hospitality Management* within the *Lutgert College of Business* at *Florida Gulf Coast University*. Previously, Dr. Collins served as Associate Professor and Chair of the *Department of Hospitality Management* in the *School of Management* at the *University of San Francisco* and has served on the Hospitality and Resort Tourism Management faculty in the *E. Craig Wall Sr. College of Business Administration* at *Coastal Carolina University*. While at *Coastal Carolina University*, Collins also oversaw the *Wall Center for Excellence*, which provides professional development and support to students completing internships, seeking post-graduation employment, and career counseling.

This textbook, *Delivering the Guest Experience: Successful Hotel, Lodging, and Resort Management* is drawn from Dr. Collins' extensive industry experience as its foundation. Prior to embarking on a career in higher education, Dr. Collins spent 25 years in the hotel industry managing upscale, full-service hotels and resorts throughout the United States. Michael began his hotel industry career in entry-level guest service positions while attending college. Upon graduation from *Michigan*

State University in 1982, with a Bachelor of Arts in Humanities, Collins completed *Marriott's* Individual Development management training program and eventually rose to the position of General Manager with *Pickett Suite Hotels* (doing business today as *Doubletree by Hilton*). During his hotel industry career, Collins managed hotels for *Hyatt Hotels Corporation* in suburban Atlanta, San Francisco, and Chicago, as well as hotels and resorts for *Wyndham International* in Salt Lake City, Palm Springs, West Hollywood, and Myrtle Beach. He also served as Vice President and General Manager for the *Resort at Glade Springs* located in Daniels, West Virginia.

In addition to a Bachelor of Arts (BA) from *Michigan State University* (1982), Michael earned a Master of Science (MS) in Strategic Leadership from the *University of Charleston* (2001) in Beckley, West Virginia (formerly *Mountain State University*) and a Doctor of Philosophy (Ph.D.) in Hospitality Management from *The Ohio State University* in 2007.

Dr. Collins has successfully delivered workshops in the United States and in Latin America on a variety of topics including effective management, training, and development of associates; customer experience management; managing a business' online reputation; and optimizing revenue. In addition to *Delivering the Guest Experience: Successful Hotel, Lodging, and Resort Management*, Dr. Collins is also the author of *Make It Count! Getting the Most from a Hospitality Internship*, an internship handbook that guides students through a successful hospitality internship experience, also published by Kendall Hunt Publishing. *Michael may be contacted at* michaelcollins@michaeldwain.com.

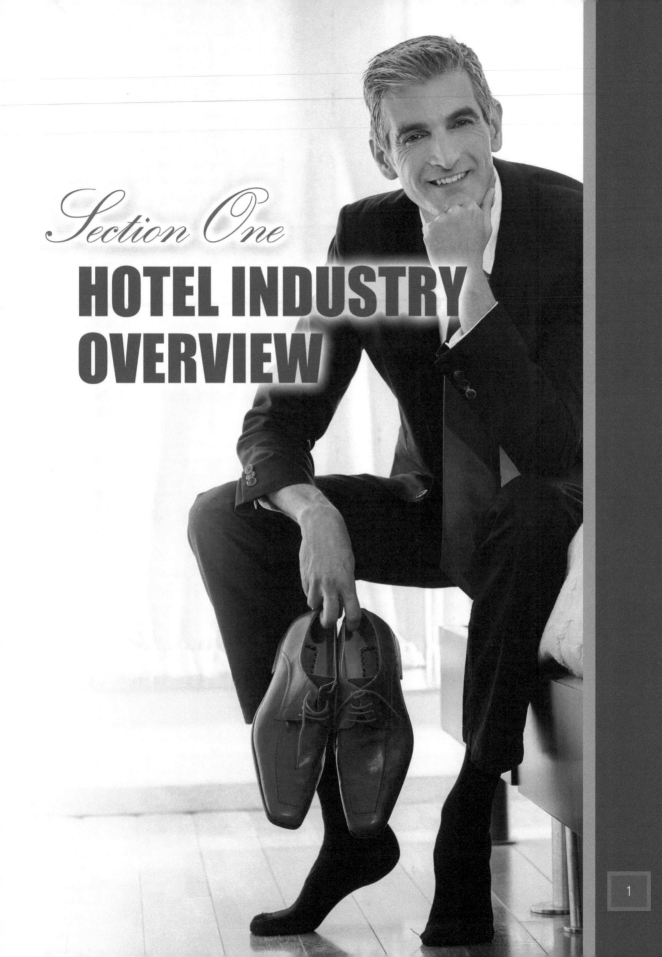

Section One

HOTEL INDUSTRY OVERVIEW

SECTION 1: HOTEL INDUSTRY OVERVIEW

Chapter 1: Introduction to the Hotel Industry

An overview of the hotel industry including its structure and the three distinct business foci within the industry—hotel branding, management, and investment (ownership)—is provided within this initial chapter.

Chapter 2: Successful Hotel Management

This chapter outlines the priorities of a successful hotel management team, introduces the "all-square" operating philosophy, and explains the organizational structure within the context of an upper-upscale hotel environment; the business-model of an upper-upscale hotel—outlining how each department contributes to a hotel's profitability—is also summarized.

Chapter 1
Introduction to the Hotel Industry

This chapter provides an overview of the hotel industry including its structure and the three distinct business foci within the industry—hotel branding, hotel management, and hotel real estate investment (ownership).

PURPOSE AND LEARNING OBJECTIVES:

This chapter will provide students with an overview of the hotel industry and introduce the range of enterprises and organizations directly engaged in the ownership, management, and branding of hotel assets. Specifically, students will be able to:

- Identify the three distinct business foci within the hotel industry.
- Explain the dynamics of the relationships that typically exist between the hotel brands, management companies, and hotel owners or investors.
- Discuss the benefits and drawbacks of hotel branding, as well as the prevalence of independent hotels within various contexts.
- Explain an asset light corporate strategy and why most hotel chains pursue such a strategy.
- Explain the important role that STR plays assisting hotels in benchmarking hotel performance.
- Identify the various segments of the lodging industry, providing examples of specific brands, as well as key business strategies employed, within each segment.
- Explain why delivering exceptional guest experiences is ultimately in every hotel organization's best interest—whether the organization is involved in the branding, management, or ownership of hotel assets.

THREE BUSINESS FOCI

There are three separate and distinct businesses functions associated with the hotel industry. These include branding, hotel ownership, and hotel management, as illustrated in *Diagram 1.1.*

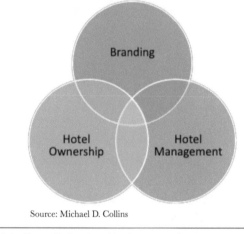

Source: Michael D. Collins

Diagram 1.1: Three distinct hotel business functions

Hotel Branding

When thinking about companies that operate businesses within the context of the hotel industry, the major hotel chains are typically the first organizations that come to mind—hotel brands including *Marriott*, *Hilton*, and *Holiday Inn*, just to name a few. In today's hotel industry, these brands are associated with a family of brands that are created and maintained by the chains' parent

Parent Company	Properties	Rooms
Marriott International	6,315	1,218,094
Hilton Worldwide	5,214	842,534
Intercontinental Hotel Group (IHG)	5,208	755,411
Wyndham Worldwide	8,341	722,163
Accor Company	4,009	588,866
Choice Hotels International	6,601	523,984
Best Western Hotels & Resorts	3,617	292,525
Hyatt	723	184,689
Radisson Hotel Group	1,158	180,638
Jinjiang Holding	1,294	161,111

Table 1.1: Global Hotel Parent Companies (Largest 10 firms by number of rooms, as of year-end 2017)

organizations. Hotel parent companies are business organizations that provide a wide-variety of support services to hotels including multiple hotel brands; design, development, and construction support; sales, marketing, and reservations services, including guest loyalty programs; clearly defined operating standards; purchasing support for acquiring furniture, fixtures, equipment, and operating supplies; information technology; and a proven, successful business model. Parent companies include *Marriott International* (www.marriott.com), *Hilton Worldwide* (www.hilton.com), *Intercontinental Hotels Group* (www.ihg.com), *Accor Company* (www.accor.com) and *Hyatt Hotels Corporation* (www.hyatt.com); a list of the 10 largest hotel parent companies in the world may be found in *Table 1.1*. Although these companies are involved in all aspects of the hotel industry to varying degrees, including hotel branding, management, and ownership, as depicted in *Diagram 1.1*, their focus is largely on branding. The primary goal of a hotel parent company is to establish and maintain a family of brands that is attractive to a variety of customer segments, as well as to hotel investors, and to then ensure that each brand is represented in

hotel parent company: a firm that provides a wide variety of support services to hotels including hotel brands

appropriate markets. The degree to which a hotel brand has widespread representation in appropriate markets is referred to as the hotel chain's level of distribution.

A hotel chain is defined as multiple lodging properties that operate under a common brand name, prominently displayed and promoted by all properties sharing the brand, in compliance with clearly defined brand operating standards. A hotel chain, brand, or flag, as to which it may also be referred, targets clearly defined segments of hotel guests by consistently offering thoughtfully designed accommodations and a specific range of peripheral services, in an effort to meet or exceed customer expectations, while providing good value for the traveler. A market or guest segment is a specific group of travelers that may be defined based upon demographic or psychographic variables (e.g. income level or lifestyle preferences) or by purpose of travel (e.g. business or leisure travel). Value is the degree to which the customer perceives that the cost of acquiring the hotel accommodations, and related peripheral services, is equitable relative to the quality of the accommodations, physical products, and support facilities, as well as the service level and overall guest experience, provided. For a hotel chain to successfully gain widespread distribution and market share, it must not only offer good value to hotel customers, it must also be designed to provide a good return on investment (ROI) for hotel developers and owners. The largest 20 hotel chains in the world are listed in *Table 1.2*.

Chain (Parent Company)	Properties	Rooms
Holiday Inn Express Hotel (IHG)	2,594	261,842
Hampton Inn (Hilton)	2,332	236,702
Holiday Inn (IHG)	1,212	223,566
Hilton (Hilton)	572	209,163
Marriott (Marriott)	555	196,113
Super 8 (Wyndham)	2,845	178,382
Courtyard (Marriott)	1,141	169,040
Best Western (Best Western)	2,139	155,195
Sheraton Hotel (Marriott)	440	154,931
Ibis Hotel (Accor)	1,100	141,639
Quality Inn (Choice)	1,656	130,318
Days Inn (Wyndham)	1,687	129,061
JinJiang Inn (JinJiang)	1,026	123,798
DoubleTree (Hilton)	512	122,757
Ramada (Wyndham)	841	117,546
Crowne Plaza (IHG)	414	114,667
Motel 6 (G6 Hospitality)	1,299	113,574
Hilton Garden Inn (Hilton)	770	111,347
Best Western Plus (Best Western)	1,204	106,123
Comfort Inn (Choice)	1,360	103,032

Table 1.2: Worldwide Hotel Chains (Largest 20 firms by number of rooms, as of year-end 2017)

Hotel Ownership

The hotel parent organizations work in partnership with well-capitalized commercial real estate investors and developers, including real estate investment trusts (REITs), to grow their family of brands; the investors that hold title to the real property associated with a hotel are in the business of hotel ownership (as illustrated in *Diagram 1.1*). To attract hotel owners to a specific brand, the hotel must be able to be constructed or converted to the targeted brand for an appropriate cost and then profitably operated to brand standards, generating operating profits that can support the construction or conversion costs, as well as any debt service associated with the investment while providing a financial return on the equity investment made in the hotel property by the hotel owners. The more consistently a hotel brand is able to meet or exceed the investment objectives of hotel owners, the more rapidly the hotel chain will be able to gain distribution. The core competencies required to create hotel brands that effectively target an appropriate mix of customer segments, while simultaneously being designed to be developed and operated efficiently and profitably, is different than the skill set necessary to raise the large amounts of capital, and managing the cost of that capital, to develop and acquire hotel assets. Hotel owners must also develop the ability to evaluate hotel markets to appropriately time their entrance into a market as well as the disposal or sale of hotel assets to profitably exit a market. Consequently, the hotel branding and ownership functions are typically performed by separate and distinct hospitality firms, as opposed to a single hospitality enterprise. *Table 1.3* provides a list of the 20 largest hotel ownership or investment groups in the world based upon number of total guestrooms owned.

real estate investment trusts (REITs): a legal entity formed to invest in income producing real estate, typically traded on a public stock exchange

hotel ownership: the investors that hold title to the real property associated with a hotel

core competencies: essential abilities

Hotel Ownership Group	Total Properties	Total Rooms
Host Hotels & Resorts	112	59,679
G6 Hospitality, LLC	473	54,584
Hospitality Properties Trust	325	49,900
Whitbread PLC	571	48,170
MGM Resorts	20	46,783
Caesars Entertainment	28	35,945
RLJ Lodging Trust	161	32,128
Colony NorthStar, Inc.	256	30,491
Ashford Hospitality Trust	134	29,004
Apa Hotel Mgtco	141	28,289
Grupo de Turismo Gaviota SA	58	24,029
Apple REIT Hospitality, Inc.	184	23,430

Table 1.3: Global Hotel Ownership Firms (12 largest firms by rooms, excluding chain owners, as of year-end 2017)

Hotel Management

A third business component of the hotel industry involves the day-to-day operation of hotels—a well-managed hotel operation is critical to the success of an individual hotel property, regardless of the brand. Managing the guest experience and hotel's service reputation; staffing and management of the human resource functions; pricing and selling (renting) of hotel accommodations and services; processing customer transactions; maintaining the hotel facilities and equipment; and maintaining and protecting operating supply inventories are just some of the myriad tasks that must be appropriately managed to ensure the success of a hotel operation. Consequently, the day-to-day operation of a hotel is typically managed by a professional hotel management firm responsible for operating the hotel to the established brand standards while maximizing profitability, to achieve the financial objectives targeted by the hotel's ownership. Examples of hotel management firms include *Interstate Hotels & Resorts* (www.interstatehotels.com) and *Evolution Hospitality* (www.evolutionhospitality.com). *Table 1.4* provides a list of the largest 25 global hotel management companies by the number of rooms under management.

hotel management firm: responsible for operating the hotel to the established brand standards, while maximizing profitability, to achieve the financial objectives targeted by the hotel's ownership

Management Company	# of Hotels	# of Rooms
MGM Resorts	19	45,666
Caesars Entertainment	30	38,255
Aimbridge Hospitality	200	34,623
Interstate Hotels	126	32,881
Crossroads Hospitality, Inc.	230	29,189
Island Hospitality Management	161	20,792
Highgate Hotels	64	20,729
HEI Hotels and Resorts	66	20,380
Pyramid Advisors, LLC	75	19,853
White Lodging	87	18,453
Pillar Hotels & Resorts	182	17,275
Remington Hotels	87	17,005
Crescent Hotels & Resorts	75	16,883
Crestline Hotels & Resorts, Inc.	110	15,854
Hersha Hospitality Management	109	15,239
Sage Hospitality	76	14,823

Table 1.4: US-based Hotel Management Companies (Largest 25 firms by number of rooms, excluding chain managed, as of year-end 2017)

From STR SHARE Center. Copyright © 2019 STR, Inc. All rights reserved. Used by permission.

Management Company	# of Hotels	# of Rooms
Two Roads Hospitality	65	14,592
TMI Hospitality	186	14,116
Columbia Sussex	39	13,736
Schulte Hospitality Group	93	12,810
Atrium Hospitality	47	12,035
The Procaccianti Group	43	11,498
Evolution Hospitality	50	11,188
Dimension Development Company	61	10,970
Davidson Hotels & Resorts	37	10,856

Table 1.4: continued...

HOTEL INDUSTRY RELATIONSHIPS

Hotel management firms gain operational control of hotel assets by virtue of a management contract or agreement with the owners of a hotel; the management contract outlines the details of the relationship between the hotel owners and the hotel management firm, including but not limited to, the term of the agreement, fee structure, operating performance requirements, budgeting procedures, expenditure limits, decision authority, indemnification, corporate expense allocation, and termination procedures. A win-win relationship is established between a hotel owner and

management contract: outlines the details of the relationship between the hotel owners and the hotel management firm, including but not limited to, the term of the agreement, fee structure, operating performance requirements, budgeting procedures, expenditure limits, decision authority, indemnification, corporate expense allocation, and termination procedures

© Syda Productions/Shutterstock.com

hotel management firm because each party brings a unique set of skills and resources to the partnership—the hotel owner brings the financial resources and commercial real estate knowledge necessary to capitalize and structure the hotel investment, while being relieved of day-to-day operating responsibilities, whereas the hotel operator brings the management expertise necessary to profitably staff and operate the hotel, maintain the hotel facilities, and deliver quality experiences to hotel guests without bearing the burden of raising the substantial sums of capital necessary to fund the development, construction, or acquisition of the hotel real estate asset.

In addition to establishing a relationship with a hotel management company, a hotel investor will typically establish a relationship with a hotel brand through a franchise or licensing agreement. A hotel franchise agreement is a contract that outlines the terms of the relationship between the hotel's owners and the parent organization or franchisor of the selected brand, granting the owner a license to operate the hotel using a specific trademark. In addition to the term of the agreement, the franchise agreement clearly outlines the responsibilities of each party as well as the fees that will be paid for the license, which are typically assessed as a percentage of revenue. Responsibilities of the franchisor or parent company, for which fees are paid by the hotel owner, include design, construction, or renovation specification and assistance; reservations services; maintaining a competitive guest loyalty program; advertising, marketing, and sales support; operating support; and brand standards. The franchisee must agree to maintain the brand's standards in terms of service quality and facilities maintenance. As a result, a hotel owner is typically required to set aside a specific portion of the hotel's revenues to be used for capital upgrades to the hotel, thereby ensuring that funds will be available to maintain the facility to brand standards.

Because brand standards must ultimately be implemented and maintained by the management team running the day-to-day operation of the hotel, it is common for the franchisor to reserve the right to approve the management firm selected by the hotel's ownership group or, in many cases, a parent organization will provide a list of approved or certified management companies that may operate their brands. At a minimum, a hotel owner will seek advice from the franchisor in selecting a management firm if one has not been selected in advance. Conversely, if a hotel investor has an established relationship with a hotel management firm, the investor may solicit recommendations from the management company on what brands the owner should consider flagging the hotel to achieve the investors' targeted financial objectives.

Branded Management Companies

As an alternative to engaging separate organizations—one to operate and a second to brand the hotel—some hotel investors may elect to establish a relationship with a branded management company or a hotel parent organization with a management services division. Many of the largest parent organizations, including *Marriott International*, *Hyatt Hotels Corporation*, and *Hilton Hotels & Resorts*, operate a management services division that may enter into a management contract or agreement with hotel owners to manage the day-to-day operation of a hotel while also including a licensing agreement to provide the hotel's brand name, marketing support, and operating standards.

branded management company:
manage the day-to-day operation of a hotel while also including a licensing agreement to provide the hotel's brand name, marketing support, and operating standards

Diagram 1.1: Three distinct hotel business functions suggest that some hotel organizations are engaged in all three aspects of the hotel industry—branding, management, and ownership; hotel parent organizations pursue a variety of strategies in this regard. For example, in comparing the strategies of a handful of the world's most recognized hotel parent organizations, some companies, such as *Choice Hotels International* and *Best Western Hotels & Resorts*, which is a membership association owned by its franchisees, do not manage a single property, choosing to franchise all (100%) of their hotels system-wide. Whereas, as of year-end 2017, *Marriott International* chose to manage 12.6% of their collective portfolio of hotels (798 of 6,315 hotels) while franchising 87.4% (5,517 of 6,315 hotels); *Hyatt Hotels Corporation* managed 8.9% (64 of 723 hotels) while franchising the remaining 91.1% (659 of 723 hotels); *Hilton Worldwide* managed 6.7% of its hotels (350 of 5,214 hotels) while franchising 93.3% (4,864 of 5,214 hotels); and luxury hotel operator *Four Seasons Hotels & Resorts* managed all (100%) of the company's 33 hotels (STR, 2018).

membership association:
a hotel brand or chain owned by its franchisees

Parent companies are more likely to directly manage hotels that provide a higher level of service—luxury or upper-upscale hotels—and larger hotels in strategically important gateway cities—such as New York City or San Francisco—as well as other high-profile markets—including Scottsdale, Arizona or Orlando, Florida. A parent company's select-service brands and full-service hotels in secondary, suburban, or tertiary markets are more likely to be franchised.

Asset Light Strategy

Most hotel management and parent companies pursue an asset light strategy, in which they avoid assuming the burden and risk of raising the large amounts of capital necessary to own the actual hotel real estate assets that they manage or brand, although they may in rare circumstances take a small, minority ownership position in a strategically important asset. Some hotel investors operate using a paired-structure, by forming a separate company to exclusively manage the day-to-day operations of hotels in which they have invested; one such example is *Windsor Capital Group* (www.wcghotels.com) and *Windsor Management Services* (www.windsor-managementservices.com) that collectively form *Windsor Hospitality Group*, which, at

asset light strategy:
a business approach through which a firm generates revenue without assuming debt or title to the real assets used to generate the revenue

paired-structure:
two closely aligned firms, one established to invest in real assets and a second to manage those assets

the time of this writing, operate 10 hotels, eight of which are licensed as *Embassy Suites* (Hilton) franchises.

By employing an asset light strategy, the hotel brands may expand their distribution, or number of locations, more quickly with far less risk. In a similar way, an asset light strategy allows management companies to gain management control of an increased number of hotel assets for minimal capital outlay and to avoid the risk of assuming large amounts of debt. Additional insight into these relationships is explored in *Chapter 12: Hotel Investment*.

Branded Versus Independent Hotels

core service:
the primary service product offered to meet customers' needs common to all service providers within a specified industry

peripheral services:
ancillary services that are provided to customers to add value to the customer experience

Obviously, not all hotels are branded, particularly hotels outside the United States. Seventy-two percent (72%) of hotel rooms are brand-affiliated in the United States, while forty-six percent (46%) of hotel accommodations outside of the United States (US) are estimated to be brand-affiliated. Independent hotels tend to be smaller, select-service properties, although this is not always the case—over seventy-five percent (75.1%) of independent hotels in the United States are economy (63.6%) or midscale (11.5%) properties, with 85.7% having 100 or fewer guestrooms (STR, 2018). With independent hotels, only a two-party relationship is necessary—between a hotel owner and a management company; however, in the case of many independent hotels, the owner may directly operate the property.

© Jacques PALUT/Shutterstock.com

LODGING SEGMENTS

The core service offered by all hotels is overnight accommodations; however, the range of peripheral services provided, such as food and beverage (F&B) services, meetings and conference services, and transportation, vary widely. Hotels may be categorized into segments based upon a combination of qualitative and quantitative factors, which include the range of peripheral services that are offered, service quality, service environment, size or location of the hotel, and pricing, just to name a few.

Full-Service Versus Select-Service

A hotel may offer a full range of services including overnight accommodations; food and beverage (F&B) services, including breakfast, lunch, and dinner service, as well as the availability of alcoholic beverages; meetings and event space, including conference support services; and more, which may include transportation, business services, concierge, and luggage assistance—such hotels are generally referred to as full-service hotels. Hotels that offer overnight accommodations and no, or only a limited degree of peripheral services, are broadly referred to as select-service hotels.

full-service hotels: offer, at a minimum, overnight accommodations; F&B services for breakfast, lunch, and dinner; and conference space and meeting services

Traditionally, full-service hotels have been further categorized primarily as luxury, upper-upscale, or upscale hotels, although there are some upper-midscale and midscale properties that offer a full range of services. Select-service hotels have been typically categorized as upper-midscale, midscale, or economy hotels, based upon the service quality delivered to customers, coupled with the quality of the service environment and the hotel's pricing strategies; however, some select-service hotels provide an upscale service environment, attentive service, with pricing comparable to their upscale, full-service peers. Consequently, it is difficult to neatly categorize hotels into distinct, clearly defined segments based upon multiple criteria simultaneously, including service quality, service environment, range of services, and price.

select-service hotels: offer overnight accommodations and no, or only a limited degree of peripheral services

Six Categories of Hotels

Hotels are categorized into one of the following six class categories: economy, midscale, upper-midscale, upscale, upper-upscale, and luxury. These categories are established by STR, which is profiled in *Box 1.1: STR: Data-Source for the Hotel Industry.* STR assigns hotels to the appropriate category based upon a hotel brand's system worldwide year-end average daily rate (ADR) or the average price paid for a guestroom per night.

average daily rate (ADR): the average price paid by guests for an individual guestroom per night

Although descriptions are provided on the following pages of the various hotel segments that include details regarding service quality, the range of peripheral services provided, service environment, and other qualitative factors commonly associated with hotels within each specific segment, the defining characteristic that determines the category to which a hotel is assigned is the ADR paid by guests. The qualitative descriptions of each segment may be provided, because hotels charging similar prices, within similar geographic markets, must present similar value propositions to their customers to be competitive. Although there may be some variation between hotels within each category, relative to the qualitative variables, the enriched descriptions of hotels within each segment provided here describe characteristics common to many, if not the great majority of hotels, within each respective category.

When reporting the annual occupancy and ADR of hotels within the descriptions of each hotel category, "chain-scale" statistics are used for hotels in the United States, while the statistics for international hotels are based upon "class"; the difference between chain-scale and class is the inclusion of independent hotels. STR's chain-scale calculations of ADR and annual occupancy break the independent hotels out into a separate, seventh category.

Approximately twenty-eight percent (28%) of hotels in the United States are independent, many of which are small economy or midscale hotels, as previously reported; many of these independent properties do not report operating statistics to STR. Consequently, using statistics that include independent hotels to quantify the market performance of hotel segments within the United States may portray an inaccurate picture. Chain-affiliated hotels, managed by professional hotel management firms, dominate the major hotel markets, and serve most business, leisure, and convention travelers in the United States.

Globally, independent hotels must be included in the performance statistics because, in a great many markets, independent properties represent most hotels and hotel rooms—excluding them would inaccurately portray the market performance of the various segments within the global hotel industry. Because the two taxonomies have been developed by STR using similar methodologies, thereby producing comparable statistics, the comparison of chain-scale annual occupancy and ADR for hotels in the United States with class annual occupancy and ADR statistics for international hotels is meaningful.

Luxury hotels offer the highest level of personalized service and a full range of services designed to satisfy the most demanding guests; staff are highly trained professionals prepared to respond to any guest request or need and feature a concierge staff, bell service, and twice-daily guestroom servicing. Many luxury hotels, particularly in resort settings, also offer spa services and all luxury hotels will, at a minimum, provide quality exercise facilities, with many providing access to a full-service fitness club. The service environment is created using only high-quality finishes and furnishings—including marble, granite, and fine, hardwood surfaces; custom-designed, classic furnishings; original artwork; oversized, high-resolution televisions; and high thread-count linens. Luxury hotels typically cater to the top 5% of

taxonomies:
sets of categories used to classify items that are mutually exclusive and collectively exhaustive

luxury hotels:
offer the highest level of personalized service and a full-range of services designed to satisfy the most demanding guests

spa services:
personalized services intended to contribute to a guest's well-being, including massage, facial, body, and beauty treatments

© Shahid Khan/Shutterstock.com

STR, founded as Smith Travel Research, is the largest supplier of market data to the hotel industry. STR tracks the occupancy, ADR, and revenue of tens of thousands of hotels, comprised of millions of hotel rooms, worldwide. Many hotels and parent companies also elect to report information regarding the profitability of their hotels and a variety of additional statistics. This global hotel industry market and performance data is then used to benchmark hotel market performance; the myriad reports that can be purchased from STR may be used by hotel investors, hotel parent companies, and hotel managers to make informed, prudent decisions regarding their hotel investments, marketing strategies, and operations. STR sorts and organizes this massive database to provide customized reports and market intelligence on-demand. In addition to hotel parent companies, management firms, and investors, many Destination Marketing Organizations (DMOs) or Convention and Visitors Bureaus (CVBs), government agencies, travel industry partners, and academic researchers rely upon STR for accurate, specific, and timely data.

STR was founded in 1985 by Randy and Carolyn Smith and is headquartered in Hendersonville, Tennessee; STR's international headquarters is based in London, England, with regional headquarter offices in Singapore (Asia Pacific), Dubai, United Arab Emirates (Middle East & Africa) and Bogota, Columbia (Latin America). Its presence has expanded to 19 countries over STR's 33-year history. In addition to premium global data that is provided for benchmarking, analytics, and marketplace insights, STR also supports the digital media platform Hotel News Now (HNN) in Ohio and a Consulting and Analytics team in Colorado. STR's SHARE Center provides data to support hospitality research and education. Detailed information about how STR data are used to benchmark a hotel's financial performance is provided in *Chapter 5: Optimizing Revenue*. For more information, explore www.str.com.

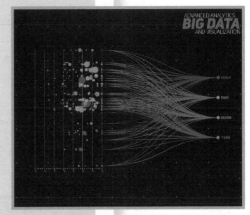

© GarryKillian/Shutterstock.com

STR:
the largest supplier of market data to the hotel industry

occupany:
the proportion of available hotel rooms sold (rented) during a specified time period

revenue:
payments received in exchange for products, services, or experiences

benchmark:
a reference point against which a meaningful comparison can be made to assess performance

the traveling public, whether traveling for business or pleasure. Meetings and events are hosted in elegant spaces with attendees tended to by a highly attentive staff. F&B services are available at any time, either in a sophisticated restaurant environment, lounge, meeting room, or in the privacy of a guest's hotel room; F&B products are prepared to order and dramatically presented, using only the finest, freshest ingredients. Fine wines and premium beverages are available.

The ADR, or the average price paid for the overnight use of a hotel room, for luxury hotels in 2017 worldwide (excluding the United States) was $270.69 (US dollars), while in the United States luxury chain-scale hotels averaged $323.71 per night, although it is not uncommon for the rental price for a luxury hotel room in a gateway city to run well in excess of $500 on any given night. Luxury hotels are located primarily in major, urban markets and high-end, destination resort markets—they are not typically found in suburban or tertiary markets. Six-and-seven-tenths percent of the global hotel room inventory and 3.3% of chain-affiliated hotel rooms located in the United States are classified as luxury hotels. Globally, luxury hotels ran an annual occupancy percentage of 68.1%, whereas in the United States the utilization rate was 75.2% in 2017. The average size or overnight service capacity of a luxury hotel in terms of room count is 151 guestrooms worldwide; however, branded luxury hotels located in the United States tend to be larger, with 320 guestrooms per hotel (STR, 2018). Examples of luxury hotel brands include *Four Seasons* (Four Seasons), *Intercontinental* (IHG), *Ritz Carlton* (Marriott), *St. Regis* (Marriott), and *Waldorf Astoria* (Hilton).

Upper-upscale hotels are also full-service hotels, offering a full range of services to include F&B services, featuring at least one three-meal restaurant; meeting and event space; and a full range of guest, meeting, and business services; as well as access to quality exercise facilities or a full-service fitness club. Like luxury hotels, upper-upscale hotels also strive to provide a high level of personalized service, as well as a quality service environment, but at a price point that is more appealing to a broader audience. The ADR of an upper-upscale hotel globally was $165.26, whereas in the United States this segment averaged $182.05, in 2017. Upper-upscale hotels represent 14.2% of the global guestroom inventory and 16.3% of the branded hotel room inventory in the United States.

© jiawangkun/Shutterstock.com

Upper-upscale hotels are typically larger than luxury hotels with an average of 159 guestrooms per property worldwide (excluding the United States) and 343 rooms typically found in a branded, upper-upscale hotel located within the United States. Global occupancy for the upper-upscale segment was 70.9% in 2017 and 74.2% for branded, upper-upscale hotels in the United States (STR, 2018). Upper-upscale brands include the core-brands for many of the parent companies, including *Hilton Hotels & Resorts*, *Hyatt Hotels & Resorts*, *Marriott Hotels & Resorts*, and *Wyndham Hotels & Resorts*, as well as a variety of additional brands, including *Embassy Suites* (Hilton), *Hyatt Regency* (Hyatt), *Kimpton* (IHG), *Renaissance Hotels & Resorts* (Marriott), *Sheraton Hotels & Resorts* (Marriott),

© lou armor/Shutterstock.com

and *Westin Hotels & Resorts* (Marriott). Upper-upscale hotels are located in a variety of locations—including urban centers, international airport locations, suburban office parks, and resort destinations, although they are not typically found in small towns or rural locations.

Upscale hotels are also typically, but not always, full-service hotels; however, the style of service is typically more casual and the service environment less sophisticated. The marble, granite and hardwood finishes found in luxury and upper-upscale hotels may be replaced with ceramic, laminate, and vinyl surfaces, although not in all cases. Some form of F&B services will be offered, although they may offer less variety and not be available, or at a minimum severely limited, for some meal periods as well as between meal periods. More prepared foods, versus "from scratch" per order food preparation, may be used. Less labor-intensive self-service food options—including buffet, counter-service, or "grab-and-go" options—are more common, often replacing the *a la carte* table service found in upper-upscale and luxury properties; in-room dining (room service) may not be available. Meeting spaces are more utilitarian and less elegant. At a minimum, access to basic exercise equipment is typically provided.

upscale hotels: typically, but not always, full-service hotels; however, the style of service is more casual and the service environment less sophisticated than in upper-upscale properties

Just over twenty-one percent (21.0%) of the global hotel guestroom inventory is classified as upscale, with 20.6% of chain-affiliated hotels in the United States falling into this category; upscale hotels average 112 rooms per hotel worldwide and 152 guestrooms in the United States. The ADR in this segment was $124.58 globally and $140.19 in the United States, with occupancy percentages of 71.0% and 73.8%, respectively, in 2017 (STR, 2018). Examples of brands in the upscale segment include *Aloft* (Marriott), *Courtyard* (Marriott), *Crowne Plaza* (IHG), *Doubletree* (Hilton), *Four Points by Sheraton* (Marriott), *Hilton Garden Inn* (Hilton), *Hyatt Place* (Hyatt), *Radisson Hotels & Resorts* (Carlson Rezidor), and *Residence Inn* (Marriott). Like upper-upscale hotels, upscale hotels are typically located in urban centers, suburban office parks, resort destinations, and close to major airports, but are also common in university/college towns or along major transportation corridors in large-to-mid-sized metropolitan areas.

Upper-midscale hotels are typically select-service hotels, although some upper-midscale properties may offer a range of peripheral services and all will include some form of food service, at least for the breakfast meal period. Any meeting space or conference services provided will be limited—perhaps one small conference or board room. Typically, what separates an upper-midscale hotel from midscale and economy properties is the quality of the hotel's guestrooms—an upper-midscale hotel aspires to provide the traveler with a guestroom that is comparable to an upscale or even an upper-upscale hotel room in terms of size, comfort, and detail, but at a lower price point. Consequently, the quality of the bedding, linens, furnishings, finishes, and guestroom amenities (soaps, shampoo, lotion, and other in-room convenience items) may be comparable to those found in an upscale or an upper-upscale hotel; however, the staffing level at the hotel will be substantially lower and public spaces may be limited. The operation of a three-meal restaurant and the provision of beverage service, extensive conference support, banquet services, in-room dining, concierge services, luggage assistance, and other labor-intensive peripheral services is avoided. Guests in an upper-midscale hotel will typically have access to a small swimming pool and a simple exercise room with a treadmill or other basic exercise equipment.

Because the required capital investment to develop an upper-midscale hotel is lower than with luxury, upper-upscale, and upscale hotels, coupled with lower labor costs, which dramatically lowers operating costs, upper-midscale hotels can be located in a wider variety of locations, including a suburban office park; adjacent to an airport, shopping district, college/university, tourism site, or other demand generator, or in a smaller town or tertiary market, including a more rural setting along a major highway. They also may be found in urban areas. Globally, upper-midscale hotels ran 67.8% occupancy in 2017 with an ADR of $102.71, while in the United States occupancy for this segment was 67.9% with an ADR of $112.95. Upper-midscale hotels contain 21.9% of hotel guestrooms globally and 25.6% of branded hotel guestrooms in the United States. The typical upper mid-scale hotel

upper-midscale hotels: typically select-service hotels, although some upper-midscale properties may offer a range of peripheral services and all will include some form of food service, at least for the breakfast meal period

guestroom amenities: soaps, shampoo, lotion, and other in-room convenience items

demand generator: an attraction, facility, or event that motivates travelers to travel to a specific destination to visit, conduct business, or attend

has approximately 100 guestrooms—99 rooms globally and 97 rooms in the United States (STR, 2018). Examples of brands in the upper-midscale segment include *Best Western Plus* (Best Western), *Comfort Inn & Suites* (Choice), *Country Inn & Suites* (Carlson Rezidor), *Fairfield Inn* (Marriott), *Hampton Inns & Suites* (Hilton), *Holiday Inn* and *Holiday Inn Express* (IHG), *TownePlace Suites* (Marriott), and *Wyndham Garden Hotels* (Wyndham).

Midscale hotels are select-service properties that provide overnight accommodations and typically some form of a morning breakfast buffet, although the availability of hot breakfast items may be limited. These hotels provide clean, comfortable accommodations, but few frills. The service environment is basic—the use of synthetic materials throughout the guestrooms, including vinyl, laminate, and fiberglass surfaces, is common. Bedding and linens are of moderate quality. Only essential hotel personnel are employed to register and check-out guests; set-up, maintain, and clear a very basic, limited breakfast buffet; clean the guestrooms; and maintain and secure the property.

Examples of brands in the midscale segment include *Baymont Inns & Suites* (Wyndham), *Best Western* (Best Western), *Candlewood Suites* (IHG), *Quality Inn* (Choice), *Hotel Ibis* (Accor), *LaQuinta Inn* (LaQuinta), *Ramada* (Wyndham), *Sleep Inn* (Choice), and *Wingate by Wyndham* (Wyndham). Midscale hotels, which average 76 rooms per property globally, comprise 15.3% of the global hotel room inventory and were 64.3% occupied, with an ADR of $82.44 in 2017. In the United States, mid-scale chain hotels average 84 rooms per property, comprise 13.1% of the available room inventory, and generated an ADR of $86.88 while running 60.0% occupancy in 2017 (STR, 2018). Like upper-midscale hotels, midscale hotels are located in many secondary or tertiary markets and along major transportation corridors.

© Supannee_Hickman/Shutterstock.com

Economy hotels are very basic hotels that provide overnight accommodations—a bedroom with a private bathroom—and are typically absent of public spaces, other than perhaps a small registration lobby. Peripheral services, including F&B services, are not typically provided, although morning coffee service may be available. Staffing levels are minimized, thereby reducing the service level that is provided to guests. Fiberglass tub and/or shower surrounds; vinyl versus ceramic or natural surface flooring; painted versus vinyl-covered wall surfaces; the absence of closet doors; the use of durable, versus elegant, furnishings and light fixtures; and a number of additional cost savings measures are used to minimize the development and construction costs of an economy hotel, leading to a very utilitarian service environment. Basic quality bedding, linens, and only essential in-room guest amenities are provided.

Due to lower construction and operating costs, an economy hotel may be located wherever there is demand for hotel accommodations, although the lower ADR generated by an economy hotel may discourage the construction of or conversion to an economy branded hotel in a high cost real estate market, such as a gateway urban or high-end resort market. Nearly twenty-one percent (20.8%) of the global hotel supply is in the economy segment, running an occupancy of 62.3% globally with an ADR of $65.39 in 2017. In the United States, a similar percentage (21.0%) of chain-affiliated hotel rooms also fall within this segment, which realized occupancy of 58.1% with an ADR of $62.47 in 2017. Globally, the typical economy hotel averages 61 rooms, whereas in the United States branded economy hotels contain 75 guestrooms per property (STR, 2018). Economy brands include *Days Inn* (Wyndham), *Econo Lodge* (Choice), *Howard Johnson* (Wyndham), *LaQuinta Inn* (LaQuinta), *Motel 6* (G6 Hospitality), *Rodeway Inn* (Choice), *Super 8* (Wyndham), and *Travelodge* (Wyndham).

Pricing and Service Strategies

Hotels targeting higher paying guests, which are luxury and upper-upscale hotels, generally price their services *a la carte*. F&B services, premium high-speed internet access, and the wide variety of additional services offered will each be priced and paid for separately. As the price of hotel accommodations decreases, the price of hotel accommodations is more likely to include complimentary items, such as a morning breakfast buffet, internet access, or an evening reception with snacks and beverages, particularly in the upper-midscale segment. This is due to the fact that guests that choose to stay in luxury or upper-upscale properties are willing to pay premium prices to have access to the specific food and beverage products and additional peripheral services that they desire upon request, while guests likely to select a more moderately priced option are seeking a strong value proposition. In addition, luxury and upper-upscale hotel guests are generally less sensitive to price, particularly those traveling on an employer reimbursed expense account. Although an upscale hotel may offer some products and services on an *a la carte* basis, the variety and availability of peripheral service products may be more limited because these guests may not be willing to pay the premium price necessary for the hotel to profitably offer the service upon demand. Meanwhile, economy hotels are designed to appeal to guests traveling on a tight budget, rarely offering any peripheral services.

Specialty Segments

As previously discussed, there are a variety of additional ways to segment hotels. STR maintains in their database a variety of detailed information regarding each hotel property so that hotels may be identified, categorized, and compared based upon a range of criteria and specific features; in addition to geographic location, some additional examples include boutique hotels, conference center hotels, destination resorts, extended stay hotels, type of location, size of meeting space, or availability of spa services, just to name a few. Consequently, hotels can also be classified based upon alternative criteria, although segmenting hotels based upon these criteria will often generate segments that may not be mutually exclusive, in terms of class or chain-scale. For example, the guestroom inventory of most hotels consists of traditional hotel rooms, approximately 250 square feet in size, with a bedroom and a private bath; however, all-suite hotels provide exclusively oversized accommodations or suites that may range in size from 350 to over 600 square feet and, in addition to a bedroom and private bathroom, may provide additional functional areas such as separate living/work areas, wet bars, or small kitchens, depending upon the specific segments of travelers that the hotel may be targeting. All-suite hotels, however, cannot all be categorized into a single class or chain-scale; rather, all-suite hotels are distributed across all categories or segments of hotels, as previously defined. *Candlewood Suites* (midscale), *Comfort Suites* (upper-midscale), *Element* (upscale), *Embassy Suites* (upper-upscale), *Extended Stay America* (economy), *MainStay Suites* (midscale), *Hawthorne Suites by Wyndham* (midscale), *Home2 Suites by Hilton* (upper-midscale), *Residence Inn* (upscale), *Springhill Suites* (upscale), *Staybridge Suites* (upscale), *Studio 6* (economy), and *TownePlace Suites* (upper midscale) all qualify as all-suite hotels but fall into a variety of chain-scale segments, as indicated. So, while all all-suite properties have oversized accommodations, relative to traditional hotels, all-suite hotels may have more in common with traditional hotels from the same chain-scale segment than with all-suite hotels from other segments, particularly in terms of service level, peripheral services, service environment, and price.

all-suite hotels: provide exclusively oversized accommodations or suites that may range in size from 350 to over 600 square feet and, in addition to a bedroom and private bathroom, may provide additional functional areas such as separate living/work areas, wet bars, or a small kitchens

It should also be noted that many hotel specialty segments emerge and evolve over time as new trends and concepts are developed. In the 1990s, for example, it became popular in large urban markets for developers to renovate previously closed hotels and to redevelop abandoned commercial buildings into unique, upscale hotels as downtown neighborhoods were revitalized—this trend continues today. At the start of this trend, these hotels were commonly labeled boutique hotels, which are typically small-er, historic hotels that have been renewed into stylish, upscale properties providing personalized service, many of which also feature signature restaurants—*Kimpton Ho-tels*, now an IHG brand, was one of the innovators that originally pioneered this hotel segment. As boutique hotels further evolved and worked to distinguish themselves from competitors by promoting special events planned at their hotels through social media and engaging in socially responsible corporate behavior, boutique brands such as *Joie de Vivre*, *Park Hotels of India*, and others began to market themselves as lifestyle hotels. Today, a lifestyle hotel may be newly constructed, a redeveloped commercial building, or a renovated historic hotel that offers a carefully selected array of services, coupled with unique design elements, aesthetics, service environment, and customer experience intended to appeal to a specific customer niche based upon demographic and psychographic variables. Consequently, many boutique hotels of the past may prefer to be considered lifestyle hotels in today's hotel landscape. Unlike all-suite hotels that may fall into all class or chain-scale categories, boutique and lifestyle hotels tend to be concentrated in the upper-upscale, upscale, and upper-midscale segments. Since Marriott developed the first *Courtyard by Marriott* hotel in the mid-1980s, the various hotel parent companies have introduced a steady stream of new brands in an effort to define new, distinct categories of hotels that are uniquely positioned to attract specific segments of customers. Therefore, the evolution of existing specialty segments—as well as the emergence of new segments—is expected to continue.

The Future of Independent Versus Branded Hotels

STR has identified that the trend globally is for an increasing proportion of hotel accommodations to become brand-affiliated each year, which has long been common practice in the United States. Due to widespread use of the Internet by consumers, starting in the late 1990s, coupled with the exponential growth in the use of mobile technology in the 21st Century, it seemed plausible that more hotels in the United States might drop their franchise agreements to avoid the franchise fees associated with brand affiliation because independent hotels are now more easily able to com-pete for market-share with branded hotels through the various channels of electronic distribution. Furthermore, many boutique and lifestyle hotels found it beneficial, in many respects, to operate as unique, one-of-a-kind independent hotels, because these hotels were specifically positioned as an alternative to the "all rooms are the same," "cookie-cutter" hotel chains that proliferated in the 1970s through the 1990s; however, these independent hotels had to sacrifice the many benefits of being brand affiliated—including the benefit of being connected to a productive reservation system, strong guest loyalty program, large purchasing network, and network of comparable hotels. To allow a hotel to enjoy the benefits of brand affiliation while simultaneously allow-ing management to position the property as a unique, one-of-a-kind hotel, many hotel parent companies have created soft brands, such as the *Ascend Hotel Collection* (Choice), *Autograph Collection* (Marriott), *Curio Collection (Hilton)*, *Kimpton Hotels* (IHG), *The Luxury Collection* (Marriott), and *Tribute Portfolio* (Marriott). Each hotel affiliated with a soft brand may maintain its individual name and reputation while also promoting itself to guests loyal to the parent company's brands—providing these hotels with the ability to maximize revenue and investor return.

EXCEPTIONAL GUEST EXPERIENCES—THE CORE SERVICE

Ultimately, the success of any hotel is determined one guest experience or moment of truth at a time—whether the hotel is a luxury, resort hotel or an economy roadside property. Each guest ultimately decides if the hotel's service quality, service environment, range of services, and amenities deliver an overall experience that provides an appropriate value in relation to the room rate that was paid. If customers perceive that the hotel provides positive experiences and good value, then the hotel will enjoy repeat patronage and guest loyalty, which are critical to a hotel's long-term success. If not, the hotel will flounder and struggle to generate the targeted ROI. In other words, regardless of the amount of investment made by a hotel's owners to develop, acquire, renovate, or reposition a hotel real estate asset—regardless of the brand that is chosen—or the management company that is contracted—a hotel's financial success is ultimately determined by how well the hotel's team of associates is able to consistently meet or exceed customers' expectations. Consequently, the title of this textbook: *Delivering the Guest Experience: Successful Hotel, Lodging, and Resort Management*.

© XiXinXing/Shutterstock.com

CHAPTER SUMMARY

The hotel industry is comprised of three primary business foci—hotel branding, hotel management, and hotel ownership. Although there may be some overlap, these three functions are generally performed by three separate types of hotel firms. Hotel parent companies focus on branding hotels—their priority is to develop and grow the distribution of a network of hotels that target specific segments of travelers. Hotel management firms manage the day-to-day operation of hotels, whereas hotel investors raise the large amounts of capital necessary to develop, acquire, and maintain hotel real estate assets. The mutually beneficial relationships formed between these organizations are articulated in franchise agreements and management contracts. Although all hotels provide overnight accommodations as their core service, hotels that provide a full-range of peripheral services, including F&B services, meeting and conference support services, exercise facilities, and possibly additional services, are typically referred to as full-service hotels; hotels that provide overnight accommodations and only a limited range of peripheral services are often referred to as select-service hotels. Hotels may be categorized into segments based upon a variety of qualitative factors; however, the ADR is the most efficient way to assign hotels to a taxonomy of hotel segments. Using ADR as the defining criteria, STR, the largest provider of market performance data to the hotel industry, assigns hotels to one of six classes—luxury, upper-upscale, upscale, upper-midscale, midscale, and economy. Regardless of the segment, a hotel is only successful if it consistently delivers positive, memorable experiences to its guests, which builds guest loyalty and drives profitability.

KEY TERMS AND CONCEPTS

all-suite hotels	hotel management firm	return-on-investment (ROI)
asset light strategy	hotel ownership	revenue
average daily rate (ADR)	hotel parent company	select-service hotels
benchmark	lifestyle hotels	service capacity
boutique hotels	luxury hotels	soft brands
branded management company	management contract/agreement	spa services
core competencies	market or guest segment	STR
core service	membership association	taxonomies
demand generator	midscale hotels	upper-midscale hotels
distribution	moment of truth	upper-upscale hotels
economy hotels	occupancy	upscale hotels
franchise or licensing agreement	occupancy percentage	utilization rate
full-service hotels	paired-structure	value
guestroom amenities	peripheral services	
hotel chain	real estate investment trusts (REITs)	

DISCUSSION QUESTIONS

1. Identify the three distinct business foci within the hotel industry. Why are these roles commonly separated?
2. Discuss the relationships that typically exist between the hotel brands, management companies, and hotel owners or investors.
3. If you were to develop a hotel in your local market, would you develop a branded or independent hotel? Explain your decision.
4. What is an asset light corporate strategy and why do most hotel chains pursue such a strategy?
5. Explain the role that STR plays in the hotel industry.
6. Describe the various segments of the lodging industry, providing examples of specific brands within each segment. What are the key factors that differentiate the various lodging segments?
7. Explain why delivering exceptional guest experiences is ultimately in every hotel organization's best interest—whether the organization is involved in the branding, management, or ownership of hotel assets.

ENDNOTES

STR (2018). Hotel Industry Analytical Foundations. *SHARE Center: Certified Hotel Industry Analyst* training materials.

HOTEL DEVELOPMENT PROJECT

Students completing a course in hotel, lodging, or resort management are encouraged to complete a hotel development project over the course of the semester/term; students are encouraged to work in small groups of 3 to 5 students. *Appendix A* outlines the project in its entirety.

Assignment 1: Understanding the Location and Market

Utilize content from: Chapter 1: Introduction to the Hotel Industry

The course instructor will provide students with the specific street address at which the proposed hotel will be developed. This address is selected at the discretion of the instructor and may or may not actually be available for development, although instructors may find it beneficial to select an available site. Ideally, this address will be located in the same city or town as the college or university at which the course is being delivered (or a nearby city or town) so that students are familiar with the market and can potentially visit the proposed hotel site.

Upon the conclusion of Chapter 1, instructors should provide the following information, which is available from the STR SHARE Center:
1. Property census for the market in which the address is located including a "radial" report using the proposed hotel site's address.
2. A hotel pipeline report listing hotels currently under consideration or development in the market (e.g. planning stage, final planning, or under construction).

From these reports, students should identify the following information:
1. The hotel supply in the market in terms of the number of hotels and the number of hotel rooms (from which students may also calculate the average size of the hotel).
2. The distribution of the existing hotel supply by class or chain scale.
3. What parent companies and brands have the largest distribution within the market? Which parent companies and brands have weak distribution or are not represented in the market?
4. How prevalent are independent hotels within the market?
5. Which 10 to 12 hotels are in closest proximity to the proposed site?
6. How many hotels are currently being planned or constructed in the market? What brands are represented in this hotel "pipeline"? How will the possible addition of these hotel properties impact the distribution of supply in terms of chain scale or class?

Chapter 2
Successful Hotel Management

This chapter identifies the priorities of a successful hotel management team, through the introduction of the "all-square" operating
philosophy; explains how an effective management team applies
basic service management strategies to successfully deliver meaningful outcomes to stakeholders; and illustrates the functional organizational structure typically used in a full-service hotel environment.

PURPOSE AND LEARNING OBJECTIVES:

This chapter provides students with an overview of how an effective management
team ensures that the needs and objectives of key stakeholders—hotel guests,
associates, investors, and community members in which the hotel operates—are
successfully fulfilled by the hotel operation. Specifically, students will be able to:

- Outline the priorities and focus of a successful hotel management team
  through an explanation of the "all-square" operating philosophy.
- Identify the key service management concepts that guide the activities of an
  effective management team, explaining how these concepts are effectively
  implemented in a hotel operation.
- Identify the various divisions and operating departments within an upper-
  upscale or luxury hotel.
- Draw an organization chart that illustrates the structure of a hotel's management team.
- Explain the role of each department, within the context of an upper-upscale
  hotel, in contributing to a property's ability to meet the needs and exceed the
  expectations of hotel guests, as well as its respective impact on profitability.
- Summarize the business model of an upper-upscale hotel, identifying the
  key drivers of profitability.
- Describe the leadership responsibilities fulfilled by a hotel's general
  manager (GM).

27

MANAGEMENT PRIORITIES AND FOCUS

A successful hotel management team understands that there are four primary stakeholders that must be considered when prioritizing their responsibilities; a stakeholder is any individual or group

> stakeholder:
> any individual or group that is impacted by the actions of the organization

that is impacted by the actions of the organization. In the case of a hotel, these stakeholders include hotel guests, associates, investors, and the community or society in which the hotel is operated. *Diagram 2.1* illustrates the all-square management philosophy, which much be considered whenever decisions are made that impact one or more of the four primary stakeholders. A successful management team realizes that the operation of a hotel enterprise impacts each of these four stakeholders and ensures that the strategies executed by the hotel and its associates successfully respects and fulfills the needs of each of these constituencies, as outlined below:

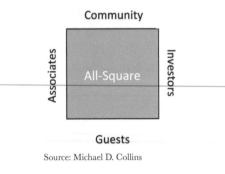

Source: Michael D. Collins

Diagram 2.1: The all-square operating philosophy

1. ***Hotel guests*** are at the base of the square because they are the foundation upon which the success of the hotel must be built. Ultimately, a hotel exists to provide hotel accommodations and other services to hotel guests. Hotel guests are the primary source of revenue for a hotel and without an adequate volume of loyal, satisfied guests, a hotel will simply not survive. In exchange for the payments made to the hotel by guests, customers expect quality products, services, and experiences that facilitate the achievement of their personal or professional objectives.

2. ***Associates*** of the hotel include all employees and managers employed by the hotel. Effective hotel managers appreciate the commitment that associates have made to the hotel and, in return, work diligently to provide associates with both extrinsic and intrinsic job satisfaction. Extrinsic satisfiers, also referred to as hygiene factors, include equitable compensation, a pleasant workplace environment, job security, and competent supervision. Examples of intrinsic satisfiers or motivators include meaningful work, opportunities for career growth, and recognition, just to name a few (Herzberg, 1959).

3. Without ***investors,*** a hotel would not exist. Investors, which in many cases are real estate investment trusts (REITs), choose to invest in hotels to achieve specific investment objectives that include earning a return on their investment (ROI). Therefore, management of the hotel has a fiduciary responsibility to engage in activities that responsibly optimize the return that investors will receive over the term of their investment in the hotel.

4. Finally, a hotel cannot operate in a vacuum—it must operate within a **community**. Many communities employ a range of strategies to attract and support hotel investments within their communities, which include building convention centers and supporting Destination Marketing Organizations (DMOs) or Convention and Visitor Bureaus (CVBs). This is because a hotel drives economic activity. Guests of the hotel generally travel from outside the local area, bringing money into a community that is spent on accommodations, meals, retail

revenue:
payments received in exchange for products, services, and experiences

extrinsic job satisfiers (hygiene factors):
essential rewards provided in exchange for an employee's labor, including compensation

intrinsic job satisfiers (motivators):
workplace rewards that add value to an employee's experience, including meaningful work and career growth

real estate investment trusts (REITs):
a legal entity formed to invest in income producing real estate, typically traded on a public stock exchange

destination marketing organization (DMO)/ convention and visitor bureaus (CVB):
a government or non-profit entity formed to promote in-bound travel to a community

corporate social responsibilities:
the requirement that a business enterprise operates as a good citizen within the community

sustainability:
eliminating or minimizing negative environmental impacts, while maintaining a long-term perspective

hotel parent company:
a firm that provides a wide variety of support services to hotels including hotel brands

hotel management firms:
firms that oversee the day-to-day operation of hotels

vision statement:
an aspirational expression of the impact the firm strives to have on society

mission statement:
defines the goals of the organization more specifically, typically in terms of the core products, services, and/or outcomes the organization plans to deliver to each key stakeholder

value statements:
moral code or core principles that govern the behavior of all associates of the firm

shopping, and much more, which supports hundreds, if not thousands, of jobs while generating substantial tax revenues. In many communities, tax revenues from hotel and accommodation taxes are the largest single source of tax revenue for the municipality's general tax fund (Bay Area Economic Institute, 2013). In addition to serving as an economic engine within a local community, a hotel also has a significant environmental footprint. Consequently, hotel managers must ensure that the enterprise fulfills its corporate social responsibilities, which includes appropriately managing sustainability issues.

There may be times when conflicts may arise between stakeholders due to limited resources. As an example, hotel facilities need to be renovated periodically, requiring an additional investment by the hotel's investors, which increases the amount of profit required to generate a reasonable ROI for investors. Employees expect their wages to increase over time, particularly as the cost of living rises. A community may implement strategies to reduce the amount of waste being transferred to area landfills, increasing the cost of waste removal. To remain competitive in the market, hotels cannot always solve these financial pressures by simply charging customers higher prices. Consequently, management is required to effectively balance the needs of each of these key stakeholders, which is the foundation of the all-square management philosophy. A square has four equal sides—an effective manager must "maintain the square" to ensure that management decisions balance the often-competing needs of stakeholders.

Vision, Mission, and Values

To effectively fulfill the needs of stakeholders, all associates employed by a hotel must work cooperatively to accomplish organizational objectives. Consequently, hotel parent companies and professional hotel management firms establish vision, mission, and value statements to clarify organizational goals and responsibilities, and to define how the hotel's associates are expected to behave. A vision statement is an aspirational expression of the impact the firm strives to have on society. For example, *Hilton's* vision statement is: "To fill the earth with the light and warmth of hospitality—by delivering exceptional experiences—every hotel, every guest, every time" (www.hilton.com, 2018). A mission statement defines the goals of the organization more specifically, typically in terms of the core products, services, and/or outcomes the organization plans to deliver to each key stakeholder. Again, *Hilton* is used as an example: "To be the most hospitable company in the world – by creating heartfelt experiences for Guests, meaningful opportunities for Team Members, high value for Owners and a positive impact in our Communities" (www.hilton.com, 2018). Finally, a successful organization will outline the core values that govern the behavior of all associates—value statements set clear expectations and establish a foundation upon which a constructive corporate or organizational culture may be built. *Hilton's* core values include the following:

> *Hospitality:* We're passionate about delivering exceptional guest experiences.
> *Integrity:* We do the right thing, all the time.
> *Leadership:* We're leaders in our industry and our community.
> *Teamwork:* We're team players in everything that we do.
> *Ownership:* We're the owners of our actions and decisions.
> *Now:* We operate with a sense of urgency and discipline (www.hilton.com, 2018).

The corporate culture of a specific hotel property is determined, in large part, by how effectively the hotel's management team models and reinforces the values espoused by the company. Associates notice if management is focused upon realizing the vision and achieving the mission that has been established or if they are not. By focusing on the achievement of these goals, managers create a healthy culture that is stable and predictable—associates have clear direction and share common goals. This improves communication and cooperation between different areas of the operation. In addition, employees have a defined set of values that regulate their interactions with co-workers, managers, guests, and other stakeholders. Consequently, establishing vision, mission, and value statements are much more than an academic exercise. If a hotel manager works at an independent hotel or for a firm that does not have a company-wide operating philosophy established, then these should be established by the management team at the property-level.

Customer-Focus: External and Internal

Although the all-square operating philosophy stresses the need to balance the needs of key stakeholders—guests, associates, investors, and the community—a successful management team realizes that every business must fulfill its economic objective, which is to operate profitably or the business will cease to exist. The needs of investors *must* be fulfilled. In addition, a business has a legal responsibility to respect and comply with laws and regulations, an ethical responsibility to do what is morally right, and a social responsibility to serve as a responsible corporate citizen; however, to fulfill these subsequent responsibilities, a hotel must first operate profitably. The key to profitability is to consistently meet or exceed guest expectations. Guests are the source of a hotel's revenue and because profit is the degree to which revenue exceeds expenses, or the costs incurred to generate the corresponding revenue, guests are the source of profitability. Consequently, management must evaluate each activity in which the business engages in terms of its contribution to this primary goal of delivering exceptional customer experiences, which in turn drives guest loyalty and hotel profitability.

---

corporate or organizational culture: organically developed beliefs and behaviors that determine how employees interact with internal and external stakeholders

economic objective: the requirement for a business to operate profitably

legal responsibility: the requirement to comply with laws and regulations

ethical reponsibility: the requirement to do what is morally right

social responsibility: the requirement to serve as a good corporate citizen

corporate citizen: the concept that a firm, like any citizen, is required to meet its economic, ethical, legal, and social responsibilities

profit: the degree to which revenue exceeds expenses

expense: a cost incurred to provide products, services, or experiences

value:
the customer's perception of the benefits received, coupled with the quality of the acquisition process, in relationship to the total cost of purchase

value equation:
a formula conceptualizing how customers calculate the perceived worth of a product, service, or experience

It is important to note that hotels of all service levels and at all price points, from economy to luxury hotels, can deliver exceptional customer experiences because customers evaluate an experience in terms of its value. Value is defined as the customer's perception of the benefits received, coupled with the quality of the acquisition process, in relationship to the total cost of purchase. This definition may be expressed in an equation, which is referred to as the value equation.

$$Value = \frac{Results\ produced\ for\ customers\ +\ Process\ quality}{Price\ to\ the\ customer\ +\ Cost\ of\ acquiring\ the\ service}$$

Formula 2.1: The value equation (Heskett, Sasser & Schlessinger, 1997)

The value equation was developed by business researchers (Heskett, Sasser, and Schlessinger, 1997) during their in-depth study of a variety of successful service firms, which included Ritz Carlton Hotels, Southwest Airlines, Federal Express, Intuit, and several additional firms; the purpose of their study was to determine how these firms consistently generate superior financial results in their respective industries. After an in-depth analysis of the business practices of these highly successful firms, Heskett and his colleagues (1997) developed a model that illustrates how these firms achieve superior profitability by focusing on internal service quality. How this internal service quality focus is translated into profitability is outlined in the service-profit chain (*Diagram 2.2*).

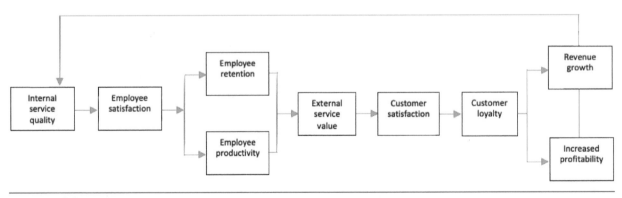

Diagram 2.2: The service profit chain (Heskett, Jones, Loveman, Sasser, & Schlesinger, 1994)

As illustrated in the Service Profit Chain (*Diagram 2.2*), service firms that provide good internal service quality, which means that associates have convenient access to the tools, training, and support necessary to perform their responsibilities, will have highly satisfied employees. Highly satisfied employees will be retained by the firm (stay longer) and be more productive, which will contribute to increased external service value, resulting in customer satisfaction. Satisfied customers will be more loyal to the firm. This, in turn, will allow the firm to increase revenue because loyal customers visit a business more frequently and, in many instances, spend more than newly acquired customers when they do visit—loyal customers may also be less price sensitive. Although some of the increase in revenue will result in improved profitability, a portion of the added revenue may be invested back into improving internal service quality. In the 20+ years since the service profit chain was first theorized, the degree to which businesses consistently satisfy customers has improved due to intense management focus on customer satisfaction, particularly in the hotel industry. As a result, customer satisfaction has become a basic expectation and hotels today must consistently *exceed* customer expectations—versus merely meeting expectations—to drive customer loyalty. Research shows that customer loyalty dramatically increases only when the satisfaction level of hotel guests is at the highest level possible versus being merely adequate to simply meet customers' needs (Bowen & Chen, 2001).

Key relationships identified by the service profit chain include the satisfaction mirror, which states that employee satisfaction drives customer satisfaction and vice versa—customer satisfaction is essential for employees to be satisfied. Bill Marriott, son of Marriott International's founders J. Williard and Alice Marriott and Marriott Chairman of the Board, states, "If a business takes care of its employees, its employees will take care of its customers" (Marriott & Brown, 1997). The goal of any successful service organization is to establish mutually profitable, personalized, and memorable relationships with its customers. Whereas customers may perceive that they have a relationship with a firm or other organization, it is impossible to have a personal relationship with a corporate entity—the relationship that exists is between the *associates* that *represent* the firm and the guests of the firm. So, the satisfaction mirror is also reflected in the relationship found within highly successful service organizations between employee loyalty and customer loyalty.

> satisfaction mirror: employee satisfaction drives customer satisfaction and vice versa

Cycle of Success

Building upon the research of Heskett, Sasser, & Schlesinger (1997), coupled with the in-depth study of leading hotel operators over a 25-year period, the "cycle of success" identifies the key activities in which management must engage to ensure that hotels consistently deliver mutually profitable, memorable, and personalized experiences to key stakeholders. These activities are illustrated in *Diagram 2.3: The Cycle of Success*.

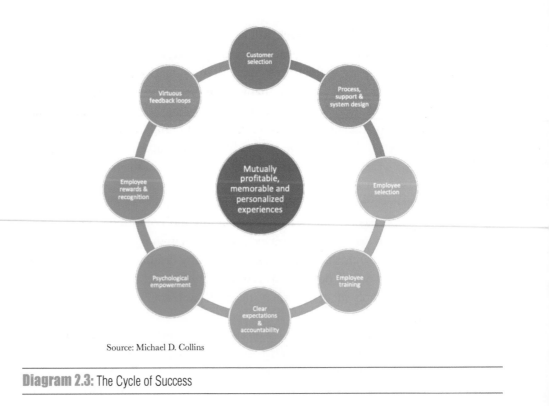

Source: Michael D. Collins

Diagram 2.3: The Cycle of Success

Careful Customer Selection

The cycle of success starts with careful customer selection. A hotel uses a variety of tools and techniques to carefully select its customers, which is the emphasis of *Chapter 3: Defining Guest Segments, Chapter 4: Effective Sales and Marketing,* and *Chapter 5: Optimizing Revenue.* A hotel has limited service capacity, which is defined as "the maximum number of customers that may be appropriately served in a specified time period. For example, a hotel with 400 rooms can only accommodate 400 overnight parties of hotel guests. Consequently, it is important that a hotel sells its limited service capacity to the most profitable guests possible, as opposed to accommodating guests on a first-come-first-served basis. To ensure that the hotel provides value to guests, as defined in the value equation (*Formula 2.1*), it is important that the guests the hotel chooses to serve will perceive that their experiences, combined with guests' perceptions of service quality, will be perceived as equitable in relationship to the price paid or cost of acquiring the overnight accommodations.

> service capacity:
> the maximum number of customers that may be appropriately served in a specified time period

Process, Support, and System Design

Successful hotel managers engage in systems-thinking; they realize that establishing a network of effective and efficient subsystems that consistently generate the targeted

> systems-thinking:
> processes and procedures designed to ensure consistent outcomes

outcomes will ensure that the larger system—or the hotel operation as a whole—achieves the targeted business objectives. Within each chapter of *Delivering the Guest Experience: Successful Hotel, Lodging, and Resort Management*, key systems and processes within each area or department of a hotel operation are outlined to provide readers with an understanding of the various subsystems—both linear and non-linear—to explain how they contribute to the overall system or the hotel's overall operation. Each subsystem must be designed and evaluated in terms of both effectiveness and efficiency. Effectiveness refers to the system's or process' ability to consistently deliver the targeted outcome or result. Efficiency refers to the degree to which a system or process is designed to deliver the targeted outcome at the lowest reasonable cost. Ultimately, all systems and processes exist to ensure the hotel consistently delivers results that meet or exceed the expectations of key stakeholders, and all processes, including internal processes designed to support associates of the hotel, must contribute to the hotel's ability to meet its obligations to hotel guests while ensuring the profitability of the hotel. Consequently, all processes and systems must be designed to ensure both effectiveness and efficiency as illustrated in *Diagram 2.4*.

linear system: thoughtfully designed process or procedure that must be executed in the specified sequence to consistently produce the targeted outcome

non-linear system: a set of guidelines or a procedure that must be continuously supported by all associates to achieve the targeted outcome

effectiveness: the degree to which a system or process consistently delivers the targeted outcome or result

efficiency: the degree to which a system or process consistently delivers the targeted outcome at the lowest reasonable cost

Source: Michael D. Collins

Diagram 2.4: Systems-thinking: All hotel systems and processes must be designed to deliver positive customer outcomes (effectiveness), while also ensuring profitability (efficiency).

Successful managers develop detailed policies and procedures that ensure exceptional customer experiences are consistently and efficiently delivered by hotel associates. The first step in creating an effective and efficient service process is to diagram the process using a service blueprint, which is a detailed, step-by-step illustration of a process or service experience that clearly identifies each step in a process and the sequence in which the steps are to be performed. Please refer to *Box 2.1: Creating a Service Blueprint* to see how one is developed and analyzed. Throughout each chapter of *Delivering the Guest Experience: Successful Hotel, Lodging, and Resort Management*, service blueprints are provided to illustrate the key functions and processes performed by the various hotel departments.

service blueprint: a detailed, step-by-step illustration of a process or service experience that clearly identifies each step in a process and the sequence in which the steps are to be performed

BOX 2.1: CREATING A SERVICE BLUEPRINT: THE HOTEL ARRIVAL EXPERIENCE

The guest arrival experience, starting with the guest's arrival at the front entrance of the hotel and ending with the guest's departure from the hotel lobby (or being left in his/her guestroom by the bell staff to enjoy his/her stay), is outlined in the service blueprint provided below. Ovals are used to designate the guests' arrival at the start of the process and to identify the end of the process, which may include one of the three possible outcomes indicated in this example. Rectangles are used to detail each step in the process and arrows designate the flow of the process, indicating the sequence in which the various steps must be completed. Diamonds indicate divergent paths in the process, for example, when the guest is asked if they have a hotel reservation; and inverted triangles identify support processes, which may be diagramed separately, such as the valet parking of the guest's vehicle. These "warning signs" also often identify potential bottlenecks in a process.

line-of-visibility: separates the processes that are executed in view of the customer

line-of-interaction: indicates points at which guests interact with staff to provide input into the service process

line-of-support: identifies the processes that may be fulfilled by support personnel within the organization, by other departments, or by vendors or sub-contractors

standard operating procedures (SOPs): detailed processes designed to ensure that guests consistently receive quality experiences that meet or exceed their expectations, to make certain that appropriate control procedures are in place, and to ensure effective, efficient internal processes to support the operation

A line-of-visibility illustrates the processes that are executed in view of the customer, a line-of-interaction indicates points at which the guests interact and provide input into the process, and a line-of-support identifies the processes that may be fulfilled by support personnel within the organization, by other departments, or by vendors or sub-contractors. In the example illustrated, the items to the left of the line-of-visibility are performed in view of guests, items to the left of the line-of-interaction require input from the guest or engagement between the service provider and the guests, whereas processes positioned to the right of the line-of-support are performed by supporting personnel or departments, typically out of view from the guest.

Service blueprints are not a replacement for detailed policies and procedures; however, they are a good first step when creating an effective policy. Quality organizations establish standard operating procedures (SOPs) to ensure that guests consistently receive quality experiences that meet or exceed their expectations, to make certain that appropriate control procedures are in place, and to ensure effective, efficient internal processes to support the operation. In addition, SOPs establish clear expectations for employees and help drive labor productivity. A service blueprint will identify all the steps included in the procedure, designate the sequence of those steps, and illustrate the flow of a process; the SOP fills in the details regarding each step of the process and is much more descriptive, often providing a suggested script for an associate to follow when interacting with guests. A service blueprint, used in conjunction with a detailed SOP, is an effective training tool because it helps an employee visualize a process step-by-step. To use an analogy, a service blueprint is like a skeleton, which frames out the process, whereas the SOP fills in the details and is like the flesh on the bones. By creating service blueprints, a hotel manager can dissect, analyze, and improve service processes—a skill critical to ensuring effective and efficient processes are established.

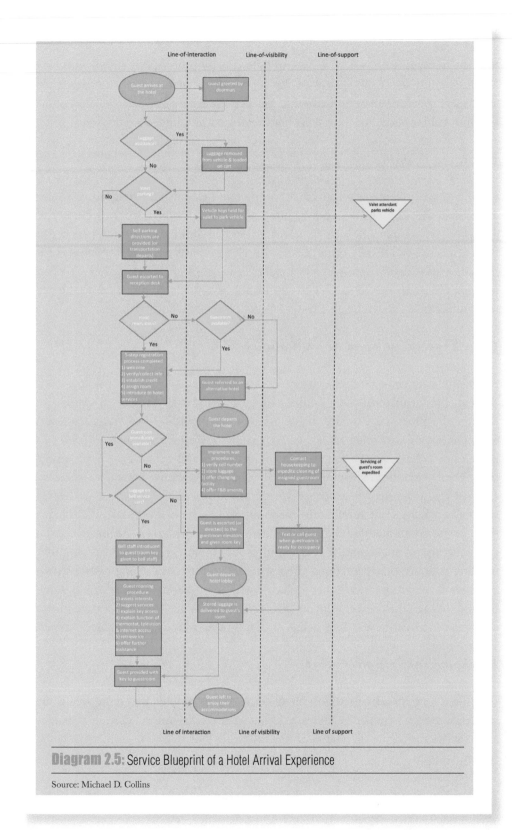

Diagram 2.5: Service Blueprint of a Hotel Arrival Experience

Source: Michael D. Collins

Employee Selection

Just as a hospitality enterprise must carefully select its guests, it is equally critical that hotels carefully select the associates that represent the firm. *Chapter 11: Administration and Control: Human Resources, Accounting, and Loss Prevention*, provides detailed information and guidance on how a hotel effectively selects and hires its employees.

Employee Training

Once team members are selected, a thorough and effective training process must be established that indoctrinates newly hired associates into the corporate culture while also providing employees with the knowledge, skills, and abilities to be successful in their respective positions. Again, *Chapter 11: Administration and Control: Human Resources, Accounting, and Loss Prevention* provides detailed insight into the design of an effective training program, as well as how to successfully assimilate employees into the corporate culture.

Clear Expectations and Accountability

service standards: succinct, clearly stated rules of behavior to be followed by all associates of the firm

line-ups: pre-shift meetings that provide updated information to associates while reinforcing corporate values, service standards, and expectations

Successful managers establish clear expectations for associates and hold associates accountable for the consistent delivery of those standards. As outlined earlier in the chapter, this process starts with the creation of vision and mission statements, as well as by identifying corporate values. Service standards, which are succinct, clearly stated rules of behavior to be followed by all associates of the firm, are also commonly established in a hotel environment to ensure that guests receive consistent, memorable experiences. The use of line-ups, or pre-shift meetings that provide updated information to associates while reinforcing corporate values, service standards, and expectations, is one additional tool that clarifies expected performance. Although a primary responsibility of management is to ensure that employees are held accountable for meeting established expectations, the corporate culture is so strong within truly successful hotel environments that compliance with these expectations is largely achieved through self-regulation—employees put forth the effort to "do things right" to avoid disappointing themselves, their peers, and, most importantly, their valued guests.

Psychological Empowerment

psychological empowerment: the degree to which an employee is intrinsically motivated to make a difference in the work environment

Psychological empowerment is defined as the degree to which an employee is intrinsically motivated to make a difference in the work environment, which is impacted by an associate's perceptions relative to the following four questions about his/her work responsibilities:

1. Is my work meaningful or important?
2. Am I competent and fully able to perform my responsibilities?

3. Do I have a degree of autonomy? In other words, can I put my own "personal touch" on my work?

4. Do I make an impact or a difference at work? (Spreitzer, 1996)

Consequently, effective hotel managers provide clear guidance and structure, but also trust their associates to deviate from the prescribed policies and procedures to respond to individual customer needs. In a healthy work environment, employees are given some latitude, based upon their assessment of specific situations, provided the guests' or employees' safety or required control procedures are not jeopardized. By encouraging associates to think and respond creatively, continuous improvement and innovation is likely to occur, which will often delight customers, as more effective or efficient processes are discovered.

Employee Rewards and Recognition

Associates that choose to work in the hotel industry do so to earn more than a paycheck; many hotel employees take great satisfaction in delighting hotel guests. To perpetuate and enhance the corporate culture, it is important that the management team rewards and recognizes associates for fulfilling the hotel's mission. Consequently, formal employee recognition programs are established in successful hotel operations, in addition to less formal ongoing forms of recognition to ensure that associates do not feel that they are taken for granted. Associates of a well-managed hotel feel valued and appreciated each day. *Chapter 11: Administration and Control: Human Resources, Accounting, and Loss Prevention* provides details regarding how effective recognition programs that enhance the corporate culture, while ensuring that associates of the firm are intrinsically satisfied, may be established.

Virtuous Feedback Loop

Effective hotel management teams are constantly assessing the performance of the hotel through a variety of virtuous feedback loops. A virtuous feedback loop, illustrated in *Diagram 2.6*, is defined as a system that seeks continuous input from stakeholders to assess, evaluate, and enhance the effectiveness of systems, processes, procedures, and tactics, thereby ensuring the continuous improvement of business outcomes. Virtuous feedback loops are used by effective management teams to continuously monitor guest satisfaction as well as associate satisfaction. The term *virtuous* is used because to be effective, management must collect feedback with a sincere intention to enhance operations; the strategies resulting from the analysis of guest and associate feedback must be focused on improving guest and associate satisfaction, not merely to improve feedback scores to achieve some arbitrary goal. Example of virtuous feedback loops include the guest survey process outlined in *Box 6.1: Guest Service Index (GSI) scores*, found in *Chapter 6: Guest Services Operations*, as well as the *Second Effort Program* which

virtuous feedback loops:
a system that seeks continuous input from stakeholders to assess, evaluate, and enhance the effectiveness of systems, processes, procedures, and tactics, thereby ensuring the continuous improvement of business outcomes

is also described in *Chapter 6* in the *Guest Communications* section. Another example is found in *Chapter 11: Administration and Control: Human Resources, Accounting, and Loss Prevention* in the discussion regarding the *Employee Opinion Survey*.

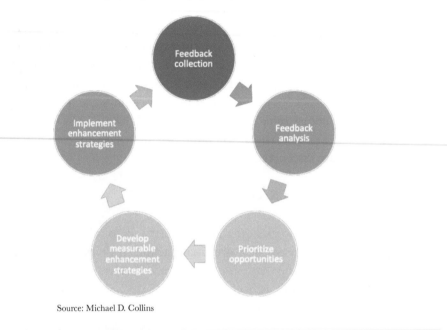

Source: Michael D. Collins

Diagram 2.6: Virtuous Feedback Loop: By continuously collecting and evaluating stakeholder feedback, a successful hotel management team continuously improves the guest experience, associate satisfaction, and operational effectiveness.

BUSINESS MODEL OF AN UPPER-UPSCALE HOTEL

sustainable competitive advantage:
a system, process, or asset that allows a firm to operate more effectively or efficiently than its competitive firms, which may not be quickly replicated by competitors

market equilibrium:
when demand for a product or service is equal to supply

In a capitalistic society, a business model develops, and continues to evolve over time, which ensures that the needs of key stakeholders are efficiently fulfilled. Because of the competitive nature of the business environment, businesses are constantly seeking to improve the efficiency of their operations to gain a sustainable competitive advantage over firms offering similar products, services, and experiences, as well as those competing for the same share of consumers' incomes. As firms identify and leverage sustainable competitive advantages, other firms work to incorporate similar enhancements into their operations to compete; once this occurs, a practice that may have served as a competitive advantage at one time has become a new industry standard. Market equilibrium is reached when demand for a product or service is equal to supply. In a market that has reached equilibrium, the cost margins at which all firms in an industry are simultaneously providing value to customers, competitive compensation to associates, and reasonable returns to investors while fulfilling their citizenship obligations to society represents the business model of the industry, which is the economic formula that most firms within a specific industry use, in terms of the revenue generated per available unit of service capacity and the corresponding expense ratios necessary, to fulfill the needs of the four key stakeholders.

business model: the economic formula commonly used by firms in a specific industry that allow the needs of the four key stakeholders to be simultaneously fulfilled

Market equilibrium, of course, is a theoretical concept and is rarely achieved in any industry or consumer market, including the hotel industry or a specific hotel market. Fluctuations in consumer demand; innovations that raise or lower the cost of providing the product, service, or experience; new entrants into or firms withdrawing from the market; the introduction of new technologies that improve employee productivity; and a variety of additional factors impact the economics of all industries; however, the general business model evolves slowly over time, particularly in mature industries such as the hotel industry.

By evaluating the performance of a sample of hotels over an entire year, distributed across a variety of markets and market conditions, the typical operating margins necessary for hotels to fulfill their economic objectives may be reasonably estimated. Consequently, the financial operating results for a large sample (n = 966) of upper-upscale hotels located in a variety of markets within the United States, comprised of 393,421 guestrooms, are presented in *Table 2.1: Financial Performance of a Typical Upper-Upscale Hotel* (STR, 2017) and will be used to define the business model of an upper-upscale hotel operation. The business model defines the typical revenue generated per available and occupied hotel guestroom and the corresponding expense ratios and profit margins, as both dollar amounts and as percentages of revenue; values are also presented for a "typical" upper-upscale hotel of 400 guestrooms.

As outlined in *Table 2.1*, the typical upper-upscale hotel in the United States generates nearly $50,000 in rooms revenue per guestroom per year or just over $180 per occupied guestroom per night (also referred to as a room night), which represents 63.2% of total revenue. Food and beverage revenues of $23,721 per year per available room ($87.10 per room night) represent 30.2% of total revenue. The remaining 6.6% of revenue or $5,138 per available room per year ($18.91 per room night) are generated by other operating revenues, which include items such as parking and communications, and from miscellaneous sources such as retail leases or interest on bank deposits. In total, a typical upper-upscale hotel in the United States generates nearly $80,000 in total revenue per available guestroom annually, or nearly $300 per room night.

room night: a hotel accommodation occupied by a guest or guests for a single night

The rooms division generates the largest contribution margin and is the primary source of a hotel's profit. With departmental expenses of only 25.8% of revenue, the typical hotel generates a departmental profit of 74.2% of guestroom revenue. In many high demand markets, with higher than typical average daily rates (ADRs), rooms division profits may run as high as 80% of rooms revenue or more. The Food and Beverage (F&B) division of an upper-upscale hotel in the United States averages a

contribution margin: revenue minus the variable costs necessary to generate the corresponding revenue

| | Amount | | | Sales |
	Per Available Room	Per Occupied Room	Annual for a 'Typical' 400-room Hotel	Sales Ratio
Revenue	$	$	$	%
Rooms	$49,598	$182.12	$19,888,961	63.2%
Food	$14,689	$53.94	$5,890,680	18.7%
Beverage	$3,938	$14.46	$1,579,148	5.0%
Other Food and Beverage	$5,094	$18.70	$2,042,190	6.5%
Other Operating Departments	$2,890	$10.61	$1,158,697	3.7%
Miscellaneous Income	$2,249	$8.30	$906,426	2.9%
Total Revenue	$78,458	$288.13	$31,466,101	100.0%
Departmental Expenses				
Rooms	$12,791	$46.97	$5,129,500	25.8%
Food and Beverage	$16,329	$59.96	$6,548,112	68.8%
Other Operating Departments	$1,860	$6.83	$745,891	64.4%
Total Departmental Expenses	$30,981	$113.76	$12,423,502	39.5%
Departmental Contribution Margin				
Rooms	$36,806	$135.15	$14,759,461	74.2%
Food and Beverage	$7,392	$27.14	$2,963,905	31.2%
Other Operating Departments	$1,030	$3.78	$412,806	35.6%
Total Departmental Operating Margin	$47,478	$174.37	$19,042,599	60.5%
Undistributed Operating Expenses				
Administrative and General	$5,875	$21.57	$2,355,617	7.5%
Information and telecommunications systems	$867	$3.18	$347,281	1.1%
Sales and Marketing (excluding franchise fees)	$5,673	$20.83	$2,274,803	7.2%
Franchise fees (royalty, guest loyalty and marketing)	$866	$3.18	$347,281	1.1%
Utility Costs	$2,557	$9.39	$1,025,463	3.3%
Property Operations and Maintenance	$3,260	$11.97	$1,307,220	4.2%
Total Undistributed Operating Expenses	$19,098	$70.12	$7,657,665	24.3%
Gross Operating Profit (GOP)	$28,380	$104.25	$11,384,934	36.2%
Base Management Fees	$2,067	$7.59	$828,889	2.6%
Incentive Management Fees	$215	$0.79	$86,274	0.3%
Income Before Fixed Charges	$26,098	$95.87	$10,469,771	33.3%
Operating Statistics:				
		Occupancy Percentage (%)	74.8%	
		Available Rooms	146,000	
		Occupied Rooms	109,208	
		Average Daily Rate (ADR)	$182.12	
		(Room) Revenue Per Available Room (RevPAR)	$136.23	
		F&B Revenue Per Occupied Room (F&BPOR)	$87.10	
		Total Revenue Per Occupied Room (TRPOR)	$288.13	
		GOP Per Occupied Room (GOPPOR)	$104.25	
		GOP Per Available Room (GOPPAR)	$77.98	

Table 2.1: Financial Performance of a 'Typical' Upper-Upscale Hotel. Based upon a sample of 966 hotels comprised of 393,421 guestrooms (407 average number of rooms per hotel) located in the United States. 2015 results as reported by STR (2017)

contribution margin of 31.2%, although the margin varies more widely from property to property, depending upon many factors including the proportion of F&B revenues that are generated from banquet operations, as opposed to restaurant or outlet sales. The departmental profit associated with the other operating departments will vary widely depending upon the source of the revenue and the complexity of the operations necessary to support the corresponding revenue; for example, valet parking revenue may be more expensive to generate than self-parking revenue because it is much more labor intensive. The overall contribution margin of the combined operating departments will total approximately 60.5% of revenue.

Undistributed operating expenses include the costs incurred at a hotel property that support the entire hotel operation and are not directly associated with just a single operating division. For example, the Administrative and General (A&G) department provides administrative, accounting, human resources, and loss prevention support to the rooms division, the food and beverage operation, and other operating departments. Total undistributed operating expenses average 24.3% of total hotel revenue overall and are comprised of A&G expenses (7.5% of total revenue), information and telecommunications system expenses (1.1%), sales and marketing (S&M) expense (7.2%), franchise fees (1.1%), utility costs (3.3%), and property operations and maintenance (POM) expenses (4.2%). The gross operating profit (GOP) of a typical upper-upscale hotel in the United States is 36.2% of total hotel revenue or nearly $30,000 per available room per year—$104.25 per room night. Management fees, paid to the hotel management firm responsible for the day-to-day operation of the hotel, total 2.9% of total hotel revenue, which brings income before fixed charges to just over $25,000 per available room per year, $95.87 per room night, or 33.3% of total hotel revenue. It should be noted that GOP and income before fixed charges may vary substantially for many hotels depending upon a variety of factors; it is not uncommon for hotels in strong hotel markets, enjoying high occupancy and ADRs, to enjoy GOPs of well over 50% of total hotel revenue.

undistributed operating expenses:
the costs incurred at a hotel property that support the entire hotel operation and are not directly associated with a single operating division

Income before fixed charges does not represent the amount of net profit or income enjoyed by hotel investors. Capital lease payments, capital reserves, and other direct ownership expenses, including property taxes and casualty insurance, must be deducted from income before fixed charges before earnings before interest, taxes, depreciation and amortization (EBITDA) may be calculated. EBITDA represents the cash flow that is generated by the hotel operation, available to hotel ownership, and may be used to estimate the value of a hotel as an operating business. Hotel investors use EBITDA to cover any debt service or mortgages that they carry on the hotel and to generate a return on their investment.

THE ROLE OF AN EFFECTIVE HOTEL GENERAL MANAGER

Ultimately, the role of a hotel GM is to ensure that hotel investors receive an equitable return on their investment. In other words, a GM must optimize EBITDA; however, an effective GM realizes that to do so, he/she must first focus on internal service quality—the first step in the service-profit chain. Consequently, an effective GM takes a servant leadership approach to his/her management responsibilities, which are to ensure that the associates throughout the hotel have the necessary tools, knowledge, skills, and abilities to effectively serve guests in a clean, well-designed, and maintained environment. Managers perform four functions: planning, organizing, directing, and controlling. An effective hotel GM works with his/her hotel managers to plan the wide variety of activities necessary to ensure that the hotel employs a team of competent hospitality professionals and that these associates have the tools, training, and equipment necessary to consistently exceed customer expectations. He/she directs the activities of the management team and associates—ensuring that everyone is working efficiently and that the various subsystems work interdependently to safeguard the effectiveness of the operation in terms of stakeholder outcomes. A successful GM realizes that he/she will only deliver positive outcomes to stakeholders if he/she effectively serves his/her associates well. In response to being well-served by the GM, associates serve guests effectively, which ultimately results in positive outcomes for all four key stakeholders—guests, associates, investors, and the community. Because an effective GM realizes that he/she can only accomplish these goals through the activities of others, he/she takes a values-based approach to guiding behavior as outlined in *Diagram 2.7*.

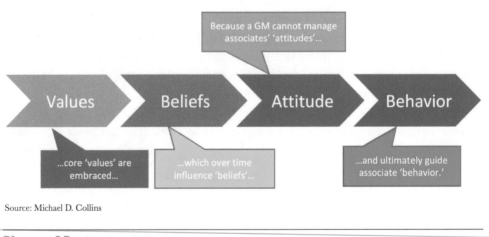

Source: Michael D. Collins

Diagram 2.7: Values-based management

Because employee attitudes drive behavior, and an employee's attitude cannot be managed by anyone but the employee himself/herself, effective GMs strictly adhere to organizational values in all that they do. They hold managers and associates within the hotel accountable for supporting and engaging in behaviors that comply with the hotel's core values. By doing so, employees more consistently comply with the hotel's values as they perform their responsibilities, which positively impact their beliefs—employees quickly recognize that compliance with the core values drives positive stakeholder outcomes. Consequently, their behavior is impacted, and behaving in a manner consistent with the hotel's core values becomes a "way of life" for all associates. The degree to which a GM behaves in a manner that is consistent with organizational values is directly related to his/her level of success in effectively leading his/her team. A hotel GM that merely talks about core values—but fails to behave in a manner consistent with the organization's values—does so at his/her own peril!

OPERATIONAL STRUCTURE OF A FULL-SERVICE HOTEL

A hotel GM cannot possibly serve the needs of guests, associates, investors, or the community alone. A hotel must employ a team of dedicated hospitality professionals possessing a wide variety of knowledge, skills, and abilities. The operational structure of an upper-upscale hotel is outlined in *Diagram 2.8* and provides an overview of how associates within a hotel are organized into work groups or teams. Most employees serve in one of the two primary operating divisions: the rooms division or the F&B division. In a resort setting, there may also be a recreation or resort services division, although resort services are often leased out or operated by a third party through a contractual relationship. The remaining associates serve in one of the support departments: S&M, A&G, or POM, sometimes simply referred to as engineering.

The structure outlined represents the departmental structure found within the context of an upper-upscale hotel, although the structure used will be influenced by the complexity and location of the operation, as well as the range of services offered by the specific hotel or resort. The functions performed by each of the various divisions and departments are self-explanatory; however, the successful management of each function is described in detail in the respective chapters of *Delivering the Guest Experience: Successful Hotel, Lodging, and Resort Management*. An upper-upscale hotel or resort will typically employ between 0.5 and 1.25 full-time equivalents (FTEs) per guestroom; an FTE refers to an associate that works an average of 40 hours per week or approximately 2,000 hours annually. Many hotels, of course, employ many part-time associates that average less than 32 hours per week; however, a more precise measure of the number of jobs supported by a hotel is indicated by referring to FTEs as opposed to the total number of associates employed by a hotel. The wide variation is due to several factors but is primarily impacted by the sales volume and complexity of the F&B operation because it is most labor-intensive. The rooms division employs approximately 0.15 of an FTE per guestroom, which contributes to its much more favorable contribution margin.

> full-time equivalent (FTE):
> an associate that works an average of 40 hours per week or approximately 2,000 hours annually

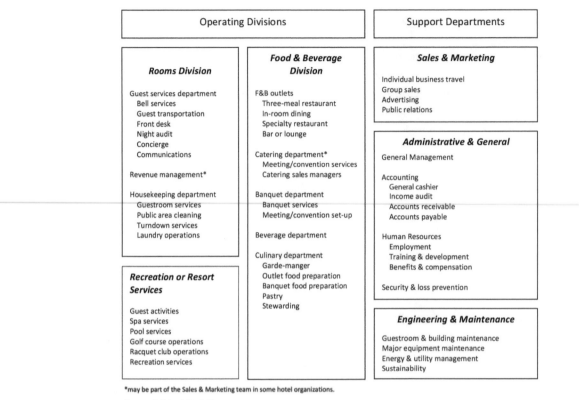

Operating Divisions			Support Departments

Rooms Division

Guest services department
  Bell services
  Guest transportation
  Front desk
  Night audit
  Concierge
  Communications

Revenue management*

Housekeeping department
  Guestroom services
  Public area cleaning
  Turndown services
  Laundry operations

Recreation or Resort Services

Guest activities
Spa services
Pool services
Golf course operations
Racquet club operations
Recreation services

Food & Beverage Division

F&B outlets
  Three-meal restaurant
  In-room dining
  Specialty restaurant
  Bar or lounge

Catering department*
  Meeting/convention services
  Catering sales managers

Banquet department
  Banquet services
  Meeting/convention set-up

Beverage department

Culinary department
  Garde-manger
  Outlet food preparation
  Banquet food preparation
  Pastry
  Stewarding

Sales & Marketing

Individual business travel
Group sales
Advertising
Public relations

Administrative & General

General Management

Accounting
  General cashier
  Income audit
  Accounts receivable
  Accounts payable

Human Resources
  Employment
  Training & development
  Benefits & compensation

Security & loss prevention

Engineering & Maintenance

Guestroom & building maintenance
Major equipment maintenance
Energy & utility management
Sustainability

**may be part of the Sales & Marketing team in some hotel organizations.*

Source: Michael D. Collins

Diagram 2.8: Operational structure of an upper-scale hotel or resort

MANAGEMENT STRUCTURE

functional organization structure:
work groups or teams of associates are supervised based upon the type of work that they do

executive operating committee (EOC):
the senior management team responsible for achieving the hotel's strategic objectives

Hotels typically use a functional organization structure, which means that work groups or teams of associates are supervised based upon the type of work that they do. An upper-upscale hotel typically employs one manager or supervisor for every 10–15 hourly-compensated FTEs using a management structure as depicted in *Diagram 2.9*. The senior management team is often referred to as the Executive Operating Committee (EOC) and includes the GM, Rooms Division Manager or Assistant General Manager, Director of F&B, Director of S&M, Controller, Director of Human Resources, and the Director of Engineering; in some organizations, the Executive Chef serves as a member of the EOC. The EOC establishes the strategic plan for the hotel and the annual budget or forecast, and is focused on long-term planning—often looking 6–12 months forward—to ensure that the operation has the necessary workforce, equipment, and strategic direction to achieve its objectives.

Reporting directly to each respective executive committee member are the department heads; this level of management includes the Guest Services Director or Front Office Manager, Director of Revenue Management, Executive Housekeeper or Director of Services, Director of Restaurants (or F&B outlets), Executive Chef (if not serving on the EOC), Banquet Manager, and the Director of Catering (or Conference Services). These managers are fully immersed in the day-to-day operation of the hotel—typically focused on the anticipated needs of hotel guests and associates within the upcoming 2–8 weeks; department heads are responsible for ensuring that the front-line associates are properly trained, efficiently scheduled, and that they have the supplies they need to effectively serve the needs of guests. Assistant department heads and hourly supervisors are employed, as needed, to ensure the successful operation of each department and are typically considered entry-level management positions. Assistant department heads are on-the-floor for most of their scheduled shifts and provide hands-on support directly to associates and guests. Assistant department heads and supervisors are focused upon the needs of hotel guests and associates today, tomorrow, and through the next week.

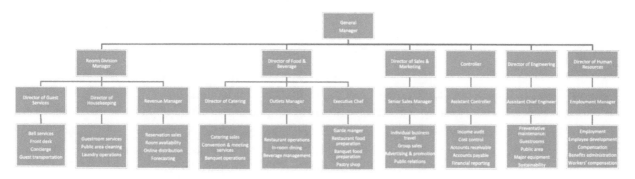

Source: Michael D. Collins

Diagram 2.9: Organization Chart for an Upper-Upscale Hotel

CHAPTER SUMMARY

A successful management team performs their responsibilities using an all-square operating philosophy, appropriately balancing the needs of four key stakeholders—guests, associates, investors, and the community. To help prioritize the competing needs of these stakeholders, an effective management team establishes vision and mission statements, in addition to defining organizational values that ultimately guide the behaviors of associates. To achieve a hotel's economic objective, hotel associates must consistently exceed guest expectations and deliver value to hotel guests as defined in the value equation (*Formula 2.1*). The service-profit chain (*Diagram 2.2*) is a conceptual model that illustrates how a focus upon internal service quality may eventually lead to increased revenues and profitability. A closely related construct, the cycle of success (*Diagram 2.3*), outlines the activities in which management must engage to ensure that a hotel is successfully operated. Included in the cycle of success is the development of effective and efficient processes and service systems; sequential processes may be outlined by service blueprints (*Box 2.1*), which is a tool that may be used to design, modify, or streamline service processes. Virtuous Feedback Loops (*Diagram 2.6*) are used by managers to ensure continuous improvement within the operation based upon both guest and associate feedback.

The role of an effective hotel GM is to spearhead planning efforts and, working closely with the EOC, ensure that all associates have the tools, training, and equipment necessary to deliver memorable experiences to hotel guests, which ultimately drives the economic success of the business, resulting in a favorable return for hotel investors. Each EOC member oversees one of the primary operating or support divisions of a hotel operation, as illustrated in the functional organizational structure found in *Diagram 2.9*. *Table 2.1* outlines the typical business model of an upper-upscale hotel. The rooms division of a hotel operation is the primary source of a hotel's profitability—typically, generating 77.5% of a hotel's departmental contribution margin. Consequently, achieving financial success in the rooms division is critical to generating a favorable cash-flow for the hotel's investors, which is measured by EBITDA. The profitability of F&B operations vary widely among upper-upscale hotels, but typically generate a departmental profit of 31.2% of corresponding revenue. Undistributed operating expenses include A&G, S&M, POM, utility expenses, and franchise fees, which combine to average 24.2% of total hotel revenue. After deducting 2.9% in management fees, the typical upper-upscale hotel in the United States enjoys an operating income before fixed charges of 33 cents for every one dollar in revenue (33.3%) or $26,098 in income per available room per year on revenues of $78,458 per available room per year.

KEY TERMS AND CONCEPTS

business model	destination marketing	efficiency
contribution margin	organizations (DMO)/convention	ethical responsibility
corporate citizen	and visitor bureaus (CVB)	executive operating committee
corporate/organizational culture	economic objective	(EOC)
corporate social responsibilities	effectiveness	expense

extrinsic job satisfaction	mission statement	social responsibility
full-time equivalent (FTE)	motivators	stakeholder
functional organization structure	non-linear system	standard operating procedures
hotel management firms	organizational culture	(SOPs)
hotel parent company	profit	sustainability
hygiene factors	psychological empowerment	sustainable competitive advantage
intrinsic job satisfaction	real estate investment trusts (REITs)	systems-thinking
legal responsibility	revenue	undistributed operating expenses
linear system	room night	value
line-of-interaction	satisfaction mirror	value equation
line-of-support	servant leadership	value statements
line-of-visibility	service blueprint	virtuous feedback loops
line-ups	service capacity	vision statement
market equilibrium	service standards	

DISCUSSION QUESTIONS

1. Explain why the service-profit chain starts with internal service quality; include the concepts of the satisfaction mirror and external service value in your explanation.
2. At the center of the cycle of success is "mutually profitable, memorable, and personalized experiences." Explain the meaning of this phrase and why it is at the center of the cycle.
3. Discuss the concept of systems-thinking. What is the difference between a non-linear and linear system? Provide an example of each. How do service blueprints relate to the concept of systems-thinking?
4. Identify a linear process for a current or past job. Create a service blueprint that illustrates the process.
5. Define each element of the cycle of success and explain the importance of each.
6. What is a virtuous feedback loop? Provide an example how a virtuous feedback loop may be used to enhance business outcomes.
7. Discuss the profitability of a full-service hotel. Which operating division produces the highest contribution margin? Why? What are undistributed operating expenses? What is the typical GOP achieved in an upper-upscale hotel in the United States?
8. Discuss why a hotel's GM must be "values-focused." Explain how corporate values ultimately impact employee behavior. Identify four corporate values that are important to include when identifying the corporate values for a hotel management firm; explain why each value was selected.
9. Why does a hotel use a functional organizational structure? Identify the EOC members for a large upper-upscale or luxury hotel. Explain the role of each.

ENDNOTES

Bay Area Economic Institute (2013). *The Economic Impact of San Francisco Hotels.* Hotel Council of San Francisco, California.

Bowen, J. T. & Chen, S. L. (2001). The relationship between customer loyalty and customer satisfaction. *International Journal of Contemporary Hospitality Management*; *13*(4/5), 213–217.

Herzberg, F.; Mausner, B.; & Synderman, B.B. (1959). *The Motivation to Work*; Wiley Publishing; New York, New York.

Heskett, J.L.; Jones, T.O.; Loveman, G.W.; Sasser J.E., & Schlesinger, L.A. (1994). Putting the service-profit chain to work. *Harvard Business Review*; *72*(2), 164–174.

Heskett, J. L.; Sasser, W. E.; & Schlesinger, L. A. (1997). *The Service Profit Chain: How Leading Companies Link Profit and Growth to Loyalty, Satisfaction, and Value.* The Free Press, New York, New York.

Marriott, Jr., J.W.; & Brown, K.A. (1997). *The Spirit to Serve: Marriott's Way.* HarperCollins Publishers, New York, NY.

Spreitzer, G. M. (1996). Social structural characteristics of psychological empowerment. *Academy of Management Journal*; *39*(2), 483 – 504.

STR (2017). *Host report: Upper-upscale hotels for year-ending 2015.* SHARE Center.

www.hilton.com (2018). Hilton vision, mission, and value statements. Accessed online at: https://www.hilton.com/en/corporate/

HOTEL DEVELOPMENT PROJECT

Students completing a course in hotel, lodging, or resort management are encouraged to complete a hotel development project over the course of the semester/term; students are encouraged to work in small groups of 3 – 5 students. *Appendix A* outlines the project in its entirety.

Assignment 2: Vision, Mission, and Values

Use content from: Chapter 2: Successful Hotel Management

Assume the proposed hotel that your team is developing will be managed by a hotel management firm that your team will establish. Based upon the information provided within this chapter, please develop the following for this newly established hospitality management company:

1. Create an aspirational corporate vision statement.
2. Keeping the all-square operating philosophy in mind, create a mission statement.
3. Define the corporate values that will be used to guide the beliefs and behaviors of associates employed by the firm.
4. Describe the corporate culture that you will strive to create and preserve.
5. Based upon this vision, mission, and values, create a name for your hospitality or hotel management firm.

Section Two

BUILDING GUEST AND CLIENT RELATIONSHIPS

SECTION 2: BUILDING GUEST AND CLIENT RELATIONSHIPS

Chapter 3: Defining Guest Segments

This chapter defines the various guest or customer segments served by hotels. By effectively segmenting guests into clearly defined market segments, hoteliers can employ specific strategies to build mutually-beneficial relationships and deliver value to each segment targeted.

Chapter 4: Effective Sales and Marketing

This chapter outlines the sales and marketing activities in which a hotel may engage to generate strong demand for its accommodations, products, and experiences with an emphasis on direct sales.

Chapter 5: Optimizing Revenue

This chapter examines the role of a successful revenue management team and identifies how benchmarking, hotel pricing strategies, careful customer selection, and revenue protection strategies are used to optimize hotel revenue.

Section 2 Supplement: Sales Team Deployment: A Tale of Two Markets

This supplement to Section 2: Building Guest and Client Relationships provides insight into how a professional sales team may be deployed, based upon specific market characteristics, to optimize their productivity. This case-study style reading contrasts two significantly different markets—Fort Myers, Florida and San Francisco, California.

Chapter 3
Defining Guest Segments

Consumers of hotel services are seeking hotel accommodations—a hotel's core service—often in combination with a range of peripheral services, including food, beverage, and conference services. This chapter defines the various guest or customer segments served by hotels. By effectively segmenting guests into clearly defined market segments, hoteliers can employ specific strategies to build mutually-beneficial relationships with targeted segments of hotel guests through the delivery of value to these customers.

PURPOSE AND LEARNING OBJECTIVES:

This chapter will provide readers with an in-depth understanding as to how an effective hotel management team defines guest segments and bundles its services to successfully deliver value to these segments. At the conclusion of this chapter, students will be able to:

- Explain the core and peripheral services offered by various types of hotels.
- Describe how hotels bundle services to provide value to guests.
- Define various segments of individual travelers or transient guests.
- Define various segments of group guests.
- Explain how meeting space is used by a hotel to optimize profitability.
- Estimate the amount of meeting space required by a hotel to achieve targeted group occupancy.
- Define contract guests.
- Calculate a minimum acceptable rate (MAR) for potential contract business using a displacement analysis.

CORE AND PERIPHERAL SERVICES

As introduced in *Chapter 1: Introduction to the Hotel Industry*, a core service is the primary service product offered to meet customers' needs common to all service providers within a specified industry. In the hotel industry, the core service is overnight accommodations—all hotels provide, at a minimum, a place for guests to sleep overnight, bathe or shower, and prepare for the day. Peripheral services are ancillary services that are provided to customers to add value to the customer experience. In the hotel industry, peripheral services that are commonly available to overnight hotel guests include Food and Beverage (F&B) services, meeting space and conference services, exercise facilities, business services, parking, and transportation. The specific range of peripheral services offered by a hotel is dependent upon a variety of factors including the hotel's pricing strategy and location. For example, a hotel in an urban location may not have parking available on-the-premises, whereas a suburban hotel may offer complimentary parking, and a hotel located at a large international airport may offer parking for a fee or as part of a park-and-fly package or service bundle. A service bundle is two or more service products that are offered for purchase in combination with one another for a sin-

core service:
the primary service product offered to meet customers' needs common to all service providers within a specified industry

peripheral services:
ancillary services that are provided to customers to add value to the customer experience

service bundle:
two or more service products that are offered for purchase in combination with one another for a single price

gle price. The most popular service bundle offered in the hotel industry is overnight accommodations together with breakfast. When service products are bundled, it is not clear to the consumer the price that is being charged for each service individually and the customer pays the agreed-upon price whether he/she consumes the entire collection of bundled services or not. In many cases, as with the hotel room and breakfast, customers may perceive that the ancillary service is provided on a complimentary basis (for free).

Many hotels offer a full range of services to its guests including hotel accommodations; F&B services; meeting space and conference services; business services; concierge services; luggage assistance; exercise facilities, often including a pool; wi-fi internet access; in-room entertainment; and airport transportation or transportation to nearby offices and attractions. Hotels that offer, at a minimum, hotel accommodations; F&B services for breakfast, lunch, and dinner; and conference space and meeting services are referred to as full-service hotels. Hotels that offer less than this full range of services are referred to as select-service hotels. Many select-service hotels employ a value-driven strategy and provide guests with overnight accommodations and access to a complimentary breakfast buffet for a specified time period each morning (typically, a 3-hour time frame). Breakfast is the most commonly consumed meal in a hotel and the cost of providing breakfast is reasonable, particularly in relationship to guests' perception of the value added by breakfast. In other words, guests may perceive that a complimentary breakfast is worth $10 to $15 or more in out-of-pocket savings to the customer per guest staying in the room, depending upon the specific items offered on the buffet; yet the cost of providing the buffet may only run $3 to $5 in actual food cost per guest. Consequently, the inclusion of breakfast, bundled together with overnight accommodations, is an effective way to add value, as defined in the value equation (*Formula 2.1*), to the guest experience. Hotel segments—from economy hotels at the low end of the scale to luxury hotels at the high end—are defined largely based upon their average daily rates (ADR) as outlined in *Chapter 1: Introduction to the Hotel Industry.*

full-service hotels: offer, at a minimum, overnight accommodations; F&B services for breakfast, lunch, and dinner; and conference space and meeting services

select-service hotels: offer overnight accommodations and no, or only a limited degree of peripheral services

value equation: a formula conceptualizing how customers calculate the perceived worth of a product, service, or experience

a la carte:
the pricing and sale of products and services individually

individual or transient guests:
a party of guests requiring fewer than 10 total room nights during a single stay

room night:
a hotel accommodation occupied by a guest or guests for a single night

individual business travelers (IBT):
transient guests traveling for work-related purposes

corporate travelers
IBTs that do not qualify for a specific discounted room rate

volume accounts
organizations that negotiate a discounted room rate in exchange for generating a specified number of room nights annually

corporate rate
a room rate offered to IBTs that do not qualify for a discount

The range of services offered to guests, and the quality of those offerings, expand as the ADR increases. Guests that pay higher room rates are generally less price sensitive and, as a result, the services offered in full-service hotels are commonly priced individually or *a la carte* as opposed to being bundled, as is common in select-service hotels. Guests staying in upper-upscale and luxury hotels are seeking specific services and experiences and are typically willing to pay for those services and experiences individually. There is typically some overlap in the mid-priced upper-midscale and upscale segments of the industry—both segments include some select-service and full-service hotels in many markets; however, hotels in the less expensive economy and mid-scale segments are typically select-service hotels, whereas more expensive upper-upscale and luxury hotels are almost exclusively full-service hotels.

INDIVIDUAL (TRANSIENT) GUEST SEGMENTS

Hotel guests may be segmented based upon whether they are traveling individually or with others as part of a larger group. As a rule, a party of guests requiring fewer than 10 total room nights during a single stay is defined as individual or transient guests; recall from *Chapter 2* that a room night is defined as one night's accommodations (one room for one night). Furthermore, transient guests may be further segmented based upon the purpose of their travel—business, pleasure (often referred to as leisure), or a combination of both. Consequently, the individual travel segments are broadly categorized as business travelers or leisure travelers. Generally speaking, business travelers are less price sensitive than leisure travelers because their employer is typically covering their travel costs.

Individual business travelers (IBT) are further segmented into corporate travelers, guests that are traveling for work-related purposes and do not qualify for any specific discounted room rates, and volume accounts. The corporate rate is a room rate at or near the top of all room rates offered because it is generally offered to any guest traveling on business. Although an IBT guest may be less price sensitive personally than a leisure traveler because they are traveling on a company expense account, business travel costs are a large expense item for many firms. As a result, many firms negotiate discounts with specific hotels located near their offices or other corporate facilities or with the hotel brands that are most popular with their

© LightField Studios/Shutterstock.com

employees that travel on behalf of their firm, often committing to generate a specified number of room nights on a monthly or annual basis to justify the discount. Business travelers that are either employed by or conducting business with these volume accounts qualify for the discounted rates. Another source of a high volume of room nights is the US government. Government travelers employed by the federal government are reimbursed for their travel based upon a *per diem* reimbursement rate; *per diem* is a Latin phrase, which means "by the day." The US government establishes *per diem* room rates for all hotel markets in the United States based upon market conditions and the ADR within each market; federal government per diem room rates are substantially lower than corporate rates and may be found online for any specific market using the following URL: https://www.gsa.gov/travel/plan-book/per-diem-rates/per-diem-rates-lookup. A government traveler that pays a room rate higher than the government *per diem* will only be reimbursed the *per diem* amount, which results in the employee subsidizing his/her work-related travel costs. Consequently, a hotel must set the government room rate at or below the *per diem* rate to generate a substantial volume of government business. State governments also establish *per diem* rates, which are typically even lower than the federal *per diem*; again, a hotel that wants to enjoy a substantial volume of state government business, which is particularly true if a hotel is located in a state capitol or near a state facility that generates in-bound travel, will need to charge a room rate at or below the state *per diem* to state employees. Travelers requesting government *per diem* rates will typically be asked to show government or military identification upon registration to confirm that they qualify to receive the deeply discounted government *per diem* guestroom rate. As a result, a government per diem rate is further defined as a qualified discount because the traveler must qualify or provide evidence of his/her eligibility to receive the discount.

Other qualified discounts, or discounted guestroom rates to which guests are entitled due to their affiliation with a specific company, organization, club, or other clearly-defined, verifiable criterion, include the American Automobile Association (AAA) rate; American Association of Retired Persons (AARP) rate or senior citizen discount; travel industry rate, often offered to verified travel agents or airline employees for their personal travel; and others depending upon the specific hotel and its location. In addition, hotels extend discounted rates to many high-volume travel agencies, which include the Online Travel Agents (OTAs), such as Expedia, Travelocity, and Priceline, as well as the major travel consortia including American Express Travel, Carlson Wagonlit Travel, and Christopherson Business Travel. A travel consortium is a group of travel agencies that form a voluntary alliance to leverage their collective purchasing power to obtain more deeply discounted pricing for their clients on travel services than the agency or their clients could obtain independently. In the case of OTAs and consortia, travelers that book their travel through the respective distribution channel receive the discounted room rate. Although many of the qualified discounts are intended to attract leisure travelers, qualified discounts must be extended to any qualified traveler when it is offered.

per diem:
the daily reimbursement rate for travel expenses, including hotel accommodations, for government travelers

qualified discount:
a discount offered to guests that can provide evidence of their eligibility to receive the discount

online travel agents (OTAs):
intermediaries that market and sell travel products and services Online and through mobile applications

travel consortium:
a group of travel agencies that form a voluntary alliance to leverage their collective purchasing power to obtain more deeply discounted pricing for their clients on travel services

distribution channel:
a chain of intermediaries through which a product or service passes from the provider to the end user

© dotshock/Shutterstock.com

leisure guests:
transient travelers traveling for personal reasons

packages:
service bundles that improve the value proposition by providing discounted access to desired services or activities

Consequently, many business travelers, as well as smaller firms that may not generate enough volume to qualify for discounted room rates on their own, establish relationships with travel consortia, use OTAs, and employ other strategies to lower their travel costs. Please refer to *Chapter 5: Optimizing Revenue*, to better understand how hotels establish, control, and monitor these discounted guestroom rates.

Leisure guests are transient travelers traveling for personal reasons—to spend time with family or friends, to explore new places, or to participate in specific cultural, sightseeing, or other recreational activities; they are also typically paying for their own travel costs. Consequently, leisure guests may be more price sensitive and are more likely to purchase packages or service bundles that improve the value proposition by providing discounted access to desired services or activities. As previously explained, hotels offer a range of qualified discounts to attract more price sensitive customers. For example, many hotels extend the federal government *per diem* to military personnel traveling on leave to capture this segment of leisure travel. In addition, hotels often leverage the volume of business that their guests may generate for an in-house amenity or popular local attraction to facilitate obtaining discounted pricing that may be used to build an attractive package or service bundle. For example, a hotel located within a resort community may create a golf package that includes overnight accommodations and two rounds of golf on a nearby 18-hole championship golf course for a price that is less expensive than what the guests would spend if the hotel room and two rounds of golf were booked individually. To provide further value, the hotel may also include a complimentary breakfast buffet in the hotel's restaurant for each guest; as previously mentioned, breakfast adds substantial value in terms of guests' perceptions for a relatively low cost. Offering packages is a strategy that is often deployed by a hotel because it offers increased value to the guest without forcing the hotel to deeply discount the guestroom rate. Another common package offered to leisure guests is a "romance package," which typically includes a bottle of champagne upon check-in, which often costs the hotel less than $10 in additional costs, and breakfast in the morning, which also adds minimal cost per guest ($3–$5 in food cost), yet the guest may perceive that these two additional amenities add $50 or more in value to the stay if purchased separately (*Box 3.1: How Packaging Adds Value*). Finally, hotels often offer weekend, holiday, or other promotional rates to leisure travelers during time periods when business travel is weak; it is not uncommon for a business guest to extend his/ her stay at a lower promotional rate after concluding the business portion of a trip.

BOX 3.1: HOW PACKAGING ADDS VALUE

A service bundle is two or more service products that are offered for purchase in combination with one another for a single price. Hotels often offer packages, or service bundles, to provide a more attractive value proposition to guests, while reducing the need to deeply discount the hotel room rate. Outlined in Table 3.1 is the retail value of services offered to guests of a hotel, along with the direct cost of providing each of the additional services or amenities. By offering the services as a service bundle—at a package price—guests will often perceive that they are being extended a lower rate for the hotel accommodations even though the hotel may not actually discount the room rate. In this example of a *"Romance Package,"* the hotel increases the price of the package an additional $20 above the standard room rate available, yet the guests still perceive that they are being offered a "deal" because the retail value of the additional services bundled together with the hotel room total $71.90—adding more than $50 of value from the guests' perspective.

© Africa Studio/Shutterstock.com

Services included in a "Romance Package"	Retail price	Direct cost of additional amenities
Hotel accommodations	$ 179.00	
Chilled bottle of champagne (delivered to room)	$ 40.00	$ 10.00
Breakfast buffet for 2 guests ($15.95 each)	$ 31.90	$ 10.00
Total price paid, if purchased individually	$ 250.90	
Package price	$ 199.00	
"Value-added" as perceived by the guest	*$ 51.90*	
Total added direct cost to the hotel		*$ 20.00*

Table 3.1: Quantifying the Value Added through Packaging

In other words, when purchasing this *"Romance Package,"* the guests receive $71.90 in additional services for only $20.00 and perceive that they are being given $51.90 of free or complimentary amenities/services (champagne and breakfast), although the hotel is actually adding the $20.00 to cover the direct costs of providing the added amenities to the $179 price of the guestroom. Consequently, the hotel can provide the value-added amenities without discounting the actual room rate—a "win-win" proposition for both the hotel and its guests!

Within the preceding paragraphs regarding individual or transient guest segments, there has been much discussion about discounted rates. Non-discounted rates are commonly referred to as the best available rate (BAR), published, or rack rate. The term *rack rate* originated when hotels maintained the status of their guestroom inventory by using a room rack; a room rack is a large display that was historically maintained behind the front desk that indicated the status of each guestroom. On this rack, there was a slot for each guestroom in the hotel; a color-coded "rack card" was inserted into each slot that indicated the room number, bedding configuration within the room, and the standard room rate (or rack rate) charged for the room. Cards were inserted backwards into the slot, when rooms were "on change" or in the process of being serviced; occupied rooms had a "rack slip" placed in front of the respective room's rack card with the guest's name, actual room rate, and dates of occupancy noted on the rack slip. Although the room rack has now been replaced by automated property management (computer) systems in most hotels, the term "rack rate" is still used by some in the industry to refer to the full, published room rate for a given room type, particularly for a hotel that uses rate fences.

Best available or rack rates are determined based upon the hotel's location, the room rates of a hotel's direct competitors, an assessment of product and service quality relative to the hotel's direct competitors, and market conditions. If a hotel uses a rate fence pricing strategy, rack rates are generally charged to a small proportion of total guests, often less than 10% to 15% of a hotel's guests; however, establishing appropriate rack rates is critically important because these rates serve as the basis from which discounts are taken. Rack rates represent the maximum rates that are charged when demand in a market is at its peak and, in many jurisdictions, hotel or innkeeper laws require that the maximum rate that will be charged for a room is posted within the guestroom to prevent over-charging or price gouging. Today, many hotels implement a dynamic pricing strategy. With a dynamic strategy a higher proportion of guests will pay the published rate than with a more traditional rate fence pricing strategy; however, the rate is typically referred to as the BAR and the rate varies based upon anticipated demand within the market. A full, detailed discussion on how BAR, published, and rack rates, as well as discounts, are established and managed is included in *Chapter 5: Optimizing Revenue*.

To summarize, transient guests typically require less than 10 room nights per stay and are traveling on business, for leisure purposes, or a combination of both. A portion of hotel guests will pay the rack or BAR for their rooms; however, many guests seek some form of a discount. A business traveler will often be offered a corporate rate, which is a non-qualified discount that offers, at most, a modest discount off the rack or published rate. Because business guests tend to be less rate sensitive, many hotels simply offer a BAR that is offered to any guest, business or leisure, that does not qualify for a discounted rate. Firms that generate a large volume of room nights on a monthly or annual basis for an individual hotel property or a hotel chain or parent company will often

best available rate (BAR):
non-discounted room rate offered to travelers for their requested dates

published rate:
room rate being marketed by the hotel through a specific distribution channel

rack rate:
the highest non-discounted room rate offered by a hotel

rate fence:
a pricing strategy that prohibits guestrooms from being sold (rented) to guest segments priced below a specific room rate (fence) based upon anticipated demand each day

price gouging:
taking advantage of strong demand to charge excessive room rates that fail to offer equitable value

dynamic pricing strategy:
a pricing approach in which room rates fluctuate based upon anticipated demand

negotiate a volume discount, and transient guests that are employed by the firm, or are conducting business with the firm, will qualify for the discount. The federal and state governments are also large consumers of hotel room nights. Consequently, they establish government *per diems*, which is the amount that they reimburse government employees per day when traveling on government-related business; hotels must offer room rates at or below the government *per diem* rates to enjoy a substantial volume of room nights from transient government guests. Transient guests, both business and leisure, may also qualify for discounts by meeting specified criteria or by booking through a specific distribution channel, such as an OTA or travel consortia. Leisure guests are much more likely than business travelers to book packages, which include hotel accommodations bundled with additional services for a single price, to maximize value. Leisure guests will also take advantage of weekend, holiday, and other promotional rates that may be offered during time periods when business travel declines. The transient guest segments are summarized in *Diagram 3.1*.

Individual Business Travel (IBT)
Best Available Rate (BAR)
Corporate
Volume accounts
Government (Federal & State)
Consortia
Online Travel Agents (OTAs)

Leisure Travel
Best Available Rate (BAR)
Qualified discounts
Military
Packages
Weekend/Promotional
Consortia
Online Travel Agents (OTAs)

Diagram 3.1: Transient Guest Segments

GROUP GUEST SEGMENTS

Group guests typically consume 10 room nights or more in a single visit, although a more specific definition will vary by property, management company, or parent company. For example, some hotels or hotel organizations require a minimum of 10 rooms for a single date, whereas others consider any group requiring a minimum of

10 room nights, in any combination of room and night multiples, to be managed as a group, particularly if the group is using hotel meeting space. Group segments include corporate, government, association, and social, military, educational, religious, and fraternal (SMERF) guests.

Corporate group guest segments may be further divided by specific industries—such as financial services, technology, biomedical, legal, etc.—depending upon the specific market and the range of firms that operate within the destination. Many industries tend to concentrate in a handful of geographic markets. For example, many technology firms operate in the Silicon Valley, south of San Francisco; the entertainment industry is focused in Southern California; the automobile industry in Detroit; and several large national banks operate out of Charlotte, North Carolina. Consequently, it is often important for a hotel to track business from a specific industry and to develop expertise in accommodating groups from these major corporate sub-segments. Hotels will also track groups booked by volume accounts as a separate group segment as well as small groups, often referred to as "express meetings," which are typically defined as groups requiring 50 room nights or less. Corporate groups typically meet and require accommodations during the weekdays (Sunday through Thursday night stays) because they are work-related. Another group segment that typically meets during the weekdays is the government segment. Government groups typically prefer to book group meetings in hotels that will offer the government *per diem*; however, if a government group is unable to find a suitable hotel with availability that will offer the *per diem* rate to the group, a government agency may contract to pay a higher rate.

association:
an organization of people with a common purpose and a formal structure

An association is an organization of people with a common purpose and a formal structure. Countless associations exist to serve the needs of specific professions, industries, and special interest groups. Examples include the American Medical Association, American Bar Association, National Automobile Dealers Association, American Hotel and Lodging Association, National Restaurant Association, and the American Quarter Horse Association, just to name a few. Association group guests are subdivided into international, national, state, and regional categories, depending upon the scope of the organization. The offices for many national associations in the United States are in the Washington, D.C. area because a major role for many associations is to advocate for the industry or people served by the organization with government representatives—a practice referred to as lobbying. For similar reasons, many

lobbying:
advocating for an industry or members of an association with government representatives

state-level associations have offices located in their respective state capitol. A major source of revenue for most associations is their annual conference; associations also use this opportunity to keep their members engaged with the mission and activities of the association. Many associations also hold regional meetings, as well as continuing education and training workshops. As a result, associations are a major source of group guests for many hotels. Because many associations are business-related, while others are more socially-oriented or centered on avocations, some associations prefer to meet during weekdays, whereas others will meet on weekends.

SMERF groups include weddings, reunions (school, family, and military), educational groups, youth organizations, religious organizations, sports tournaments, service clubs, bar and bat mitzvahs, fraternal organizations, and many others. These social events typically occur on the weekends or during holidays and, because participants are paying the cost of attending these events out-of-pocket, these groups tend to be very rate sensitive. Because SMERF clients are typically seeking deeply discounted rates, SMERF groups are used by hotels to fill low demand periods when business and association travel soften, such as during weekends and holiday periods in many markets.

SMERF groups: guests with a social, military, educational, religious or fraternal affiliation generating 10 or more room nights

Corporate groups
Industry specific
Volume accounts
Express meetings (< 50 room nights)

Government
Federal
State
Local (municipal or county)

Association groups
Industry advocacy
Professional
Avocation or special interest
Scope: International, national, state or regional

Social, Military, Educational, Religious and Fraternal (SMERF)
Weddings
Reunions (school, family, & military)
Educational groups
Youth organizations
Religious organizations
Sports tournaments
Service clubs

Citywide Conventions
Corporate
Government
Association
SMERF

Diagram 3.2: Group Guest Segments

© Matej Kastelic/Shutterstock.com

MEETING AND CONFERENCE SPACE

The financial success of a hotel is dependent upon the success of the guestroom operation—the rooms division generates the greatest contribution margin and the largest portion of a hotel's profit, as outlined in *Chapter 2: Successful Hotel Management*. Consequently, the meeting and conference space within a hotel exists, first and foremost, to increase the demand for hotel guestrooms. It is almost always preferable to use the hotel's meeting space to accommodate groups that will generate hotel room revenue versus simply generating meeting room rental or catering revenue alone, because the contribution margin generated by hotel room revenue is much greater than the contribution margin generated by meetings and banquets; the rare exception is over dates during which the entire inventory of hotel accommodations may be sold to transient guests, in which case the meeting room rental and catering revenues may be considered incremental revenue because the hotel's guestrooms are already fully occupied.

To bolster demand for a hotel's accommodations, many upscale, and most upper-upscale and luxury hotels, offer meeting and conference space, in addition to a full range of conference and catering services. The exact amount of meeting space, as well as the configuration of that space, is dependent upon several factors, including the total number of hotel rooms within the hotel as well as the anticipated transient demand for overnight accommodations within the market. For example, the developer of a 400-room upper-upscale hotel may determine that the hotel may be able to consistently attract demand from 100 transient guests or more per night; therefore, the developer many want to include sufficient meeting space within the hotel to support groups requiring as many as 300 guestrooms per night to fill the hotel's total guestroom service capacity. To support groups requiring 300 rooms per night, the hotel would require a

service capacity:
the maximum number of customers that may be appropriately served in a specified time period

minimum of 3,000 square feet of meeting space and, ideally, would contain 12,000 square feet or more of meeting space, along with appropriate pre-function space. Pre-function space consists of lobbies and corridors outside of the meeting space that may be used to hold guests waiting to enter a scheduled meeting or event, for registration tables, and for coffee breaks, receptions, and other group events that do not require an enclosed, private conference room; the amount of pre-function space in a hotel typically consists of approximately 25% to 50% of the total enclosed, private meeting space available within the property. In other words, a hotel with 12,000 square feet of conference space will typically have an additional 3,000 to 6,000 square feet of pre-function space. Meeting space is typically configured so that it may be subdivided into spaces of various dimensions and sizes using operable walls or airwalls.

pre-function space: consists of lobbies and corridors outside of the meeting space that may be used to hold guests waiting to enter a scheduled meeting or event, for registration tables, and for coffee breaks, receptions, and other group events that do not require an enclosed, private conference room

operable walls or airwalls: mechanical walls that may be used to subdivide a large meeting space into smaller rooms

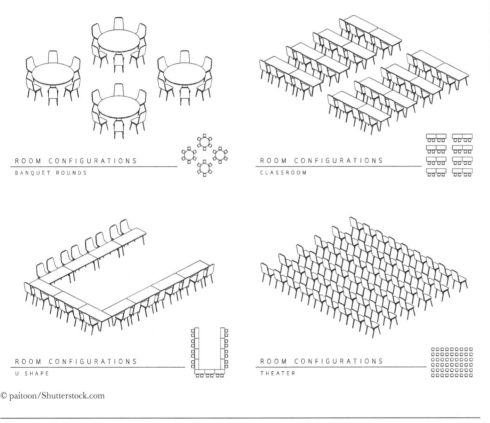

ROOM CONFIGURATIONS
BANQUET ROUNDS

ROOM CONFIGURATIONS
CLASSROOM

ROOM CONFIGURATIONS
U SHAPE

ROOM CONFIGURATIONS
THEATER

© paitoon/Shutterstock.com

Diagram 3.3: Common Conference Room Layouts

Returning to our example, a single occupancy group occupying 300 rooms would require approximately 3,000 square feet of meeting space to host a conference in which the participants were all participating in a single session while seated in a theater configuration, as illustrated in *Diagram 3.3: Common Conference Room Layouts*; however, most conferences require more than a single meeting room, in addition to requiring more

theater configuration: the most efficient group seating arrangement with a seat for each meeting attendee arranged in rows

classroom configuration:
a group seating arrangement with meeting attendees seated at rectangular tables set up in parallel rows

plenary session:
a single meeting at a conference expected to be attended by all conference participants

breakout sessions:
meetings held at a conference that are attended by subsets of the conference participants

banquet rounds:
large, round tables that may seat 8 - 12 guests

meeting space intensive:
groups that require a larger amount of meeting space per group room night relative to alternative groups

complex conference room layouts. A theater configuration is among the most efficient meeting room configurations, requiring just 9 to 10 square feet of meeting space per participant. If a group requires a classroom conference room configuration, then the space requirements increase to 18 to 24 square feet per attendee, depending if the conference planner specifies an 18 or 30 inch table depth; this would expand the minimum space required for an event with 300 attendees to as much as 7,200 square feet. Many conferences require a conference room for a plenary session, set theater style, and then additional rooms for breakout sessions during which the conference attendees split into smaller sub-groups to attend sessions on specialized topics of interest. In addition, many groups require a separate space in which meals may be served because lunch service, for example, needs to be set-up while the morning meetings are in session. A meal function for 300 guests, served at banquet rounds, may require nearly 3,600 square feet of meeting space. Consequently, it is not unreasonable to expect that accommodating a conference for 300 attendees—requiring a 300-attendee plenary session set theater style (10 square feet [sf] per attendee or 3,000 sf); three 100-person breakouts set classroom (18 sf per attendee or 5,400 sf); and a separate room set with banquet rounds for breakfast and lunch for 300 guests (12 sf per attendee or 3,600 sf)—to require a total of 12,000 square feet of meeting space. If the 300 rooms, or a significant portion of these rooms, are sold to groups that generate double, triple, or even quadruple-occupancy per guestroom, then the square footage of meeting space required to support the group may double to 24,000 sf, triple to 36,000 sf, or quadruple to 48,000 sf.

The key point relative to understanding guest segmentation and relationships is that a hotel that aspires to attract group guests will need to target the guest segments that the hotel is able to accommodate within its meeting space. Association groups are typically more meeting space intensive, which means that they often require a large amount of meeting space per group room night, whereas SMERF groups often require a more moderate amount of meeting space, and government and corporate groups may, in some cases, not require any meeting space because their respective meetings may take place at government or corporate facilities located in close proximity to the host hotel, although this is not always the case. Additional discussions regarding meeting space requirements, configurations, and usage, are included in *Chapter 5: Optimizing Revenue*, and *Chapter 8: Food and Beverage Operations*.

Finally, it should be noted that many government organizations construct convention centers and employ additional strategies to attract meetings and other large-scale events to a destination to increase demand for hotel accommodations. Because hotel occupancy taxes represent a large source of tax revenue in many jurisdictions, municipal, county, and state governments often subsidize the operation of a convention center that accommodates the less profitable activity of providing meeting and event space for conferences, in addition to providing financial support to Destination

Marketing Organizations (DMOs), also referred to as Convention and Visitors Bureaus (CVBs), because the hotel taxes generated by hotel guests attending these events more than offset the cost of these subsidies (*Box 3.2: The Moscone Convention Center*). Conferences and events that take place in a municipality's convention center and generate room nights for multiple hotels within the destination are referred to as citywide conventions. Many hotels that rent blocks of rooms to these large, citywide conventions classify these room nights as a separate group market segment. Although citywide groups are very often association or SMERF groups, they may come from any segment including the corporate or government segments. Consequently, citywides may be further sub-categorized as appropriate based upon the specific nature of the group. The various group guest segments are summarized in *Diagram 3.2*.

destination marketing organization (DMO)/ convention and visitors bureaus (CVB): a government or non-profit entity formed to promote in-bound travel to a community

citywide conventions: conferences and events that take place in a municipality's convention center and generate room nights for multiple hotels within the destination

CONTRACT GUESTS

The final guest segment defined is contract guests. Firms and organizations that require hotel accommodations over an extended period, typically a minimum of 30 days, may enter into a contract with a hotel to secure a specific number of hotel rooms over a specific set of dates. The contract establishes the terms for a long-term lease on a specified number of hotel rooms and the client is charged for the hotel rooms each night for the duration of the contract, regardless of whether the rooms are fully occupied. A common example is the rental of accommodations for airline flight crews.

contract guests: clients that secure a specific number of rooms over a continuous set of dates of 30-days or longer

Airlines enter into contracts with hotels to acquire hotel accommodations for the pilots and flight attendants employed by the airline that arrive to various destinations and are unable to return to their home airport due to flight safety restrictions. The Federal Aviation Administration (FAA) restricts pilots from operating an aircraft in flight for longer than 8 to 9 hours within a 24-hour period, depending upon various circumstances; once the maximum number of flight hours has been reached, the pilot and crew must rest for a minimum of 10 hours before their next flight (www.faa.gov, n.d.). Consequently, the major airlines secure dozens of hotel rooms in many locations on an annual basis to accommodate its flight crews. Because of the large volume of room nights generated by the airlines through these contracts, coupled with the long-term nature of the rentals, airlines typically receive deeply discounted hotel room rates. The room rate charged for these rooms is determined through the execution of a displacement analysis, which is explained in *Box 3.3: Displacement Analysis for Contract Rooms*.

displacement analysis: analysis conducted to determine the MAR that a hotel should accept for a long-term room contract

Contracted rooms may be occupied by different guests for single night stays, as in the case of the airlines, or by the same guests for extended stays. Many firms, including law, construction, consulting, and auditing firms, may rent blocks of rooms for 30 days or longer to accommodate employees that are working in the destination on a

BOX 3.2: THE MOSCONE CONVENTION CENTER

© Sheila Fitzgerald

The Moscone Convention Center, located in San Francisco, California, is comprised of over two million square feet of building area that includes over 700,000 square feet of exhibit space, 106 meeting rooms, and nearly 123,000 square feet of pre-function lobbies. The original Center, now referred to as Moscone South, was completed in 1981. The first major expansion of the Center occurred in 1991 and 1992, which included the Esplanade Ballroom and Moscone North. Eleven years later, in 2003, Moscone West opened its doors for business. A third expansion of Moscone is just being completed (2018) that adds over 305,000 square feet of functional area, including new exhibition space, meeting room and pre-function space, and an additional ballroom, as well as support areas. Proponents of the most recent expansion boast that hotel tax revenues directly generated as a result of this third expansion will total more than $20 million annually. The project is expected to create 3,400 permanent new jobs and is anticipated to generate a net economic impact of over $734 million through 2026 (www.mosconeexpansion.com, n.d.). The Moscone Convention Center is named to honor the former Mayor of San Francisco, George R. Moscone, who was an advocate for the construction of the Center, which was funded and is still owned by the City and County of San Francisco.

The Moscone Convention Center was built with one purpose in mind—to generate demand for hotel accommodations in San Francisco. Mayor Moscone and the City's leadership recognized the benefits of a vibrant, tourism-driven economy. The hotel industry in San Francisco is an economic juggernaut—generating an annual economic impact in the Bay Area of over $6.0 billion each year, which supports 62,000 jobs, and tax revenues of more than $250 million annually (see *Tables 3.2* through *3.4*). Of the $250+ million in occupancy taxes generated by hotel guests, two-thirds (67%) of the tax revenue, or over $170 million, is contributed to the City's general fund, which is used to fund the general operation of the City and County of San Francisco, making the hotel industry the largest single source of tax revenue for the "City by the Bay" (Bay Area Economic Council, 2013).

Source	Direct impact	%	Indirect impact	%	Total impact	%
Hotel revenues	2,100,000,000	48%	1,356,000,000	61%	3,456,000,000	52%
Capital expenditures	0	0%	160,000,000	7%	160,000,000	2%
Visitor spending	2,300,000,000	52%	718,000,000	32%	3,018,000,000	45%
Total	**4,400,000,000**	**66%**	**2,234,000,000**	**34%**	**6,634,000,000**	**100%**

Table 3.2: Economic Impact of San Francisco Hotels

Source	San Francisco	%	Rest of Bay Area	%	Total	%
Hotel revenues	24,312	41%	1,624	50%	25,936	42%
Capital expenditures	1,331	2%	79	2%	1,410	2%
Visitor spending	33,269	56%	1,538	47%	34,807	56%
Total	**58,912**	**95%**	**3,241**	**5%**	**62,153**	**100%**

Table 3.3: Jobs Supported by San Francisco Hotels

From *The Economic Impact of San Francisco Hotels.* Copyright © 2013 by Hotel Council of San Francisco. Used by permission.

Moscone Center hosts a wide variety of conferences—for associations, corporations, government, and SMERF groups. Moscone's state-of-the-art facilities are specifically designed to host technology-focused conferences due to the high concentration of bio-technology and technology firms located in the San Francisco Bay Area, which includes the Silicon Valley. The Moscone Center is professionally managed by SMG Worldwide Entertainment & Convention Venue Management (www.smgworld.com); however, the facility actually operates at a loss despite the more than $10 million in operating revenues and additional $35.6 million in F&B revenues generated by the Center each year. To offset this loss, 13.5% of the hotel taxes collected, totaling over $34 million, are used to offset this operating loss. In addition, convention delegates attending events at Moscone Center also pay taxes to the City and County on restaurant meals, admission fees to tourism and cultural venues, as well as through their retail shopping activities. Consequently, the Center's operating losses are dwarfed by the tax revenues gained by the City and County—not to mention the jobs and additional economic benefits indirectly resulting from the Moscone Convention Center's operation.

The fact that the Moscone Center operates at a loss illustrates why hotel developers are reluctant to invest in conference and banquet facilities when developing a hotel. Although developers will invest in building some meeting and banquet facilities when constructing a new hotel, hotel investors prefer to invest as large a proportion of their investment as possible in the construction of hotel rooms because the contribution margin on hotel rooms is 75% to 80% of room revenue versus 40% or less on food, beverage, and conference services revenues. Plus, guests will spend $150 to $350 or more per day on an upper-upscale or luxury hotel room versus often just a fraction of that on banquets and conference services each day of a conference—further increasing the financial benefit of investing in hotel rooms versus conference facilities. As a result, many local governments, such as the City and County of San Francisco, realize that investments by the public sector in conference facilities like the Moscone Center will be followed by private investment in the hotels, restaurants, and retail shopping facilities necessary to serve the convention delegates attracted each year. Ultimately, well-planned investments in public infrastructure to support conferences and tourism will typically generate the economic activity and tax revenues necessary to provide the community with a net return on their investments.

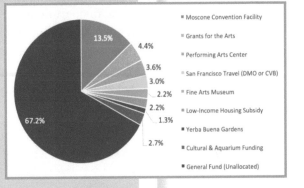

- Moscone Convention Facility
- Grants for the Arts
- Performing Arts Center
- San Francisco Travel (DMO or CVB)
- Fine Arts Museum
- Low-Income Housing Subsidy
- Yerba Buena Gardens
- Cultural & Aquarium Funding
- General Fund (Unallocated)

Table 3.4: Distribution of the $250 million+ in Tax Revenues Generated by San Francisco Hotels

From *The Economic Impact of San Francisco Hotels.* Copyright © 2013 by Hotel Council of San Francisco. Used by permission.

specific case or project. The hotel becomes the guests' home-away-from-home as they complete the project on behalf of their employer. Even if the employee occasionally vacates the room to return home for a weekend or other brief period, the firm will pay the rental for the room on a continuous basis. This is because the deeply discounted rate that is typically extended to the firm is based upon a continuous rental. In addition, if a hotel room is rented for longer than 30 days in most jurisdictions, the guest is not required to pay hotel occupancy taxes, which are typically between 10% and 15% of the room revenue; once a room is rented for over 30 days, it is equivalent to renting an apartment or other long-term housing and is not subject to accommodation taxes. By renting the rooms continuously, this also allows the occupant of the room the convenience of leaving his/her personal items in the guest room during any brief absences because guests staying for 30 days or longer will typically have a substantial amount of clothing and other personal items stored in their hotel rooms.

BOX 3.3: DISPLACEMENT ANALYSIS FOR CONTRACT ROOMS

© ESB Professional/
Shutterstock.com

Firms seeking to secure hotel accommodations for an extended period are typically able to obtain deep discounts because the incremental cost of servicing one additional room is minimal and, for many of the nights during the term of the contract, the guestroom may go vacant should the contract not be secured. To determine the MAR that a hotel should accept for a long-term contracted room, a displacement analysis may be conducted.

To determine the MAR for potential contract business, the hotel manager must estimate the number of nights during the term of the contract during which the contracted rooms will displace higher paying customers. Then, using the rate that will potentially be paid by the highest paying customers on nights higher paying customers may be displaced, the amount of incremental revenue that must be generated on nights during which no displacement takes place may be estimated to determine the MAR or break-even point. The formula that should be used is represented in *Formula 3.1: The Displacement Formula*:

$$m = \frac{d\,(p - m)}{(n - d)}$$

Where:

m = minimum acceptable rate
n = number of contracted room nights
d = number of higher rated room nights displaced
p = price obtained for the displaced room nights

Formula 3.1: The Displacement Formula

To clarify the concept, the use of the *displacement formula* to solve for *"m"* or the MAR is illustrated in the following example:

- An airline would like to book 10 rooms for flight crew use for the upcoming calendar year, which will generate 3,650 room nights (10 rooms X 365 nights). Consequently, $n = 3,650$.

- Based upon historical occupancy data, the hotel manager anticipates that the hotel will sell-out or fill all available hotel rooms for 100 nights during the upcoming calendar year or contract period. As a result, the contract with the airline will result in 1,000 higher-rated room nights being displaced (10 rooms X 100 nights) or $d = 1,000$.

- The hotel manager anticipates that the highest-priced rooms on these high demand nights will be sold for $229 each. Consequently, $p = \$229$.

- These values are then inserted into the displacement formula as outlined below:

$$m = \frac{1,000\ (229 - m)}{(3,650 - 1,000)}$$

- The formula is then solved for *"m"* and it is determined that the MAR for the contract is $62.74, which means that the contract should be accepted by the hotel if a room rate may be negotiated with the airline that exceeds $62.74.

To look at it another way, should the contract be accepted at $62.74 per room per night, the contract with the airline will generate $166,261 in revenue on the 265 dates during the year that the hotel is not sold out ($62.74 X 10 rooms X 265 days), which is the same amount of revenue that will be lost from the 10 higher paying customers that will be displaced on the 100 nights that the hotel is anticipated to sell all of its available service capacity [($229 - $62.74) X 10 rooms X 100 nights].

Although some hotel managers may be reluctant to offer such low room rates to contract clients, it simply makes financial sense to secure contract business above the break-even or MAR because accommodating the business increases a hotel's overall revenue. In addition, the increased occupancy assists the hotel in generating higher rates on peak demand nights and may also lower overall marketing costs because the hotel has fewer rooms to market and sell. If a 400-room hotel contracts to sell 30 to 40 rooms per night to contract guests, then the hotel's available service capacity is reduced by between 7.5% and 10%. This will allow the hotel to be more selective with the guests that it elects to accommodate on a greater number of nights throughout the contract period, which will assist the hotel in increasing the ADR charged to non-contract guest segments.

CHAPTER SUMMARY

Hotel managers clearly define various segments of customers or guests based upon the purpose of their travel and further segment these clients based upon the guests' level of rate sensitivity, business volume, and services required. Guest segments are broadly categorized as either transient (individual) or group travelers, which are defined as a group of guests requiring 10 or more room nights on a single visit. Transient travelers are further subdivided into IBT or leisure travelers. IBT guests tend to be less rate sensitive because the cost of their travel is typically covered by their employer, although many firms employ various strategies to lower their corporate travel costs. Leisure travelers tend to be more rate sensitive because they are typically paying their own travel expenses; many hotels create service bundles or packages that provide added-value to leisure travelers, which helps minimize the need to offer as many deeply discounted room rates. Hotels that seek group business typically use in-house meeting space to attract meetings and conferences. Although conference and catering revenue is an important source of incremental revenue for many hotels, the priority of a hotel is to use its meeting space to generate demand for hotel guestrooms because the contribution margin earned on hotel rooms is substantially higher than the margin earned on conference and banquet revenues. Due to the lower margins earned hosting conferences, coupled with the substantial hotel occupancy taxes generated by hotel room revenue—often taxed at between 10% and 15%—many government municipal, county, and state governments subsidize the hotel industry by using a portion of hotel tax revenues to build and operate convention centers, as well as to fund DMOs or CVBs. The in-bound travel resulting from these efforts generates economic activity that further increases tax revenues and employment opportunities and provides additional economic benefits within the destination. Although many hotels may be reluctant to establish contractual relationships to rent rooms on a long-term basis at deeply discounted rates, a displacement analysis may be conducted to determine the MARs above which it makes financial sense to accommodate these contract clients.

KEY TERMS AND CONCEPTS

a la carte
association
banquet rounds
best available rate (BAR)
breakout sessions
citywide conventions
classroom configuration
contract
convention and visitors bureaus
    (CVBs)

core service
corporate rate
corporate travelers
destination marketing
    organizations (DMOs)
displacement analysis
distribution channel
dynamic pricing strategy
full-service hotels
individual business travelers (IBT)

individual/transient guest
leisure guests
lobbying
meeting space intensive
online travel agents (OTAs)
operable walls/airwalls
packages
per diem
peripheral services
plenary session

pre-function space	rate fence	SMERF groups
price gouging	room night	theater configuration
published rate	select-service hotels	travel consortium
qualified discount	service bundle	value equation
rack rate	service capacity	volume accounts

DISCUSSION QUESTIONS

1. Identify the two most profitable transient guest segments and the two most profitable group guest segments. Explain the reasons for selecting each segment.

2. Identify the two least profitable transient guest segments and the two least profitable group guest segments. Again, explain the reasons for selecting each segment.

3. Assume that a hotel developer plans to develop a 500-room upper-upscale hotel; he/she wants a recommendation on how much meeting space to include in the hotel to support a 400-group room ceiling. How many square feet of meeting space is needed? How should the space be configured? Justify your answers.

4. Explain why many municipal, county, and state governments invest in tourism promotion and convention facilities. How are funds raised by these agencies to make these investments? What are the economic benefits of such investments?

5. The headquarters of a multinational corporation is near a hotel. The accounting firm that audits the corporation requires hotel rooms for weeks at a time and has requested a contract room rate at the hotel for eight rooms per night on an annual basis. A review of the hotel's projected occupancy indicates that the hotel will sell-out approximately 58 nights during the year. The BAR typically charged on sell-out nights is $219. Calculate the break-even rate for the potential contract. Explain how the break-even rate is used by the hotel.

ENDNOTES

Bay Area Economic Institute (2013). *The Economic Impact of San Francisco Hotels.* Hotel Council of San Francisco, California.

www.faa.gov (n.d.). Information retrieved from the Federal Aviation Administration website maintained by the *United States Department of Transportation*; accessed May 14, 2018.

www.mosconeexpansion.com (n.d.). Information retrieved from the Moscone Expansion website maintained by the *City and County of San Francisco, California*; accessed May 12, 2018.

HOTEL DEVELOPMENT PROJECT

Students completing a course in hotel, lodging, or resort management are encouraged to complete a hotel development project over the course of the semester/term; students are encouraged to work in small groups of 3 to 5 students. *Appendix A* outlines the project in its entirety.

The next *hotel development assignment* may be found at the conclusion of *Chapter 5: Optimizing Revenue.*

Chapter 4
Effective Sales and Marketing

Once a hotel has identified the specific guest segments that it is prepared to appropriately accommodate, an effective sales and marketing strategy must be identified to attract and secure relationships with these customers. This chapter outlines the sales and marketing activities in which hotel management may engage to generate strong demand for its accommodations, products, and experiences.

PURPOSE AND LEARNING OBJECTIVES:

An effective marketing strategy in a hotel environment includes an aggressive direct sales effort by a professional sales team that develops relationships with key clients within the local hotel market while simultaneously employing a variety of additional marketing strategies. The content within this chapter will prepare readers to:

- Identify key demand generators and sources of business for hotels.
- Explain why direct sales is a necessary and highly effective component of a hotel's marketing mix.
- Create a staffing plan for a hotel sales department and recommend a deployment strategy for the sales team.
- Define "prime selling time" and explain its importance.
- Outline strategies that may be used to effectively supervise sales professionals.
- Explain the marketing support that is provided by parent companies or the hotel's brand.
- List the components of an effective integrated marketing communications program.
- Define consumer generated content and explain the marketing opportunities and challenges it creates.
- Provide examples of cooperative marketing partnerships.
- Identify the components of a hotel marketing plan.

DEMAND GENERATORS AND SOURCES OF BUSINESS FOR HOTELS

Chapter 3: Defining Guest Segments identified a wide range of travelers that seek both the core service of overnight accommodations, as well as the peripheral services, including food, beverage, and conference services, offered by hotels. The challenge faced by hoteliers is how to attract the desired volume of travelers at the desired guestroom rates from the guest segments available within the market. When a traveler selects a hotel, one of the primary factors considered is the hotel's location—a traveler typically desires to stay in a hotel that is in proximity to the primary purpose of his/her visit. Consequently, a hotel marketer must identify key demand generators within a reasonable distance from the hotel. A *demand generator* is defined as an attraction, facility, or event that motivates travelers to journey to a specific destination to visit, conduct business, or attend. The specific guest segments that a hotel will pursue is determined by the specific nature of the demand generators located or that take place within the hotel's local market.

> demand generator: an attraction, facility, or event that motivates travelers to journey to a specific destination to visit, conduct business, or attend

A hotel located in an urban market will typically pursue individual business travelers (IBT) conducting business in neighboring and nearby office buildings during the traditional work week. On weekends, the same urban hotel may pursue leisure travelers looking to visit cultural attractions in the city or shop in a nearby urban shopping district. A hotel located in a sub-

© Angel DiBilio/Shutterstock.com

urban office park will also pursue IBT guests from the nearby office buildings, but an example of a primary demand generator for weekend business may be a local youth sports facility that hosts weekend tournaments, which will generate overnight stays by youth sports teams and their families (part of the social, military, educational, religious, and fraternal [SMERF] segment). Of course, a hotel cannot rely on just one or two, or even a handful, of demand generators to meet its revenue goals.

Fortunately, there are dozens of quality sources of business in most markets—particularly markets in which upscale, upper-upscale, and luxury hotels are developed. Examples of demand generators include, but are not limited to, airports; art galleries; churches and religious venues; citywide conventions; colleges and universities; conference centers; concert venues; courthouses; federal, state, county, and municipal government facilities; expressways and major transportation arteries; festivals; hospitals and medical facilities; manufacturing plants; museums; natural attractions including beaches, parks, lakes, and rivers; office and commercial buildings; recreational facilities, such as golf courses and ski areas; spas, personal care, and wellness facilities; sports arenas and stadiums; shopping districts and malls; theaters; tourism and historic sites; and trade and exposition centers. This list may be expanded almost endlessly and includes both the physical facilities and locations or venues, as well as the events or activities that take place within these various locations.

DIRECT SALES

To attract and pursue the potential hotel business that may be generated by the events and activities taking place in these various locations, a

© totojang1977/Shutterstock.com

hotel marketer must research each demand generator. Customers' needs for overnight accommodations, and the various peripheral services offered by the hotel, must be determined and the primary decision-maker that determines which hotel(s) is (are) used to fulfill these needs must be identified. A hotel representative may then engage in discussions with the decision-maker, or his/her designee, to fully assess the potential client's needs and evaluate the value of the potential client to the hotel. The hotel marketer then must determine if there is a good match between the potential client and the hotel in terms of the quality and range of services offered by the hotel; the hotel's pricing for guestrooms and the additional services required; the typical arrival and departure patterns of the overnight hotel guests; and many other factors. How the value of potential business is evaluated, and customers are selected, is discussed in detail in *Chapter 5: Optimizing Revenue*; however, the important point to recognize in this current chapter is that the process of sales prospecting involves a bit of detective work, research, evaluation, judgment, tenacity, and the ability to build trusted relationships—all qualities that may only be found in a professional salesperson. As a result, a primary marketing method used, particularly by upscale, upper-upscale, and luxury full-service hotels, is direct sales. Direct sales is defined as one-to-one marketing of products, services, and experiences through the development of trusted relationships between buyers and a representative of the supplier. Direct sales is most effective in the sale of complex and highly customized products. Because a client planning a conference, special event, or arranging overnight accommodations for hundreds or even thousands of travelers annually may have a variety of very specific needs, direct sales is the most effective and efficient way to assess each potential client's needs and to negotiate the potential relationship.

The number of sales representatives employed by a hotel at the individual property level will vary depending upon the chain-scale or class of the hotel (e.g. economy, mid-scale, upper-mid-scale, upscale, upper-upscale, or luxury), the number of rooms, the square footage of available conference space, the range of peripheral services offered, and the variety of guest segments pursued. An economy hotel with less than 100 rooms located along a major expressway, for example, may not employ any dedicated sales representatives but may require the hotel's general manager or assistant to perform the direct sales function; however, mid-scale hotels and above will typically employ one or more sales representatives. A hotel typically employs one sales representative per 75 to 100 available rooms—in other words, a 100-room hotel will employ one sales representative whereas a 400-room hotel may employ four to five representatives and a 1,000-room property 10 sales representatives or more. In addition to sales representatives, which are typically referred to as sales managers, more sales professionals may also be employed dependent, primarily, on the amount of meeting space within the hotel and the number of available guestrooms. As the number of available hotel rooms and square footage of available meeting space increases, the complexity of the conferences, meetings, and events hosted by the hotel increases. As a result, many

sales prospecting: the process of identifying potential clients, assessing their needs, and evaluating the fit between these needs and the services, products, and experiences offered by the firm

direct sales: one-to-one marketing of products, services, and experiences through the development of trusted relationships between buyers and a representative of the supplier

hotels will add conference service managers and catering sales managers to sell food, beverage, and conference support services, while also managing the details of the events taking place in the hotel's conference and meeting space; the deployment of conference service managers to support the sales managers is common in hotels with over 350 rooms and more than 15,000 square feet of meeting space. It is common for these typically upscale, upper-upscale, or luxury hotels to employ one conference service manager for every two sales managers that prospect and *book*, a term commonly used in the industry in lieu of "execute a contract for" group business. The number of catering sales managers employed by a hotel will vary based upon the number and scope of events that the hotel books into its meeting space that do not require overnight accommodations.

book:
a term commonly used whenever a hotel room is rented (sold) or group contract is executed

Roles of the Various Sales Professionals

Sales Manager

A *sales manager*, sometimes referred to as a *sales executive* or *sales representative*, is responsible for identifying potential customers in their assigned guest segment(s) and assessing their needs to see if the hotel is a good fit for the client. If so, the sales manager will work to establish and maintain a productive relationship with the client by negotiating and securing mutually beneficial contracts between the client and the hotel. Most sales managers will be employed to pursue group business requiring 50 room nights or more, although one or more sales managers may be assigned to pursue IBT by identifying, contracting, and maintaining relationships with volume accounts within the market. Once a client has signed a group contract for 50 room nights or more, the client is turned over to a conference services manager to manage the details of the meeting, conference, or event to allow the sales manager's primary focus to be on prospecting and booking additional group business.

Meetings Express Manager

The *meetings express* or *small meetings manager* focuses on group business requiring between 10 and 50 room nights. Because these groups are less complex than larger conferences, and these clients tend to book with shorter lead times, the express meetings manager negotiates the contract and arranges all the details of the meeting—it is often said that the small meetings or express sales manager both "books and cooks" the meeting. Although the express meetings manager may seem, at first glance, to have a wider scope of responsibility, these smaller meetings generally require substantially less negotiation because many of these meetings are booked by volume accounts with established guestroom rates, are offered the best available rate (BAR) for the dates requested, or are extended the corporate rate, if one is available; hotels will also create express meetings packages that simplify menu planning and pricing for small groups. Because much of this business is the result of in-bound inquiries initiated by the client, eliminating the need for a substantial amount of prospecting by the small meetings manager, coupled with the fact that much less revenue is generated by a small meeting as compared with a large, complex conference, the express meetings manager position is often used as an entry-level sales position.

Conference Services Manager

© zhu difeng/Shutterstock.com

The role of the *conference services manager* is to manage the details of the meetings or conferences booked into the hotel while ensuring compliance with the terms of the contracts that are established by the respective sales manager. Following the negotiation of the contract, each executed contract will specify the dates of the conference, the number of room nights required each night, the guestroom rates, the square footage of meeting space required, and a basic outline of each group's Food and Beverage (F&B) requirements, which results in an estimate of the overall value of the F&B catering revenue that must be generated by each group. Based upon the estimate of F&B revenue, an "F&B minimum" is established; the conference services manager sells each assigned client detailed menus for each catered event during their respective conference with the goal of ensuring that the total F&B purchased by each group meets, or ideally exceeds, the established F&B minimum. The conference services manager also communicates each group's needs to the various operating departments throughout the hotel to ensure that every department is prepared to meet and exceed each group's expectations. For many conferences, the conference services manager will host a pre-convention meeting with key department heads from throughout the hotel and the client's primary contacts to ensure that all operating departments are adequately informed of the group's needs and are prepared to exceed their expectations.

Catering Sales Manager

A *catering sales manager* pursues F&B business generated by events that do not require overnight accommodations. The primary purpose of meeting space in a hotel is to generate demand for overnight accommodations because the contribution margin on hotel room revenue is substantially higher (74.2% from *Table 2.1*) than the contribution margin on F&B revenue (31.2% from *Table 2.1*); however, there may be times during which the hotel's meeting and conference space may be idle. As a result, a catering sales manager's role is to prospect for and book catering-only events during times when in-house guests are not using the event space to generate incremental F&B revenue. To prevent a catering-only group from displacing a multi-day conference that will book hotel rooms, in addition to F&B and conference revenue, producing more total revenue and profit for the hotel, restrictions are established on the type and timing of catering-only business that the catering sales manager may book. For example, events may only be booked if they are taking place within the upcoming 6 months, generate a minimum amount of F&B revenue per square foot of meeting space used, and take place during specified time periods (e.g. after noon on a Sunday; after 6 p.m. on a Monday, Thursday, or Friday; or during a holiday period). Obviously, the restrictions will vary based upon the specific demand and booking patterns for transient and group business within a specific hotel. A more in-depth discussion about evaluating business and selecting which specific clients a hotel should accommodate may be found in *Chapter 5: Optimizing Revenue*.

Director of Catering and Conference Services

The *director of catering and conference services* serves a dual role. This sales professional will be assigned the responsibility of managing specific group clients—working as a conference service manager—or, in some hotels, he/she may fulfill the role of the catering sales manager; however, this seasoned professional will also oversee the catering and conference services managers department by directly supervising and mentoring the other conference services and the catering sales manager, if applicable. As outlined in *Chapter 2: Successful Hotel Management*, the director of catering and conference services may report directly to the director of sales and marketing or to the director of F&B, because the department serves both a sales and operational function. This decision is typically made by the hotel management firm operating the hotel; however, regardless of the management structure, the director of catering and conference services will work closely with both the sales team and the F&B operations team.

Director of Sales and Marketing

The *director of sales and marketing* may be assigned to prospect and book business within a specific guest segment or may simply be assigned specific client accounts to manage; however, this sales professional also oversees and manages the sales and marketing department. In small, select-service hotels, the hotel may only employ a director of sales, whereas in large, complex hotel operations this role may be split, with a director of marketing overseeing the entire sales and marketing effort while the director of sales oversees the sales managers and the direct sales activities. The director of sales and marketing reports directly to the hotel's general manager.

Sales Assistant

The *sales assistant* serves an administrative support role within the sales office. Whether a hotel employs one or more sales assistants is dependent upon the number of sales professionals employed by the hotel, coupled with the level of automation, although a ratio of one assistant for as many as four or five sales professionals is not uncommon. Most sales offices use a sophisticated sales management system (SMS) in which client information is maintained and the activities of the sales professionals are tracked; this SMS also generates contracts, using various boilerplate contracts for specific client segments (e.g. volume accounts, express meetings [< 50 room nights], large conferences [> 50 room nights], etc.) that are modified, as appropriate, based upon the specific needs of the client. A sales assistant may also maintain the hotel's social media accounts and/or serve as the system administrator for the SMS. An efficient sales assistant is an invaluable asset to a sales professional because he/she can manage many of the routine responsibilities of the sales managers and conference services manager, as well as interface directly with clients to collect or exchange information; this frees up the sales professionals to focus on their most important function—booking business and driving revenue.

© fizkes/Shutterstock.com

distribution channel:
a chain of intermediaries
through which a product
or service passes from the
provider to the end user

Revenue Manager

The *revenue manager* is responsible for optimizing hotel revenue, working as an integral part of the sales team. The revenue manager oversees the on-property reservations sales agents; communicates BARs to the guest services (front office) team; ensures appropriate guestroom pricing and availability strategies are in place for each distribution channel; ensures the accuracy and proper management of group room blocks; and maintains a statistical database that is used for forecasting revenue and evaluating potential business. Although the focus of revenue managers has traditionally been on optimizing guestroom revenue, progressive revenue managers have shifted their focus to total hotel revenue, including food, beverage, and ancillary revenue. A capable revenue manager can substantially increase the profitability of a hotel, while also enhancing the customer experience, by providing valuable insights and accurate forecasts, which will lead to prudent decision-making by the sales team and appropriate staffing levels throughout the operation. Due to this broad impact, the revenue manager will often report directly to the general manager, which will also allow him/her to maintain objectivity when debates occur among the

BOX 4.1: A CAREER IN HOTEL SALES

Imagine creating memorable celebrations to help guests commemorate the most important moments in their lives, negotiating a contract to host an art or food festival, or orchestrating a large corporate event attended by several hundred guests. These are just some of the activities enjoyed by hotel sales professionals!

To begin a career in hotel sales, the first step is simply getting a "foot in the door," whether at the front desk, in the hotel's reservations office, or as part of the banquet services team. Most hotel sales professionals start their careers on the front-lines because a good understanding of hotel operations is critical to the success of a hotel sales professional. In addition, the director of sales and marketing, as well as the hotel's general manager, typically prefer to bring personnel into the sales office that are familiar with the hotel—its corporate culture, values, guest service standards, and inner-workings—and that have demonstrated a commitment to enthusiastically providing exceptional customer experiences.

The first position that many sales professionals secure within the sales department is as a sales assistant. In this capacity, an aspiring sales, conference services, or catering sales manager can become familiar with the sales process and responsibilities of the various positions within the office, as well as the SMS and sales contracts. Sales assistants also interact frequently and establish relationships with clients of the hotel.

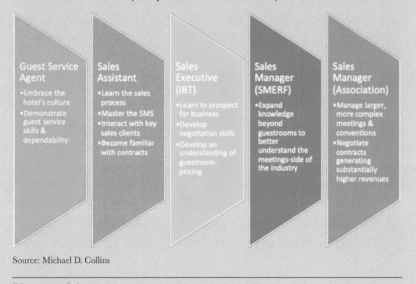

Guest Service Agent
- Embrace the hotel's culture
- Demonstrate guest service skills & dependability

Sales Assistant
- Learn the sales process
- Master the SMS
- Interact with key sales clients
- Become familiar with contracts

Sales Executive (IBT)
- Learn to prospect for business
- Develop negotiation skills
- Develop an understanding of guestroom pricing

Sales Manager (SMERF)
- Expand knowledge beyond guestrooms to better understand the meetings-side of the industry

Sales Manager (Association)
- Manage larger, more complex meetings & conventions
- Negotiate contracts generating substantially higher revenues

Source: Michael D. Collins

Diagram 4.1: One Possible Career Path in Hotel Sales

Following a tenure as a sales assistant, the next career move is often into an express sales manager's position, managing groups that require 10 to 50 room nights. Because an express sales manager "books and cooks" the meeting, this position provides a recently promoted sales professional with exposure to both the booking (sales) side and the service (conference services) side of the sales process; yet, because the meetings managed are small—often with just 10 to 15 attendees—they are rarely overwhelming. Another possible move is into the role of an IBT sales manager or sales executive. In this capacity, a recently promoted sales professional will learn the valuable skills of prospecting and negotiation. Because the focus of this sales role is on generating transient business, negotiations are less complex and the needs of the client more straightforward—overnight accommodations for the clients' in-bound employees, vendors, and customers.

After serving in one of these two entry-level sales roles, an upwardly mobile sales professional may elect to move into a sales, conference services, or catering sales manager role, depending upon his/her specific career interests, serving, over time, clients with more complex needs that generate increasing amounts of revenue. Many sales professionals enjoy the challenge associated with locating, negotiating, and booking group businesses and choose to spend their entire careers in sales management positions, whereas others may aspire to one day manage the entire sales department, as a director of sales and marketing, or to advance to the position of general manager. There are also regional sales director roles, overseeing the sales teams at multiple hotels, and opportunities in national and international sales offices that supply sales leads to hotels within the company's family of brands. Some successful sales managers even venture off on their own to start their own representation firm, which signs contracts with multiple hotels, many of which are non-branded, independent hotels, and uses their established relationships to generate group business for the hotels they represent.

sales team members regarding which clients should be accommodated by the hotel and when managing group room blocks. Recall that a hotel has limited service capacity and, as a result, the hotel management team has a fiduciary responsibility to optimize revenue; the revenue manager plays a lead role in fulfilling this responsibility. In some organizations, the revenue manager may report to the rooms division manager or director of sales and marketing, as opposed to the general manager.

service capacity:
the maximum number of customers that may be appropriately served in a specified time period

Sales Team Deployment

Sales team deployment refers to the specific guest segments that will be assigned to each sales manager and for which he/she will be held accountable. As previously discussed, the demand generators located within proximity to the hotel will determine the guest segments that are available in the market; however, further research will need to be conducted to identify the potential volume the hotel may expect to enjoy from each segment. Once a hotel has been operating for several years, historical data may be used to assess the potential of each segment; however, markets are continually evolving with firms moving into and out of the market, changes in economic conditions impacting the volume of business travel, and disruptors causing shifts in how business is conducted in many industries and, in some cases, creating entirely new industries. Consequently, it is critical that a hotel's sales managers spend as much time as possible communicating with clients and conducting market intelligence to keep abreast of changing market conditions, as well as changes in the hotel needs and booking patterns of current clients of the hotel. Please refer to the *Section 2 Supplement: Sales Team Deployment: A Tale of Two Markets* for a detailed discussion as to how the characteristics of a market impacts the deployment of a hotel's sales team.

> **sales team demployment:** the specific guest segments that will be assigned to each sales manager and for which he/she will be held accountable

> **disruptor:** an innovation or new technology that fundamentally changes the status quo in an industry

Effective Supervision of Sales Professionals

Prime selling time is generally between the hours of 9:00 a.m. and 4:00 p.m., in the clients' respective time zone, Monday through Friday, because it is during these hours that professional meeting planners and others assigned with the responsibility of booking hotel accommodations or planning meetings and events are conducting their business affairs. Consequently, it is during these hours that sales professionals have the best opportunity to interact with their clients. As a result, it is imperative that sales managers focus on meeting, communicating, and interacting with their existing clients, as well as prospecting for new clients, during this prime selling time. As a general rule, meetings with other hotel personnel, planning, and administrative work should be completed prior to 9:00 a.m. or after 4:00 p.m. to maximize the use of a sales manager's most valuable resource—prime selling time.

> **prime selling time:** generally the hours between 9:00 a.m. and 4:00 p.m., in the clients' respective time zone, Monday through Friday

Effective directors of sales and general managers will protect their sales managers from distractions during prime selling time. They will also create systems and processes to ensure that sales managers use this time effectively to engage in productive interactions with clients and potential clients. For example, it is common to start each day with a morning sales meeting, which should be concluded by 8:30 a.m. During this meeting, each member of the team will review any potential business discovered during the preceding day, re-cap the previous day's primary activities, and share his/her planned sales activities for the current day. By sharing this information, sales professionals are held accountable for their use of prime selling time. In addition, the entire sales team will take this time to discuss strategies to capture prime pieces of business and to exceed the hotel's revenue goals. Sales managers are also expected to entertain clients on property as often as possible, which allows the director of sales and general manager to personally meet clients, enhancing the relationships that are established with key clients. After 4 p.m., members of the sales team are expected to respond to any emails, text messages, or telephone calls they may have missed while they were with clients; complete any administrative tasks, which includes ensuring that all the day's activities were logged into the SMS; and prepare for the following morning's sales meeting by reviewing the day's key activities, as well as the sales professional's plans for tomorrow. Please refer to *Box 4.2* for the *"One Question You Should NEVER Ask!"* a hotel sales manager.

BOX 4.2: "THE ONE QUESTION YOU SHOULD NEVER ASK!"

© fizkes/Shutterstock.com

A sales manager's productivity is determined by one primary factor—how well he/she uses prime selling time. There are 168 hours in a week (24 X 7), but a maximum of only 35 hours of prime selling time, which is **less than 21% of the total hours available!** Sales managers should be encouraged to spend as much of this time as possible interacting with clients.

A sales manager's productivity is determined by his/her **activities**; however, many hotel general managers and directors of sales focus on a sales manager's production. They believe that by focusing on results, members of their sales team will produce better results; however, worrying about how much business a sales manager has booked month-to-date, or how much more he/she needs to produce for the remainder of the month to achieve his/her goal, has no impact on production. Instead, a wise sales team leader focuses on activities.

James Evans, the retired Senior Vice President of Sales and Marketing for *Hyatt Hotels Corporation*, advised general managers to *never* walk into a hotel sales office and ask, "What did you book today?" Jim felt that this question was counterproductive and failed to provide the general manager with any insight as to which sales team members were performing and which were struggling.

"Just because a sales manager happened to receive a signed contract from a client today does not mean that he is being productive today," Jim would explain. "Instead, ask your sales managers probing questions about their activities: 'Who have you spoken with today?' 'Have you uncovered any new leads today?' 'What are your plans for the day?' 'Are you having challenges with any of your clients that I may assist you with?' By focusing on their activities, you let your sales team know that you are interested in what they are doing and that you are available to assist them!" (Collins, 1990).

Sales is a numbers game—the more qualified clients with whom a sales manager speaks and the more proposals that a salesperson sends out, the more business he/she will typically book. Of course, to use time productively, a sales manager must "work smart." Sales managers need to develop good sources of leads, focus on the leads with the most potential, plan their activities, and then work their plan. Most certainly, sales production needs to be reviewed at least weekly with each member of the sales team; however, sales activities should be reviewed daily. If a sales manager is not meeting production goals, then his/her activities should be evaluated first—how much prospecting is being done; how many sales calls are being made; how many clients are being entertained; and how many proposals are being sent out. If the number of sales activities are in-line with the productive members of the sales team, then the sources and quality of the leads, as well as the sales manager's sales techniques and tactics, may need to be reviewed; the director of sales should accompany the non-performing sales manager on sales calls and jointly entertain clients to verify the quality of the sales activities. Most importantly, the director of sales should establish sales activity goals for an under-performing member of the sales team. Undoubtedly, if the activity goals are achieved, the production will follow.

This guidance does not only apply to sales. Success in any aspect of life is based upon *activities*—not a singular focus on *results*. Certainly, goals must be set and progress toward achieving these goals must be measured; however, the purpose of tracking progress is to assess whether the current activities are effective. If positive progress is being made, stay on course. If not, the **activities** must be modified!

MARKETING SUPPORT PROVIDED BY THE HOTEL'S BRAND

As outlined in *Chapter 1: Introduction to the Hotel Industry*, hotel parent companies provide a wide variety of support services to their franchised and managed hotels; marketing support is one of the key benefits of brand affiliation. Over seventy percent of available hotel rooms in the United States, and nearly 50% of available hotel rooms outside of the United States are brand-affiliated (STR, 2018). Many guests are loyal to specific hotel brands because they are confident that they will enjoy a hotel

© walterericsy/Shutterstock.com

experience that provides value, as defined by the value equation (*Formula 2.1*). Brands provide a range of marketing support services as outlined below.

Electronic Media Platform

A fully-functional internet website and mobile application is provided for the family of brands that link seamlessly with the website for each specific brand supported by the parent company. Each brand-affiliated hotel is provided with a template upon which hotel and location-specific information may be added. Collectively, the web-pages contain a specific hotel's information from the property's website. These websites and mobile apps are continuously monitored, secured, and updated periodically as technology and guest expectations change. Independent hotels must develop their own websites, mobile apps, and electronic media platform, typically by using an outside web development professional.

Brand Advertising

Brand-affiliated hotels typically pay a marketing fee of between 1% and 2% of guestroom revenue, averaging 1.6% for the major brands based in the United States, to the parent company (Russell & Kim, 2016). The marketing fees paid by the hotels are typically restricted and may only be used to advertise the brand per the franchise agreement. By pooling advertising resources, branded-hotels have substantially more purchasing power to communicate the brand's value-proposition to a broader audience of potential customers than they could on their own. In addition, branded hotels benefit from the pooled marketing resources of all hotels supported by the parent company because the collective advertising by all brands within the family of brands drives customer traffic to the firm's website where brand-switching may occur. Independent hotels, conversely, may not reach as many customers; however, every dollar of advertising investment is used to advertise their specific property. Consequently, independent hotels can precisely target every dollar of their media investment while also fully customizing their message.

Central Reservations Office

The central reservations office (CRO) provides complete reservations support to brand-affiliated hotels. Due to the widespread use of mobile applications and the internet, most reservations are booked electronically through the central reservation system (CRS), which are seamlessly received at the individual properties; however, the CRO also supports "online chats" and telephone reservations, 24-hours per day, 7-days per week. Approximately 11% to 13% of reservations for a brand affiliated hotel come through the CRO, whereas another 25% to 40% are booked directly through the brand's mobile app or website, which means that between 36% to 50% or more of a brand-affiliated hotel's reservations are typically received through the CRS, depending upon the specific property. Most brands charge a specified fee per reservation, with reservation fees averaging approximately 2% of guestroom revenue across all major US-based brands (Russell & Kim, 2016).

Loyalty Program

As outlined in the service-profit chain, customer loyalty drives the profitability of a service enterprise. Loyalty programs allow guests to accumulate points to qualify for complimentary hotel accommodations and to receive additional perks and benefits while staying at brand-affiliated hotels. Because guests can typically accumulate or redeem points at any hotel affiliated with the family of brands, loyalty programs are more effective for a brand or collection of hotels than for an independent hotel property. An individual branded hotel is generally charged for points earned by loyalty members accommodated by the hotel, while being reimbursed by the parent company, at a discounted rate, for points that are redeemed at the hotel; the cost of the points is intended to cover the costs of operating the loyalty program. Loyalty fees range from between 1% and 2.4% of guestroom revenue (Russell & Kim, 2016).

Regional, National, and International Sales Offices

Parent companies operate regional, national, and international sales offices in strategic locations; these offices employ an appropriate team of sales professionals that provide sales leads for brand-affiliated hotels. As previously mentioned, many upscale, upper-upscale, and luxury hotels host conventions and conferences for national associations. Consequently, many parent companies or hotel brands operate sales offices in Northern Virginia or Washington D.C., for example, where many national associations are headquartered. Again, the goal of these offices is to provide qualified sales leads to the individual properties where they are assigned to the appropriate member of the hotel's direct sales team; however, the relationship maintained with the client by the sales professional at the brand's sales office may be instrumental in helping a property book a specific piece of business. The cost of operating these offices is covered by the variety of franchise and reservation fees generated from the incremental revenue generated by these sales offices and, in some cases, by commissions that are paid on business realized from the sales leads that are furnished to the individual properties, depending upon the brand.

BRAND RELATIONSHIPS

The hotel brands, through their networks of sales offices and marketing activities, establish countless relationships that benefit brand-affiliated hotels. These include relationships with corporate accounts, travel consortia, online travel agents (OTAs), and other high-volume consumers of hotel services. Because a brand can often offer these high-volume producers of hotel reservations with access to hundreds, or even thousands, of hotels in hundreds of locations, and at which each reliably provides a consistent guest experience, these high-volume customers are able to simplify their acquisition of hotel services because they avoid negotiating individual contracts with hundreds of individual hotel properties. Many times, individual properties may opt in or out of specific relationships established by the brand. For example, a hotel operating in a market enjoying consistently strong demand may decide not to participate in an opportunity to offer a deep discount to a specific OTA solicited by the parent company. At a minimum, an individual hotel property always can control the availability of its guestroom inventory through the various distribution channels even if they are required to participate in a chain-wide agreement.

Property Referrals

Another marketing benefit of brand-affiliation are property-to-property referrals. Many professional meeting planners plan conferences in multiple locations. Following the successful execution of a meeting at one property, it is not uncommon for the meeting professional to ask their sales or conference services manager for a referral to a hotel of the same brand in another location. Many conferences change or rotate locations each year; however, it is time consuming for the planner to communicate the specific needs of the group to an entirely new hotel management team. By using the same hotel brand, the meeting planner can anticipate that his/her group's specific needs may be communicated directly to the recommended hotel. In addition, the receiving hotel uses similar processes and systems, which will allow for a consistent guest experience. Granted, the meeting planner will still need to communicate extensively with the receiving hotel's conference services manager to finalize the details of the meeting; however, the process of negotiating a contract, as well as the initial planning, is greatly simplified.

CREATING AN EFFECTIVE INTEGRATED MARKETING COMMUNICATIONS PROGRAM

A consistent image and message are critical to successful marketing. By ensuring that all marketing efforts convey a similar look and feel, a more memorable impression will be made on consumers. For brand-affiliated hotels, the parent company takes the lead on establishing the essence of the brand. Property specific marketing should be consistent with the image established by the brand to leverage the brand's marketing efforts. Because it takes multiple impressions to impact a potential customer through advertising, for example, advertising by a specific hotel property will be more effective if the consumer im-

© Georgejmclittle/Shutterstock.com

mediately connects the image and message communicated by the property with the brand's advertising, as well as advertising initiated by other hotels within the chain. An independent hotel has much more limited resources than a hotel brand, so it is just as critical that all marketing communications executed by an independent hotel conveys a consistent image and message.

Traditional Media

Advertising through traditional media channels, which includes both print and broadcast media, is rarely used by individual hotel properties. Due to its high cost and broad audience, these media channels are generally too expensive to include in the marketing budget of an individual hotel. Opportunities do exist for an individual hotel to create marketing partnerships with television or radio stations in local or feeder markets as described in the *marketing partnerships* section below; however, most traditional media expenditures—for television, radio, and print media advertising—will be made and executed by the parent company on behalf of the brand. Independent hotels, in some cases, may execute some traditional media purchases in strong feeder markets; however, they must be very targeted, such as a print ad in a regional lifestyle publication or broadcast advertising through cable television systems or radio stations in select feeder markets.

Electronic Media

As previously explained, the parent company will provide an electronic media platform upon which a branded hotel will construct its hotel website and webpages, which may also be accessed through the parent company's or brand's mobile app. Individual properties should not deviate from the prescribed brand format or establish separate sites or apps, which may only confuse consumers. Independent hotels should ensure that the look, feel, and image conveyed by the hotel's website or mobile app are consistent with the overall marketing communications program. Specific electronic media communication channels include the following.

Email Communications

Repeat patronage is critical to the success of a hotel. Consequently, the best source of potential future guests is past guests. Every hotel—branded or independent—has a database of past guests that may be used to solicit future business; however, the message communicated through email solicitations must be consistent with the marketing image conveyed by the brand or independent hotel through other marketing channels. Hotels must also be careful to allow guests to control the frequency and types of messages received from the hotel for email marketing communications to be effective.

Online Advertising

Online advertising has become extremely sophisticated in recent years. Advertising that reaches consumers through web browsers, search engines, individual websites, social media sites, and mobile applications can target specific customers based upon websites viewed, past searches, and a variety of additional metrics tracked by the various electronic media channels. In addition, the cost of the advertising, in many cases, is based upon the number of consumers that actually "click through" the advertising and are delivered to the brand's or hotel's website. Consequently, online or mobile advertising is an increasingly flexible, cost-effective, and measurable marketing communications channel.

Social Media

The previous forms of advertising and marketing communications discussed are entirely controlled by the hotel or parent company—the advertiser produces and has complete control of the message. When a hotel marketer uses social media to convey its message to consumers, control of the marketing message is shared with hotel guests or members of the social network. The use of user-generated content by marketers presents several opportunities, but also presents some challenges. User-generated content is more trusted by consumers because it is viewed as more authentic. Many consumers have become skeptical of picture-perfect photographs with smiling hotel employees serving seemingly delighted guests. As a result, customers appreciate photographs taken by actual guests of the hotel and descriptions of guest experiences expressed in a guest's own words. Creating social media sites will allow hotel marketers to share these powerful messages. The benefit of a social media site is that the hotel can control the content that is shared through the site; however, it is important that a member of the hotel's marketing team is assigned to closely monitor the site and to keep it up-to-date with recent postings and information on hotel happenings, promotions, and events. A well-managed social media site is critical to maintaining relationships with many guest segments, particularly in leisure-driven markets.

> **user-generated content:**
> any form of communication media, including photographs, videos, audio files, descriptions, or reviews, created by the consumers of a product or service

Review Sites

Review sites, such as TripAdvisor and Yelp, are driven by user-generated content; however, hotel management may respond to content posted by users on the sites. Again, a member of the hotel's marketing team should be assigned to closely monitor key review sites and should respond, preferably within hours, to guest postings—both positive and negative. A quick response sends an indication to potential guests that the hotel staff is responsive to guest feedback. A management account may be established for most review sites that allows a representative of the business to respond to reviews that are posted; requests can also be made through this portal to have erroneous or malicious reviews removed. Hotel management should not become distressed regarding an occasional negative review—consumers actually expect a business to receive a mixture of positive, mixed, and an occasional negative review. Please review *Box 4.3: Responding to Online Reviews* for more information on how effective hotel marketers manage their online reputations.

BOX 4.3: RESPONDING TO ONLINE REVIEWS

© chrisdorney/Shutterstock.com

Whether positive or negative, the most important thing a hotel marketer can do is to respond quickly to online reviews—preferably within hours and within 24 hours maximum. By responding quickly to online reviews, prospective customers are assured that the hotel is responsive to guest concerns.

Online reviews are referred to by marketers as user-generated content, which is more trusted by consumers because it is viewed as authentic—providing an actual indication as to what a potential customer is likely to experience when doing business with the firm. Consequently, a positive guest review sends potential hotel guests a powerful message; whereas, a negative review may cause a potential guest and a hotel manager distress! Hotel managers can relax—hotel consumers expect an occasional negative or mixed review. As a matter of fact, a negative review may sometimes be turned into a positive marketing message (read on).

When responding to any review—positive, negative, or mixed—there are a couple of rules that apply. In addition to responding quickly, write the response in an informal, conversational tone and do not post a scripted response—in other words, do not "cut and paste" the same response to multiple review postings. Many hotel managers tend to use formal language when addressing guests—this is inconsistent with the informal nature of social networks and online communities. Even when providing a short response to express appreciation for a positive review, customize each posting by responding to a comment made within the review, such as, "Thanks for sharing your experience at our resort. Glad to hear that your kids enjoyed the waterslide in our pool! Hope that you and your family will be able to make it back soon."

With negative reviews, it is most important that a hotel manager does not become defensive or offer too much of an explanation within the response regarding the guest's concerns. And always show respect for the guest's opinion. In the response, acknowledge the guest's comments by, again, responding to one or two specific comments within the review and expressing concern for the situation—an apology is perceived as being more sincere if empathy is expressed prior to the apology. Any reparation made to the guest should not be posted within the response but extended through direct communication. For example, "Thanks for taking the time to share your experience at our resort. I can imagine your frustration when you returned late in the afternoon to find that your room had not yet been serviced. I understand your disappointment and look forward to speaking with you to apologize personally and to fully resolve your concerns." Then be certain to contact the guest quickly to follow-up.

When possible, a response should clarify guest expectations or provide additional information about the hotel—this often allows a hotel manager to turn a negative review into helpful insights for potential future guests that may read the review. At a recent *HX: The Hotel Experience*, an annual industry tradeshow held in New York City, a TripAdvisor representative described an online review posted for a Caribbean resort in which a mother with young children complained that her children were tremendously bored while staying at the resort because there were no family activities and the adults around the pool constantly complained about her children shouting and splashing water while enjoying the resort's pool. The general manager of the resort showed empathy, respect, and concern for the guest in his response. After offering a sincere apology, he went on to clarify that the resort was not a family-oriented property but strived to provide a romantic oasis for newlyweds and couples celebrating anniversaries.

Although TripAdvisor will not disclose the details of the algorithm used to rank hotel properties within their respective markets, the TripAdvisor representative did provide the following guidance to hotel marketers that would like to improve their rankings:
1. Generate positive reviews. The most important factor, obviously, is the quality of online reviews—how guests rate the hotel.
2. Ensure that reviews are current. The "freshness" of the reviews matter—reviews that are months old may not accurately reflect the current quality of the guest experience.
3. Increase the number of reviews. A hotel with a half-dozen exceptional reviews, even if void of any negative reviews, will not earn a high ranking—the sample size is simply too small.

To accomplish these goals, a hotel manager must, first and foremost, ensure sound operational practices are in place and that associates are guest-focused—there is no other way to consistently generate positive reviews. To ensure that reviews are current, a hotelier must focus on item number 3—increasing the number of reviews. An increased number of reviews will also minimize the impact of any negative reviews that may be received.

To increase the number of reviews, hotels are encouraged to provide guests with a link to the TripAdvisor review site; however, fabricated reviews are strictly forbidden. Different review sites have different rules regarding how customer reviews may be encouraged. Wise hotel marketers will be aware of the different protocols for the various review sites most commonly viewed by their guests and potential guests.

Marketing Partnerships

In addition to the marketing support provided by the hotel brands, hotels—both brand-affiliated and independent—establish relationships with other marketing partners, including Destination Marketing Organizations (DMOs).

Destination Marketing Organizations

DMO or convention and visitors bureau (CVB): a government or non-profit entity formed to promote in-bound travel to a community

DMOs or Convention and Visitors Bureaus (CVBs) are non-profit associations or government agencies, funded by a specified proportion of the hotel occupancy and other tourism-related taxes collected in the area served, that promote in-bound travel and tourism into a local community, county, state, or country. The exact structure of the organization and its funding is determined, in the United States, by state and local legislation. The DMO concept was introduced in *Chapter 3: Defining Guest Segments,* and is discussed in *Box 3.2: The Moscone Convention Center* as well as in *Box 4.4: The Beaches of Fort Myers and Sanibel.* As defined, DMOs operate on the municipal, county, state, or national level and hotels may elect to partner with DMOs on multiple levels simultaneously. For example, most hotel marketers will work very closely with the local DMO or CVB but may also elect to participate in some cooperative advertising opportunities within the state-level organization.

cooperative (co-op) advertising: marketing communications that promote two or more entities simultaneously, for their mutual benefit, allowing the entities to share the cost of the promotion

In most markets, a hotelier's relationship with the local or regional DMO is his/her most valuable and important strategic marketing relationship. As a result, both a hotel's general manager and the director of sales and marketing will typically be engaged in this relationship. DMOs are a valuable source of sales leads for group business while also providing opportunities for hotel marketers to co-brand their property with the destination through cooperative (co-op) advertising, which is marketing communications that promote two or more entities simultaneously, for their mutual benefit, allowing the entities to share the cost of the promotion. Co-op advertising and marketing partnerships allow an individual hotel property to make the most of its finite marketing budget and are particularly important to independent hotels.

Strategic Partnerships

Additional strategic partnerships will be formed by hotel marketers with a variety of local demand generators, including adjacent golf courses, cultural venues, local festivals, and the like, for the mutual benefits of both organizations. For a strategic partnership to work, both entities must be pursuing the same customer segments, which will allow for an appropriate value proposition to be offered to the intended audience. Through these partnerships, each of the organizations involved will lower their marketing costs by leveraging their available marketing resources with others.

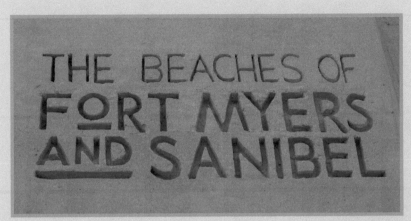

© Lynn Hristov/Shutterstock.com

The Lee County Visitors and Convention Bureau is a government agency that works to promote the county as a premier destination for leisure and business travel. Because the community does not support a large publicly owned convention center—Fort Myers' River District is served by the 42,000 square foot *Harborside Event Center*—this agency labels itself as a "Visitors and Convention Bureau (VCB)" as opposed to a CVB, whereas other similar organizations may label themselves as a DMO; however, the terms are essentially synonymous.

The Lee County VCB is a government agency funded by a 5% tax on short-term accommodations that supports a staff of over 30 full-time employees, in addition to operating five off-site sales offices located in the Northeastern United States, Midwestern United States, Canada, United Kingdom, Scandinavia, and Germany. The Bureau looks to develop promotional and public relations campaigns; build relationships through direct sales; and work with local service providers to develop products, services, and experiences that support tourism in Lee County, Florida. The county markets itself as *The Beaches of Fort Myers and Sanibel* and promotes the destination across multiple platforms including through the Bureau's website, broadcast media (television and radio), print media (newspapers and magazines), digital media (mobile and online), social media, electronic customer relationship management (ERCM), and out-of-home (OOH) marketing, which is supported by the off-site sales offices. *The Economic Impact of Tourism in Lee County, Florida USA* is summarized in *Table 4.1*.

Please explore the following URLs for specific information about the Lee County Visitor and Convention Bureau's current marketing campaign—*That's "Islandology"*:

www.fortmyers-sanibel.com
https://www.youtube.com/watch?time_continue=30&v=Ld--4mXrvi4
https://www.youtube.com/watch?v=vf6Kbqb2EQk&feature=youtu.be

The Lee County Visitors and Convention Bureau's "Brand Promise"

The Beaches of Fort Myers and Sanibel provides visitors with an authentic vacation experience that creates connections between people and nature, surrounding them with the things they value most.

Visitors 2016	3,009,619
Visitor Expenditures 2016	$3.03 billion
Tourist Tax Revenue (short-term accommodations) FY 2015 – 2016	$39.7 million
Tourism-related Employment (Lee County) 2016	41,319

Table 4.1: The Economic Impact of Tourism in Lee County, Florida

Source: Lee County Visitors and Convention Bureau (2017)

trade-outs, barter, or sponsorship agreements: marketing services or promotion provided in exchange for products or services

Trade-outs, barter, or sponsorship agreements allow a hotel to contribute hotel services in exchange for marketing exposure. For example, a hotel may serve as a corporate sponsor for a local event. In exchange for providing overnight accommodations for use by event organizers, the hotel is listed as a corporate sponsor for the event and the hotel's logo is included on all promotional materials produced to market the event. Hotels may also acquire broadcast media exposure by providing overnight accommodations, a meal in the hotel's restaurant, or even a wedding/catering package for a contest or promotion being offered by a radio or television station in the local or feeder market. When evaluating these opportunities, the hotel marketer must compare the retail cost of purchasing the broadcast media advertising with the hotel's costs of providing the services to ensure a favorable exchange. These types of strategic relationships are particularly important for independent hotels.

In some circumstances, a hotel marketer may decide to forge a relationship with a representation firm or wholesaler. A representation firm is a sales organization that provides direct sales support to suppliers in exchange for a fee—to put it simply, it is a sales team for hire. There are specific representation firms that specialize in the tourism, travel, and conference services industries. Many of the sales professionals with these firms are former hotel and DMO sales managers that have strong relationships with tour operators and professional meeting planners; these relationships are used to feed sales leads to the hotels and other service providers that the firm represents. The contractual relationship typically requires the payment of a monthly retainer to the representation firm as well as a specified commission on guestroom revenue earned from any bookings that are secured from the sales leads provided.

> **representation firm:**
> a sales organization that provides direct sales support to suppliers in exchange for a fee

> **wholesaler:**
> a travel intermediary that purchases hotel accommodations and other travel services at deep discounts, bundling them into vacation packages sold at a single price

A wholesaler purchases hotel accommodations and other travel services, such as airline tickets, in bulk at deep discounts; these travel services are then bundled into vacation packages and re-sold at a single price. The wholesaler earns the breakage, which is the difference between the retail price paid by the consumer and the wholesale cost of the services paid by the wholesaler. There are also wholesalers that focus on providing conference services to clients, including overnight guestrooms and conference support.

> **breakage:**
> the difference between the retail price paid by the consumer and the cost of the services

THE HOTEL MARKETING PLAN

The sales and marketing strategies and tactics that will be deployed for the upcoming calendar or fiscal year are outlined in an annual marketing plan. Creating a marketing plan is an integral component of preparing the hotel's financial forecast and annual budget and identifying the specific activities that must be executed for the hotel to achieve its revenue goals. Because many conferences and events, particularly citywide conventions and large conferences, book several years in advance, the marketing plan will include targeted booking goals for group room nights and revenue for several years into the future—typically, a minimum of 5 years—as well as the sales and marketing activities necessary to realize these established room nights, ADR, and revenue goals for future years.

The following content is contained in the annual marketing plan for an individual hotel:

Market Analysis

A current market analysis that assesses general economic conditions, the local business environment, an analysis of competitors, assessment of new hotels entering the market, and the market conditions and prospects for the hotel's key clients; the analysis also identifies potential clients the hotel plans to target. The analysis should review the status of and outlook for each guest segment available within the market. This compilation of this information will result in marketing-focused strengths, weaknesses, opportunities, and threats (SWOT) analysis, which identifies the hotel's internal strengths and weaknesses, as well as external opportunities and threats.

Revenue Optimization Strategies

Broad strategies are identified to enhance revenues in response to the market analysis. For example, the analysis may reveal that there is an opportunity to drive the average daily rate (ADR) on weekdays or to increase weekend occupancy in the summer months, mid-June through mid-August. Although these strategies tend to focus on driving guestroom revenue, strategies to drive food, beverage, and ancillary revenues should also be included.

Projected Room Nights, ADR, and Rooms Revenue

A forecast of the total number of room nights, ADR, and room revenue that will be generated for the following year, broken down by the guest segment, is included. This forecast will reflect the revenue optimization strategies that have been identified in the previous section. This forecast will typically be subject to further review and change; however, this initial forecast provides a solid basis upon which booking goals may be established for the sales team. A detailed description of the critically important forecasting process is provided in *Chapter 5: Optimizing Revenue*.

Group Booking Goals

Booking goals for each group segment are included for the upcoming and future years; these goals must reflect the various booking patterns for each segment (e.g. city-wide conventions and association groups typically book further in advance; corporate group business books more short-term, etc.). Again, further discussion regarding how these goals are established is provided in *Chapter 5: Optimizing Revenue*.

Food, Beverage, and Ancillary Revenue Forecast

Another item included in the marketing plan is an estimate of food, beverage, and ancillary revenues. Forecasted room nights by guest segment (e.g. leisure transient, IBT, corporate group, association group, SMERF, etc.) drives this process because the composition of in-house hotel guests impacts the amount of food, beverage, and ancillary revenue that may be anticipated. Expected banquet revenue per group room (BRGR) is used to generate revenue production goals for the conference services sales team for the upcoming year, as well as for future group contracts issued by the sales managers, although BRGRs for future-year contracts must be adjusted, as appropriate, using an inflation factor. Revenue goals are also established for the director of catering and/or the catering sales manager for catering-only bookings.

Analyses of Changes in Revenue and the Guest Segment Mix

Statements that summarize the anticipated changes compared with previous years in terms of revenues, as well as the guest segment mix, may also be included in the plan. These statements serve to identify the key factors that are driving the projected changes in revenues year-over-year; they also confirm that the broad revenue enhancement strategies previously identified have been properly considered when forecasting revenue and establishing booking goals for the sales team. An example of these analytical statements includes,

> "Room night production from volume accounts is expected to increase 6.2%, which is consistent with annual trends, while the ADR will increase a more modest 1.2%, resulting in a $145,440 (7.3%) increase in room revenue from volume accounts. While the ADR increase within the volume account segment is modest, the increase in volume account room nights will reduce the hotel's dependence on deeply discounted OTA and Travel Consortia room nights during the week, which will help achieve the targeted increase in the overall ADR."

To this point, marketing plan components have focused on setting appropriate goals, as well as identifying strategies to achieve these goals—in other words, plans have been made. Recall that sales success is dependent upon a focus upon activities—not goals. Consequently, the next section of the marketing plan, the *sales and marketing action plan*, is most critical to achieving the revenue and booking goals that have been established. This section must be a working game plan that guides the activities of the sales team, each day, over the course of the upcoming year.

Sales and Marketing Action Plan

The sales and marketing action plan will include a listing of all activities that must be executed by a member of the sales team to achieve revenue and booking goals.

This plan must be comprehensive and include all marketing activities—direct sales, brand-supported initiatives, co-op marketing and strategic partnerships, traditional media, electronic media, social media, public relations, and email campaigns. Whereas not all marketing activities initiated by the parent company for the brand may be included in a property-level plan, it is important to include any initiatives that require property involvement. For example, the action plan may include "update property-specific information included on webpages on the branded website" or "submit property-specific rates for national corporate accounts." For each activity, the following must be identified: the guest segment(s) or revenue category(ies) impacted; the objective or goal; the sales team member responsible; the targeted completion date (or dates, for recurring activities); and the expense budgeted to execute the activity, if applicable. Each member of the sales team must be involved in creating the action plan to ensure ownership and accountability for the plan. To facilitate its execution, the action plan should be maintained electronically using the SMS or database management software so that activities may be sorted by guest segment, revenue category, targeted completion date, and by team member responsible; this will allow the director of sales (DOS) to ensure that all activities are executed on a timely basis and to hold team members accountable for their specific responsibilities.

Sales and Marketing Budget

The final section of the marketing plan includes the sales and marketing budget. As outlined in *Table 2.1*, sales and marketing expenditures typically total just over seven percent (7.2%) of total hotel revenue, excluding franchise fees, which include royalty, marketing, and guest loyalty fees. Reservation fees that support the CRO and CRS are included in the rooms division's expenses. Consequently, the expenses included in the sales and marketing budget will include the anticipated payroll expense to support the direct sales, conference services, and support team, as well as funding to cover the marketing activities initiated at the property level. As previously explained, the CRO and CRS will typically generate from 35% to over 50% of a hotel's reservations; these guests are attracted to the hotel, in large part, by its brand-affiliation and the marketing support provided by the brand. The remaining 50% to 65% of reservations, as well as most catering and conference-related revenue, is generated by the aggressive direct sales effort, strategic marketing partnerships, and additional marketing activities that are spearheaded and funded at the hotel level. The sales and marketing budget of an independent hotel will typically run higher than a brand-affiliated hotel. At a minimum, the money saved due to the lack of franchise, brand-marketing, and guest loyalty fees will be invested into marketing activities, which may increase the sales and marketing expense budget at an independent hotel to between 8% and 10% of total hotel revenue.

CHAPTER SUMMARY

To develop an effective sales and marketing strategy for a hotel, demand generators within the local market must be identified, which determine the guest segments that are available. The potential of each guest segment must then be evaluated, strategies formulated, and relationships established to attract business from the most desirable guest segments; these activities are most effectively executed by a direct sales team. To manage the efficacy of the direct sales team, management must focus on the activities of the hotel's sales professionals during prime selling time. Brand-affiliated properties are supported by a wide range of marketing activities initiated by the parent company. Although results will vary by property, the CRO and the CRS may generate up to 50% of a hotel's reservations for a branded hotel. Electronic media, particularly social media and email campaigns, can be a cost-effective marketing tool; however, a hotel must closely monitor its online reputation by responding quickly and appropriately to online reviews. Strategic partnerships in the local market, particularly with the local DMO or CVB, may also generate productive results. The marketing plan establishes revenue targets and booking goals for the hotel's sales team, in addition to identifying the specific activities in which each sales professional must engage to achieve these goals.

KEY TERMS AND CONCEPTS

book
breakage
cooperative (co-op) advertising
demand generator
direct sales
disruptor
distribution channel

DMOs/convention and visitors bureaus (CVBs)
prime selling time
representation firm
sales prospecting
sales team deployment
service capacity

social, military, educational, religious, and fraternal (SMERF)
trade-outs, barter, or sponsorship agreements
user-generated content
wholesaler

DISCUSSION QUESTIONS

1. What is a demand generator? Identify at least a dozen demand generators within your local market.
2. Define direct sales. Discuss why direct sales is the most effective marketing method for an upper-upscale hotel product.
3. Discuss the roles of the various sales professionals. How do the roles differ and why are the roles separated? Discuss a possible career-path in hotel sales.

4. What strategies may be employed to ensure the productivity of the sales team? Discuss how the sales team may be deployed in an upper-upscale or luxury hotel in your local market.

5. What marketing support is provided to a hotel by a parent organization or the brand? Identify at least a half dozen forms of brand support.

6. Discuss the importance of electronic media in hotel marketing. Identify a minimum of three specific electronic media strategies that may be effective in marketing a hotel.

7. Explain how customer review sites have impacted hotel marketing. Why is user-generated content perceived as more meaningful to potential hotel guests? How should a hotel manager respond to online reviews, particularly negative reviews? What strategies may be employed to improve a hotel's online ranking or reputation?

8. Discuss the marketing partnerships that are formed between hotels and DMOs. Why do many municipal, county, state, and national governments support and promote tourism?

9. Discuss the components of a comprehensive marketing plan. What are the sales and marketing expense levels and largest marketing disbursements in a typical upper-upscale hotel?

ENDNOTES

Collins, M.D. (1990). Recollection of guidance provided by Mr. James Evans, Senior Vice President of Sales, during a property visit to the Hyatt Regency San Francisco; Hyatt Hotels Corporation, Chicago, Illinois.

Lee County Visitors and Convention Bureau (2017). Information retrieved from the *Lee County Visitors and Convention Bureau* website at www.fortmyers-sanibel.com. Accessed May 16, 2018.

Russell, K. M.; & Kim, B. (2016). *Hotel Franchise Fee Guide (2015/16 United States)*. HVS; Mineola, NY.

STR (2018). Hotel Industry Analytical Foundations. *SHARE Center: Certified Hotel Industry Analyst* training materials.

HOTEL DEVELOPMENT PROJECT

Students completing a course in hotel, lodging, or resort management are encouraged to complete a hotel development project over the course of the semester/term; students are encouraged to work in small groups of 3 – 5 students. *Appendix A* outlines the project in its entirety.

The next *hotel development assignment* may be found at the conclusion of *Chapter 5: Optimizing Revenue.*

Chapter 5
Optimizing Revenue

This chapter examines the role of a successful revenue management team and identifies how hotel pricing strategies, careful customer selection, yield management, benchmarking, and revenue protection strategies are used to optimize hotel revenue.

PURPOSE AND LEARNING OBJECTIVES:

A hotel has limited service capacity; consequently, an effective process must be established to ensure that the hotel carefully selects customers to optimize revenue. Upon the conclusion of this chapter, readers will be able to:

- Explain why hotel management's goal is to optimize versus maximize revenue.
- Identify the five conditions that must be in place to employ optimization strategies.
- Identify the core members of the revenue management team and discuss their respective roles.
- Define and calculate key performance indicators (KPIs), including average daily rate (ADR), demand, occupancy percentage, revenue, revenue per available room (RevPAR), room nights, service capacity, supply, utilization rate, and yield.
- Describe the process of establishing hotel room rates.
- Explain dynamic guestroom pricing strategies.
- Describe how hotels manage their available service capacity by using stay restrictions.
- Explain how group business is evaluated and selected by a hotel.
- Explain how food, beverage, and ancillary revenue goals are established for meetings and events hosted by a hotel.
- Explain the key components of a sales contract, identifying the sections within the contract that are designed to protect the hotel from the loss of contracted revenue.
- Describe the process of forecasting hotel occupancy, ADR, and room revenue, as well as food, beverage, and ancillary revenue.
- Identify the data and data analysis techniques used to guide revenue optimization processes and decision-making.
- Explain the concept of benchmarking, as well as the role STR plays in providing competitive market data.

OPTIMIZING REVENUE

The management team of a hotel property has a fiduciary responsibility to optimize revenue. In *Chapter 3: Defining Guest Segments*, the categories of guests that consume hotel services are defined. In *Chapter 4: Effective Sales and Marketing*, strategies are outlined to generate demand for a hotel's products, services, and experiences. The current chapter explores strategies to manage the demand created by the hotel sales and marketing team to optimize hotel revenue. Ideally, the marketing strategies employed will identify and generate more demand for services than the hotel can accommodate. Under such circumstances hotel management may be selective when choosing which customers to serve, allowing hotel management to optimize revenue.

> fiduciary responsibility: a legal and ethical obligation to work in the best interest of the employer

Optimizing Versus Maximizing Revenue

The term *optimizing* is specifically chosen, rather than *maximizing*, because it may not always be in a hotel's best long-term interest to maximize revenue. Recall from *Chapter 4: Effective Sales and Marketing* that the sales team works to establish trusted relationships with key clients. For trusted relationships to be established, clients must feel that their relationship with a hotel is mutually beneficial. There may be times when a hotel marketer may be able to sell its available guestroom inventory to guests

©TijanaM/shutterstock.com

willing and able to pay a higher room rate for a given night, thereby maximizing revenue; however, there may be volume accounts that provide the hotel with a substantial number of room nights throughout the year, even during periods of low demand. Wise hotel managers will set aside a portion of their inventory during high demand periods, such as during citywide conventions and the peak season in the market, to be able to accommodate requests for accommodations from volume accounts. In addition, recall from *Chapter 2: Successful Hotel Management* the discussion regarding the *all-square operating philosophy*; there may be times when hotel management offers accommodations at a discounted rate for a community event due to the hotel's responsibility to be a good corporate citizen. Finally, some group bookings may impact the ability of guests from other segments staying in the hotel to enjoy their hotel experience, such as a large youth group, for example; under such circumstances, hotel management must consider the impact of the group booking on the ability of other guests in the hotel to enjoy their respective experiences—hotel management cannot always evaluate business from a strictly financial perspective.

Five Necessary Conditions

To successfully optimize revenue, hotel managers employ various pricing, yield management, and customer selection strategies. Although the primary focus of these strategies center on optimizing a hotel's guestroom revenue, which typically accounts for the largest share of a hotel's revenue and produces the highest contribution margin, the revenue optimization strategies described within this chapter may be applied in a variety of contexts—not solely in a hotel setting—provided the five following conditions are met:

1. *Perishable service product:* If an enterprise provides a service product that cannot be stored or sold on an alternative date or time, which results in unused inventory being forever lost, then the service product is perishable. Examples include hotel accommodations; cruise ship cabins; airline seats; tickets to performances or sporting events; and access to recreational facilities, such as golf course tee times or tennis court reservations. Simply put, a hotel room that is vacant tonight forever loses the opportunity to produce revenue for tonight's date—it perishes.

2. *High fixed and low variable costs:* The largest costs associated with providing the service product do not vary with volume, while the incremental costs associated with the sale of an additional unit of the service product are low. For example, the high capital costs of constructing or acquiring, as well as financing, a multi-million-dollar hotel facility are not impacted by the hotel's occupancy, while the cost of accommodating one additional overnight guest is minimal—typically, just the housekeeping labor and additional costs of servicing the guestroom. Therefore, provided that a hotel receives more revenue by selling an additional room night than the low, variable costs incurred by selling the additional room night, then the incremental revenue received contributes toward fixed costs. In other words, it is prudent to sell the room night, even if fixed costs are not fully covered by the transaction.

3. *Stochastic demand:* Demand for the service product is a random variable that fluctuates over time based upon a variety of identifiable factors that allow anticipated business volumes to be estimated but not precisely predicted. Although a hotel operator does not know the precise number of rooms that will be occupied for any future date, a hotel manager can accurately estimate hotel occupancy for future dates based upon historical trends, day-of-the-week, group bookings, and market conditions. This allows a hotel manager to adjust guestroom pricing and availability, based upon these factors, to optimize revenue.

4. *Elastic demand:* Demand for the product is inversely related to price—as the price increases, demand decreases and vice versa. Many guests may be interested in enjoying a weekend escape to a tropical island resort, for example, but as the price of that weekend escape increases, fewer guests are willing or able to pay the price necessary to enjoy the resort—as the price decreases, more guests are interested in purchasing the experience. This phenomenon is directly related to the value equation (*Formula 2.1*).

5. *Multiple guest segments:* Finally, the business must be able to access multiple customer segments willing and able to pay different prices. In other words, a variety of customers seek the service product—many of which have different price sensitivities. A business traveler on a company expense account that must attend a meeting in the destination, for example, may be less price sensitive than a col-

lege student traveling to the same destination simply to explore the city or to visit friends. It is common for these various customers to purchase the product through different distribution channels.

REVENUE MANAGEMENT TEAM

The revenue management team responsible for optimizing revenue is spearheaded by the hotel's general manager (GM). Because optimizing revenue is critical to a hotel management team's ability to maximize profitability, the GM takes a leadership role in optimizing revenue and is ultimately held accountable for the hotel's pricing and optimization strategies. The GM relies heavily on input received from the revenue manager. The revenue manager's primary responsibility is to monitor and manage the hotel's revenue performance. Consequently, the revenue manager often has the greatest awareness of the competitive forces within the hotel's marketplace, as well as the hotel's booking pace, availability, and market performance. The director of sales also closely monitors demand, room rates, and booking pace within the market, although in many hotels, particularly in upper-upscale and luxury hotels, the director of sales often focuses upon group bookings. Another hotel executive with a strong interest in optimizing room revenue is the rooms director. Obviously, a hotel must meet or exceed targeted guestroom revenue for the rooms division to meet its financial goals. Finally, the director of food and beverage (F&B) and director of catering and conference services also perform an important role on the revenue optimization team by ensuring that the F&B revenues generated by guests selected to stay in the hotel, particularly group guests using the hotel's meeting space, meet forecast F&B revenue targets.

The revenue management team meets daily, during the traditional workweek, to review booking pace for the upcoming 8 to 12 weeks and to assess whether the revenue optimization strategies in place are producing the desired results. In addition, individual hotel sales managers will present potential group bookings during the daily business review to ensure that group business is being appropriately vetted and contracted. The guest service or front office manager will also receive direction on room rates to be offered to potential walk-in guests, or guests without reservations, during this important business review meeting typically held each morning.

BASIC REVENUE MANAGEMENT CONCEPTS

The following revenue management terms and concepts are essential to understanding revenue optimization strategies:

Revenue, Expenses, and Profit

revenue:
payments received in exchange for products, services, and experiences

profit:
the amount by which revenue exceeds expenses

expense:
a cost incurred to provide products, services, or experiences

loss:
when expenses exceed revenue

Revenue is defined as payments received in exchange for products, services, and experiences. Although a simple concept, this term is sometimes mistaken with profit. Profit is the amount by which revenue exceeds expenses. An expense is a cost incurred that is necessary to delivering a product, service, or experience to a customer. Consequently, revenue and profit are closely related; however, revenue is not impacted by expenses, although revenue typically causes expenses to be incurred. Profit is a general term and there are different levels or types of profit, depending upon the source of the revenues and the specific expenses included when calculating profit. For example, gross operating profit (GOP) is equal to operating revenues minus operating expenses, but GOP does not include overhead expenses, such as debt service or the mortgage payments that hotel owners must pay when financing a hotel. If revenues fail to fully cover expenses, there is no profit and a loss is incurred. The focus of this chapter is on optimizing revenue, which directly impacts profit, although consideration must also be given to the profitability or contribution margin of each specific category of revenue. Contribution margin is the amount of incremental profit generated for each unit increase in revenue and is calculated by subtracting the variable costs incurred because of an increase in revenue from the amount of the revenue increase.

Service Capacity (Supply)

service capacity:
the maximum number of customers that may be appropriately served in a specified time period

supply:
the number of available hotel rooms for a specified time period; STR's equivalent to hotel service capacity

Service capacity is defined as the maximum number of customers that may be appropriately served in a specified time period. A hotel has a daily service capacity that is equivalent to the number of guestrooms available for overnight rental to potential guests each day; to obtain the service capacity for a longer time period, the daily service capacity is multiplied by the number of days in the time period of interest. For example, a 400-room hotel has a service capacity of 400 room revenue generating opportunities daily, 1,200 (= 400 X 30) revenue generating opportunities in a 30-day month, or 146,000 (= 400 X 365) opportunities annually. The concept of service capacity also applies to many of the peripheral services offered by a hotel—a restaurant, bar, and conference facilities each have a limited service capacity. STR refers to service capacity as supply (STR, 2018); this term has the equivalent meaning and is used interchangeably with service capacity throughout this textbook.

Room Nights (Demand)

room night:
a hotel accommodation occupied by a guest or guests for a single night

A room night is defined as one hotel guestroom occupied for one single night. A guest that stays five nights in a hotel generates five room nights. A group client that uses 15 guestrooms for three nights generates 45 room nights. STR defines the number of guest parties seeking accommodations for a specified set of dates within a defined market as demand. Demand and hotel room nights are directly related—demand generates room nights. STR quantifies demand in terms of the number of room nights sold by hotels within a specified time period within a defined market (STR, 2018). Consequently, demand and room nights may be used interchangeably when discussing demand for hotel accommodations.

Utilization Rate (Occupancy)

Utilization rate is the proportion of service capacity that is consumed during a specified time period. In the hotel industry, the utilization rate is commonly referred to as the occupancy, occupancy rate, or occupancy percentage; however, the more general term is defined because it applies in other contexts, such as a restaurant or conference center. The utilization rate is calculated by dividing the number of units sold for a specific time frame by the available service capacity for the equivalent period—or demand divided by supply, to use STR's terminology.

Average Price (Average Daily Rate)

The average price may be calculated by dividing revenue by demand. In the hotel business, the average price is referred to as the average daily rate (ADR) and represents the amount of revenue generated by the typical customer each night of his/her stay; it is the average amount paid by a guest to rent a hotel room. In a F&B setting, the average price is referred to as the average check.

Yield (Revenue per Available Room)

Revenue divided by service capacity is referred to as yield, which is the amount of revenue generated per revenue producing opportunity. Yield is the most meaningful measure of revenue performance because it is impacted by both utilization rate and average price. In hotels, the yield is referred to as revenue per available room (RevPAR); in the restaurant industry, it is referred to as revenue per available seat hour (RevPASH); and in the conference services area, yield may be measured in terms of revenue per square foot (RSF) of meeting space used per day or banquet revenue per group room night (BRGR).

To better understand the application of these concepts to assess the revenue performance of a hotel, please review *Box 5.1: Key Performance Indicators*.

---

demand:
a term utilized by STR equivalent to the number of room nights rented (sold) for a specific time period

utilization rate:
the proportion of service capacity that is consumed during a specified time period

occupancy, occupancy rate, or occupancy percentage:
the proportion of available hotel rooms sold (rented) during a specified time period

average price:
the arithmetic mean of the amounts paid by customers for a single unit of a service, product, or experience

average daily rate (ADR):
the average price paid by guests for an individual guestroom per night

yield:
the amount of revenue generated per revenue producing opportunity

RevPAR:
the amount of room revenue generated per available hotel room for a specified time period

RevPASH:
the amount of F&B revenue generated per available seat per hour for a specified time period

BOX 5.1: KEY PERFORMANCE INDICATORS

© wavebreakmedia/shutterstock.com

key performance indicators (KPIs): used to assess the performance of the revenue optimization team; include occupancy (%), average daily rate (ADR), and RevPAR

To measure the effectiveness of the revenue optimization strategies employed by a hotel, three key performance indicators (KPIs) are used to assess the performance of the revenue optimization team. These include occupancy (%), average daily rate (ADR), and RevPAR.

The formulas for calculating the KPIs are as follows:

Formula 5.1: Hotel Occupancy (%): $\% = (d \div s) \times 100$

Formula 5.2: Average Daily Rate: $ADR = r \div d$

Formula 5.3: Revenue per Available Room: $RevPAR = r \div s$

Where: d = demand (room nights sold)
s = supply (service capacity)
r = revenue (guestroom revenue)

As an example, assume a 400-room hotel sells 104,392 room nights in a year producing $22,563,427 in annual guestroom revenue. Using this information, the following values may be calculated:

d = 104,392
s = 146,000 = 400 X 365
r = $22,563,427

Consequently: $\% = \mathbf{71.5\%} = 104{,}392 \div 146{,}000 \times 100$
$ADR = \mathbf{\$216.14} = 22{,}563{,}427 \div 104{,}392$
$RevPAR = \mathbf{\$154.54} = 22{,}563{,}427 \div 146{,}000$
(RevPAR also may be calculated as, $\mathbf{\$154.54} = 216.14 \times .715$)

Hotel occupancy, expressed as a percentage, will always be less-than-or-equal-to one-hundred percent (100%), except in the rare circumstance where a hotel sells out and rents one or more of its guestrooms twice within one 24-hour period. It is expressed as a percentage because it represents the percentage of available rooms that were sold or rented during the time period specified. In other words, the occupancy percentage represents the utilization rate of available service capacity.

While running a high occupancy indicates positive performance, high occupancy alone is not the primary goal of a successful hotelier. Occupancy must be balanced with ADR. If a hotel is running a high occupancy level consistently (80% to 90% or better), then it may be more profitable for a hotel to take measures to increase its ADR at the risk of losing some occupancy points. Strong occupancy is an indication of strong demand and, typically, favorable market conditions; however, it should be noted that additional occupancy adds additional expense. Good financial performance begins with strong occupancy to achieve economies of scale. Consequently, a successful hotel seeks to maintain an annual occupancy level, in most markets, of over 70% to 75%.

ADR, expressed as a dollar amount, is an indication of the average price that customers are paying to the hotel in exchange for overnight accommodations during a specified time period. ADRs vary substantially from market to market and hotel to hotel. Consequently, it is difficult to define good performance as a dollar amount in general terms. The location and service level of the hotel, as well as the quality of the physical asset and range of services and amenities offered to guests by the hotel, all impact ADR.

Obviously, hotels generate higher ADRs in markets that are enjoying strong demand, which is indicated by consistently high occupancy levels among all hotels within a market. In addition to the prices that are charged by the hotel, the mix of customers from each segment, as defined in *Chapter 3: Defining Guest Segments*, impacts the ADR substantially. Increasing the ADR has minimal impact on a hotel's expenses. As a result, increasing the ADR has a dramatic and positive impact on the profitability of a hotel—for every additional dollar gained in ADR, a hotel's profit increases by nearly one dollar for each room night sold. In the example noted, just a $1.00 increase in the annual ADR from $216.14 to $217.14, would increase the revenues and profits of this 400-room hotel by over $100,000 for the year because there are 104,392 room nights occupied annually.

RevPAR, expressed as a dollar amount, is the KPI that provides the best indication of a hotel's overall revenue performance. RevPAR is influenced by both occupancy and ADR and increases as either occupancy or the ADR increases. Conversely, a drop in either occupancy or ADR can negatively impact RevPAR. RevPAR indicates the amount of revenue generated by the hotel for each available room in the hotel per night within a specified time frame. RevPAR will always be less-than-or-equal-to the ADR. RevPAR equals the ADR when the hotel is fully occupied (100% occupancy). Another way of conceptualizing RevPAR is to think of it as the ADR that would be achieved if each vacant room is included in the ADR calculation at a zero-dollar room rate. An alternative way of calculating RevPAR is to multiply the ADR by the hotel's occupancy (RevPAR = ADR x %).

RevPAR represents the yield, which is the amount of revenue generated per revenue-generating opportunity. Therefore, it is the most important KPI because it is a "blended" value, blending both occupancy (utilization rate) and ADR (average price). Very often, a hotel manager can become overly focused on either driving occupancy (utilization rate) or ADR (average price); however, a wise hotelier realizes that you cannot deposit your occupancy percentage or ADR into a bank account—a hotel deposits its total revenue. Therefore, appropriately balancing occupancy with ADR, to maximize RevPAR, must be the goal!

economies of scale: cost advantages received when a business enjoys a sufficient volume of business to operate efficiently

ESTABLISHING GUESTROOM RATES

Hotels must establish room rates that are attractive to the guest segments that the hotel has chosen to pursue. Guests desire to receive the best value possible. Consequently, hotel marketers must be cognizant of the value equation, which was introduced in *Chapter 2: Successful Hotel Management* in *Formula 2.1* when establishing prices; therefore, it is important to review this equation again, which is found below in *Formula 2.1: The Value Equation*:

$$Value = \frac{Results\ produced\ for\ customers\ +\ Process\ quality}{Price\ to\ the\ customer\ +\ Cost\ of\ acquiring\ the\ service}$$

Review of Formula 2.1: The Value Equation

(Heskett, Sasser & Schlessinger, 1997)

Ultimately, the price paid for hotel accommodations by a guest has a substantial impact on the value that a customer perceives receiving from his/her hotel experience. Because the price paid by the customer is contained within the denominator of the value equation, the perception of value has an inverse relationship with the price; value perceptions decrease as the price increases and vice versa. Consequently, hotel management must ensure that hotel associates consistently deliver positive customer outcomes through the execution of high-quality service processes to optimize revenue. In addition to the quality of the hotel experience, guests often determine the price at which the hotel delivers an equitable value by comparing the hotel's pricing with room rates previously paid at hotels that deliver a similar experience, as well as with the rates of competitive hotels within the hotel's marketplace. As a result, a competitive rate survey provides valuable information to the revenue management team when pricing hotel rooms.

Establishing Best Available Rates

In many markets, hotel room rates are priced higher during the week, Sunday through Thursday, than on the weekends, Friday and Saturday, because weekday business travelers are typically willing and able to pay higher rates—plus demand is stronger during the week due to the demand generated by business travelers. Therefore, hotels typically survey weekday and weekend rates separately. Whether collected manually or through the use of technology, room rates at competitive hotels may be collected for a variety of future dates and lengths-of-stay (e.g. stays for one, two, three, or more nights), depending upon the lengths-of-stays typical within the market, and sorted into weekday and weekend prices. The arithmetic mean or average as well as the standard deviation of the samples may then be calculated to provide a starting point for rate discussions, as explained in the following example:

Assume that a hotel collects a sample of 1,300 non-qualified or best available rate (BAR) room rates being offered by competitive hotels in market for future dates, representing a total of 1,600 room nights. Eight hundred of the hotel stays, representing 1,000 room nights, are for weekday stays, whereas 500 of the hotel stays, representing 600 room nights, are for weekend stays. In addition to the above values, the average length-of-stay, ADR, standard deviation, minimum value, and maximum value for the weekday and weekend samples, respectively, have been calculated and provided in *Table 5.1: Room Rate Distribution Analysis* based upon the samples. This data may be used to create a BAR framework.

	Weekday	Weekend
Stays	800	500
Room nights	1,000	600
Average Length-of-Stay	1.25	1.20
ADR	**$ 187.02**	**$ 140.50**
Standard Deviation	**$ 21.23**	**$ 17.70**
Minimum rate	$ 149.00	$ 99.00
Maximum rate	$ 229.00	$ 199.00

Table 5.1: Room Rate Distribution Analysis

When creating this framework, the revenue management team should be cognizant of the empirical rule, which states that, if a random sample is selected from a population in which the observations are normally distributed, then 68.2% of observations will be found within one standard deviation of the mean, whereas 95.4% of observations will be within two standard deviations of the mean, and virtually all observations (99.7%) will be within three standard deviation units of the mean; this rule is illustrated in *Diagram 5.1: Empirical Rule*. Although the distribution of all room rates offered by competitive hotels in a market may not be normally distributed, if a large enough sample is collected, the distribution of room rates observed is likely to approximate a normal distribution closely enough that the empirical rule may be applied to estimate the distribution of observations found within the market. In other words, approximately two out of every three room rates offered to guests by competitive hotels will be within one standard deviation of the average of all room rates observed and approximately 95% of room rates offered within the market will be within two standard deviations of the average rate observed.

empirical rule:
if a random sample is selected from a population in which the observations are normally distributed, then 68.2% of observations will be found within one standard deviation of the mean, whereas 95.4% of observations will be within two standard deviations of the mean, and virtually all observations (99.7%) will be within three standard deviation units of the mean

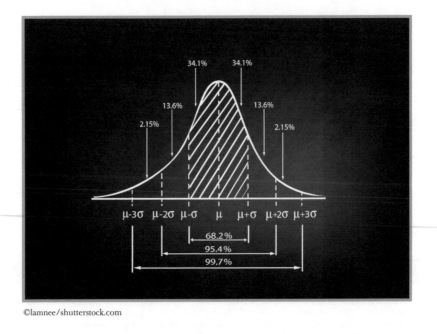

Diagram 5.1: Empirical Rule

Applying the empirical rule to the data analyzed in *Table 5.1*, this means that two of every three guests, or approximately 68% of guests shopping for a hotel room from a competitive hotel in this market for a weekday stay are being offered room rates of between $165.79 (= $187.02 – $21.23) and $208.25 (= $187.02 + $21.23), and the great majority of guests, or approximately 95% of guests, are being offered room rates of between $144.56 (= $187.02 – [2 x $21.23]) and $229.48 (= $187.02 + [2 x $21.23]). On the weekends, two of three, or 68%, of potential guests are being offered rates of between $122.80 (= $140.50 – $17.70) and $158.20 (= $140.50 + $17.70) and approximately 95% of guests are being offered rates of between $105.10 (= $140.50 – [2 x $17.70]) and $175.90 (= $140.50 + [2 x $17.70]). The total range of rates offered to guests by competitive hotels during the week is $80.00, running from between a low rate of $149.00 and a $229.00 maximum rate, whereas the rates run from $99.00 to $199.00, representing a range of $100.00, on weekends. From this information, the mid-point and a recommended increment to be used for rate adjustments may be suggested, which are outlined in *Table 5.2a: Initial BAR Framework*. It should be noted that the actual distribution of rates may vary slightly from these quick rules-of-thumb; however, there will not typically be a substantial variation. For detailed instructions on calculating the mean and standard deviation of the sample, and verifying that the distribution is approximately normal, please refer to the ***Special supplement: Calculating the Mean, Standard Deviation, and Skewness of a Sample*** located at the end of this chapter.

	Weekday	Weekend
BAR mid-point	$189	$139
Ideal increment for premiums or discounts	$ 20	$ 20

Table 5.2a: Initial BAR Framework

The initial BAR framework suggested in *Table 5.2a*, assumes that the hotel for which rates are being established offers service quality and facilities that are competitive within its market and comparable to the hotels included in the room rates sampled. Consequently, the BAR mid-points suggested in *Table 5.2a* of $189 (weekday) and $139 (weekend) are in-line with the average rates depicted in Table 5.1 of $187.02 (weekday) and $140.50 (weekend). Keeping *Equation 2.1: The Value Equation* in mind, a hotel can charge higher rates if its service quality and facilities are superior to those of its competition, while still delivering value to guests. Whereas, if a hotel is inferior to its competition in terms of the outcomes delivered to customers or the quality of processes and facilities, then the hotel may need to offer lower guestroom rates to improve customers' perceptions of value. Recall that a hotel must deliver value to its guests to build customer loyalty. To optimize revenue, a revenue management team must also take full advantage of the dispersion or spread of room rates offered within the market, as opposed to simply offering a mid-range room rate aligned with the average or arithmetic mean of the rate sample, which leads successful hotel managers to execute a dynamic pricing strategy.

Dynamic Pricing

Most travelers understand the concept of dynamic pricing, particularly because it was introduced to the travel industry over four decades ago by the airline industry. A dynamic pricing strategy takes advantage of the basic economic principle of supply and demand to charge higher prices during periods of higher demand, while leveraging the concept of elasticity of demand by lowering prices during periods of lower demand.

dynamic pricing: takes advantage of the basic economic principle of supply and demand to charge higher prices during periods of higher demand, while leveraging the concept of elasticity of demand by lowering prices during periods of lower demand

Historically, as outlined in *Chapter 3: Defining Guest Segments*, hotels established rack or published rates and a range of discounts. A rate fencing strategy was then used by hoteliers to restrict access to the various discounts based upon anticipated demand. In the past, it was common for hotels to sell a very small proportion of their total available room inventory at the rack rate except during periods of very high demand—the rack rate was merely a reference point used to establish the various discounted guestroom rates. Today, most hotel marketers have replaced their rack or published rates with a BAR; however, the BAR is not a static, fixed value—it fluctuates based upon anticipated demand—and it is dynamic.

rate fence: a pricing strategy that prohibits guestrooms from being sold (rented) to guest segments priced below a specific room rate based upon anticipated demand each day

A well-executed dynamic pricing strategy allows the revenue management team to substantially reduce the number of discounted rates that are offered or, in some cases, to eliminate discounts. The goal is to sell the BAR to most individual travelers staying in the hotel on any given night, thereby ensuring rate parity. Rate parity is achieved when the price for a hotel room for a specific date does not vary depending upon the distribution channel or the booking site where the reservation is made. Many hotel parent companies guarantee that the lowest room rate available will always be offered through their brand's proprietary website or mobile app. A dynamic pricing strategy helps hotel marketers to deliver on this promise, which builds brand loyalty.

rate parity:
when the price for a hotel room for a specific date does not vary depending upon the distribution channel or the booking site where the reservation is made

As previously mentioned, the BAR must always offer travelers an equitable value. Taking advantage of guests by charging excessive rates that fail to offer an equitable value is an unethical practice referred to as price gouging; however, guests understand that demand for hotel accommodations fluctuate. Therefore, sophisticated travelers understand and expect hotel room rates to fluctuate on a daily, weekly, or seasonal basis.

price gouging:
taking advantage of strong demand to charge excessive room rates that fail to offer equitable value

When using a dynamic pricing strategy, hotels establish room rates based upon the guestroom rates of key competitors, coupled with factors that impact demand within the market. These rates are then periodically adjusted by reasonable increments, so that the hotel still provides value to the customer, based upon the changing dynamics within the market. Factors that impact the rate include anticipated demand, pricing adjustments made by competitors, and booking pace. As previously explained, a measure of room rate dispersion within the market, such as the standard deviation of the room rate sample, provides the room revenue management team with guidance regarding the specific amount the rate may be reasonably adjusted, while still providing value.

booking pace:
a measure of how quickly available guestrooms are being sold (rented) for future dates

Returning to our example, the initial BAR framework suggested in *Table 5.2a* recommends mid-point values of $189 on weekdays and $139 on weekends, as well as a $20 increment when changing prices in response to market conditions. This recommendation is based upon the standard deviation calculated from the rate sample of $21.23 on weekdays and $17.70 on weekends, as outlined in *Table 5.1: Room Rate Distribution Analysis*. By increasing or decreasing room rates by no more than approximately two standard deviation units, the full range of BARs offered by the hotel will remain competitive within the marketplace, as explained in *Table 5.2b: BAR Dynamic Pricing Model*, because approximately 95% of room rates offered by competitive hotels are within two standard deviations of the average or mean rate.

BAR-level	Weekday	Weekend	When offered	Implications*
Highest BAR (limited availability)	$229	$179	Demand clearly exceeds supply; the availability of rooms in the market is extremely limited.	Less than 2.5% of guests typically pay higher than this room rate in this market.
High BAR (strong demand)	$209	$159	Demand is moderately higher than is typical; availability is somewhat limited.	16% of hotel guests typically pay more than this room rate in this market.
BAR (standard rate)	$189	$139	Standard rate offered during periods of moderate or typical demand.	50% of hotel guests typically pay this rate or higher and 50% would typically pay this or lower rates.
Low BAR (soft demand)	$169	$119	Demand is weaker than normally experienced; plenty of room availability in the market.	84% of guests typically pay room rates higher than this and only 16% pay this rate or less.
Lowest BAR (weak demand)	$149	$ 99	Demand is extremely weak; accommodations are widely available.	Most guests (97.5%) typically pay this rate or higher when traveling to this market.

*The approximate proportion of potential hotel guests traveling to the market that would typically pay higher or lower room rates than the respective BAR, based upon the empirical rule.

Table 5.2b: BAR Dynamic Pricing Model

Psychological or Just-Below Pricing

Research has consistently demonstrated that a psychological or just-below pricing strategy is an effective way to maximize revenue, including within the hotel industry (Collins & Parsa, 2006). When a price is established, the left-most digits are most meaningful in determining a customer's perception of the price offered, because these values are most significant. For example, with the $189 standard BAR offered in *Table 5.2b*, the hundreds-digit, "1" in this case, is most significant—the "1" indicates that the rate is over $100, but less than $200; the "8" and "9" that follow the "1" are less significant because these values are placed in the tens-digit and singles-digit positions, respectively. In other words, the "1" adds $100 to the price, the "8" adds $80 to the price, and the "9" adds just $9 to the price. Therefore, the digits further to the left within the room rate have the most substantial impact on whether a potential guest determines if the rate offers acceptable value, resulting in a booking, or not. Quite frankly, most guests willing and able to pay $180 for an overnight hotel experience, for example, will not be deterred from paying $189—the additional $9 will not result in a lost booking. Consequently, revenue is usually optimized when rates end with a "9," as reflected in *Table 5.2b: BAR Dynamic Pricing Model*. It should be noted, however, that when rates are below $100 per night, and the dispersion of rates is modest with a standard deviation of $10 or less in the rate sample, it may be appropriate to tier rates in increments of less than $10, resulting in

> **psychological or just-below pricing strategy:**
> the use of prices that end with a "9" in the singles-digit position

rates that end in values other than $9. This circumstance is most likely to occur in the economy and midscale segments, where guests are more rate sensitive.

Qualified Rates

As outlined in *Chapter 3: Defining Guest Segments*, hotel marketers pursue a variety of guest segments that are often willing and able to pay a variety of hotel room rates. The dynamic pricing strategy, as previously discussed, provide attractive yet competitive rates to many guest segments; however, some guest segments will require specifically negotiated or more deeply discounted guestroom rates. For example, if the revenue management team determines that revenue may be optimized by accommodating government travelers under specific circumstances, then the hotel may extend the government *per diem* rate on select dates; recall from *Chapter 3* that the government *per diem* guestroom rate is specific to each market and determined by an annual hotel rate study conducted by the General Services Administration of the United States government. *Per diem* rates are updated each October and available online at: https://www.gsa.gov/travel/plan-book/per-diem-rates/per-diem-rates-lookup.

last room availability: provides a client with access to a negotiated or volume discount on dates when discounted room rates are not being offered

Hotel marketers may also choose to negotiate rates with corporate or institutional clients within their specific market that generate large volumes of overnight hotel guests on an annual basis. Many of these organizations may also host meetings for employees, clients, franchisees, or vendors. Rates for these local volume accounts are negotiated based upon the total number of room nights generated each year, as well as the typical arrival and departure patterns of each account's overnight travelers, and whether the client expects to receive last room availability, which requires that the client be sold a room at the client's volume rate even if no discounted rates are being extended for the specific date(s) requested. Qualified rates, as outlined in *Chapter 3*, are rates extended only to guests that meet a specific requirement or qualification (e.g. government employees; employees of or travelers conducting business with a firm or organization with a volume account agreement; members of specified membership organizations, such as AAA or AARP; travelers booking through a specific Online Travel Agent (OTA) site or travel consortia; etc.). Qualified rates may offer discounts of 10% to 50% less than the standard BAR rate, depending upon the specific needs of the client, travel pattern of the travelers, and overall market conditions, although these rates are most commonly expressed as a specific dollar amount versus a percentage discount. The revenue management team will often perform a displacement analysis, as explained in *Box 3.3: Displacement Analysis for Contract Rooms* in *Chapter 3: Defining Guest Segments*, to assess the potential revenue impact of a deeply discounted rate.

It should be noted that many negotiated rates will not use a just-below or psychological pricing strategy, as previously recommended. Clients that generate a substantial volume of hotel room nights annually use their purchasing power to negotiate the lowest rate possible because each dollar increase in rate may represent a considerable increase in the client's annual lodging costs. For example, a client generating an average of 100 room nights per month, or 1,200 room nights per year, saves over $10,000 annually by negotiating a $9.00 decrease in the rate paid ($10,800 = $9 X 1,200). In addition, many OTAs, travel consortia, and wholesalers mark-up their negotiated rate, typically by 20% or more, when re-selling the accommodations to their clients.

For example, a negotiated OTA rate of $150 represents the net rate received by the hotel, which is typically marked-up or priced higher by the OTA. The guest reserves the room through the OTA website or app, pays the room rate established by the OTA directly to the travel agent at time of booking, which may be marked-up to $179 or $189 on the OTA's website or app, while the OTA pays the hotel the negotiated $150 rate following the guest's stay, retaining the price difference as the OTA's share of the revenue; this OTA business model is referred to as the merchant model. Travel agents or sites that accept a commission, typically of 10% of room revenue, allowing the guest to book at the hotel's BAR or non-discounted rate and pay the hotel directly, are using a commission model. It is not uncommon for a hotel that extends a deeply discounted rate to an OTA to require them to mark-up the price of the room a minimum percentage amount to prevent potential guests from knowing how deeply the hotel is willing and able to discount its room rates.

Guest Mix

The guestroom prices or rates extended by a hotel are not the only factor that determine the overall ADR realized by a hotel. The ADR is determined, in large part, by its guest mix or the proportion of total guests that are paying each of the various rates that are offered by the hotel. The following example illustrates the dramatic impact that guest mix has on a hotel's ADR.

Assume a hotel sells 200 guestrooms for a specific night and extends to guests one of four room rates—BAR, corporate volume, government, or a travel consortia rate. The guest segments, number of rooms sold to each segment, room rate extended to each segment, and the total revenue produced, as well as the overall ADR, is indicated in *Table 5.3a: Impact of Guest Mix (1st night)* below:

	Rooms sold	%	Rate	Room revenue	%
Best Available Rate (BAR)	80	40.0%	$209.00	$16,720	45.8%
Corporate volume	60	30.0%	$185.00	$11,100	30.4%
Government	20	10.0%	$134.00	$2,680	7.3%
Travel consortia	40	20.0%	$150.00	$6,000	16.4%
Total	**200**	**100.0%**	**$182.50**	**$36,500**	**100.0%**

Table 5.3a: Impact of Guest Mix (1st night)

merchant model: travel agents or sites that price and market hotel accommodations, collect payment for the accommodations directly from guests, while paying hotels deeply discounted negotiated room rates

commission model: travel agents or sites that accept a commission from a hotel, allowing the guest to book at the hotel's BAR or non-discounted rate while paying the hotel directly

guest mix: the proportion of total guests that are paying each of the various room rates offered by the hotel, synonymous with market mix

Now, assume that on a second night the hotel experiences lower demand from guests that are willing and able to pay the BAR rate and that the number of accommodations requested from corporate volume accounts also is reduced. Guests from these segments are replaced for the second night with guests paying the lower government and travel consortia rates. The hotel still manages to sell 200 guestrooms; however, the guest mix and resulting room revenue and ADR is outlined in *Table 5.3b: Impact of Guest Mix (2nd night)*.

	Rooms sold	%	Rate	Room revenue	%
Best Available Rate (BAR)	40	20.0%	$209.00	$8,360	26.0%
Corporate volume	20	10.0%	$185.00	$3,700	11.5%
Government	60	30.0%	$134.00	$8,040	25.0%
Travel consortia	80	40.0%	$150.00	$12,000	37.4%
Total	**200**	**100.0%**	**$160.50**	**$32,100**	**100.0%**

Table 5.3b: Impact of Guest Mix (2nd night)

market mix:
the proportion of total guests that are paying each of the various room rates offered by the hotel, synonymous with guest mix

Despite offering identical room rates, as well as selling the same number of room nights, the hotel on the second night, detailed in *Table 5.3b*, generates $4,400, or 12.1% less in guestroom revenue (= $36,500 - $32,100) and an ADR of just $160.50 as compared to an ADR of $182.50 on the initial night, depicted in *Table 5.3a*. This $22.00 or 12.1% drop in the ADR on the second night is due entirely to a shift in the guest mix—also commonly referred to as market mix.

©Kzenon/shutterstock.com

MANAGING THE AVAILABILITY OF ROOM RATES

Because a variety of rates is offered by a hotel revenue management team—including BARs, volume rates, government rates, and OTA and travel consortia rates, in addition to other discounts—the availability of these various room rates must be controlled. A rate fencing strategy is commonly used to control access to discounted guestroom rates. The concept of rate fencing involves prioritizing access to accommodations to the various guest segments based upon the room rates that each segment is willing and able to pay for overnight accommodations. To effectively use a rate fencing strategy, a hotel marketer restricts access to its available guestroom service capacity based upon anticipated demand from each guest segment. Guest segments that pay higher guestroom rates, such as the guests paying BAR and corporate volume rates in the guest mix example provided in *Tables 5.3a* and *5.3b*, are given priority over guests from the lower-rated government and travel consortia segments. Implementation of this strategy requires that a hotel limit or *fence-off* the number of accommodations to be sold to each specific segment of customers based upon anticipated demand. In some instances, it may be appropriate to eliminate access to any guests from a specific segment if demand from higher priced segments is adequate to sell-out the hotel's remaining available service capacity.

Distribution Channels

Many qualified discounts, including deeply discounted OTA and travel consortia rates, are sold through specific distribution channels. A distribution channel is a chain of intermediaries through which a product or service passes from the provider to the end user. One of the primary distribution channels within the travel industry is the global distribution system (GDS)—a computer network originally established by the airline industry to facilitate flight reservations—which is now a primary distribution channel for a variety of travel products, including hotel accommodations and rental cars. In addition to the hotel parent companies, through their brand websites, apps, and central reservation system (CRS), distribution channels within the hotel industry include the previously mentioned GDS, including the Amadeus, Apollo, Galileo, Sabre, and Worldspan computer networks; travel agents and travel consortia, including American Express Travel Service, Carlson Wagonlit, and Thomas Cook Travel; OTAs, such as Expedia, Orbitz, and Travelocity; and metasearch sites, including Kayak, Google Travel, TripAdvisor, and Trivago; as well as countless travel wholesalers, tour operators, and more.

Because hotels often offer deeply discounted guestroom rates only through specific distribution channels, a hotel may restrict access to discounted rates by controlling the availability of its accommodations through these various distribution channels. In other words, a hotel may offer accommodations through all available distribution channels when demand is low, while limiting the distribution channels through which its accommodations are offered when guestroom availability is limited or demand is strong. In addition to the room rate offered, a hotel's decision to sell accommodations through a specific distribution channel is impacted by the cost incurred when a reservation is booked through the respective channel; a single reservation may also flow through multiple channels, incurring multiple fees. For example, a reservation

distribution channel: a chain of intermediaries through which a product or service passes from the provider to the end user

global distribution system (GDS): a computer network used to facilitate the electronic distribution of travel services

metasearch sites: travel sites that allow the side-by-side comparison of prices offered for identical travel services through multiple electronic distribution channels simultaneously may be booked through a travel agent, which accesses the hotel's availability and rate information, and relays the reservation, through the Sabre (GDS) reservation system; the reservation is then forwarded by the GDS to the individual hotel through the hotel parent company's CRS. Consequently, the individual hotel will pay a 10% commission to the travel agent, a fee to Sabre, and an additional reservation fee to the parent company (brand) on that single reservation. Fees may be calculated as a percentage of the total room revenue associated with the reservation, a flat fee per reservation, or a combination of both. It is not uncommon for a hotel to incur fees as high as 25% to 30% of the total value of the reservation in some instances.

Length-of-Stay and Day-of-the-Week Considerations

The amount of room revenue generated by a specific guest is impacted by more than the room rate that is paid; it is also impacted by the number of nights the guest is planning to stay in the hotel. As a result, the number of nights requested, as well as the specific dates requested, must also be considered when determining whether a reservation request should be accepted by the hotel. Refer to the guest mix example, illustrated in *Tables 5.3a* and *5.3b*, and it is not difficult to understand that a government traveler staying for two nights, at a rate of $134 per night, generates more total revenue, $268, than a guest staying at a BAR of $209 for just one night. Furthermore, the specific nights that the guest is requesting must also be considered. Demand for accommodations is lower in many markets, for example, on Sunday nights and much higher on Wednesday nights. Consequently, a guest's stay that includes a Sunday night is more valuable to a hotel, and can be offered a deeper discount, than a guest planning to stay only on a Wednesday night, under such circumstance.

Consider the following regarding the typical weekend travel patterns experienced by many hotels:
- Many hotels enjoy strong weekend demand from leisure travelers.
- Virtually all weekend hotel stays, on non-holiday weekends, will include a Saturday night because many people work a traditional Monday through Friday workweek.
- Only a portion of weekend guests will arrive on a Friday evening, because many guests will work on Friday and may not begin their weekend activities until Saturday morning.
- Because many weekend guests will return to work on Monday morning, following a weekend excursion, very few weekend travelers will stay on Sunday night.

Because of these factors, weekend demand for leisure travelers will peak on Saturday night for most non-holiday weekends. If reservation requests are honored on a first-come-first-served basis, then the hotel's service capacity or guestroom inventory will sell-out for Saturday prior to Friday night, resulting in the displacement of guests seeking a two-night (Friday and Saturday night) weekend stay. Therefore, a stay restriction must be put in place to prevent Saturday night from filling with one-night stays and displacing revenue on Friday night.

Stay Restrictions

Stay restrictions are controls established to ensure that any available guestroom inventory sold to transient or individual guests complies with the current revenue optimization strategies. In other words, the revenue management team establishes specific criteria that a transient reservation must meet, or the business will be turned away. The most common stay restriction is a minimum-length-of-stay (MLOS); a MLOS restriction requires that any reservation request for the restricted night must stay the specified number of nights or longer to be accepted by the hotel. So, for example, if a hotel has a typical weekend booking pattern in which demand peaks for Saturday nights, a hotel may place an MLSO2 restriction on Saturday night, which requires that any additional reservations booked for a Saturday arrival are staying for at least two nights—this restriction also prevents the displacement of two-night or longer stays arriving prior to Saturday that include Saturday night, because one night Saturday-only stays will be turned away. A full description of how stay restrictions are used to optimize revenue is outlined in *Box 5.2: Effective Yield Management*.

Building upon a Group Base

The focus of managing an effective sell strategy is upon optimizing the room revenue generated by individual travelers, both business and leisure, that often book their accommodations during the final 6 weeks prior to their arrival, as well as short-term group business, which tend to be small groups of less than 50 room nights. In many hotels, particularly select-select service economy, midscale, upper-midscale, and smaller upscale hotels, with limited meeting space, individual travel represents the lion's share of the hotel's occupancy and revenue. In larger hotels, particularly upscale, upper-upscale, and luxury hotels with a substantial amount of meeting space, group guests generate the majority, or at least a substantial share, of the hotel's guestroom revenue. In addition, group business—clients that occupy 10 or more rooms per night—often generate a substantial amount of food, beverage, and ancillary revenue, which is critical to the hotel's financial success. In larger, group-oriented hotels, it is critical that a significant base of group business is contracted well in advance to allow the hotel to effectively optimize revenue.

stay restriction: reservation controls established to ensure that the sale of available guestroom inventory optimizes revenue

minimum-length-of-stay (MLOS): any reservation request for the restricted night must stay the specified number of nights or longer to be accepted by the hotel

BOX 5.2: EFFECTIVE YIELD MANAGEMENT

yield management:
the practice of optimizing revenue by carefully selecting the guests to whom available service capacity is sold based upon specific factors

minimum acceptable rate (MAR):
a room rate specified for each night below which a hotel will not accept a reservation

Yield management is the practice of optimizing revenue by carefully selecting the guests to whom available service capacity is sold based upon specific factors. Some may question whether this practice is ethical, or even legal, because it is a form of discrimination; however, it is not only ethical, management has a fiduciary responsibility to optimize revenue. A business cannot discriminate based upon a guest's ethnic or religious background, nationality or country of origin, race, gender, age, or other demographic factors; however, a business may sell its available service capacity in a manner that optimizes the revenue generated in exchange for its available products and services.

Stay restrictions are controls established to ensure that any available guestroom inventory sold to individual travelers complies with the hotel's current revenue optimization strategies. A minimum acceptable rate (MAR) is established for each night by the revenue management team to ensure that no room nights are sold at a room rate below the established minimum. Additional stay restrictions are used to control the length of a guest's stay or arrival and departure pattern; commonly used stay restrictions, as well as their intended purposes, are outlined in *Table 5.4: Commonly Used Hotel Stay Restrictions*. Stay restrictions controlling length-of-stay or arrival-and-departure patterns are applied to a reservation request based upon the guest's requested date of arrival. Hotel policies vary on how BARs and MARs are applied; however, it is becoming increasingly common for revenue management teams to charge guests paying BAR the BAR corresponding to each night of the guest's stay, even if it causes the guest's rate to fluctuate over the course of the stay. Discounted rates are commonly offered over the entirety of a guest's stay, if the reservation is accepted, particularly if last room availability has been negotiated with the client. In other words, a guest that books the non-qualified BAR rate may experience a rate change during their stay; however, a guest that qualifies to receive the government *per diem* is typically extended the government *per diem* rate for the guest's entire length-of-stay if the reservation is accepted. The exception may be if a hotel uses a "no-discount" restriction.

The use of stay restrictions is illustrated in the following example:

Assume that a 400-room hotel has the availability outlined in the third and fourth rows of *Table 5.5: Guestroom Availability, MARs, and Stay Restrictions* for the 7-day period specified approximately 1 month in advance. In the fifth row, the anticipated numbers of room nights that are expected to be sold or picked-up in the 30 days immediately preceding each date, based upon a 6-week average for the corresponding day-of-the-week, are indicated. In the sixth row, the historical demand for the corresponding day-of-the-year (e.g. first Sunday in May, first Monday in May, etc.), based upon a 2-year

Stay restriction	Description	Impact or purpose
MAR	All guests must pay a room rate greater than or equal to the MAR.	Optimizes the guestroom rate or price charged.
MLOS#[1]	Identifies the minimum number of nights a guest must stay if stay includes the restricted date.	Limits the number of reservations accepted for a peak night and increases occupancy on the shoulder[2] nights.
Minimum-Maximum (MIN#-MAX#)[3]	Guest may stay more than a stated minimum number of nights or no more than a maximum number of nights.	Eliminates a mid-range stay while permitting either a long stay (longer than the minimum-value) or a short stay (shorter than the maximum-value).
Closed-to-Arrival (CTA)	No reservations are to be taken for guests that will arrive on the restricted date.	Prevents the hotel from accepting more arriving guests on the restricted date; used when arrivals far outnumber expected departures following a night projected to sell-out to prevent excessive overbooking.
One-Night-Only (ONO)	Reservations are being accepted for 1 night only when arriving on the restricted date.	Offered the night prior to a severely over-sold night to prevent guest relocations (walks).
No-Discounts (NO-DISC)	No-discounts available on this night under any conditions.	This is a special stay restriction that applied to all reservations, including stay throughs, to prevent discounts from being accommodated on high demand nights.
No room type (e.g. NO double-queens, NO kings, etc.)	Used when a specific room type is sold-out or oversold.	Used when a specific room type is in high demand to prevent the hotel from being unable to honor room type commitments; particularly useful when an event generates strong demand for multiple occupancy guestrooms and double-doubles or double queen-bedded rooms are sold-out.
50% rule[4]	If a potential guest stay qualifies for **more** than half (50%) of the requested dates, then the reservation should be accepted.	Ensures that a guest reservation with a long duration is not turned away due to short-term considerations, because any displaced revenue on restricted nights is more than offset by the additional nights of incremental revenue.

[1]The # symbol is to be replaced with the number of nights required (e.g. MLOS2, MLOS3, etc.).
[2]Shoulder nights are the nights on either side, the night before or after, the restricted date.
[3]Again, the # symbol is replaced with a specific number of nights (e.g. MIN3-MAX1; MIN5-MAX2; etc.).
[4]The 50% rule recognizes that the incremental revenue generated on the non-restricted nights more than offsets any revenue displaced on the restricted nights provided the reservation complies with the stay restrictions in place on MORE than half of the requested dates.

Table 5.4: Commonly Used Hotel Stay Restrictions

average, is noted. The hotel offers a volume rate of $185, a government rate of $134, and a travel consortia or OTA net rate of $150, in addition to a BAR, which runs from $149 to $229 on weekdays and $99 to $179 on weekends, adjusted in $20 increments, as outlined in *Table 5.2b: Dynamic Pricing Model*. BARs have been established for each day as specified in the 7th row and MARs are identified in the 8th row. Finally, the stay restrictions established are indicated in the 9th row of *Table 5.5*, as specified, based upon anticipated demand.

Row	Day	Sun	Mon	Tue	Wed	Thu	Fri	Sat
2nd	*Date*	*5/5/2019*	*5/6/2019*	*5/7/2019*	*5/8/2019*	*5/9/2019*	*5/10/2019*	*5/11/2019*
3rd	Rooms available	79	75	22	17	106	215	21
4th	Rooms on-the-books	321	325	378	383	294	185	379
5th	30-day pick-up (6-week average)	41	72	94	112	81	67	78
6th	Historical demand (2-year average)	184	365	392	397	342	227	354
7th	BAR	$189	$209	$229	$229	$189	$139	$179
8th	MAR	$134	$134	$229	$229	$134	$134	$179
9th	Stay restrictions		MIN4-MAX1	MLOS3	MLOS2			MLOS2

Table 5.5: Guestroom Availability, MARs, and Stay Restrictions

The explanation of the room rates and stay restrictions specified in *Table 5.5* are as follows:

- ***Sunday, May 5:*** All reservations are accepted for guests requesting to arrive on Sunday at any guestroom rate, including the government *per diem*. Because Sunday is not anticipated to sell-out (79 rooms available with a 30-day pick-up of just 41 room nights anticipated) and the hotel will struggle to fill all available rooms on Monday, the 6th of May (75 rooms available with a 72-room night pick-up anticipated), all anticipated reservation requests must be accommodated to optimize revenue on these two nights, including discounts, which is why the MAR is set at $134. Even a stay of three or four nights, arriving on Sunday evening at the government *per diem* rate, will enhance hotel revenue because a four-night stay at *per diem* generates $536 (= $134 x 4) in revenue, although it potentially displaces a guest at the BAR of $229 on Tuesday, the 7th of May, and on Wednesday, the 8th. If this displacement occurs, the displacement cost is $190 (= [$229 - $134] x 2);

displacement cost: room revenue lost when a reservation is accepted at a lower room rate than an alternative reservation for specific dates

the incremental revenue generated by accepting the 4-night *per diem* guest, arriving on Sunday for a 4-night stay, is $268 (= $134 x 2), because the guestroom would not otherwise be sold on Sunday (5) or Monday (6) nights. This results in net revenue being enhanced by $78 (= $268 - $190). Because the hotel will still enjoy a reasonable level of occupancy on Sunday night, and availability is limited on the surrounding dates, the BAR is set at the "standard," mid-point level (refer to *Table 5.2b*). This helps the hotel maintain price or rate integrity, ensuring that guests that stay multiple nights at BAR experience reasonable increases or reductions in their room rates when rate changes occur.

- **Monday, May 6:** Reservations arriving on Monday, the 6 of May, will be accommodated for 1-night stays or for 4-night or longer stays. All anticipated reservation requests are needed Monday evening to optimize revenue; 2- or 3-night reservations, particularly at discounted rates, are likely to displace other guests, whereas stays of four or five nights enhance net revenue. As a result, the MAR is set at $134 because stays that meet the minimum-maximum (MIN4-MAX1) restriction enhance net revenue, as previously explained. The BAR is increased to $209, the "high BAR" rate (refer to *Table 5.2b*), because limited guestroom inventory remains available and anticipated demand is sufficient to sell nearly all of the remaining service-capacity (75 rooms available with anticipated demand of 72 rooms). Even if the hotel experiences some resistance to the $209 (high BAR) rate, the higher BAR may potentially generate incremental revenue of $1,500, which is estimated by multiplying the remaining 75 rooms available by the $20 (= $209 - $189) rate premium enjoyed. Consequently, net revenue is enhanced unless more than 7 (= $1,500 ÷ $209) potential reservations are lost for Monday night due to resistance to the "high BAR" room rate of $209.

- **Tuesday, May 7, and Wednesday, May 8:** Demand for accommodations far exceeds supply for Tuesday and Wednesday night (demand of 94 and 112 room nights, respectively, are estimated whereas only 22 rooms remain available on Tuesday and 17 available on Wednesday). Therefore, the BAR Is set at its highest-level of $229 (refer to *Table 5.2b*), which is also the MAR. Guests arriving on either of these dates must stay through Thursday night due to the MLOS3 and MLOS2 restrictions on the 7th and 8th of May, respectively. The revenue management team may consider placing a no-discounts (NO-DISC) restriction on these nights; however, any discounts staying through these two nights will generate incremental revenue on both Monday and Thursday nights, and possibly on additional nights when the revenue is needed, resulting in a net revenue gain even if accommodated at a qualified discount.

- **Thursday, May 9, and Friday, May 10:** Demand is not anticipated to be adequate to sell the remaining rooms available on Thursday, May 9 (available service capacity of 106 with anticipated demand of 81 room nights), or on Friday, May 10 (215 rooms available with demand of 67 rooms estimated). Consequently, the MAR is set at $134 and the BAR at the "standard BAR" of $189 on Thursday and $139 on Friday (refer to *Table 5.2b*).

- **Saturday, May 11th:** Demand (78 room nights anticipated) far exceeds supply (21 rooms available), resulting in a "highest BAR" rate of $179 (refer to *Table 5.2b*)

incremental revenue:
the room revenue gained when accepting one reservation over an alternative reservation

net revenue:
the incremental revenue gained less the displacement cost

price or rate integrity:
the practice of maintaining relatively consistent room rates, avoiding wide dispersion in pricing, to manage guests' perceptions of value

also being set as the MAR. In addition, guests arriving on Saturday must stay through Sunday night. Guests arriving prior to Saturday that pay the BAR will experience a rate increase to the $179 "highest BAR." No discounted guestroom rates will be permitted to stay-through Saturday night.

Effectively placed stay restrictions slow down the booking pace on nights with high demand, without impacting the sale of available guestrooms on nights with lower demand, with the ultimate goal of leveling day-to-day occupancy by limiting peaks and valleys. Many hotel markets experience strong mid-week demand (Tuesday and Wednesday), softer demand on shoulder nights (Monday and Thursday), and weak demand at the beginning and end of the workweek (Sunday and Friday). Likewise, it is common for hotels to experience stronger leisure demand on Saturday night, with weaker demand on Friday and Sunday. The revenue management team's objective is to sell every available room, at the highest room rate possible, each-and-every night, each week. Therefore, stay restrictions are placed on nights with peak demand to save rooms, in effect, for guests that also desire to stay on shoulder nights and nights with weak demand; however, the revenue management team must be cognizant of typical travel patterns when placing stay restrictions. For example, while the revenue management team may desire to sell their remaining guestroom inventory only to guests requesting to stay Friday, Saturday, *and* Sunday nights, for a specific high-demand weekend, there may be very few guests that will request such an arrival and departure pattern. Consequently, establishing stay restrictions that require a 3-night stay, Friday through Sunday night, during a non-holiday weekend may be a futile exercise—negatively impacting revenue optimization efforts.

sell strategy:
a combination of BARs, MARs, and stay restrictions put in place by the revenue optimization team to optimize room revenue each night

Finally, it must be noted that the sell strategy or combination of BARs, MARs, and stay restrictions recommended to optimize revenue over the 7-day period illustrated within this example is based upon the limited information provided. Additional information is typically available in an actual hotel setting, which may include anticipated demand by guest segment (versus overall demand as provided in this example); availability and BARs of competitive hotels; awareness of special events taking place in the market; and much more. This additional information may lead the revenue management team to execute more aggressive optimization strategies. Hotel marketers that use a revenue management system (RMS) often rely upon sell strategy recommendations that are provided by this technology, which uses complex algorithms that track, monitor, and analyze the wealth of information available regarding supply, demand, and pricing dynamics within the hotel's marketplace. A more detailed explanation of these algorithms is provided in *Box 5.4: Understanding RMS Algorithms*.

©ID1974/Shutterstock.com

Chapter 3: Defining Guest Segments provides detailed descriptions of the various group segments, their booking patterns, and room rate sensitivities; the chapter also discusses how meeting space is used to generate group business. *Chapter 4: Effective Sales and Marketing*, as well as the *Section 2 Supplement: Sales Team Deployment: A Tale of Two Markets*, outline how a hotel marketer deploys the hotel sales team to pursue the most profitable group segments for a specific property. As discussed earlier in this chapter, the revenue management team typically meets with the entire sales team each morning for a daily business review meeting during which all potential group bookings are discussed with the revenue management team. In addition to maintaining BARs and MARs for transient or individual travelers, the revenue management team also establishes and maintains MARs for group bookings, for the upcoming 12-month period, which provide guidance to the hotel's sales managers as they negotiate with clients. Group bookings contracted for dates further than 12 months in advance are typically quoted the current year's rate, for the equivalent date, plus a maximum percentage mark-up or adjustment per year to allow some flexibility because economic conditions, and therefore demand, may change prior to the group's arrival, particularly if the meeting is booked 3 to 5 years in advance (e.g. $189 + 3% maximum per year).

Sales managers are also well aware of preferred booking patterns and are often armed with a variety of tools to incentivize groups to adjust their meeting dates or day-of-the-week arrival and departure patterns for the benefit of the hotel. For example, a group looking to book a weekend meeting or event in May may be offered a lower room rate if they book for Mother's Day or Memorial Day weekend, because these weekends often experience lower demand. Or a group willing to alter its plans to arrive on a Sunday evening may be offered a complimentary welcome reception on Sunday evening or continental breakfast hosted by the hotel each morning. The goal of these strategies is to ensure that group booking patterns establish a solid base of group business that complement the typical travel patterns of individual travelers, helping the hotel achieve level occupancy without peaks and valleys. It is often said that the effectiveness of a sales manager is not determined by the amount of business he/she books, but by the amount of business he/she is able to move to alternative dates!

Group Contracts

Group contracts must contain a variety of clauses to protect the hotel against the loss of revenue. A detailed discussion of a group contract from a legal perspective is outside the scope of this textbook; however, hotel managers must ensure that appropriate protections are included in the contract to prevent the loss of contracted revenue. A group contract contains, at a minimum, the details regarding the client's commitment to purchase and the hotel's responsibility to provide a range of service products and experiences, including the dates of the event; number of overnight accommodations each night; guestroom rate; meeting space requirements; estimated number of attendees; and food, beverage, and ancillary revenue minimums. Within the context of this agreement, the following clauses are designed to protect the hotel from loss of revenue:

- *Cancellation fee*: Once a contract has been executed and signed by both parties, a cancellation of the meeting, event, or the use of overnight accommodations results in a cancellation fee. The amount of the fee typically varies depending how far in advance the event is cancelled because, as the date of the event approaches, it becomes more difficult for the hotel to replace the booking. A last-minute cancellation, typically within 30 days, often requires a payment of 50% to 100% of the estimated revenue to be generated by the group, depending upon the mix of rooms and F&B revenue.

cancellation fee:
fee imposed by a hotel on a client that cancels a group contract

- *Attrition clause*: An attrition clause is a fee that is incurred if a group fails to pick up its contracted guestroom block. A group is provided with a cut-off date, typically 30 days prior to the group's arrival. The group may release a portion of its contracted rooms, typically up to 25%, without penalty prior to the cut-off date. If the group fails to pick-up a specified minimum proportion of the contracted room nights, often 75%, then the group is obligated to pay an attrition charge to make-up for the shortfall in rooms revenue. The hotel may release any rooms not picked-up by the group's cut-off date for sale to individual travelers or other groups to allow the hotel to mitigate its loss, although some clients may choose to guarantee full payment of the remaining rooms in the block. Attrition charges may run as high as 75% to 100% of the room revenue shortfall due to the high contribution margin generated by room revenue. Although a hotel may be legally

attrition clause:
a fee that is incurred if a group fails to pick up its contracted guestroom block

cut-off date:
the date until which a group's room block will be retained

entitled to collect the full attrition charges due from a group client, many hoteliers consider it unethical to charge attrition to a group if the hotel is able to re-sell the rooms; waiving all or a portion of an attrition fee, under such circumstances, also demonstrates goodwill toward the client.

- *F&B minimum*: An F&B minimum represents the minimum amount of F&B revenue that must be generated by the group, meeting, or event. Because a hotel has limited service capacity, including a limited amount of meeting and conference space, each square foot of space used by a group must produce a minimum amount of revenue for the hotel to achieve its financial targets. The F&B minimum is commonly estimated based upon a BRGR. Consequently, when the revenue management team evaluates the value of a potential group booking, BRGR is considered in addition to the guestroom rate that is charged; the amount of meeting space needed by the group to hold its various meetings and events also must be considered by evaluating the amount of F&B revenue generated per-square-foot. This is discussed in detail in *Chapter 3: Defining Guest Segments*. Often groups that generate a high-volume of F&B revenue will not be charged meeting room rental or set-up fees, which cover the labor costs associated with setting up the meeting rooms; however, groups that fail to meet their F&B minimum will often be charged meeting room rental or set-up fees to offset the contribution margin lost due to the F&B revenue shortfall. Because the contribution margin of F&B revenue is more modest than with guestroom revenue, the meeting room rental or set-up fees are typically 50% to 75% of the F&B revenue shortfall because no food or beverage cost of goods sold (COGS) is incurred by the hotel on this alternative revenue.

> **F&B minimum:**
> the minimum amount of F&B revenue that must be generated by the group, meeting, or event

> **set-up fees:**
> fees that cover the labor costs associated with setting up meeting rooms

Options

Once a group contract is signed, a hotel blocks the required number of hotel rooms and the meeting space required by the group from sale to other groups or individual guests. As a result, revenue may potentially be turned away by the hotel because the hotel's guestrooms or conference space is already committed. Cancellation fees, attrition charges, and F&B minimums are all designed to prevent the loss of revenue by contractually obligating the client to generate the contracted revenue or to make up any shortfall; however, the hotel always has the responsibility to mitigate any losses by attempting to re-sell any unsold guestrooms or meeting space to alternative groups or guests. In addition, hotels often book multiple groups for the same date using options to prevent turning away alternative clients prior to securing a fully-executed contract. An option provides a group client that requests dates for which a contract has already been issued the ability to book their guestrooms, meeting, or event over the same dates should the client in the primary position opt to not execute or fulfill the contract that has been issued.

> **options:**
> provides a group client that requests dates for which a contract has already been issued the ability to book their guestrooms, meeting, or event over the same dates should the client in the primary position opt to not execute or fulfill the contract that has been issued

Group meetings and conventions, particularly large events, involve an immense amount of pre-planning; multiple people are often involved in the final decisions regarding the location, dates, and details of the event. Many meetings, particularly association meetings and citywide conventions, are booked years in advance. Consequently, a tentative agreement may be established with a hotel pending approval by the final decision-makers, which is often a board or committee. Once a contract is issued, the contract must be signed and fully executed by a date specified within the contract, which may be months after the contract has been issued. As a result, another group may express interest in the same dates and sign a contract that allows them the opportunity to book their meeting, conference, or event should the initially contracted business not materialize. It is not uncommon for a large convention hotel to be discussing the possible accommodation of two or three different groups for the same dates—the first group to be issued a contract for the specified dates is in the primary position, the second group is holding first option, and the third group holds a second option contract.

FORECASTING HOTEL REVENUE

Throughout this chapter, there has been much discussion regarding anticipated demand—the revenue management team, as well as the hotel sales team, make pricing and customer selection decisions based upon anticipated demand. Consequently, the ability to accurately forecast room nights and revenues is critical to successful revenue management processes.

Hotels complete an annual forecast or budget each year that serves as a benchmark over the course of the subsequent year for long-term planning. It is typically during the annual forecasting process that the revenue management team evaluates the ideal mix of business between individual travelers and group clients. Based upon this analysis, a hotel establishes a group ceiling, which is the targeted number of group room nights that are to be sold each day, with the remaining inventory set aside for sale to transient guest segments. In some markets, the group ceiling may be static over the course of the entire year; however, in other markets, particularly markets with large seasonal swings in transient demand, the group ceiling may vary by month or season.

group ceiling:
the targeted number of group room nights that are to be sold each day, with the remaining inventory set aside for sale to transient guest segments

Annual Forecasting Process

The annual forecasting process begins as early as June and culminates between mid-September and mid-October with a forecast review meeting at which the hotel's management team, executives from the hotel's management company, and hotel ownership agree on financial goals for the upcoming calendar year. The KPIs established during the forecasting process will guide the revenue management team's revenue optimization efforts over the course of the upcoming year—serving as benchmarks against which the hotel's financial performance will be assessed. Consequently, the importance of creating an accurate revenue forecast cannot be underestimated.

Diagram 5.2: Annual Revenue Forecast Process illustrates the process of forecasting a hotel's revenues. This tedious process, once completed, results in an initial revenue forecast that will be reviewed by the entire revenue management team, often leading to a spirited discussion through which revisions and refinements are made. Once the revenue forecast has been approved by the hotel's general manager, as well as corporate executives from the hotel's management firm, labor costs, food and beverage costs, other controllable expenses, and profitability may then be projected. The completed revenue forecast and operating budget is then presented to the hotel's ownership for final approval, which provides hotel management with a complete set of financial goals or benchmarks for the upcoming calendar year.

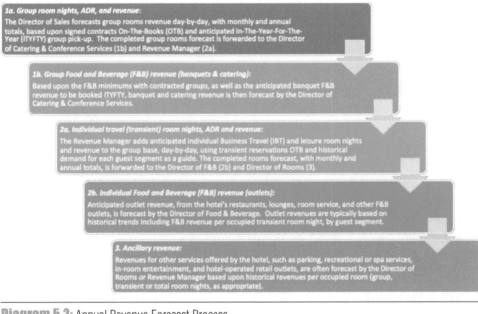

1a. Group room nights, ADR, and revenue:
The Director of Sales forecasts group rooms revenue day-by-day, with monthly and annual totals, based upon signed contracts On-The-Books (OTB) and anticipated In-The-Year-For-The-Year (ITYFTY) group pick-up. The completed group rooms forecast is forwarded to the Director of Catering & Conference Services (1b) and Revenue Manager (2a).

1b. Group Food and Beverage (F&B) revenue (banquets & catering):
Based upon the F&B minimums with contracted groups, as well as the anticipated banquet F&B revenue to be booked ITYFTY, banquet and catering revenue is then forecast by the Director of Catering & Conference Services.

2a. Individual travel (transient) room nights, ADR and revenue:
The Revenue Manager adds anticipated Individual Business Travel (IBT) and leisure room nights and revenue to the group base, day-by-day, using transient reservations OTB and historical demand for each guest segment as a guide. The completed rooms forecast, with monthly and annual totals, is forwarded to the Director of F&B (2b) and Director of Rooms (3).

2b. Individual Food and Beverage (F&B) revenue (outlets):
Anticipated outlet revenue, from the hotel's restaurants, lounges, room service, and other F&B outlets, is forecast by the Director of Food & Beverage. Outlet revenues are typically based on historical trends including F&B revenue per occupied transient room night, by guest segment.

3. Ancillary revenue:
Revenues for other services offered by the hotel, such as parking, recreational or spa services, in-room entertainment, and hotel-operated retail outlets, are often forecast by the Director of Rooms or Revenue Manager based upon historical revenues per occupied room (group, transient or total room nights, as appropriate).

Diagram 5.2: Annual Revenue Forecast Process

It must be noted that no short-cuts should be taken when generating the annual revenue forecast. Hotel occupancy, ADR, and revenue must be forecast day-by-day and segment-by-segment for each of the 365 days in the upcoming year. Attempting to forecast revenues by starting with monthly totals for each of the previous 12 months, and then adjusting these monthly totals based upon anticipated changes in demand, ultimately leads to an inaccurate and unachievable forecast. Although historical trends are often used in forecasting—such as the average number of BARs sold on a Saturday night in October, for example—individual months, year over year, are not always comparable. The number of peak midweek nights, the number of weekends, and other factors, including the exact dates of various holidays or special events that may not recur in subsequent years, will all impact demand within a given month. Consequently, revenue forecasts must be completed day-by-day to ensure that all relevant factors are considered and accurately reflected in the annual revenue forecast.

Short-Term Forecasts

In addition to the annual forecast, the revenue manager provides a 10-day forecast each week that is used for short-term planning, such as scheduling hotel employees, as well as an updated annual forecast each month, for mid-range planning, such as ordering operating supplies for the upcoming month. The updated annual forecast includes actual results year-to-date, an updated forecast for the upcoming 1 to 3 months, and the annual forecast for the remainder of the year, assuming there is no indication that a significant variation is likely to occur. By looking at the week ahead, the upcoming 30 to 90 days, and through the end of the current year, the revenue management team may more effectively adjust revenue optimization and hotel marketing strategies based upon anticipated demand. *Box 5.3: Updating the Annual Forecast* provides additional insight into the forecasting process.

BOX 5.3: UPDATING THE ANNUAL FORECAST

The revenue manager spearheads the updating of the annual forecast by the middle of each month. To complete this update, hotel occupancy must first be estimated for the upcoming month. Assume that it is currently Wednesday, September 11, 2019 and the revenue manager is forecasting occupancy for the upcoming month—October 2019—for a 400-room hotel using three primary sets of data: A *3-Year Demand Tracking* report; *6-Week Pick-Up Trends*; and the number of room nights on-the-books (OTB), which includes the sum of group rooms picked-up and individual reservations currently booked, for each night in October.

Diagram 5.3: 3-Year Demand Tracking is a report commonly used as a guideline to forecast hotel occupancy. This report charts the average number of transient, group, contract, and total rooms occupied by day-of-the-week, for the month specified, based upon a 3-year average. The *3-year Demand Tracking* graph is a valuable revenue optimization and forecasting tool because it clearly identifies the peaks and valleys that an effective revenue management team attempts to minimize by leveling demand, using stay restrictions, as previously described in *Box 5.2: Effective Yield Management*. This visual depiction of historical demand is also used when creating the annual revenue forecast, specifically when forecasting group room nights (*Step 1a*) and transient room nights (*Step 2a*) as outlined in *Diagram 5.2: Annual Revenue Forecast Process*.

Diagram 5.3: 3-Year Demand Tracking reveals the following:
- The busiest night of the week during the month of October is typically Wednesday, with a 3-year average of 387 room nights occupied, representing 96.8% occupancy.
- The slowest night during October is typically Sunday, with just 162 or 40.5% or available rooms rented.
- Tuesday night is the strongest night for group rooms, with 248 rooms typically occupied by group guests.
- The hotel has averaged six contract rooms per night in October over the past 3 years.
- Occupancy during the month of October, over the past 3 years, has averaged 293 rooms per night, or 73.3%.

A second forecasting tool, illustrated in *Diagram 5.4: 6-Week Pick-Up Trends*, identifies the number of room reservations picked-up, or booked in addition to the room nights already OTB, by day-of-the-week, for the most recent historical 6-week period. The pick-up trends in *Diagram 5.3: 6-Week Pick-Up Trends*, are based upon the actual number of room nights realized less the number of reservations that were OTB at the time the equivalent monthly forecast was produced. In this example, the revenue manager is forecasting occupancy for the month of October 2019, creating the forecast on September 11, 2019, which is a Wednesday positioned approximately 3 weeks prior to the start of the month. Consequently, the most recently completed equivalent forecast period for which actual occupancy will be available, to be compared with the number of room nights that were OTB at the time the forecast was generated, is the previous month—August of 2019. Therefore, the data used in *Table 5.6: 6-Week Pick-Up History* and illustrated in *Diagram 5.4: 6-Week Pick-Up Trends* is based upon the reservations that were OTB on Wednesday, July 10, when the August 2019 forecast was generated, and the actual number of room nights occupied in August. The pick-up is the difference between these two values—the actual rooms occupied for each respective date minus the number of rooms OTB for the corresponding date. These values are calculated in *Table 5.6: 6-Week Pick-Up History*.

Note that the number of rooms picked-up are negatively impacted (less than the actual demand) if a larger than usual number of rooms are booked farther in advance. For

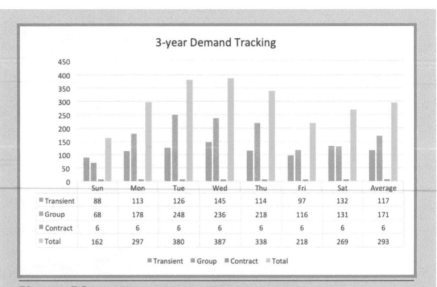

3-year Demand Tracking

	Sun	Mon	Tue	Wed	Thu	Fri	Sat	Average
▪ Transient	88	113	126	145	114	97	132	117
▪ Group	68	178	248	236	218	116	131	171
▪ Contract	6	6	6	6	6	6	6	6
▪ Total	162	297	380	387	338	218	269	293

▪ Transient ▪ Group ▪ Contract ▪ Total

Diagram 5.3: 3-Year Demand Tracking (October 2016 – 2018)

6-Week Pick-Up Trend Report   **OTB as of:**   12-Jun-19

	Rooms	%	ADR	Revenue	RevPAR
August statistics:	10,131	81.7%	$ 242.12	$2,452,918	$ 197.82

2-weeks out	Sun	Mon	Tue	Wed	Thu	Fri	Sat	Week's	Occupancy
Date	7/29/2019	7/30/2019	7/31/2019	8/1/2019	8/2/2019	8/3/2019	8/4/2019	Total	Points
OTB	172	283	362	364	327	201	248	1,957	69.9%
Actual	174	290	373	379	340	225	282	2,063	73.7%
2-week p/u	2	7	11	15	13	24	34	106	3.8%

3-weeks out	Sun	Mon	Tue	Wed	Thu	Fri	Sat	Week's	Occupancy
Date	8/5/2019	8/6/2019	8/7/2019	8/8/2019	8/9/2019	8/10/2019	8/11/2019	Total	Points
OTB	160	243	302	287	268	171	241	1,672	59.7%
Actual	187	282	383	359	342	227	302	2,082	74.4%
3-week p/u	27	39	81	72	74	56	61	410	14.6%

4-weeks out	Sun	Mon	Tue	Wed	Thu	Fri	Sat	Week's	Occupancy
Date	8/12/2019	8/13/2019	8/14/2019	8/15/2019	8/16/2019	8/17/2019	8/18/2019	Total	Points
OTB	141	221	276	262	241	159	219	1,519	54.3%
Actual	197	275	372	363	350	228	318	2,103	75.1%
4-week p/u	56	54	96	101	109	69	99	584	20.9%

5-weeks out	Sun	Mon	Tue	Wed	Thu	Fri	Sat	Week's	Occupancy
Date	8/19/2019	8/20/2019	8/21/2019	8/22/2019	8/23/2019	8/24/2019	8/25/2019	Total	Points
OTB	112	201	233	242	218	137	191	1,334	47.6%
Actual	163	268	375	349	338	212	299	2,004	71.6%
5 week p/u	51	67	142	107	120	75	108	670	23.9%

6-weeks out	Sun	Mon	Tue	Wed	Thu	Fri	Sat	Week's	Occupancy
Date	8/26/2019	8/27/2019	8/28/2019	8/29/2019	8/30/2019	8/31/2019	9/1/2019	Total	Points
OTB	186	273	308	314	205	126	185	1,597	57.0%
Actual	218	353	400	395	363	241	310	2,280	81.4%
6-week p/u	32	80	92	81	158	115	125	683	24.4%

Table 5.6: 6-Week Pick-up History

example, advance bookings were higher than usual for Tuesday, August 28, and Wednesday, Augusts 29, 6-weeks out, with 308 and 314 of 400-rooms already sold for each night respectively. Consequently, limited inventory was available for sale, which resulted in fewer rooms being picked up on Tuesday and Wednesday nights, 6-weeks out, than were picked-up on the Tuesday and Wednesday nights, just 5-weeks out (81 rooms picked up 6-weeks out versus 107 rooms picked up 5-weeks out on Tuesday, and 92 rooms 6-weeks out versus 142 5-weeks out on Wednesday). Also note that these pick-up trends are net values, which include room nights gained less room nights lost.

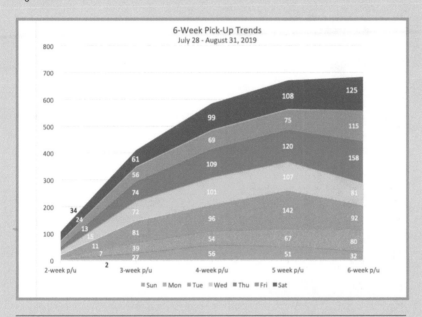

Diagram 5.4: 6-Week Pick-Up Trends

Although *Diagram 5.3: Historical Demand Tracking* illustrates historical trends from past years, *Diagram 5.4: 6-Week Pick-Up Trends* provides information from the current year so that the historical trends may be adjusted based upon the current economic realities and trends in the market. These two reports, combined with the actual number of reservations OTB for the upcoming month, October 2019, may then be used to forecast occupancy for each night of the upcoming month, as outlined in *Table 5.7: Updated 30-day Occupancy Forecast*. The updated 30-day occupancy forecast can be generated by simply adding the number of rooms OTB on September 11, 2019 to the anticipated pick-up trends for the corresponding weeks (2-weeks out through 6-weeks out) and then making minor adjustments to address any anomalies. This process has been completed in *Table 5.7: Updated 30-day Occupancy Forecast*.

Looking at *Table 5.7: Updated 30-day Occupancy Forecast*, note that occupancy each night is simply the addition of room nights OTB and the expected pick-up, which is transferred directly from the 6-week pick-up trend report illustrated in *Diagram 5.4: 6-Week Pick-Up Trends*. Refer to Tuesday, October 1, for example; there are 351 room nights currently on the books and the 2-week pick-up for a Tuesday night is anticipated to be 11 room nights, resulting in a projection of 362 (= 351 + 11) room nights for October 1, 2019. The same process applies to each night of the month (e.g. 372 + 15 = 387 for October 2; 314 + 13 = 327 for October 3; 263 + 24 = 287 for October 4; etc.). Anomalies occur October 15–17, which are highlighted in gold in *Table 5.7: Updated 30-day Occupancy Forecast*, because the number of room nights OTB plus the expected pick-up values exceed 400 rooms or the hotel's total service capacity (e.g. 319 + 96 = 415 on October 15; 307 + 101 = 408 on October 16; and 318 + 109 = 427 on October 17). As a result, the number of anticipated rooms occupied have been recorded as 400 or 100% occupancy. In addition, the Revenue Manager has only forecasted two of these three nights to fill because, quite candidly, it can be challenging to completely fill every guestroom within a hotel three nights in succession due to unanticipated early departures, no-show reservations, and other factors—in other words, the revenue manager has used his/her personal judgment to allow a small margin for error. If the revenue manager forecasts three consecutive sell-outs and the hotel fails to sell its complete guestroom inventory by just one or two rooms for one or more of these three nights, then the hotel will miss achieving the revised forecast. This illustrates that, although data is used to drive the forecasting and revenue optimization processes, human judgment must sometimes be used to modify or adjust expectations based upon non-quantitative factors.

Anomalies in the forecast occur again—October 29–31 (highlighted in blue). Recall that the 6-week pick-up trend reflected that fewer rooms were picked up 6-weeks out than 5-weeks out, which is not logical because there is one additional week to book rooms. This anomaly occurred in the 6-week pick-up trend report (refer to *Table 5.6: 6-Week Pick-Up History*) because there were more reservations OTB 6-weeks out than 5-weeks out (e.g. 308 and 304 room nights, respectively, OTB for Tuesday, August 28 and Wednesday, the 29, versus 233 for Tuesday, August 21 and 242 for Wednesday, August 22). Consequently, some of the demand for accommodations 6-weeks out may have been displaced due to the lack of available rooms. As a result, it is logical for the revenue manager to expect that pick-up during the current forecast period may be stronger than the 92 room nights picked up on Tuesday night 6-weeks out and the 81 room nights picked up for Wednesday night 6-weeks out. As a result, the revenue manager has forecast sell-outs for Tuesday and Wednesday nights, the 29th and 30th of October. On Thursday, October 31, a sell-out may also be possible, particularly because the 6-week pick-up trend for Thursday night projects a 158-room night pick-up; however, again, the revenue manager moderates these expectations, assuming the hotel will not fill for three consecutive nights.   Currently, there is a 28-room night difference between room nights OTB for Wednesday, October 30 (301 rooms) and Thursday, October 31 (273 rooms); the revenue manager maintains this disparity by forecasting 373 occupied rooms on the 31—a 27 room night difference from Wednesday to Thursday. Once the day-by-day forecast is complete, the revenue manager will analyze the forecast based upon monthly totals to ensure that the forecast is realistic and achievable.

A quick check of the overall numbers by day-of-the-week and in total, which may be found on the final two rows of *Table 5.7: Updated 30-day Occupancy Forecast*, reveals the following:

- Overall occupancy is forecast to run 79.3% or 317 per night, which is higher than the 3-year average of 73.3% or 293 rooms per night.
- This increase is due, primarily, to higher occupancy on the weekend nights—an average of 301 room nights versus 269 room nights on Friday nights and a 301 versus 269 average on Saturday nights.
- Shoulder nights are also stronger with 184 room nights forecast on Sunday nights, on average, versus a 3-year historical average of 162 room nights, as well as 354 forecast on Thursday versus a 3-year historical average of 338 room nights.

After making these observations, the revenue manager must verify that these deviations from the 3-year trend can be substantiated. Perhaps there are more group rooms on-the-books for the weekend and shoulder nights going into October of 2019 than experienced in past years; or maybe weekend or shoulder night occupancy has simply been stronger this year over previous years; the higher weekend and shoulder night occupancy could also be attributed to the more effective use of stay restrictions and other revenue optimization strategies. If the deviations cannot be substantiated, then further adjustments will be made to the 30-day forecast for October.

Once the occupancy forecast has been locked-in for October, the ADR may then be estimated. Because 7,706 room nights or 78.4% of the anticipated 9,828 room nights to be consumed during the month are already OTB, the ADR for the business already booked serves as the starting point for estimating the overall ADR that will be realized for the month. The guestroom rates at which the remaining 2,122 room nights are anticipated to be booked in the month for the month will determine the actual ADR that will be realized. The ADR for these remaining 2,122 room nights may be estimated by breaking them into weekday (1,649) and weekend (473) room nights and applying the appropriate ADR to each of these room night totals based upon the BARs and various qualified and discounted rates that may be made available for the respective weekday and weekend nights. Assuming that this process results in an ADR forecast of $187.42 for the month, this leads to a rooms revenue forecast in October of $1,841,964 and a RevPAR of $148.55.

October 2019 Forecast   **OTB as of:** 11-Sep-19

	Rooms	%	ADR	Revenue	RevPAR
October* forecast:	9,828	79.3%	$ 187.42	$ 1,841,964	$ 148.55

*note that the first two dates (September 29 & 30) and final two dates on the forecast (November 1 & 2) are not included in the October monthly totals.

2-weeks out	Sun	Mon	Tue	Wed	Thu	Fri	Sat	Week's Total	Occupancy Points
Date	9/29/2019	9/30/2019	10/1/2019	10/2/2019	10/3/2019	10/4/2019	10/5/2019		
OTB	157	225	351	372	314	263	270	1,952	69.7%
Expected p/u	2	7	11	15	13	24	34	106	3.8%
Forecast	159	232	362	387	327	287	304	2,058	73.5%

3-weeks out	Sun	Mon	Tue	Wed	Thu	Fri	Sat	Week's Total	Occupancy Points
Date	10/6/2019	10/7/2019	10/8/2019	10/9/2019	10/10/2019	10/11/2019	10/12/2019		
OTB	173	225	319	302	256	189	227	1,691	60.4%
Expected p/u	27	39	81	72	74	56	61	410	14.6%
Forecast	200	264	400	374	330	245	288	2,101	75.0%

4-weeks out	Sun	Mon	Tue	Wed	Thu	Fri	Sat	Week's Total	Occupancy Points
Date	10/13/2019	10/14/2019	10/15/2019	10/16/2019	10/17/2019	10/18/2019	10/19/2019		
OTB	154	312	319	307	318	172	220	1,802	64.4%
Expected p/u	56	54	96	101	109	69	99	584	20.9%
Forecast	210	366	400	400	395	241	319	2,331	83.3%

5-weeks out	Sun	Mon	Tue	Wed	Thu	Fri	Sat	Week's Total	Occupancy Points
Date	10/20/2019	10/21/2019	10/22/2019	10/23/2019	10/24/2019	10/25/2019	10/26/2019		
OTB	119	212	240	262	225	124	184	1,366	48.8%
Expected p/u	51	67	142	107	120	75	108	670	23.9%
Forecast	170	279	382	369	345	199	292	2,036	72.7%

6-weeks out	Sun	Mon	Tue	Wed	Thu	Fri	Sat	Week's Total	Occupancy Points
Date	10/27/2019	10/28/2019	10/29/2019	10/30/2019	10/31/2019	11/1/2019	11/2/2019		
OTB	125	283	295	301	273	142	191	1,610	57.5%
Expected p/u	32	80	105	99	100	115	125	656	23.4%
Forecast	157	363	400	400	373	257	316	2,266	80.9%

October *(3-year historical demand tracking)*

Forecast average	184	318	389	386	354	243	301	317	79.3%
3-year average	162	297	380	387	338	218	269	293	73.3%

Table 5.7: Updated 30-day Occupancy Forecast

DATA

The ability to accurately forecast occupancy and revenue, as well as to optimize revenue, relies on data availability, as outlined in *Box 5.3: Updating the Annual Forecast*. Some of the data that is helpful in forecasting anticipated demand includes the following:

- *Historical demand*: Historical demand by segment is recorded and tracked by guest segment and by day-of-the-year, day-of-the-week, monthly, and annually, based upon the number of guestrooms occupied each night. This information may then be appropriately sorted and analyzed to ensure accurate forecasts and to guide marketing and revenue optimization decision-making. *Box 5.3: Monthly Update of the Annual Forecast* illustrates how historical demand may be used during the forecasting process.

    > historical demand: actual room nights sold (rented), by guest segment and in total, for previous dates

- *Booking pace*: The concept of booking pace compares how strong demand is for specific future dates as compared to same-time-last-year (STLY) based upon reservations or contracted group rooms currently on-the-books. In other words, it provides an indication if more guests, fewer guests, or about the same number of guests have made reservations for future dates as had at the STLY, which provides a hotel marketer with insight regarding fluctuations in demand year-over-year. For example, if a hotel had 150 room reservations OTB for the third Thursday in August, as of July 1 of last year, and this year the hotel has 165 room reservations

OTB for the third Thursday in August, as of July 1, then the hotel is 15 room nights or 10% ahead of pace—an indication that there is stronger demand year-over-year. Conversely, if the hotel only has 135 rooms on-the-books on July 1, then the hotel is 10% or 15 rooms behind pace and may be experiencing weaker demand. Hotels carefully track booking pace for individual, group, and total travel—it is critically important market intelligence.

- *6-week pick-up trends*: A 6-week pick-up trends report provides an indication as to how many reservations are being sold during the final 6-week booking window immediately preceding an arrival date—when most individual reservations are typically sold. Again, this forecasting tool is explained in additional detail in *Box 5.3: Monthly Update of the Annual Forecast.*

- *Turn-aways*: A turn-away, also referred to as a denial, represents a reservation inquiry for one or more specific dates that is not booked because the guest's request did comply with the stay restrictions in place for the date(s) requested. A turn-away is recorded for each night of the guest's potential stay. By tracking the number of guests that are turned away by the hotel, the revenue management team can estimate total demand and quantify the number of room nights that are potentially lost or displaced due to the hotel's yield management strategies for the respective dates. Ideally, the specific guest segment affected by each turn-away is recorded so that demand may be more accurately forecast and anticipated for each guest segment.

- *Turn-downs*: When a guest is offered the opportunity to book accommodations, at a specific rate, but chooses not to make the reservation, then a turn-down is recorded for each night requested. These are sometimes referred to as abandons, because the potential guest often abandons the reservation process mid-stream. Turn-downs or abandons, like turn-aways, assist in tracking total demand by segment. Turn-downs also provide insight on guests' perceptions of the BAR and other pricing decisions made by the revenue management team.

- *Total demand*: In addition to historical demand, total demand may be tracked by recording the number of reservation inquiries received for each specific date. Total demand may also be estimated by adding the number of turn-aways (or denials) and turn-downs (including abandons), as previously defined, to the historical demand. At a minimum, a hotel will track monthly historical demand because the number of occupied rooms and occupancy level is recorded on financial statements; however, a measure of total demand provides more meaningful insight to the revenue management team.

- *Rates and availability at competitive hotels*: The availability of accommodations at a hotel's direct competitors, as well as the room rates being offered by these competitors, is also closely monitored. Traditionally, hotels attempted to shop their competitors by calling other hotels or by shopping online to track their availability and the guestroom rates being offered. In today's business environment, many

---

6-week pick-up trends: provides an indication as to how many reservations are being sold during the final 6-week booking window immediately preceding an arrival date

turn-away (denial): a reservation inquiry for one or more specific dates that is not booked because the guest's request did comply with the stay restrictions in place for the date(s) requested

turn-down: when a guest is offered the opportunity to book accommodations, at a specific rate, but chooses not to make the reservation

abandons: when potential guests abandon the reservation process mid-stream, which are also counted as turn-downs

inquiry: a reservation request where a specific date or dates have been shopped by a potential guest

hotels use automation, and outside services such as TravelClick (www.travelclick.com), to gather market intelligence through the various distribution channels, including brand websites, the GDS, OTAs, and metasearch sites.

Revenue Management Systems

RMS, such as IDeaS, Duetto, and Kriya, are sophisticated information systems that may be used to guide the revenue optimization process. An RMS typically interfaces with the property management system (PMS), sales management system (SMS), CRS, and GDS to monitor sales activity and demand for the hotel's accommodations. Depending upon its level of sophistication, the system will assist in monitoring and forecasting demand to ensure that prudent decisions are made by the hotel management team relative to pricing, stay restrictions, and in the selection of business that will be accommodated by the hotel. An effective RMS also considers the impact of F&B and ancillary revenues likely to be generated by a guest or group client when guiding customer selection decisions.

The sheer volume of data that must be collected, as well as the data analysis required to effectively use this data, can be overwhelming. In addition, hotel markets are dynamic and rapidly changing. Consequently, attempting to manually collect and analyze the data necessary to make timely and prudent decisions to optimize revenue is nearly impossible. Many of the examples used within this chapter, including *Table 5.1: Room Rate Distribution Analysis*; *Box 5.2: Effective Yield Management*; *Diagram 5.3: 3-Year Demand Tracking*; and *Diagram 5.4: 6-Week Pick-Up Trends* are simplified examples of the data that is collected and the analysis that is executed to support revenue optimization processes. Data availability drives the ability of a RMS to accurately forecast demand, which is essential to successfully optimizing revenue (Weatherford & Pölt, 2002). In other words, hotels that collect, update, and analyze large amounts of data on an ongoing basis are at a competitive advantage. Consequently, successful hotel marketers often use outside vendors, such as STR and TravelClick, to provide competitive market information.

TravelClick, for example, collects over 10 billion hotel room rates through the GDS and online distribution channels and tracks actual reservation bookings at over 22,000 hotels to provide its Hotelligence360 product, which allows a hotel to more accurately assess its competitive position within its market. A detailed description of the types of analysis that may be performed by a RMS that has access to large amounts of data to generate recommended optimization strategies is provided in *Box 5.4: Understanding RMS Algorithms*.

```
73  temp_file.write(buff)  import shutil if os.path.exists("Input4RTAVIES
74  content = f.read().splitlines() for line in content:  searchObj = re.
75  mapFid2Type[searchObj.group(1)] = searchObj.group(2) for filename in
76  searchObjfName = re.search( r'(\w+)\.', str(fName), re.M|re.I) if sea
77  wb = load_workbook(filename)  print ("--------------------------------
78  filename4createFolder = fileN filename4createFolder = filename4create
79  numberOfColumn = ws.max_column numberOfRow = ws.max_row idNumber = 1
80  for row in ws.rows: for cell in row:   if (pivotCell==1):  temp=str(c
81  pivotCell=+2 else:item_ID = cell.value if(pivotCell==2): item_Event =
82   if(item_Event == "RT_EVENT" and pivotCell==3): item_RICname = cell.v
83   if(item_Event == "RT_EVENT" and pivotCell>=5):  if(pivotCell%2 == 1 a
84   else: if(str(cell.value) != "None"):  valueDict = cell.value item_Fic
85   if(item_Event == "RT_CHAIN_EVENT" and pivotCell==4): item_Template =
86   if(pivotCell%2 == 1 and str(cell.value) != "None"): keyDict = cell.va
87   pathOfTemplate = "templateFolder\\" + item_Template  if(item_Event ==
88   if(item_Event == "RT_OUTPUT" and pivotCell>=4):  if(pivotCell%2 == 0
89
90   tempString = template_type_buffer tempString = tempString.replace("c
91   dataCal = datetime.date.strftime(d,'%Y-%m-%d') tempString = template
92  tempString = tempString.replace("czDataType",typeOfFID.capitalize())
93   elif(typeOfFID == "TIME"):  dataCal = str(value) searchObj = re.sea
94   searchObj2 = re.search( r'(\d+)-(\d+)-(.*)', dataCal, re.M|re.I) if
95   FormatValueOfTime = 0  searchObj3 = re.search( r'(\d+)\.(\d+)', temp
```

©Vintage Tone/Shutterstock.com

algorithm:
sequence of steps or rules to be followed when solving a problem

binomial probability distribution function:
allows the probability of a given number of successes out of a given number of trials to be calculated based upon the probability of achieving a single successful outcome provided there are only two possible outcomes

An algorithm is sequence of steps or rules to be followed when solving a problem. RMS use algorithms to guide the revenue management team toward the optimal solution. Although algorithms are often complex, requiring hundreds or even thousands of calculations to determine ideal solutions, this simplified example is intended to provide insight into how RMS programmers create the algorithms that use the large amount of data collected by the system to analyze the revenue impact of alternative revenue optimization strategies.

The binomial probability distribution function serves as the statistical foundation for many RMS algorithms. Although the mathematical formula may be complex, the concept supported by the formula is quite simple. Think of the process of booking a reservation like tossing a coin—there are only two possible outcomes. With a coin toss, the coin lands with either the "head" or the "tail" side of the coin in view; with a reservation request, a guest either books a reservation or does not book a reservation. This is why the binomial distribution—"bi" meaning "two"—is the statistical foundation of many RMS algorithms.

The binomial probability distribution formula allows the probability of a given number of successes out of a given number of trials to be calculated based upon the probability of achieving a single successful outcome. Relating this statement back to a coin toss, assume that a "head" is defined as a success and a fair coin has a 50% chance of landing with the "head" of the coin in view. So, the probability of a successful outcome on a single trial is 50%. If a fair coin is tossed 10 times, it follows that a successful outcome will occur on five of the 10 tosses; however, in reality, five successes may or may not occur. Although there is a 0.50 probability or 50% chance that a coin will land with a "head" in view each time the coin is tossed, making it reasonable to think that five "heads" are *likely* to occur if a coin is tossed 10 times, the likelihood that this actually occurs is far from certain (100%)!

If a fair coin is tossed 10 times, there are actually 11 possible outcomes from no "heads" up to and including 10 "heads." The binomial probability distribution formula may be used to estimate the probability of any one of these possible outcomes. And because one of these possible outcomes must occur, the sum of these 11 probabilities (e.g. the probability of no "heads," plus the probability of one "head," plus the probability of two "heads," plus the probability of three "heads," etc., up to and including the probability of 10 "heads") will total one or 100%, which is the foundation of the cumulative binomial probability formula. The cumulative binomial probability distribution formula, *Formula 5.4*, is as follows:

$$P(X \leq x \mid n) = \sum_{k=0}^{x} \left(\frac{n!}{(n-k)!\,k!} \right) p^k q^{n-k}$$

Where: $P(X \leq x \mid n)$ = the probability that the value of discrete random variable X is less than or equal to a specified value of x given n trials.

n = number of trials
k = possible values of x
p = probability of success on a single trial
q = probability of failure on a single trial or $(1 - p)$
x = number of desired successes
X = actual number of successes

Such that: $[P(X = 0) + P(X = 1) + P(X = 2)\ldots P(X = n)] = 1$

Meaning that: The number of successful outcomes realized, X, will be a discrete random variable between 0 and n, inclusive, and the sum of the probabilities of all possible values of x is equal to 1. In other words, X will equal 0 or 1 or 2 or 3 or any other discrete value up to an including the total number of trials, represented by n.

This further implies: $P(X \geq x) = \{1 - P[X < (x-1) \mid n]\}$

Meaning that: The probability that the number of successful outcomes realized, X, is greater than or equal to x is equal to the complement of (or 1 minus) the probability that X is less than $x - 1$.

Formula 5.4: Cumulative Binomial Probability Distribution Formula

---

Using this formula, the probability of five or more "heads" being realized when a coin is tossed 10 times may be calculated as follows:

$$P(X \geq 5 \mid 10) = 1 - \left[\sum_{k=0}^{4} \left(\frac{10!}{(10-k)!\,k!} \right) .5^k (.5^{10-k}) \right]$$

The solution to this equation is 0.623, which is the probability that five or more "heads" are viewed when tossing a coin 10 times—in other words, five or more heads will occur 62.3% of the time.

From Tossing Coins to Selling Rooms

How does this example of tossing a coin 10 times relate to optimizing revenue? Imagine that five rooms remain available in the hotel for a given night and 10 additional reservation inquiries are anticipated to be received for this date requesting the BAR. The revenue management team is debating whether the BAR should be set at its highest level of $229, high level of $209 or, perhaps, at the standard BAR of $189, to make certain the five remaining rooms are sold and revenue is optimized.

Assume the historical data collected by the RMS shows that 50% of guests that are offered the highest BAR rate of $229 will accept the rate offered and book the reservation; if the BAR is reduced to $209, historical data shows that three out of four guests or 75% of guests will book the reservation; and if the BAR is set at $189, eight out of 10 or 80% of guests will book the room. Translating this information into the variables necessary to calculate the probability of selling the remaining five rooms using the cumulative binomial probability distribution formula reveals the following:

If the BAR is set at $229, the values are the same as with the coin toss example previously described: the number of trials is 10; the probability of a single successful outcome is 50%; and the number of successful outcomes desired is five or more. Consequently, the probability of selling all five rooms at a $229 BAR, using the cumulative binomial probability distribution formula, is 0.623—the same as the coin toss. But, what if the BAR is lowered?

The number of trials and the number of successful outcomes desired remains the same for all BAR categories, at 10 and 5, respectively; however, assume RMS data further reveals that the probability of success improves to 75% if the BAR is set at $209 and to 80% if the BAR is $189. Substituting these revised probabilities of a single success into the binomial probability distribution formula reveals that the probability of selling all five rooms increases to 0.980 if the rate is dropped to $209 and to 0.994 if the BAR is set at $189. Consequently, setting the BAR at $229 will often result in the sale of fewer than five guestrooms—which will occur 37.7% of the time—whereas setting the BAR at $209 or less will almost always result in all five remaining rooms being sold—this will occur 98.0% of the time.

To evaluate the revenue potential of each decision, a revenue factor may be calculated by multiplying the five rooms remaining available, by each BAR, and by the probability of selling all five remaining rooms available at the respective BAR; these revenue factors may then be compared to determine which rate will typically generate the most room revenue. The revenue factor projects the average amount of revenue that would be produced by each respective choice over the long run if the same decision was made when facing the identical situation on multiple occasions. These values are reflected in *Table 5.8: Evaluating BAR Options*.

Rate category	Guestroom rate	Conversion rate	Probability of selling 5 or more rooms*	Revenue factor
Highest BAR	$ 229	50%	0.623	$ 713.39
High BAR	$ 209	75%	0.980	$ 1,024.38
Standard BAR	$ 189	80%	0.994	$ 938.98

*using the cumulative binomial probability distribution formula

Table 5.8: Evaluating BAR Options

Initially, the revenue management team may think—five rooms remain available, 50% of guests book at $229, so the remaining five rooms should sell if the BAR is set at $229 because 10 inquiries are anticipated—after all, 50% of 10 is 5; however, the above analysis establishes that, by setting the BAR at $209, the hotel is likely to earn approximately $300 more in revenue than if the BAR is set at $229. Three rooms sold at $229 produces $687 (= 3 X $229) in room revenue, whereas five rooms sold at $209 generates $1,045 (= 5 X $209) in room revenue—an increase of $358. Even if four rooms are sold at the highest BAR of $229, $916 (= 4 X $229) in revenue is generated, which is still $129 (= $1,045 - $916) less than the $1,045 generated by selling all five rooms at $209.

Another way to assess the situation, particularly if the priority is to sell the remaining guestroom inventory, is to evaluate the change in the probability of selling the remaining five rooms as a result of lowering the guestroom rate. When the rate is dropped from $229 to $209, the probability of selling all five rooms rises substantially from 0.623 to 0.980, nearly a 26 percentage point increase; however, dropping the rate an additional $20 to $189 only improves the likelihood of selling all five rooms to 0.994, less than a 2 percentage point improvement. Consequently, the first rate decrease is clearly justified, while the second reduction is not warranted.

Using Technology to Do the Math

Fortunately, technology is available to help the revenue management team execute the calculations necessary to make prudent revenue optimization decisions. As an alternative to calculating these probabilities manually, which is tedious, the *"binomdist"* function within *Microsoft Excel* may be used. Simply type the following into a cell within an *Excel* spreadsheet: =1-binomdist(4,10,.5,true). The binomial distribution parameters within *Excel* (within the parentheses) are defined as follows: number of successes, number of trials, probability of success, and "true" because a cumulative function is desired versus the probability of an *exact* number of successes (e.g. *exactly* 5). Note that the cumulative binomial distribution function within *Excel* calculates the sum the probabilities of zero successes up through the number of successes defined by the first parameter entered (number of successes). Consequently, the complement of the cumulative binomial distribution function is the desired result of the calculation in this instance, which results in "=1-" being entered in *Excel* within the cell prior to the "*binomdist*" function. And because the probability of five or more heads is the desired value, the number of successes is set at four, or one less than five, because the resulting value will be one minus the probability of four or fewer "heads," which is equivalent to five or more "heads" out of 10 trials.

Embracing Technology

To effectively optimize revenue, the revenue management team must make decisions regarding which guests to accept, at which rates, and which guests to turn away. The simple example illustrated here is just one minor decision out of literally hundreds of decisions that must be made each month to effectively optimize revenue. This example also illustrates that the optimal decision may not be as simple and straight-forward as may initially appear—data and data analysis must drive decisions.

Even the simple decision illustrated within this example—the BAR that should be established for a specific date when only five rooms remain available—requires a significant amount of data be collected and analyzed to support the decision. The RMS must track the number of reservation inquiries by guest segment to allow it to accurately estimate the number of inquiries expected from the guest segments that will be offered the BAR, as well as the conversion rates of reservation inquiries at the various BARs. This data must then be used to determine the probability of converting five or more of the anticipated inquiries into actual reservations. Even if the required data is available and the revenue manager has the knowledge to calculate the probability of converting five or more reservation inquiries, will the revenue manager consistently take the time to gather the data and make the necessary calculations to ensure that the optimal decision is made, particularly with a seemingly minor decision? Will the other members of the revenue management team trust and follow the revenue manager's recommendation? Consequently, the use of a RMS programmed with an algorithm that systematically gathers the appropriate data, analyzes the data, and accurately calculates the probabilities and revenue factors, as outlined in *Table 5.8: Evaluating BAR Options* to allow the optimal strategy to be employed, is invaluable.

As previously explained, massive amounts of data are available through a wide variety of information systems that support hotel operations, as well as the sale and distribution of hotel accommodations and services. Consequently, the wealth of information available to improve revenue optimization decision-making is nearly limitless. Hotel sales, revenue management, and marketing professionals, working in partnership with data scientists and computer programmers, have developed algorithms that break revenue optimization decisions down into step-by-step sequences of commands that retrieve the relevant data, complete the appropriate analyses, and communicate recommendations or, in some cases, even execute the optimal strategies to maximize revenue. Wise hotel marketers will take full advantage of these tools and embrace this available technology.

The law of large numbers states that the accuracy of an estimate of a value within a population, based upon a sample, improves as the sample size increases. Using a coin toss example, once again, a coin that is tossed 1,000 times is more likely to accurately estimate the proportion of "heads" at closer to 0.50 or 50%—the true value—than if the estimate is based upon just 10 tosses or even 100 tosses. Consequently, a RMS that collects and tracks a large amount of data can more accurately estimate values that will provide meaningful insights to the revenue management team. In addition, markets are dynamic and ever-changing. As a result, data must constantly be updated and analyzed on a continuous basis. The conversion rate of inquiries to bookings at a specific guestroom rate will change over time, for example, particularly if demand in a market is increasing and room rates are being increased at competitive hotels. So, data must be current. An effective RMS will constantly collect and update the data upon which optimization recommendations are made—a revenue manager, regardless of how capable, simply cannot collect and analyze the most current and relevant data as quickly and efficiently as a properly programmed RMS.

law of large numbers: the accuracy of an estimate of a value within a population, based upon a sample, improves as the sample size increases

The pricing, forecasting, yield management, and data analysis examples provided within this chapter are simplified to assist readers in understanding the basic concepts behind pricing, forecasting, and effective revenue optimization decision-making. In practice, the revenue management team must embrace and learn to trust technology to guide these processes. To do so, it is important that revenue management professionals ensure that accurate, reliable data are being collected by or input into the RMS; they must understand the types of analyses that are being performed by the system; and how to evaluate their revenue and market performance to ensure the effectiveness of the algorithms driving optimization recommendations and strategies. The most sophisticated RMS include algorithms that review the accuracy of past forecasts, evaluating the effectiveness of previous revenue optimization strategies generated by the system, and may even allow the system to self-regulate or modify how data is used to drive future optimization recommendations. These forms of machine learning or artificial intelligence (AI) are undoubtedly the future of revenue management—propelling the hotels that embrace this technology to new levels of success.

THE LAST HOTEL TO SELL-OUT

Although hotels desire to sell every available guestroom, every night possible, being the first hotel to sell-out within the market provides no benefit. As a matter of fact, it may be more profitable to be the last hotel within a market to sell all available service capacity. As demand for accommodations increases within the market, room rates also rise. A hotel with available rooms, while all other hotels are full, will be able to command a premium guestroom rate for the final several rooms that are sold. Of course, the value equation must be considered; however, a wise revenue management team will manage the pace at which rooms are sold, particularly when the market is anticipated to be sold-out, to optimize ADR and to protect rooms for relationship-building opportunities with key clients.

ASSESSING REVENUE PERFORMANCE

benchmark:
a meaningful reference point against which current performance may be compared

To evaluate the revenue management team's effectiveness, a process must be established to benchmark market performance. A benchmark is a meaningful reference point against which current performance may be compared to assess performance. As previously discussed, two commonly used benchmarks include the annual forecast and year-over-year performance; however, even if a hotel is outperforming last year's financial results, or achieving its forecasted financial goals, the hotel's true performance in the marketplace—relative to its competitors—is still unknown.

Although KPIs provide important insight about a hotel's revenue performance, these KPIs must be compared against the overall performance of the hotel's direct competitors to assess the effectiveness of the revenue management team's optimization strategies. This is commonly done using a STAR report, provided by STR. The STAR report allows a hotel to compare its revenue performance against a competitive set of hotels in terms of occupancy, ADR, and RevPAR. For STR to generate a STAR report, the revenue management team must first identify a competitive set of hotels whose aggregate KPIs will serve as the benchmark.

competitive set:
a group of hotels against which a hotel competes for guests and market share

A competitive set is a group of hotels against which a hotel competes for guests and market share. STR suggests that competitive sets be established based upon four primary factors: proximity, price, product, and participation. A hotel will want to include hotels within its competitive set that are located within a reasonable distance to the subject hotel and its demand generators (proximity), as well as hotels that charge similar guestroom rates to the various guest segments that the hotels compete to attract (pricing). It is also common for hotels within the competitive set to provide a similar range of services and service level (product). Finally, the hotel under consideration for inclusion in the competitive set must provide its data to STR so that its KPI statistics may be used to calculate market performance (participation). Many hotel managers create more than one competitive set against which to compare their performance, particularly if the hotel competes against different hotels for different guest segments. Please refer to *Box 5.5: Benchmarking a Hotel's Performance* for additional details.

Once competitive sets are established, an index is calculated for each KPI that allows a hotel's performance in the market to be assessed. These include the penetration (occupancy) index, the ADR index, and the yield (RevPAR) index, defined and calculated as follows:

Penetration Index

The penetration index evaluates market penetration by comparing the hotel's occupancy with the occupancy of the hotels included within the competitive set; it may also be referred to as the occupancy index. It is calculated by dividing the hotel's occupancy by the occupancy for the competitive set of hotels and multiplying by 100 and is expressed as a percentage. A score that exceeds 100% indicates strong market performance—the hotel is enjoying more than its fair share of demand or room nights in the market. A score of less than 100% indicates that the hotel may not be performing to its potential.

penetration index (or occupany index): a measure of a hotel's market penetration, which compares the hotel's occupancy with the occupancy of hotels within its competitive set

fair share: when the proportion of room nights or revenue sold by a hotel is equal to the hotel's proportion of available rooms within its competitive set

ADR Index

Like the penetration index, the ADR index compares the hotel's ADR with the ADR for the competitive set. It is expressed as a percentage and is calculated by dividing the ADR of the hotel by the ADR for the competitive set of hotels and multiplying the resulting ratio by 100. A hotel that is outperforming its competitors in terms of ADR will have an ADR index exceeding 100%, whereas a hotel that is priced lower, on average, than its competitors will have an index of less than 100%.

ADR index: a measure of a hotel's pricing performance, which compares the hotel's ADR with the ADR of hotels within its competitive set

Yield (RevPAR) index

A hotel's RevPAR index is calculated by dividing the RevPAR for a hotel by the cumulative RevPAR generated by hotels in the competitive set and multiplying the result by 100. Again, a hotel that enjoys a RevPAR or yield index of over 100% is outperforming its competitive set of hotels in terms of room revenue generated per revenue producing opportunity. The RevPAR index is the best measure of a hotel's overall revenue performance.

yield index (or RevPAR index): a measure of a hotel's revenue performance, which compares the hotel's RevPAR with the RevPAR of hotels within its competitve set

Box 5.5: Benchmarking a Hotel's Performance provides additional details about the use of these benchmarks.

BOX 5.5:

©wavebreakmedia/
Shutterstock.com

To measure the effectiveness of a hotel's revenue optimization strategies, KPIs must be compared against the KPIs of the hotel's competitors. STR, the primary supplier of competitive market data for the hotel industry (profiled in *Chapter 1: Introduction to the Hotel Industry, Box 1.1*), collects data from thousands of hotels on a regularly scheduled basis. Most parent companies provide revenue performance data to STR for their brand-affiliated hotels; many independent hotels also report their revenue statistics to STR, which compiles this data and prepares customized reports for each hotel based upon its specific competitive set(s).

To protect the proprietary nature and confidentiality of the data, STR only reports the statistics in aggregate. This means that STR will only provide statistics for multiple hotels combined into a competitive set (comp set) of properties or from a specific destination or market. STR requires a minimum of three properties be identified in a competitive set, in addition to the participating hotel, and strongly suggests that hotels include four or more hotels in its competitive set(s); the average number of hotels in a comp set is between five and six properties. There are also restrictions on the composition of the competitive set in terms of the proportion of the available rooms within a competitive set that can be affiliated with a single parent company or hotel management firm. This ensures that a firm cannot create a comp set that would allow the firm to isolate an individual property's performance by backing out the performance of hotels under the company's control. These sufficiency requirements ensure that STR does not inadvertently disclose a hotel's individual market performance to its competitors.

sufficiency requirements: guidelines established by STR that hotels must follow when identifying its competitive set to protect the confidentiality of each property's individual data

Three indices are used to compare a hotel's performance against its competitors; these indices include the penetration or occupancy index; the ADR index; and the RevPAR index as previously defined. These indices are calculated as follows:

Formula 5.5: Penetration index: Occupancy index = Hotel's occupancy ÷ Competition's occupancy x 100

Formula 5.6: ADR index: ADR index = Hotel's ADR ÷ Competition's ADR x 100

Formula 5.7: RevPAR index: RevPAR index = Hotel's RevPAR ÷ Competition's RevPAR x 100

The following example serves to illustrate how these indices may be used by the revenue management team of an individual property to assess their property's performance and the impact of this information on the hotel's revenue optimization strategies.

The Hotel Don Francisco, part of the Curio Collection by Hilton, is a boutique hotel with 112-guestrooms that competes with the six following primary competitors:

Best Western Plus	242-guestrooms
Hampton Inn by Hilton	90-guestrooms
Hyatt Place	85-guestrooms
Kimpton Tuscan (IHG)	84-guestrooms
Marriott Midtown	350-guestrooms
Wyndham Garden Hotel	98-guestrooms

There are 30 days in June, which means there were 31,830 room nights available among the hotels in the competitive set, including the Hotel Don Francisco, which represents the supply in the comp set. Demand in the market totaled 22,830 room nights sold, which represents 71.7% occupancy (= 22,830 ÷ 31,830). The ADR in the market was $198.78, which resulted in total room revenue of $4,538,201 (= 22,830 X $198.78) and RevPAR for the competitive set of $142.58 (= $4,538,201 ÷ 31,830).

The Hotel Don Francisco, Curio Collection by Hilton, enjoyed occupancy of 71.5% with an ADR of $214.63, which resulted in 2,402 occupied room nights (= 112 X 30 X 71.5%) and guestroom revenue of $515,541 (= 2,402 X $214.63). RevPAR for the Don Francisco for June was $153.43 (= $515,541 ÷ 3,360). Consequently, the following penetration, ADR, and RevPAR indices were experienced by the hotel for the month of June:

Penetration index:	99.7% = 71.5% ÷ 71.7%
ADR index:	108.0% = $214.63 ÷ $198.78
RevPAR index:	107.6% = $153.43 ÷ $142.58

Overall, the revenue management team for the Don Francisco Hotel would be likely to interpret this as a strong performance for the month of June. The hotel's occupancy was in-line with the market at 99.7% of fair share (71.5% versus 71.7% for the comp set), whereas the hotel was able to achieve a higher ADR than its competitors collectively, achieving 108% of fair market share ($214.63 versus $198.78); this resulted in the hotel earning 107.6% of RevPAR or revenue share ($153.43 versus $142.58). Fair market share is achieved when a hotel's share of occupied room nights is equal to its proportion of available rooms in the comp set—in other words, when a hotel achieves a penetration index score of 100%. Likewise, when a hotel's ADR is in-line with its competitors, achieving a 100% ADR index, it achieves fair rate share; and a 100% RevPar index indicates the hotel has achieved fair revenue share.

Although it is likely that the Hotel Don Francisco's revenue management team would be pleased by their June performance, the perception of their performance is impacted by how well the hotel has performed relative to its competitive set in recent months, as well as in June the previous year. Every hotel enjoys a unique position within its competitive set based upon various qualitative factors. These factors may include the chain-scale of the various hotels within the comp set; guests' perceptions of the quality of the various brands represented in the market; the age and maintenance of each hotel's physical facilities; the size of each hotel's guestrooms; the peripheral services

fair market share: achieved when a hotel's share of occupied room nights is equal to its proportion of available rooms in the comp set, achieving a 100% occupancy index

fair rate share: achieved when a hotel's ADR is in-line with its competitors, achieving a 100% ADR index

fair revenue share: achieved when a hotel's RevPAR is in-line with its competitors, achieving a 100% RevPAR index

available at each hotel; guests' perceptions of each hotel's service quality; and other factors. Consequently, some hotels—particularly many luxury and upper-upscale hotels competing in markets with few direct competitors—may fully expect to achieve ADR and RevPAR indices well in excess of 100%. Conversely, other hotels may simply not have the facilities and services to achieve 100% indices in ADR and RevPAR and may be content receiving less than fair share in these areas.

For example, if the Hotel Don Francisco, Curio Collection by Hilton, typically achieves a 110% ADR index, coupled with a penetration index of 100% or higher, resulting in a RevPAR index of 110% or higher, then the revenue management team may be disappointed with its June performance of 107.6% of revenue share. This may very well be the case because the Best Western Plus (242 rooms), Hampton Inn by Hilton (90 rooms), the Wyndham Garden Hotel (98 rooms), and the Hyatt Place (85 rooms), representing nearly half (48.5%) of the total available hotel rooms (1,061 rooms) in the comp set, are likely to be positioned and priced lower than the Hotel Don Francisco. The number of hotel rooms within each property impacts the influence that each hotel's performance has on the performance of the comp set—in other words, in this example, the Marriott Midtown, with 350 rooms or nearly one-third (33.0%) of the 1,061 total available rooms in the comp set, has the most substantial impact on the performance of the comp set, whereas the Kimpton Tuscan (IHG) has the least impact due to its 84 rooms (7.9% of available rooms). Finally, the performance of the target hotel—the Hotel Don Francisco, in this example—is included when calculating the performance of the comp set.

Each hotel selects its own comp set. The management team of the Hotel Don Francisco, Curio Collection by Hilton, usually in partnership with corporate leadership and the hotel's ownership, would have selected the six specific properties included in its comp set; however, each of these six properties may or may not include the Hotel Don Francisco in their respective comp sets—it's left to the discretion of each individual property. Many hotels create one comp set to assess its performance in terms of individual or transient guests, while selecting a separate comp set to assess its group room revenue performance. A hotel with a significant amount of meeting space may want to compare itself to hotels with similar meeting space capacity, as well as a similar number of available guestrooms. This may result in the inclusion of hotels that are a further distance from the hotel and even hotels located in different markets or tracts.

certified hotel industry analyst (CHIA): an industry certification that identifies hotel revenue management professionals capable of accurately assessing a hotel's market performance

Aspiring revenue managers and other hotel professionals that desire to gain additional insight into benchmarking performance may want to consider pursuing certification as a *certified hotel industry analyst* (CHIA). CHIA certification is offered by *STR*, in partnership with the *Educational Institute* of the *American Hotel and Lodging Association* (*AHLA*), and the *International Council on Hotel, Restaurant, and Institutional Education* (*ICHRIE*).

CHAPTER SUMMARY

Hotel managers have a fiduciary responsibility to optimize revenue. Because a hotel has limited service capacity, the revenue management team, which includes the hotel's general manager, revenue manager, director of sales and others, must effectively balance the goal of driving occupancy, while maximizing the ADR, to optimize yield, which is measured as revenue per available room (RevPAR). To accomplish this goal, a hotel must offer competitive guestroom rates, as well as a range of discounted rates, while successfully executing a dynamic pricing strategy that restricts availability to guest segments seeking lower rates during periods of high demand. Hotel services are marketed through a variety of distribution channels that are closely monitored by the revenue management team, which use stay restrictions to manage guest arrival and departure patterns to level occupancy and control booking pace, particularly on peak demand nights.

Group bookings account for a substantial share of occupied room nights, particularly in upper-upscale and luxury hotels with a substantial amount of meeting space. Consequently, the group sales managers apply similar yield management strategies when negotiating and contracting group business. The entire revenue management team is often involved in vetting potential group business, which includes assessing the amount of ancillary and BRGR that will potentially be generated to help guide the group selection process during daily sales review meetings. Group contracts include F&B minimums, as well as cancellation and attrition clauses to protect a hotel from unexpectedly losing revenue due to a group that falls short of its revenue commitments.

The revenue management team must accurately forecast revenue and anticipate demand, by market segment, to effectively optimize revenue and to select the most profitable guests possible. Consequently, the availability of data, coupled with the ability to effectively analyze data, is critical. Many hotels use technology, including sophisticated RMS, to collect, analyze and evaluate the wide variety and overwhelming volume of data available through both internal and external sources. Data analysis is not only used proactively to manage rates and availability for future dates, it is also used to evaluate the effectiveness of a hotel's revenue optimization strategies historically. STR provides market data on a hotel's direct competitors, allowing a hotel to compare its KPIs—occupancy, ADR, and RevPAR—to those of its key competitors and to calculate revenue-share within the hotel's specific market. By keeping score, the revenue management team may assess their performance and improve their effectiveness.

KEY TERMS AND CONCEPTS

6-week pick-up trends
abandons
ADR index
algorithm
attrition clause
average daily rate (ADR)
average price
benchmark
binomial probability distribution
    function
booking pace
cancellation fee
certified hotel industry analyst
    (CHIA)
commission model
competitive set (comp set)
contribution margin
cut-off date
demand
denial
displacement cost
distribution channel
dynamic pricing
economies of scale
empirical rule
expense

F&B minimum
fair market share
fair revenue share
fair rate share
fair share
fiduciary responsibility
global distribution system (GDS)
group ceiling
guest mix
historical demand
incremental revenue
inquiries
key performance indicators (KPIs)
last room availability
law of large numbers
loss
market mix
merchant model
metasearch
minimum acceptable rate (MAR)
minimum-length-of-stay (MLOS)
net revenue
occupancy index
occupancy
occupancy rate/occupancy
    percentage

options
penetration index
price/rate integrity
price gouging
profit
psychological/just-below pricing
    strategy
rate fence
rate parity
revenue
RevPAR
RevPAR index
RevPASH
room night
sell strategy
service capacity
set-up fees
stay restriction
sufficiency requirements
supply
turn-away
turn-down
utilization rate
yield
yield index
yield management

SPECIAL SUPPLEMENT: CALCULATING THE MEAN, STANDARD DEVIATION, AND SKEWNESS OF A SAMPLE

Earlier in this chapter, it is suggested that a sample of hotel room rates from competitive hotels be used to calculate the ADR within the market by calculating the mean $(\overline{X})$ of the observations; it is further suggested that the standard deviation of the sample, s, be used to estimate the amount of dispersion within the sample. These values may be calculated using the following formulas:

Mean: $\quad \overline{X} = \dfrac{\Sigma x}{n}$ $\qquad\qquad$ Standard deviation: $\quad s = \sqrt{\dfrac{\Sigma(x - \overline{X})^2}{n - 1}}$

Where,

$\quad x$ = each observed value

$\quad n$ = number of observations

It is also suggested that the empirical rule be applied to estimate the proportion of observations that occur within one, two, or three standard deviations of the mean (refer to *Figure 5.1: Empirical Rule*) assuming the observations approximate the normal distribution. To expedite these calculations while simultaneously evaluating if the observations approximate the normal distribution, the revenue management team may use the *Data Analysis* tool available in *Microsoft Office Excel*.

To use *Excel* to make these calculations, the optional *Analysis Toolpak* must be installed as an *Add-in* feature. Once this feature has been installed, click on *Data*, then *Data Analysis*, followed by *Descriptive Statistics*, and *OK*. Highlight the sample data using the dialog box that appears requesting the *Data Range* to be entered; check the *Summary statistics* box, and then click *OK* a final time. *Excel* will generate the summary statistics in the format below, which was created using the data set that produced the statistics found in *Table 5.1: Room Rate Distribution Analysis*:

Weekday		Weekend	
Mean	187.0238	Mean	140.5
Standard Error	0.750724	Standard Error	0.791576
Median	179	Median	139
Mode	175	Mode	139
Standard Deviation	21.23368	Standard Deviation	17.70019
Sample Variance	450.8693	Sample Variance	313.2966
Kurtosis	-0.69777	Kurtosis	0.894353
Skewness	0.480131	Skewness	0.386999
Range	80	Range	100
Minimum	149	Minimum	99
Maximum	229	Maximum	199
Sum	149619	Sum	70250
Count	800	Count	500

The *Skewness* statistic may be used to determine if the data set approximates the normal distribution; the closer the statistic is to zero, the more closely it approximates the normal distribution. Sample sets with a *Skewness* value between -1 and 1 approximate the normal distribution. If the value is below -1, then there may be more extreme observations (room rates) at the lower end of the distribution, whereas there may be more extreme observations (room rates) at the higher end of the distribution if the skewness statistic is greater than 1.

DISCUSSION QUESTIONS

1. Discuss the difference between maximizing and optimizing hotel revenue. Under what conditions might a revenue management team select a guest or group that does not maximize hotel revenues over a specific set of dates.
2. Explain the concept of yield and why maximizing price (ADR) or utilization rate (occupancy %) must not be the primary goal of the revenue management team.
3. Explain the value equation and why it must be considered when a hotel establishes its guestroom rates. How does the dispersion of hotel room rates within the market impact pricing decisions? Include *Diagram 5.1: The Empirical Rule* in the conversation.
4. Discuss the use of a dynamic pricing strategy, as well as the concepts of rate fencing and market mix, on ADR and RevPAR.
5. Using the stay restrictions outlined in *Table 5.4: Commonly Used Hotel Stay Restrictions*, discuss the stay restrictions applied in *Table 5.5: Guestroom Availability, Minimum Acceptable Rates (MARs), and Stay Restrictions*; identify and explain alternative strategies to those recommended. Looking at *Table 5.7: Updated 30-Day Occupancy Forecast*, in *Box 5.3: Updating the Annual Forecast*, suggest stay restrictions for the upcoming month of October 2019.
6. Define the term algorithm. Identify the types of internal and external data, including specific variables, that may be useful when evaluating alternative revenue optimization strategies. Explain how algorithms are created and used to support decision-making and customer selection.
7. Discuss the performance of the Hotel Don Francisco, Curio Collection by Hilton, based upon the information provided in *Box 5.5: Benchmarking a Hotel's Performance*. What opportunities may exist for the hotel to improve its market performance? Explain.

ENDNOTES

Collins, M. D., & Parsa, H.G. (2006). Pricing strategies to maximize revenues in the lodging industry. *International Journal of Hospitality Management*, 25(1), 91-107.

Heskett, J. L.; Sasser, W. E.; & Schlesinger, L. A. (1997). *The Service Profit Chain: How Leading Companies Link Profit and Growth to Loyalty, Satisfaction, and Value*. The Free Press, New York, New York.

STR (2018). Hotel Industry Analytical Foundations. *SHARE Center: Certified Hotel Industry Analyst* training materials.

Weatherford, L. R., & Pölt, S. (2002). Better unconstraining of airline demand data in revenue management systems for improved forecast accuracy and greater revenues. *Journal of Revenue & Pricing Management*, 1(3), 234.

HOTEL DEVELOPMENT PROJECT

Students completing a course in hotel, lodging, or resort management are encouraged to complete a hotel development project over the course of the semester/term; students are encouraged to work in small groups of 3 – 5 students. *Appendix A* outlines the project in its entirety.

Upon the conclusion of *Chapter 5: Optimizing Revenue*, students are prepared to complete the following assignment.

ASSIGNMENT 3: DEFINING THE HOTEL: BRAND, GUESTROOM COUNT, FACILITIES, AND EXPERIENCES

Use content from: Chapter 3: Defining Customer Segments; Chapter 4: Effective Sales and Marketing; and Chapter 5: Optimizing Revenue.

Based upon the key demand generators identified within the market, the current mix of hotel accommodations, and hotels in the pipeline, please identify the following information about the proposed hotel for the site:

1. The key guest segments that the hotel will target. Be certain to identify a variety of customer segments that will use the hotel during the week, as well as on weekends and during holiday periods.
2. Based upon the guest segments targeted, describe the guest experience that will be delivered to guests of the hotel, as well as the brand and chain-scale that has been selected for the hotel. Provide an overview of the brand's parent company and its family of brands. Explain how the brand standards of the specific brand selected align with the targeted guest experience for the various customer segments the hotel will serve.
3. Using the STR data provided by the course instructor, which is based upon the property's preliminary comp set identified in *Assignment 1: Understanding the Location and Market*, estimate the hotel's annual occupancy, ADR, and RevPAR. Identify the number of hotel guestrooms, proposed rate structure, and market mix for the hotel that is designed to generate the targeted occupancy, ADR, and RevPAR (e.g. rack rate or range of BARs; corporate and volume rates; government; leisure and discounted rates; and weekday and weekend group rooms).
4. Modify the comp set, as necessary, based upon the brand and parent company proposed. If the comp set changes, the instructor will acquire modified benchmark data from STR's SHARE Center, which will be used for *Assignment 6: Hotel Development Proposal Presentation*.

Section 2 Supplement:
Sales Team Deployment:
A Tale of Two Markets

To understand the factors that impact sales team deployment, imagine two identical hotels, in-terms of guestroom count, square footage of meeting space, and chain-scale, but located in two very different markets. Both hotels are upper-upscale, 400-room hotels, with 30,000 square feet of total meeting space, including a 12,000 square foot ballroom, a 9,000 square foot junior ballroom, and 9,000 square feet in break-out and small function space. Consequently, the hotels may accommodate approximately 1,000 guests in its ballroom for an in-house function and still have 18,000 square feet of available space for additional functions and break-out meetings. One hotel is located in Fort Myers, Florida and the second in San Francisco, California—two substantially different markets.

Fort Myers, Florida is home to just over 130 hotels with nearly 12,000 hotel rooms; the average hotel in Fort Myers has 88 guestrooms (STR, 2017). The historic River District, located on the southern shore of the Caloosahatchee River, serves as Fort Myers' downtown area; however, it far from a typical urban landscape. 'Downtown' Fort Myers is more of a quaint, southern town and is home to the historic Edison and Ford Winter Estates, a few blocks down the river from the restaurants and night life of the River District. The River District also is home to the Harborside Event Center, a modest conference center with just nine meeting rooms comprising 42,000 square feet of total meeting space; there are just a handful of hotels in the District, including a 122-room Holiday Inn and 67-room Hotel Indigo. Construction is underway on the 12-story, 243-room Luminary Hotel and there are plans to expand and renovate the Harborside Event Center to attract more meetings to the River District; however, the strongest demand generator in Southwest Florida is the beautiful coastline along the Gulf of Mexico, which is located approximately 20-miles west of the River District. As a matter of fact, the Lee County Visitors and Convention Bureau markets the area as *The Beaches of Fort Myers and Sanibel* (www.fortmyers-sanibel.com); please refer to **Box 4.4: The Beaches of Fort Myers and Sanibel** for additional information.

Each winter, 'snowbirds,' retirees and affluent leisure travelers from the Northeastern and Midwestern United States, as well as Canada, flock to the Southwest Florida coast to enjoy the warm winter temperatures, sun-filled days, and warm waters of the Gulf of Mexico. In addition, two Major League Baseball (MLB) teams, the Boston Red Sox and Minnesota Twins, conduct their spring training at two stadiums in the area—Century Link Park and JetBlue Park (a.k.a. 'Fenway South'). Peak demand for accommodations runs from mid-November through late-April during which time, accommodations in the Fort Myers area and extending south through the more upscale Naples and Marco Island hotel market are difficult to locate. Naples, located 40 miles to the south of Fort Myers, is home to two Ritz Carlton Resorts—the 450-room Beachfront Resort, with 42,000 square feet of meeting space and the 291-room Golf Resort, with 16,500 of meeting space and a 36-hole championship golf course designed by Greg Norman. Further to the south is the 726-room JW Marriott Marco Island Beach Resort, which boasts 62 meeting rooms containing 140,000 square-feet of meeting space, ten restaurants, and two 18-hole championship golf courses. The largest properties in the Fort Myers area, represented by the Lee County Visitors and Convention Bureau, include the 458-room South Seas Island Resort, a luxury-scale hotel with nearly 30,000 square feet of indoor and outdoor meeting space located on Captiva Island; the 454-room Hyatt Regency Coconut Point Resort with 82,500 square feet of indoor and outdoor event space, as well as water slides, multiple pools, and beach access; the 347-room Marriott Sanibel Harbour Resort & Spa, with 30,000 square feet of meeting

space; and the 263-room Westin Cape Coral Resort at Marina Village with 50,000 square feet of meeting space.

The Fort Myers – Cape Coral, Florida metropolitan area is ranked in the top ten areas in the United States in terms of anticipated economic growth in 2018. The area enjoyed the second highest population growth in the nation in 2017 (2.77%) and is expected to enjoy the highest growth in population in 2018 (3.37%). Despite this growth in population, job growth was stagnant in 2017 at 0.21%, ranking the area 91st in the nation; however, employment is expected to grow at a more robust 2.52% in 2018, which should place it closer to the top ten (projected 12th in the nation) in terms of job growth (Sharf, 2018). The growth in population is driven, primarily, by retirees relocating to the area, which explains the weak job growth. The top five non-government employers in the market include three health care providers that support the health care needs of the aging population, in addition to two grocery retailers (Table 5.1). Fort Myers is home to Florida Gulf Coast University, a rapidly growing regional university that has grown its enrollment to over 15,000 students in just 20-years; the University continues to expand its academic programs and has established a business incubator, working with local officials to diversify the regional economy. The Southwest Florida International Airport provides direct flights to a variety of major and secondary markets in the Northeast, Mid-Atlantic, Southeast, Midwest, and Great Lakes regions; as well as Houston, Dallas, Denver, and Colorado Springs. Direct international flights are available to three cities each in Canada (Montreal, Ottawa and Toronto) and Germany (Cologne/Bonn, Dusseldorf, and Munich).

According to STR (2017), there are more than 33,000 hotel rooms in over 200 hotels in the city of San Francisco, excluding the airport, suburban, and surrounding areas such as the 'Silicon Valley'—home to Apple, Google, Facebook and many additional technology firms, which is approximately forty miles to the south of San Francisco. The majority of these hotels are located within a four by five mile (20 square mile)

© kropic1/Shutterstock.com

San Francisco, California USA

area located in the heart of the city, which includes the Financial District, Union Square, and Knob Hill. The average hotel has just over 150 rooms; however, there are dozens of large hotels including the San Francisco Hilton at Union Square with nearly 2,000 rooms and the 1,500-room Marriott Marquis, which is connected via underground tunnel to the 2.0 million square-foot Moscone Convention Center (please refer to *Box 3.2: The Moscone Convention Center*), as well as iconic hotels, including the Fairmont, Intercontinental Mark Hopkins, Westin St. Francis, and the Ritz-Carlton San Francisco. There are also dozens of boutique hotels with less than 100 rooms each that dot the San Francisco hotel landscape.

San Francisco is an international tourism destination, premier convention site, home to major league sports franchises, and boasts a vibrant business community. Leading industries include biotechnology, tourism, technology, and banking and finance, which includes a strong venture capital market. The Bay Area is home to several large and prestigious universities, including the University of California San Francisco—a highly ranked medical school located in the heart of the city that works in close partnership with the biotechnology industry. In recent years, the San Francisco market has enjoyed exceptional hotel industry performance with annual hotel occupancy in excess of 80% and an Average Daily Rate (ADR) in excess of $250.00 per night. With an annual occupancy of over 80%, San Francisco cannot be considered a 'seasonal' market, although rates do peak in the spring and fall during the peak convention season. San Francisco Travel (www.sftravel.com), a non-profit, Destination

Marketing Organization (DMO), aggressively markets San Francisco as a convention, leisure and business destination.

Table S.1 summarizes key information about the two markets.

	Fort Myers, Florida USA	San Francisco, California USA
Hotels	133	216
Hotel guestrooms	11,721	33,376
Average rooms per hotel	88	154
Occupancy percentage (approximate)	70%	80%
Average Daily Rate (ADR) (approximate)	$150	$250
Revenue Per Available Room (RevPAR)	$105	$200
*Above statistics are furnished by the STR SHARE Center (2017)		
Tourism expenditures	$3.0 billion	$10.7 billion
Lodging	23.3%	20.0%
Food & beverage	25.1%	23.1%
Shopping	24.7%	15.9%
Ground transportation	9.0%	21.9%
Sightseeing, entertainment & other	16.8%	19.3%
Hotel taxes generated (approximate per year)	$40 million	$250 million
*Above statistics are furnished by the Lee County Visitors & Convention Bureau and San Francisco Travel Association for each of the two destinations respectively (2017)		
Five (5) Largest Private Employers (number of local employees; industry)		
Fort Myers, Florida USA	**San Francisco, California USA**	
Lee Health (13,595; health care)	Wells Fargo & Co. (8,195; banking)	
Publix Super Market (7,183; retail grocer)	Salesforce (6,600; technology)	
NCH Healthcare System (7,017; health care)	California Pacific Medical Center (6,000; health care)	
Walmart Supercenters (5,271; general retailer)	PG&E Corp. (4,325; utility)	
Bayfront Health (3,060; health care)	Gap Inc. (4,268; clothing retailer)	
*Above statistics are furnished by the Southwest Florida Economic Development Alliance (accessed online on May 14, 2018 at https://swfleda.com/top-100-employers/) and the San Francisco Business Times (accessed May 14, 2018 online at https://www.bizjournals.com/sanfrancisco/subscriber-only/2016/12/30/employers-san-francisco.html) for the Fort Myers and San Francisco markets respectively.		

Table S.1: Tale of Two Markets: Market Comparisons

STRATEGIC OVERVIEW

Fort Myers is largely a leisure-driven destination with relatively weak local corporate demand, but strong leisure demand across the entire week during the peak season (mid-November through late-April). Corporate group business must be attracted from outside of the local market, primarily from the Northeast and Midwest. Due to the tropical, resort environment, much of the corporate business coming out of these markets will be incentive business, utilized to reward top-performers with their respective organizations. In addition, national associations may be attracted to the market, particularly during the prime season, while state associations may take advantage of lower guestroom rates that may be available during the off-season (May through October). High-end groups coming out of the major markets, including New York City, Washington D.C. and Chicago, may be attracted to the higher end properties in the Naples region, while more price-sensitive groups may find a better value in a Fort Myers property. During the off-season, the Fort Myers area hotels need to open their doors to government business, attract SMERF groups, and offer special promotional rates to capture 'stay-cations' and guests from the east coast of Florida, since many locals and Floridians from the Fort Lauderdale and Miami area, just a 2-hour drive, as well as land-locked Orlando, 3-hours by car, enjoy the unspoiled beauty of Southwest Florida's Gulf Coast beaches.

In comparing the two markets, San Francisco is a more traditional urban market with a high concentration of corporate clients and a major convention center that accommodates a variety of high profile conventions, attracting delegates from across the country and around the world. So, the focus is on driving the average daily rate (ADR) with high-end corporate groups that will utilize the hotel's meeting space. During citywides, 'contingent' groups that meet in conjunction with the parent organization hosting the convention will be targeted that will utilize the hotel's in-house meeting space for meetings and catered events. Fortunately, strong leisure demand may be utilized to fill available weekend and holiday periods when corporate demand softens; due to its high price-point, government and most SMERF groups may be priced out of the San Francisco market.

Table S.2 summarizes a possible approach to deploying sales managers in a 450-room hotel with 30,000 square feet of meeting space within each market. Based upon a ratio of one sales manager per 75 – 100 rooms, each hotel would typically employ four-and-one-half to six sales managers, plus the appropriate support personnel.

Position	Primary Market Assignments	
	Fort Myers, Florida USA	San Francisco, California USA
Director of Sales & Marketing (a)	Local accounts; international	City-wide conventions
Senior Sales Manager (b)	National & state associations	Corporate (SoMa: biotech & tech)
Sales Manager (c)	Corporate & incentive groups	Corporate (Financial District, East Bay)
Sales Manager (d)	SMERF, government	National & state associations
Express Meetings Manager	10 – 50 room nights	10 – 50 room nights
Account Executive	---	Local corporate volume accounts
Director of Catering & Conference Services	Conference services (a & c)	Catering only
Catering Sales Manager	Catering-only including weddings	---
Conference Services Manager (1)	Conference services (b & d)	Conference services (a & d)
Conference Services Manager (2)	---	Conference services (b & c)
Sales Intern (local university)	Seasonally	Year-round
Sales Assistant	Support (a, c, & DCCS) & social media	Support (a, d & CS1) & SMS
Sales Assistant	Support (b, d, & CS1) & SMS	Support (b, c, DCCS & CS2)

Table S.2: Tale of Two Markets: Proposed Sales Team Deployment

SALES TEAM DEPLOYMENT

In Fort Myers, the director of sales & marketing (DOS) will need to spend most of his/her time in the local market to be available to support and manage the sales team, in addition to implementing marketing strategies to drive leisure business. The local Lee County Visitors & Convention Bureau (VCB) focuses its efforts on driving leisure business into the market and the DOS will be the hotel's primary contact with the Bureau. So, the DOS will focus on Fort Myers and building relationships with local business leaders to attract local accounts and the VCB to drive business into the hotel. Since the Lee County VCB also operates off-site sales offices in Canada, Germany, and Scandinavia (please refer to **Box 4.4**), the DOS will also manage in-bound international travel. The senior sales manager will pursue national and state association business, spending a great deal of his/her time in Northern Virginia/Washington D.C., home to many national associations, and Tallahassee, home to many state associations. The corporate sales manager will pursue corporate incentive and training business with a focus on the Midwest; sales trips to Chicago, Columbus, Detroit, Indianapolis, St. Louis, as well as New York, will be a regular part of this sales professional's activities—insurance companies, financial firms, automakers, health care, pharmaceutical, and other firms looking to reward and train their sales professionals, dealers, and distributors of their products and services will be targeted. The SMERF sales manager will pursue, primarily, off-season business from the SMERF and government segments, while the express meetings manager will handle inquiries that come into the sales office for small groups with 10 – 50 room nights, which tend to book short-term. This deployment calls for five direct sales positions.

On the service side, the director of catering & conference services (DCCS) will manage the catering and convention services team in addition to servicing the DOS and corporate sales manager's bookings, although some of the smaller groups may be delegated to the express meetings manager. A conference services manager will service the association and SMERF sales managers' groups. The hotel may also want to employ a catering sales manager. Many resort markets, such as Fort Myers, enjoy strong weddings business, which require minimal in-house guestrooms; this sales professional will be responsible for the weddings market and seek catering only business to drive incremental business into the hotel's conference and event space.

The 'half-time' person may be utilized to bring a student intern to the hotel from the School of Resort & Hospitality Management at the local university that can help prospect for off-season business and assist the service team during the busy season—gaining exposure to both the sales and service aspects of the sales function. Two sales assistants will be employed—one will oversee the hotel's social media sites and the second will serve as the systems administrator for the Sales Management System (SMS). The sales assistants' respective administrative support roles may be aligned as specified (within the parentheses) in Table S.2.

In San Francisco, much more of the business will be driven locally. Again, in addition to managing the direct sales team, the DOS will serve as the primary contact with San Francisco Travel, the local Destination Marketing Organization. Consequently, the DOS will manage the citywide convention blocks; however, it may be in the hotel's best interest not to participate in a great majority of the citywide guestroom blocks since the hotel may be able to book more profitable corporate business that also utilizes the hotel's meeting space, driving food, beverage and ancillary revenue. The two corporate sales managers are deployed geographically since Market Street divides the commercial district of the city into two halves. South of Market (SoMa) is an area that has gone through a re-vitalization effort over the past 20 – 30 years and is the site of San Francisco's 'new economy,' including many technology start-ups, biotechnology firms, and the new medical school campus of the University of California San

Francisco. The city's second largest employer, Salesforce, recently constructed the tallest office tower in San Francisco (70 stories) to house its workforce and business operations South of Market. Consequently, the SoMa sales manager will focus on bio-tech and technology accounts, primarily, prospecting and booking business South of Market and down through the Silicon Valley. North of Market Street is referred to as the Financial District, which is home to San Francisco's 'traditional economy,' which includes banking and financial services, international trade, retail business, and tourism. The Financial District is home to San Francisco's largest employer Wells Fargo. This corporate sales manager will prospect for and book business generated from within the Financial District and will also be responsible for accounts north of the Golden Gate Bridge in Marin County, the Sonoma and Napa wine valleys, and the East Bay, which includes Oakland, which may be accessed via a 10 – 15-minute rapid transit ride under San Francisco Bay.

An additional sales manager may be deployed to pursue national and state association business, splitting time in Northern Virginia/Washington D.C. and Sacramento; the primary reason for this is due to the different travel patterns associated with association business, although it may be tempting to deploy this third sales manager on corporate accounts due to the sheer volume of corporate business. In addition, there may be association groups that schedule meetings in conjunction with some citywide conventions but are 'outside of the block' that will hold meetings in the hotel's conference space. An express meetings manager will serve as an in-house sales professional, responsible for groups requiring 10 – 50 room nights that typically book short-term. An account executive will round out the direct sales team, focusing on high-volume corporate accounts that generate IBT.

The DCCS will oversee the sales services team that includes two conference services managers. Opportunities to accommodate catering-only and social events will be limited due to the heavy use of the hotel's meeting and conference space by in-house groups. As a result, the DCCS will manage catering-only events personally, while the conference services managers will each be assigned to support two sales managers—perhaps one handling the citywides and associations, supporting the DOS and the association sales manager, and the second supporting the two corporate sales managers.

Again, it is suggested that the hotel employ a sales intern from one of the hospitality management programs in the area that may assist with prospecting, servicing, and the hotel's social media program. It is always good to have a pipeline of sales professionals being developed since revenue is the lifeblood of a hotel or any business. Two sales assistants will be employed; one will be assigned to support three sales professionals and will also serve as systems administrator for the SMS, while the second will support four sales professionals. The social media program may be overseen by the revenue manager or guest services manager and assisted by the sales intern.

DISCUSSION QUESTIONS

1. Discuss the deployment of the sales managers within each of the two markets. What changes might you recommend to the deployment strategies suggested? How might the deployment be modified, in each of the two markets, for a hotel with double the facilities (800-rooms with 60,000 square feet of meeting space) or a luxury hotel with half the facilities (200-rooms with 15,000 square feet of meeting space)?

2. Research a market of choice—perhaps your hometown or a city in which you aspire to someday live. Outline a deployment strategy for the market researched for a similar hotel described in this supplemental reading (upper-upscale, 400-room with 30,000 square feet of meeting space) or modify the available facilities as described in discussion question #1.

3. In which market might you prefer to work? Identify both professional and personal reasons for your decision. Describe the biggest opportunities and challenges you might face as a DOS within each market.

4. Based upon the information provided above, coupled with the knowledge and skills learned in Chapters 3 – 5 of *Delivering the Guest Experience*, approximate the KRIs and total annual guestroom revenue for the hotel within each of the two (2) markets. How do the revenues and KRIs compare?

5. Based upon the salaries and wages of sales professionals within each market, project the total payroll expense for each sales team as suggested. Based upon the room revenue estimated in discussion question #4, calculate the sales payroll to room revenue ratio as well as the sales payroll expense per occupied room and per available room. Discuss the implications. The following website may be helpful in obtaining salary information for each market: www.bls.gov.

END NOTE

Sharf, S. (2018). Full List: America's Fastest Growing Cities 2018. *Forbes* (online version, February 28, 2018); accessed May 14, 2018 at https://www.forbes.com/sites/samanthasharf/2018/02/28/full-list-americas-fastest-growing-cities-2018/#220a83467feb.

Section Three

DELIVERING THE CORE SERVICE:
THE ROOMS DIVISION

SECTION 3: DELIVERING THE CORE SERVICE: THE ROOMS DIVISION

Chapter 6: Guest Services Operations

This chapter outlines the role, function, and successful management of the front office or guest services operations.

Chapter 7: Housekeeping and Laundry Operations

This chapter outlines the role, function, and successful management strategies employed within the housekeeping and laundry operation.

Chapter 6
Guest Services Operations

The core service delivered by a hotel is overnight accommodations. Guests' consumption of overnight accommodations typically starts and ends with interactions with the hotel's front office associates, which dramatically influence guests' perceptions of the hotel's service quality. This chapter outlines the role, function, and key management strategies essential to the successful management of front office operations, commonly referred to as guest services.

PURPOSE AND LEARNING OBJECTIVES:

Upon the conclusion of this chapter, students will be able to:
- Explain the role of the guest services department, including the guest experiences delivered by the department.
- Identify key linear and non-linear processes critical to effective and efficient guest service operations.
- Diagram and explain the reservations sales function.
- Explain strategies employed to successfully manage a hotel's guestroom inventory.
- Identify the key elements of effective arrival and departure experiences.
- Discuss the role of the communications or "at your service" team.
- Discuss the role of the bell staff, concierge, and guest activities team.
- Identify factors that impact a hotel's transportation services.
- Explain the parking options that may be available to guests, including the factors that contribute to the selection of a hotel's parking service options.
- Explain how guest service index (GSI) scores are typically calculated and how they may be used to improve a hotel's performance.
- Recommend staffing levels and project labor costs for a hotel's guest service operation based upon room count and service level.
- Identify tactics and strategies that contribute to the effective management of guest services operations.

KEY FUNCTIONS, SERVICE PROCESSES, AND EXPERIENCES

The guest experience commonly begins and ends with interactions between hotel guests and the guest services team. These interactions ultimately determine the guests' perceptions regarding the quality of service and customer care delivered by the hotel. Although most guests reserve their accommodations through a mobile application or online, some guests prefer to contact the property directly to speak with a member of the reservation sales team—particularly leisure guests, guests with specific needs or requests, guests traveling to resort destinations, or guests seeking a special or group rate. Regardless of the

© YAKOBCHUK VIACHESLAV/Shutterstock.com

method of booking their hotel reservations, all guests are impacted by their arrival experience at a hotel property, which is a primary responsibility of the guest services team. Many hoteliers believe that guests form an opinion regarding the hotel's service quality within the first 10 minutes of their arrival and this initial impression or imprint determines the guests' attitude and response to circumstances that they encounter throughout the remainder of their stay—as the adage states, you only have one opportunity to make a positive first impression!

This chapter explains the role and functions of the guest services team, which include reservation sales; the arrival experience and guest registration process; guestroom inventory control; guest account management and departure experience; communications; rooming and luggage support; concierge services and guest activities; business services; transportation services; and parking operations.

Systems-Thinking with a Customer Focus

As previously depicted in *Diagram 2.4: Systems-Thinking*, management must create linear and non-linear systems to ensure that the activities executed by hotel associates are both effective, delivering positive guest experiences, and efficient, ensuring the profitable operation of the hotel. Because the entire role of the guest services team is to directly interface and attend to both the expressed and unexpressed wishes of hotel guests, it is particularly important that every front office process is designed with the guest experience in mind. In addition, recall that the value equation, defined in *Formula 2.1*, includes in its numerator *process quality*, which means that the quality of the service processes in which a guest participates directly influences their perceptions of the value delivered by the hotel enterprise. Consequently, guest service process design must prioritize guest convenience or process quality.

Reservations Sales Function

The reservation process is a sales function that is delivered by the revenue manager and reservation sales agents. As outlined in *Chapter 5: Optimizing Revenue*, the reservations sales team must assess customers' needs and sell the hotel's guestroom inventory based upon the current sales strategy and availability of guestrooms, as illustrated in *Diagram 6.1: Reservations Sales Process*. Individual travelers are offered available accommodations at the best available rate or a qualified discount, if available, provided the requested arrival and departure pattern does not conflict with any stay restrictions that may be in place. If a guest's reservation request does not comply with the yield management strategies in place for the requested date(s), the guest is informed that the accommodations requested by the guest are not available for the date(s) or at the rate requested. Explaining any restrictions that may be in place or attempting to alter the guest's travel plans to conform to these restrictions is typically counterproductive. The reservation is simply turned away. Many travelers appreciate being referred to an alternative property that may be able to honor the guest's request—this is a particularly effective strategy if the hotel management firm or parent organization has another affiliated hotel in the market.

Group reservation requests are honored if the request is received prior to the client's contracted cutoff date and there are remaining rooms available in the group's room block. Group reservations, particularly from corporate clients, are often received on rooming lists, although many associations and social, military, educational, religious, and fraternal (SMERF) groups require the individual attendees of the meeting or event to book and guarantee their reservations individually. It is incumbent upon the revenue manager to ensure that all group contracts, in terms of room rate, dates of group rate availability, and the number of rooms blocked for each night specified are fulfilled in a manner that is consistent with the group sales contract because this represents a legally binding agreement between the hotel and the group client.

Once it is determined that a reservation request may be honored, the mobile app, website, or reservation sales agent will attempt to close the sale by asking if the guest would like to book the reservation. If the guest elects to book the reservation, the guest's arrival and departure dates, room type request, and room rate will have already been recorded while the guest's needs were assessed during the initial steps of the reservation sales process; however, additional information, including the guest's name, address, cellular telephone number, email address, and anticipated arrival time or flight information will then be collected, as well as any special requests the guest may have. Once the guest's contact information has been collected, it is important that the hotel's cancellation and no-show policy is clearly communicated prior to requesting the guest to provide credit card information to guarantee the reservation; many hotels require that reservations are guaranteed. A guaranteed reservation is

guaranteed reservation: a hotel reservation for which the hotel is guaranteed the first night's payment if a guest fails to arrive as scheduled

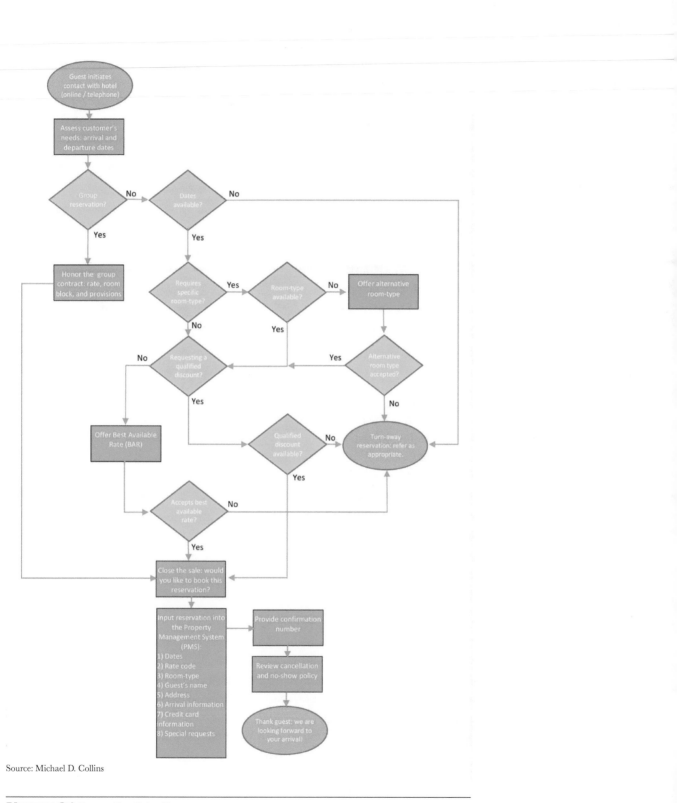

Source: Michael D. Collins

Diagram 6.1: Reservation Sales Process

a hotel reservation for which the hotel is guaranteed the first night's payment, using an approved credit card, if a guest fails to arrive as scheduled. A deposited reservation is a reservation that is guaranteed through the payment of an advanced deposit equivalent to the first night's room and tax charges. If the hotel receives payment for the estimated room and tax charges for a guest's entire stay, then the reservation is referred to as a pre-paid reservation. Some hotels offer a substantial discount if a guest pre-pays for the entire stay, particularly if the pre-payment is non-refundable.

Reservation sales are more complex in a resort environment. In addition to overnight accommodations, many resort guests will schedule peripheral services including golf tee times and spa services at the time of booking. When booking packages, the availability of these services often must be confirmed at the time the reservation is sold. Resort guests also tend to be more concerned with the guestroom's layout, location, and view. Consequently, guests booking a stay at a resort or spa are more likely to contact the property directly to make a voice reservation with a reservation sales agent.

Reservation sales agents must be well-informed and have immediate access to information—not only relative to the peripheral services offered by the hotel, but regarding the local area and activities taking place within the hotel and community. Agents must be able to explain packages, take reservations for additional services offered by the hotel and its industry partners, and be fully aware of groups scheduled to hold events at the hotel, as well as other hotel properties nearby. Reservation sales agents must be able to succinctly articulate cancellation policies and fees, as well as effectively and diplomatically resolve disputes regarding these policies and fees. As a result, reservation sales agents must be effective, persuasive communicators and possess the soft skills of tact and diplomacy.

No-Shows, Cancellations, and Overbooking

A guest that is scheduled to arrive on a specific date and fails to arrive as scheduled is referred to as a no-show; no-shows and late cancellations are typically subject to a charge of one night's room and room tax charges, although policies vary by hotel. Cancellation policies, particularly in busy urban, suburban, and airport locations, often allow cancellation up until 6 p.m. on the day of arrival, although it is becoming increasingly common to require 24-hour, 48-hour, or 72-hour notice, particularly in resort destinations. Wise hoteliers provide their guest service team members with some flexibility and latitude in enforcing cancellation and no-show charges to protect long-term guest relationships and the hotel's goodwill. An effective strategy is to charge no-show and cancellation charges, or to require forfeiture of pre-payments, but to offer the guest the opportunity to apply these payments to a future reservation,

© Cheng Wei/Shutterstock.com

within a specified time frame, because this will encourage the guest's repeat patronage. Cancellation policies and no-show charges are intended to prevent the loss of revenue resulting from guests that do not arrive to the hotel as scheduled; however, hotels must balance collection of these fees with the management of positive long-term guest relationships. As a result, many hotels engage in the practice of modestly overbooking the hotel based upon historical no-show statistics, as discussed in *Chapter 5: Optimizing Revenue*.

Managing Guestroom Inventory

The revenue manager directly supervises the reservation sales agents and has the primary responsibility of managing the hotel's guestroom inventory or service capacity—a hotel's most valuable revenue-producing asset. As discussed in *Chapter 5: Optimizing Revenue*, the revenue manager is a key member of the revenue optimization team, often serving as the chief statistician and historical recordkeeper for the hotel; his/her ability to accurately forecast demand, through a comprehensive awareness of historical performance, coupled with current guestroom availability, market conditions, and trends, allows the revenue management team to make prudent yield management and pricing decisions. As a result, the revenue manager is responsible for managing the availability of accommodations through the various distribution channels. To assist with this process, many hotels use a channel manager, which automates the communication of a hotel's room rates and guestroom availability from the property management system (PMS) or brand's proprietary reservation or revenue management system (RMS) to the various online travel agent (OTA) sites and the global distribution system (GDS), to ensure that the hotel is selling its available hotel accommodations to the appropriate guest segments, on each respective date, and at the optimal price.

> **channel manager:** information technology that monitors a hotel's guestroom availability to optimize room revenue by controlling access and room rates through the various distribution channels

Although many guests merely require a run-of-the-house guestroom, defined as any available overnight accommodation, others require a specific room configuration, such as a king-bedded, double-queen, or double-double guestroom with two full-size beds. Still others may require two adjacent rooms, two adjoining rooms with internal connecting doors, a room on a high-floor or a low-floor, an accessible guestroom, or a suite. Some groups may request that all their guestrooms be located on the same floor or within a specific area of the hotel. These specific needs and requests—and countless others—require advanced planning to accommodate. Consequently, the revenue manager must carefully monitor special requests, as well as the availability of specific room types. This will ensure that the hotel is not over-committed relative to a specific room-type or configuration of guestrooms, while allowing as many special requests as possible to be honored. Most guests are assigned a specific guestroom upon check-in, to facilitate the availability of guestrooms for early arrivals; however, the revenue manager or reservation sales agent may pre-block a specific guestroom for some reservations at the time the reservation is received to maximize the likelihood that requests are honored.

The revenue manager is also responsible for managing group room blocks. Once a fully executed group contract is received by a hotel, the revenue manager will ensure that the booking is reflected as a definite group within the property management, reservation, and revenue management system (RMS). He/she will then assess the impact of the group on the general availability of guestrooms, as well as the availability of specific room types, particularly if the group requires a large number of a specific type of guestrooms (e.g. kings, double-queens, etc.). If necessary, appropriate adjustments will be made to the hotel's sell strategy over the group's dates of stay. Later, as a group client's cut-off date approaches, typically one-to-two weeks in advance of the 30-day or alternatively negotiated cut-off date, which is when the group's remaining group room block is scheduled to be released, the revenue manager will review a group's guestroom pick-up; the revenue manager will determine if the group is on pace to pick-up their entire room block, whether they may need additional rooms, or if the group may fall short of using their entire contracted room block and discuss the group's status with the sales team. The sales manager or director of sales may be asked to reach out to the client at this time to discuss these observations or any concerns. If there is an attrition clause in the contract, and the group is short of fulfilling its group rooms commitment, the client may take steps to encourage attendees to book reservations or the hotel may be in the position to offer to reduce the block at a reduced or even no cost, particularly if the hotel may be able to sell the rooms to alternative guest segments. For more details on attrition charges and policies, please refer to *Chapter 5: Optimizing Revenue*.

Guest Arrival Experience

Recall from *Chapter 2: Successful Hotel Management*, the diagram in *Box 2.1: Creating a Service Blueprint: The Hotel Arrival Experience*, which illustrates the guest's arrival experience at an upper-upscale or luxury hotel. The execution of the arrival experience is a primary responsibility of the doorperson, bell staff, and guest service agents (GSAs) at the front desk of the hotel. This experience forms a guest's first impression of the hotel. As a result, hotels employ a range of tactics and strategies to make the arrival experience memorable.

©Monkey Business Images/Shutterstock.com

A simple, yet effective strategy to consistently deliver memorable arrival experiences is to ensure that all guest service team members use the guest's name throughout the arrival process—when a guest is consistently called by their name (e.g. "Welcome Ms. Garcia"), he/she simply feels more welcome and valued by the hotel. Consequently, the guest services team will develop a variety of systems and processes to ensure that the front office team is made aware of guests' names, which facilitates the execution of this simple, yet effective, strategy. Some examples of these tactics include the following:

- When a guest requests an airport pick-up from a hotel that provides airport transportation, the dispatcher (typically the Public Broadcast eXchange [PBX] operator or at-your-service agent) will inform the van driver of the guest's name prior to pick-up so the guest may be greeted by name; this also helps the driver ensure that he/she has picked up all guests waiting for transportation from the airport to the hotel.
- When a vehicle transporting an arriving guest arrives at the hotel, the doorperson will retrieve the guests' luggage and read the guests' names from the luggage tag on the guests' baggage, facilitating his/her ability to address the guest by name.
- The dispatcher or van driver may advise the GSAs at the front desk of the guest's name in advance of their arrival or the doorperson or bell staff will escort guests to the front desk and introduce the guest by name to the front desk reception team (e.g. "Good afternoon, Rita, this is Ms. Garcia who has just arrived and would like to register").
- When a guest presents a credit card to pay for hotel services, hotel associates are trained to retrieve guests' names from the credit card and to then use it consistently throughout their remaining interaction with the guest.

doorperson:
a non-exempt associate responsible for assisting guests arriving and departing the hotel

bell staff:
non-exempt associates, including doorpersons, bellpersons, and transportation drivers, responsible for providing personalized and memorable arrival experiences, as well as luggage and transportation assistance, to hotel guests

guest service agent (GSA):
a non-exempt associate responsible for registering arriving guests, checking-out departing guests, and providing guests with personalized, memorable experiences

PBX operator or at-your-service (AYS) agent:
a non-exempt associate responsible for providing communications services for hotel guests and staff

- More sophisticated hotels use technology to identify guests. For example, many hotels have property management and point-of-sale systems that display guests' names whenever a key card is swiped, room number is entered, or with Radio Frequency Identification (RFID) technology.
- A non-linear system that may be established to encourage the use of the guests' names is to set a service standard that all hotel staff members "strive for five," which means that hotel associates will attempt to work guests' names into each interaction as many as five different times. This may seem a bit excessive; however, if the staff is "striving for five," each team member is more likely to use the guests' names at least a handful of times within each interaction.

Many hotels provide a special welcome amenity upon registration. One of the most iconic examples of an effective welcome amenity program is the warm, freshly-baked chocolate-chip cookies that are provided to guests when registering at a *Doubletree by Hilton* hotel. Large, thick chocolate-chip cookies, with walnuts, are baked, bagged, and delivered to the front desk each hour and provided to every overnight hotel guest upon check-in; *Doubletree's* goal is to remind guests that each of their hotels serves as a home-away-from-home during travelers' time "on-the-road", complete with cookies "like mom used to bake" (or even better!). *Marriott International* provides each of their most frequent, "elite-status" guests with his/her favorite beverage upon check-in at Marriott-branded hotels; when guests reach elite-status, after staying a specified number of room nights within a calendar year at a *Marriott*-branded hotel, they are asked to record their preferred beverage (or other arrival amenity) in the company's *Bonvoy* program database, along with other guestroom preferences. A final example, executed at many resort hotels in Hawaii, is to greet guests with the traditional Hawaiian lei. To be meaningful, welcome amenities should be thoughtful, unique to the location, or personalized, and the strategy must be implemented consistently.

An arrival amenity—particularly for leisure guests or in an upper-upscale or luxury class resort setting—is just one effective way to ensure a hotel demonstrates a strong, customer-focused service culture within the first 10 minutes of guests' arrival. Another simple strategy, particularly applicable in upper-upscale and luxury hotels, is to always "assume service," which means that staff must be trained to immediately offer guests assistance rather than to ask if guests want assistance (e.g. "Would you like assistance with your luggage?" or "Do you want to valet park your car?"). Guests typically elect to stay in upper-upscale and luxury properties because of these added services and never should be required to seek or to ask for assistance—it should be offered or simply assumed. If a guest does not desire the assistance offered, then the guest will inform the staff that will graciously retreat (e.g. "Yes, Mr. Jones, you may park your own vehicle on the second or third floors of our garage. Thank you for staying with us.").

Regardless the class or chain-scale of the hotel, the registration or check-in process involves five steps, whether the process is completed personally at the hotel's registration desk or electronically through a mobile application. These include the following:

1. Greet or welcome the guest;
2. Verify the accuracy of the guest's information within the reservation system or collect the guest's contact information, if the guest has not made a reservation in advance;
3. Assign the guest appropriate accommodations or room type;
4. Assist the guest in establishing credit or a form of payment for the guest's account;
5. Introduce the guest to the hotel's services (e.g. food & beverage [F&B] offerings and hours of operation, business services, transportation services, etc.).

The guest's room key is then presented to the bell staff, who will implement the guest rooming procedure, or handed directly to the guest if bell services are not desired by the guest or offered by the hotel.

If the appropriate accommodations or an acceptable alternative is not immediately available for the guest upon registration, then the hotel's wait procedure will be implemented. When a guest is required to wait for an appropriate guestroom to be cleaned and made available to the guest, which may occur when a guest arrives prior to the hotel's scheduled check-in time, a guest-focused hotel will have a wait procedure in place that does not delay the guest's ability to begin accomplishing the objectives that motivated the trip. Recall that a guest typically elects to stay in a hotel to accomplish specific objectives—build personal or business relationships, attend a meeting or event, or any number of other specific purposes. When guests arrive at a hotel prior to the availability of their accommodations, wise hotel managers will provide guests with options while they are waiting, which may include some of the following:

- In a resort-setting, changing rooms may be made available so that guests may freshen-up from their trip and change their attire to facilitate the use of the hotel's pool and other recreational facilities.
- The guest may be offered a complimentary beverage or discount on food items in the hotel's F&B outlets.
- Many hotels create waiting areas with complimentary snacks, beverages, and activities—such as the availability of video and/or board games or the broadcast of major league or college sporting events on a large screen television.
- Groups arriving may be provided with an area in which the group may begin to congregate and interact with one another.
- Transportation may be provided to a nearby shopping or entertainment district.

Regardless of the specific strategy employed, the goal must be to allow guests' vacations, celebrations, or business activities to begin without delay; this will minimize the inconvenience of being required to wait prior to being provided access to a

rooming procedure: the linear-process of assisting a guest to their room, while introducing hotel services and technology, and attending to any initial needs

wait procedure: a linear-process implemented when a guest's accommodations are not immediately available upon check-in

check-in time: a time specified by the hotel after which guests can expect their accommodations to be immediately available following the registration process

guestroom. At a minimum, luggage storage needs to be provided and a cellular telephone number obtained so that guests may be contacted when their respective guestroom becomes available. In addition, the cleaning of the specific guestroom required to accommodate the guest should be expedited; however, guests are not typically traveling simply to sleep overnight in a hotel room. Consequently, providing guests with the ability to begin the pursuit of the personal or professional objectives that motivated them to travel to the destination will create a positive first impression. Once a guest's room is available, the guest's luggage should be automatically transferred to the guest's room, particularly in an upper-upscale or luxury hotel setting; the guest should be contacted; and the guest's room key delivered to the guest. A well-executed wait procedure provides the opportunity to "wow" the guest.

© XiXinXing/Shutterstock.com

Guest Rooming Procedure

An upper-upscale or luxury hotel must also ensure that a consistent rooming procedure is in place. The key elements of an effective rooming procedure are illustrated in *Diagram 6.2: Guest Rooming Procedure*. The procedure begins with the introduction of the bell staff to the guest by the GSA upon the guest's registration. The bell staff should take a personal interest in the guest by asking questions, which may include learning from where the guest traveled today or what brings them to the destination. These initial inquiries may allow the hotel associate to determine some of the guest's specific interests so that he/she may highlight amenities or services of interest offered by the hotel on the way to the guestroom. Once the bell staff and guest arrive at the guest's accommodations, the guest services team member should explain the operation of the guestroom's key, thermostat, television, and WiFi services and offer to set the guestroom thermostat at a temperature at which the guest feels comfortable. Finally, the bell staff should assume service and set up the luggage rack and retrieve the ice bucket to fill it for the guest using the ice machine located nearest the guest's room. The rooming procedure is typically the guest services team's final opportunity to ensure a positive first-impression is made.

departure experience: a process that ensures a guest's efficient departure from the hotel, allowing the hotel to express appreciation for the guest's patronage

Guest Departure Experience

Another opportunity to ensure that a guest forms a positive impression of a hotel's service culture is during the guest's departure experience. There are two key elements of a departure experience—efficiency and appreciation. First, guests are often on a tight

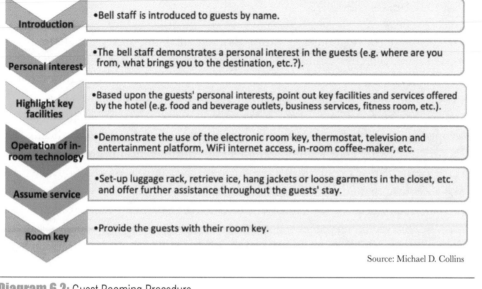

Introduction	• Bell staff is introduced to guests by name.
Personal interest	• The bell staff demonstrates a personal interest in the guests (e.g. where are you from, what brings you to the destination, etc.?).
Highlight key facilities	• Based upon the guests' personal interests, point out key facilities and services offered by the hotel (e.g. food and beverage outlets, business services, fitness room, etc.).
Operation of in-room technology	• Demonstrate the use of the electronic room key, thermostat, television and entertainment platform, WiFi internet access, in-room coffee-maker, etc.
Assume service	• Set-up luggage rack, retrieve ice, hang jackets or loose garments in the closet, etc. and offer further assistance throughout the guests' stay.
Room key	• Provide the guests with their room key.

Source: Michael D. Collins

Diagram 6.2: Guest Rooming Procedure

schedule on the day of their departure; they typically have flights to catch or long road trips ahead of them, as well as possibly having some last-minute business items to which they need to attend. As a result, many guests will take advantage of an express checkout process, which may be expedited by the application of technology, whether that be via mobile app, lobby kiosk, or the guestroom television. Many hotels deliver printed copies of guests' room accounts or folios, sliding them under each respective guestroom door very early on the morning of each guest's scheduled departure date for review and to provide guests with printed receipts. Hotels also typically email electronic copies of the guests' settled guestroom folios to the email addresses that the hotel has on file, along with a link to an online survey requesting feedback regarding guests' hotel experiences. Because guests establish credit upon registration, there is no need for guests to be required to stop by the front desk to personally checkout of the hotel—hotel room keys may be left in guestrooms or a drop-box is often provided at the main entrance of the hotel.

express checkout: allows guests to depart the hotel without requiring them to complete the transaction at the front desk of the hotel

folio: an itemized accounting record of a guest's stay at a hotel

The Park Hotels in India (www.theparkhotels.com) differentiates their collection of boutique hotels through stunning, unique contemporary design, coupled with signature F&B services at the forefront of current culinary trends. To make an indelible impression on their guests, *The Park Hotels* also focuses on delivering memorable departure experiences, whether by providing chocolates or another departure gift unique to the respective hotel's location—or by simply waving to guests as their vehicles depart the hotel until the guests are completely out-of-sight (Ramachandran & Gupta, 2012). Guest loyalty is critical to a hotel's financial success; therefore, successful hotel managers are always seeking creative ways to earn a guest's repeat patronage, as illustrated by this example.

Guest Experience Mapping

guest experience mapping:
the macro-level analysis of the series of processes that collectively comprise the entire guest experience, from initial awareness through post-departure communication

guest loyalty loop:
post-departure communication and other activities designed to maintain guest engagement, encouraging repeat patronage and loyalty

To build long-term relationships with customers, it is important that hotel parent companies, management companies, and individual hotel properties understand and design the guest experience from a wholistic perspective—starting with the guests' initial awareness of the hotel through the guests' post-departure interfaces, as illustrated in *Diagram 6.3: Guest Experience Mapping*. Although service blueprints may be developed to ensure that each individual service process is designed to be effective and efficient, guest experience mapping considers how these various processes interface and their cumulative impact over the course of the entire customer journey. The goal is to ensure that guests' perceptions of the process quality delivered throughout their journey are positive, which is critical to delivering value to the customer. The consistent delivery of customer value generates customer loyalty, which is reflected in *Diagram 6.3* by the guest loyalty loop. Following a guest's departure from the hotel, effective hotel marketers strive to keep the customer engaged with the hotel through social media and other forms of electronic and traditional media. This ensures that the hotel and the hotel's brand remain top-of-mind the next time the traveler requires hotel accommodations.

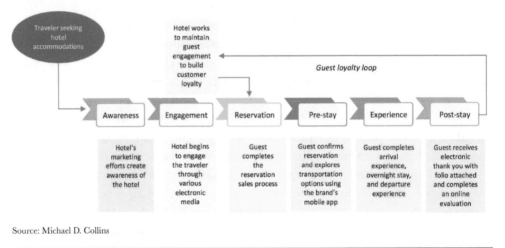

Source: Michael D. Collins

Diagram 6.3: Guest Experience Mapping

Guest Communications

The hotel's communications (**PBX**) operators, dispatchers, or at-your-service team are responsible for operating the hotel communications systems, including the telephone and radio systems. Due to the widespread use of cellular telephones, the call volume through hotels' traditional switchboard or telephone system has been reduced substantially in recent decades; however, there remain many critically important communications functions that must be managed and executed to ensure the effective and efficient operation of a hotel, including life-safety and security responsibilities. In many larger hotels, particularly those in excess of 400 rooms, these functions continue to be performed by dedicated PBX operators, dispatchers, or at-your-service agents, although these duties may be performed by guest service (front desk) agents in many smaller properties or during periods of low occupancy or call volume.

The first responsibility of communications personnel is to respond to incoming telephone inquiries. Theoretically, a communications operator wants to always maintain an open switchboard—the goal of the communications team is to answer incoming calls and to transfer each call to the appropriate hotel department as quickly as possible. In other words, an effective PBX operator strives to avoid lengthy conversations with incoming callers on the switchboard. When incoming calls are received, the hotel is identified, the employee identifies themselves by first name, and the caller is asked, "To where may I director your call?" After assessing the needs of the caller, the PBX operator is often scripted to respond, "My pleasure to connect you," prior to transferring the call.

Another important role served by the communications team is tracking all guest needs and requests, which includes following through with guests to ensure their complete satisfaction. The guest services department maintains a guest request log, either manually or electronically. Many hotels now include a special request feature on their mobile app, in addition to promoting a specific telephone extension, such as #55, that guests may use to communicate any special needs, requests, or problems that may be encountered (e.g. extra pillows or amenities, luggage assistance, a problem with television reception in the guest's room, etc.). The communications department logs the call or incoming electronic request, contacts and dispatches the appropriate team member to address the request (e.g. housekeeping, bell staff, engineering, etc.), and then, after the responding department has notified the communications specialist that the request has been resolved, he/she contacts the guest to ensure that the matter has been resolved to the guest's complete satisfaction. This follow-up process is often referred to as a second effort program. Recording and tracking guest requests, as well as dispatching personnel to respond the requests, is commonly managed in today's hotels using an electronic system such as HOTSOS.

Each month, the communications department summarizes requests received through the second effort program and prepares a Pareto chart that identifies the *"Top 5" Guest*

second effort program: a system to ensure guest satisfaction that requires guest services personnel to verify guest satisfaction following the resolution of a guest request by hotel personnel

Pareto chart: a graph that identifies the number of observations on the primary y-axis and the cumulative proportion of total observations on the secondary y-axis, listing the items observed from most-to-least frequent on the x-axis

Requests, as illustrated in *Diagram 6.4: "Top 5" Pareto chart*. A Pareto chart identifies the number of observations, from most frequent to least, on the primary y-axis and the cumulative proportion of the observations on the secondary y-axis. By reviewing this information on a monthly basis, senior management can evaluate guest needs and address frequently recurring guest requests or problems.

For example, many hotels now provide an iron and ironing board within each guestroom—they are standard equipment that are stored on an iron-rack mounted within the closet of each guestroom. This added guestroom feature is a direct result of just this type of analysis. In many hotels, the timely delivery and the retrieval of irons loaned to guests upon request resulted in increased labor costs, many lost irons, and guest complaints. As a result, many hotel managers decided it is more convenient to guests and cost efficient in the long-run if irons and ironing boards are simply placed within each guestroom. Consequently, this guestroom amenity is now a standard item in many hotels and is no longer a frequently recurring service complaint within these hotels.

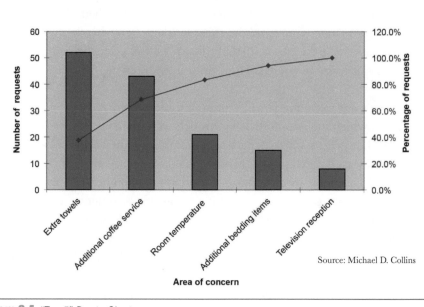

Source: Michael D. Collins

Diagram 6.4: "Top 5" Pareto Chart

Many hotels offering in-room dining assign the at-your-service agents with the responsibility of selling room service meals to guests. The communications department is typically staffed whenever in-room dining is available, eliminating the need for the in-room dining personnel to provide continual telephone coverage within the department—delivering meals to guestrooms takes the in-room dining servers away from the department for considerable periods of time, making continual telephone coverage challenging. To facilitate this strategy, a separate dedicated room service telephone line is installed within the communications department, as well as a F&B point-of-sale (POS) terminal. PBX operators learn the intricacies of the room service menu and are instructed on various upselling techniques—such as suggesting an appropriate wine with dinner. Following the delivery of a room service meal, the PBX operator contacts the guest, obtains customer feedback regarding the meal, arranges for the retrieval of the room service tray and service items, and may also suggest coffee and dessert, particularly after an evening meal has been served. A wise director of F&B will encourage the sale of wine, dessert, and other room service items that enhance the guest experience while increasing revenue by offering incentives to the at-your-service agents for upselling and follow-up sales.

Emergency Communications

At-your-service agents must be prepared to respond quickly and calmly in an emergency. The communications team maintain a variety of back-up reports if the hotel's PMS becomes inoperable due to a power outage or other technical issue. Although technology is extremely reliable in today's highly automated environment, the hotel must have accurate records immediately available regarding the guests that are registered within the hotel, their current account balances, and the status of each guestroom. Consequently, back-up reports are run on a scheduled basis in the unlikely event that the system is unavailable for any reason. These reports may include a guestroom status report, sorted in guestroom order, as well as a listing of guests, along with their contact information, arrival and departure information, guestroom rates, and account balances, sorted in alphabetical order. In addition, the PBX operators maintain a printed list of guests that may need special assistance in the event of an emergency—this list may include guests with different abilities as well as elderly guests allowing hotel staff or emergency personnel to be dispatched to these guestrooms as appropriate.

In the event of an emergency, the communications team dispatches loss prevention officers, as well as the manager-on-duty (MOD), to the scene of the situation to investigate the matter using the hotel's two-way radio communications; typically, the hotel has a code system established, using colors or numbers (e.g. "code blue" for a medical emergency, "code red" for a fire emergency, etc.) to avoid alarming guests that may overhear the radio transmission. The PBX operators also contact first responders external to the hotel by accessing the local 911 emergency communications dispatcher. In the event of an automated fire alarm, the operator immediately contacts the 911 dispatcher alerting him/her of a fire alarm at the hotel, providing the hotel's address, and the specific location of the alarm; security personnel or the door/bell staff are sent to meet the emergency responders and to direct them to the appropriate location within the hotel. In emergency situations other than fire, the PBX operator waits for the loss prevention officer or MOD to assess the situation so that the nature of the emergency can be accurately communicated to the 911 dispatcher; this ensures the appropriate first responders (fire, police, or emergency medical service [EMS] professionals) are dispatched. It is critical that PBX Operators respond calmly and immediately to ensure the most efficient response possible and the optimal outcome for the guests and hotel associates impacted by the emergency; this will also minimize the hotel's liability. Emergency procedures are explained in additional detail in *Chapter 11: Administration and Control: Human Resource Management, Accounting, and Loss Prevention.*

© Olivier Le Moal/
Shutterstock.com

concierge:
a non-exempt associate that tends to guests' special needs including dining reservations, arranging sightseeing tours, acquiring theater tickets, and other specific requests

pre-stage:
the advanced preparation of a guestroom prior to the guest's arrival, or a sales tour, to ensure the guestroom is welcoming

Concierge and Guest Activities

A dedicated concierge staff is maintained by upper-upscale and luxury hotels, which tend to guests' special needs including dining reservations, arranging sightseeing tours, acquiring theater tickets, and other specific requests. An effective concierge maintains relationships with a variety of hospitality, tourism, entertainment, and transportation professionals within the local community to not only ensure his/her awareness of activities that may delight hotel guests, but to facilitate the ability to obtain guest access to these activities. The concierge is often assigned the responsibility of preparing for VIP guests by ensuring that premium guestrooms, with preferred views, are pre-blocked for VIP guests scheduled to arrive each day. The concierge will ensure that in-room dining places a special arrival amenity in VIP guestrooms (he/she may also research the VIP guests' preferences); that these pre-blocked rooms are appropriately pre-staged with drapes drawn, soft lighting, and elegant music playing in the room; and by preparing hand-written welcome notes from the concierge offering his/her services during each guest's respective stay to be placed within each VIP's guestroom. The concierge may also place a telephone call to each VIP guest on each day of their stay to see if he/she may attend to any special needs or requests.

Many upper-upscale and luxury hotels operate a Club or Concierge-level floor. Typically placed on the upper floors of the hotel, due to the superior view, a Club floor must be accessed by using a guest's room key within the elevator. A Concierge Clubroom may be located on the floor where a light breakfast, evening snacks, wine, beverages, and perhaps late night coffee, tea, and desserts are served. The Clubroom will also provide comfortable seating areas, televisions, and a small conference table; the Clubroom provides a comfortable, residential-style area where guests may congregate, conduct business, or simply relax. Concierge staff is often available within the Clubroom during the early morning and evening hours, when guests are most likely to visit the Club. VIP guests, as well as the hotel's most frequent travelers, often receive complimentary upgrades to the Concierge-level, although guests may also purchase access by paying a premium Club-level guestroom rate.

Hotels, particularly in resort settings, may employ a guest activities team. These associates work as part of the concierge staff and are responsible for scheduling and executing a range of activities for guests. Depending upon the specific nature of the destination, these activities may include cooking or craft classes; activities focused upon health, wellness, and nutrition; nature or beach walks; cultural activities; shopping excursions; sports; and various family activities. Many hotels offer children's activities or Kids' Camps, particularly during the summer or on weekends. At a minimum, the concierge may arrange in-room childcare services from a certified provider.

Business services may also fall under the purview of the concierge team, although some hotels—particularly those that host many large conventions, corporate meetings, and events—may house a commercial business center that may be operated by a sub-contractor such as *FedEx Office*. Business travelers have online access to software and files through their cellular telephones and tablet computers; however, travelers may prefer access to a full-size computer and keyboard, or require access to printers or scanners, particularly if attempting to complete a large project while on the road. Guests attending meetings or conventions may find it more convenient or cost-effective to produce some materials for their meeting on-site rather than shipping the items to the meeting destination. In-house business centers also may be used to fulfill unanticipated printing, copying, signage, and other production needs.

Transportation Services

The transportation services offered by a hotel will vary significantly by location. Most hotels located near a major airport will provide, at a minimum, a complimentary airport shuttle; some hotels located adjacent or very close to one another may elect to co-operate an airport shuttle, particularly if the hotels are affiliated by brand (hotel parent organization), operated by the same management firm, or share common ownership. In a suburban-setting, a hotel may provide transportation to specific demand generators within the local market, including

© James R. Martin/Shutterstock.com

the offices or facilities of the hotel's volume accounts, a shopping or entertainment district, or a transportation hub, such as a nearby commuter train station. In an urban center, complimentary transportation services provided by the hotel may be very limited or not offered at all, because the hotel will typically be within walking distance to many demand generators, in addition to being serviced by taxi and limousine services, public transportation, and ride-sharing services, including *Lyft* and *Uber*. Many resort hotels are served by a resort shuttle that provides guest transportation between the various recreational amenities; lodging facilities; and shopping, dining, and entertainment centers located on the resort. The cost of operating a shuttle that provides transportation for multiple hotels or tourism venues, such as in a resort-setting, is often split among the participating venues; however, hotels that provide transportation services only for the convenience of in-house guests bear the cost entirely. Some hotels may elect to provide retail space for a car rental agency as an added convenience to guests, particularly if the parking capacity at the hotel is adequate.

Parking Services

Parking services available at a hotel vary and are impacted by the location, the number of parking spaces available, the mix of hotel guests, the hotel's service level, and the local market. Hotels in airport and urban locations, where demand for parking often exceeds the available number of parking spaces, generate parking revenue with their parking facilities. In these congested locations, guests expect to be charged for parking. Conversely, guests that do not park a vehicle at a hotel should not be expected to subsidize the staffing and maintenance of a parking facility through higher guestroom rates; instead, the cost of parking should be allocated to the guests that use parking services through the direct assessment of parking fees. Hotels with a substantial amount of meeting space, or that house popular restaurants, bars, or other retail outlets, may experience particularly high demand for parking, which may necessitate installing parking gates and hiring staff to control access to parking facilities, particularly during high demand periods. In these settings, parking often becomes a significant profit-center for the hotel. Parking may also be leveraged as a marketing tool. Examples include offering 2 hours of complimentary parking for guests that dine in the hotel's restaurant; the offering of a park-and-fly package by an airport hotel, which may allow guests up to 5 days of complimentary parking, as well as airport shuttle transportation if the guest stays in the hotel one night or more prior to his/her scheduled flight; or its use as a bargaining chip by a sales or catering sales manager when negotiating a group or catering contract.

The hourly rate for parking and the daily maximum is impacted by parking rates within the local market, although many hotels enjoy a premium price due to the convenience to guests of parking in the hotel's in-house garage or parking lot, particularly if demand for parking exceeds the available service capacity. Upper-upscale and luxury hotels may also offer valet parking. In addition to enhancing the guest experience, valet parking allows hotels to increase parking service capacity, because cars may be tandem-parked unlike in a self-park setting, as well as to increase parking revenues through higher fees. Hotels without a garage or parking lot often form a relationship with a nearby parking facility or may contract with a parking service to provide valet parking; hotel guests using the off-the-premises or contracted parking services are typically charged parking fees by the hotel, which retains a commission prior to compensating the parking vendor.

ORGANIZATIONAL STRUCTURE

The guest services department is managed by the director of guest services or front office manager. One or more assistant guest service or assistant front office managers provide shift coverage at the front desk because the department operates 24-hours per day, 7-days per week. The revenue manager, whose role is described in detail in *Chapter 5: Optimizing Revenue*, is an integral member of the guest services or front office team; however, the revenue manager typically reports directly to the hotel's general manager, rooms division manager, or director of sales. Consequently, a dotted-line or indirect reporting relationship is reflected between the revenue manager and the director of guest services in *Diagram 6.5: Guest Services Departmental Structure*. The bell captain and chef concierge round out the guest services or front office supervisory team, although these associates are generally directly supervised by non-exempt, hourly supervisors.

director of guest services or front office manager:
an exempt manager that oversees the entire guest services or front office operation, including front desk, concierge, bell services, transportation, and communications

revenue manager:
an exempt manager responsible for optimizing hotel revenue that directly supervises the reservations sales agents

bell captain:
non-exempt supervisor that oversees the bell and transportation staff

chef concierge:
a non-exempt supervisor that oversees the concierge and guest activities associates

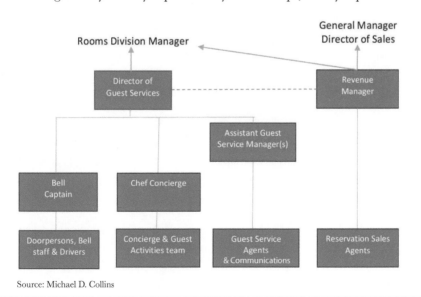

Source: Michael D. Collins

Diagram 6.5: Guest Services Departmental Structure

© Robert Kneschke/
Shutterstock.com

guest service index (GSI):
a measure of guests' perceptions of service quality, calculated within many hotel organizations as the percentage of positive responses from guests that complete service quality surveys

As has been emphasized throughout this textbook, the consistent delivery of exceptional guest experiences is critical to a hotel's financial success. Hotel management keeps track of its guest service performance by closely monitoring its guest service index (GSI) scores, which are calculated within many hotel organizations as the percentage of positive responses from guests that complete service quality surveys. A positive response is either an affirmative response to a direct "yes" or "no" question or a response higher than "neutral" if an evaluative or scaled-response is requested.

Guest surveys are collected through a variety of methods, including electronic, post-departure surveys, the link to which is emailed to guests, and guest comment cards that may be distributed on property. These surveys often include questions regarding each aspect of a guest's stay—the arrival experience, cleanliness and maintenance of the guestroom, F&B services, the efficiency of the checkout process, and more. Guests are also asked multiple questions about their general experience and rating of the hotel, such as, "How do you rate your overall experience at this hotel?" commonly using a five-point scale consisting of "Excellent," "Good," "Fair," "Poor," or "Very poor;" in such cases, only ratings of "Excellent" or "Good" are classified as positive responses. Each area of the hotel, as well as the hotel's overall rating, is typically assessed using multiple questions to ensure that the survey is reliable and valid. Many hotel managers consider the most important question on the guest service quality survey to be one that assesses whether a guest intends to return to the hotel if he/she returns to the same destination in the future. Ultimately, this is the primary goal of a hotel's associates—to consistently deliver guest experiences that result in guests returning to the hotel on their subsequent visits to the destination.

Hotel associates must strive to deliver complete guest satisfaction 100% of the time! Many hotel managers consider guest responses in excess of 90% positive acceptable; however, a negative response from just 3% to 4% of guests may translate into the potential loss of thousands of customers annually. For example, a 400-room hotel running a 70% annual occupancy, with an average of 1.25 guests per room night and an average length-of-stay of 1.5 nights, will serve 85,167 (= 400 x 0.7 x 365 x 1.25 ÷ 1.5) unique customers per year. If between three and four percent (3.5%) of these customers have a negative experience at the hotel, indicating that they will not return to the hotel on a future visit, the hotel will lose nearly 3,000 customers annually (85,167 x 0.035 = 2,981). In other words, a 96.5% success rate results in the loss of nearly 3,000 guests annually! Many of these guests may also share their negative experiences with family, friends, and through online travel review-sites—amplifying the impact of those negative guest experiences.

Guest survey responses may be analyzed to provide the hotel's management team with valuable information and insight. Hotels will generally group the responses by department and calculate composite scores for each area of the hotel operation. For example, survey questions related to the friendliness of the front desk associates, the efficiency of the registration and checkout processes, and the responsiveness of guest service personnel to guest requests will be combined to generate an overall GSI score for the front desk associates; questions related to the cleanliness of the guestrooms and courtesy of housekeeping personnel encountered during the guest's stay will be used to calculate an overall GSI score for the housekeeping department, etc. Department managers are challenged to ensure that scores are maintained or improved as appropriate. In addition, regression analysis may be used to determine the specific factors that contribute most to a guest's overall satisfaction with the hotel. By using the composite GSI scores for guests' overall rating of the hotel's service quality as the dependent variable, hotel managers may determine which specific factors—staff friendliness, employee efficiency, or cleanliness, for example—most accurately predict a guest's overall satisfaction or likelihood to return. Although a hotel's location is a critical factor in a guest's initial selection of a hotel, the guest's perception of the cleanliness of the hotel is a critical factor in determining whether a guest will return to a specific hotel (Rauch, Collins, Nale, & Barr, 2015).

Most hotel parent organizations provide GSI surveys, scores, and rankings as part of the support services provided to franchised and managed hotels. Tracking each branded hotel's performance, in terms of consistently meeting and exceeding customer expectations, is essential to building, improving, and protecting the reputation of the hotel company's brands. Hotel parent companies recognize the best performing hotels and work closely with a property's management team to address challenges at hotels with poor GSI performance. Each hotel's GSI performance is typically compared and ranked among comparable hotels—hotels that carry the same brand name, located in similar markets (e.g. airport, urban, resort, etc.), or of similar size in terms of room count. Although it is important for hotel managers to employ strategies to maximize the number of surveys that are completed by hotel guests, a wise manager stops short of attempting to influence or sway the results. A higher response rate from guests not only yields more accurate scores, it generally improves GSI scores because the majority of guests motivated to complete surveys by a hotel's efforts to increase the response rate, will have had positive experiences at the hotel, while guests with negative experiences are already motivated to respond to survey requests; however, the most successful hotel managers are genuinely interested in using GSI results to recognize departments and individual team members for their strong performance, as well as to identify opportunities to improve the guest experience.

Guest Services Staffing and Labor Costs

non-exempt or hourly associate:
a front-line associate or supervisor that is eligible to receive overtime compensation

exempt or salaried associate:
an administrative, management, or sales associate that is not eligible to receive overtime compensation

In the United States, the Fair Labor Standards Act (FLSA) regulates the employment relationship. The US Department of Labor categorizes employees as either non-exempt or exempt. The great majority of workers employed by a hotel are non-exempt; non-exempt employees, commonly referred to as hourly associates, must be compensated at a higher hourly wage rate of at least 1.5 times the associate's standard hourly wage rate, for hours worked in excess of 40 hours per workweek. The day-of-the-week that starts the workweek is defined by the employer but must run for 7 consecutive, 24-hour days. An employer is not required to pay overtime wages to an exempt employee that may work in excess of 40 hours within the employer defined workweek. To qualify for exempt status, which is also often referred to as being salaried, an employee must earn $455 or more per week and be assigned responsibilities that are considered administrative, executive, professional, computer, or outside sales, as defined by the US Department of Labor (2018).

The director of guest services, or front office manager, assistant guest service manager (GSM), and the revenue manager typically qualify for the executive exemption because their primary duty is to manage a "customarily recognized department or subdivision of the enterprise" (US Department of Labor, 2008). These managers also "regularly direct the work of at least two or more other full-time employees or their equivalent" and "have the authority to hire or fire other employees" or their "suggestions and recommendations as to the hiring, firing, advancement, promotion or any other change of status of other employees [is] given particular weight" (US Department of Labor, 2008). The remaining guest service positions—including the bell, door, and transportation staff; concierge; GSAs; and reservation sales agents, as outlined in *Diagram 6.5*, are non-exempt positions.

staffing guide:
a tool that uses measures of labor productivity to manage payroll costs

labor productivity:
a measure of the amount of output generated or work completed per unit of an employee's compensated work time

hours-per-occupied-room (HPOR):
a labor productivity ratio using labor hours as the measure of work time and room nights as the measure of output

cost-per-occupied-room (CPOR):
a ratio used to measure efficiency, calculated by dividing an expense by the corresponding number of room nights serviced

Management has the responsibility to schedule a suitable number of associates to ensure that adequate staff members are available to meet the guests' needs, while responsibly controlling payroll costs. Consequently, staffing guides are created that provide a specific labor productivity factor for each position. Labor productivity is a measure of the amount of output generated or work completed per unit of an employee's compensated work time. Two common productivity factors used to effectively schedule and manage labor costs within a hotel operation are hours-per-occupied-room (HPOR) and cost-per-occupied-room (CPOR). The HPOR productivity factor uses labor hours as the measure of compensated work time and room nights as the measure of output or work produced; HPOR is calculated by dividing the number of worked or to-be-scheduled hours with the corresponding number of room nights that are supported by these labor hours. CPOR is calculated by dividing wages, which represents a measure of compensated work time by associates, with the corresponding number of room nights, representing a measure of output supported by these wages.

Common staffing guidelines for each guest service position are provided in *Table 6.1: Guest Services Staffing Guidelines*, along with the average wage for each position; annual salaries and hourly wage rates are obtained from the Bureau of Labor Statistics website, which is maintained by the US Department of Labor (www.bls.gov, 2018). *Column 2 of Table 6.1* indicates the *staffing requirements* for each guest service position within an upper-upscale hotel of approximately 400 rooms. For example, GSAs, excluding the overnight shift, are typically scheduled between 8 hours per 75 occupied rooms and 8 hours per 150 occupied rooms, depending upon the specific hotel, its annual occupancy, and seasonal fluctuations in occupancy; a hotel may need to allow for lower employee productivity during extended periods of low occupancy to ensure minimum coverage. To calculate the corresponding productivity factors for GSAs in *Table 6.1*, the midpoint of this range is used, which is 8 hours per 112.5 occupied rooms, or $[(75 + 150) \div 2]$. Consequently, HPOR is 0.071 or 8 hours $\div$ 112.5 room nights. CPOR is $1.13 or $[(8$ hours X $15.92) \div 112.5$ room nights] with $15.92 representing the average wage rate for GSAs from *column 4*. These productivity factors indicate that for each guestroom rented, the hotel uses 0.071-of-an-hour of GSA labor and incurs $1.13 in GSA labor cost. More details on how staffing guides and productivity factors are used to schedule associates and control labor costs are outlined in *Box 6.2: Scheduling the Guest Services Team.*

In the example provided in *Table 6.1*, exempt, salaried mangers include the GSM, revenue manager, and two assistant GSMs. The number of assistant GSMs employed at a hotel will vary depending upon the number of rooms and occupancy-level enjoyed by the hotel; an upper-upscale hotel with 400 rooms, consistent with a "typical" hotel as defined in *Table 2.1: Financial Performance of a "Typical" Upper-Upscale Hotel*, will often employ two assistant managers so that continual management coverage may be provided at the front desk of the hotel from 7 a.m. until 11 p.m. daily, although smaller properties, as well as properties with less activity, may cover some shifts using hourly supervisors in lieu of salaried managers. Many hotel management firms and parent organizations, particularly firms that are anticipating growth through the addition of new properties, use the assistant guest service management position to develop and cultivate management talent internally.

Because salaried managers are not compensated on an hourly basis, an HPOR productivity factor is not applicable to exempt associates; however, management salaries for a specified period of time may be divided by the number of room nights sold for the corresponding time period to determine the CPOR for guest services management coverage. For example, recall that a typical upper-upscale hotel with 400 rooms generates 109,208 room nights annually, or 74.8% x 400 x 365 (STR, 2017). Consequently, a manager earning an annual salary of $50,520 incurs a cost of $0.46 per occupied room, or $50,520 $\div$ 109,208 room nights, whereas two assistant GSMs earning an average salary of $43,350 each generate a CPOR of $0.79 or $[(\$43,350 \times 2) \div 109,208$ room nights]. The total CPOR of guest services management payroll

1.	2.	3.	4.	5.	6.
Position	Staffing requirements	Exempt or non-exempt (FLSA)	Wage rate[1]	Hours per occupied room (HPOR)[2]	Cost per occupied room (CPOR)[3]
Director of Guest Services	5 – 6 shifts per week	Exempt	$ 50,520	n/a	$ 0.46
Revenue Manager	5 – 6 shifts per week	Exempt	$ 50,520	n/a	$ 0.46
Assistant Guest Service Manager (2)	10 – 12 shifts per week	Exempt	$ 43,350	n/a	$ 0.79
Guest Service AgentS	8 hours per 75 – 150 room nights	Non-exempt	$ 15.92[4]	0.071	$ 1.13
Guest Service Agents (overnight)	8 hours per day	Non-exempt	$ 16.92[5]	0.027	$ 0.46
'At Your Service' Agents	8 – 16 hours daily	Non-exempt	$ 11.63	0.040	$ 0.47
Concierge team	8 – 16 hours daily	Non-exempt	$ 15.92	0.040	$ 0.64
Door staff	16 hours daily	Non-exempt	$12.67	0.053	$ 0.67
Bell staff	8 hours per 150 – 200 room nights	Non-exempt	$ 12.67	0.046	$ 0.58
Drivers	8 – 16 hours daily	Non-exempt	$ 12.67	0.040	$ 0.51
Reservations Sales Agents	40 – 120 hours per week	Non-exempt	$ 17.25	0.038	$ 0.66
				Total CPOR =	$ 6.83

[1]Actual salaries and wage rates may vary significantly from these national averages, provided by the Bureau of Labor Statistics (2018), depending upon a hotel's room-count, service-level, location and the responsibilities and qualifications of the specific manager or employee. Management salaries displayed are annual amounts per manager; non-exempt wage rates are per hour.

[2]HPOR is calculated based upon the mid-point value of the staffing requirement specified in column 2, assuming a 400-room hotel operating at a 74.8% annual occupancy rate consistent with *Table 2.1: Financial performance of a 'typical' upper-upscale hotel in the United States.* For example, HPOR for Guest Service Agents = 8 ÷ [(75 + 150) ÷ 2] = 0.071 hours per occupied room; CPOR = [(8 x $15.92) ÷ 112.5] or 0.071 X $15.92 = $ 1.13 per occupied room.

[3]CPOR calculations are estimated based upon the wage rates and hours per occupied room provided assuming a 400-room hotel operating at 74.8% annual occupancy, consistent with *Table 2.1: Financial performance of a 'typical' upper-upscale hotel in the United States.*

[4]The average wage for Guest Service Agents is $11.63 nationally; however, this includes many small, roadside properties in rural areas. Since this guide is provided for an upper-upscale or luxury hotel, which are typically located in urban and resort areas, the average wage for hotel a Concierge is utilized as the average Guest Service Agent wage since these two positions typically pay a comparable wage rate.

[5]Assume $1.00 per hour wage premium for overnight Guest Service Agent (11 p.m. – 7 a.m. shift).

Table 6.1: Guest Services Staffing Guidelines

is projected to total $1.71, which equals 0.46 + 0.46 + 0.79, or [$50,520 + $50,520 + ($43,350 X 2)] ÷ 109,208 room nights.

In practice, a hotel's annual forecast or budget provides guidelines regarding the HPOR and CPOR anticipated to be incurred for each position, each month. These values are multiplied by the number of rooms forecast by the revenue manager each week to determine the number of total hours that may be scheduled by position during the respective week; this process ensures that the hotel is properly staffed to meet guest needs while also making certain that payroll costs are appropriate. HPOR and CPOR ratios may be used to manage staffing needs and estimate payroll costs. For example, a 400-room hotel experiencing 74.8% annual occupancy would require 7,754 (= 109,208 x 0.071) hours of GSA labor annually and incur $123,405 (=109,208 x $ 1.13) in GSA wages for the year, excluding overnight coverage. To provide this level of staffing, assuming that a full-time employee works approximately 2,000 hours annually, the hotel would require 3.9 full-time equivalent (FTE) employees, although the hotel would be likely to employ three full-time and two or more part-time GSAs to provide more scheduling flexibility and coverage during periods of peak occupancy.

full-time equivalent (FTE):
"an associate that works an average of 40 hours per week or approximately 2,000 hours annually

Finally, it should be noted that the payroll information and staffing guide provided in *Table 6.1* is provided for illustrative purposes only. A hotel must establish an appropriate staffing guide based upon the hotel's class (luxury, upper-upscale, upscale, upper-midscale, midscale, or economy); layout or design; guest expectations; competition; and wage rates and cost-of-living within the hotel's specific market. Obviously, wages are higher in major cities, such as New York City and San Francisco, than at a hotel along an interstate highway in the Midwestern United States. Management salaries also vary widely, based upon the size of the operation (number of guestrooms), location, and qualifications of the manager. For example, the average salary for a lodging manager in the United States, which may be used to estimate the rooms division manager's salary, is $58,610, while in California, the average is $66,790. In San Francisco, specifically, it is $85,590 (Bureau of Labor Statistics, 2018)—not only is San Francisco a high cost-of-living area, it also has a higher proportion of luxury and upper-upscale hotels, as well as larger hotels, than in the United States in general. *Table 6.1* may be used as a starting point for establishing guest services staffing guidelines for a hotel, but the values must be adjusted based upon the characteristics of the specific hotel and the wage rates within the hotel's local market.

© Flamingo Images/Shutterstock.com

© Nong Mars/
Shutterstock.com

The GSM is responsible for scheduling the guest service associates each week to ensure that the department operates effectively by consistently meeting and exceeding guest expectations, and efficiently within the budgeted staffing guidelines. Achieving these two objectives simultaneously is only possible through pre-planning and the proper use of staffing guidelines.

Assume that the hotel's senior management team has determined that the staffing guidelines outlined in *Table 6.1*, specifically the HPOR labor productivity guidelines found in *column 5* and CPOR in *column 6*, provide the appropriate staffing level to ensure the effective and efficient operation of the guest services department. Each week, the revenue manager prepares a 10-day forecast, which includes a revised projection for the upcoming weekend (allowing staffing adjustments to be made to the current week's schedule), while also providing an estimate to serve as the basis for scheduling associates for the upcoming 7-day workweek, which runs Monday through Sunday.

The 10-day forecast provided to the GSM by the revenue manager is as follows:

	Fri 10/5/2018	Sat 10/6/2018	Sun 10/7/2018	Mon 10/9/2018	Tue 10/10/2018	Wed 10/11/2018	Thu 10/12/2018	Fri 10/13/2018	Sat 10/14/2018	Sun 10/15/2018	Total Mon - Sun
Room nights	312	388	212	284	391	400	354	297	318	197	2,241
Occupancy	78.0%	97.0%	53.0%	71.0%	97.8%	100.0%	88.5%	74.3%	79.5%	49.3%	80.0%
Arrivals	284	92	187	118	147	27	42	204	73	174	785
Departures	262	16	363	46	40	18	88	261	52	295	800
ADR	$ 142.48	$ 143.67	$ 184.13	$ 197.83	$ 203.14	$ 205.12	$ 198.17	$ 138.98	$ 139.72	$ 190.47	$ 183.42
Revenue	$ 44,454	$ 55,744	$ 39,036	$ 56,184	$ 79,428	$ 82,048	$ 70,152	$ 41,277	$ 44,431	$ 37,523	$ 411,042
RevPAR	$ 111.13	$ 139.36	$ 97.59	$ 140.46	$ 198.57	$ 205.12	$ 175.38	$ 103.19	$ 111.08	$ 93.81	$ 146.80

Please note that the total column, located to the far right, only includes the totals for the upcoming workweek for which the schedule is being prepared (Monday through Sunday) and does not include the immediate weekend's revised forecast.

The hours that may be scheduled for each guest service position are calculated by multiplying the HPOR for each position, found in *column 5* of *Table 6.1*, by the number of occupied rooms forecast for the week, which in this example is 2,241 room nights. The hours to be scheduled by position may then be divided by 8 to calculate the number of shifts that may be scheduled for each position. These calculations reveal the following:

Position	Hours Per Occupied Room	Hours to be scheduled	Shifts to be scheduled
Guest Service Agents	0.071	159	20
Overnight GSAs	0.027	61	7
At-your-service Agents	0.040	90	11
Concierge team	0.040	90	11
Door staff	0.053	119	13
Bell staff	0.046	103	14
Transportation	0.040	90	11
Total guest service team (hourly)	**0.317**	**700**	**87**

Please note that the reservations sales agents are scheduled separately by the revenue manager and are not included on this guest services schedule or in the number of hours or shifts available within this example.

The GSM also collects additional supplemental information to complete the weekly schedule, such as an arrival manifest for individual travelers, which is a listing of each day's anticipated check-ins listed in sequential order based upon the projected arrival times recorded on each guest's reservation, providing insight on the flow of guest traffic that may be expected at the hotel's entrance door and front desk. For this specific week, the GSM has been informed that the department must be prepared to accommodate the specific needs of a corporate group that will be using the hotel during the week for an in-house conference. The group is using 200 guestrooms, single occupancy; the group's initial meeting is scheduled for 2 p.m. on Tuesday, with an optional luncheon buffet that will be made available to group guests prior to this meeting from 11 a.m. until 1 p.m. Group guests traveling longer distances, estimated to be about half the group, will arrive on Monday with the remaining guests arriving on Tuesday morning. The groups' meetings end in the late-afternoon on Thursday, with approximately one-third of the group scheduled to leave on flights Thursday evening, with the remaining two-thirds leaving on Friday morning. Almost the entire group will be arriving to and departing from the nearby airport, using the hotel's airport transportation service to transfer to and from the hotel.

arrival manifest:
a listing of each day's anticipated check-ins listed in sequential order based upon the projected arrival times

After the GSM has determined the number of labor hours and shifts available for each position, based upon the week's forecast, and collected any additional pertinent information, the remaining steps in completing the employees' work schedule are as follows:
1.   Schedule management coverage for the guest services department.

2. Schedule basic or minimum shift coverage for each position within the department.
3. Determine the number of remaining shifts available by position.
4. Add additional shifts to the schedule for each position, based upon forecasted arrival and departure patterns, as well as any anticipated special circumstances.
5. Project the department's total payroll hours and projected labor expense to ensure compliance with budgeted labor guidelines.

The completed schedule is outlined in the following table:

Day	Mon	Tue	Wed	Thu	Fri	Sat	Sun	
Date	10/9/2018	10/10/2018	10/11/2018	10/12/2018	10/13/2018	10/14/2018	10/15/2018	Total
Occupied rooms	284	391	400	354	297	318	197	2,241
Occupancy %	71.0%	97.8%	100.0%	88.5%	74.3%	79.5%	49.3%	80.0%
Arrivals	118	147	27	42	204	73	174	785
Departures	46	40	18	88	261	52	295	800
Position:								Hours-for-the-week
Management								
Guest Service Manager	6 am – 4 pm	9 am – 7 pm	2 pm – 12 am	1 pm – 11 pm	Off	Off	6 am – 4 pm	Exempt
Assistant GSM AM	Off	6 am – 4 pm	6 am – 4 pm	6 am – 4 pm	6 am – 4 pm	6 am – 4 pm	Off	Exempt
Assistant GSM PM	2 pm – 12 am	2 pm – 12 am	Off	Off	2 pm – 12 am	2 pm – 12 am	2 pm – 12 am	Exempt
Front Desk								
Guest Service Agent 1	7 am – 3 pm	7 am – 3 pm	7 am – 3 pm	Off	7 am – 3 pm	Off	7 am – 3 pm	40
Guest Service Agent 2	3 pm – 11 pm	3 pm – 11 pm	Off	Off	7 am – 3 pm	7 am – 3 pm	8 am – 4 pm	40
Guest Service Agent 3	12 pm – 8 pm	9 am – 5 pm	3 pm – 11 pm	3 pm – 11 pm	3 pm – 11 pm	Off	Off	40
Guest Service Agent 4	Off	Off	10 am – 6 pm	7 am – 3 pm	3 pm – 11 pm	Off	3 pm – 11 pm	32
Guest Service Agent/AYS	11 pm – 7 am	11 pm – 7 am	Off	Off	3 pm – 11 pm (AYS)	3 pm – 11 pm	4 pm – 12 am	32 + 8 (AYS)
Overnight GSA	Off	Off	11 pm – 7 am	11 pm – 7 am	11 pm – 7 am	11 pm – 7 am	11 pm – 7 am	40
						Total GSA hours:		168
						Total Overnight GSA hours:		56
						AYS hours:		8
Communications								
At Your Service 1	7 am – 3 pm	7 am – 3 pm	Off	Off	7 am – 3 pm	10 am – 6 pm	7 am – 3 pm	40
At Your Service 2	3 pm – 11 pm	3 pm – 11 pm	10 am – 6 pm	10 am – 6 pm	Off	Off	3 pm – 11 pm	40
						Total AYS hours:		88

Concierge/Club								
Chef Concierge	6 am – 2 pm	6 am – 2 pm	6 am – 2 pm	6 am – 2 pm	6 am – 2 pm	Off	Off	40
Concierge	2 pm – 10 pm	2 pm – 10 pm	2 pm – 10 pm	2 pm – 10 pm	Off	9 am – 5 pm	Off	40
							Total Concierge hours:	**80**

Bell service								
Doorperson 1	Off	7 am – 3 pm	7 am – 3 pm	7 am – 3 pm	7 am – 3 pm	7 am – 3 pm	Off	40
Doorperson 2	3 pm – 11 pm	3 pm – 11 pm	3 pm – 11 pm	3 pm – 11 pm	Off	Off	7 am – 3 pm	40
Doorperson 3	7 am – 3 pm	Off	Off	Off	3 pm – 11 pm	3 pm – 11 pm	3 pm – 11 pm	32
Bell Captain	7 am – 3 pm	7 am – 3 pm	8 am – 4 pm (Bell + Van)	7 am – 3 pm	7 am – 3 pm	Off	Off	40
Bellperson 1	3 pm – 11 pm	3 pm – 11 pm	Off	Off	Off	9 am – 5 pm	7 am – 3 pm	32
Bellperson 2	Off	10 am – 6 pm	Off	12 pm – 8 pm	3 pm – 11 pm	Off	3 pm – 11 pm	32
							Total Door hours: **Total Bell hours:**	**112** **104**

Transportation								
Van Driver 1	6 am – 2 pm	6 am – 2 pm	Off	6 am – 2 pm	6 am – 2 pm	8 am – 4 pm	Off	40
Van Driver 2	4 pm – 12 am	4 pm – 12 am	Off	4 pm – 12 am	Off	Off	4 pm – 12 am	32
Van Driver 3	Off	Off	4 pm – 12 am (Bell + Van)	2 pm – 10 pm	8 am – 4 pm	Off	Off	24
							Total Transportation hours:	**96**

The following considerations were made when creating the schedule:

1. **Management coverage:** The GSM will cover the morning assistant GSM's days off on Monday and Sunday and the evening Assistant GSM's days off on Wednesday and Thursday; this allows the GSM to work with all associates, across all shifts. The GSM will also work across the day on Tuesday, which will be busy due to the corporate group's early arrival, which is anticipated to cause a "wait" situation. The GSM will also work the evening on Wednesday to manage the sell-out and resolve any guest relocations (walks) that may occur.

2. **Front desk coverage:** One or more GSAs are on duty 24-hours daily, which ensures minimum coverage. On the days with the heaviest arrivals, 204 on Friday, October 13, and 174 on Sunday, October 15, two GSAs are scheduled on the evening shift, along with a dedicated at-your-service agent. These same 2 days of the week will also experience a heavy number of departures, 261 on Friday and 295 on Sunday; therefore, a team of two dedicated GSAs will be scheduled at the front desk, complemented by a dedicated at-your-service agent covering the communications area. Note that one of the two GSAs on each shift for Sunday are scheduled 1-hour later than the typical shift because, on Sundays, guests tend to check out later in the morning and to arrive later in the evening.

guest relocations (walks): circumstances created by a hotel's inability to honor a guest's reservation, resulting in the transfer of the guest to a nearby, comparable hotel

3. **Tuesday coverage:** Front desk staffing may initially appear to be light at the front desk on Tuesday, particularly with 147 arrivals; however, both assistant GSMs are scheduled to work, in addition to the GSM who will arrive mid-morning to help manage the anticipated wait situation resulting from the group's early arrival. The front desk will be covered with a GSA on each shift—morning and evening—and a third GSA is scheduled to work across the day, arriving at 9 a.m. and working until 5 p.m., which will allow this third agent to help with the group arrival, because approximately 100 of the 147 arrivals will check in prior to the group's initial meeting at 2 p.m. The communications area is also covered with a dedicated at-your-service agent during each shift on Tuesday to allow the GSAs to be focused solely on the guest traffic at the front desk.

4. **Communications:** The communications area is covered by two at-your-service agents 16 hours per day, one each morning and evening, except for Wednesday, Thursday, and Saturday, due to a lower turn-of-the-house on these 3 days.

5. **Concierge coverage:** The concierge staff covers the Concierge Club lounge, which is available to qualifying guests Monday through Friday mornings, as well as Monday through Thursday evenings. The Club lounge provides a light breakfast each of these mornings, as well as appetizers, beverages, coffee, tea, and desserts in the evenings. The concierge team also tends to any hotel guests with special needs during the week and is typically scheduled to provide lobby coverage across-the-day on Saturday to provide leisure guests with tourist information and other recommendations.

6. **Bell service:** Doorpersons are scheduled from 7:00 a.m. until 11:00 p.m. daily to maintain a positive arrival experience for guests. Bellperson coverage is also scheduled from 7:00 a.m. until 11:00 p.m. on Monday, Tuesday, Friday, and Sunday to facilitate providing baggage assistance on these 4 days with heavy check-ins and checkouts. An additional bellperson is scheduled on Tuesday, from 10:00 a.m. until 6:00 p.m. because group guests that arrive early may need to place their baggage into storage, which must then be delivered to guestrooms later in the day as rooms become available. Minimal bell service coverage is scheduled on Wednesday and Saturday due to the low turn-of-the-house, although luggage assistance will be provided to guests, as needed, by the van drivers, loss prevention personnel, or GSAs or managers in the absence of a dedicated bellperson.

7. **Transportation:** Van drivers are typically scheduled to provide transportation services from 6:00 a.m. until midnight Monday through Thursday, as well as from 6:00 a.m. until 2:00 p.m. on Friday and 4 p.m. until midnight on Sunday. On the weekend, the clientele shifts from business travelers, many of which fly into the destination, to leisure guests, most of which drive to the destination. Therefore, demand for transportation is greatly reduced from Friday evening through Sunday morning. Because the 200 corporate group guests will be departing the hotel, requiring airport transportation on Thursday evening and Friday morning, an

turn-of-the-house: refers to the number of guests arriving and departing on a specific date

additional van driver is scheduled for each of these shifts. The van drivers and bell staff cover for one another as needed; a bellperson, or other available and qualified guest service personnel, will provide transportation if required by a guest if a van driver is not available, or the hotel may use local transportation (e.g. limousine, taxi, commercial shuttle, or ride-share). This strategy will be employed on Wednesday because there is a low turn-of-the-house with just a single bellman or van driver scheduled for each shift to cover both positions.

Managing Payroll Costs

The final step in scheduling is to confirm that the projected payroll cost reflected on the schedule is within budgeted guidelines. Based upon the schedule outlined above, the following guest services payroll hours and costs are projected for the week ending October 15, 2018:

Position	Hours scheduled	Hours budgeted	Variance	Average wage	Payroll projected	Payroll budgeted	Variance	Actual HPOR	Budgeted HPOR	Actual CPOR	Budgeted CPOR
Guest Service Agents	168	159	9	$ 15.92	$ 2,674.56	$ 2,532.33	$ 142.23	0.075	0.071	$ 0.87	$ 1.13
Overnight GSAs	56	61	(5)	$ 16.92	$ 947.52	$ 1,030.86	$ (83.34)	0.025	0.027	$ 0.32	$ 0.46
At Your Service Agents	88	90	(2)	$ 11.63	$ 1,023.44	$ 1,053.27	$ (29.83)	0.039	0.040	$ 0.46	$ 0.47
Concierge	80	90	(10)	$ 15.92	$ 1,273.60	$ 1,434.24	$ (160.64)	0.043	0.040	$ 0.57	$ 0.64
Door staff	112	119	(7)	$ 12.67	$ 1,419.04	$ 1,501.47	$ (82.43)	0.046	0.053	$ 0.59	$ 0.67
Bell staff	104	103	1	$ 12.67	$ 1,317.68	$ 1,299.78	$ 17.90	0.050	0.046	$ 0.63	$ 0.58
Transportation staff	96	90	6	$ 12.67	$ 1,216.32	$ 1,142.91	$ 73.41	0.043	0.040	$ 0.54	$ 0.51
Total department	**704**	**712**	**(8)**	**$ 14.02**	**$9,872.16**	**$ 9,994.86**	**$ (122.70)**	**0.321**	**0.317**	**$ 3.98**	**$ 4.46**

Overall, the guest services department is scheduling $9,872 in payroll compared with a budget of $9,995, resulting in $123 in savings; however, this is a projection and not based upon actual hours worked, which will not be known until after the work week is completed. As a percentage of revenue, guest services payroll is projected to run 2.4% of revenue or $9,872 in payroll ÷ $411,042 in revenue, which is in-line with budget.

Due to the strong occupancy forecasted for the week, of 80%, the department is enjoying the benefit of economies-of-scale. Notice how the concierge position is staffed with two full-time associates that typically work 80 hours per week. Based upon the staffing guide of 0.040 hours per occupied room, 84 hours of concierge staffing is permitted per week based upon the hotel's annual occupancy of 74.8%, or 0.040 HPOR

economies-of-scale: cost advantages received when a business enjoys a sufficient volume of business to operate efficiently

x 400 rooms x 7 days x 0.748 occupancy, and 90 hours is permitted during the current week, or 0.040 HPOR x 2,241 occupied rooms. Because the staffing of the concierge lounge during the week, coupled with 8-hours of lobby coverage on Saturday, is generally static, the concierge position will not use all available hours during busy weeks of 74.8% occupancy or higher, but may use more hours than budgeted, on an HPOR basis, during slower weeks when occupancy runs below 74.8%. To ensure that wages for the concierge position remain in-line on a monthly and annual basis, a bit fewer hours will be scheduled than the budget allows, based upon HPOR, during busy weeks, although a bit more hours than the budget may allow may be needed during slower weeks. In addition, the guest services management team may reduce hours or even close the Concierge club during low-demand periods, such as holidays.

Economies-of-scale also result in some savings in other job categories during the current week, including overnight GSAs, where a flat 56-hours per week is generally required, and doorman, which is typically staffed at a flat 112-hours per week. For the week ending October 15, the GSM has decided to invest a few of the hours saved due to these economies-of-scale into 9 additional GSA hours and 6 hours of additional van driver hours to accommodate the specific needs of the primary in-house group. Finally, it should be noted that employees are scheduled to work 8-hour shifts and payroll is projected based upon 8-hour shifts; however, associates receive a 30-minute non-paid meal break, which often brings their actual work hours down to 7½ hours per shift. Some employees, particularly GSAs, may need to work this additional half-an-hour at the end of their shift to close out their cashier's bank or due to other business demands. Guest service management often trims payroll costs by allowing staff to depart as scheduled, after 7½ hours of paid work time, provided there is no negative impact on the operation or guest experience. This ensures that payroll costs are kept in-line with budgeted guidelines.

KEYS TO EFFECTIVE MANAGEMENT

A successful GSM must, first and foremost, be passionately committed to the consistent delivery of exceptional guest experiences. This passion for the customer must not be exhibited by words alone, but through action—an effective GSM will demonstrate his/her commitment to the customer through genuine, empathetic guest interactions that consistently deliver positive outcomes for customers. Leading by example is guest service management's first step in establishing an exceptional guest service culture. The GSM and the entire guest service supervisory team can only hold the remaining guest service associates accountable if they are "walking the talk"—not merely "talking the talk."

A second key to successful management is to ensure that a guest-focused culture is established and maintained within the front office and throughout the entire hotel. An effective guest services management team will consistently hold a daily line-up at the start of each shift. A line-up is a quick, 5- to 10-minute gathering of all guest service associates preparing for their respective shift during which management will review hotel service standards, on a rotating basis, and discuss any special situations or information of which guest service employees need to be aware to be prepared to meet and exceed customer expectations. After ensuring that everyone is in proper uniform, the manager will review the guest service standard-of-the-day while also informing the guest service team about any groups or VIP guests expected to arrive, the best available rate that is to be extended to walk-in guests, and any other pertinent information for the upcoming shift.

> **daily line-up:** pre-shift meetings that provide updated information to associates while reinforcing corporate values, service standards, and expectations

Hotel service standards that are typically reviewed during the line-up are succinct, clearly stated rules of behavior to be followed by all associates within the hotel; examples of service standards include the following:

> **service standards:** succinct, clearly stated rules of behavior to be followed by all associates of the firm

1. *20/10 rule:* Always acknowledge a guest within 20-feet through eye-contact and within 10-feet with a verbal acknowledgment such as, "Good morning" or "Good evening."
2. *Strive for five:* Always use the guest's name in every interaction, striving to use it at least five times when practical.
3. *My pleasure:* When asked to perform a service by a guest, respond with a sincere, "My pleasure" as opposed to saying, "You're welcome."
4. *Escort the guest:* When a guest requests direction, escort the guest to the desired location versus pointing and providing verbal direction alone.
5. *Express appreciation:* When concluding guest interactions, thank the guest for choosing to stay at our hotel.

These suggested service standards represent just a handful of possibilities, although it is important to limit standards to a manageable list of no more than a dozen standards. Service standards universally apply to all hotel associates and must be emphasized daily, throughout the hotel, to ensure they are an effective non-linear system ingrained within the culture of the firm.

Guest service associates must also be empowered—they must be given latitude to respond to guest's needs. "When service employees perceive themselves to be in control of situations they encounter in their jobs, they experience less stress. Lower levels of stress, in turn, lead to higher performance. When employees perceive that they can act flexibly rather than by rote in problem situations…control increases and performance improves" (Zeithaml, Berry, & Parasuraman, 1988). Consequently, associates must be armed with multiple strategies and options that may be presented to guests to rectify problems that do occur. Presenting guests with options when resolving their concerns leads to increased satisfaction because they have more control over the service recovery process (Joosten, Bloemer, & Hillebrand, 2017). Although effective GSMs delegate the responsibility of responding to guest needs and rectifying problems to front-line associates, they do not abdicate responsibility. They stand behind the decisions of guest service team members and are accessible to provide assistance to staff, if needed; effective managers also recognize associates by showing appreciation for situations that have been creatively resolved by front office staff, while using situations that did not produce favorable outcomes as teachable moments to improve the skills of their associates.

Finally, effective GSMs engage in anticipatory management by embracing their roles as servant leaders. Their focus is on ensuring that the guest service associates have the training, tools, and guidance necessary to consistently meet and exceed customer expectations, delivering a high level of internal service quality, which in turn drives employee satisfaction and productivity, critical to providing value to guests. To deliver a high-level of internal service quality, GSMs use the wealth of information that is available—including the 10-day rooms forecast; daily trace files and reminder logs; group details provided by the sales and conference services team; arrivals manifest; data maintained in the customer relationship management system; and guest insights received through virtuous feedback loops—to facilitate the guest services team's ability to anticipate the needs of hotel guests, ensuring successful business outcomes. Daily processes are created, and checklists are used, to ensure specific guestrooms are pre-blocked for arriving guests with special needs and requests; to protect pre-blocks from being removed on reservations for upcoming dates, particularly on sold-out nights; to ensure key packets, welcome letters, and amenities are prepared for VIP and frequent guests; to ensure credit checks are completed on guest accounts that extend their stays; to check each day's arrivals list for duplicate reservations; to confirm the room status of vacant rooms from the previous night; and to complete the wide variety of additional activities each day necessary to ensure exceptional guest experiences, optimize and protect revenue, and prevent errors.

CHAPTER SUMMARY

The guest services team is typically the first and the final point of contact for hotel guests and includes the reservations sales, bell and transportation, front desk, concierge, and communications associates. Interactions between guest services personnel and guests are critical in defining guests' perceptions of service quality and value. The guest experience journey typically begins with the reservations sales process, through which guests are selected whose needs align with the hotel's positioning and sales strategy. Guests' first impressions of the service quality provided by a hotel property are determined by their arrival experiences—many hotel executives believe that the first 10 minutes of a guest's experience are the most critical. Consequently, well-managed front office operations consistently execute well-orchestrated linear processes to ensure the quality of the guest registration and rooming processes. Because process quality is a salient factor within the value equation, guest experience mapping is used to ensure that the cumulative impact of all service processes result in positive guest perceptions. GSI scores are used to assess guests' perceptions of service quality. A metric commonly used to assess a hotel's overall GSI performance is the percentage of guests that report that they will return to or recommend the hotel to others; however, even a small percentage of negative responses may translate into the loss of thousands of hotel guests annually. Consequently, hotel associates must strive to achieve 100% guest satisfaction.

The guest services department is managed by the director of guest services, GSM, or front office manager; the revenue manager works closely with the director of guest services but often reports directly to the general manager. One or more assistant GSMs are often employed, particularly in upper-upscale or luxury hotels, to ensure daily management coverage of the department from 7 a.m. until midnight. Although most guest services associates are non-exempt, hourly associates, the guest services management team is exempt from receiving overtime compensation for hours worked in excess of 40 hours per 7-day workweek. HPOR and CPOR productivity factors are used to ensure that guest service areas are staffed to be effective, yet efficient.

An effective guest services management team must be passionately committed to consistently delivering exceptional guest experiences by personally engaging in genuine, empathetic guest interactions. Additional keys critical to the effective management of the guest services department include the following:

1. *Daily line-up:* An information exchange through which the guest service management team reinforces service standards and processes, while ensuring that guest service team members have all information necessary to effectively anticipate guests' needs.
2. *Service standards:* Succinct, clearly stated rules of behavior to be followed by all associates within the hotel; guest services management must hold associates accountable for consistently executing the standards.
3. *Empowerment:* Guest service associates must be given latitude to respond to guests needs; this allows associates to respond flexibly to a guest's specific situation and to offer the guest alternative solutions which, in turn, leads to more satisfactory service recovery.

4. *Anticipatory management:* Daily routines must be established, and checklists used, to ensure that guest service associates adequately plan for the anticipated needs of arriving and in-house guests; through proper advanced planning, the guest services team may eliminate being forced to react to guest challenges later.

In summary, effective GSMs embrace their roles as servant-leaders, ensuring that the guest services department is properly staffed, associates are properly trained, and that associates have the information, tools, and support necessary to consistently deliver exceptional guest experiences.

KEY TERMS AND CONCEPTS

accessible guestroom

arrival manifest

attrition clause

bell captain

bell staff

channel manager

check-in time

chef concierge

concierge

cost-per-occupied-room (CPOR)

cut-off date

daily line-up

departure experience

deposited reservation

director of guest services/front
   office manager

doorman

economies-of-scale

exempt or salaried associate

express checkout

folio

full-time equivalent (FTE)

guaranteed reservation

guest experience mapping

guest loyalty loop

guest relocations (walks)

guest service agent (GSA)

guest service index (GSI)

hours-per-occupied-room (HPOR)

labor productivity

labor productivity factor

no-show

non-exempt or hourly associate

Pareto chart

PBX operator or at-your-service
   (AYS) agent

pre-block

pre-paid reservation

pre-stage

revenue manager

rooming procedure

run-of-the-house

second effort program

sell strategy

service standards

staffing guide

turn-of-the-house

wait procedure

DISCUSSION QUESTIONS

1. Explain the key functions, service processes, and guest experiences delivered by the guest services team.

2. Why is systems-thinking important within the guest services area? Identify and create a service blueprint for a linear guest service process. Identify and explain a non-linear system critical to successful guest service operations.

3. Explain why it is important for a hotel to select its guests; include the concept of service capacity in the explanation. Outline how the reservation sales process leads to the appropriate selection of hotel guests.

4. Why is it important to establish reservation guarantee, no-show, cancellation, and overbooking policies? How do these policies impact guest services operation?

5. What role does guest service management perform in terms of managing the hotel's guestroom inventory? When does responsibility of managing the guestroom inventory transfer from the revenue manager to the GSM and assistant GSMs?

6. Describe the impact of the guest's arrival experience. Outline tactics that may be employed to ensure positive arrival experiences; include a discussion of the registration process, rooming, and wait procedures. Discuss the concept of guest experience mapping.

7. Explain the role of guest communications or at-your-service agents; include a discussion of a second effort program, guest request tracking, and emergency communications.

8. Discuss the role of the concierge team. Explain the services typically offered on a hotel's Concierge Club level or floor.

9. Explain how GSI scores are used to assess a hotel's performance in terms of service quality. Why must hotel associates strive to deliver 100% positive guest satisfaction? Is this a realistic goal?

10. Discuss the staffing and structure of the guest services department within an upper-upscale or luxury hotel; identify the exempt and non-exempt positions. Explain the concept of labor productivity; identify two measures of labor productivity and explain how these measures are calculated. Review the guest service schedule created in *Box 6.2: Scheduling the Guest Services Team;* how might you suggest modifying this schedule to improve effectiveness or efficiency?

11. What is a service standard? Suggest a set of eight or more service standards to be used within a hotel setting. Explain what is meant by the comment that GSMs must "walk the talk" versus merely "talking the talk" to be effective.

12. Identify four key tactics that may be employed to ensure the effective management of the guest services department; explain the concepts of internal service, empowerment, and anticipatory management. Why is it important to apply these concepts in a guest service context?

ENDNOTES

Bureau of Labor Statistics (2018). *Occupational Employment and Wages, May 2017.* Accessed online July 11, 2018 at: https://www.bls.gov/oes/2015/may/naics4_721100.htm

Joosten, H., Bloemer, J., & Hillebrand, B. (2017). Consumer control in service recovery: beyond decisional control. *Journal of Service Management, 28*(3), 499-519. doi:10.1108/JOSM-07-2016-0192

Ramachandran, J. & Gupta, S. (2012). *The Park Hotels: Designing Experience*; Indian Institute of Management; Bangalore, India; available through *Harvard Business School Publishing*, Cambridge, MA; www.hbsp.harvard.edu.

Rauch, D. A., Collins, M. D., Nale, R. D., & Barr, P. B. (2015). Measuring service quality in midscale hotels. *International Journal of Contemporary Hospitality Management, 27*(1), 87-106. doi:10.1108/IJCHM-06-2013-0254

STR (2017). *Host report: Upper-upscale hotels for year-ending 2015.* SHARE Center.

United States Department of Labor (2018). *Fact Sheet #17G: Salary Basis Requirement and the Part 541 Exemptions Under the Fair Labor Standards Act (FSLA)*; accessed online on August 27, 2018 at: https://www.dol.gov/whd/overtime/fs17g_salary.htm.

Zeithaml, V. A., Berry, L. L., & Parasuraman, A. (1988). Communication and control processes in the delivery of service quality. *Journal of Marketing, 52*(2), 35–48.

Chapter 7
Housekeeping and Laundry Operations

This chapter outlines the role, function, and successful management strategies within the housekeeping and laundry operation, which is a significant responsibility. The director of services or executive housekeeper is ultimately responsible for maintaining the cleanliness and quality of the hotel's guestrooms and public areas. This chapter provides an overview of these responsibilities.

PURPOSE AND LEARNING OBJECTIVES:

This chapter prepares readers to:
- Identify the responsibilities and priorities of the housekeeping and laundry operations.
- Describe the responsibilities of the heart-of-the-house rooms division associates and the organizational structure of the department.
- Create a staffing plan, schedule, and labor budget for a housekeeping department.
- Explain how guestroom amenities, cleaning chemicals, and other supplies are ordered, inventoried, and controlled.
- Explain the linear and non-linear processes essential to ensuring the cleanliness, quality, and maintenance of the hotel's guestrooms and public areas.
- Describe evening turndown services.
- Explain the housekeeping department's role in protecting hotel rooms revenue.
- Establish an appropriate linen par for a hotel operation, explaining the impact of dropping below a 3-par of guestroom linen.
- Explain how laundry is processed within the hotel, identifying the differences in processing guestroom terry and pool towels, bed linens, food and beverage linens, and rags.
- Estimate the laundry production capacity required in a hotel and describe the primary equipment used.

PRIMARY ROLE OF THE HOUSEKEEPING DEPARTMENT

Cleanliness—if a hotel is not clean, guests will not return. Therefore, exceptional, well-managed housekeeping services are essential to the success of a hotel enterprise. Each day, the housekeeping associates must turn-the-house, which entails servicing each and every occupied guestroom within the hotel, while also impeccably maintaining the public areas of the property. The hotel management team also oversees the laundry operation, which services thousands of pounds

> turn-the-house: providing housekeeping service to each and every guestroom within the hotel occupied the previous night

©Africa Studio/Shutterstock.com

of linen each day. Because the housekeeping team is cleaning every square inch of the property, as well as accessing each guestroom each day, the housekeeping department is a key source of work orders for the property operations and maintenance (POM) or engineering team—ensuring that all areas of the hotel are properly maintained.

ORGANIZATIONAL STRUCTURE

The organizational structure of the housekeeping department is illustrated in *Diagram 7.1: Housekeeping Organization Chart*.

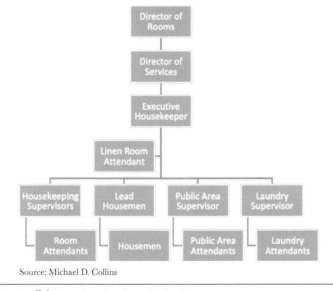

Source: Michael D. Collins

Diagram 7.1: Housekeeping Organization Chart

Housekeeping Management and Supervision

Supervision of the housekeeping operation is overseen by the director of services, who is assisted by the executive housekeeper, although some hotel organizations refer to these exempt managers as the executive housekeeper and assistant executive housekeeper, respectively. A team of non-exempt supervisors assist this management team, including housekeeping supervisors, lead housemen, and a laundry supervisor, although large hotels (i.e. > 500 guestrooms with > 30,000 square feet of meeting space) may employ an exempt laundry manager. The director of services reports directly to the director of rooms, director of operations, or assistant general manager, although he/she may report directly to the general manager in a smaller property (i.e. < 300 rooms). Housekeeping managers must be highly organized, possess strong leadership skills, and pay meticulous attention to detail.

The linen room attendant serves in an administrative capacity for the housekeeping operation. The linen room attendant controls access to the housekeeping department's storeroom, issuing supplies, guestroom amenities, and master key cards to housekeeping personnel. The linen room attendant also serves as a communications hub, as a liaison with guest services and other departments, relaying requests for the servicing of specific rooms, the need to service a specific public area restroom, a request for additional towels at the pool or in the health club, and other guest-driven requests to the appropriate housekeeping personnel or supervisor.

Housekeeping supervisors serve as the eyes and ears of management throughout the hotel. Housekeeping personnel are spread throughout the entire hotel facility, from room attendants up on the guestroom floors cleaning hotel rooms to public area attendants cleaning lobbies and restrooms throughout the public areas of the hotel. Consequently, supervisors constantly roam their assigned areas of the hotel inspecting and verifying that high standards of cleanliness are being maintained. Housekeeping supervisors on the guest floors, often referred to as inspectors or inspectresses, are assigned specific floors or wings of the hotel for which they are responsible—randomly inspecting and scoring a designated portion of their assigned guestrooms daily. A public area supervisor works side-by-side with the public area attendants. The laundry supervisor also works hands-on, alongside the laundry attendants, but is responsible for prioritizing laundry production, managing labor productivity, and ordering laundry chemicals and supplies. Supervisory staffing levels are generally one supervisor for every 10 to 12 housekeeping associates.

Line Positions and Responsibilities

Room attendants are the backbone of the housekeeping department. These hard-working hospitality professionals service the hotel guestrooms each day, preparing vacated guestrooms for newly arriving guests while refreshing stayovers, which is a term used to refer to guests staying for multiple nights. The servicing or cleaning of the hotel guestrooms is physical, tedious work ideal for associates that enjoy a very structured work environment and have a keen eye for detail. Many luxury hotels provide a twice daily housekeeping service—with the evening service referred to as turndown service and the staff providing this service referred to as turndown attendants. For more information about the work completed by room attendants, please refer to *Box 7.1: **R E S P E C T***.

Housemen fulfill a variety of roles in the housekeeping department. Most housemen are assigned to the guest floors—typically one housemen for every four or five room attendants, depending upon the specific lay-out of the hotel guestrooms. Housemen assist the room attendants by periodically pulling used linens from the room attendants' carts and depositing used linen in a laundry chute or taking it directly to the laundry; housemen also restock the room attendant carts with fresh linen while removing trash, debris, and used glassware from the carts. Keeping room attendants' carts properly cleared of used linens, trash, and glassware removed from guestrooms, while stocking fresh linens and sanitized glassware back onto the carts, helps maintain room attendant productivity. Housemen also vacuum guestroom corridors, clean stairwells and elevator landings, and assist room attendants with any heavy lifting, as required, such as moving furniture or rotating mattresses. Housemen serve an important role on deep cleaning teams and many are trained floor-care experts, allowing them to strip and wax floors and to shampoo carpets.

Public area attendants maintain the cleanliness of the hotel's public areas, including lobbies, public restrooms, and pre-function space, although food and beverage (F&B) personnel are responsible for the removal and policing of all F&B china, glass, and service-ware. The routine cleaning of the meeting rooms, restaurants, and F&B outlets is the responsibility of F&B associates—including banquet housemen and food servers, as side-work; however, housekeeping personnel, including public area attendants and housemen, will be called upon to assist with special projects and the deep cleaning of meeting rooms and F&B outlets on a scheduled, typically quarterly, basis. In a similar way, the bell staff will keep the front entrance and lobby free of debris and trash; however, the public area team will routinely clean the area, including vacuuming, dusting, and polishing of floors and other hard surfaces. The public area attendants are also commonly called upon to service the associate locker-rooms and other heart-of-the-house areas, including office areas.

Laundry attendants maintain the hotel's linen, including guestroom terry, terry from the pool, health club, or spa, bed linens, and F&B linens. The laundry may also service wash-and-wear uniforms in-house, in addition to rags, used by room attendants and a variety of F&B personnel.

laundry supervisor:
a non-exempt housekeeping supervisor responsible for ensuring the quality of linen production and productivity of laundry associates

room attendant:
a non-exempt associate responsible for effectively and efficiently servicing assigned guestrooms each day

stayover:
a registered guest that is not scheduled to depart

turndown service:
evening housekeeping service during which the room is refreshed and bedding is turned down for the guest

turndown attendant:
a non-exempt associate that provides evening turndown and other housekeeping services to guests

houseman:
a non-exempt associate that assists the room attendants by running linen and supplies, while maintaining guestroom corridors and other assigned areas

public area attendant:
a non-exempt associate that maintains the cleanliness of public areas, including lobbies and restrooms

laundry attendant:
a non-exempt associate that effectively and efficiently processes hotel linens

BOX 7.1:

© Andrey_Popov/
Shutterstock.com

At the onset of my management career in the hospitality industry, I completed *Marriott International's Individual Development (ID) Management Training* program—the equivalent to today's *Voyage Leadership Development* program. As a rooms division management trainee, the director of rooms ensured that I quickly gained respect for the housekeeping team by assigning me, on my very first day of work, to the housekeeping department. I was instructed to go back to the housekeeping department and to exchange my business-suit-and-tie for a houseman's uniform.

Jorge Gonzalez, the hotel's executive housekeeper, informed me that my assignment was quite simple—all I needed to do to complete the housekeeping portion of the *ID* training program was to clean 18 rooms in an 8-hour day, *Marriott's* standard at the time, and the rooms needed to pass his personal inspection. Once I was able to accomplish this, I could then move on to train in other departments. I thought to myself, "How hard can this be?"

Following nearly 2 weeks of training, one thing became crystal clear—I would never be able to clean 18 rooms, each passing inspection, in an 8-hour work day. It was simply too much work and the attention-to-detail required was overwhelming—the logos on the shampoo and conditioner bottles needed to be properly aligned; the toilet paper roll required a triangle fold on the end; the bath soap must be placed at the correct angle on a properly folded and positioned bath matt; and the list goes on! I also remember the anxiety, distress, and disappointment I felt as Jorge went through the room—noting the dust on the top of a picture frame, the smudge that I missed on the guestroom window, the debris in the corner of the room behind the curtain, the stray hair remaining in the bathtub, or the improper placement of the television's remote control on the nightstand. Plus, I went home at the end of each day with an aching back, which left me struggling to get out of bed the next morning.

To this day, over 36 years later, this housekeeping experience remains the most valuable training activity I ever experienced as a leader—it taught me one absolutely critical lesson: ***I need my associates MUCH MORE than they need me!***

My job as a leader or manager is a support role—to ensure that my associates have the tools, training, and support that they need to get the job accomplished. I must properly schedule associates and maintain a safe and productive work environment in which associates are treated with respect. Although important, my job is certainly not *more* important—it is merely a different role. Both jobs—the role of the manager and the role of the line-worker—must be accomplished.

And the bottom-line is this: Whether the manager makes it to work on any given day is typically of little consequence to hotel guests—the staff will make it through the day and get the work accomplished with or without me; however, if the staff does not show up, I cannot possibly get the job done without them—the guest experience *will* be negatively impacted.

Because of this experience, I have a true appreciation and respect for room attendants (and all my hotel co-workers) that has endured throughout my life-long career in the hospitality industry.

Sincerely,
Michael Collins, Author
Delivering the Guest Experience

HOUSEKEEPING STAFFING

Maintaining the cleanliness of a hotel is a labor-intensive process. Rooms division profitability is determined, in large part, by how well the housekeeping management team manages labor productivity. Recall from *Chapter 6: Guest Services Operations* that productivity is defined by the amount of work accomplished per unit of labor. Adequate housekeeping personnel must be scheduled to ensure the effectiveness of the department—resulting in impeccably clean facilities—while simultaneously managing the efficiency of the staff to ensure that financial goals are achieved.

© Dima Sidelnikov/
Shutterstock.com

Managing Labor Productivity

The productivity measures commonly used to schedule and assess the efficiency of housekeeping associates are hours per occupied room (HPOR) and cost per occupied room (CPOR). The staffing guides used to ensure productivity targets are met are defined in terms of guestrooms serviced per hour or per full-time equivalent (per 8-hour shift). Another important measure of labor productivity is the labor or payroll percentage, which is a cost ratio that reflects labor costs as a proportion of corresponding room revenue. A productivity measure expressed as a measure of labor hours relative to occupied guestrooms, or vice versa, is a pure measure of productivity because it strictly evaluates the amount of work accomplished per labor hour. Labor percentages are not pure measures of productivity because they are also impacted by wage rates and overtime premiums that may be incurred on the labor side of the equation, as well as the average daily guestroom rate on the revenue side. Labor costs per occupied room are also impacted by these factors and therefore is not a pure measure of productivity, although it does provide an indication of the effectiveness of housekeeping management in managing labor productivity, coupled with overtime wages.

> **pure measure of productivity:**
> a labor productivity measure expressed as a ratio of labor hours relative to occupied guestrooms

Recall that these measures of productivity used within the rooms division, HPOR, rooms per labor hour (RPLH), CPOR, and payroll percentage, were introduced in *Chapter 6: Guest Services Operations,* and are calculated as follows:

Formula 7.1: Hours Per Occupied Room

$$h = \frac{n}{r}$$

Where: h = *hours per occupied room*
n = *number of hours worked for a specified time frame*
r = *number of rooms occupied for the equivalent time frame*

Formula 7.2: Rooms Per Labor Hour

$$l = \frac{r}{n}$$

Where: l = *rooms per labor hour*
n = *number of hours worked for a specified time frame*
r = *number of rooms occupied for the equivalent time frame*

Formula 7.3: Labor Percentage (%)

$$p = \frac{w}{s}$$

Where: p = *labor cost percentage*

w = *total wages for a specified time frame*

s = *department revenue (sales) for the equivalent time frame*

Formula 7.4: Cost Per Occupied Room

$$c = \frac{w}{r}$$

Where: c = *labor cost per occupied room*

w = *total wages for a specified time frame*

r = *number of rooms occupied for the equivalent time frame*

Calculating Labor Productivity

Assume that a typical 400-room upper-upscale hotel running 74.8% annual occupancy with a $182.12 average daily rate (ADR), as outlined in *Table 2.1: Financial Performance of a "Typical" Upper-Upscale Hotel*, incurred the housekeeping labor expenses and hours, for each non-exempt position, as outlined in *Table 7.1: Non-Exempt Housekeeping Labor*.

Annual totals		
Occupied rooms	109,208	
Average Daily Rate (ADR)	$ 182.12	
Room revenue	$ 19,888,961	
Occupancy %	74.8%	
RevPAR	$ 136.23	
Housekeeping labor statistics	*Labor expense*	*Labor hours*
Housekeeping Supervisors	108,912	5,926
Room Attendants	649,093	54,348
Public Area Attendants	126,787	10,770
Housemen	137,998	11,652
Laundry Attendants	189,640	15,891
Total Salaries & Wages	**$ 1,212,430**	**98,587**

Table 7.1: Non-Exempt Housekeeping Labor

HPOR, or h for each non-exempt, variable housekeeping position is calculated as follows, using the *Formula 7.1* or $n \div r$, which represents the number of hours divided by the number of room nights:

Housekeeping Supervisor: $0.054 = 5,926 \div 109,208$
Room Attendant: $0.498 = 54,348 \div 109,208$
Public Area Attendant: $0.099 = 10,770 \div 109,208$
Houseman: $0.107 = 11,652 \div 109,208$
Laundry Attendant: $0.146 = 15,891 \div 109,208$

Interpreting this value, HPOR indicates that for each room occupied, approximately one-half (0.498) hour of room attendant labor is required to clean and service each occupied guestroom. Total non-exempt housekeeping and laundry productivity is 0.903 labor hours per occupied room night, or $98,587 \div 109,208$. This is a pure measure of labor productivity because it defines a specific relationship between actual labor hours and units of work. The HPOR for the room attendant, 0.498, may also be multiplied by 60, because there are 60 minutes in an hour, to determine how much time it takes room attendants, on average, to service a guestroom, which is nearly thirty, or 29.88, minutes.

RPLH, or l, for each non-exempt housekeeping position, is calculated, using *Formula 7.2* or $r \div n$, which represents the number of occupied room nights divided by the number of labor hours, as follows:

Housekeeping Supervisor: $18.43 = 109,208 \div 5,926$
Room Attendant: $2.01 = 109,208 \div 54,348$
Public Area Attendant: $10.14 = 109,208 \div 10,770$
Houseman: $9.37 = 109,208 \div 11,652$
Laundry Attendant: $6.87 = 109,208 \div 15,891$

This measure of productivity is merely the reciprocal of HPOR and indicates that room attendants, for example, service approximately two guestrooms for each hour of room attendant labor, while the total non-exempt (hourly) housekeeping and laundry department collectively serviced 1.11 rooms for each hour of labor, or $109,208 \div 98,587$.

Total non-exempt housekeeping payroll, as a percentage of revenue, totaled just over 6.09% of room revenue, which is calculated as $1,212,430 \div $19,888,961. The payroll percentage or p for each non-exempt housekeeping position is calculated as follows, using *Formula 7.3: $w \div s$*, or wages divided by room revenue:

Housekeeping Supervisor: $0.55\% = \$108,912 \div \$19,888,961$
Room Attendant: $3.26\% = \$649,093 \div \$19,888,961$

Public Area Attendant: 0.64% = $126,787 ÷ $19,888,961
Houseman: 0.69% = $137,998 ÷ $19,888,961
Laundry Attendant: 0.95% = $189,640 ÷ $19,888,961

Wages as a sales ratio indicate that for each dollar in room revenue, approximately 6% or 6 cents are incurred in non-exempt (hourly) housekeeping and laundry wages.

Finally, the CPOR or c, as defined in *Formula 7.4*, may be calculated by dividing wages by number of occupied room nights or $w \div r$:

Housekeeping Supervisor: $1.00 = $108,912 ÷ 109,208
Room Attendant: $5.94 = $649,093 ÷ 109,208
Public Area Attendant: $1.16 = $126,787 ÷ 109,208
Houseman: $1.26 = $137,998 ÷ 109,208
Laundry Attendant: $1.73 = $189,640 ÷ 109,208

Including all non-exempt housekeeping and laundry labor, the housekeeping department incurred $11.10 in wages for each room night sold, or $1,212,430 ÷ 109,208.

These annual statistics for a "typical" 400-room upper-upscale hotel may be used to create a staffing guide and annual staffing plan for a hotel, as explained in *Box 7.2: Creating an Annual Staffing Plan*.

CONTROLLING HOUSEKEEPING SUPPLIES, INVENTORIES, AND COSTS

In addition to managing staffing levels, the director of services and executive housekeeper are responsible for ensuring that housekeeping personnel have the tools, equipment, and supplies necessary to execute their responsibilities. Internal service quality is critical to employee satisfaction and productivity and, to be efficient and productive, housekeeping personnel must have the supplies and equipment essential to completing their assigned duties.

The supplies and equipment that housekeeping personnel require fall into four primary categories: guestroom amenities; cleaning supplies; operating supplies, including linen and glassware; and operating equipment. The description and control of each of these items is discussed beginning on page 235.

BOX 7.2: CREATING AN ANNUAL STAFFING PLAN

To effectively manage labor costs, staffing guides must be established that may be used to guide the scheduling of housekeeping personnel. Historical measures of productivity, from an effectively and efficiently managed housekeeping operation, may be used to create the staffing guides. An example of a housekeeping staffing guide is outlined in *Table 7.2: Housekeeping Staffing Guide*.

© Andrey_Popov/Shutterstock.com

1.	2.	3.	4.	5.	6.
Position	**Staffing requirements**	**Exempt or non-exempt (FLSA)**	**Wage rate[1]**	**Hours per occupied room (HPOR)[2]**	**Cost per occupied room (CPOR)[3]**
Director of Services	5 – 6 shifts per week	Exempt	$ 58,610	n/a	$ 0.54
Executive Housekeeper	5 – 6 shifts per week	Exempt	$ 42,380	n/a	$ 0.39
Linen Room Attendant	8 hours per day	Non-exempt	$ 18.21	0.027	$ 0.49
Housekeeping Supervisors	8 hours per 150 room nights	Non-exempt	$ 18.21	0.053	$ 0.97
Room Attendants	8 hours per 16 room nights	Non-exempt	$ 11.74	0.500	$ 5.87
Turndown Attendants	8 – 16 hours per day (> 60%)[4]	Non-exempt	$ 12.74[5]	0.047	$ 0.60
Housemen	8 hours per 75 occupied rooms	Non-exempt	$ 11.74	0.107	$ 1.26
Public Area Attendants	16 – 32 hours daily (< 50% or > 70%)[6]	Non-exempt	$11.74	0.099	$ 1.16
Laundry Attendants	32 – 40 hours daily	Non-exempt	$ 12.58[7]	0.146	$ 1.71
				Total CPOR =	**$ 12.99**

[1]Actual salaries and wage rates may vary significantly from these national averages, obtained from the Bureau of Labor Statistics (2018), depending upon a hotel's room-count, service-level, location and the responsibilities and qualifications of the specific manager or employee. Management salaries displayed are annual amounts per manager; non-exempt wage rates are per hour.

[2]HPOR is calculated based upon the staffing requirements specified in column 2, which are derived from the values in *Table 7.1: Non-Exempt Housekeeping Labor* and calculated within this chapter. Minor differences are due to rounding and variations in wage rates from overtime, merit increases, etc. impacting wages in *Table 7.1*.

[3]CPOR calculations are estimated based upon the wage rates and hours per occupied room provided assuming a 400-room hotel operating at 74.8% annual occupancy, consistent with *Table 2.1: Financial performance of a 'typical' upper-upscale hotel in the United States*.

[4]Turndown Attendants are staffed at 8-hours on days occupancy is less than 60% and at 16-hours per day when occupancy exceeds 60%.

[5]Assume $1.00 per hour wage premium for evening shift Turndown Attendants (3 p.m. – 11 p.m. shift).

[6]Public Area Attendants are staffed at 16-hours daily when occupancy is less than 50%, 24-hours when occupancy is between 50% and 70%, and at 32-hours when occupancy exceeds 70%.

[7]Laundry Attendant wage rate includes 40-hours per week at $18.21 for the Laundry Supervisor; remaining Laundry Attendant wage is $11.74 consistent with additional housekeeping positions.

Table 7.2: Housekeeping Staffing Guidelines

The staffing guidelines outlined in *Table 7.2* provide housekeeping management with clear direction on how to schedule housekeeping associates to ensure that the department operates effectively and efficiently. This staffing guideline may be used to create the department's schedule each week as explained in *Box 6.2: Scheduling the Guest Services Team* in *Chapter 6: Guest Services Operations*. The process is identical, as outlined below:

1. Housekeeping associates are scheduled based upon the staffing guidelines outlined in *Table 7.2*, coupled with the hotel's anticipated occupancy each day, as identified in the weekly forecast.
2. Once the schedule is complete, the total number of hours scheduled for each non-exempt position is calculated by job category (e.g. housekeeping supervisor, room attendant, houseman, etc.).
3. The number of occupied rooms forecast for the week is multiplied by the HPOR identified in column 5 of *Table 7.2* above to identify the number of hours allotted by position.
4. The total number of hours scheduled for each non-exempt position, identified in step #2 above, are compared with the number of hours allotted for each position, identified in step #3 above, to ensure that the staffing levels scheduled are aligned with the allotted number of hours by position. Adjustments are made to the schedule as appropriate.

The staffing guide may also be used to create an annual staffing plan. Occupancy within many hotels fluctuates by season. Because housekeeping's most labor intensive positions, including room attendants, housemen, and housekeeping supervisors, are completely variable—no room attendants are needed if no rooms are occupied, where-as 25 room attendants are required on a full-house, in this example, with the number of room attendants varying directly with the number of rooms occupied. Consequently, the total number of associates that will need to be employed within each of these positions will vary by season. To ensure that the department has an adequate number of associates throughout the year, a staffing plan must be created.

Assume that the hotel's occupancy by month is forecast as outlined in *Table 7.3: Hotel Occupancy and Housekeeping Staffing by Month*. Using the HPOR specified in column 5 of *Table 7.2*, the number of hours required to provide housekeeping services to hotel guests, based upon each month's anticipated occupancy, is calculated for each non-exempt housekeeping position by multiplying HPOR by the number of room nights forecast. The required number of hours for each position are then divided by 4.33, to estimate the number of hours required for each position on a weekly basis for the respective month. Note that for February, 4 versus 4.33 is used because there are exactly 4 weeks versus 4.33 as in the remaining 11 months. The resulting number of hours is then divided by 40, because a full-time associate is scheduled to work 40 hours per week; this provides the number of employees or full-time equivalents (FTEs) the hotel must employ in each position to properly staff the hotel. For example, the hotel will need to employ an average of 26.5 room attendants over the course of the year, employing a maximum of 32.9 room attendants during the busiest month of January and just 21 FTEs in July, the lowest occupancy month.

By completing this analysis and creating an annual staffing plan, the housekeeping management team can determine how to best staff the housekeeping department and anticipate staffing needs. For example, the department requires one full-time linen room attendant and a second attendant to cover the full-time attendant's 2 days off per week. Rather than hire a second part-time attendant, the department may decide to hire, or most likely promote from within, a team member that covers the linen room attendant position 2 days per week and then splits time as a housekeeping supervisor because two full-time and one part-time supervisors are needed; this will allow one FTE to fill both part-time positions. To accommodate the busiest months of the year, when three housekeeping supervisors are needed, the management team may consider bringing in a student intern from a hospitality management program to fill this role or they may elect to start developing one of the hotel's room attendants with leadership potential as a part-time housekeeping supervisor.

Although the staffing plan indicates that the department requires an average of 26 full-time and one part-time room attendant, the department is more likely to employ 20 to 30 full-time room attendants, depending upon the season, while maintaining a minimum of three to five additional part-time room attendants on the payroll to allow for week-to-week fluctuations in hotel occupancy. The staffing plan developed in *Table 7.3* splits occupancy evenly over the 4.33 weeks in a typical month; however, occupancy may vary substantially week-to-week, particularly in hotels that enjoy a substantial amount of group business. During a lower occupancy month, for example, occupancy may vary by 10 to 20 occupancy points or more from one week to the next. Consequently, housekeeping management must have an adequate number of trained staff members available to meet customer demand during a busy week, even when overall occupancy for the month may be low-to-moderate. Although the hotel in this example requires no more than 25 room attendants on any given day, adequate staff must be employed to accommodate multiple sell-outs within a single workweek, as well as to allow for providing each associate with 2 days off each week.

Finally, the hiring and training of personnel takes time. As a result, it is important that the housekeeping management team, working with the hotel's human resource professionals, is proactive. Staffing needs must be anticipated, and personnel requisitions submitted 4 to 6 weeks prior to when additional associates are actually needed on the job because staff will need to be recruited, screened, interviewed, hired, and trained prior to being productive members of the department. Consequently, housekeeping management may issue requisitions to hire additional housekeeping personnel in mid-to-late August to allow staff to be hired and trained in September for the upcoming season. Hiring may continue from October through November so that, by year's end, the housekeeping department is fully staffed for the peak-season, which runs January through April inclusive. Any staff attrition or positions that are vacated starting in April will not be replaced due to the lower levels of occupancy anticipated during the shoulder-months of May and June and lower-occupancy, or off-season months, of June through August. Housekeeping personnel will be encouraged to use their vacation hours during the months of June through August. In mid-August, the staffing cycle will repeat and the staffing process for the upcoming season will begin.

"Selling" Guestrooms

The training of room attendants is typically a 2-week process before a newly hired room attendant is prepared and able to service a full-board of guestrooms. During their first 2 weeks on-the-job, newly hired room attendants will often shadow experienced room attendants as they learn the proper procedures and techniques necessary to effectively and efficiently service hotel guestrooms. A pair of room attendants working together have much lower productivity; as a matter of fact, their productivity may be cut in half if the pair—trainer and trainee—services one full board of guestrooms during a shift. The productivity of a newly hired room attendant may also be below the department standard for as long as 2 weeks, as his/her efficiency improves, and he/she is assigned progressively more rooms each day during the training period. Consequently, a system must be in place to ensure that housekeeping productivity standards are achieved, despite room attendant turnover and the subsequent training of replacements. Many housekeeping departments maintain productivity standards through the practice of selling guestrooms.

selling guestrooms: in a housekeeping context, refers to compensating room attendants for servicing additional guestrooms, above the standard allotment, during their scheduled shift

Selling guestrooms allows experienced room attendants to receive additional compensation for cleaning additional guestrooms, above-and-beyond the department standard, during their standard 8-hour shift. The productivity standard for room attendants identified in *Table 7.2* is 16 guestrooms per 8-hour shift; however, some experienced, efficient room attendants may be able to clean 18 to 20 guestrooms in an 8-hour shift that fully meet housekeeping standards. Consequently, housekeeping management may allow experienced room attendants that have a track-record of earning high inspection scores (please refer to the *Room Inspections* section later in this chapter) to service additional guestrooms in exchange for additional compensation on a per-room basis.

Assume that, after all room attendants are scheduled a full-board of 16 rooms, several guestrooms remain unassigned to specific housekeeping personnel for cleaning. Housekeeping management may announce during the morning line-up that there are additional guestrooms available for sale for room attendants that complete their initial board of rooms early. Later in the day, as the room attendants are nearing the completion of their work, housekeeping supervisors may begin "selling" the additional rooms to room attendants that are projected to finish their initial boards in less than 8 hours. Room attendants may be paid $3 to $5 or more per additional room serviced, which often is less than the typical

CPOR incurred. If room attendants receive wages of $12 per hour, for example, and are allowed 30-minutes per room, the CPOR for room attendant labor is $6 per room. This strategy also assists management in covering rooms that are left unassigned due to employee call-offs. The "selling" of guestrooms is a win-win proposition—all guestrooms are properly serviced on-time, efficient room attendants earn additional compensation during their scheduled shift, and room attendant productivity standards are maintained.

	Total	Jan	Feb	Mar	Apr	May	Jun	Jul	Aug	Sep	Oct	Nov	Dec
Room nights	109,208	11,412	9,947	10,712	9,954	8,865	7,616	7,262	7,349	8,353	9,682	8,914	9,142
Occupancy	74.8%	92.0%	88.8%	86.4%	83.0%	71.5%	63.5%	58.6%	59.3%	69.6%	78.1%	74.3%	73.7%
Linen Room Attendant	2,949	308	269	289	269	239	206	196	198	226	261	241	247
Housekeeping Supervisor	5,788	605	527	568	528	470	404	385	389	443	513	472	485
Room Attendant	54,604	5,706	4,974	5,356	4,977	4,433	3,808	3,631	3,675	4,177	4,841	4,457	4,571
Turndown Attendant	5,133	536	468	503	468	417	358	341	345	393	455	419	430
Houseman	11,685	1,221	1,064	1,146	1,065	949	815	777	786	894	1,036	954	978
Public Area Attendant	10,812	1,130	985	1,060	985	878	754	719	728	827	959	882	905
Laundry Attendant	15,944	1,666	1,452	1,564	1,453	1,294	1,112	1,060	1,073	1,220	1,414	1,301	1,335
Required FTEs	Average	Jan	Feb	Mar	Apr	May	Jun	Jul	Aug	Sep	Oct	Nov	Dec
Linen Room Attendant	1.4	1.8	1.7	1.7	1.6	1.4	1.2	1.1	1.1	1.3	1.5	1.4	1.4
Housekeeping Supervisor	2.8	3.5	3.3	3.3	3.0	2.7	2.3	2.2	2.2	2.6	3.0	2.7	2.8
Room Attendant	26.5	32.9	31.1	30.9	28.7	25.6	22.0	21.0	21.2	24.1	28.0	25.7	26.4
Turndown Attendant	2.5	3.1	2.9	2.9	2.7	2.4	2.1	2.0	2.0	2.3	2.6	2.4	2.5
Houseman	5.7	7.1	6.7	6.6	6.1	5.5	4.7	4.5	4.5	5.2	6.0	5.5	5.6
Public Area Attendant	5.2	6.5	6.2	6.1	5.7	5.1	4.4	4.2	4.2	4.8	5.5	5.1	5.2
Laundry Attendant	7.7	9.6	9.1	9.0	8.4	7.5	6.4	6.1	6.2	7.0	8.2	7.5	7.7

Table 7.3: Hotel Occupancy and Housekeeping Staffing by Month

Guestroom Amenities

Guestroom amenities include the soap, shampoo, conditioner, lotion, and other in-room amenities provided to overnight guests. Appropriate inventories of these items must be maintained to ensure that they may be provided to guests on a consistent basis; however, access to these guestroom supplies must be tightly controlled to prevent pilferage and to manage costs. Steps that must be taken to control the inventory of guest supplies include the following:

© Siyanight/Shutterstock.com

1. *Secured storage:* Guestroom amenities should be stored in a secured storage area with tightly controlled access.
2. *One case at a time:* Only a single case of any guestroom amenity should be opened at a time until it is empty, at which time a new case may be opened.
3. *Monthly ordering:* Inventory of guestroom amenities should be completed once each month, at which time an order may be prepared to bring the inventory up to a 6-week supply, assuming a lead time of less than 2-weeks on receiving shipments once an order is placed. The specific amount ordered may be adjusted based upon the specific setting, but it should represent 1 month's inventory, plus 1 to 3 weeks of additional inventory, depending upon the lead time for delivery.
4. *Usage factors:* Usage factors are calculated and adjusted each month based upon the actual number of each amenity item consumed during the prior month, coupled with the number of guestrooms occupied during the corresponding month. The number of items consumed is equal to the opening inventory, plus purchases received during the month, minus the ending inventory. Once the consumption of each amenity is calculated, this value may be divided by the number of room nights occupied during the corresponding month to calculate the usage rate for each amenity. A detailed example is provided in *Box 7.3: Calculating Guestroom Amenity Usage Factors*.

   usage factor:
   the number of a specific guestroom amenity consumed per room night

5. *Amenity caddies:* Each room attendant is issued, each morning, a supply of guestroom amenities adequate to service his/her assigned guestrooms. No more than one amenity item for each guestroom is provided, although the number may be adjusted based upon the usage factor for each amenity item.

6. *Re-stocking caddies:* Amenity caddies should be re-stocked by designated personnel at the conclusion of each day, typically by the evening turndown attendants, housemen, or public area attendants, as side work. The assigned personnel will be issued an adequate inventory of guestroom amenities to re-stock the caddies, as opposed to being given access to the full, secured inventory.

A common error made by an inexperienced housekeeping manager is to open multiple cases of facial soap, bath soap, shampoo, conditioner, lotion, and other guestroom amenities and to place these cases in multiple linen rooms and housekeeping storage areas throughout the property. The objective of the well-meaning housekeeping manager is to ensure that housekeeping staff have easy access to these essential guestroom supplies; however, once multiple cases are opened and dispersed throughout the hotel or resort, the manager has lost control of the inventory, making it difficult to estimate how many cases of each item remain in-house and how much to order for the subsequent month. Ultimately, this practice will lead to the complete and rapid depletion of the inventory of one or more guest amenity items—negatively impacting internal service quality and the guest experience.

Cleaning Chemicals and Supplies

primary cleaning chemicals: chemicals used in a variety of cleaning applications, including glass and all-purpose cleaners, and disinfectants

specialty cleaning chemicals: chemicals required for specific cleaning applications

material safety data sheets (MSDS): provide information regarding the proper use and remedies to address improper exposure to chemicals

Primary cleaning chemicals are purchased in bulk, mixed, and dispensed electronically; large drums of concentrate are received and connected to an electronic dispenser that mixes each chemical with the appropriate amount of water to properly dilute the concentrate. Primary cleaning chemicals must only be dispensed into properly labeled, spray-top containers. The primary chemicals used by housekeeping personnel include a multi-purpose cleaner, glass cleaner, and a disinfectant cleaner, which is used in restrooms. Furniture polishes, stainless steel, floor-care products, and other specialty cleaners are purchased as needed. Because many chemicals are toxic, housekeeping personnel must wear proper eye and skin protection, have access to eye-wash and hand-washing stations, and be properly trained in the use of each chemical. Material safety data sheets (MSDS) must be available in a three-ring binder or electronically in proximity to the chemical dispensing station, which explains the risks and remedies to improper exposure to each cleaning chemical used within the hotel.

Chemical vendors are a valuable source of information; cleaning challenges encountered by housekeeping management may be presented to chemical vendors for possible solutions. In addition, chemical suppliers will often conduct in-service training programs during which they will train hotel personnel in the proper use of their chemicals and equipment to obtain the desired outcome. For example, chemical vendors may be used to train housemen on how to properly strip and wax a hard-surface floor or to properly shampoo a carpet.

Operating Supplies, Including Linen and Glassware

Linen, glassware, china, and service-ware are inventoried quarterly, or every 3 months. Although the focus of the housekeeping department is on the linen, glassware, and any china or service-ware required in the guestrooms, housekeeping management often works with the executive steward from the F&B division to execute a complete inventory of these big four inventory items. Because these items are not consumed by guests but are eventually depleted over time due to normal wear-and-tear, damage, loss, or breakage, hotel management must periodically inventory these items and order replacements to ensure that an adequate working inventory is maintained. The inventory required of each operating supply is referred to as its par-level. An adequate number of other guestroom operating supplies, such as in-room directories, must also be maintained to allow for their replacement, as needed. Please refer to *Box 7.4: Maintaining a 3-Par of Guestroom Linen* for more information on the importance of maintaining adequate inventories of operating supplies, particularly linen.

big four inventory: the quarterly inventory of 4 operating supplies, including linen, glassware, china, and service-ware, that require periodic replacement

par-level: the inventory required of each operating supply

Operating Equipment

Room attendant carts, vacuum cleaners, mops, mop buckets, brooms, squeegees, and a host of additional equipment is required by housekeeping personnel. Much of this operating equipment, such as room attendant carts and vacuum cleaners, are numbered and assigned to specific areas of the hotel. For example, room attendant carts may be numbered sequentially and assigned to specific guest floors; the vacuum cleaners used by room attendants may also be numbered, which correspond with the specific cart number to which the vacuum cleaner is assigned. Additional vacuum cleaners and operating equipment may be assigned to public area custodial closets. The goal is to ensure accountability. In other words, it is important that individual housekeeping associates are held accountable for the care and maintenance of the equipment that has been assigned to them for their use. This will help ensure that carts and operating equipment are kept clean and in good operating condition, minimizing the misuse of these essential housekeeping tools.

BOX 7.3: CALCULATING GUESTROOM AMENITY USAGE FACTORS

© Devil007/Shutterstock.com

Assume a 400-room upper-upscale hotel runs 83% occupancy or 9,954 room nights in April and is anticipating 71.5% occupancy or 8,865 room nights to be occupied during the month of May. The hotel opened the month of April with the inventories of guestroom amenities indicated as the month ending March 31, 2019 inventory in *Table 7.4a: Guestroom Amenities: Inventory, Usage Factors, and CPOR* (column 2) and ended the month with the April 30, 2019 inventory (column 4) remaining in-stock; additional cases of guestroom amenities were received during the month, as indicated in column 3, based upon an order that was placed on Tuesday, April 2, 2019.

1.	2.	3.	4.	5.	6.	7.	8.	9.	10.
Amenity[1]	**Opening** (March 31, 2019)	**Purchases** (received in April)	**Ending** (April 30, 2019)	**Consumption** Cases	Each	**Usage factor**	**Cost per case**	**Total expense**	**CPOR**
Shampoo	15	28	14	29	8,352	0.839	$137.14	$3,977.06	$0.40
Conditioner	11	20	9	22	6,336	0.637	137.14	3,017.08	0.30
Lotion	10	20	9	21	6,048	0.608	137.14	2,879.94	0.29
Facial soap	12	24	10	26	7,488	0.752	55.20	1,435.20	0.14
Bath soap[2]	28	38	19	47	6,768	0.680	32.40	1,522.80	0.15
Shower caps	6	5	4	7	2,016	0.203	54.71	382.97	0.04
[1]All amenities, except bath soap, package 24-dozen or 288-items per case. [2]Bath soap packaged 12-dozen or 144-per case.							**Total**	**$13,215.05**	**$1.33**

Table 7.4a: Guestroom Amenities: Inventory, Usage Factors, and CPOR (April 2019)

To calculate the number of cases of each guestroom amenity item consumed during the month of April, the opening inventory, from March 31 (column 1), is added to purchases received in April (column 2), and the ending inventory, from April 30 (column 3), is subtracted; the result is recorded as cases consumed, which is found in column 5 of *Table 7.4a*. The formula for this calculation is provided in *Formula 7.5: Inventory Consumed*. Because all guestroom amenities, except for bath soap, are packaged 24-dozen or 288-items per case, the number of cases consumed can be multiplied by 288 to calculate the number of individual amenities consumed; bath soap is packaged 12-dozen per case, so the factor used to calculate the number of bars of bath soap consumed during the month is 144. The total number of each guestroom amenity item consumed in April 2019 is recorded in column 6.

Formula 7.5: Inventory Consumed

$$c = o + p - e$$

Where: c = consumption

o = opening inventory

p = purchases received

e = ending inventory

To calculate the usage factor for each guestroom amenity, found in column 7, the quantity of each amenity item consumed during the month (column 6) is divided by the number of occupied room nights during the corresponding month, which for April is 9,954 room nights. The usage factor represents the number of items consumed per occupied room or the proportion of guests that consumed each amenity item each night of their stay. In other words, 0.839 bottles of shampoo were consumed per room night, or 83.9% of guests used a bottle of shampoo each night of their stay. The formula for this calculation is noted in *Formula 7.6: Usage Rate.*

Formula 7.6: Usage Rate

$$u = \frac{c}{r}$$

Where: u = usage rate

c = consumption for a specified time frame

r = occupied guestrooms for the equivalent time frame

To calculate the total cost of providing guestroom amenities for the month, the number of cases consumed of each guestroom amenity, noted in column 5 of *Table 7.4a*, is multiplied by the price per case of each respective amenity item, which is listed in column 8; the total expense of providing each guestroom amenity item is recorded in column 9, and the total cost of providing all guestroom amenities is represented by the sum of the values in column 9, which is $13,215.05 for April 2019.

If the expense incurred to provide guestroom amenities, found in column 9, is divided by the number of room nights occupied during the month—9,954 for the month of April 2019—the result is the CPOR for guestroom amenities. Recall that the CPOR formula was provided earlier in *Formula 7.4*; however, the cost of amenities replaces wages in the numerator of this ratio because the cost of guest amenities is now being calculated versus labor CPOR. These costs have been placed in column 10 of *Table 7.4a*. CPOR is used to forecast or budget the expense of providing guestroom amenities, which tends to be a stable value month-over-month. By calculating usage factors, as well as CPOR each month, the housekeeping management team can ensure that there are no unusual fluctuations in the consumption patterns of guests or in the cost of providing guestroom amenities, which may indicate a problem with inventory control.

Re-Ordering Amenities

Based upon the ending April 30, 2019 inventory, coupled with the usage rates calculated in *Table 7.4a*, an amenity order must be prepared to replenish guestroom amenities to ensure an adequate supply of amenities for the month of May. The additional formula needed to prepare an accurate order is *Formula 7.7: Forecast Consumption*.

Formula 7.7: Forecast Consumption:

$$f = (r)(u)$$

Where: f = forecast consumption
r = room nights forecast
u = usage rate

The calculations necessary to prepare this order have been completed and are recorded in *Table 7.4b: Guestroom Amenities to be Ordered*. The values in each column are calculated as follows:

1. First, the number of guestroom amenities required to service guestrooms for the month of May must be calculated using *Formula 7.7*. Because occupancy in May is projected to run 71.5% or 8,865 room nights, the r value in *Formula 7.7* is 8,865, which must be multiplied by the corresponding usage rate, u, found in column 2 of *Table 7.4b* for each amenity item. The resulting quantities of amenities required are found in column 3 of *Table 7.4b*.

2. The number of individual amenity items required, found in column 3 of *Table 7.4b*, must then be divided by 288 or 144, as appropriate, based upon the packaging per case, to convert the number of each amenity item required to the number of cases required, which is recorded in column 4.

3. The ending inventory from April 30, 2019 becomes the opening inventory in May and is recorded in column 5.

4. The number of cases in the opening inventory (column 5) is subtracted from the number of cases required, found in column 4, to determine the number of additional cases required to fulfill the needs of guests during the month of May 2019, which is recorded in column 6.

5. To allow a 2-week lead time for delivery, the additional number of cases required for the month is multiplied by 1.5 to ensure that an additional one-half month of inventory is on-hand. This value represents the recommended quantity to order, which is found in column 7.

6. Because partial cases cannot be ordered, the number of cases recommended is typically rounded up to the next whole number of cases; however, because, in this example, the month of June is projected to be slower than May, with occupancy expected to drop to 63.5% or 7,616 room nights, the number of actual cases to be ordered are rounded down (as recorded in column 8). This will allow the housekeeping management team to reduce the inventory as the hotel moves into the slower summer season.

7. The total cost of the order is recorded in column 10, which represents the number of cases actually ordered (column 8) multiplied by the price per case recorded in column 9.

1.	2.	3.		4.	5.	6.	7.		8.	9.	10.
Amenity[1]	Usage factor	Amenities required Each		Cases	Opening (April 30, 2019)	Additional required	To be ordered Recommended	Actual		Price per case	Cost of order
Shampoo	0.839	7,438		25.8	14	11.8	17.7	17		$137.14	$2,331.38
Conditioner	0.637	5,643		19.6	9	10.6	15.9	15		137.14	2,057.10
Lotion	0.608	5,386		18.7	9	9.7	14.6	14		137.14	1,919.96
Facial soap	0.752	6,669		23.2	10	13.2	19.7	19		55.20	1,048.80
Bath soap[2]	0.564	5,002		34.7	20	14.7	22.1	21		32.40	972.00
Shower caps	0.203	1,795		6.2	4	2.2	3.4	3		54.71	164.13
[1]All amenities, except bath soap, packaged 24-dozen or 288-items per case. [2]Bath soap packaged 12-dozen or 144-items per case.										Total	$8,493.37

Table 7.4b: Guestroom Amenities to be Ordered (May 2019)

This procedure is designed to ensure that amenities are ordered and secured based upon anticipated demand. Some hotels, particularly hotels that experience only small fluctuations in occupancy month-to-month, may elect to use a standard par system and to order enough amenities each month to bring inventories back to an established par level; however, this alternative method does not adjust the inventory each month based upon forecast room nights, which may result in a shortage of amenities during a high demand month.

A Few Additional Notes Regarding Amenity Inventories and Controls

Partial cases of guestroom amenities are not typically counted when the inventory is taken; once a case is opened, it is quickly consumed, particularly in a larger property with a room-count that exceeds the number of individual amenity items within a single case. Unopened, sealed cases should be stored in a single locked storeroom with tightly controlled access. The evening or overnight shift personnel that are responsible for re-stocking the guest amenity caddies for the room attendants should be provided with just one or two cases of each amenity item—only the number of cases necessary to fill each caddy with no more amenities than the total number of guestrooms serviced by a room attendant daily. Amenity items with lower usage factors may be stocked in proportionally smaller quantities. The focus of this example is on the control of guest bathroom amenities; however, other guestroom amenities and in-room paper supplies, such as coffee, tea, condiments, and disposable coffee cups and lids, for use with an in-room coffeemaker, for example, should be managed in the same manner.

Maintaining an adequate number of guestroom amenities to ensure that room attendants have the necessary items to service each of their assigned rooms is critical. Running short on amenities is simply poor management, which negatively impacts associate productivity and morale, as well as guest satisfaction. As a result, it is best to err on the side of ordering an extra case or two rather than to possibly run short—after all, soap and shampoo are not perishable items, provided they are properly stored and secured.

LINEAR AND NON-LINEAR PROCESSES

A variety of linear processes and non-linear systems must be in place to ensure the successful management of the housekeeping and laundry operations. These processes include the following:

Breaking-Out-the-House

The first employee to arrive in the housekeeping department each morning is typically the director of services or executive housekeeper and the first task to be completed is to break-out-the-house, which must be completed prior to the arrival of the room attendants. Breaking-out-the-house involves sub-dividing the guestrooms occupied the previous night into sections for each scheduled room attendant to service. In some hotels, this process is completed manually; however, this task is often an automated function of the property management system (PMS). Although it is common sense that room attendants should be assigned to clean guestrooms in proximity to one another, other factors must be considered including the number of check-outs, which take additional time, and the configuration of the rooms—double-queens, kings, suites, etc.—to ensure an even distribution of the workload. Hotels with rooms of

breaking-out-the-house:
sub-dividing the guestrooms occupied the previous night into sections for each scheduled room attendant to service

various sizes may use a point-system, assigning added points to guestrooms that require additional time, to ensure that work assignments are equitable and rooms will be completed on time.

© Dusan Petkovic/ Shutterstock.com

Hotels that use a manual system print out the attendants' room assignments and place the assignments on clip-boards with appropriate notations recorded, identifying which rooms are check-outs and which are stayovers, while noting any special guest requests. Guests' names should not be included on the manual lists because it may jeopardize guests' privacy. Many hotels now issue tablet computers to the room attendants, which provide the room attendant with much more details regarding the rooms that have been assigned, including the guests' names, because accessing the tablet may be password protected. The use of technology, versus a manual listing, also allows the room attendant to be notified once a departing guest has checked out of the room, while also facilitating communication with room attendants. Requests for early service, late service, no service, or the expediting of a vacated room can be communicated seamlessly to the room attendant by housekeeping management or directly by the guest services department.

Daily Discrepancy Report

Prior to 10:00 a.m., the housekeeping supervisors must physically check each guestroom reported as vacant the previous evening; this allows the daily discrepancy report to be completed, which ensures that all room revenue has been properly recorded for the previous day. The night audit staff posts room and tax charges to each occupied guestroom during the overnight shift. In the morning, a list of vacant rooms—for which no room revenue was recorded—is provided to the housekeeping department. These rooms are physically checked to ensure that they are indeed empty, clean, and ready-to-occupy, ensuring that someone did not use the room without revenue being posted. Any discrepant rooms—rooms that are reported vacant but are actually occupied or require servicing—must be reported by the housekeeping department to the front office. It is then the responsibility of the guest services manager on-duty to resolve the discrepancy.

daily discrepancy report:
a physical check of all guestrooms for which no room revenue was posted to prevent the loss of revenue

discrepant room:
a room recorded as vacant by the front office (night audit) the previous night that is actually occupied or requires servicing

This daily process ensures that the guest services team does not provide a guest with a key to a room, while failing to check the guest into the computer system and charging the guest for the accommodations. Quite frankly, this procedure is designed to protect room revenue, preventing the theft of overnight accommodations because guest services personnel could potentially collect payment from a cash-paying guest, pocket the cash, and provide the guest with a room key; by then changing the room to an "on-change" versus "vacant-ready" status, the room is not likely to be rented by another guest services associate. Of course, the theft of hotel services will rarely occur in a well-managed hotel; however, this is an important check-and-balance to prevent registration errors. In most cases, when a discrepancy is found, it is due to a guest that changed rooms, due to a specific request or maintenance issue, and guest services personnel simply forgot to change the guest's room number within the PMS.

Morning Line-Up

line-up:
pre-shift meetings that provide updated information to associates while reinforcing corporate values, service standards, and expectations

Line-up occurs at the beginning of each shift, with the primary line-up occurring in the morning when the room attendants start their days. The morning line-up is a quick 10-minute process during which the following occurs:

1. *Staff presentation:* The presentation of the staff is quickly inspected by the housekeeping management team to ensure proper grooming, uniforms, and name tags are in place for all housekeeping personnel.

2. *Service standards:* Although housekeeping personnel are considered heart-of-the-house associates that work primarily behind the scenes, they do work on the guestroom floors and public areas of the hotel. Consequently, it is important that they understand and consistently execute the hotel's service standards in their interactions with hotel guests. Recall that service standards are defined as succinct, clearly stated rules of behavior to be followed by all associates within the hotel. Typically, a service-standard-of-the-day is reviewed each day during line-up.

daily special:
a specific priority item to be covered in each guestroom when it is serviced that specific day

3. *Daily special:* The daily special is a specific priority item to be covered in each guestroom when it is serviced that specific day; the daily special may include items such as high-dusting, vacuuming in corners or under chairs, checking guestroom windows for smudges, cleaning television remote controls, checking room service menus for stains, sweeping balconies, or cleaning bathroom floors under the vanity or between the toilet and the wall, just to mention a few examples. The executive housekeeper may rotate through a list of regular daily specials or prioritize concerns that have been commonly discovered during recent room inspections.

4. *Announcements and team-building:* The morning line-up is an ideal time to make general announcements to the staff and to build *esprit de corps*. Housekeeping is challenging, tedious work that is often under-appreciated. Morning line-up is an ideal time to recognize associates for superior performance or simply to allow management to let the entire housekeeping staff know that they are sincerely appreciated.

Following the morning line-up, room attendants are assigned their boards and sign out their electronic master key cards, which are secured in the director of service's office.

Each room attendant is also issued a caddy by the linen room attendant with the appropriate quantities of guestroom amenities.

Guestroom Cleaning Procedure

As with all hotel processes, designing an appropriate guestroom servicing procedure begins with the creation of a service blueprint. The blueprint should outline the cleaning process step-by-step, ensuring that the procedure is both effective and efficient. The housekeeping novice may believe that cleaning a hotel room is a common-sense proposition that does not need to be completed the same way by each room attendant every time; however, a well-designed process that is consistently executed will ensure that rooms are properly cleaned and serviced in the most efficient manner possible. Some factors that must be considered when designing this process include the following:

© Dean Drobot/
Shutterstock.com

- The room attendant should be required to turn on all lighting within the room upon entering; this ensures that all light bulbs are checked for proper operation, plus it improves visibility during the cleaning process.
- Next, all trash and debris must be removed from the room, including emptying coffee grounds or packets from the coffee maker; by removing all trash from the room in a single pass, valuable time is saved by the room attendant.
- All soiled or used linen should also be removed in a single pass, while placing the duvet cover and pillows on a chair, sofa, or ottoman to prevent them being stepped upon, keeping them out of the path of the room attendant while the room is serviced.
- All glassware should also be removed from the guestroom early in the process; by placing trash, used linen, and dirty glassware on the cart at the start of the process, more time is allowed for the housemen supporting the room attendant to pull these items from the room attendants' carts for disposal or servicing.
- The bathroom is typically cleaned first—again, a specific sequence of steps is to be followed, which ends with the replacement of bathroom linens and amenities, as required, followed by the mopping of the bathroom floor, which allows time for the floor to dry while the bedroom is serviced.
- Bed linens are brought into the guestroom, often following the general cleaning and dusting of the guestroom, so the bed can be made. It is customary to triple-sheet beds in hotels, which is a tradition that extends back to when heavy wool blankets were used. Because wool blankets tended to be rough and irritating to the skin, fine hotels placed a base sheet on the bed to cover the mattress along with two top sheets on the bed—one below the blanket and a second on top

triple-sheet:
the use of three sheets on a bed, including a base sheet and two top sheets placed on each side of the blanket

of the blanket to protect guests from encountering the blanket. Although wool blankets are no longer used in hotels today, the tradition of triple-sheeting beds in upper-midscale through luxury hotels continues.

- The process typically ends with the vacuuming of the guestroom carpet, which ensures no footprints are left behind in the guestroom.

Room attendants are typically more productive when working alone in the guestrooms, which also improves accountability, allowing individual room attendants to be recognized for the high-quality work that they perform in their assigned rooms. In addition, room attendants must not be permitted to listen to music or to watch television while cleaning guestrooms, although the operation of the television remote control may be quickly checked by turning on and back off the television during the cleaning process. Work standards must be established that ensure room attendants are free from any distractions that may impede their ability to respond to guests or to work efficiently.

Room Attendant Safety

Room attendants often work alone, isolated in guestrooms; their safety is a top concern for hotel management. Consequently, room attendants should be permitted to keep guestroom doors closed and secured while servicing guestrooms—although it should not be latched with the night latch. This prevents room attendants from being surprised or assaulted by a guest or any other person that may enter a guestroom while it is being serviced. If the door is secured, only the registered guest or a housekeeping supervisor is able to enter the room using an electronic key card. Electronic door lock systems allow guestroom locks to be audited so that management can determine exactly which keys have been used to access a room, including the specific time and date of entry. This is an important protection for room attendants.

If a guest knocks on the door while it is being serviced, requesting to enter the room, the guest should be kindly requested to open the door with his/her electronic key card. If the guest does not have a key, he/she must be referred to the front desk so that guest services personnel may verify the identity of the guest and issue a replacement room key; the guest should be informed that this procedure is for the guest's own protection. Finally, if firearms, illegal drugs, or other suspicious items are found in a hotel guestroom, the room attendant should leave the room immediately and notify housekeeping management. For the safety of hotel staff and guests, firearms are not permitted in hotel rooms, unless permission is granted by the hotel's general manager, which is usually only provided to verified law enforcement officers.

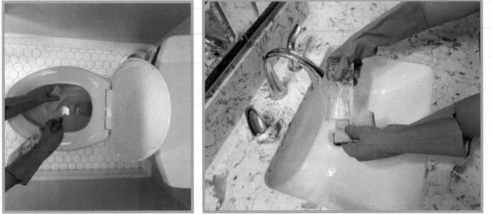

Cleaning guestroom glassware: A clearly defined process for servicing in-room glassware must be established and consistently enforced for the safety of hotel guests.

Glassware

A process must be established to remove glassware from hotel guestrooms so that it may be properly cleaned and sanitized prior to being returned to service, ideally in a commercial dish machine. Most health department regulations require that china, glass, and service-ware provided for guest use be cleaned and sanitized in a dish-machine with a minimum wash temperature of 140° Fahrenheit, a first rinse of 160°, and a final rinse of at least 180° Fahrenheit. As an alternative, glassware may be washed using a non-toxic, effective sanitation agent approved by the health department, although the wash temperature must be controlled and glasses air dried—glasses cannot be hand-dried using a cloth, which can contaminate the surface. This alternative process is unlikely to produce a clear, spot-free glass. Consequently, for the safety of guests, as well as the appearance of the glassware, all guestroom glasses should be machine-washed and sanitized.

To accomplish this task, many hotels stock clean glassware with stan caps on the room attendants' carts. Housemen, when making their rounds, remove soiled glassware that has been replaced with clean glassware in the guestrooms, placing the used glassware in glass racks. In mid-afternoon, following the mid-day rush in banquets and the F&B outlets, these glass racks, filled with used guestroom glassware, are taken to the steward-ing department by a team of housemen to be run through the hotel commercial dish-machine. Once the glassware is serviced, it is returned to housekeeping storage areas so that it may be used to re-stock the room attendants' carts the following day. To efficient-ly complete this process, the hotel must maintain a glassware par of at least two to three times the number of glasses required to stock all the hotel's guestrooms. Although this may be a challenging process, particularly during periods of high occupancy, relying on room attendants to properly sanitize glassware within the guestrooms may place guests in peril, while contributing to an already heavy workload.

stan cap:
a protective cover placed on glassware after it has been cleaned and sanitized

Checklists

Checklists must be provided for all public area attendants, which outline specific sequences of duties to be completed by each associate, each shift. As tasks are completed, and each time a public restroom is serviced, the time and the initials of the associate are recorded, either manually or electronically. This recordkeeping assists housekeeping management in tracking the productivity of personnel, while also allowing management to determine if the frequency with which the public areas, including restrooms, are being serviced is sufficient to maintain hotel standards. Department checklists are also maintained by the linen room attendant or housekeeping supervisor during each shift to ensure that all duties are completed and to monitor the workload, which helps verify that staffing levels are appropriate, and associates are productive over the course of their entire shift.

Heart-of-the-House Cleanliness

If hotel management wants to maintain a clean and spotless front-of-the-house, heart-of-the-house areas must also be impeccably maintained. Poorly maintained floors; damaged, marked-up walls; disorganized storage areas; dirty, finger-printed doors, door-frames, carts, and equipment; or dingy, dirty locker-rooms and employee break areas in the heart-of-the-house quickly carry over to front-of-the-house areas. Poor standards of maintenance and cleanliness in the heart-of-the-house also sends a message to hotel associates that the proper maintenance of their work environment is not as important as maintaining the guest areas of the hotel. Quite frankly, it is a sign of disrespect toward hotel associates that may negatively impact associate morale.

© fivepointsix/Shutterstock.com

Evening Turndown Service

Luxury hotels and many upper-upscale hotels provide an evening turndown service for their hotel guests; although luxury hotels may provide this second daily housekeeping service for all guestrooms, upper-upscale hotels may only provide this service for VIP guests and on the concierge or club-level floor. The following steps are taken to refresh the room during the turndown service:

1. All trash and debris are removed from the room.
2. Used bathroom linens are replaced.

3. The coffee-maker is serviced, if necessary, and coffee/tea supplies replenished.
4. The draperies and black-out curtains are drawn.
5. A nightstand lamp is turned on adjacent to the side of the bed that is turned down.
6. If the room is single-occupancy, the bed is turned down, with a triangular fold, on the side from which the guest would logically enter the bed; if the bed may be accessed from either side, then it is turned down on the side closest to the bathroom. In a double-occupancy room, both sides of a king-bed or both beds in a double-double or double-queen room should be turned down.
7. A note card from the management or the concierge, along with a chocolate (one or two, depending upon occupancy), will be placed on the bed wishing the guest a pleasant night's rest. Some properties may also lay out a robe on the edge of the bed.
8. The radio will be turned to an appropriate classical, jazz, or light music station at low volume setting.
9. The room should be vacuumed, if necessary.

Many properties, particularly in resort settings, will add their own unique signature to the turn-down process, as well as a special touch when children are occupying the room with their parents; it is an opportunity to create a lasting impression.

Deep Cleaning

Although the daily servicing of hotel rooms will maintain the overall appearance of guestrooms, a deep-cleaning program must be established to ensure that each hotel is periodically deep-cleaned. A deep-cleaning program includes many of the following tasks:

- Move all guestroom furnishings, including dressers, armoires, desks, sofas, casual chairs, ottomans and beds, to vacuum and clean under and behind these items.
- Vacuum all upholstered surfaces, lampshades, and curtains.
- Clean and dust all walls and other flat surfaces.
- Polish all wood surfaces.
- Scrub and treat grout lines in the bathrooms and other tiled areas; scrub all hard-surface flooring.
- Clean all recessed lighting fixtures; telephones; remote controls and televisions front-and-back; light switches and electrical outlets; exhaust vents; HVAC units, controls/thermostats, vents, and diffusers.
- Shampoo carpets, as required.
- Launder or dry clean duvet covers, mattress pads, bedspreads, or accent pillows, and curtains, as appropriate.
- Rotate mattress(es).

deep-clean:
the periodic, systematic, and thorough cleaning of a guestroom, tending to details that cannot be maintained through daily servicing alone

A deep-cleaning team includes a minimum of one room attendant and one house-man, although teams may consist of three or four housekeeping associates in some properties. The deep-cleaning team will be assigned a designated number of gues-trooms to service per day, depending upon the exact scope of the work. Housekeep-ing management must carefully track and monitor the deep-cleaning of guestrooms to ensure that the entire inventory of hotel rooms is deep-cleaned a designated num-ber of times per year, which is at least twice annually, although many hotels target quarterly deep cleaning depending upon the exact scope and depth of the process.

Many hotels use outside contractors for periodic shampooing of carpets, as well as drapery cleaning. In-house carpet cleaning is often done only on an emergency, as needed basis to address spills and carpet issues that occur between scheduled clean-ings. In a hotel with a largely business clientele, it is common for an outside contrac-tor to clean all guestroom and corridor carpets twice annually during holiday periods when business travel softens. For example, a hotel may bring in multiple carpet clean-ing crews with truck-mounted equipment, run their chemical, steam, and suction hose lines up the fire stairwells and efficiently shampoo all the guestroom carpets in a 4- to 7-day period; this procedure may then be duplicated twice annually, about 6-months apart, during low-demand periods, such as the 4th of July holiday and then again the first weekend of the year, following the New Year's holiday. Of course, the specific dates selected will be dependent upon the market and anticipated demand. In addition to carpet cleaning, it is also a common practice in the industry to have a truck with dry cleaning equipment clean all the hotel's draperies and sheers on site at least once annually.

Sustainability

A hotel operation makes a substantial environmental impact. Thousands of gallons of water are used daily, in addition to a high volume of electricity, cleaning chemicals, laundry detergents, and paper supplies, as well as soaps and personal care items in the guestrooms—just to mention some of the environmental impacts. The housekeeping department, in partnership with hotel guests, have many opportunities to manage a hotel's environment impact by engaging in the following activities:

- *Reusing hotel linen:* Most hotels hang a notification on a bathroom towel rack or on a bedroom pillow encouraging guests staying multiple nights to re-hang and to reuse their bathroom towels; terry linen should be placed in tub only if they would like it replaced. Guests are also informed that bed linens are changed only upon check-out or upon request.
- *Soaps, shampoo, and conditioners:* Used bars of soaps and partially used bottles of guestroom amenity items are placed into bins on the room attendants' carts, which are then collected at the end of each day in a large drum provided by a

recycling firm that purchases the partially used bars of soap and other soap products, such as shampoo, by weight from the hotel for recycling. These products are converted into other commercial cleaning products.

- *Recycling programs:* As discussed in *Chapter 8: Food and Beverage Operations*, as well as *Chapter 10: Maintaining the Hotel Asset and Sustainability*, hotels participate in several recycling programs, which typically include metal, glass, paper, and food waste recycling.

- *Energy conservation:* Another major role of the housekeeping associates is to ensure good energy conservation practices, particularly in the guestrooms. Because these associates are in every occupied guestroom each day, the room attendants and housekeeping supervisors must police thermostats to ensure they are set at the prescribed level based upon the season of the year, while also ensuring that exterior windows and doors are closed and secure after guests have left their rooms. Room attendants should also turn off televisions, radios, small appliances, and lights in the guestrooms that have been left on by guests.

Cribs, Rollaway Beds, and Other Housekeeping Requests

The housekeeping department maintains an inventory of cribs, roll-away beds, and other specific items, often including yoga mats and work-out equipment, to accommodate guest requests. These items must be stored in specified areas, so they may be retrieved and delivered efficiently. Requests made at the time of reservation for extra bedding, including cribs, roll-away beds, or the make-up of sofa beds, should be accommodated prior to the guests' arrival; a specific guestroom should be pre-assigned, and the requested item placed in the room. If a request is received upon registration, housekeeping should be notified immediately so the request may be fulfilled. Hotels that offer evening turndown service will often fulfill requests to make up sofa beds during the evening turndown process. It is important that an accurate inventory of specialty items is maintained, by storage location, so housemen are not required to search the property for this equipment.

© Phovoir/Shutterstock.com

MAINTAINING HOTEL GUESTROOMS

Overnight accommodations are the core service provided by a hotel enterprise. The quality of the overnight accommodations—including the quality of the finishes and furnishings, thread-counts of the linens, as well as the cleanliness and freshness of the guestroom—is a critical element in the overall guest experience. Consequently, the maintenance of the hotel guestrooms is essential to a hotel's success.

Room Inspections

To ensure that guestroom cleanliness and quality standards are maintained, hotel management must *inspect what they expect*. There has been much discussion throughout this chapter on accountability. And regular, detailed, systematic room inspections are critical to ensuring that standards are clear and housekeeping associates are held accountable for meeting the established standards.

To effectively reinforce the standards, there must be a three-tier inspection program.

three-tier inspection program:
the systematic inspection of a hotel's accommodations by front-line supervisors, housekeeping management, and senior management to impeccably maintain the cleanliness and quality of the hotel's core service product

Level-One Inspections

Housekeeping supervisors must randomly inspect hotel guestrooms daily, scoring the room attendants on their performance. These inspections must be documented using a standardized, thorough scorecard. Room attendants that maintain average scores that exceed a specified score, 90% or 95% for example, are often paid a higher level of compensation; these associates only have a handful of their rooms randomly inspected each week to ensure that they are maintaining their high-level of performance. The reduced cost of inspection, realized as through a reduction in housekeeping supervisor wages, will offset the premium wage these self-inspecting room attendants are paid. Room attendants that are not self-inspecting will have all their rooms inspected each day, prior to the rooms being placed into vacant ready-status, and a specific number of their rooms scored, with the results communicated by the supervisors to the respective room attendants.

Level-Two Inspections

A specified number of guestrooms are also inspected by housekeeping management, including the director of services and executive housekeeper, each week. Scores are also tabulated based upon these inspections and feedback is provided to the respective room attendant. Requiring housekeeping management to inspect rooms each week ensures that they are in-touch with the quality of the work being executed by room attendants, while also helping management to identify priorities and potential daily special items.

Senior management inspections, including regular participation by the hotel's general manager, rooms division manager, director of engineering, and the director of services or executive housekeeper, must be completed, preferably each week, but at least twice each month. Senior management should take this opportunity to interact with the room attendants on the floors and to show appreciation for the tedious, challenging work that they perform. Although the inspection team should not hesitate to point out areas that may be improved, it is equally important to point out to the room attendants what they are doing well—a simple thank you or "good job" received from the general manager or rooms director can really lift the spirits of a room attendant or supervisor.

The greatest benefit of this three-tier inspection process is that it communicates to the room attendants, housemen, and housekeeping supervisors that what they do—each and every day—is important. It is important to guests, critically important to the success of the hotel, and of great concern to senior management. People sincerely appreciate being held to high standards—it encourages them to take pride in their work. By spending time each week on the guestroom floors—inspecting rooms and interacting with the housekeeping team—the general manager and other senior managers send a clear message that the room attendants, housemen, and housekeeping supervisors are valued members of the team. The impact of senior management's engagement with the housekeeping team will be reflected in the quality of their work, their productivity, and employee morale throughout the entire property.

Property Operations and Maintenance Partnership

Although the housekeeping department is responsible for the cleanliness of the hotel and its guestrooms, the POM or engineering department must ensure that the building and all equipment is in good repair and proper working order. Because the housekeeping team inspects and cleans the entire hotel each day, they will often be the first associates to identify maintenance needs throughout the hotel. As a result, they must work in close partnership with the engineering team. Room attendants must have access to work orders, which can be manually completed and turned into the linen room attendant during breaks or at the end of the day for further processing, or they may enter work orders directly into the facilities management system (FMS) through their tablets, if electronic boards are used to assign guestrooms. Hand-held, two-way radios are used by public area attendants and housekeeping supervisors, which allows engineering management to be quickly made aware of any immediate concerns.

Because POM departmental priorities and associates' productivity must be managed by the director of engineering, work orders should be completed and submitted—either manually or electronically—to avoid disrupting the work of the hotel's engineers, which are assigned to other specific projects and repairs as prioritized by the director of engineering or chief engineer. It is then left to the discretion of engineering management to determine if a maintenance item requires immediate attention. Completing work orders for all maintenance items is critical to ensure follow-through; it allows housekeeping management to follow-up and hold the POM team accountable, making certain that maintenance items are not left unaddressed. Housekeeping management should meet with the director of engineering or chief engineer to discuss work orders that appear to be languishing in the system or delayed. With an electronic FMS, housekeeping management is often able to check to see if a work order has been assigned to an engineer for follow-up or if there is some form of delay, such as the repair of a piece of equipment that is awaiting parts.

The weekly walk-through with senior management, as previously described, is often an opportunity to discuss maintenance priorities and the timely completion of work orders. It must be understood that the POM department receives requests from all areas of the hotel, in addition to being required to complete preventative maintenance tasks and must prioritize the many maintenance requests received based upon their potential impact on the guest experience, the efficient operation of the hotel, and the priorities of senior management.

LAUNDRY OPERATIONS

The hotel's in-house laundry operation supports both the rooms division as well as the F&B division of the hotel. Its effective and efficient operation is critical to internal service quality. Room attendants, banquet housemen, food servers, and the culinary team all rely upon the laundry department to provide clean linen, which is essential to their ability to efficiently perform their respective duties.

Types of Linen

Linen falls into a taxonomy of five categories: terry, bed, F&B, rags, and wash-and-wear uniforms. Each category requires a unique blend of chemicals and its own unique cleaning process. The specific standard for each category of guestroom linen is typically specified by the brand, parent company, or management firm, including the thread-count required, fabric content, dimensions, and color.

© Lopolo/Shutterstock.com

Terry Linen

Terry includes guestroom towels and in-room robes, if provided to guests, as well as towels and robes used at the pool or in wellness facilities, including the health club or spa. Terry is typically serviced using a laundry detergent, and perhaps a small amount of bleach, during the wash cycle and a fabric softener during the rinse cycle. It is dried in a commercial dryer and folded using an automatic folder or by hand. Guestroom terry is typically folded in thirds, and again in half, to expedite its proper placement on towel racks in the guestrooms. White terry linen is commonly used in hotel guestrooms because colored linens will fade over time, resulting in towels with inconsistent coloration due to the respective age of the towels, which appears untidy in guestrooms. In addition, guests generally perceive white towels as being cleaner and fresher. Luxury hotels and upper-upscale hotels may often provide four sizes of in-house terry, including washcloths, hand-towels, bath-towels, and oversized bath-sheets. Terry for wellness facilities are also commonly white, although colored beach towels may be provided at a hotel swimming pool, particularly in resort settings. Terry is typically 100% cotton to maximize absorbency, although some polyester content may be permitted, particularly in economy and mid-scale properties, to increase durability.

Figure 7.1: High-Temperature Flatwork Roller Iron

Bed Linens

thread-count:
a measure of a linen's
quality indicating the
number of threads per
square inch

Quality bed linens, including sheets and pillow cases, are critical to ensuring the comfort of guests, sending an immediate message regarding the quality and cleanliness of the hotel's facilities. Immaculate, crisply-pressed, fresh-smelling sheets allow hotel guests to sleep in comfort, confident that the guestroom environment is clean and sanitary. High thread-count linens, often of 400-threads per square inch or higher, are used in luxury and many upper-upscale hotels; thread-counts are typically specified by the hotel's brand, as is the fabric content; the dimensions specified must consider mattress specifications to allow for an adequate tuck when beds are made. Lower thread-counts and cotton quality, or the use cotton-polyester blends, result in bed linen with a rougher texture, which is found in lower-end economy and mid-scale properties. Hotels that use high quality linens process bed linens by washing them with detergent and perhaps a small quantity of bleach; followed by a fabric softener, to provide a fresh scent, coupled with starch during the rinse cycle; bed linens are removed from commercial washing machines and, while still damp, processed through a high-temperature flatwork roller iron, such as the one pictured in *Figure 7.1*, which quickly dries the bed linens, producing crisp, wrinkle-free bed linens with a luxurious feel. Many large flatwork ironers include a folding mechanism that makes a minimum of three to four folds in bed sheets to reduce them to a manageable dimension. Again, hotels most commonly use white linens to ensure a consistent appearance.

Smaller hotels, particularly economy and mid-scale hotels, do not typically have flat-work ironers and, as an alternative, dry their sheets in a commercial dryer. Consequently, starch is not included in the mix of laundry chemicals used to process bed linens. A permanent press, cotton-polyester fabric content may be best in these settings. Small high-end luxury, upper-upscale, and upscale properties without an in-house roll ironer may elect to contract out the servicing of their linen to a commercial laundry.

Food and Beverage Linen

The processing of F&B linen also avoids the use of commercial dryers and is processed using commercial washing machines and a high-temperature flatwork roller iron, as pictured in *Figure 7.1*. Laundry detergent and a degreaser are used in the wash cycle and starch is added during the rinse cycle so that F&B linens appear crisp and wrinkle-free after being dried, ironed, and folded by the high-temperature roller iron. Many F&B operations use linen of a variety of colors. Each F&B outlet may have a unique color, based upon the theme and décor of the outlet, and multiple colors of banquet linen may be available, based upon the colors of fabrics and carpets in the conference center, and to accommodate frequent client requests. Hotel laundries that do not have a high-temperature roller iron use permanent press F&B linens with a high polyester content that may be tumble dried, although F&B linens with a higher cotton content and thread-count offer more absorbency, while providing a more luxurious feel.

Rags

Housekeeping, culinary, and food service personnel use rags for cleaning purposes. Although hotels may purchase rags, as needed, stained, torn, and other discarded terry linen may also be converted to rags. It is important that a strict policy is enforced throughout the hotel that prevents guestroom terry from being used as rags. It is common for room attendants and others to use washcloths or hand towels like rags, because they have convenient access to them; however, this will quickly inflate a hotel's linen replacement expense. When a towel is stained or torn, and cannot be reclaimed, then it may be converted to a rag instead of being discarded. Unrepairable terry should be collected in a single location and then, on occasion, this linen should be dyed a specific color to identify these items as rags. This allows hotel management to quickly identify if an associate is using guestroom terry as rags and to take corrective action. Rags must be processed with a laundry detergent and degreaser and tumbled dry.

Uniforms

Although many front-of-the-house uniforms must be dry cleaned or laundered and pressed, many heart-of-the-house uniforms may be wash-and-wear uniforms that may be processed in-house. These uniforms may be washed using a detergent, rinsed with a fabric softener, and tumble dried; culinary uniforms may require the use of a degreasing agent.

Reclaiming Linen

Laundry attendants must be trained to set aside linen that is stained or in need of repair as it is processed. Allowing linen to be placed back into service that does not meet hotel standards is inefficient because associates in the operating departments, including housekeeping or food service personnel, must notice the deficiency and pull the item, which is often placed with soiled linens into a laundry bag or cart for re-servicing. The linen item will often then be processed again, even if it was not used by a guest, prior to being pulled from service. Linen that requires additional attention must be accumulated and inspected by housekeeping or laundry management to determine if it can possibly be reclaimed through an additional stain removing or repair process. Terry that cannot be reclaimed may be dyed and converted to rags, as previously described, whereas bed and F&B linens may often be donated to appropriate charitable organizations.

Laundry Chemicals

Throughout the description of the various linen processing methodologies, the use of specific laundry chemicals—including detergents, bleach, fabric softeners, starch, and degreasing agents—is mentioned. In a commercial laundry, the chemicals required to clean and process linen are purchased in bulk, typically in large drums, and dispensed into the wash cycles electronically. The dispensing controls are programmed so that the laundry attendants simply load the machines and press the appropriate control button based upon the type of linen being processed; the machine is programmed to dispense the proper chemicals, at the appropriate time, while regulating the duration of each cycle. Any concerns with the quality of the processed linens should be discussed with the laundry's chemical vendor; the vendor shares a mutual concern that the laundry processes produce high-quality outcomes. The overuse of chemicals will not produce an ideal finished product. The hotel's chemical vendor often has expertise that he/she will share with laundry management and staff through in-service training programs; a professional chemical representative may also assist with the proper programming of laundry equipment for each linen type processed.

Laundry Equipment

Hotel laundries generally process a minimum of 8 and up to 16 pounds or more of laundry, per room night, per day, depending upon the complexity of the specific hotel operation. An economy or mid-scale hotel with no F&B operation or pool facility operate at the low end of this scale, whereas upper-upscale and luxury hotels, with conference space and multiple F&B outlets, operate at the high end; resort properties that offer extensive recreational and wellness facilities, such as a spa, may process even more. This translates into laundry production that may exceed 4,200 pounds per day, nearly 30,000 pounds per week, and 126,000 pounds per month in a typical 400-room upper-scale hotel. The capacity of the laundry equipment required to accommodate this level of production can be estimated as follows:

1. *Maximum daily production:* Estimate the number of pounds of linen that will be processed daily, per guestroom, using *Table 7.5: Estimating Laundry Weight Processed per Guestroom*. Multiply the corresponding value, based upon the description of the hotel, by the total number of hotel guestrooms.

2. *Multiply this value by 7 days:* This value represents the typical weekly laundry production. This value is typically not based upon hotel occupancy, because a hotel must be able to process all in-house linen generated by a sold-out house in a single day; however, it may be reduced if the hotel is running under a 60% occupancy annually by multiplying the typical weekly laundry production by 0.8.

3. *Divide by number of hours of operation per week:* Typically, a hotel laundry will be operated 7-hours daily, 7-days per week, for a total of 49-hours per week. This allows one-half hour at the start and end of each day for the starting-up, shutting-down, cleaning, and organizing of the laundry. Some laundries may operate a second-shift during high occupancy periods; however, the vibration and noise associated with operating laundry equipment may not make this possible in many hotel settings.

4. *Divide this value by 1.5, which represents the number of loads per hour:* Loads that are lightly soiled, such as most bed linens, may be processed at the rate of two loads per hour (30 minutes per load), whereas heavily soiled linen, such as F&B linen, may only be processed at a rate of 1.2 loads per-hour (50 minutes per load). A 1.5 loads per hour factor (40 minutes per load) is typically appropriate for moderately soiled linen or for hotels that process a blend of guestroom and F&B linen. The resulting value from this four-step calculation is the total washing capacity that is required within the hotel's laundry operation (www.commerciallaundryequip.com, 2018).

A hotel always requires a minimum of two washing machines, in the event of a machine malfunction, and to allow multiple categories of linen to be serviced simultaneously. A mid-size hotel may want to split the total capacity required between three machines, whereas a large hotel may split the total wash capacity between four or more machines. Consequently, the total washing capacity calculated above may then be divided by two for a smaller hotel, under 200-rooms, by three for a mid-sized hotel (201 to 500 guestrooms), or by four or more for a larger property with over 501-rooms—this provides the approximate capacity of each washer-extractor that is needed for the hotel's laundry operation. To simplify training, the primary washer-extractor machines should be of the same capacity, although some laundries may add one supplemental, smaller capacity machine for small loads, including uniforms.

Drying capacity should be established at a ratio of 2:1 for standard washer-extractors, or 1.25:1 if high G-force washer-extractors are purchased. This ratio may be reduced by one-third to one-half if a high-temperature flatwork roller iron and folder is used to process bed and F&B linens, depending upon the typical proportion of total laundry that is comprised of guestroom, health club, spa, or pool terry, which must be tumble dried in commercial dryers.

Hotel Segment	Guestroom linens	F&B linens	Pool/spa linens	Estimated pounds per guestroom
Economy	√			8 lbs
Midscale	√			9 lbs
Upper-midscale	√+		√	10 lbs
Upscale	√+	√	√	12 lbs
Upper-upscale	√++	√+	√	14 lbs
Luxury	√++	√+	√+	16 lbs
Upper-upscale or luxury resort	√++	√++	√++	18+ lbs

√ = basic linen
+ = increase in linen quantity and/or quality, which each add weight.

Table 7.5: Estimating Laundry Weight Processed per Guestroom

As an example, assume a 400-room, upper-upscale hotel, running well in excess of 60% occupancy annually, with a pool, in addition to a significant F&B banquet operation, is adding an in-house laundry, moving laundry production in-house. Based upon *Table 7.5*, it is estimated that the hotel will process 14 pounds of linen per day. This value (14) is multiplied by 400 (number of guestrooms), then by 7 (number of days in a week); the result is then divided by 49 (the number of hours the laundry will be operated each week) and again by 1.5 (the number of loads run per hour). Consequently, the laundry's required washing capacity is 533.3 pounds (= 14 x 400 x 7 ÷ 49 ÷ 1.5). If this capacity is split between three machines, then the hotel may want to purchase three 175- to 200- pound capacity washer-extractor machines. Assume the hotel purchases three 175-pound washer-extractors with high G-force, plus one 80-pound capacity standard washer-extractor for small loads. The decision may also be made to purchase three 225-pound capacity dryers, providing 675-pounds of drying capacity (1.12:1 dryer-to-washer ratio) because the hotel will also install a flatwork roller ironer, with folder, to process bed and banquet linens to upper-upscale hotel quality standards.

BOX 7.4: MAINTAINING A 3-PAR OF GUESTROOM LINEN

A well-managed housekeeping and laundry operation will maintain a 3-par of guestroom linen. A par of guestroom linen is defined as the quantity of each linen item that is required to properly supply each guestroom in the hotel one time. Consequently, a 3-par of linen is a supply adequate to stock each guestroom with linen three times.

© Lubos Chlubny/Shutterstock.com

To operate at peak efficiency, a housekeeping department requires the following:
- *Par-1: In-service:* All hotel guestrooms must be adequately supplied with linen for guest use; this is referred to as the in-service linen.
- *Par-2: At-rest:* A second par of linen must be available to room attendants to be placed into the guestrooms as the rooms are serviced over the course of the day; this is referred to as the rested linen, because it was processed by the laundry the previous day and has rested overnight in the linen storage closets.
- *Par-3: In-process:* The third par of linen is currently being processed by the laundry associates; this par is referred to as the in-process linen and is the linen that was removed from the guestrooms during the previous day's turn-of-the-house.

Room attendants have a heavy workload and must not be required to wait for guestroom linen; the linen that room attendants require to perform their work must be readily available on their carts or in the linen closets on the guestroom floors, if carts are not used. This is the rested linen that is ready each morning to be placed into guestrooms as soiled and used linens are removed from the hotel's guestrooms.

Laundry attendants, to be productive, must have laundry to begin processing as soon as they arrive on-site each morning. Consequently, laundry attendants start their day by opening the laundry chute, in a high-rise setting, or emptying laundry carts received in the laundry during the previous day, to begin sorting linen for processing. The

par:
the quantity of each linen item that is required to properly supply each guestroom in the hotel one time

in-service linen:
linen currently in the guestrooms for guest use

rested linen:
linen processed by the laundry the previous day that has been shelved overnight

in-process linen:
linen currently being processed by the laundry associates

chute is then closed, or the linen carts removed from the processing areas so the linen removed from the guestrooms over the course of the current day may be collected for processing the following day. By having the laundry removed from guestrooms the previous day immediately available for processing upon their arrival, laundry attendants can get to work without delay and laundry equipment can be operated at full capacity, which is critical to minimizing laundry costs and maximizing production.

An inexperienced housekeeping manager may believe that he/she is saving money by tightly managing the linen budget and operating with less than a 3-par of guestroom linen; however, the manager may only be fooling themselves! The lost productivity, in terms of room attendant labor—because they are forced to wait for linen to be processed and to then return to guestrooms a second time to re-stock towels or pillow-cases—coupled with the higher costs associated with operating a laundry that is running partial loads—while laundry associates wait for linen to be retrieved from the guestrooms for processing—will more than offset any savings in linen expenditures. Plus, the condition of linen that is not processed and allowed to rest overnight, prior to being placed back into service, will deteriorate more quickly, necessitating more frequent replacement.

To maintain a 3-par, a linen inventory is taken quarterly, as part of the big-4 inventory process, which includes china, glassware, silverware (or service-ware), and linen. An appropriate order is placed to bring the complete guestroom linen inventory up to a full 3-par. To avoid spikes in linen expense when these orders are placed, a hotel typically accrues linen expense at a CPOR determined by the previous year's actual annual CPOR, plus an inflation factor, during the non-inventory months. Then, each quarter, the accrual is adjusted based upon the actual order that is placed. For more information about accruals and how they work, please refer to *Chapter 11: Administration and Control: Human Resources, Accounting, and Loss Prevention.*

Prioritizing Laundry Workload

Housekeeping and laundry management must appropriately manage and prioritize laundry production. Although the cleaning of guestroom linen is a daily, routine activity, demands placed on the laundry by the F&B division may vary much more substantially on a day-to-day basis. Therefore, it is critical that an open line of communication be established between the banquet manager or set-up manager and the laundry supervisor. Linens cannot be turned around quickly—it can take hours to process the linen needed for a large banquet event. Therefore, the F&B

division must be proactive and communicate with the laundry supervisor, executive housekeeper, or director of services if a large quantity of a specific color of F&B linen is required for a special event or if specific items must be processed quickly. For example, it is too late if, on Saturday morning, the laundry supervisor finds out that the white banquet linens used at a large Friday evening dinner function the previous night is needed an hour from now to re-set the ballroom for a Saturday afternoon wedding reception. This also reinforces the need to maintain a 3-par of guestroom linen so that today's guestroom linen production—which is not needed until tomorrow—may be used to fill in the production schedule around any pressing F&B linen needs. This also illustrates the need to maintain an appropriate inventory of F&B linen as well.

Allocating Laundry Expenses

Although the bulk of the linen processed by a hotel laundry is often used in the guestrooms, a considerable amount of the laundry workload involves processing F&B linens—particularly in a hotel with a large banquet operation. As a result, the entire expense of the laundry operation should not be borne by the rooms division and an appropriate allocation of laundry expenses should be charged to the F&B division. Rather than track the actual expenses associated with processing rooms versus F&B linens, expenses should be closely monitored and tracked during a 2-week period each year. The specific weeks selected should be typical weeks during which the rooms

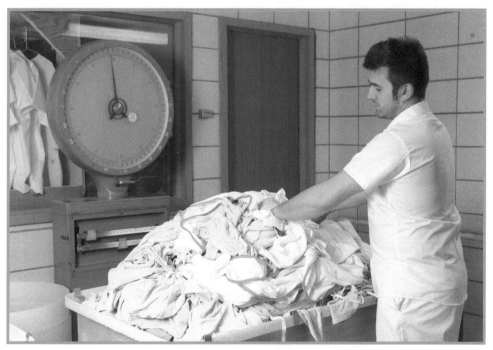

© Lopolo/Shutterstock.com

division's and F&B division's demand for linen is typical—in other words, a 2-week period should be selected during which rooms occupancy and F&B revenues are close to the annual weekly averages. This will ensure an equitable allocation of laundry expenses.

During this 2-week period, the weight of all linen processed should be closely monitored and recorded as it is placed into the washing machines. This will allow housekeeping and laundry management to determine the proportion of the total wash load that is comprised of rooms linen versus F&B linen. As a double-check on the allocation, or simply as an alternative methodology, laundry attendants may be asked to record the amount of their time that is spent feeding guestroom bed linens and F&B linens, respectively, into the high-temperature roller iron, as well as the time spent pulling terry from the dryers and folding towels, because labor comprises the majority share of laundry operations costs. The proportion of labor spent processing guestroom linen versus F&B linen may then be calculated. The cost of operating the laundry is typically recorded on a separate page of the profit and loss (P&L) statement, which includes labor costs, payroll taxes and employee benefits (PT&EB), and other controllable laundry expenses, including chemicals. The total cost of operating the laundry may then be split and added to the divisional P&L statement for each major operating division—the rooms division and the F&B division—based upon this analysis (e.g. 70%/30%, 60%/40%, etc.). To be candid, this allocation has no overall impact on the hotel's earnings before interest, taxes, depreciation, and amortization (EBITDA). Consequently, precise accuracy in the allocation is not necessary, but ensures that the rooms division and F&B division P&Ls accurately reflect, within reason, the contribution margins earned on each division's respective revenue.

CHAPTER SUMMARY

The effective and efficient operation of the housekeeping and laundry departments is critical to the success of a hotel enterprise—a guest will not return to a hotel that is not clean and well-maintained. The housekeeping and laundry operation are managed by the director of services and executive housekeeper, with assistance provided by a team of non-exempt supervisors. Room attendants are responsible for the daily cleaning of hotel rooms, which is tedious, strenuous work. Public area attendants maintain the lobbies and public areas of the hotel, including public restrooms. The provision of housekeeping services is labor-intensive work; therefore, a primary responsibility of the housekeeping management team is to ensure that labor productivity standards are achieved. In addition to controlling payroll costs, housekeeping management must strictly control access to large inventories of guestroom amenities, cleaning supplies, linen, glassware, and operating equipment. Processes must be established to ensure that all guestrooms and public areas of the hotel are properly serviced, while allowing housekeeping associates to be held accountable for fulfilling their individual responsibilities despite being dispersed throughout the hotel. A three-tier room inspection program must be in place to ensure that established housekeeping standards are being maintained, while verifying the timely completion of maintenance work orders. The laundry operation must efficiently process both guestroom and F&B linens daily to ensure that room attendants and F&B associates have the linen necessary to effectively and efficiently fulfill their duties.

KEY TERMS AND CONCEPTS

assistant executive housekeeper	inspector or inspectress	room attendant
big four inventory	public area supervisor	selling guestrooms
breaking-out-the-house	laundry attendant	specialty cleaning chemicals
daily discrepancy report	laundry manager	stan cap
daily special	laundry supervisor	stayover
deep-clean	line-up	thread-count
director of services	linen room attendant	three-tier inspection program
discrepant room	material safety data sheets (MSDS)	triple-sheet
executive housekeeper	par	turn-the-house
guestroom amenities	par-level	turndown attendant
housekeeping supervisor	primary cleaning chemicals	turndown service
housemen	public area attendant	usage factor
in-process linen	pure measure of productivity	
in-service linen	rested linen	

DISCUSSION QUESTIONS

1. Discuss how the scope and staffing of a hotel's housekeeping and laundry operation is impacted by its scale (e.g. economy, midscale, upper-midscale, upscale, upper-upscale, or luxury).

2. Explain strategies that may be employed to ensure that housekeeping productivity standards are maintained—include the concepts of HPOR, CPOR, and "selling" rooms in the explanation.

3. Using the 10-day forecast provided in *Box 6.2: Scheduling the Guest Services Team*, create a weekly work schedule for the housekeeping department based upon the housekeeping staffing guidelines identified in *Table 7.2*.

4. Using the hotel occupancy forecast in *Table 7.3*, coupled with the usage rates for April 2019 found in *Box 7.3*, project the number of cases of each guestroom amenity that will be consumed, as well as the total cost of the guestroom amenities, for each month in 2019; calculate the total annual cost of all guest amenities.

5. Describe the morning line-up process and explain its importance.

6. Discuss the importance and process of properly servicing in-room glassware.

7. Identify the different types of hotel linen and explain how each is serviced, including a discussion of the laundry chemicals and equipment needed to properly service each type.

8. Assume a 400-room hotel is split half-and-half between king-bedded and double-queen guestrooms. All beds are triple-sheeted. Identify the total quantity of each linen item required to maintain a 3-par of guestroom linen assuming that king-bedded rooms have three pillows on each bed; three each of washcloths, hand-towels, and bath-towels; while double-queen rooms have two pillows per bed (four per room); four each of washcloths, hand-towels, and bath-towels. All rooms have a terry bath mat and an extra hypo-allergenic pillow in the closet, encased in a pillow-case and plastic, zippered sleeve.

ENDNOTES

Bureau of Labor Statistics (2018). *Occupational Employment and Wages, May 2017*. Accessed online November 12, 2018 at: https://www.bls.gov/oes/2015/may/naics4_721100.htm

www.commerciallaundryequip.com; (2018). General Laundry Planning Calculation Methods; PDF file retrieved online on November 14, 2018 at: https://www.google.com/url?sa=t&rct=j&q=&esrc=s&source=web&cd=4&ved=2ahUKEwiawv6eqdXeAhWyq1k-KHST-Cj4QFjADegQIBhAC&url=https%3A%2F%2Fcommerciallaundryequip.com%2F-wp-content%2Fuploads%2F2014%2F07%2Fequipment-sizing-guide.pdf&usg=AOvVaw0l2L-DwqQ6IU9fZrLm-wxPj

HOTEL DEVELOPMENT PROJECT

Students completing a course in hotel, lodging, or resort management are encouraged to complete a hotel development project over the course of the semester/term; students are encouraged to work in small groups of 3 – 5 students. *Appendix A* outlines the project in its entirety.

Upon the conclusion of *Chapter 7: Housekeeping and Laundry Operations*, students are prepared to complete the following assignment.

Assignment 4: Rooms Division: Service and Staffing

Use content from: Chapter 6: Guest Services Operations and *Chapter 7: Housekeeping and Laundry Operations.*

With the hotel room count, brand, and rate structure for the hotel identified, a rooms division P&L statement may be created. The following information may be presented in an Excel spreadsheet:

1. Occupied room nights, occupancy, ADR, room revenue, and revenue per available room by month for the hotel's first 12 months of operation, including annual totals. Room nights, ADR, and revenue should be broken out by guest segment.

2. Rooms division payroll expenses, by position, including hours, wage or salary rates, and total wages, broken out by month. Include an additional 35% for PT&EB. For each position, identify if staffing is determined based upon a fixed or variable staffing level and include at least one productivity factor used for any positions that are variably staffed. Calculate the number of rooms division associates or FTEs needed to staff the rooms division.

3. Forecast other controllable expenses for the hotel rooms division as a percentage of revenue or on a CPOR basis, based upon the hotel's chain-scale, month-by-month, including an annual total.

4. Rooms division departmental profit or contribution margin is also to be provided, as a dollar amount and as a percentage of hotel revenue, month-by-month, and on an annual basis.

Section Four

DELIVERING THE PERIPHERAL SERVICES:
FOOD, BEVERAGE, CONFERENCE SERVICES, AND RECREATION

SECTION 4: DELIVERING PERIPHERAL SERVICES: FOOD, BEVERAGE, CONFERENCE SERVICES AND RECREATION

Chapter 8: Food and Beverage Operations

This chapter provides an overview of outlet (restaurant, bar, and in-room dining) operations; banquets, catering, and conference services; as well as culinary arts and food production.

Chapter 9: Resort Operations

The focus of this chapter is on the unique characteristics of a resort lodging operation, typically located in a beach; golf; racquet sport; or mountain location. This chapter explores the variety of accommodation types and ownership structures, which creates a different dynamic between ownership and lodging management, as well as the characteristics unique to many resort communities and their impact on resort operations.

Chapter 8
Food and Beverage Operations

This chapter provides an overview of outlet (restaurant, bar, and in-room dining) operations; banquets, catering, and conference services; as well as culinary arts and food production.

PURPOSE AND LEARNING OBJECTIVES:

Hotel managers working in a full-service hotel environment, particularly in upper-upscale and luxury hotels, deliver food and beverage (F&B) products and experiences to support the overall guest experience. In a select-service hotel context, an F&B component may be included within the service bundle delivered to hotel guests. This chapter delivers the following learning outcomes to ensure that readers understand basic F&B concepts critical to supporting a successful hotel operation:

- Discuss the role of the F&B operation in delivering meaningful outcomes for the key stakeholders identified in the all-square operating philosophy: hotel guests, associates, investors, and the local community.
- Define the scope of an F&B operation within the context of an upper-upscale or luxury hotel, explaining how the F&B operation may serve as the "personality" of the hotel.
- Explain ways in which the F&B division supports the guestroom operation and how this influences management decision-making.
- Discuss F&B profitability, defining prime costs and typical contribution margins within the F&B division.
- Describe the organizational structure of the F&B division, identifying key department heads, managers, and line-level associates.
- Identify and define labor productivity measures, as well as labor offsets, used to manage F&B labor costs.
- Forecast food and beverage revenue.
- Identify and explain control systems established to manage and control food and beverage inventories and costs of goods sold (COGS).
- Identify both linear and non-linear processes established to ensure guest experiences that consistently exceed customers' expectations.
- Identify strategies employed to ensure the responsible sale of alcoholic beverages.

CHAPTER OUTLINE:

The purpose of this chapter is to provide insight into food and beverage (F&B) operations within the context of an upper-upscale or luxury hotel environment. This chapter will not cover all F&B management concepts in depth—there are many academic texts on F&B operations—but it will provide an overview of how a hotel general manager (GM), supported by a qualified F&B management team, effectively manage F&B operations to successfully deliver consistent and memorable F&B products and experiences, adding value to the overall guest experience.

The "all-square" operating philosophy, introduced in *Chapter 2: Successful Hotel Management*, applies to the management of the F&B operation, just as it does to all areas of the hotel. The man-

© wavebreakmedia/Shutterstock.com

© Petar Djordjevic/Shutterstock.com

agement team, to be successful, must provide guests with value, as defined by the value equation (please refer to *Formula 2.1: Value Equation*), while also contributing to the hotel management team's overall effort to deliver a return on investment to the hotel's investors or owners. Of course, these goals can only be successfully achieved through the proper management and oversight of the hotel's associates because it is ultimately the F&B associates that deliver experiences to guests. As has been reiterated throughout *Delivering the Guest Experience*, the customer or guest must always be the focus of attention because hotel guests are the source of all revenue, and strong revenues are essential to the hotel's ability to provide both extrinsic and intrinsic job satisfaction to associates while delivering a return on investment (**ROI**) for investors, which supports the hotel's ability to be a good corporate citizen.

SCOPE OF FOOD AND BEVERAGE OPERATIONS

The core services provided by the F&B division—designed to fulfill guests' primary needs—include food service, beverage service, and meeting support services; secondary or peripheral services provided include audio-visual services, entertainment, special event support, and minibar services within the guestrooms, if offered. The F&B division also provides employee meals to the hotel's associates.

The primary departments within the F&B division include the following:

Food and Beverage Outlets

Outlet operations are comprised of the hotel's restaurants; any food or beverage carts; grab-and-go operations; deli operations; bars, lounges, or taverns; as well as in-room dining or room service, which is typically available in upper-upscale and luxury hotel environments. The number and variety of F&B outlets is determined by the number of guestrooms within the property, as well as the location, average length-of-stay, and positioning of the hotel. A hotel in an urban area, or a suburban office park or retail/entertainment district, may provide guests with easy access to a variety of independent or nationally-recognized chain restaurants, including casual service, fine dining, and quick service operations. Consequently, the variety of F&B outlets operated within the hotel may be limited in such an environment. Conversely, a destination resort, luxury hotel, or a hotel in a more isolated location—particularly if the average length-of-stay exceeds three or four nights—may offer a variety of F&B outlets, providing guests with a range of cuisines, service levels, and customer experiences to enjoy over the duration of their stay.

Conference Services, Catering, and Banquet Operations

The catering, conference services, or meeting support department includes two areas—the catering or conference services team, which serves as the banquet department's sales force, selling the catered meals and events that take place in the hotel's meeting space; and the banquet and conference set-up team, which is the operations team that executes meal service and events in the hotel's conference facilities.

As discussed in detail in *Chapter 3: Defining Guest Segments*, the amount of conference and event space within a hotel is determined by the number of guestrooms, coupled with the proportion of hotel rooms ideally allocated for use by in-house groups. To summarize, a hotel requires enough space to accommodate guests within the group room allotment for a meeting and a meal in two separate meeting rooms, at a minimum. Meeting room set-ups typically require between 10 and 24 square feet of meeting space per guest, depending upon the configuration of the room, whereas meals require approximately 12 square feet per guest. Many conferences also include both general and break-out sessions, increasing the amount of meeting space required per guest. Consequently, a hotel's conference center requires a minimum of 22 and, ideally, 36+ square feet of meeting space per meeting guest, plus adequate pre-function space—outside of the enclosed meeting rooms—for receptions and assembly areas between events; this basic meeting space allotment per guest must then be doubled, to between 44 and 72 square feet per group guestroom, to allow for double occupancy within the group guestroom allotment.

If these meeting space requirements are applied to a "typical" 400-room, upper-up-scale hotel, with an 80% or 320-group-room allotment, the resulting hotel may offer between just over 14,000 square feet and nearly 24,000 square feet of conference and event space. Many large conference hotels and destination resorts have guestroom counts that exceed 500, 800, or even 1,000 guestrooms. In these mammoth hotels, it is not uncommon for the hotel to offer well over 100,000 square feet of event space. For a more detailed discussion regarding meeting space requirements, please refer to *Chapter 3: Defining Guest Segments*.

Beverage Department

The beverage department provides support to all F&B personnel involved in the sale and service of alcoholic beverages throughout the hotel. The beverage department serves both F&B outlets and the banquet department and, in a resort, setting may support recreational areas including a pool, beach, or golf club.

Food Production Department

The culinary or food production department is responsible for preparing all food served throughout the property, supported by the stewards, which maintain the cleanliness of all the heart-of-the-house F&B areas and equipment. The stewards also manage the delivery of prepared food products from the food preparation or kitchen areas to the function space or other remote foodservice locations within the hotel or resort.

The "Personality" of the Hotel or Resort

Although a hotel's décor, including its guestroom furnishings and the quality of its interior finishes, provide guests with an indication of the hotel's market position and service level, the quality and creativity of the hotel's F&B operation can distinguish a hotel significantly from its competitors—in other words, it defines the "personality" of the hotel. Creative menus, artistically presented using quality ingredients, provide guests with memorable experiences, leaving the lasting impressions critical to building customer loyalty. The inclusion of regional dishes—locally sourced when possible—in addition to providing the familiar, comfort foods that many travelers desire, ensure that the F&B operation contributes to the overall success of the hospitality enterprise, while meeting guests' most basic biological need—nourishment.

Supporting the Guestroom Operation

A hotel's F&B operation must, first and foremost, support the guestroom operation. Consistent with the value equation (refer to *Formula 2.1*), a high quality F&B operation provides additional value to hotel guests, which may positively impact the hotel's ADR. In addition, specific F&B services—such as a three-meal restaurant or in-room dining—are expected in many hotel operations, particularly upper-upscale and luxury hotels. Although a room service operation is rarely profitable, a high-end upper-upscale or luxury hotel is expected to offer an in-room dining option to guests; quite frankly, it is difficult to position a hotel property at the top of the market—charging premium guestroom rates—without a quality F&B operation. For branded hotels, the hotel parent companies dictate the scope of F&B services that must be provided to guests through the brand standards established by the chain.

Although full-service hotels—offering a range of F&B services in addition to overnight accommodations—often operate profitable F&B operations, the profitability of the F&B operation does not completely drive management decision-making in a hotel context. The impact of each decision must be weighed against its impact on the overall guest experience and the hotel's market position. For example, as *Box 8.1: The Future of In-Room Dining* outlines, hotel room service operations are rarely profitable, despite higher menu prices and delivery charges; however, most upper-upscale and luxury hotels offer some form of in-room dining. This is because a business traveler paying a premium room rate that would like to order dinner, while working on a project or watching a sporting event in the privacy of his/her guestroom, expects to be able to do so. In the same way, a couple staying in a luxury resort to celebrate their wedding anniversary expects to be able to order breakfast delivered to their room in the morning. In a similar way, it may not enhance the profitability of the F&B division to operate a hotel's restaurant 24-hours per day; however, a large, upper-upscale hotel located in proximity to a major international airport, accommodating guests arriving from destinations from around the globe, may determine that offering food-service around-the-clock provides the hotel with a competitive advantage. Consequently, although the impact of F&B operations on profitability is certainly a major consideration in decision-making, the impact of a specific management decision on the F&B division's profitability may not always be the primary concern.

The F&B division must also support a variety of additional areas of the hotel operation, particularly in a resort environment. In a full-service resort, for example, the recreation and wellness areas of the operation—including the pool, golf course, or spa—may each require some level of support from the F&B division. Again, some F&B support operations may negatively impact the operating margin of the F&B division; however, a wise hotel manager looks at the big picture, evaluating how each support function delivered by the F&B division contributes value to the overall guest

© Igor Meshkov/Shutterstock.com

experience. Although actions must be taken to optimize the profitability of the F&B division, steps to drive the profitability of the F&B operation alone should not be implemented without considering the impact on the hotel's average daily rate (ADR), market position, or the guest experience.

Food and Beverage Profitability

As previously outlined in *Table 2.1: Financial Performance of a "Typical" Upper-Upscale Hotel*, based upon a sample of 966 hotels, comprised of 393,421 hotel guestrooms, the typical upper-upscale hotel in 2015 generated $53.94 in food revenue per occupied guestroom, $14.46 in beverage revenue, and $18.70 in additional ancillary F&B revenue, including meeting room rental, audio-visual equipment rental, and other miscellaneous F&B-related revenue; this accounted for just over thirty percent (30.2%) of total hotel revenue. The contribution margin—revenue minus the direct expenses incurred to generate the corresponding revenue—was 31.2%, which translates into an increase of nearly $3 million in annual profit from F&B operations for a "typical" 400-room upper-upscale hotel located in the United States (STR, 2017); please refer to *Table 8.1a: F&B Profitability* for more detail. This leaves little doubt that the F&B division can potentially be a substantial source of profit for a hotel; however, profitability varies widely, depending upon the specific circumstances of an individual hotel property.

	Per occupied room[1]		Annual for a "typical" 400-room hotel[2]		Sales ratio (%)
Revenue					
Food	$	53.94	$	5,890,680	61.9%
Beverage		14.46		1,579,148	16.6%
Miscellaneous		18.70		2,042,190	21.5%
Total	**$**	**87.10**	**$**	**9,512,017**	**100.0%**
Total F&B expenses	**$**	**59.96**	**$**	**6,548,112**	**68.8%**
F&B contribution margin	**$**	**27.14**	**$**	**2,963,905**	**31.2%**
[1]Based upon a sample of 966 upper-upscale hotels comprised of 393,421 guestrooms (407 average number of rooms per hotel) located in the United States (STR, 2017).					
[2]Annual values assuming 74.8% occupancy.					

Table 8.1a: F&B Profitability

Table 8.1b: Common F&B Expense Levels and Operating Margin outlines expense levels commonly encountered within an upper-upscale hotel F&B operation, although the actual values may vary substantially for an individual hotel, based upon the scope and scale of its F&B operation. The F&B division's profitability is much lower than the rooms division, which typically earns a 75% to 80% contribution margin, due in part to the cost of goods sold (COGS). Food cost may run as high as 32% to 35% of food revenue in the F&B outlets department; however, a hotel's overall food cost will typically run in the high twenties (27% to 29%) as a percentage of food revenue, particularly in an upper-upscale hotel with a large amount of meeting and conference space, due to the strong proportion of food revenue contributed by the banquet operation.

Beverage cost will typically run in the mid-twenty percent range (23% to 27%), as a percentage of beverage revenue, although it may run closer to 30% in an F&B operation that generates a high proportion of its beverage revenue through the sale of wine. Payroll in the F&B division will often run around 30% of total F&B revenue, whereas payroll taxes and employee benefits (PT&EB) may be close to thirty percent (28% to 32%) of total salaries and wages for the F&B division, depending upon the proportion of full-time associates receiving benefits. Other controllable expenses, including paper supplies, cleaning chemicals, and a range of other miscellaneous operating supplies, typically run between 7% to 10% of total F&B revenues. These expense levels lead to an F&B division contribution margin of just over thirty percent (31.2%) in many hotels.

	Per occupied room	Annual for a "Typical" 400-room Hotel	Sales ratio (%)
Food revenue	$ 53.94	$ 5,890,680	61.9%
Beverage revenue	14.46	1,579,148	16.6%
Miscellaneous revenue	18.70	2,042,190	21.5%
Total F&B revenue	$ 87.10	$ 9,512,017	100.0%
Cost of Goods Sold (COGS):			
Food cost[1]	$ 15.37	$ 1,678,844	28.5%
Beverage cost[2]	3.47	378,995	24.0%
Total Cost of Goods Sold (COGS)	$ 18.84	$ 2,057,839	27.5%
Labor:			
Salaries & wages	$ 26.13	$ 2,853,605	30.0%
Payroll taxes & employee benefits[3]	$ 7.58	827,545	29.0%
Total payroll & related	$ 33.71	$ 3,681,151	38.7%
Other controllable expenses	$ 7.41	$ 809,122	8.5%
Contribution Margin:	$ 27.14	$ 2,963,905	31.2%
[1]Percentage of food revenue only.			
[2]Percentage of beverage revenue only.			
[3]Perentage of F&B payroll. All other ratios are expressed as a percentage of total F&B revenue.			

Table 8.1b: Common F&B Expense Levels and Operating Margin

Although *Table 8.1b: Common F&B Expense Levels and Operating Margin* may outline a reasonable expectation of the expense levels and contribution margin generated by the F&B division of an upper-upscale or luxury hotel, expenses and margins will vary significantly from property-to-property depending, in large part, upon the mix of sales between F&B outlets and the banquet department. As described in *Box 8.1: The Future of In-Room Dining*, room service operations—one component of the F&B outlets department—are inherently inefficient. Contribution margins are often lower in hotel restaurants, even though many guests expect to pay a modest premium for the convenience of dining in the hotel, due to wide fluctuations in business volumes, coupled with the need to operate a hotel restaurant during periods of low demand to provide the availability of foodservice to hotel guests, further hampering the profitability of

F&B outlets. Food production—in terms of both culinary labor and food cost—is often less efficient in the outlets than in the banquet department.

Conversely, food and labor costs may be managed very efficiently within the banquet operation—a handful of culinary professionals can prepare meals for hundreds of guests and there is little food waste or overproduction in the banquet department; the executive chef knows the precise needs of group clients in advance—enabling him/her to staff and order food product accordingly. In a similar way, the banquet manager can schedule the precise amount of labor necessary to effectively and efficiently service a group event. Consequently, F&B operations accommodating a substantial amount of banquet business may commonly enjoy contribution margins in the F&B division that exceed 40% or even 50% of revenue.

As the proportion of F&B revenue shifts from the outlets to the banquet departments, food cost typically decreases while payroll often increases, as an absolute dollar amount. Prices are often higher for banquet meals because a private ballroom or function space must be set up for the meal function, which requires a significant amount of labor; the banquet room must also be cleared and cleaned following the event. Therefore, the higher prices generate a higher gross margin—food revenue less food cost—which helps offset the labor cost associated with the turning or set-up and clearing of the banquet room. Hotels may also charge service charges—or standard gratuities—as well as meeting room rental or set-up fees on catered events to offset labor costs, which ultimately lower labor costs as a percentage of revenue.

turning meeting, function or banquet space: the clearing, cleaning, and re-setting of a hotel function room

In summary, the profitability of hotel F&B operations vary widely. Some hotel F&B operations fail to generate a department profit—they operate at a loss, as an amenity for hotel guests. A select-service hotel that provides a complimentary breakfast buffet, for example, typically operates its F&B operation as an expense center only to add value to the guest experience; this added expense is anticipated to be offset by a higher ADR, occupancy, and revenue per available room (RevPAR) enjoyed by the rooms division. Many full-service hotels, supporting both outlet and banquet operations, may operate at a loss, at close to break-even, or with a modest profit depending upon the size, scope, and nature of the F&B operation. Although the typical upper-upscale hotel F&B division operates with a contribution margin of approximately 30% of total F&B revenue, upper-upscale and luxury hotels with large, high-volume conference centers may generate a substantial contribution margin that exceeds 40% of total F&B revenue—adding millions of dollars to the hotel's bottom-line.

Regardless of the scope of the operation, a wise hotel management team recognizes the value that a well-managed F&B operation adds to the guest experience, potentially allowing the hotel to command a higher ADR while building customer loyalty. To accomplish this goal, F&B outlets must be designed to effectively compete with local independent foodservice operations, as well as the national chains, in terms of food quality, menu creativity, service, décor, and value. Conference support and banquet operations must consistently and efficiently deliver exceptional and memorable experiences to group guests, with an emphasis on ensuring successful outcomes for group clients that plan these meetings and events. Although the contribution margin generated by the rooms division may drive the overall profitability of a hotel enterprise, a well-managed F&B division potentially adds increased profitability, while also providing a hotel with "personality." And this "personality" is essential to driving repeat business from individual guests, as well as meeting and event planners—critical to a hotel's long-term success.

BOX 8.1: THE FUTURE OF IN-ROOM DINING

In 2013, the *New York Hilton Midtown* in New York City, after 50 years of operation, announced that room service would no longer be available in its nearly 2,000 guestrooms (Bignewsnetwork.com, 2013). Imagine operating a restaurant, spread over a 47-floor building that covers an entire city block with each of the 1,900+ tables located behind a locked door in a separate room. Imagine, as well, that on a busy morning, hundreds of guests, in hundreds of rooms scattered throughout this 47-story building order breakfast to be delivered—hot and fresh—to their individual rooms, primarily between the hours of 7 and 8 a.m. That is the reality of operating room service in the *New York Hilton Midtown*!

© BestStockFoto/Shutterstock.com

Operating a room service or in-room dining operation is a challenge. It is an inherently labor-intensive, inefficient proposition. Hotel personnel must be available to sell the orders, which typically are sold through a telephone conversation with hotel guests, although hotels are increasingly using cell phone apps and in-room entertainment systems, accessible on the guestroom televisions, to facilitate and streamline the order-taking process. Many hotels also place printed room service menu cards, which may be filled out by guests and hung on the guestroom doorknobs at night prior to retiring, to order breakfast for delivery the following morning. Room service meals must be properly prepared in the hotel kitchen and then carefully assembled—with all the appropriate condiments and service-ware—on a tray or cart for delivery to the guestroom. A check must also be printed for presentation to the guest. Access to guestrooms is typically via a service elevator, which is also being used by housekeeping and other hotel personnel to access the guest floors; a hotel often has only a single, or certainly no more than two or three service elevators, depending upon the size, design, and lay-out of the hotel. Hot food must be kept warm in a hot box—commonly heated by an open flame burning in a can of fuel gel.

The trip to a guestroom from the kitchen may take 5 to 15 minutes or longer depending upon the distance, coupled with the length of the wait and subsequent ride on the hotel's service elevator. After announcing his/her arrival at the guestroom, the server must wait for the guest to respond, open the door, and give the server permission to enter the room, allowing the server to place and serve the meal within the guestroom. The accuracy of the meal must be confirmed, instructions provided to the guest to request tray removal, and the guest must be given time to review the accuracy of the order/guest-check and sign the check. If there is any item or condiment missing from the delivery, the time required for the server to correct the error is substantial because it may require a round-trip to the hotel's kitchen. After the guest has consumed the meal, room service personnel must return to the floor to retrieve the foodservice equipment, china, glassware, linen, and service-ware from the guest's room or corridor, if the guest elects to place the tray outside of their door.

Due to the inherent inefficiency of the in-room dining process, hotels typically charge 10% to 20% higher prices on the room service menu than for the equivalent menu items when ordered in the hotel's dining room. In addition, there is less variety on the room service menu due, in part, to a consideration of how well each menu item may travel to a hotel guestroom from the kitchen. Hotels also include a flat delivery fee of $5 to $10 per order, as well as an automatic service charge of 18% to 24% of the cost of the F&B items ordered. These fees are intended to help offset the high labor costs associated with the room service operation. The higher price of in-room dining is also intended to encourage guests to dine in a hotel F&B outlet, where F&B services may be more efficiently provided.

The *New York Hilton Midtown* cited the high cost of labor as a major factor when deciding to shut-down its room service operation; however, hotel officials also made it clear that the elimination of room service did not mean that in-room dining would no longer be available within the hotel. Like many hotels, the *New York Hilton Midtown* has introduced grab-and-go operations at the property. Grab-and-go operations include kiosks, food carts, and other quick service operations that provide guests with conveniently packaged F&B products that may be purchased and carried by the guest to their guestroom or simply consumed within the public spaces of the hotel. Many grab-and-go and quick service operations are branded—such as Starbucks licensed stores that are successfully operated in hundreds of hotels worldwide—whereas many other hotel-based, quick-service F&B operations are developed by hotel parent companies, hotel management firms, and individual hotel operators. Quick service operations are much less labor intensive and provide guests with convenient access to familiar foods, which often include muffins, bagels, deli-style sandwiches, salads, flatbreads, and more. These items may often be prepared and pre-packaged—or quickly prepared and packaged—in biodegradable or recyclable disposable containers, eliminating the need for hotel staff to retrieve, clean, and sanitize dishes and service-ware.

Another alternative to room service that is gaining ground, particularly in urban areas in which a wide-variety of high-quality restaurants operate, is the use of restaurant delivery services such as *Uber Eats* and *GrubHub*. Many hotel guests now use these services when they are home or in their offices. Consequently, it is only natural that guests are turning to these services to have food delivered to the privacy of their hotel guestrooms while on-the-road. An increasing number of hotel restaurants are also partnering with food delivery services to augment food outlet revenues, enabling them to provide meals to nearby residents and businesses while, in effect, subcontracting the food delivery component of the transaction to an outside vendor. This allows the hotel to provide guests with the convenience of in-room dining while avoiding the operational challenges and high costs of providing a traditional room service experience.

DIVISIONAL STRUCTURE

The F&B division is overseen by the director of F&B, who serves on the executive operating committee (EOC) of the hotel, which in some hotel organizations also includes the executive chef. The full management structure of the F&B division, within an upper-upscale or luxury hotel, is illustrated in *Diagram 8.1a: Food and Beverage Organization Chart (Operations)*. The F&B director reports directly to the GM and typically has four direct reports that oversee the four primary operating departments within the division. These department heads include the director of F&B outlets, beverage manager, banquet manager, and executive chef.

The director of outlets oversees service execution in all F&B outlets serving prepared foods to guests. This includes restaurants, F&B carts and kiosks, grab-and-go operations, as well as in-room dining. The director of outlets is assisted by outlet or restaurant managers and assistants that are assigned responsibilities for specific outlets or shifts. The F&B outlets department employs food servers, assistant food servers (or bussers), food runners, hosts, and cashiers, as appropriate, to staff the various F&B outlets operated by the hotel.

director of F&B:
an exempt manager that oversees the F&B operating division and serves on the executive operating committee

director of outlets:
an exempt department head that oversees all F&B outlets, including in-room dining

outlet or restaurant manager:
an exempt manager that oversees the operation of a specific F&B outlet or shift

food server:
a non-exempt associate that sells and serves prepared foods to guests

assistant food server (busser):
a non-exempt associate that assists food servers in providing guest service in a high volume or high service quality F&B outlet

food runner:
a non-exempt associate that assists in delivering prepared foods to guests in a high volume F&B outlet

host:
a non-exempt associate that greets, seats, and performs other guest service functions in an F&B outlet

cashier:
a non-exempt associate that collects payments from guests for hotel services, products, and experiences

The beverage manager oversees the distribution and sale of alcoholic beverages throughout the entire hotel operation. In some hotels, the beverage department may be assigned to one of the outlet managers, assistant outlet managers, or the assistant banquet manager, depending upon the size, scope, and specific characteristics of the beverage operation. For example, if the lion's share of beverage revenue is generated through catering or banquet operations, then the assistant banquet manager may be assigned the beverage management responsibilities; however, if the beverage operation includes a high volume beverage outlet—such as a sports bar or entertainment venue—then the outlet manager responsible for this outlet may be assigned beverage management responsibilities. If a hotel generates a substantial volume of beverage revenue, then a separate beverage manager may be employed. As discussed later in the chapter, it is critical that a single manager is held responsible for the management of the beverage inventory and beverage COGS. In addition to the beverage inventory and COGS, the beverage manager often is assigned the responsibility of re-stocking guestroom minibars, if available, as well as managing and supervising any entertainment contracted by the hotel—including bands, comedy acts, or disc jockeys (DJs). Line-level associates employed by the beverage department include outlet and banquet bartenders; barbacks, responsible for stocking bars with ice, glassware, and supplies; and cocktail servers.

The banquet manager oversees the execution of all food service within the hotel's conference, meeting and event space. The set-up manager, often referred to as the convention service manager, oversees the banquet housemen responsible for setting the tables, chairs, staging, dance floors, and other equipment required by conference guests within the hotel's meeting space; the banquet set-up team is also responsible for breaking down this equipment, cleaning, and vacuuming the room following any scheduled events. When setting a room for a meeting or event that does not involve serving a meal, the set-up team will also place linens, table skirts, pens and pads, glassware, water service, hard candies, and other meeting room guest amenities in the conference rooms. When a meal is served, the banquet housemen will set the tables, chairs, buffet line, staging, dance floor, and other items required by the client; however, the banquet servers will cloth the tables with appropriate linen and set the them for the meal service with china, glassware, service-ware, and the additional table-top items required for the service of the meal. Following the meal, the banquet servers are responsible for clearing the tables, following each course of the meal, down to the table-clothes. The set-up manager also works closely with the audio-visual vendor or department, as well as the special events department or exhibition service vendors, including florists and lighting contractors, to ensure that clients' needs for audio-visual support, pipe-and-drape, lighting and special effects, and centerpieces are fulfilled.

The banquet servers, responsible for serving meals, are supervised directly by the assistant banquet manager and banquet captains. Banquet captains are non-exempt (hourly) supervisors that are assigned the responsibility of overseeing a specific meal function to ensure impeccable service that exceeds clients' expectations. In addition to providing traditional plated-meal service, banquet servers may also be assigned the responsibility of maintaining buffet lines and serving coffee and meeting breaks, which typically include coffee and tea service, iced beverages, and a variety of snack items, often including fresh fruit or baked goods.

banquet captain:
a non-exempt supervisor that oversees the delivery of F&B services in the hotel's meeting and event space

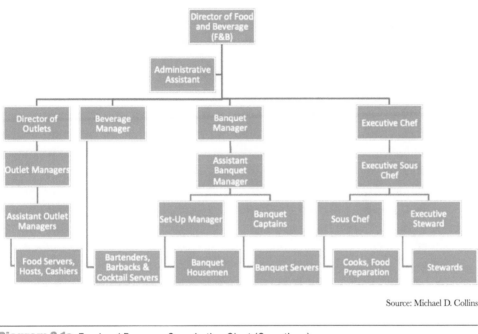

Source: Michael D. Collins

Diagram 8.1a: Food and Beverage Organization Chart (Operations)

The executive chef is responsible for all food production. With the support of the executive sous chef and sous chefs, the executive chef oversees the creation of all menus throughout the hotel operation—both in the outlets and those offered by the catering sales team to banquet clients. The structure of the supervisory support team within the food production or culinary department is dependent upon the size and scope of the various food operations. Although the executive sous chef clearly serves the lead support role to the executive chef, he/she may focus on banquet food production in a large banquet house or on a hotel's signature restaurant, if the hotel operates a high-profile restaurant; however, in many operations the executive sous chef will rotate throughout the operation, providing coverage for sous chefs on their scheduled days off, to help ensure consistent food quality and the efficiency of food production operations throughout the hotel.

Sous chefs may be assigned to specific outlets or banquet food production, depending upon the respective food sales volume of each area, as well as the physical layout of

executive chef:
an exempt manager responsible for all food production that may serve on the executive operating committee

executive sous chef:
an exempt manager responsible for overseeing the food production or culinary department

sous chef:
an exempt manager responsible for overseeing food production for a specific outlet or during an assigned shift

pastry chef:
an exempt manager that
oversees the production
of baked goods, desserts,
and confections

lead cook:
a non-exempt associate
that supervises food
production personnel

line cook:
a non-exempt associate
that prepares food prod-
ucts and meals for guests

saucier:
a non-exempt culinary
associate that prepares hot
food items, particularly
dishes including sauces

grill cook:
a non-exempt culinary
associate that specializes
in grilling meats and
vegetables

short-order cook:
a non-exempt culinary as-
sociate that prepares fresh
meals, particularly in the
hotel's 3-meal restaurant

garde manger:
a non-exempt culinary
associate specializing in the
preparation of cold foods

baker:
a non-exempt culinary
associate that prepares
breads, pastries, and
confections

banquet cook:
a non-exempt culinary
associate assigned to
prepare food and meals for
consumption in the hotel's
meeting and event space

executive steward:
an exempt manager that
oversees the inventories
and cleanliness of all
food production areas,
equipment, china, glass,
and service-ware

the food production facilities. In some hotel environments, all food items are prepared in a centrally located kitchen, while in others, separate kitchens may be operated for one or more individual outlets or for banquets—making it necessary for a separate sous chef to be assigned responsibility for overseeing each remote food production area. Although it is becoming less common for a hotel to operate a pastry shop, due to the availability of high-quality breads, pastries, cakes, and specialty dessert items through local bakeries or commercial food suppliers, as frozen items, some hotels, particularly luxury hotels, employ a pastry chef and operate an in-house bakery shop. The various chefs oversee teams of lead cooks; line cooks, including sauciers, grill, and short-order cooks; other food production personnel, including garde mangers, bakers, and banquet cooks; and other culinary professionals.

The executive steward, supported by a team of stewards, is responsible for maintaining the cleanliness of all food production areas. In addition to the operation of all dishwashing stations, the stewards clean all pots, pans, and cookware, while maintaining the cleanliness of the kitchen floors and service areas throughout each day. At the end of each day, the entire culinary team will work in partnership with the stewards, through their assigned side-duties, to thoroughly clean the kitchen, including the food production tables, walk-in coolers, freezers, and equipment prior to shutting down food production operations each day. The stewards also assist with plate-ups, during which banquet meals are plated, covered, and placed in a warmer or hot-box for transport from the banquet kitchen to the banquet and event space. The executive steward is also responsible for maintaining the hotel's inventory of china, glassware, service-ware, and food service equipment, and spearheads the F&B division's recycling efforts.

Although *Diagram 8.1a: Food and Beverage Organization Chart (Operations)* outlines the management structure for the operations managers and associates within the F&B division, *Diagram 8.2b: Food and Beverage (F&B) Organization Chart (Sales)* identifies the sales professionals responsible for selling F&B products and services to group clients, as well as an alternative placement of the banquet operations team found in some hotels. Recall from *Chapter 3: Effective Sales and Marketing* that many hotels, particularly upper-upscale and luxury hotels with substantial meeting space, employ a team of sales professionals that include a director of catering and conference services that oversees the catering sales manager(s)—who book events in the hotel's meeting and conference space for clients that require few, if any, overnight accommodations—as well as conference service managers—who sell F&B and meeting support services to group clients generating 10 or more room nights. These sales professionals commonly report to the director of sales because they perform a sales function; however, in some hotel environments, these sales professionals may report instead to the director of F&B.

Some hotel management firms believe the alternative structure, as illustrated in *Diagram 8.1b*, provides the director of F&B increased input into how the hotel's meeting space is used to optimize F&B revenue. As previously explained, strong banquet and catering revenue can significantly impact the profitability of the F&B division—therefore, this alternative structure may contribute to a more profitable F&B division. It is also not uncommon—when the catering and conference services sales team does report directly to the director of F&B—to include the banquet operations team as part of the catering and conference services department, also as illustrated and noted in *Diagram 8.1b*. This alternative structure may assist in improving communication, coordination, and the level of engagement between the catering sales and operations teams, ultimately enhancing the experience of conference and banquet guests.

steward:
a non-exempt associate that maintains the cleanliness of food production areas, equipment, china, glass, and service-ware

Food and Beverage Staffing Guides

As outlined in *Chapter 6: Guest Services Operations* and *Chapter 7: Housekeeping and Laundry Operations*, staffing guides must be established to ensure that hotel personnel are properly scheduled to ensure effective and efficient operations—the same principle applies to the F&B division. Staffing allowances must be adequate to ensure that guests needs may be effectively fulfilled; however, targeted F&B contribution margins cannot be achieved if the F&B service and production teams are not scheduled efficiently. Establishing generic staffing guides that may be applied within any

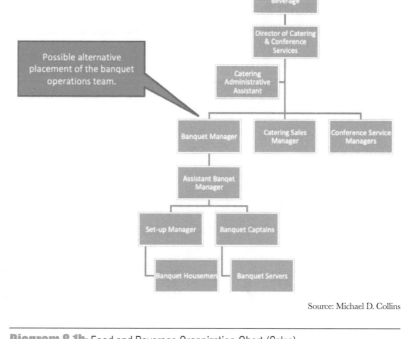

Source: Michael D. Collins

Diagram 8.1b: Food and Beverage Organization Chart (Sales)

hotel F&B setting is difficult due to the many variables that impact F&B staffing—the size and scope of the banquet operation, the number and types of F&B outlets, and the sophistication of the menus delivered to guests, which impact the degree to which items are freshly prepared from scratch in-house. Consequently, F&B staffing guides must be constructed for each component of the F&B operation and these various components are aggregated to identify the overall staffing needs of the operation. Broad guidelines commonly applied when staffing F&B operations are identified in *Table 8.2: General F&B Staffing Guidelines*, whereas a description as to how labor costs are managed within the F&B division are outlined in *Box 8.2: Managing F&B Labor Productivity: Banquet Labor Offsets*.

Fixed, Exempt Staff			
Position	**General guidelines**	**Salary or wage rate[1]**	**Comments**
Director of F&B	Full-time exempt position	$ 87,410	May be combined with the rooms division manager position, serving as an assistant general manager or director of operations, in a smaller property (350-rooms or less).
Assistant Director of F&B	Full-time exempt position	$ 67,720	Optional position in large hotels with substantial F&B operations (500 + guestrooms, multiple outlets, 30,000+ square foot conference center); F&B-director-in-development.
Director of Outlets	Full-time exempt position	$ 67,720	Optional position in large hotels with multiple, high-volume F&B outlets.
Outlet Manager	One or more full-time exempt positions	$ 67,720	Job title may reflect the actual name of the outlet managed (e.g. Bay Street Tavern manager, in-room dining manager, etc.), unless managing multiple outlets; may serve as department chair if three or fewer outlets, in lieu of a director of outlets.
Assistant Outlet Managers	One or more full-time exempt positions	$ 41,240	Again, job title may reflect the actual name of the outlet managed; may be assigned responsibility for multiple F&B outlets for a specific shift or meal period.
Beverage Manager	Full-time exempt position	$ 41,240	Optional position in hotels with a large beverage operation; responsibilities of this position may be performed by an outlet manager or assistant banquet manager in a smaller F&B operation.
Banquet Manager	Full-time exempt position	$ 67,720	Position may be eliminated in a hotel with limited meeting and conference space (10,000 square feet or less); in a small banquet house, banquet operation may be an extension of the outlet operation, overseen by an F&B manager.
Assistant Banquet Manager	One or more full-time exempt positions.	$ 41,240	Typically, a single position, except in a hotel with a very large banquet operation (50,000+ square feet); position may be eliminated in a smaller banquet house (< 20,000 square feet).
Set-Up Manager	Full-time exempt position or hourly supervisor	$ 41,240	Typically, a full-time exempt position; however, the responsibilities may be assigned to the banquet manager, assistant banquet manager, or a non-exempt supervisor in a smaller banquet house.

Position	General guidelines	Salary or wage rate[1]	Comments
Executive Chef	Full-time exempt position	$ 67,720	Often the most highly compensated members of the F&B management team, requiring creativity and culinary knowledge, coupled with strong business management and interpersonal skills.
Executive Sous Chef	Full-time exempt position	$ 58,170	Optional position in large hotels with substantial F&B operations (500 + guestrooms, multiple outlets, 30,000+ square foot conference center); executive-chef-in-development.
Sous Chef	One or more full-time exempt positions	$ 58,170	Number of positions dependent upon the size and scope of the F&B operation, coupled with the design and layout of food production areas; may include a pastry chef if baked goods prepared in-house.
Executive Steward	Full-time exempt position	$ 41,240	Typically, a full-time exempt position; however, the responsibilities may be assigned to a non-exempt supervisor or a sous chef in a small F&B operation.

Non-Exempt, Variable Staff				
Position	General Guidelines	Salary or wage rate[1]	Productivity measure	Comments
Hosts, Greeters, Food Assemblers, Baristas, and Cashiers	Multiple non-exempt positions scheduled per meal period	$12.38	Sales volume ($) per labor hour	Scheduling is dependent upon the number of outlets and corresponding sales volume; food assemblers, baristas or cashiers typically required in grab-and-go and quick service outlets; cashier may also be scheduled during breakfast shift in 3-meal restaurant.
Banquet & Outlet Food Servers	Multiple non-exempt, tipped positions	$13.74	Hours-per-cover	Food servers are typically scheduled based upon the anticipated number of covers, while ensuring minimum coverage. The exact productivity ratio is determined by the style-of-service provided at the banquet event or within the specific outlet.
Bartenders, Barbacks and Cocktail Servers	Multiple non-exempt, tipped positions	$14.80	Beverage-revenue-per-labor-hour	Scheduling is dependent upon the number of beverage outlets and hours of operation for each outlet; banquet bartenders are scheduled by function with bartender fee offsets, as appropriate.

Position	General Guidelines	Salary or wage rate[1]	Productivity measure	Comments
Banquet Housemen	Multiple non-exempt positions	$ 12.73	Banquet-revenue-per-labor-hour (including meeting room rental and set-up fees)	Scheduling is dependent upon the anticipated needs in terms of setting and turning meeting and conference space; a large proportion of the hours are scheduled overnight, because the meeting and conference space must be cleaned and re-set following each day's events, including evening functions, and prior to the next morning's events. Meeting room rental and set-up fees may be charged to offset banquet houseman labor if banquet F&B revenue generated by a set-up is inadequate to meet productivity target.
Culinary, including Food Preparation, Line Cooks, and Bakers	Multiple, non-exempt positions	$ 15.63	Food-revenue-per-labor-hour	Culinary staffing will vary widely. Typically, a minimum fixed staffing level or base-staff is required to operate the kitchen; this will include the culinarians needed to complete routine food preparation work and to provide basic coverage of the food preparation line for the three-meal outlet and in-room dining. Additional variable staffing is then added to cover banquet food preparation needs and outlet food preparation above an established minimum volume.
Stewards	Multiple, non-exempt positions	$ 12.88	Food-revenue-per-labor-hour or hours-per-day	Stewards are scheduled to cover the various dish stations, pots-and-pans-washing areas, and to perform routine kitchen cleaning processes; additional stewarding hours will be scheduled to support large banquet functions and on days with a high volume of food sales.

[1]Actual salaries and wage rates may vary significantly from these national averages, provided by the Bureau of Labor Statistics (BLS; 2018), based upon the size, scope, and service-level of the F&B operation, location of the hotel, and the responsibilities and qualifications of the specific manager or employee. Management salaries displayed are annual amounts per manager; non-exempt wages are per hour, including tips, gratuities, and service charges, where applicable.

Table 8.2: General F&B staffing guidelines

As outlined in *Table 8.1b: Common F&B Expense Levels and Operating Margin*, salaries and wages in the F&B division typically total approximately 30% of F&B revenue, although the precise value will vary based upon a variety of factors. As explained in *Chapter 6: Guest Services Operations* and *Chapter 7: Housekeeping and Laundry Operations*, hotel staff must be carefully scheduled to ensure the effective and efficient operation of the hotel, which is accomplished using staffing guides. A similar process—including the use of staffing guides—takes place within the F&B division.

© Andrey_Popov/Shutterstock.com

Table 8.2: General F&B Staffing Guidelines identifies productivity measures that are commonly used to guide staffing levels for each position within the F&B division. Recall that labor productivity is defined as the amount of work that is accomplished per unit of labor. Within the rooms division, as outlined in *Chapters 6: Guest Services Operations* and *7: Housekeeping and Laundry Operations*, nearly all variable staffing is determined using hours-per-occupied-room (HPOR) as the productivity measure. In the F&B division, a single measure cannot be universally applied. Instead, F&B revenue must be divided, and labor productivity measures applied for each specific position relative to the corresponding amount of food or beverage revenue served by the respective associates. In other words, banquet food revenue, and the corresponding banquet cover counts, must be used to manage the productivity of the banquet associates, while F&B revenue and cover counts for each outlet must be used to determine staffing needs within each corresponding outlet.

If a single kitchen is used to prepare foods for all F&B outlets and banquet functions, then total food sales may be used to identify staffing needs in the food production area; however, if remote kitchens are operated for specific outlets or banquet food preparation, then culinary labor must be evaluated based upon the appropriate portion of food revenue. As an example, assume a hotel operates a single, primary kitchen to support banquet operations, the three-meal restaurant, and in-room dining operation. A second, remote kitchen is operated in the hotel's specialty restaurant, which operates Tuesday through Saturday evening for dinner only. Total food revenue, less food revenue generated by the specialty restaurant, will serve as the basis for scheduling culinary and stewarding labor in the main kitchen, while food revenue generated in the specialty restaurant will be used to schedule and assess culinary and stewarding labor costs that support the specialty restaurant.

Labor Offsets

A hotel F&B operation employs a variety of labor offsets to help manage the cost of providing F&B services to its guests. Labor offsets in a hotel F&B operation come in various forms including gratuities, service charges, direct labor charges, set-up fees, and meeting room rental. Each of these labor offsets is defined below:

- *Tips and gratuities:* The most common form of labor offsets are gratuities. It is customary in restaurants in the United States, including F&B outlets located in hotels that provide table service, for the food servers to be tipped by patrons of the restaurant. This enables the hotel to deduct a tip credit from the food servers' hourly wage rate, provided the employees' total compensation per hour exceeds the federal and state minimum wage. Although the average wage for food servers in the United States is $13.74 per hour (BLS, 2018), in a hotel setting the cost-per-hour incurred by the hotel for employing a food server may be as low as $2.13 per hour, depending upon the amount of the tip credit allowance applied by the hotel; the employer must simply ensure that each server's total wage-per-hour exceeds the federal minimum wage of $7.25, or the state minimum in which the hotel is located, if higher (Nagele-Piazza, 2018).

- *Service charges:* Pricing for banquet functions typically are quoted plus-plus (++), which refers to taxes and service charge. Tax rates on prepared foods are set by the local and state taxing authorities, whereas service charges are set by hotel management at between 18% and 24% of banquet F&B revenue. Banquet food servers are compensated in one of two ways—either at a flat hourly wage, with the service charge retained by the house (which refers to the hotel) to offset all or a portion of the hourly wages paid, or at a lower wage rate, with the service charge being distributed to the banquet food servers. In many hotels, the service charge may be split three ways, between the banquet servers, banquet management, and the house, or a two-way split between the servers and either banquet management or the house. In many states, the hotel (or house) is not legally permitted to retain any service charges, gratuities, or tips that are paid by a client or guest—100% of these payments to the hotel must be distributed directly to the employees. State tax regulations also determine if service charges are subject to sales tax. Hotel management must be aware of regulations related to service charges within the state in which the hotel operates.

- *Direct labor charges:* When a client requests an action-station on a food buffet, such as a meat carving, omelet, or pasta station, the hotel will charge a fee or direct labor charge to cover the cost of the culinary professional that will cover the action station on the buffet line. Another example of a direct labor charge is a bartender fee that may be charged to a client that requests alcoholic beverage service, including cocktails, but the hotel does not anticipate serving a volume substantial enough to cover the cost of the bartender's wages, including the bar set-up and break-down time.

- *Set-up fees* or *meeting room rental:* If a client using a hotel's meeting space fails to generate an acceptable volume of F&B revenue-per-square-foot of meeting space used, or banquet-revenue-per-group room (BRGR), then the client may be charged a set-up fee or meeting room rental; this revenue is intended to cover the cost of banquet housemen to set-up, break-down, and clean the room for the event, as well as to offset any banquet F&B contribution margin lost when meeting space is used for a meeting or event with no or only minimal food or beverage service, which potentially displaces banquet F&B that may have been generated from an alternative group or catered function.

set-up fee:
a fee charged to a client to offset the cost of setting up and breaking down a meeting room

meeting room rental:
a fee charged to a client in exchange for the use of a meeting room or event space

Labor Offsets: An Example

To illustrate how labor offsets impact total F&B labor costs, assume that a "typical" 400-room upper-upscale hotel running an annual occupancy of 74.8% is a 65% group house; in other words, group clients generate 70,985 room nights of the 109,208 room nights sold annually. If $48.73 in BRGR is generated in banquet food revenue alone, then the hotel will enjoy $3,458,790 in banquet food revenue for the year. Assume that this revenue breaks down, in terms of category, average check, and covers, as outlined in *Table 8.3a: Banquet Food, Beverage, and Miscellaneous Revenue*; banquet-related beverage and miscellaneous revenues are also provided.

Table 8.3b: Impact of Labor Offsets (Banquets) provides a breakdown of all banquet-related salaries and wages necessary to generate the $4,122,441 in total banquet F&B revenue. These labor costs do not include the director of F&B, F&B outlet service labor, F&B outlet culinary labor, or conference services and catering sales team salaries, nor are the PT&EB to supplement these wages included; these labor statistics represent the direct labor costs associated only with the preparation and service of banquet food and beverages. For illustrative purposes, all wages, including wages for the banquet service team, are calculated using the hourly wages obtained from the Bureau of Labor Statistics (BLS, 2018) rather than lowering wages to allow for the direct distribution of banquet service charges to the banquet service team; also note that the banquet captains are compensated at a $2.00 per hour premium over banquet servers ($15.74 versus $13.74). Based upon the staffing guides provided, the total direct labor cost required to deliver the $4,122,441 in banquet food and beverage revenue is $1,401,171 in salary and wages, or 34% of banquet F&B revenue.

Table 8.3b: Impact of Labor Offsets (Banquets) also identifies $1,350,084 in labor offsets comprised of $989,386 in banquet service charges, which are assessed at 24% of banquet food and beverage revenue, as well as $360,698 in meeting room rental, set-up, and director labor fees. In this specific example, the labor offsets cover nearly all (96.4%) of the direct labor expense incurred in the preparation and service of banquet food and beverages. Without these labor offsets, labor costs total 34% of banquet F&B revenue; however, as a result of these labor off-set charges, hotel management collects the direct cost of banquet-related labor directly from the hotel's banquet clients.

	Room nights	%		
Transient rooms	38,223	35.0%		
Group rooms	70,985	65.0%	BRGR[1] = $48.73	
Total room nights	109,208	74.8%	Annual occupancy %	
Banquet food revenue:	**Revenue**	**%**	**Average check**	**Covers**
Breakfast	$ 871,521	14.1%	$ 16.37	53,239
Lunch	$ 840,820	13.6%	$ 23.69	35,493
Dinner	$ 456,293	7.4%	$ 32.14	14,197
Reception/breaks	$ 1,290,156	20.9%	$ 14.54	88,732
Sub-total banquet food revenue:	**$ 3,458,790**	**56.1%**	**$ 18.05**	**191,660**
Banquet beverage revenue:	**Revenue**	**%**	**RGR[2]**	
Banquet beverage revenue	$ 663,651	10.8%	$ 9.35	
Sub-total banquet F&B revenue:	**$ 4,122,441**	**66.9%**	**$ 58.07**	
Other F&B banquet-related revenue:				
Banquet service charges[3]	$ 989,386	16.0%	$ 13.94	
Meeting room rental, set-up & labor fees	$ 360,698	5.9%	$ 5.08	
Audio visual & other commissions	$ 372,672	6.0%	$ 5.25	
F&B miscellaneous	$ 319,434	5.2%	$ 4.50	
Sub-total other banquet-related F&B revenue:	**$ 2,042,190**	**33.1%**	**$ 28.77**	
Total banquet-related F&B revenue:	**$ 6,164,631**	**100.0%**	**$ 86.84**	

[1]BRGR represents banquet food revenue per group room night.
[2]RGR represents the corresponding category of revenue per group room night.
[3]Banquet service charges commonly distributed directly to hotel associates through payroll versus being recorded as revenue.

Table 8.3a: Banquet Food, Beverage, and Miscellaneous Revenue

	Hours	Wage rate[1]	Salaries & wages	%[2]	Staffing guidelines	
Banquet management	*exempt*	$ 50,067	$ 150,200	3.6%	Three managers: banquet manager, assistant, & set-up manager (3 FTEs)	
Culinary management	*exempt*	$ 49,922	$ 124,805	3.6%	One-half (½) each of executive chef, executive sous chef, and executive steward, plus one sous chef (2.5 FTEs)	
Management sub-total:	***exempt***	**$ 50,000**	**$ 275,005**	**6.7%**		
Banquet service team:						
Banquet Captains	6,133	$ 15.74	$ 96,535	2.3%	4-hours-per-125-banquet-covers or 0.032 hours-per-cover	
Banquet Food Servers	40,391	$ 13.74	$ 554,967	13.5%	4-hours-per-20-buffet-covers or 15-plated-covers	
Banquet Bartenders	3,792	$ 14.80	$ 56,126	1.4%	4-hours-per-$350-banquet-beverage-revenue (bars only)	
Banquet Housemen	1,612	$ 12.73	$ 20,521	0.5%	32 - 72 hours daily, depending upon scheduled conference activity	
Banquet service team sub-total:	**51,928**	**$ 14.02**	**$ 728,149**	**17.7%**		
Banquet culinary team:						
Cooks & Food Preparation	19,765	$ 15.63	$ 308,919	8.9%	$175-banquet-food-revenue-per-labor-hour	
Stewarding	6,918	$ 12.88	$ 89,098	2.6%	$500-banquet-food-revenue-per-labor-hour	
Culinary & stewarding sub-total:	**26,682**	**$ 14.92**	**$ 398,017**	**11.5%**		
Total banquet salaries & wages (before labor offsets):			**$1,401,171**	**34.0%**	Total salaries & wages excluding PT&EB[4]	
Less labor offsets:				%[3]		
Banquet service charges			$ 989,386	70.6%	24% of banquet F&B revenue	
Meeting room rental, set-up & direct labor fees			$ 360,698	25.7%		
Total labor offsets:			**$1,350,084**	**96.4%**		

[1]Average annual salary or hourly wage rate obtained from the BLS statistics (refer to *Table 8.2*).
[2]Represents percentage (%) of banquet food and beverage revenue for banquet management & service; percentage (%) calculated of banquet food revenue only for culinary management, culinary & stewarding.
[3]Labor offset percentage (%) presents percentage of total banquet salaries & wages.
[4]Payroll Taxes and Employee Benefits.

Table 8.3b: Impact of Labor Offsets (Banquets)

pool gratuities:
the distribution of all
service charges for the pay
period among all banquet
service associates based
upon the proportion of
total hours worked by
each banquet associate

When banquet service charges are distributed directly, the distribution may be distributed to banquet servers, banquet bartenders, and banquet captains based upon the actual functions that each respective associate works; however, it is common in many banquet operations to pool gratuities and distribute all service charges for the pay period among all banquet service associates based upon the proportion of total hours worked by each banquet associate. This ensures that associates are not penalized when scheduled to work a banquet event that generates a smaller gratuity or service charge per-hour-worked; this also simplifies scheduling. One benefit of distributing a portion of banquet service hours to the banquet management team is that it provides incentive pay during very busy times, such as during the holiday party season in early-to-mid-December, when the banquet managers may be required to work long days and extra shifts.

Overall Labor Costs: F&B Division

Again, the typical F&B operation incurs a labor cost of approximately 30% of total F&B revenue. Because catered events are contracted in advance, the labor to prepare and serve banquets may be precisely anticipated and scheduled. Although banquet events are labor-intensive, labor offsets are typically employed to manage the cost of banquet labor, allocating this expense directly to banquet clients, as illustrated above. Labor costs are often more challenging to manage in the F&B outlets where demand is more stochastic—outlet revenue may be estimated but not precisely predicted. In addition, a hotel's restaurant may be scheduled to operate during periods of low demand to support the rooms operation—recall that guests often expect an upper-upscale or luxury hotel to offer the availability of F&B services at their convenience. A room service operation may also be in place to support the guestroom operation, despite its inherent inefficiency, as explained in *Box 8.1: The Future of In-Room Dining*. Although some labor offsets may be employed in the outlets—guests of the hotel's F&B outlets typically tip restaurant food servers an average of 15% to 20% of their total check, and room service employs delivery fees, coupled with automatic service charges—a larger proportion of the hotel's direct outlet labor expense, including management and kitchen labor, will be borne by the hotel. Consequently, although labor offsets substantially lower the cost of labor within the F&B division, covering the lion's share of service labor, overall labor costs in the F&B division are typically 30% of total F&B revenue.

© Marius Pirvu/Shutterstock.com

FORECASTING F&B REVENUE

As has been discussed in previous chapters, including *Chapter 4: Effective Sales and Marketing* and *Chapter 5: Optimizing Revenue*, revenue within the F&B division is forecast using revenue-per-occupied-room ratios, as illustrated to estimate total hotel F&B revenues in *Table 8.1a: F&B Profitability*. Outlet revenues are most commonly forecast based upon outlet-revenue-per-transient-room-night, while banquet revenues are based upon BRGR sold, as illustrated in *Box 8.2: Managing F&B Labor Productivity: Banquet Labor Offsets*. If a significant portion of in-house group guests do not have a meal function scheduled for a specific meal period, these group room nights may be added to the individual or transient travelers in-house to estimate traffic in the restaurant, room service, and other outlets for the corresponding meal period. Alternatively, cover counts may be estimated using capture ratios—or the percentage of in-house guests that are anticipated to use a specific F&B outlet; for example, history may show that 8% of all in-house guests use in-room dining for breakfast. Consequently, in-room dining covers for breakfast may be estimated by multiplying the number of room nights occupied by 0.08 and the corresponding revenue estimated by multiplying the resulting value—the number of covers anticipated—by the amount of the average room service breakfast check.

capture ratios:
the percentage of in-house guests that are anticipated to use a specific F&B outlet

Even outlets that receive a significant proportion of their guest traffic from outside of the hotel may find the use of revenue-per-occupied-room statistics an accurate method of forecasting revenue. Typically, guest traffic within a specific outlet will vary by day-of-the-week and by season; guestroom occupancy also varies by these same day-of-the-week and seasonal factors. Consequently, revenue projections estimated using the relationship between covers or revenue and occupied room nights will often prove to be accurate.

Beverage revenue is most commonly forecast as a percentage of corresponding food revenue. Referring to *Table 8.1a: F&B Profitability*, food revenue for the typical upper-upscale hotel in the United States is $53.94 per occupied room, whereas beverage revenue totals $14.46; this indicates the beverage revenue runs 26.8% (= $14.46 ÷ $53.49) of corresponding food revenue. On an annual basis, the typical 400-room upper-upscale hotel, running 74.8% occupancy, generates $5,890,680 in food revenue and $1,579,148 (= $5,890,680 X 26.8%) in beverage revenue. Beverage ratios as a proportion of food revenue are typically very stable within individual F&B outlets. Beverage revenue may also be forecast on a per-occupied-room basis for a beverage-only outlet, such as a lobby bar, while alcoholic beverage service in the conference and event space is prearranged and included in the catering or group sales contract; therefore, banquet beverage revenue may be forecast based upon the amount of contracted revenue anticipated. Total beverage revenue may be forecast by aggregating the beverage revenue anticipated as a percentage of food revenue in each of the food outlets, plus any anticipated beverage revenue per occupied guestroom for any beverage-only outlets, and contracted banquet beverage amounts.

Accurate forecasting of F&B revenue is critical to the effective management of the F&B division. As discussed in *Chapter 5: Optimizing Revenue*, data availability and quality directly impact forecast accuracy. Fortunately, the data available from the F&B point-of-sale (POS) system, sales management software, and hotel financial statements, enable F&B managers to estimate revenues using an array of statistics, including revenue-per-room-night (transient, group, or total); historical capture ratios within the various F&B outlets; or from catering contracts on-the-books. Accurate forecasts serve as the foundation for staffing each area of the F&B operation to ensure that guests' needs may be effectively and efficiently fulfilled, while also ensuring that associates have the food, beverage, and supplies required.

PRIME COST

prime cost:
the cost of labor, coupled with the cost of food

The cost of labor, coupled with the cost of food, is referred to as the prime cost; in most commercial food service operations, prime cost runs between 55% and 60% of food revenue, with each component accounting for about half of the total prime cost. In other words, labor cost and food cost will each run approximately 30% of food revenue. If an operation uses more highly processed ingredients and food products, then food cost will run a bit higher than 30%, whereas labor costs will run a bit below 30%. If more raw ingredients or less processed food products are used in production, then food cost will run a bit lower; however, more labor will typically be incurred because more food processing will need to take place on-the-premises. The executive chef must determine if it is more cost effective to purchase a more highly processed product (shredded cheese, for example) or to buy a lower cost item (such as a block of cheese) and to then process it (or shred it, in this example) in-house.

In high-end food operations—particularly in luxury hotels—it is often preferred to process food items in-house. For example, marinara sauce may be made in-house in an upper-upscale or luxury hotel versus using a canned or bottled tomato sauce, which may be preferred in an upscale or select-service property. In a similar way, luxury hotels are more likely to operate an in-house pastry shop. Although the cost of raw ingredients to produce breads, pastries, and dessert items, including flour, eggs, fruit, and dairy products, are much less expensive than purchasing freshly baked breads, pastries, and fully-prepared, frozen dessert items, the labor cost necessary to produce breads, pastries, and dessert items in-house will more than offset any savings in food cost. Although the prime cost of many food items prepared in-house may be higher, due to the high cost of labor, food quality must also be considered, as well as the hotel's ability to offset these higher costs with higher pricing. Higher volume operations can also afford to prepare more food products in-house.

Strategies to manage labor costs have already been discussed; however, labor only accounts for approximately half of prime cost. Consequently, controlling COGS is also critical to the financial success of the F&B division.

Food, booze, and money: F&B managers must establish tight control systems to protect these three valuable assets—food, alcoholic beverages, and cash.

CONTROLLING F&B INVENTORIES AND COST OF GOODS SOLD

There is a simple rule in the business of F&B—never trust *anyone* with food, booze, or money. Although the F&B management team works to build a culture of mutual respect and trust, managers and associates alike need food and financial resources to live. Many people also enjoy the consumption of alcoholic beverages, which can be expensive, and may take advantage of weak beverage control systems to pilfer alcoholic beverages. Consequently, these items must be tightly controlled, and processes established to protect these valuable assets.

Restricting Access

All hotel associates must be required to enter and leave the hotel through the employee entrance, which is typically adjacent to the receiving area; the point of egress must be monitored by loss prevention officers and the use of a security camera may be highly effective at deterring losses. The hotel must reserve the right to inspect bags, backpacks, and packages that hotel associates carry out of the hotel when departing; the routine inspection of every associate's bag, backpack, or package—every time, every day—creates an atmosphere of business-as-usual, reducing conflicts that may arise if bags are only inspected randomly.

Deliveries of food, beverage, and other supplies to the hotel should only be permitted during specified time periods, during which a receiving agent or other designated associate must be available to verify deliveries to ensure that all items included on the packing slip are included in the delivery. An industrial scale should be located on the receiving dock so that food products may be weighed upon receipt to verify weights and quantities. Once an order of food, beverage, or other supplies is received and verified, it must be entered into the purchasing or inventory management system and immediately stored. Frozen items must be stored in a secure freezer, refrigerated items in a walk-in cooler, and the remaining food items in a locked dry goods storage room. High cost food items—including premium seafood and beef items—may be secured in a meat or valuables locker within the walk-in cooler or freezer. Alcoholic beverages must be checked in and secured immediately in the beverage storeroom, which typically contains a cooler to store beer and other beverages requiring refrigeration; the beverage manager **must** be involved in the receipt of beverage inventory. Bottles of liquor (e.g. alcoholic beverages other than wine or beer) must be tagged immediately upon receipt and prior to storage with beverage control stickers that identify the bottles as property of the hotel; this ensures that bartenders cannot "sell" their own bottles of liquor to cash-paying guests. The use of a purchasing or inventory management system allows the hotel to maintain a perpetual inventory of food, beverage, and supplies.

meat or valuables locker:
a secured area within a food or beverage storage area for high-cost food and beverage products

Checks and Balances

Responsibility for ordering F&B items, receiving F&B items, completing the monthly inventories, approving invoices, and disbursing payment must be separated among various hotel personnel. This division of duties provides a system of checks and balances to ensure that all F&B products ordered, received, and paid for by the hotel are used to support the hotel's F&B operation. The executive chef is responsible for providing the food specifications—in terms of grade or quality, quantities, level-of-processing, and packaging—which is communicated to the purchasing agent or specified vendor. Many hotel parent companies and management companies establish relationships with external purchasing management firms, such as *Avendra, LLC* (www.avendra.com), and develop an in-house purchasing infrastructure to support the properties that fly their flags or are under their management control, taking advantage of volume pricing to manage the cost of food and other essential operating supplies. Relationships are also established with national food service suppliers, such as *Sysco Corporation* (www.sysco.com) and *US Foods* (www.usfoods.com); the parent or management company often receive rebates based upon volume, minimizing the number of deliveries each week, and for the timely payment of invoices. Direct ACH payment relationships with food vendors also ensures that food costs are accurately reflected on hotel financial statements.

Access to F&B inventories must be tightly controlled; once received, F&B products must be secured and access to these storage areas restricted. Food products needed on the cooking line in the outlets, for processing or distribution through quick-service and grab-and-go outlets, as well as for banquet events, must be requisitioned. As food products are moved from the secured storage areas to the front lines of the F&B operation, they are considered in-process and consumed—no longer part of the hotel's F&B inventory, unless returned to inventory. At the start of each shift, the sous chef overseeing each area of the food production operation requisitions the specific quantity of food products that he/she anticipates will be required during the upcoming shift or meal period; the food products requisitioned will be placed in reach in coolers, refrigerated drawers, and other appropriate locations to provide the culinary team with access only to the food product required to prepare guest meals. Alcoholic beverages needed in food production are requisitioned by the executive chef or executive sous chef, issued by the beverage manager, and stored in a secured alcohol locker.

Outlet bartenders arrive 30 minutes prior to the start of their assigned shift and complete an inventory of their assigned bar; a requisition is then completed to bring the bar up to the established par-level. The par-level includes an adequate inventory of beer, wine, and liquor to accommodate guest demands based upon historical consumption levels during a given shift. Because beer and wine bottles are discarded for recycling as they are consumed, a bottle-for-bottle exchange is not required; however, empty liquor bottles are retained by the bartender and exchanged bottle-for-bottle due to their high value and slower consumption. Banquet bartenders may be scheduled 60 minutes or more prior to the start of beverage service because they must fully assemble and stock their portable banquet bars. Banquet bartenders complete beverage requisitions

division of duties: the requirement that specific duties, including the ordering, receiving, and payment for F&B products, be performed by different hotel associates to prevent theft

par-level: the inventory required of each operating supply

bottle-for-bottle exchange: a policy that requires an empty beverage bottle be provided by the bartender to acquire a replacement bottle based upon the beverages requested by clients; the appropriate beverages are then issued by the beverage manager to each bartender. Over the course of the event, any additional product issued by the beverage manager to support a banquet bar is recorded on the requisition and acknowledged by the bartender; at the end of the evening, any unused alcoholic beverage products are returned to the beverage storage area and recorded by the beverage manager as they are returned to inventory so that the requisition reflects the actual beverage consumption for the event. Wine served in a banquet setting, by banquet food servers, will be requisitioned by banquet management or the assigned banquet captain, who will be held responsible for its service, as well as for returning any unused inventory. It is critical that a minimum of two people confirm the transfer of alcoholic beverages to any area of the hotel—the beverage manager and the associate responsible for the service of the alcohol.

Menu Engineering

© frantic00/
Shutterstock.com

recipe card:
a detailed record of a menu item that includes a photograph of the prepared food item; a list of all ingredients; the cost of each ingredient; a 5% allowance of the total cost of individual ingredients to cover kitchen costs; and a step-by-step description of the item's preparation method

Another key to controlling food cost is to ensure that menus are efficiently designed. In addition to including menu items that produce an adequate sales volume, which reduces spoilage, menus must be designed so that ingredients may be cross-utilized. For example, a 6-ounce boneless chicken breast may be used on the lunch menu for a chicken sandwich, on the dinner menu for a chicken picatta, and on both menus, grilled, sliced, and served on top of a Caesar salad. Items must be priced and laid-out graphically on the menu to produce a favorable mix-of-sales and a reasonable overall food cost percentage. Recipe cards are created that include a photograph of the prepared food item, to ensure the consistency of the presentation; a list of all ingredients in order of inclusion in the recipe; the cost of each ingredient; a 5% allowance of the total cost of individual ingredients to cover kitchen costs, which includes the cost of oils, seasonings, and condiments; and a step-by-step description of the item's preparation method. The recipe card is used to price the menu item, by dividing the total cost of ingredients, including kitchen costs, by the desired food cost percentage; the resulting price may be compared to pricing at competitive restaurants or banquet facilities to ensure that the resulting price provides a value to guests.

As a general rule, higher priced items, such as steaks or seafood, will run a higher food cost ratio, whereas lower priced items, such as pasta dishes or entrée salads, will run a lower food cost ratio; however, it is important to remember that higher or lower food cost ratio may not correspond to the contribution margin generated by a menu item. For example, a steak dinner priced at $32 that runs a 35% food cost generates a gross contribution margin of $20.80 or [$32 – ($32 x 35%)], whereas a pasta primavera dish priced at $18, while only running a 22% food cost percentage, contributes just $14.04 or [$18 – ($18 x 22%)]. A well-engineered menu accounts for a variety of factors, including that fewer higher-priced items and more low-to-moderately priced items will be sold; that higher-priced items can be sold at a higher food cost ratio because the dollar contributed per unit sold will be more (as in the example above); and that a mix of items—over a broad range of prices—may attract a higher proportion of hotel guests to dine in the hotel's restaurant.

Menus are created for each outlet, as well as for banquet operations. Although the executive chef typically spearheads menu production—based upon his/her culinary knowledge, coupled with the capabilities of the food production team—the director of F&B, outlet managers and food servers, catering sales, conference services managers, and banquet managers also provide valuable input. Customized menus may be provided for catering clients—often tested during a client tasting or chef's table event—although these menus must also be costed through the creation of recipe cards to ensure that appropriate COGS are realized. In many organizations, it is increasingly common for hotel parent companies and hotel management firms to produce menus and recipe cards at the corporate level or, at a minimum, provide a database of recipe cards from which affiliated properties may select individual menu items. Many hotel brands require that hotels offer a core menu of select menu items—produced to clearly specified brand standards—to ensure a level of consistency within food operations across all hotels affiliated with the brand; these core menus are often supplemented with signature items that are added at the property level.

client tasting:
a sales technique that allows a potential client to sample various items available on the banquet menu

chef's table:
a sales technique and relationship-building event during which clients watch the chef prepare their meal, which is often served at a table set-up in the kitchen

Potential Food Cost

Once menus have been costed, potential food cost may be estimated by anticipating the quantity of each menu item that will be sold throughout the F&B operation. The POS provides detailed data regarding the menu mix to project the potential food cost; please refer to *Box 8.3: The Point of Sale System: Control Critical* for further detail. Potential or theoretical food cost is the expected total cost of the food ingredients necessary to prepare all food items sold during a specified time period; it is calculated by multiplying the quantities of each menu item sold by the cost of ingredients required to produce the corresponding quantities of each menu item respectively, based upon the costed recipe card. The potential food cost is a financial benchmark that is used to assess the efficiency of food production operations.

menu mix:
the quantities of each menu item sold and the proportion of total food revenue generated by each item

potential or theoretical food cost:
the expected total cost of the food ingredients necessary to prepare all food items sold during a specified time period

Formula 8.1: Potential food cost ratio more clearly defines this calculation:

$$f\% = \frac{\sum cq}{\sum pq} \times 100$$

Where: $f\%$ = potential food cost ratio
c = total cost of ingredients from the recipe card for each menu item sold
p = price of each menu item sold
q = quantity of each menu item sold

Formula 8.1: Potential Food Cost Ratio

beverage cost ratio:
calculated by dividing the cost of the beverage by its retail price

Potential Beverage Cost

Alcoholic beverage sales are divided into three categories: beer, wine, and liquor. The COGS for each category of alcohol vary substantially. The cost of a standard 12-ounce pour of draft beer will generally fall between 15% and 20% of the retail price, whereas the cost of bottled beer, as a percentage of the retail price, will generally be set at approximately 22% to 25%. Wine costs run substantially higher as a percentage of the retail price, generally running between 30% and 40% for a 5 to 6 ounce pour, whereas a standard 1.5-ounce shot of liquor within a cocktail will run in the mid-to-high teens (16% to 19%) as a percentage of revenue.

on-tap:
refers to beer that is served from a keg using a beer glass or mug

house pour wine:
the standard wine served when a specific varietal is ordered by a guest

premium pour wine:
higher priced wines sold to guests using the vintner's label

The potential beverage cost ratio is calculated by dividing the cost of the beverage by its retail price. Retail drink prices are established by category of drink. Because the cost of providing specific beverages within each category varies, sub-categories are also established. For example, draft beers are priced based upon the specific beers that are offered by the hotel on-tap, whereas bottled beers are often sub-categorized and priced as either a domestic beer, which are produced in the United States, or as a higher-priced imported beer; hotels seeking to create more memorable guest experiences often offer a third category of beer—beers produced in local microbreweries. Wine sold by-the-bottle are priced individually, whereas wines-by-the-glass are priced as a house pour or as a premium pour, that typically is marketed to guests using the vintner's label.

well liquor:
a beverage served using the hotel's least expensive brand of liquor

call liquor:
a beverage served using the brand of liquor requested by the guest and priced accordingly

premium liquor:
a beverage served utilizing the hotel's most expensive liquor available for which a higher price is charged

Liquor is generally sub-categorized as well, call, or premium. A well drink is mixed using the hotel's least expensive brand of liquor and is served when the customer has not identified a preference for a specific brand of alcohol; when a guest specifies a specific brand of liquor, the brand called will be provided and priced higher than a similar drink using the well brand. Premium liquors are the most expensive liquor selections available within the hotel—premium liquors are served upon request and require higher pricing to maintain a reasonable beverage cost. Finally, specialty cocktails and signature drinks are priced as appropriate, based upon the cost of the specific ingredients necessary to create the beverage—this sub-category of alcoholic beverages includes cocktails that require more than a standard 1.5-ounce pour of liquor, such as a Long Island iced tea, or other more expensive mixes and garnishes, such as those used in a Bloody Mary, Pina Colada, or strawberry daiquiri. It should be noted that the sale of non-alcoholic beverages—including coffee, tea, soft drinks, fruit juices, bottled waters, and milk—are recorded as food sales and included in the food cost; however, the specialty mixes and garnishes needed to prepare specialty cocktails and signature drinks, as well as virgin (non-alcoholic) cocktails, are recorded on the beverage cost ledger because these costs must be aligned with the corresponding beverage revenue.

The potential or theoretical beverage cost assumes that all drinks sold and served have been accurately prepared and precisely measured to include the appropriate amount of alcohol, mixes, and other ingredients. In other words, the potential beverage cost does not allow for waste or pilferage and serves as a benchmark against which actual beverage cost may be compared. It is calculated by applying the estimated beverage cost ratio for each category of beverage sales—beer, wine, and liquor—to the respective amount of beverage revenue generated within each category.

Formula 8.2: Potential beverage cost ratio more clearly defines this calculation:

$$a\% = \left[\frac{(br_1 + wr_2 + lr_3 + m)}{b + w + l}\right] \times 100$$

Where: $a\%$ = potential alcoholic beverage cost ratio
b = beer revenue
l = liquor revenue
w = wine revenue
m = cost of required mixes and garnishes for beverages sold
r = targeted cost ratio for corresponding category of alcohol
(r_1 = beer cost ratio; r_2 = wine cost ratio; r_3 = liquor cost ratio)

Formula 8.2: Potential Beverage Cost Ratio

Calculating the Actual Cost of Goods Sold

On the final day of each month, at the close of business, an inventory is taken of all food products within the hotel's food storage areas. A separate inventory is taken of all alcoholic beverages, including specialty mixes, within the beverage storeroom and

specialty or signature cocktail:
a mixed drink that requires more than a standard 1.5-ounce pour of liquor, specialty mixes and garnishes, or is served in specialized or commemorative glassware

virgin (non-alcoholic) cocktails:
specialty beverages designed to mimic alcoholic cocktails that do not include alcohol

potential or theoretical beverage cost:
the cost of ingredients for all alcoholic beverages served assuming all drinks are accurately prepared and precisely measured

secured behind all retail and service bars. These inventories represent the closing inventory for food and beverage, respectively. The opening inventory, which is listed as a current asset on the previous month's balance sheet, is the month-end inventory from the previous month. Food purchases and beverage purchases received during the month are each added to the opening inventory for the respective cost ledger—food cost or beverage cost—and the closing inventories, also referred to as ending inventories, are deducted; the resulting values represent the COGS for each respective category of revenue—food cost or beverage cost.

Formula 8.3: Actual Cost of Goods Sold Value and Ratio defines how this value, as well as the corresponding cost ratio, are calculated:

$$COGS = o + p - e$$

$$COGS\% = \left(\frac{COGS}{T}\right) \times 100$$

Where: $COGS$ = Cost of Goods Sold
o = opening inventory
p = purchases
e = closing inventory
$COGS\%$ = Cost of Goods Sold ratio
T = total corresponding revenue (food or beverage)

Formula 8.3: Actual Cost of Goods Sold Value and Ratio

Theoretically, there should be no variance between the potential and the actual food cost or the potential and actual beverage cost; any discrepancy that does exist at month-end must be researched and analyzed by F&B management. Most importantly, corrective action must be taken to address the causes identified. In a well-managed F&B operation, COGS, including month-to-date (MTD) food cost and MTD beverage cost are monitored daily, based upon purchases received MTD and the perpetual inventory system, if available—if a perpetual inventory is not maintained, food cost and beverage cost may be estimated assuming each respective inventory is stable. By monitoring food cost and beverage cost daily, using a daily revenue and control report or online financial dashboard, F&B management, including the executive chef and beverage manager, may take corrective action as soon as a potential problem is identified.

To minimize the likelihood of a discrepancy, F&B products must be tightly controlled, as previously outlined. In addition, food portions must be carefully controlled, while waste and spoilage are minimized. In terms of beverage control, pours must be carefully measured. Alcoholic beverages must be served in the appropriate glassware and the pours accurately measured—12-ounce beers; 5-ounce glasses of wine, which equates to five glasses per standard bottle (750 ml); and 1.5-ounce shots of liquor, or 16 drinks per standard bottle (1/5 or 750 ml). There are a variety of products and techniques that may be employed to ensure that bartenders are measuring and serving alcoholic beverages to patrons—including the use of posi-pours, random bottle counts, and shopping services. The accurate portioning of alcohol served to guests extends beyond merely minimizing the discrepancy between the potential and actual beverage cost, it is also critical to ensuring the alcoholic beverages are served responsibly. Controlling food portions and beverage pours only addresses the cost-side of the equation; it is equally important that all revenue is accurately recorded.

Protecting Revenue

As outlined in *Box 8.3: The Point-of-Sale System: Control Critical*, the POS system is critically important in controlling food and beverage COGS. All F&B associates responsible for food or beverage production must be instructed to only produce a food or beverage product when an order is received through the POS system. In other words, culinary associates must only produce a food item if a chit is received on the POS order printer located on the food production line and a bartender may only draw a beer, pour a glass of wine, or mix a cocktail *after* entering a drink order into the POS system or if a chit is received on the POS printer located behind the bar. This ensures that all F&B revenue is posted prior to production. Please refer to *Box 8.3* for further detail.

chit:
a paper ticket printed by the POS system authorizing the production of a food or beverage product

BOX 8.3: THE POINT-OF-SALE SYSTEM: CONTROL CRITICAL

A POS system is an information system that records the sale of all F&B revenue. Terminals are located throughout the F&B outlets—at each service station—and behind the bar; some systems also employ the use of hand-held terminals. The scope of functions managed by POS systems vary; however, at a minimum, the F&B POS system is used to record customers' F&B orders, to relay the details of each order to F&B production areas, to produce a guest-check that may be presented to guests for payment, and to then process the guests' payments to close the check, whether the check is settled with cash, credit card, as a guestroom charge, or billed to a group or company master account. To facilitate the processing of room charges and

© Aleksei Lazukov/ Shutterstock.com

F&B revenue posted to master accounts, the POS system typically interfaces with the property management system (PMS) in which guestroom accounts and group master accounts are maintained.

As soon as a guest's food or beverage order is taken, the first step is to enter the order into the POS system—this initiates the production of the food or beverage order because a chit, or small slip of paper with the details of the order, will be automatically printed in the appropriate production area, whether that is the hot food line, cold food line, or behind the bar. In some environments, a monitor on the food production line displays the order rather than creating a paper chit. If food production personnel are not permitted to fire-up an order or bartenders permitted to pour or mix a drink without the order being entered into the POS system, management is assured that no food or beverage products will be produced or served without the revenue being posted; this policy must be strictly enforced. When an order is placed within the POS system, a check is created that must be settled by the associate that placed the order, ensuring accountability. If a food order is being re-cooked due to a preparation error, the order still must be entered into the POS system to authorize its production; the check is then settled to an account used to track errors and guest service courtesies.

In addition to posting F&B orders, and expediting their settlement, most POS systems in use today include several F&B cost control features. The cost of producing each menu item may be entered into the system, which allows the system to automatically calculate the potential food cost and potential beverage cost based upon the actual mix of sales, both MTD or for a specified time period. Many POS systems include or interface with purchasing, receiving, and inventory management software, maintaining a perpetual inventory of F&B products in storage; this helps reduce pilferage because actual inventories, particularly of high-cost items, may be spot-checked by F&B management against the perpetual inventory maintained by the POS or inventory management system at any time. These systems may also produce purchasing recommendations, as well as relay orders directly to the hotel's preferred vendors with a few clicks of a mouse.

menu abstract:
provides a detailed listing of the quantities sold of each menu item by date or for a specified time period

The use of a menu abstract, which provides a detailed listing of the quantities sold of each menu item by date or for a specified time period, is a critical tool when evaluating and re-engineering menus. It is also helpful when forecasting revenue or budgeting F&B COGS. Although the needs of meetings and banquet guests are generally communicated via banquet event orders (BEOs), referred to by some hoteliers as banquet prospectuses (BPs), the POS system is used in many hotels to process banquet checks due to the cost control and inventory features associated with many systems. Finally, the POS system may provide essential real-time data regarding F&B revenues and COGS to the enterprise management system, or other accounting systems, including online financial dashboards, which is critical to the successful management of the F&B operation.

Pre-Shift Routines

F&B control procedures contribute to the successful delivery of exceptional customer service—controlling costs and delivering exceptional customer experiences are not mutually exclusive goals. As with other areas of the hotel operation, management must anticipate customer needs and pay meticulous attention to detail. Appropriate pre-shift processes must be executed prior to each meal or service period. Inventories must be checked on the food production lines in advance of each shift to ensure that culinary associates have the necessary food products on-hand—a cook supporting an F&B outlet cannot be expected to requisition additional steaks or seafood items, for example, during the middle of the dinner rush. A bartender, in a similar fashion, must check the beverage inventory behind the bar prior to opening so that the liquor storeroom does not need to be accessed mid-shift. These pre-shift procedures allow access to F&B storage areas to be tightly controlled—controlling costs, while simultaneously ensuring effective guest service.

DELIVERING EXCEPTIONAL GUEST EXPERIENCES

As has been reiterated throughout *Delivering the Guest Experience*, the successful delivery of both effective and efficient services, as illustrated in *Diagram 2.4: Systems Thinking*, begins with the creation and execution of well-designed service processes or linear systems, as well as non-linear systems.

Linear Systems

Service blueprints or process flow-charts must serve as the foundation of standard operating procedures (SOPs), as well as the employee training programs, developed by F&B managers to ensure the consistent delivery of F&B services. Please refer to *Box 8.4: A Service Blueprint of a Dining Experience* for a discussion regarding the design of linear food service processes.

Non-Linear Systems

In addition to linear service processes, non-linear systems must also be in place, such as the use of service standards and continuous feedback loops, to ensure the consistent delivery of exceptional customer outcomes. Recall, as discussed in *Chapter 2: Successful Hotel Management*, that service standards are succinct, clearly stated rules of behavior to be followed by all associates of the firm, designed to ensure that guests receive

BOX 8.4: A SERVICE BLUEPRINT OF A DINING EXPERIENCE

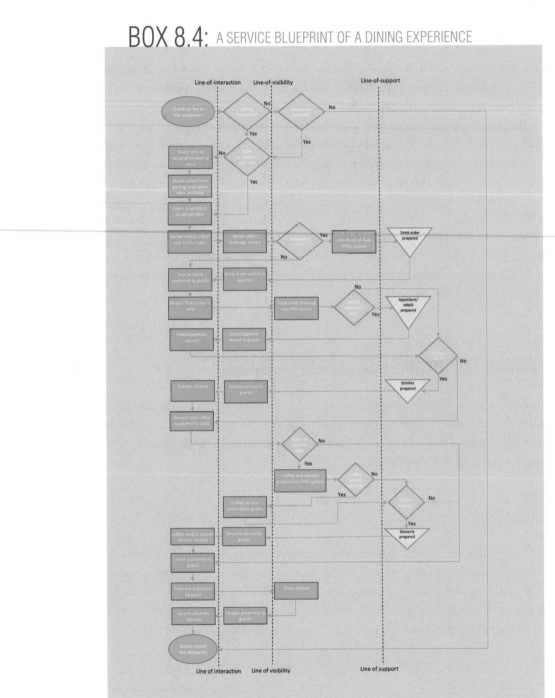

Whether in the hotel's dining room or ballroom, a successful upscale, upper-upscale, or luxury hotel will often serve meals to hundreds, if not thousands, of guests each day. To ensure the consistent execution of these dining experiences, F&B management must thoughtfully design a service process for each F&B outlet and banquet service.

The dining process, typically delivered in an upscale table-service restaurant, is illustrated in *Diagram 8.2: Dining Service Blueprint.* Many of the elements included within this process must be included in any dining experience delivered by the F&B outlets department, including greeting the customer, selling the food order, entering the order into the POS system, delivering the F&B products, collecting payment, clearing the meal following consumption, and thanking the customer; however, the exact steps, and the sequence of the steps, may change. In addition, steps not included in the dining blueprint illustrated may need to be added for "grab-and-go" operations, in which food products are sold, quickly prepared, and packaged for carry-out. Therefore, a separate blueprint is typically required for each outlet.

Service processes may also need to be modified by meal period. For example, while it is customary to present guest checks for payment after the complete meal has been delivered and consumed by guests during the evening meal period, as illustrated in *Diagram 8.2*, it is not uncommon for guest checks to be presented immediately following the delivery of the food, prior to its consumption, during breakfast service. To further expedite breakfast service, buffet service may be offered because the morning meal period is typically the hotel's busiest. A cashier stationed at the entrance to the restaurant may also process guest payments during the breakfast period, while servers process guest payments during lunch and dinner service. The key is to ensure that the process is carefully planned—for each outlet and each meal period—with the guest's convenience in mind.

In a banquet setting, individual guest orders are not taken, but meals are pre-arranged by the client and a menu pre-selected. In addition, payment arrangements are made in advance of the function and a guaranteed guest count is provided to the hotel, typically 72 hours in advance. The production of the meal is authorized through the kitchen's receipt of a BEO or BP from which a guest check is produced and presented to the client. Consequently, the service blueprint for the execution of a banquet meal may be simplified, relative to the flow-chart provided in *Diagram 8.2*, because it will not include the sales processes or the entry of individual orders into the POS system; however, service blueprints for commonly executed banquet service styles—buffet; plated with pre-set salads or desserts; and full, multiple-course plated meal service—should be developed.

A service blueprint is a valuable management tool, ensuring a service process is clearly defined, efficiently designed, and consistently executed by associates to deliver positive guest experiences. It is an excellent training and diagnostic tool, serving as the foundation for developing effective SOPs.

consistent, memorable experiences; examples of service standards are outlined in *Chapter 6: Guest Services Operations,* and include such items as the 20/10 rule, striving for five, using the phrase "my pleasure," escorting guests to their requested destination, and expressing appreciation. Service standards must be consistently applied in all areas of the hotel, including the F&B division, by reinforcing the standards during pre-shift line-ups as well as by holding associates accountable for executing the standards while performing their duties. Virtuous feedback loops must be designed to solicit guest feedback on F&B operations, including the availability of F&B services, F&B quality, menu selection, service execution, pricing, and guests' perceptions of the value delivered by the F&B division. Management must analyze customer feedback, respond appropriately, and adjust F&B operations, based upon the feedback received from guests, to ensure continuous improvement within the F&B division.

F&B Outlets

banquet event order (BEO) or banquet prospectus (BP): a printed or electronic document that fully details the needs of a client for a meeting, banquet, or event to include the space assigned and set-up required; style-of-service; food menu; beverage requirements; and any additional client needs, including audio-visual

Providing exceptional guest service in the F&B outlets requires accurate forecasting so that guest demands may be anticipated; this allows the outlet managers to appropriately staff the service team and the outlet sous chef to properly schedule food production personnel, while also stocking the food production lines with ample inventory to meet guest needs. A pre-shift line-up must be held to review service standards; introduce any special menu items available to guests; discuss the anticipated flow and volume of business, based upon hotel occupancy and groups in-house; and to assign service stations and side-work responsibilities. Employee incentive programs, guest feedback, and other topics relevant to outlet operations may also be discussed at this time; it is also the ideal time to ensure that grooming and uniform standards are being maintained by associates. As previously discussed, the bartender must also complete a pre-shift beverage inventory prior to the start of any shift during which alcoholic beverage service will be offered to ensure that an adequate par of alcoholic beverages is on-hand to accommodate anticipated demand.

Banquet Operations

Conference services and catering sales managers communicate the needs of meetings and banquet guests using BEOs, also commonly referred to as BPs. A separate BEO is completed for each scheduled function. There are five sections on a banquet event order. The first section, typically included as a header or footer on the page, includes the basic information regarding the group or organization hosting the event, including the name of the client, company, or organization; the name of the primary hotel contact; the address; telephone; email; and billing instructions. The remainder of the form is divided into quadrants with each of the four quadrants including specific information, as outlined below:

1. *Room set-up requirements:* The first, upper-left-hand quadrant, directed to the banquet set-up team, includes details regarding the meeting room set-up; number of seats; table or seating configuration; linen specifications; and any additional client needs, such as a dance floor, staging, pipe-and-drape, head tables, buffet lines, etc. A diagram may be included, as necessary.

2. *Banquet service requirements:* The second, upper-right-hand quadrant will include all details the banquet managers require to support or properly serve the function. This will include the style-of-service (e.g. plated meal, buffet meal, hand-passed hors d'oeuvres, pre-set salads or desserts, etc.) as well as any beverage needs, including a cash or host bar, service of wine with dinner, etc. The pricing of the function may also be provided within this quadrant of the BEO.

3. *Menu and food production requirements:* The third, bottom-left-hand quadrant will include all food production requirements, including the complete menu; the anticipated guest count will often be re-stated within this section, particularly if there is a split menu (e.g. 400 total guests, 250 beef and 150 seafood). This section provides the executive chef and culinary management team with the details regarding the food that must be prepared to successfully execute the function, including hors d'oeuvres, appetizers, entrées, and desserts.

4. *Additional requirements:* Any additional details regarding the event, particularly those provided by outside vendors, such as audio-visual requirements, floral or other centerpieces, and any additional information not included elsewhere on the BEO may be provided in this fourth, bottom-right-hand quadrant.

The director of catering or conference services will typically hold a minimum of two BEO review meetings per week to review scheduled functions for the upcoming week. Although BEOs contain approximate guest counts, banquet clients are typically required to provide a guarantee 72 hours prior to an event. Once a guaranteed count is provided to the hotel, the client is contractually obligated to pay for the number of guests guaranteed, even if fewer guests partake in the meal, although the client is invoiced for guests above the guaranteed count. As a result, the hotel must be prepared to serve an additional 10% of the number of guests guaranteed because savvy meeting planners tend to underestimate the guarantee. During BEO meetings, guarantees are provided for functions within the 72-hour window; this is also the ideal time for the culinary and banquet management teams to seek clarification regarding any information provided or details that may not be adequately specified on a BEO. For complex, multi-day conferences, the conference service manager servicing the group may also schedule a pre-convention meeting during which the conference

BEO review meeting: a gathering of the managers and supervisors involved in the execution of meetings, banquets, and events with the catering and conference sales team to review and plan for upcoming functions

guarantee: the number of guests a client anticipates will participate in a scheduled banquet, meeting, or event

pre-convention meeting: a meeting held with a client, conference services manager, and key hotel managers to review the client's expectations and prepare for the group's conference

details, including BEOs, are reviewed with the hotel management team while the client is present; this allows the client to clarify the group's expectations directly with the operations management team that will be executing their conference or event.

Responsible Sale of Alcoholic Beverages

The sale of alcoholic beverages represents a potential liability for a hotel operator and its ownership. Dram shop laws, which are in place in 48 of the 50 States and two US territories, allow employees that serve alcohol, hotel managers, and the ownership of the hotel with an on-premise liquor license to each be held personally liable for the injury or death of any person resulting from the service of alcoholic beverages to persons under the age of 21 years, patrons served to the point of intoxication, or guests that are served alcohol that appear intoxicated at the time of service. Consequently, management has a responsibility to train all associates assigned the responsibility of serving alcoholic beverages in the responsible service of alcohol. Several programs are available, including *ServSafe* (www.servsafe.com/ServSafe-Alcohol) and *TIPS* (www.gettips.com/index.html), to provide this instruction to F&B employees, which provide turnkey training solutions, including assessments and certification of associates. Training must be completed on a routine, quarterly basis, and responsible service should be continually reviewed during the daily pre-shift employee line-ups with alcohol-serving associates. Accurately measuring pours, and posting drinks within the POS system, not only help control the beverage cost, but also allow beverage-serving associates to track the amount of alcohol that is being consumed by each guest to prevent associates from over-serving guests. By responsibly serving alcohol, hotel associates help ensure that guests leave the property with only positive memories of their hotel experience.

dram shop laws: allow employees that serve alcohol, hotel managers, and the ownership of the hotel with an on-premise liquor license to each be held personally liable for the injury or death of any person resulting from the service of alcoholic beverages to persons under the age of 21 years, patrons served to the point of intoxication, or guests that are served alcohol that appear intoxicated at the time of service

CHAPTER SUMMARY

F&B operations are a critical element of a successful hotel operation, particularly in an upper-upscale or luxury hotel environment, providing a hotel with "personality"—critical to delivering memorable guest experiences that enhance customer loyalty. The scope of a typical F&B operation includes F&B outlets, the banquet department, and the food production or culinary department, which is supported by the stewarding department. Although the profitability of the F&B division varies widely, based upon the size and scope of the F&B operation, a well-managed, high-volume operation in an upper-upscale hotel typically generates a departmental operating margin of approximately 30% of total F&B revenue, potentially adding millions of dollars to the bottom-line of an upper-upscale or luxury hotel. Although the profit generated by the F&B division is often substantial, optimizing profit is not the sole goal of management—the F&B operation must, first-and-foremost, support the rooms operations, which drives the overall profitability of the hotel. The availability of quality F&B services within a hotel allows the property to optimize guestroom revenue by positively impacting occupancy, ADR, and RevPAR. Controlling prime cost, which consists of COGS and labor costs combined, is critical to achieving financial success—prime cost typically runs just under 60% of food revenue; however, maintaining tight cost controls and delivering exceptional customer experiences are not mutually exclusive goals.

A well-managed F&B operation ensures that guest needs are anticipated by management, which allows F&B inventories to be effectively managed and staff to be efficiently scheduled; this, in turn, results in effective service execution. The use of linear systems, driven by well-designed service processes, coupled with the non-linear systems, including service standards, pre-shift line-ups, and virtuous feedback loops, allow F&B associates, led by the director of F&B, to consistently deliver memorable experiences and value to guests.

KEY TERMS AND CONCEPTS

action-station	barback	chef's table
assistant food server (or busser)	bartender fee	chit
baker	bartender	client tasting
banquet captain	BEO review meeting	closing inventory
banquet cook	beverage cost ratio	cocktail server
banquet event order (BEO) or banquet prospectus (BP)	beverage manager	convention service manager
	bottle-for-bottle exchange	direct labor charge
banquet houseman	call liquor	director of F&B
banquet manager	capture ratio	director of outlets
banquet server	cashier	division of duties

dram shop laws	meeting room rental	prime cost
executive chef	menu abstract	recipe card
executive sous chef	menu mix	saucier
executive steward	on-tap	service charge
food runner	opening inventory	set-up fee
food server	outlet or restaurant managers	set-up manager
garde manger	par-level	short-order cook
gratuities	pastry chef	sous chefs
grill	plus-plus (++)	specialty or signature cocktail
guarantee	pool gratuities	steward
host	potential food cost	turning meeting, function or
house pour wine	potential or theoretical beverage cost	banquet space
labor offsets	potential or theoretical food cost	virgin (non-alcoholic) cocktail
lead cooks	pre-convention meeting	well liquor
line cooks	premium liquor	
meat or valuables locker	premium pour wine	

DISCUSSION QUESTIONS

1. Discuss how a successful F&B operation may contribute to the hotel's ability to serve key stakeholders, including hotel guests, associates, investors, and the local community.
2. Draw an organization chart for a typical F&B operation within an upper-upscale hotel; explain the role of each manager within the F&B division.
3. Explain how the F&B division potentially serves as the "personality" of a hotel property; identify the specific components of the F&B operation or factors that define the hotel's personality.
4. Identify ways in which the F&B division supports the guestroom operation; how does this impact the hotel's key result indicators, including occupancy, ADR, and RevPAR?
5. What is the "typical" departmental profit for the F&B division? What is prime cost? What does the prime cost, and the two primary components of prime cost, typically run in a commercial food service operation?
6. Explain how a hotel's F&B operation is staffed. What factors are used to determine staffing levels within each department within the F&B division? What is a labor offset? Provide specific examples of labor offsets and explain the purpose of each.
7. Based upon the month-by-month and annual hotel occupancy identified in *Table 7.3: Hotel Occupancy and Housekeeping Staffing by Month*, forecast F&B revenues, including outlet food revenue (assume a single three-meal outlet), banquet food revenue, outlet beverage revenue, banquet beverage revenue, and miscellaneous F&B revenues. Assume a 70%/30% group-to-transient ratio. Explain your methodology.
8. Explain how to calculate potential food cost and actual food cost. Identify potential causes of discrepancies between the two values.

9. Identify the typical COGS for the different categories of alcoholic beverages. Explain how to calculate potential beverage cost and actual beverage cost. Identify potential causes of discrepancies between the two values.

10. What is menu engineering? How is it used in a hotel setting? Explain factors that should be considered when creating an outlet food menu.

11. Identify linear processes and non-linear systems established to ensure guest experiences that consistently exceed customers' expectations within the F&B division. Discuss the application of these systems in the outlets, banquet, and food production area.

12. Why is the responsible service of alcohol important? Identify key strategies that must be employed to ensure the responsible sale of alcoholic beverages.

ENDNOTES:

Bignewsnetwork.com (2013). Room service comes to an end at New York Hilton. (2013, November 16). Big News Network.Com (Dubai, United Arab Emirates). Retrieved from https://login.ezproxy.fgcu.edu/login?url=http://search.ebscohost.com/login.aspx?direct=true&db=edsnbk&AN=14A1F3A7B6BA6810&site=eds-live

Bureau of Labor Statistics (2018). *Occupational Employment and Wages, May 207.* Accessed online November 16, 2018 at: https://www.bls.gov/oes/2016/may/naics3_722000.htm#00-0000.

Nagele-Piazza, L. (2018). Can employers pay tipped workers less than minimum wage? Check federal and state requirements first. Society for Human Resource Management website. Accessed online November 16, 2018 at: https://www.shrm.org/resourcesandtools/legal-and-compliance/employment-law/pages/tipped-workers-minimum-wage.aspx

STR (2017). *Host report: Upper-upscale hotels for year-ending 2015.* SHARE Center.

HOTEL DEVELOPMENT PROJECT: ASSIGNMENT 5: DEFINING THE F&B CONCEPT: OUTLETS AND SERVICES:

<u>*Uses content from:*</u> *Chapter 4: Effective Sales and Marketing; Chapter 5: Optimizing Revenue;* and *Chapter 8: Food and Beverage Operations.*

Based upon the brand and chain-scale of the proposed hotel, define the scope of the F&B operation; create a departmental profit and loss statement for the F&B operating division.

The scope of the F&B operation should include the following:
1. A list of each F&B outlet or service that will be available to guests (e.g. breakfast room with buffet-line and seating for 50 guests; a three-meal restaurant; 35-seat lobby lounge; etc.). Students are encouraged to get creative and name or assign themes to the various outlets, as appropriate.
2. The types of items and price range of F&B products made available on the menu of each F&B outlet by meal period.
3. The total square footage of meeting space and the break-down of this space (e.g. 40,000 square feet (sf) of total meeting and function space, including a 12,000-sf ballroom; a 8,000-sf junior ballroom; 10,000 sf of break-out rooms, and 10,000 sf of pre-function space).

In addition, an F&B profit and loss statement should be generated for each of the first 12 months of the hotel's operation, including the annual total, in an Excel format that includes the following:
1. The covers, average check, and revenue for each F&B outlet; use a covers-per-occupied-transient guestroom as the basis for forecasting covers.
2. The BRGR and corresponding banquet revenue forecast each month; students are encouraged to use a separate BRGR for weekday and weekend groups.
3. Beverage revenue, broken down between outlet beverage and banquet beverage, for each month and for the year.
4. F&B COGS, which will be forecast as a percentage of revenue.
5. F&B division payroll expenses, by position, including hours, wage, or salary rates, and total wages. Include an additional 35% of total salaries and wages for PT&EB costs. For each position, identify if staffing is determined based upon a fixed or variable staffing level and include at least one productivity factor used for any positions that are variably staffed. Calculate the number of associates or full-time equivalents anticipated to be employed within the F&B division.
6. Other expenses for the F&B division, which may be forecast as a percentage of revenue based upon the scope of the F&B operation and chain-scale of the brand selected.
7. F&B division departmental profit or contribution margin, as a dollar amount and as a percentage of hotel revenue.

Chapter 9
Resort Operations

The focus of this chapter are the unique characteristics of a resort lodging operation, typically located at a beach, golf course, racquet sport, or mountain location. This chapter explores the variety of accommodation types and ownership structures, which creates a different dynamic between ownership and lodging management, as well as the characteristics unique to many resort communities, including their impact on resort operations. A brief discussion regarding the marketing and operations of many resort recreational amenities—including golf and spa operations—is included.

PURPOSE AND LEARNING OBJECTIVES:

Although many day-to-day operational functions are identical, whether in a traditional commercial hotel or resort environment, managing a hotel in a resort setting presents several unique challenges. After reading this chapter, the reader will be able to do the following:

- Identify the different types of lodging commonly available in a resort setting, explaining how they differ from traditional hotel accommodations.
- Describe the various recreational facilities provided in resort contexts.
- Explain the similarities and differences between marketing and operating a hotel as compared to a recreational facility or amenity, such as a golf course, mountain resort, theme park, or spa.
- Identify specific characteristics of resort destinations that impact the successful operation of a resort hotel, explaining strategies that may be employed to manage each challenge presented.

Unlike a traditional commercial hotel, located in an urban, sub-urban, or airport environment, guests are attracted to resort destinations to engage in recreational and leisure activities; resort attractions may include a beach; golf and racquet sports; mountain-based activities, including skiing, snowboarding, and adventure activities; or theme parks. Although many of a resort hotel's day-to-day operational processes are the same as in any hotel operation, many lodging operations within a resort environment contain a wider variety of accommodation types and ownership structures, which creates a different dynamic between ownership and management. A brief discussion of the marketing and operations of resort recreational amenities—including golf and spa operations—is included. Finally, the unique characteristics of resort communities create additional challenges that may be encountered by managers working in a resort setting. This chapter explores these challenges.

TYPES OF LODGING IN A RESORT SETTING

A wide variety of lodging operations may be found in a resort setting, including traditional hotels, condominium hotels, vacation rentals, and vacation ownership resorts. Outlined below are descriptions of the various types of lodging options guests may encounter in a resort setting.

Traditional Hotels Versus Destination Resort Hotels

Traditional hotels are common in resort environments. Many of these hotels refer to themselves as a resort, as opposed to a hotel, simply because the property is located in a resort area or market. Because there are no restrictions on the use of the term *resort*, the term is not consistently applied, which often causes confusion among guests. Some self-proclaimed resort properties may be luxury, upper-upscale, or upscale hotels offering a range of peripheral services, including spa and food and beverage (F&B) services, whereas others may be select, limited-service, or even economy hotels providing only overnight accommodations.

> **traditional hotel:**
> a lodging property of any class or service-level that offers overnight accommodations owned by single ownership group or investor

A destination resort hotel is a large property designed to be a self-contained escape from the outside world. Once guests arrive at a destination resort hotel, guests do not need to leave the premises to accomplish the objectives motivating the trip. Destination resort hotels are often 1,000+ room properties with a wide-variety of room types, and often offer multiple service levels (e.g. traditional, upper-upscale hotel rooms, as well as luxurious resort suites or bungalows providing a higher level of personalized service). Destination resort hotels contain a variety of F&B outlets, offering various cuisines and service levels, in addition to recreational and wellness facilities. Multiple pools, often including water slides, a splash park, and an adults-only pool; live entertainment venues; lush landscaping; a full-service spa and salon; a game arcade; and multiple retail shops characterize a destination resort hotel. A large conference center that may include a wedding-pavilion and multiple outdoor event venues is also available to accommodate meetings, conferences, and social events. Destination resort hotels employ an activity staff that provide a full schedule of activities for hotel guests, including children's programs. Finally, a destination resort hotel may also operate a recreational facility, such as a championship golf course or racquet club, or provide its guests with preferred access to an adjacent or nearby recreational facility. An example of a destination resort hotel is the *Hilton Waikoloa Village* (www.hiltonwaikoloavillage.

> **destination resort hotel:**
> a large property designed to be a self-contained escape from the outside world offering a full-range of services including overnight accommodations, food, beverage, conference, and recreational services

com) or the *Atlantis Resort* on Paradise Island in the Bahamas (www.atlantisbahamas. com), pictured on the previous page.

Resort Communities

Many resort hotels and alternative forms of resort lodging are in resort communities. A resort community is a collection of private residences and businesses, with a focus on recreational activities, that form a cooperative in which all property owners must participate to promote and support the common interests of the community. A resort community is often a gated community that includes a variety of recreational amenities, such as a golf course or racquet club, beachfront, hotel, condominiums, villas, or single-family residences; many resort communities also include a village area with restaurants and retail shopping. The property owners form a property owners association (POA) that is governed by a board of directors, elected by the property owners. Many of the major businesses in the community, such as a hotel or a retail shopping facility, may have a permanent seat on the board. The POA assesses monthly or quarterly dues that are used to operate and maintain the community, which often includes providing security services, road maintenance, common area landscaping services, a resort shuttle or other transportation services, and marketing to the community. Commercial members of the POA may be assessed higher fees.

Unlike a private lifestyle community, which restricts access to the community—including its recreational amenities—to property owners and their guests, a resort community allows public access. Consequently, a resort community may support a wider array of businesses than a private residential lifestyle community. In addition, outside guests that support the businesses within the resort community, in effect, subsidize the lifestyle of the resort's private residents and property owners. Although some of the community's residents may reside year round in the resort, many of the property owners are part-time residents or simply vacation in the resort annually and place their condominium, villa, or home in the rental pool when they are not using their residence personally. Many resort communities require property owners that are seeking to rent out their residences to visitors to use a specified property management firm that operates exclusively within the resort, allowing the resort to have more control and background information regarding visitors staying within the community.

An example of a resort community is *Palmetto Dunes Oceanfront Resort* on Hilton Head Island in South Carolina. Explore their website at www.palmettodunes.com to learn more about resort communities, paying particular attention to the interactive map, which provides a list of all services offered at the resort. The community is home to two upper-upscale hotels—the *Marriott Resort & Spa* and the *Omni Hilton Head Oceanfront Resort*. The community also offers oceanfront condominiums, as well as con-

resort community:
a collection of private residences and businesses, with a focus on recreational activities, that form a cooperative to support common interests

private lifestyle community:
a resort community that restricts access to the community and its amenities to property owners and their guests

rental pool:
privately owned condominiums, villas, or homes that are made available as vacation rentals by outside residents

dominium rentals above the retail shops and restaurants that surround the resort's *Shelter Cove Marina,* through the resort's property management company *Sand Dollar Management,* in addition to golf villas and private home rentals. The resort boasts three 18-hole championship golf courses, a racquet club, and two spas—one located within each of the hotels on property. Boat rentals, fishing charters, and boat tours are available through the marina and there are multiple restaurants, including the *Dunes House Oceanfront Bar & Grill,* on the premises. The shops and restaurants around *Shelter Cove Marina* may be accessed by the public directly from the Island's primary highway, whereas the oceanside of the resort may only be accessed by residents, property owners, and the resort's overnight guests through a security gate. The resort also has its own fire station located on property for the safety of residents and guests.

The two hotels within *Palmetto Dunes Resort* are examples of two different types of resort hotels. The *Marriott Resort & Spa* is a traditional hotel, operated by a hotel management firm and branded through a franchise agreement with *Marriott International.* Although the *Omni Hilton Head Oceanfront Resort* is operated by a branded management company, *Omni Hotels & Resorts,* this Hilton Head Island property was originally developed as a condominium hotel, named *Mariner's Inn* at *Palmetto Dunes Resort* when it initially opened. To secure the funding necessary to develop the hotel, each of the hotel's 323 guestrooms were sold to individual investors. To purchase a unit, the owners were required to sign a contract that committed their unit to the rental pool managed by the manager of the hotel—a practice referred to as required pooling. This allows the manager of the property to operate the hotel as a traditional hotel because the hotel management firm has control of the hotel's guestrooms and public areas, as opposed to the individual unit owners; the revenue received from guests are pooled and split evenly among the various property owners, as opposed to being tracked by individual unit and distributed to each unit's specific owner. This structure also allows the hotel manager to manage the capital expenditure program for the entire property, which ensures that all guestrooms are adequately maintained and renovated to keep the quality of accommodations consistent, benefitting all investors.

> **condominium hotel:**
> a lodging operation in which the title to each individual hotel room or lodging unit is separately held

> **required pooling:**
> a condominium hotel in which owners are required to give control of their individual units to the management company hired to manage the property

Vacation Rentals and the Sharing Economy

One of the challenges with condominium, villa, or home rentals through a property management company, commonly referred to as vacation rentals within a resort setting, is often the inconsistency of the accommodations. Because each individual property owner is typically responsible for maintaining their individual unit, some of the rental properties may be well-appointed and impeccably maintained, whereas other resort residences within the same building or community may contain outdated furnishings or be poorly maintained. Housekeeping services are also not typically provided daily and peripheral services—such as valet parking, luggage assistance,

> **property management company:**
> a company employed by a property owner to rent, manage, and maintain a real estate asset

> **vacation rental:**
> a privately-owned condominium, villa, or home that may be rented by visitors for short-term visits of less than 30-days

concierge and business services, and on-premise F&B services—may not be available. As a result, condominiums, villas, and single family homes are often rented at prices that are well below the cost of renting a traditional hotel guestroom, particularly when considering that condominiums, villas, and vacation homes often contain multiple bedrooms, plus living and dining areas supported by fully-equipped kitchens within each unit. Consequently, the rental of private residences provides an excellent value and a viable lodging alternative for families and other large parties seeking to spend time together in a resort setting.

In recent years, the marketing of vacation rentals through online services such as *Airbnb* (www.airbnb.com), *Couchsurfing* (www.couchsurfing.org), *Flipkey* (www.flipkey.com), *HomeAway* (www.homeaway.com), and *Vacation Rental by Owner* (*VRBO;* www.vrbo.com) have risen in popularity in both resort and urban markets. Referred to as peer-to-peer rentals or the sharing-economy, these online services allow homeowners, or even renters with a lease on a property in some cases, to offer their entire residence or a room within their residence to travelers seeking overnight accommodations. Exclusive use of the entire residence for the requested nights may be contracted or the guest may contract to cohabitate the residence, merely contracting to use a bedroom within the home, staying as a guest simultaneously while the homeowner or leaseholder is also in the home. Although many hoteliers initially expressed alarm with the rising popularity of online booking sites and home rentals, the impact on upper-end hotels has been minor. Research shows that rentals through *Airbnb*, for example, have minimal impact on upper-upscale and luxury hotels—particularly those that cater to business travelers; the online rental of private residences primarily impact economy and midscale hotels. Furthermore, the impact is greatest during periods of high demand (Zervas, Proserpio, & Byers, 2017). In other words, many travelers turn to these online services when traditional hotels are sold-out or as a lower-cost alternative to a hotel stay.

The short-term rental of condominiums and vacation homes has always been popular in resort markets. Online services are merely an alternate way to market and facilitate condominium and home rentals; however, these services raise several challenges that must be addressed by the homeowner using the service, as well as the communities in which these short-term rentals take place. First, overnight guests must be provided with access to the unit, which can be arranged through the rental management office when a property is managed by a professional property management firm. Units must also be cleaned and inspected for pilferage or property damage following the guests' departure; this may be challenging for an absentee property owner that does not live in proximity to the vacation rental property to arrange. Many peer-to-peer vacation rental websites allow property owners to establish their own advance payment, cancellation, and security deposit policies, in addition to cleaning fees, which may cause confusion with overnight guests because these policies are often not consis-

peer-to-peer rentals or sharing-economy: the marketing and contracting of short-term, overnight real estate rentals through online services

tent property-to-property or stay-to-stay, even when the traveler uses the same site to book the accommodations. Peer-to-peer rentals also raise many concerns for neighbors and local officials.

Hotels must comply with specific regulations designed to ensure guest safety. They are equipped with life-safety systems—including fire alarms, sprinklers, and pressurized fire escape stairwells. Emergency instructions and evacuation routes are posted on the back of guestroom doors and hotel staff trained to respond in a variety of emergency situations are on the premises 24 hours per day. Vacation rentals are not required to comply with these same safety regulations. In a hotel, guest service staff collect positive identification from hotel guests upon registration and respond if a guest is creating a disturbance. Neighbors are typically unaware of the specific identity of guests that are renting a neighboring residence through an online service and, if inconvenienced by a disturbance, may be forced to get local law enforcement involved to avoid taking the matter into their own hands.

Hotels also collect hotel occupancy taxes, which may be used to market tourism or support the community's tourism infrastructure, such as a destination marketing organization (DMO) or convention center. Many communities are now requiring online booking-websites to collect and remit local occupancy taxes on short-term rentals facilitated through their sites to address this concern. Finally, many communities are concerned with the impact of short-term rentals on the cost of housing within their respective communities. Property owners can often generate more rental revenue by renting their property on a short-term basis through the sharing economy or a vacation rental property management firm, as opposed to renting it to a tenant through a long-term lease. The math is simple—$2,000 per week versus perhaps just $1,750 per month, for example. As a result, many communities are now restricting the number of nights a private residence may be rented on an annual basis to minimize the impact of short-term rentals on the cost of housing within the market (Lazo, 2015), although this type of restriction may be less likely to occur in a resort market. *Box 9.1: The Challenge of Regulating Short-Term Vacation Rentals* discusses the importance of appropriately regulating and inspecting short-term vacation rentals, particularly in terms of guest safety, while ensuring the collection of appropriate taxes from visitors within a resort environment.

© John Wollwerth/Shutterstock.com

Many families and others traveling on a budget find renting a vacation home a cost-effective alternative to staying in a full-service hotel or resort. Although such accommodations may not offer the same level of personalized service, the ability to prepare meals in a fully-equipped kitchen and convene in the living room or on the patio of an oceanfront beach home far outweigh the inconvenience of carrying one's own luggage or forgoing hotel room service; however, it is important that local communities appropriately regulate short-term rentals to ensure guest safety and that overnight visitors contribute their fair-share toward supporting the local community.

In 2007, seven college students were tragically killed by a fire that consumed their vacation rental during a weekend trip to Ocean Isle Beach, North Carolina. Six students escaped the blaze with only minor injuries by jumping from the home that was elevated one-story above the ground-level, which may have contributed to the rapid spread of the fire (Scott & O'Connor, 2007). Although the cause of the fire was not initially known, it is known that, although the home had working smoke detectors, the vacation rental was not protected by a sprinkler system—no death has ever occurred as the result of a fire in a building that is fully-protected by a fire sprinkler system. Many of the students had consumed alcohol the previous evening; in 60% of college student deaths caused by fires, at least one student had consumed alcohol the previous evening, with 40% of deadly fires occurring between 5 a.m. and 7 a.m., and

56% occurring on the weekend, mirroring the circumstances of the Ocean Isle Beach tragedy (Davis, n.d.). Because a fire-suppression sprinkler system is required in all hotels within the United States, and in many other countries worldwide, coupled with the 24-hour presence of hotel guest service and security personnel, it is unlikely that a similar tragedy would have occurred in a hotel setting. Consequently, it is important that local authorities identify appropriate safety regulations, possibly including safety inspections, for properties that are offered as short-term rentals, although regulations alone may not have prevented the Ocean Isle Beach tragedy.

Although the assessment of property taxes is one way communities collect revenue to support the maintenance of a community's infrastructure and services—including roads, police, and fire protection—property taxes alone may be inadequate to support the costs added by an influx of tourists. Therefore, local officials must determine the most effective way to collect tax revenues from tourists to ensure the community provides a safe, clean environment with an adequate infrastructure and services for tourists and residents alike. Local tax jurisdictions often collect additional revenues from tourists through hotel occupancy taxes; taxes on short-term rental properties; sales taxes on restaurant meals and prepared foods; and amusement taxes, on rounds of golf, lift tickets, theme park tickets, and admissions to other local attractions.

A single tragedy within a resort market that relies upon tourism to bolster the local economy can have lasting, negative consequences. Consequently, it is important that the local hotel and lodging community—and entire tourism industry collectively—work in partnership with local government officials to effectively regulate lodging operators of all types, while creatively promoting tourism.

Interval or Vacation Ownership

In response to demand from travelers that vacation annually and desire to purchase a partial ownership interest in resort real estate, interval or vacation ownership was created, originally referred to as a timeshare. Because many potential buyers cannot afford or may not want the responsibility of full, year-round ownership of a resort property, buyers may purchase ownership of a specific week or time interval of ownership in a specific resort property. For example, someone that may enjoy winter sports, such as snow skiing or snowboarding, may purchase vacation ownership of a one- or two-bedroom unit located at a ski resort for one-week during the destination's ski season. In some cases, ownership is offered in a specific unit, for a specific week;

interval or vacation ownership (timeshare): a partial- or shared-ownership interest in a resort real estate property, which allows exclusive access for a specified time period or the contract may specify the style and size of the unit, as well as the time frame or season of the year during which the owner is entitled access. Other vacation ownership providers sell access to their vacation ownership resorts through a point system. With a point system, points are purchased that may be redeemed at the owner's home resort, or at other vacation ownership properties managed by the vacation ownership management firm, based upon the location of the unit reserved, as well as the size of the unit, and specific dates requested. Obviously, more points must be redeemed to reserve lodging units that accommodate a larger number of overnight guests and to reserve accommodations in premium locations or during high-demand dates.

Interval or vacation ownership offers several benefits to the operator, as well as the buyer. First, the developer shifts the risk of resort real estate ownership to the vacation owners as the units of ownership in the resort are sold. With traditional lodging, such as a hotel, the developer must bear the cost of developing the hotel property and the owner is responsible for the property's debt service, regardless of how well the property performs financially; the property owner must make mortgage payments to the lender whether the hotel operation generates sufficient cash-flow to cover the debt service payments or not. With vacation ownership, if the buyer does not have the required cash to pay for the property in-full at closing, the purchaser assumes personal liability for any loan that is taken to complete the purchase. Vacation ownership developers initially invest in building the common areas of the resort—including a welcome center, recreational facilities, such as a large resort-style pool, and F&B facilities, like a poolside bar and grill—along with the first phase of lodging units. Once the initial phase of lodging units is nearly sold-out, then subsequent phases of lodging units may be built. This allows the developer to recover the cost of developing the property as the resort is constructed, lowering the risk of developing the resort.

Vacation owners enjoy the benefit of being an investor in the resort property at which they vacation—resort associates and management recognize guests as owners, frequently expressing their appreciation for the owners' investment in the resort. Service levels at a vacation ownership resort are typically higher than may be found in a traditional vacation rental or a private residence but vary based upon the positioning of the specific resort or interval ownership operator. The cost of operating the resort, including providing guest services and housekeeping personnel, is allocated to the resort's interval owners through the assessment of annual fees, although some incremental revenue for F&B and other services may help offset operating costs. Exchange fees may be assessed when an interval owner chooses to vacation in an alternative location other than the home resort. In addition, owners typically incur an annual capital expenditure assessment, which is used to maintain, update, and renovate the resort as required. Because of their ownership stake in the resort, vacation owners may enjoy some tax benefits related to their vacation ownership investment. Vaca-

exchange fees:
fees assessed to vacation owners when they elect to visit an alternative property rather than their own vacation property

capital expenditure assessment:
an annual fee charged vacation owners to maintain, update, and renovate the resort as required

tion ownership is permanent, unless sold, and may be passed on to heirs and future generations.

Some of the best-known operators in the vacation ownership industry include *Bluegreen Vacations*, *Diamond Resorts International*, *Disney Vacation Club*, *Interval International*, *Marriott Vacation Club*, *Hyatt Residence Club*, *Hilton Grand Vacations Club*, *RCI*, *The Ritz Carlton Destination Club*, and *Wyndham Vacation Resorts*. Vacation ownership brands affiliated with traditional hotel lodging parent companies are typically operated by separate companies through a licensing agreement with the namesake brand. It may be surprising to know that *Hyatt Residence Clubs* are managed by *Marriott Vacations Worldwide Corporation* after being purchased by *Interval Leisure Group (ILG), Inc.* in 2014, which in turn was purchased by *Marriott Vacations Worldwide* in 2018 (Tan & Callanan, 2018). Many of the firms listed above develop, sell, or manage interval ownership properties, while others, such as *RCI* and *Interval International*, are interval ownership exchange networks; these networks allow vacation owners to exchange their vacation ownership time with other enrolled vacation owners.

RECREATIONAL AMENITIES AND FEES

Resort hotels, particularly destination resort hotels, offer a range of recreational amenities, which may include resort-style pools and water features, golf courses, racquet sports, and mountain and adventure activities. Wellness facilities also attract guests to many resorts.

© Elena Serebryakova/Shutterstock.com

Resort-Style Pools and Water Features

Pools, splash parks, and waterslides are the most common recreational amenities found in a resort property (Wisnom, 2013); in recent years, a lazy river that allows guests to leisurely float on a tube around the perimeter of the pool area has become a must-have feature in many destinations. Properties that accommodate both families, as well as adult couples celebrating honeymoons and anniversaries, often find it necessary to operate a quiet or adults-only pool, which is typically located in a more secluded area providing a more relaxing alternative to the large, centrally located resort-style pool. Although a few resorts offer waterparks or slides that require a separate admissions fee, savvy resort operators use the hotel's pools and water features to generate incremental revenue in several ways

Resort Services Fees

Resort hotels, particularly those with a large resort-style pool that includes water features, often charge a resort services fee, which is a flat daily charge added to each guest's room account to cover the cost of providing resort services, including access to the resort's pool, chaise lounge chairs, pool towels, spritzing, and other services that may be offered poolside, as well as access to quality Internet service, the hotel's exercise facilities, morning coffee service, bottled water in the guestroom, business center access, and other services, such as live entertainment, for which the hotel does not charge *a la carte* fees. Resort service fees in the United States typically ranged between $10 and $25 per night and averaged $19.52 per night in 2016, representing nearly 10% of the hotel's room rate; approximately 7% of resort hotels reported charging a resort fee in 2014 (Manning et al, 2018). The financial impact of a resort services fee is substantial; a $20.00 per day resort services fee, added to each guest's room account in a 400-room hotel running 70% annual occupancy generates over $2.0 million annually in incremental revenue.

Consumers have pushed back against resort service fees, claiming that these fees allow resort hotels to deceive guests by setting room rates at artificially low levels to attract customers, only to bolster guestroom rates through the inclusion of a mandatory, daily resort services fee. The Federal Trade Commission (FTC) has sided with consumers, indicating that the practice is deceptive if the fee is not disclosed, in advance, at the time of booking; however, approximately half of resort guests surveyed by the *American Hotel and Lodging Association (AH&LA)* have indicated that they are willing to pay resort service fees if the fees are "worth it" and add value to the guest's stay (Manning et al, 2018). By charging guests for the myriad of services covered by the resort services fee individually, resort guests may perceive they are being "nickeled-and-dimed" over the course of their stay. Therefore, charging a fee may not only be appropriate, but may be preferred in many resort settings.

A wise hotel manager charges a resort services fee that is reasonable in relationship to the services and facilities supported by the fee. The fee must be clearly communicated at the time of booking, identifying the specific resort services that are provided in exchange for the fee. For example, a destination resort hotel may indicate through the reservation sales process that the guestroom rate is $249 per night, plus applicable hotel occupancy taxes, and a $25 per night resort services fee, which provides access to the hotel's splash park, water slides, and resort-style pool, featuring afternoon poolside entertainment; poolside towels and padded chaise lounge chairs; high-speed Wi-Fi Internet access throughout the resort; in-room bottled water, coffee, and tea service; access to the fully-equipped exercise facility; evening family activities; and a choice of daily newspapers. Finally, it should be noted that resort service fees are subject to sales tax or even hotel occupancy taxes in some states. The practice of splitting prices into components is referred to as partition-pricing. In the example cited above, the hotel marketer has decided to partition the daily guestroom rate to include a $249 nightly charge for use of the hotel guestroom, and a separate $25 daily fee for the services covered by the resort services fee, bringing the total daily price to $274 per night; some states have determined that the partitioning of a hotel room rate in this manner requires that hotel occupancy taxes are collected on the full non-partitioned room-rate of $274 versus the guestroom portion ($249) of the rate only.

> partition-pricing: the practice of splitting prices into components

Savvy hoteliers also use the resort's pool area to generate incremental retail and F&B revenues. Shops, tiki huts, or kiosks may be placed around the pool that provide swimwear, t-shirts, and tank-tops, sunglasses, hats, sunscreen, water floats, and more. A poolside bar and snack bar—possibly including a swim-up bar—can drive F&B revenue, as well as scheduling F&B servers to roam the pool deck, and may pay dividends, allowing guests to place food and beverage orders without leaving their poolside chaise lounge chairs. Casual furniture groupings, umbrellas to shield guests from the midday sun, radiant heaters for chilly mornings or evenings, and live entertainment may all be employed on the pool deck to create an inviting, comfortable environment where guests can congregate, relax, and enjoy a light meal or beverage. In addition to driving incremental revenue, such an environment generates positive experiences and memories for resort guests, further enhancing perceptions of value and guest loyalty.

Golf Resorts

Although the number of rounds of golf played in the United States declined from nearly 30 million in 2006 to just below 25 million in 2013, it has stabilized at approximately 24 million rounds per year since 2015 (Outdoor Foundation, 2018); still, 21.6% of household members in high income households within the United States, defined as the top one-third of households in terms of income, have an interest in golf (Statista, 2018). In other words, just over one-in-five high-income household members

© romakoma/Shutterstock.com

are golfers, which ultimately may drive the decision to visit a destination that includes golf among its resort amenities. Travel—particularly leisure travel—is a discretionary household expenditure that can be best-afforded by high-income households. Consequently, a resort that does not provide access to golf, during warm weather months, may possibly eliminate 20% of its potential customer-base by failing to provide its guests access to a championship golf course.

Golf courses positively contribute to a resort environment in numerous ways. First, it provides a substantial amount of aesthetically pleasing green space to the resort's environment; an 18-hole championship, par-72 golf course requires 120 to 200 acres, including tee-boxes, fairways, greens, sand bunkers, out-of-bounds areas, as well as ponds, lakes, and creeks, which provide water for course irrigation as well as serving as water hazards, making play more challenging. This green space provides pleasing vistas from the guestrooms of adjacent hotels. A golf course also adds value to any real estate development surrounding the golf course; a homesite, condominium, or resort villa built along an adjacent golf course can be sold for a premium price or rented, as a short-term vacation rental, for a premium overnight or weekly rental rate. In many cases, the cost of developing a golf course is completely or, at a minimum, partially re-captured by the premium prices commanded by the residential real estate developed along with the golf course by the resort's developer. A well-marketed, well-managed golf course is also profitable, often generating a contribution margin well in excess of 50% of revenue.

Golf courses are rarely owned by the owner of the hotel's real estate or managed by the hotel management firm that is contracted to manage an adjacent resort hotel; however, a resort golf facility often works in partnership with an on-property or adjacent resort hotel to establish a seamless experience for resort guests. Guests of the resort hotel can often play golf on the course, as part of a golf package, or may charge cart and green fees, as well as any retail charges or F&B services from the golf facility to their hotel guestroom account. Golf courses are often managed by a professional golf management firm, such as the Troon Group (www.troon.com) or ICON Management Services, Inc. (www.theiconteam.com), that prioritizes operating efficiency and the quality of the golfers' experience, while striving to achieve the financial objectives established by the owners of the course.

In a resort community or residential lifestyle community, the golf course is typically owned by the POA, although golf courses may be owned by individual investors, business partnerships, a real estate investment trust (REIT), or a government entity, such as a municipality or county. When owned by a POA, homeowner access to the course may be prioritized and included in POA assessments, although homeowners will typically be required to pay cart-and-green fees, at a member-discounted rate, or through an annual trail fee if using their own golf cart, to cover the variable costs of operating the course; in some resort communities, golf membership may be optional and assessed through a separate membership fee. Play on the course by resort guests, including guests of a hotel located within or adjacent to the resort community, is often encouraged because member play alone is inadequate to fully support the cost of operating and maintaining the course; this allows the play of resort guests that are charged premium cart-and-green fees to subsidize the cost of maintaining the property owners' lifestyle.

Optimizing revenue at a golf facility is surprisingly similar to optimizing hotel guestroom revenue. The two primary variables that impact revenue are the utilization rate and average cart-and-green fees; the manager of the course seeks to balance the utilization of available tee times or service capacity with the average price paid per golfer to optimize revenue, realizing that demand is both stochastic and elastic, concepts discussed in detail in *Chapter 5: Optimizing Revenue*. A golf course has a maximum service capacity, depending upon the number of hours of daylight and the spacing of tee-times; a golf course can typically accommodate approximately 250-rounds-per-day, although this varies by season. The number of minutes between tee times impacts both service capacity and the quality of the guest experience—the more time between foursomes, the less rushed golfers are on the course; however, this reduces service capacity. Member-owned courses prioritize the quality of play and may space tee times 12 to even 15 minutes apart. A course seeking to maximize service capacity may schedule tee times just 6 to 7 minutes apart, although courses seeking to balance quality of play without sacrificing service capacity typically schedule tee times 9 to 10 minutes apart. An 18-hole round typically takes 4 hours to complete, with some variation.

Because golfers play in groups of four, an 18-hole course may accommodate an additional 24 golfers per hour; however, many golfers prefer to tee-off early in the morning, to complete the round while it is cooler, prior to lunch and the mid-afternoon sun. As a result, some courses double-tee, which refers to sending groups off the 1st hole or front nine and the 10th hole or back nine simultaneously, maximizing the number of early morning tee-times. Of course, double-teeing does not add any additional service capacity, because 2 hours following the start of play, no tee times may be reserved for a 2-hour window as the groups that were double-teed cross-over and make-the-turn. In other words, approximately 2 hours following the time at which double-teeing began, the first

cart-and-green fees:
a payment made to a golf course that allows access to play the course utilizing a course-provided golf cart

trail fee:
a payment made annually or seasonally to allow a golfer to utilize his/her personal golf cart on a golf course

membership fee:
payments made at regular intervals that provide access to specific facilities, services, or other specified privileges

utilization rate:
the proportion of service capacity that is consumed during a specified time period

service capacity:
the maximum number of customers that may be appropriately service in a specified time period

foursome:
a group of golfers playing a course, which is typically comprised of four golfers

double-tee:
refers to sending groups off the 1st hole or front nine and the 10th hole or back nine of a golf course simultaneously

front nine:
holes 1 through 9 on a golf course

back nine:
holes 10 through 18 on a golf course

make-the-turn:
refers to a golfer or foursome moving from the 9th hole to the 10th hole on the course

foursome to tee-off on the front nine will begin play on the back nine, and the group that started their round on the 10th hole will be crossing over to the front nine. It typically takes nearly 2 hours to fill a golf course to capacity, with a foursome on each hole, when double-teeing, because eight golfers (a foursome on the 1st hole and a foursome on the 10th hole) start play every 10 minutes, or 48 golfers per hour.

A strategy commonly used to increase service capacity, which may be used when a golf tournament is scheduled on the course, is a shot-gun start. With a shot-gun start, foursomes are assigned to each of the 18 holes on the course and play begins at the same time for up to 72 golfers on the course; a shot-gun start may actually accommodate up to 144 golfers because two foursomes may be sent to each hole, with the second group, group "B," teeing off once the first group, group "A," at the same tee-box clears the fairway. In addition to tournaments, the use of a shot-gun start may be used to accommodate conference groups that want to place a golf event on their agenda, requiring every golfer in the group both start and complete their respective round of golf at approximately the same time.

The design of the course also impacts the pace-of-play. Skilled low-handicap golfers tend to keep their ball in-play, avoiding out-of-bounds areas, whereas less-skilled high-handicap golfers may frequently drive their tee-shots into the rough or out-of-bounds areas, which slows down play as golfers search for their golf balls. As a result, golf course designers tend to create out-of-bounds areas, when designing a resort course, that prevent golfers from being able to search for lost golf balls, because they are composed of thick, impenetrable brush or bounded by creeks or water hazards; this forces golfers to drop a new golf ball, take their penalty stroke, and play on, speeding the pace-of-play. Resort courses also tend to have a single-fairway design, maximizing the amount of real estate with golf course views around the perimeter of the course, as opposed to a core-course design in which multiple fairways run parallel to one another and the golf holes are clustered around a clubhouse; a core-course design requires less total real estate than with single-fairway or double-fairway designs and is more commonly used when developing a country club or municipal course.

In addition to cart-and-green fees, golf membership, and trail fees, other sources of revenue at a resort's golf course include retail revenue at the pro-shop for soft goods, such as logoed golf shirts, caps, and attire, and hard goods, including golf balls and equipment. F&B revenue includes sales from the beverage cart, which circulates on the course to provide snacks and refreshments during play, and from the clubhouse bar and grill. Golf instruction, as well as golf range ball fees, are additional sources of revenue generated by a resort's golf operation.

The director of golf or head golf professional is typically a *Class A* Golf Professional, certified by the Professional Golfers Association of America (PGA). The management

---

shot-gun start:
foursomes are assigned to each of the 18 holes on the course and play begins at the same time for up to 72 golfers on the course

pace-of-play:
the speed at which golfers are able to complete a round of golf

low-handicap golfers:
highly skilled golfers that typically require fewer strokes above par to complete their rounds

high-handicap golfers:
poorly skilled golfers that require many strokes above par to complete their rounds

single-fairway design:
a golf course at which fairways are lined with homes, villas, or condominiums versus adjacent fairways

core-course design:
multiple fairways run parallel to one another and the golf holes are clustered around a clubhouse

soft goods:
retail items that include clothing, such as logoed golf shirts, caps, and other attire

hard goods:
retail items which include golf balls, clubs, and equipment

beverage cart:
a vehicle that circulates on a golf course, providing snacks and refreshments

team also includes one or two assistant professional(s), often responsible for instruction or tournaments, and a golf course superintendent, responsible for the maintenance of the course. Non-exempt associates include pro-shop personnel; outside staff that greet golfers and load golf bags onto golf carts, in addition to picking-the-range; and a starter that controls the start-of-play at holes 1 and 10. Golf course ambassadors circle the course in golf carts, ensuring a favorable pace-of-play by monitoring golfers on the course while preventing non-golfers or non-paying golfers from entering the course; it is important that only golfers are permitted on the course because severe injury or even death may result from someone being hit by an errant golf shot. Golf course maintenance workers and an equipment mechanic round-out the non-exempt golf course staff. An F&B supervisor is often employed at the course to supervise the F&B associates, which include food servers, culinary and stewarding personnel, bartenders, and beverage cart personnel.

Racquet Sports

In addition to golf, many resorts also include tennis facilities and, increasingly, pickleball courts, which require less space; pickleball is a sport that can be learned more quickly than tennis, combining elements of tennis, table tennis, and badminton. Tennis-oriented resorts often include courts of different surfaces, including hard-surface, cushioned hard-surface, clay, natural grass, and synthetic turf; each surface impacts the speed or pace at which the ball travels, as well as the players' footing, and requires a different level of capital investment and maintenance. A tennis professional may be employed to offer instruction; additional revenue may be generated by court-rental, retail sales of tennis attire and equipment, and other services, including racquet re-stringing. Resorts that do not emphasize racquet sports may offer access to one or more hard-surface courts, including access to these facilities as a component of the resort services fee.

Mountain Resorts and Adventure Sports

Mountain resorts provide guests access to skiing, snowboarding, and snowtubing in the winter, as well as a variety of adventure sports, such as fishing, hiking, horseback riding, kayaking, mountain biking, and rafting in warm weather months, and are typically located in remote settings. Each of these activities requires a resort to employ an appropriate team of qualified personnel, and to acquire the necessary operating equipment, to manage and safely deliver exceptional guest experiences. Mountain resort operators based in the United States, such as Vail Resorts (www.vailresorts.com), Intrawest (www.intrawest.com), and Boyne Resorts USA (www.boyneresorts.com), operate multiple mountain resorts, located primarily in the Rocky Mountain region

mountain resort:
a resort that provides guests with access to skiing, snowboarding, snowtubing, and other mountain-based activities

adventure sports:
activities that involve some risk and often include interaction with nature

© Nataliya Nazarova/Shutterstock.com

of the Western United States and Canada; the Northeastern United States, including Maine, New Hampshire, and Vermont; and a handful of operations located in the Great Lakes region, including Michigan and Wisconsin. A wide variety of resort lodging—including traditional hotels, wholly-owned vacation rentals, and vacation ownership properties—are often developed and managed in partnership with or directly by these mountain resort management firms. Because the winter sports season is limited, golf courses and alpine slides are also often developed—and summer festivals are held—to encourage travel to the destination during the warm weather months of the year. Despite these efforts, many mountain resort markets experience wide swings in demand, with the lowest occupancy period typically occurring during the mud months in the spring, as the snow melts.

mud months:
the spring season at a mountain resort, during which occupancy is typically the lowest

A mountain resort requires a significant amount of real estate and capital investment, as well as access to a reliable source of water to feed snowmaking equipment; over 100 ski resorts, located in the Western United States, rent all or a portion of their skiable terrain from the United States Forest Service (USDA, n.d.). Although a detailed discussion of the development and operation of mountain resorts is outside the scope of this textbook, readers may immediately identify parallels between the development, ownership, and management of mountain resorts and the branding, ownership, and management of traditional hotel properties. Performing these three distinct functions require specific sets of business skills, which may be performed by different firms or separate divisions within a single firm, often working in partnership with well-capitalized real estate investors.

Guest experiences at a mountain resort are delivered by associates employed by a management firm, specializing in mountain resort operations, operating the resort under a contract with a real estate partner, although some services and facilities at the resort may be sub-contracted or leased out to other firms, partnerships, or individuals, as appropriate. Revenue is generated through use fees, including the sale of lift tickets, instruction, and the sales or rental of the specialized equipment and attire required to participate in the various resort activities, in addition to food, beverage, lodging, and retail revenue. A lease, commission, or combination of lease and commission is often paid to the owner of the real estate upon which the resort operates, generating income for the property owner.

Theme Park Resort

Following the success of *Disneyland* in California, Walt Disney, in partnership with his older brother Roy, quietly assembled a 43 square mile parcel of land in central Florida, just west of Orlando, to create the world's largest and most frequently visited resort destination in the world—the *Walt Disney World Resort* (disneyworld.disney.go.com). This resort consists of four theme parks—the *Magic Kingdom, Epcot Center, Disney's Hollywood Studios*, and *Disney's Animal Kingdom*—in addition to a waterpark, hotels, restaurants, vacation ownership properties, retail centers, and an extensive transportation network. Each of the resort development strategies described in this chapter have been used by the *Walt Disney Company* over the past five decades to develop and expand the *Walt Disney World Resort*.

When the initial theme park, the *Magic Kingdom*, opened in 1971, traditional hotels, including the *Contemporary Hotel* and *Polynesian Village Resort*, were constructed by *Disney*, which were operated by the *Walt Disney Company*. Later, *Disney Village* was created to allow hotel developers and leading hotel management firms to build and operate traditional hotels on property that is leased from *Disney*. *Disney* also established its own vacation ownership subsidiary, which operates interval ownership resorts on the property, as well as in other resort locations, including the Hawaiian Islands. *Disney Springs*, a large retail and entertainment complex, was also built on *Disney* grounds, leasing retail, restaurant, and entertainment space to leading retail and entertainment providers, including AMC theaters and the *Cirque du Soleil*. Golf courses, spa operations, sports complexes, and additional hotels targeting all guest segments, from value-seeking (economy) clientele to guests seeking a high-level of luxurious, personalized service, have been added to the *Walt Disney Resort* over the years. *Disney* has created a world-class resort with facilities to accommodate virtually any guest need—from a youth group seeking to combine a theme park visit with a baseball tournament to a high-end corporate group providing training for its sales force. The *Disney Institute* will even help deliver the training.

Disney is not the only operator of a multi-faceted theme park-style resort—*Universal Studios* (www.universalparks.com) competes directly with *Disney*, operating theme park resorts in Florida and California. Other theme park operators include Merlin Entertainment (www.merlinentertainments.biz), Six Flags (www.sixflags.com), and *Overseas Chinese Town Enterprises*, a state-owned theme park resort operation in China. *Disney* has also expanded globally, operating theme park resorts in Tokyo, Paris, Hong Kong, and Shanghai.

Wellness Amenities

© UfaBizPhoto/
Shutterstock.com

Resort hotels and other lodging operations in a resort setting often include wellness facilities, such as an exercise facility or spa. Health and fitness centers include cardio-equipment, such as treadmills, elliptical trainers, and exercise bikes, as well as weight machines, as opposed to free weights, to minimize the likelihood of guest injuries. As previously discussed, access to the exercise facility may be included in a resort services fee. Aerobic exercise, Pilates, yoga, spinning, and other classes may be scheduled each day, particularly in a destination resort hotel; however, a fee may be assessed to participating guests. Many resort hotels also offer an amenity spa designed to enhance and complement a guest's overall experience at the resort, by delivering highly personalized services, although an amenity spa is not typically the sole focus of a guest's visit.

Spa services are presented to a guest through a spa menu, which is organized by the type of service, to include massage, facials, body treatments, and beauty treatments. Massage is the most popular spa treatment, offered at 100% of resort spas (iSpa, 2018); a massage treatment commonly lasts 50 to 60 minutes in duration, although the total time of a guest's visit to the spa varies widely, depending upon the additional services and spa facilities used by the guest. There are a variety of massage modalities that may be offered, with resort spas commonly offering deep tissue, stone, pregnancy, aromatherapy, and relaxation massages, at a minimum. Although massage services are typically provided on an individual basis, resort spas may offer couples massages, particularly in resorts that cater to honeymoon and anniversary couples.

Facials are also popular treatments in a resort setting. Although there are a variety of facial treatments available, they typically involve the same basic steps—cleanse, exfoliate, extract, massage, mask, and finish. The purpose of a body treatment is to exfoliate the recipient's skin, through a body scrub, and to detoxify the body while

amenity spa:
a spa designed to enhance and complement a guest's overall experience at the resort, by delivering highly personalized services

spa services:
personalized services intended to contribute to a guest's well-being, including massage, facial, body, and beauty treatments

spa menu:
a listing of spa services available with pricing, organized by type of service

facial:
a treatment to cleanse and refresh the client's facial skin

body treatment:
a treatment to cleanse, detoxify, and hydrate the client's skin

hydrating the skin. Many resort spas offer signature treatments designed to highlight the spa's unique features and strengths, as well as waxing, manicures, pedicures, nail and hair services, and make-up consultations.

A destination spa is a resort in which the spa facility is a primary demand-generator for the property, often requiring guests to purchase multiple-day spa packages that include a variety of treatments. The focus of a destination spa is on wellness and lifestyle change. The services offered support and promote a healthy lifestyle, including food menus that contain healthful spa cuisine and detoxifying juices. Destination spas provide access to saunas, steam therapy, and hydrotherapy pools, sometimes fed by natural hot springs. Meditation, nutrition counseling, cooking classes, and other educational activities offered at destination spas instruct guests on how to begin and maintain lifestyles focused on wellness. Examples of destination spas include *Mii Amo* in Sedona, Arizona (www.miiamo.com); *Golden Door* in San Marcos, California (https://goldendoor.com); *Rancho La Puerta* in Tecate, Baja California, Mexico (https://rancholapuerta.com); and the *Westglow Resort & Spa* in Blowing Rock, North Carolina (www.westglowresortandspa.com).

Treatment providers in a spa include massage therapists; estheticians that perform skin care, including facials, body treatments, hair removal, and make-up application; and technicians that provide beauty-related services. Treatment providers may be compensated on an hourly basis or per treatment and commonly receive gratuities. While some resort spas may employ treatment providers as independent contractors, the spa's operator must be careful to fully comply with Internal Revenue Service (IRS) regulations regarding the employment of independent contractors, which states, "an individual is an independent contractor if the payer has the right to control or direct only the result of the work and not what will be done and how it will be done" (IRS, 2019). Spa operators that have sole control of a treatment provider's work schedule, pricing, and scheduled side-duties, may not be able to justify engaging treatment providers as independent contractors. Consequently, only 7.8% of spa employees in the United States are independent contractors (iSpa, 2018). Spas also employ guest service personnel that schedule appointments, greet guests, and process guest payments in addition to a Spa Manager or Director.

The spa industry is highly regulated. Treatment providers must pass the state board-licensing exam for their area of specialty and maintain a valid massage therapy, esthetician, or cosmetology license, as appropriate, issued by the state in which the spa operates; these individual licenses must be posted. Spas must comply with additional regulations that vary by state. Maintaining the cleanliness of spa facilities is critical to remaining in compliance with these regulations and spa operations are subject to random inspections, at any time during operating hours, by State or local health departments.

destination spa:
a resort focused on wellness and lifestyle change, with extensive spa facilities and services

treatment providers:
massage therapists; estheticians that perform skin care; and technicians that provide beauty-related services

massage therapists:
treatment providers trained and licensed to provide clients with massage treatments

estheticians:
treatment providers trained and licensed to perform skin care, hair removal, and application of cosmetics

technicians:
treatment providers trained and licensed to provide hair and beauty-related services

spa manager or director:
an exempt manager responsible for overseeing the operation of the spa, ensuring its financial success

Because treatment providers deliver treatments on an individual basis, spa operations are labor-intensive. Consequently, the contribution margin generated by a spa is modest. While 47% of resort spas in the U.S. reported a contribution margin in excess of 20% of total spa revenue in 2017, 48% reported an operating profit of less than 20%, with the remaining 5% of resort spas operating at a loss (iSpa, 2018). Due to the labor-intensive nature of a spa operation, coupled with its modest contribution margin, it is common for a resort hotel to lease out its spa facility to an independent operator. Whether leased-out or operated in-house, the primary financial benefit of the spa operation to the resort is the value that it adds to the overall guest experience versus the bottom-line profit generated by the spa itself. Like other resort amenities, the availability of spa services contributes to a resort's ability to attract guests and to command a higher ADR, ultimately impacting guest loyalty while driving guestroom revenue.

MARKETING RESORT SERVICES

In *Section 2, Building Guest and Client Relationships*, which includes *Chapter 3: Defining Guest Segments*, *Chapter 4: Effective Sales and Marketing*, and *Chapter 5: Optimizing Revenue*, an in-depth discussion is provided regarding effective marketing, pricing, and revenue optimization strategies used in a hotel or lodging operation. These same techniques and strategies are completely transferable to resort settings. Resorts—including golf, oceanfront, mountain, theme park, and destination spas—pursue many of the same guest segments, depending upon the specific facilities offered by the resort, although the mix of guests will vary.

Resort destinations typically rely on a higher proportion of leisure travel than a typical commercial hotel and much of the business travel to a resort property may be group-related, particularly if the resort includes conference facilities. Because there are typically fewer businesses that generate in-bound corporate business travel located in resort destinations, business travel to a resort market is often incentive travel, designed to reward associates for achieving specific goals, such as a company's sales professionals or independent agents marketing the company's products and services. Association groups are also attracted to resort markets because meeting attendance is often bolstered when conferences are held in a resort destination.

Many resort markets experience overwhelming demand during the peak season, while struggling to sell available service capacity during the off-season. Therefore, resorts strive to maximize revenue during the peak season, while focusing much of their marketing efforts to sell shoulder and off-season service capacity. Quite frankly, a resort's off-season financial performance often accounts for the bulk of any year-over-year performance improvement, because there may be very little room to improve peak season performance. One strategy that may be effectively employed is to shift groups requesting high-demand dates, but requiring lower pricing, into shoulder and off-season periods. Another strategy that is used is dynamic pricing.

Recall from *Chapter 5: Optimizing Revenue* the five conditions that must be present to successfully execute the dynamic pricing strategies and yield management strategies used by hotels. These include:
1. Perishable service product
2. High fixed and low variable costs
3. Stochastic demand
4. Elastic demand
5. Multiple guest segments

Each of these conditions apply to selling the recreational activities offered by golf, racquet, mountain, and theme park resorts. The lone exception may be destination spas that incur higher variable costs on spa services. Consequently, each of these resort operations must balance utilization rate with average price to optimize the yield or revenue-generated-per-opportunity, being cognizant of the impact of increased utilization or volume on service quality and the overall guest experience.

For example, *Disney* has been experimenting with dynamic pricing strategies at its theme parks, raising prices over 20% over the past 5 years, because its domestic theme parks often reach full-capacity on high-demand days. By raising prices on days with peak demand, *Disney* can reduce over-crowding, improving both the customer experience and profit margins; however, *Disney* executives want to avoid creating a public perception that they are price-gouging, which negatively impacts guests' perceptions of value. They also want to remain true to Walt Disney's fundamental goal of providing families with an affordable entertainment experience (Schwartzel, 2018).

Similar revenue optimization strategies may improve both customer experiences and profitability in golf and mountain resort settings. A golf course can increase cart-and-green fees during periods of highest demand, such as Saturday morning during the destination's peak golf season, to prevent over-crowding on the course, improving the pace-of-play while enhancing profitability. During periods of low demand, such as in the afternoon or during the week, lower prices are offered to attract more price-sensitive golfers, although minimum acceptable fees must be established to maintain price integrity. The same dynamic pricing strategy is effective in pricing lift tickets at a mountain resort, with higher prices reducing demand and improving profitability during periods of peak demand, while enhancing the skier/snowboarder experience by eliminating over-crowding and long lines to access the lifts.

One additional marketing challenge that impacts resorts, particularly those located on an island, is lift; this challenge is discussed in *Box 9.2: Working on an Island: The Challenge of Lift*.

BOX 9.2: WORKING ON AN ISLAND: THE CHALLENGE OF LIFT

© Perfect Lazybones/Shutterstock.com

One of the challenges that resort operators may face, particularly in an island location, is the availability of lift. Lift refers to the number of airline seats available into a specific destination. Because many resort destinations are in remote or island locations, it is essential that guests have access to the destination via commercial airline. Without adequate lift into a destination, a resort lodging facility is simply unable to generate enough demand for its accommodations to ensure the financial success of the property. Although this situation applies to island locations, limited transportation options also impact other remote locations. For example, accessing a mountain resort located in the Colorado Rockies may require a flight into Denver, a destination with adequate lift; however, the availability of rental cars, particularly SUVs to handle snow-covered mountain roads, may be limited or expensive, complicating travel to the resort.

Recall from *Chapter 2: Successful Hotel Management* the value equation, which states that a guest's perception of value is equal to the quality of guest outcomes delivered, plus the service process quality, divided by the price of the service product plus any additional costs of acquiring the service, as outlined below:

Formula 2.1: The Value Equation

$$Value = \frac{Results\ produced\ for\ customers\ +\ Process\ quality}{Price\ to\ the\ customer\ +\ Cost\ of\ acquiring\ the\ service}$$

The logistics and expense of travel to a resort located in an island or remote destination may potentially impact guests' perception of value in two ways. First, a traveler required to fly into a nearby location, which is then followed by a second form of transportation to transfer from the airport to the resort, may experience a reduction in "process quality," reducing value. Secondly, the cost of the airfare, coupled with other required transportation costs, increases the denominator within this equation, which also lowers the customer's perception of value. As a result, a lack of available transportation options or high transportation costs into a market may reduce the effectiveness of the resort's marketing efforts.

Many resort destinations are seasonal. Like hotels, airlines respond to the seasonal nature of a given market; however, unlike lodging operations, airlines can manage service capacity by limiting or increasing the number of flights into a market based upon seasonal fluctuations in demand. During the off-season, lift into the market may be severely limited, negatively impacting a customer's ability to book a flight into the destination. This negatively impacts both individual and group travel. Although a meeting planner may want to take advantage of the reduced costs of scheduling a conference during the resort's off-season, the meeting planner may struggle to book the flights necessary to efficiently bring the meeting's attendees into the destination for the required dates, forcing the meeting planner to plan the conference in an alternative destination.

Further complicating the issue, wholesalers and other travel intermediaries often purchase large blocks of airline tickets into resort destinations, particularly island destinations. By controlling a portion of the lift into a given resort market, the travel intermediary has increased leverage to demand lower rates for lodging, allowing the travel agent to increase their margin when packaging flights with overnight accommodations for re-sale. In other words, the travel intermediary captures a larger portion of the value associated with the vacation package transaction at the resort's expense.

In many resort destinations, resort hotels work in partnership with the DMO and other hospitality and tourism-related businesses to subsidize flights during off-season and shoulder-season periods. A portion of the DMO's budget; hotel occupancy, restaurant sales, or amusement taxes; or economic development funds may be allocated to subsidize off-season flights with low load-factors or a minimal flight schedule into the destination during low demand periods because the economic impact of inadequate lift may be devastating to the local economy. By ensuring lift is available into the market year-round, resort operators may market their resorts with confidence knowing that adequate transportation will be available for guests attracted by their off-season marketing efforts.

load-factor:
the utilization rate or proportion of airline seats sold on a specific commercial airline flight

OPERATIONAL SYSTEMS

Just as the marketing techniques and strategies apply in a resort setting, the operational strategies used in a hotel are also fully applicable to resort recreational operations. Golf, mountain, and theme park resorts, or a destination spa, must have a clearly defined vision and mission, and must operate using a value-centered philosophy, creating a guest-centered organizational culture. Resort operators must be good corporate citizens, operating in compliance with the "all-square" operating philosophy that balances the sometimes-competing interests of guests, associates, investors, and the community in which the resort operates. Service standards must be established to set clear expectations for associates. Consequently, the roadmap provided for the successful operation of a hospitality organization, outlined in *Chapter 2: Successful Hotel Management*, applies to any resort environment.

UNIQUE CHARACTERISTICS OF A RESORT MARKET

To close this discussion of resort operations, there are several factors that impact resort markets that should be noted and briefly discussed. These include seasonality; housing costs and availability; scarcity of labor; and community dynamics. Many of these factors are increasingly challenging in urban and suburban markets; however, they present particularly acute challenges in resort destinations.

Seasonality

As has been discussed, resort markets typically experience substantial swings in occupancy and pricing. During peak season, the number of guests—and demands from these guests—may overwhelm staff. Although during the off-season, low demand may require staffing to be cut-back to the point where employees are unable to earn adequate wages to cover their essential living costs. It is not uncommon for a resort operation to earn all profits for the entire year in a 2- to 3-month window, while operating at a loss for the remaining 9 or 10 months. Resorts operations must plan for these swings in business volume—completing renovations, deep-cleaning projects, and other necessary work during low demand periods, while carefully managing the resort's cash-flow to ensure the resort's financial obligations can be fulfilled. If a resort is managed by a management firm with operations in other markets, managers and other key employees may be transferred into the resort just prior to the peak season and then transferred out to other properties during the off-season, to reduce off-season payroll. In addition, specific marketing efforts—including the creation of festivals and special events—are planned to bolster demand during off-season and shoulder-season periods, which are essential to improving year-over-year performance, as previously indicated.

Housing Costs and Availability

Home prices in a resort market are often higher than in a suburban area or small town. A condominium, villa, or single-family home can also generate more rental income as a short-term vacation rental, as opposed to being offered as a long-term rental through an annual lease; plus, as a short-term vacation rental, the owner of the residence still can use the property when desired. As a result, fewer residential properties are placed on the rental market as long-term rentals, limiting the availability of housing in a resort market. As a result, many service industry workers struggle to locate affordable housing in a resort market, negatively impacting the availability of labor. The high cost of housing forces many employees working in resort markets to travel considerable distances to and from work each day.

Resorts, particularly those located in remote or island destinations, sometimes address the housing challenge by providing on-property housing or subsidizing apartment rentals for associates. Resorts also may work with other employers within the market to subsidize transportation to the destination. For example, on Hilton Head Island in South Carolina, resort hotels and other employers located on the Island support the cost of providing bus transportation from nearby towns and military bases to Hilton Head Island, transporting workers to and from the island each day from areas up to an hour away, where housing is more affordable.

Scarcity of Labor

Many of the residents within a resort area are retirees and seasonal residents. Full-time, working residents consist primarily of professionals, such as medical doctors and health professionals, real estate professionals, attorneys, financial planners, resort managers, and small business owners, due to the high cost of housing. As previously explained, line-level service workers struggle to secure affordable housing within many resort markets. Consequently, labor shortages are common in resort settings. Strategies that resorts, lodging operators, bars and restaurants, retail stores, and other businesses employ to attract front-line service workers include the following:
- Seasonal workers may be brought into the market from other seasonal markets with a complementary season, particularly if the resort's operator has operations in other markets;
- Student interns may be recruited from hospitality management, culinary programs, business schools, and other college programs to work for the season;

- Businesses may apply for H-2B visas, which may be used to employ temporary non-agricultural workers, although the United States Congress places caps on the number of workers that may be brought into the country, with half of the workers able to employed during the first half of the fiscal year (October – March) and half during the second half (April – September); the current cap is set at 66,000 workers (www.uscis.gov);
- Resorts may relax rules on nepotism or the employment of relatives, although it is important to avoid allowing family members to work in supervisory-subordinate relationships.
- When budgeting payroll in a resort setting, it may be appropriate to plan for the added expense of overtime wages; because guests are typically paying premium prices during peak season, contribution margins may be achieved even if overtime is incurred, and service levels must be maintained.

Community Dynamics

The economic base is not typically diverse in a resort destination. Hospitality and tourism-related businesses comprise the lion's share of local businesses, with many small business owners operating retail stores, bars and restaurants, and visitor-related services, including transportation, rentals, and destination services in addition to providing professional services. Large corporations are rarely based in resort markets. Consequently, large hotels and resort operations, requiring a substantial capital investment, are often the largest for-profit businesses and the major employers within the local market, except for, perhaps, the local school district or the health care system. Consequently, the local community relies upon these hospitality organizations to provide community stewardship, serving as exemplary corporate citizens within the community.

Decisions made by the operators of the largest resorts within a market impact many businesses within the local community, particularly those that depend upon the resort's guests for its customer-base. As a result, decisions made by resort operators may be closely scrutinized by the community. In addition, local officials may look to the resorts as primary sources of tax revenue to support government projects, because visitors do not vote in local elections. It is also common for many residents of the community to resent traffic congestion and crowds during the resort's peak season, failing to appreciation fully the economic impact of visitors, which subsidize community residents' quality-of-life. The availability, diversity, and quality of retail shopping; wealth of entertainment and dining options; and presence of recreational amenities, often at deeply discounted rates for locals, are often the result of tourism.

The role of community steward may be challenging, particularly during the off-season or economic downturns when many resorts struggle to meet their financial goals and obligations; however, senior management must embrace this role, providing community leadership through active involvement in the local chamber of commerce and DMO. The success of a destination's major resorts, and the community as a whole, are inter-dependent.

Finally, because the year-round population is often limited, a resort manager must recognize that resort communities are often small towns, even if a million or more tourists or conference attendees visit the destination annually. As a result, it is difficult for a resort manager to disappear into the community; senior managers are frequently recognized in public, resulting in unexpected discussions with residents about community-related issues and concerns. Managers may not be able to go the grocery store, a movie, or restaurant without encountering an associate from work. Although many may not view this as a negative consequence of working in a resort destination, it certainly creates a different dynamic than a hospitality industry manager may experience when working in a larger urban market, which potential resort managers may want to consider prior to pursuing a resort-based career opportunity.

CHAPTER SUMMARY

Resorts provide guests with access to recreational activities, such as water activities, golf, racquet sports, mountain and adventure activities, theme parks, or wellness activities. Although traditional hotels are common in resort destinations, other forms of lodging abound, including condominium hotels; vacation rental properties, often marketed and contracted through online booking sites; and vacation ownership resorts. Resort communities are often developed in resort destinations that include recreational amenities; retail shopping; multiple restaurants; and other resort services, such as a spa; as well as traditional or condominium hotels; vacation ownership properties; and individually-owned condominiums, villas, and single-family homes, often built along a golf course. A destination resort hotel is a large property, designed to serve as a self-contained escape from the outside world, which typically operates multiple F&B outlets, a conference center, and a variety of resort amenities, including a spa.

Strategies and techniques effective in ensuring the successful marketing and operation of a traditional hotel property are fully transferable to a resort, including its resort recreational amenities. Resort facilities, such as golf courses, mountain resorts, and theme parks, require a significant up-front capital investment, have high fixed costs with low variable costs, experience demand that is both stochastic and elastic, and pursue multiple customer segments. Consequently, the revenue optimization strategies outlined in *Chapter 5: Optimizing Revenue*, may be used to drive a resort's recreational revenues; a resort services fee is also effective in generating incremental revenue, provided the fee allows guests access to a variety of value-added resort amenities, including a resort-style pool with water features, exercise and wellness facilities, and high-speed Internet access. One additional marketing challenge faced by resorts, particularly those located on an island, is the availability of lift.

Resorts are typically seasonal, experiencing significant swings in business volumes. The high cost of housing, coupled with a shortage of affordable long-term rental properties in many resort areas, contribute to the challenge of finding an adequate number of qualified service employees. To fill job vacancies, many resorts transfer staff from other managed properties, recruit college students to work as interns, offer subsidies to associates to offset housing and transportation costs, and apply to bring in foreign workers through the United States Customs and Immigration Service's H-2B visa program. Despite these efforts, many resorts must plan for their associates to work overtime hours during the peak season. Senior management of major resorts often serve as community leaders because the success of these resorts, and the communities in which they operate, are intertwined. In addition to serving as major employers, many small-businesses in resort communities rely upon guest traffic at the destination's major resorts to support their businesses.

KEY TERMS AND CONCEPTS

adventure sports
amenity spa
back nine
beverage cart
body treatment
capital expenditure assessment
cart-and-green fees
condominium hotel
core-course design
destination resort hotel
destination spa
double-tee
estheticians
exchange fees
facial
foursome
front nine
hard goods
high-handicap golfers

interval or vacation ownership
  (timeshare)
lazy river
lift
load-factor
low-handicap golfers
make-the-turn
massage therapist
membership fee
mountain resort
mud months
pace-of-play
partition-pricing
peer-to-peer rentals
pools, splash parks, and
  waterslides (water features)
private lifestyle community
property management company
quiet or adults-only pool

rental pool
required pooling
resort community
resort services fee
service capacity
sharing-economy
shot-gun start
single-fairway design
soft goods
spa manager or director
spa menu
spa services
technicians
traditional hotel
trail fee
treatment providers
utilization rate
vacation rental

DISCUSSION QUESTIONS

1. Discuss the various types of lodging available in many resort settings. Identify specific guest segments that may prefer each of the lodging types identified.

2. Discuss challenges presented by the sharing economy. What challenges may a resort community homeowner experience if a neighboring home is marketed and frequently rented by visitors through an online rental site such as *Airbnb* or *VRBO*?

3. What are the risks and the benefits of purchasing a vacation ownership property?

4. Calculate the financial impact of a $25 resort services fee in a 1,000-room destination resort hotel running 72% annual occupancy with an ADR of nearly $350 per night, offering an extensive array of resort amenities including a large, resort-style pool with waterslides and a splash park. Calculate the financial impact of a $25 resort services fee in a 350-room, oceanfront resort hotel, offering beach towels, morning coffee service, a 25-meter lap pool and exercise room that runs a $184 per night ADR and 68% annual occupancy. Discuss the reaction of hotel guests to the $25 resort services fee at each of the resort hotels described.

5. Assume a major conference at a hotel located in a resort community wants to schedule a best-ball golf tournament on Saturday morning, requiring exclusive use of the resort's golf course. What challenges may be encountered if the tournament is booked? Suggest options that may be offered to the group to accommodate their golf tournament at the resort.

6. Compare and contrast managing a golf operation, a mountain resort, and a theme park. Consider operations, staffing requirements, peripheral services offered, pricing, and revenue optimization strategies for each of the three.

7. Explain the differences between a destination spa and an amenity spa. Why may salon services not be offered at a destination spa? Why may a destination spa require a multiple-day stay?

8. Identify and discuss the challenges that resort operators often encounter, particularly in island and remote destinations. Include the concept of lift in the discussion.

ENDNOTES

Davis, R. (n.d.). N.C. beach house inferno highlights well-known risks. *USA Today*. Retrieved from https://login.ezproxy.fgcu.edu/login?url=http://search.ebscohost.com/login.aspx?direct=true&db=a9h&AN=J0E162016733407&site=ehost-live

IRS (2019). *Independent Contractor Defined*. Accessed February 20, 2019 online at: https://www.irs.gov/businesses/small-businesses-self-employed/independent-contractor-defined

iSpa (2018). 2018 ISPA U.S. Spa Industry Study. *International Spa Association*; Available online at: https://experienceispa.com/resources/research.

Lazo, A. (2015, Oct 26). U.S. news: Measure targets short-term rentals. *Wall Street Journal*; Retrieved February 15, 2019 at: http://ezproxy.fgcu.edu/login?url=https://search-proquest-com.ezproxy.fgcu.edu/docview/1726673650?accountid=10919

Manning, C., deRoos, J., O'Neill, J. W., Bloom, B. A. N., Agarwal, A., & Roulac, S. (2018). Hotel/lodging real estate industry trends and innovations. *Journal of Real Estate Literature*, *26*(1), 13–41.

Outdoor Foundation. (2018). Outdoor Participation Report 2018; July 2018; p. 39; accessed February 19, 2019 through the Statista Database online at https://www.statista.com/study/17509/golf-statista-dossier/.

Scott, S., & O'Connor, A. (2007, October 31). Students' dreams ended in rush of morning fire. *New York Times*, p. A19(L).

Schwartzel, E. (2018). Disneyland's ticket to ride is $299. *Wall Street Journal*, Eastern Edition; New York, New York; 19 June; pp. B1 & B2.

Statista. (2018). Statista Global Consumer Survey 2018. June; accessed February 19, 2019 through the Statista Database online at https://www.statista.com/study/17509/golf-statista-dossier/.

Tan, G. & Callanan, N. (2018). Marriott Vacations Agrees to Buy ILG for About $4.7 Billion; *Bloomberg*; New York City, NY. Accessed online on February 13, 2019 at: https://www.bloomberg.com/news/articles/2018-04-30/marriott-vacations-agrees-to-acquire-ilg-for-about-4-7-billion.

USCIS. (2019). H-2B Temporary Non-Agricultural Workers. *United States Customs and Immigration Services*. Retrieved February 20, 2019 at: https://www.uscis.gov/working-united-states/temporary-workers/h-2b-temporary-non-agricultural-workers

USDA. (n.d.). US Forest Ski Area Program. *United States Department of Agriculture*; accessed on February 20, 2019 online at: https://www.fs.fed.us/recreation/programs/ski_water.../ski_area_program_info.pdf.

Wisnom, Mary (2013). Resort Recreation Amenity Report. *Journal of Tourism Insights*; 4(1); Article 1. Available at: https://doi.org/10.9707/2328-0824.1039.

Zervas, G., Proserpio, D., & Byers, J. W. (2017). The rise of the sharing economy: estimating the impact of Airbnb on the hotel industry. *Journal of Marketing Research* (JMR), 54(5), 687–705.

Section Five

DELIVERING A RETURN TO HOTEL INVESTORS

SECTION 5: DELIVERING A RETURN TO HOTEL INVESTORS

Chapter 10: Maintaining the Hotel Asset and Sustainability

The appropriate maintenance of the hotel, mechanical systems, and equipment is a key responsibility that protects the value of the real estate asset and is the focus of this chapter, which also includes a discussion on sustainability issues.

Chapter 11: Administration and Control: Human Resources, Accounting, and Loss Prevention

This chapter outlines strategies to successfully employ and manage a team of hospitality professionals that can deliver exceptional guest experiences, while simultaneously driving the profitability of the hotel. The chapter outlines the key human resource strategies and accounting processes necessary to deliver successful business outcomes, while also exploring the role of the loss prevention team.

Chapter 12: Hotel Investment

This chapter takes a deeper look at hotel operations from the perspective of hotel investors, including the assessment of a hotel's performance as a real estate investment.

Chapter 10

Maintaining the Hotel Asset and Sustainability

The appropriate maintenance of the hotel, mechanical systems, and equipment is a key responsibility that protects the value of the real estate asset, which is the focus of this chapter. The chapter also includes a discussion of sustainability issues.

PURPOSE AND LEARNING OBJECTIVES:

This chapter provides readers with the knowledge and ability to:

- Describe the various building systems and mechanical equipment that must be maintained in a hotel environment.
- Explain how the property operations and maintenance or engineering department is staffed, and labor productivity assured.
- Identify the categories of management information systems (MIS) commonly used to support the property operations and maintenance (POM) functions.
- Identify and describe the three categories of service calls.
- Discuss the types of support that a director of engineering may seek from outside contractors and explain why this support may benefit the hotel.
- Discuss the capital expenditure process, including the 5-year rolling capital expenditure plan.
- Calculate the payback or return on investment (ROI) from a capital expenditure.
- Describe the various sustainability programs executed by responsible hotel operators.

CHAPTER OUTLINE:

SCOPE OF THE PROPERTY OPERATIONS AND MAINTENANCE DEPARTMENT

The property operations and maintenance (POM) department, commonly referred to as the engineering department in many hotels, is responsible for the maintenance of the physical building, real estate, and equipment required to successfully operate the hotel. The scope of the director of engineering's responsibility includes the maintenance and repair of a variety of physical assets, building systems, and equipment.

property operations and maintenance (POM) or engineering department: maintains the hotel's physical assets, building systems, and equipment

director of engineering: an exempt manager that oversees the maintenance of the hotel's physical assets, building systems, and equipment, serving as a member of the executive operating committee

© industryviews/Shutterstock.com

Building Systems

Building systems in a hotel include the following:

Electrical Systems

The electric distribution system receives power from its source, typically the local electric utility, and distributes it throughout the property. It consists of transformers that receive power at extremely high voltages from the power company, reducing the voltage to appropriate levels for its distribution and use throughout the hotel. Increasingly, hotel electrical systems may be supplemented by an on-property solar energy system.

Water Systems

Like electricity, water must be received from its source, typically the local water authority, and distributed throughout the property for guest use within the hotel's guestrooms, as well as use within operational areas including the kitchen and laundry. Water may also be needed to support recreational and wellness activities—including pools, spas, and steam rooms. The life-safety system may also require water within the sprinkler system for fire-suppression. Hotels may use well-water or water from a retention pond for irrigating the grounds and landscape, requiring the maintenance of a pumping station or aeration system. Water systems may also segregate water into potable water, for human consumption, and gray water, treated or reusable water used for specific applications. A hotel water system must typically be able to heat water to different temperatures for use in the kitchen, laundry, and guestrooms. Waste water and sewage must be removed from the property for treatment. Water is also used in some heating, ventilation, and air conditioning HVAC systems.

building systems: essential equipment required to make a structure functional and safe, including electrical systems, plumbing, lighting, ventilation, and life safety systems

electric distribution system: receives power from its source, typically the local electric utility, and distributes it throughout the property

potable water: water for human consuption

gray water: treated or reusable water used for specific applications

Heating, Ventilation, and Air Conditioning Systems

Heating, ventilation, and air conditioning (HVAC) systems are designed to maintain comfortable temperatures in all areas of the hotel, including both the front-of-the-house and heart-of-the-house areas. Another important aspect of an HVAC system is to balance the interior air, ensuring that air is taken into the HVAC system for treatment and discharged from the system following treatment in a manner that does not create drafts or air pressure discrepancies between various areas or rooms within the hotel. A hotel may use a centralized heating and cooling system, which pumps hot or cold fluids through a system of pipes from a central cooling tower, chiller, or boiler to individual air handlers throughout the building; a decentralized system or network of package units, or individual heating and cooling units that each heat or cool the air independently; or a combination of both—using a centralized system in the hotel's public areas and individual package units in the hotel guestrooms, for example.

Alternative Fuel Systems

Most hotels use natural gas or other types of fuel, as opposed to electricity, as a source of heat in their commercial kitchens, laundry, HVAC, and water systems. The system to receive, store, and distribute this fuel must be routinely inspected and maintained.

Life Safety Systems

A hotel's life safety system includes a firm alarm system that alerts guests and associates, both audibly and visually, of a potential emergency; emergency relay stations or pull-stations are typically found throughout the hotel, which may be manually activated by hotel guests or associates, or the alarm system may automatically activate when water flow occurs in the

© A_stockphoto/Shutterstock.com

sprinkler or fire suppression system. The fire alarm system is connected to a fire control panel that informs the emergency response team or fire brigade of the location and nature of the alarm (e.g. "manual pull station," "west end," on the "5th guestroom floor"). The fire alarm system often includes a broadcast system that allows announcements to be made informing guests and associates the nature of the alarm. Life safety systems also include an emergency power system, supported by an emergency generator, which must be maintained and tested weekly; a fire suppression system in the kitchen; sprinkler systems throughout the public, heart-of-the-house, and guestroom areas; fire doors with automatic, electro-magnetic releases; and pressurized escape stairwells that prevent smoke from entering, leading evacuees directly outside of the building. A detailed discussion of emergency procedures may be found in the Loss Prevention section of *Chapter 11: Administration and Control: Human Resources, Accounting, and Loss Prevention.*

Lighting Systems

Lighting systems include systems that provide ambient light to supplement natural light during the daylight hours, while providing basic visual light during the evening and overnight hours, as well as more sophisticated lighting systems necessary to accommodate guests' needs in the meeting and event space. Restaurants, lounges, and other areas of the hotel often require special lighting systems to create a specific ambiance or special effects.

Wireless Service, Internet of Things, and Entertainment Systems

In today's connected world, guests demand nearly constant access to a Wi-Fi Internet connection. As a result, the bandwidth of Internet service available to guests must be adequate to support guests' desires to not only conduct their business affairs on the laptops, tablets, and smartphones, but to also stream music and movies on their devices. Many hotels, particularly upper-upscale and luxury hotels, also offer guests a wide array of entertainment offerings, including first-run movie and other pay-per-view options. Consequently, hotels are installing increasingly sophisticated Internet systems to support the use of technology throughout the hotel—by both hotel guests and associates—because technology is also being used more extensively to monitor the activities and productivity of associates and to support management control functions.

Telecommunications Systems

Although technology relies increasingly on wireless technology, guestroom televisions and telephones remain connected via wires and cables; conventional telephones are located throughout the guestrooms, offices, and heart-of-the-house areas, which may be critical in emergency situations. These systems must be maintained, not only to support emergency communications, but to provide a variety of television viewing options and services within the guestrooms, reducing demand on the hotel's wireless capacity. Guestroom telephones are still used in some hotels to relay guestroom status, to provide wake-up call service, to place in-room dining orders, or to request guests contact the guest services team at their convenience by illuminating a message light. Many guests enjoy the convenience of contacting hotel staff using the in-room telephone or to order room service, check the balance on their account, or check-out of the hotel using the television's remote control.

fire suppression system: devices including overhead sprinklers and dry chemical systems designed to extinguish a fire automatically upon being detected by the system

fire control panel: the central panel to which all fire detection and suppression devices are connected, which displays the location and cause of an alarm

emergency generator: a diesel engine that generates sufficient electricity to maintain basic lighting, the life safety system, and other essential operating systems in the event of a power outage

sprinkler systems: a network of sprinklers located throughout the public areas and guestrooms designed to extinguish a fire upon detection

fire doors: doors with a specified burn-through rating that close automatically when fire is detected to minimize the spread of a fire and the smoke produced

pressurized escape stairwells: emergency escape paths that lead guests out of the building while protecting them from smoke inhalation

lighting systems : systems that provide ambient light to supplement natural light, basic visual light, and a range of lighting options in the meeting and event space

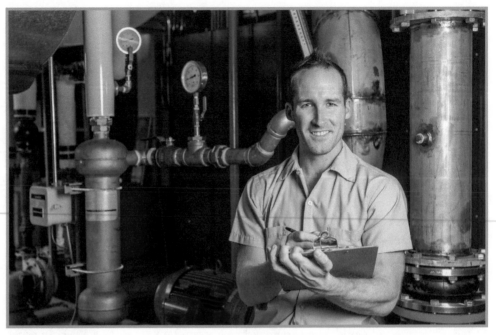

© Lopolo/Shutterstock.com

Engineering Knowledge, Skills, and Abilities

To appropriately manage and maintain the various systems within the hotel, the engineering department must assemble a team of engineers with the specific knowledge, skills, and abilities (KSAs) necessary to maintain, troubleshoot, and repair the wide-variety of operating equipment required in a hotel setting. Some of the specific KSAs that an engineering department's personnel must collectively possess include the following:

Mechanical KSAs

HVAC or refrigeration mechanic:
a non-exempt associate with the skills and certification to repair and maintain refrigeration and HVAC systems

The employment of an HVAC or refrigeration mechanic that has the skills and certification to work with refrigerants and to repair refrigerators, freezers, and HVAC systems is critically important in a hotel setting. Cooling and refrigeration equipment typically use coils filled with refrigerants under high-pressure and air flow to cool the temperature within a specific environment, whether within a walk-in or reach-in refrigerator or freezer, or a specific room or space as part of an HVAC system.

boiler mechanic:
a non-exempt associate with the skills to repair and maintain high pressure boilers and heat exchangers

Hot water is needed in a variety of applications within a hotel; boilers or heat exchangers are used to heat water in a commercial building. A boiler mechanic has the knowledge and expertise to maintain a high-pressure boiler system, as well as heat exchangers. A hotel will typically employ a minimum of two boilers or heat exchangers: one to provide hot water to the guestrooms and a second to provide hot water to the commercial areas of the hotel, including the kitchen and laundry. A third boiler may also be maintained as part of a centralized HVAC system, if hot water is used as the medium in a radiator system. With a minimum of two boilers providing potable hot water, there is redundancy, safeguarding the hotel against complete system failure, while also allowing the boiler serving the guestrooms to be set at a lower temperature, eliminating the likelihood that a guest suffers a scalding incident. Water in commercial areas may then be set at a higher temperature to improve the effective, efficient operation of laundry and other equipment; some commercial equipment, such as commercial dishwashers, require even higher water temperatures, using booster heaters to raise the water temperature even further, as required by local or state health regulations.

A kitchen mechanic is qualified to repair and maintain the wide-variety of kitchen equipment found within a hotel, including grills, flattop griddles, broilers, cooktops, deep-fryers, convection ovens, steamers, jacketed kettles, mixers, and a nearly endless variety of other equipment and small appliances, depending upon the nature and scope of the food and beverage (F&B) operation. Most of this equipment typically uses natural gas, as opposed to electricity, because its heat is instant, easily controlled, and more energy efficient.

© Taras Vyshnya/ Shutterstock.com

kitchen mechanic: a non-exempt associate qualified to repair and maintain the wide-variety of kitchen equipment found within a hotel

All heated kitchen equipment must be properly vented via a commercial exhaust hood that must be maintained, although the cleaning of the hood is routinely performed by culinary and stewarding personnel, as well as by an outside vendor quarterly. An automatic, dry-chemical fire suppression system must also be in place and properly maintained in the kitchen area, which is routinely inspected by POM, but typically maintained through an outside contract to reduce the hotel's liability. The most expensive piece of kitchen equipment in many commercial kitchens, particularly in a large upper-upscale or luxury hotel, is often the commercial dishwasher, which is typically a conveyor-style machine; however, much of the maintenance and support needed to maintain the commercial dishwasher is provided by the hotel's supplier of dishwashing chemicals.

A general mechanic may also be employed to maintain and repair the hotel's commercial laundry equipment, although this responsibility sometimes falls on the kitchen mechanic, particularly in a smaller or less complex hotel operation. As discussed in

general mechanic: a non-exempt associate qualified to repair and maintain a hotel's mechanical devices, including laundry equipment

Chapter 7: Housekeeping and Laundry Operations, most hotels operate a commercial laundry that processes thousands of pounds of laundry daily, requiring a variety of laundry equipment, including high-capacity washers/extractors, dryers, folders, and often a large, high-temperature flatwork roller iron, which often presents regular maintenance challenges. Engineering personnel with mechanical skills may also be used to repair the wide variety of smaller operating equipment used throughout the hotel, including vacuums, floor buffers, carts, mixers, blenders, motorized equipment, and the like.

Building Trades

The engineering team includes an electrician among its building tradespersons, commonly employed to troubleshoot any problems with the hotel's electrical system, to maintain the hotel's electrical equipment, and to support the electrical needs of meetings and conferences being held on property. It is not uncommon for a conference to require additional power—beyond the meeting space's capacity—be made available to conference guests, particularly if a tradeshow is taking place in the hotel's ballroom or exhibit space. Plumbers are also needed to maintain the hotel's water system, including pipes, drains, and sewage connections.

Hotels often employ engineering personnel to serve as carpenters, masons, and painters, doubling as wall vinyl technicians. Sheetrock walls within hotels are typically covered with heavy wall vinyl, particularly in guestrooms and high traffic areas, to reduce the likelihood of damage and to simplify cleaning; however, it is not uncommon to open walls or ceilings to make repairs to plumbing, electrical, or HVAC systems. Hotel rooms are routinely damaged by guests; doors and door frames are struck by carts filled with heavy loads; red wine is spilled on carpets; and delivery trucks sometimes fail to appropriately navigate tight turns, just to mention a few of the potential causes of the wide-variety of damage that occurs to a hotel's walls, ceilings, door frames, equipment, carpet, furniture, and building exterior. The engineering department must be prepared to quickly and efficiently repair any damage that occurs, maintaining the facility in the best condition possible—the more in-house skills the engineering team has among its workforce, the more quickly and efficiently the necessary repairs can be made.

Although all front-line personnel within the engineering department are typically referred to as engineers, each member of the engineering team typically falls into one of three categories: shift engineer, skilled tradesperson, or preventative maintenance personnel, as illustrated in *Diagram 10.1: POM Organizational Structure.*

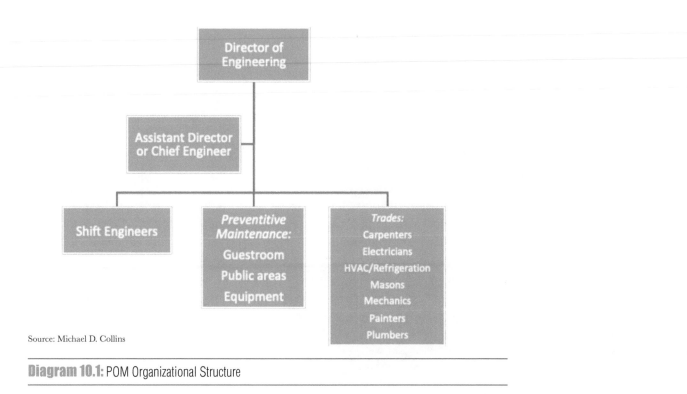

Source: Michael D. Collins

Diagram 10.1: POM Organizational Structure

The number of guestrooms, operational complexity, and annual revenue of a hotel will determine the precise number of engineers employed by a specific hotel. The department is managed by a director of engineering, a member of the hotel's executive operating committee (EOC), assisted by an exempt assistant director of engineering or a non-exempt chief engineer. In large hotels of 500-rooms or more, an exempt assistant director of engineering and a non-exempt, supervisory chief engineer may both be employed.

POM Expenses

POM expenditures total 4.2% of revenue in upper-upscale hotels in the United States, which brings total annual engineering department expenses to just over $1.3 million in a typical upper-upscale hotel with 400 guestrooms (STR, 2017). A minimum of 35% to 40% of this expenditure may be spent on engineering salaries and wages, depending upon the structure of the department and the proportion of work that is completed by in-house personnel, which may support an engineering team of 6 to 10 engineering managers, supervisors, and line associates in a typical 400-room hotel. The size and scope of the F&B operation also impacts engineering staffing. As F&B revenue increases, the hotel must add engineering personnel to support the expanded F&B facilities, meeting space, and equipment necessary to generate this added revenue.

assistant director of engineering:
an exempt manager that assists the director of engineering in overseeing the POM department

chief engineer:
a non-exempt supervisor that assists engineering management in overseeing the POM department

At a minimum, an upper-upscale or luxury hotel requires three shift engineers that provide basic coverage of the department from 7 a.m. until midnight, 7-days or 14-shifts-per-week, to ensure that maintenance personnel are available over the course of each day to respond to guest calls—addressing guest needs in their guestrooms and the hotel's conference center. The shift engineer also responds to any management or associate calls to address urgent maintenance needs throughout the hotel operation. Maintenance requests are entered into a work order system by hotel staff to communicate all maintenance requests—both urgent and non-urgent—to the engineering department. Shift engineers often complete a routine check of all light bulbs throughout the public areas of the hotel, check thermostat settings and temperature readings, test water chemical levels in pools and spas, and perform other routine duties outlined on a daily shift checklist when not responding to a specific call. Shift engineers often double-

© Alhim/Shutterstock.com

ble as tradespersons and may be assigned specific work orders to complete between calls during their scheduled shifts.

CATEGORIES OF MAINTENANCE TASKS

Guest Calls

As discussed in *Chapter 6: Guest Services*, maintenance requests from guests are often received by the PBX operator or at your service (AYS) agent stationed at the hotel's switchboard or front office. Requests are logged by guest services personnel as part of a second effort program designed to ensure that all guest requests are quickly addressed to the guest's complete satisfaction. After a guest request is received, the shift engineer is contacted via a two-way radio, and the specific request is relayed to the engineer. The engineer then gathers the tools or equipment he/she anticipates needing to address the concern prior to arriving at the guestroom or specific location of the request. The engineer announces his/her arrival before entering a guestroom and then proceeds to effectively and efficiently remedy the specific situation. After the engineer has confirmed that the guest is satisfied with the solution and corrective action, the engineer will notify guest services personnel that the matter has been resolved. The PBX Operator or AYS agent then contacts the guest to confirm complete satisfaction with the resolution of the concern. Appropriate notations are made in the second effort log. At the end of each month, maintenance requests received from guests are summarized in a Pareto chart so that frequently occurring maintenance requests may be eliminated or reduced.

Work Orders

Internal maintenance requests, generated by hotel associates, are entered into the work order system, which are reviewed and prioritized each shift by engineering management. These tasks are assigned to the various engineers based upon each team member's specific KSAs. The shift engineer may be notified of an urgent request—which directly impacts guests, associates, or the effective and efficient operation of the hotel—via two-way radio. The assigned engineer records the time he/she starts working on the maintenance request; the parts and resources used to make the necessary repair, adjustment, or correction to address the request; and the time he/she completes the request. This allows the director of engineering to track the cost of completing a specific repair, while also monitoring the productivity of each member of the engineering team. If a request cannot be immediately addressed—because parts or additional time is needed—then the engineer notes this in the system so that the parts can be ordered, and the work can be rescheduled.

For example, a work order may be submitted noting that an air handler within a meeting room makes a "squeaking noise" at its initial start-up. An HVAC mechanic is assigned the work request and, after initially assessing the situation, determines that the fan belt needs to be replaced; however, the belt needed is not in stock and the repair will take 45 to 60 minutes to complete. Therefore, to complete the request, the belt must be ordered and, once received, the work must be scheduled during a 1-hour window during which this specific meeting room is not in use. As a result, the engineer changes the status of the work order to "parts on order" and moves on to the next assigned work order. Once the fan belt arrives, the repair may be scheduled for completion while the room is not in use; the HVAC mechanic re-opens the request, makes the necessary repair, and closes the request, as "complete," following the repair.

Preventative Maintenance

preventative maintenance (PM): routine tasks that must be completed at scheduled intervals to maintain the hotel, building systems, and equipment

The preventative maintenance (PM) team falls into three categories: guestroom, public area, and equipment. The guestroom PM technician methodically progresses through each guestroom on a scheduled basis to inspect the room from top-to-bottom, using a prescribed checklist, looking for any maintenance-related concerns, while completing any necessary repairs. The guestroom PM cart has the equipment and spare parts necessary to address many common problems found in the guestrooms, such as repairing a small tear in the wall vinyl, removing a water ring on a guestroom table, replacing a lampshade finial, adjusting the valve-and-float in the toilet tank, repairing a dripping faucet, or replacing a curtain's pull rod. The PM technician may also be responsible for changing guestroom HVAC filters and performing other

guestroom PM technician: a non-exempt POM associate that routinely inspects guestrooms, completing necessary PM tasks and other repairs as required

routine maintenance items in the guestrooms or guestroom corridors, such as touching-up interior closet paint or nicks on chair-rails and doorframes.

Public area PM involves completing a routine, systematic inspection of a hotel's public areas, including lobbies, public restrooms, exercise and recreational facilities, pre-function, and meeting space. As these areas are inspected by the public area PM technician; this engineering professional typically has a background in general construction enabling him/her to make a wide range of basic repairs to furniture, carpet, plumbing fixtures, and wall vinyl.

The equipment PM technicians perform preventative maintenance tasks on mechanical equipment and building systems, as assigned. Tasks may include changing the fan belt or repacking the bearings on an air handler; checking the gas-flow or thermostat calibration on a specific piece of laundry or kitchen equipment; cleaning or replacing filters for the hotel's pool or whirlpool; or routine flushing or testing of back-flow valves in a floor drain system. Because a hotel operates 24-hours per day, 7-days per week, it is important that PM is performed on all the hotel's operating system, as required, to prevent systems from failing, which may result in guest inconvenience or impede hotel associates from effectively and efficiently performing their assigned responsibilities. *Box 10.1: PM Before It's Too Late!* emphasizes the importance of routine maintenance processes.

SAFETY

Engineers must take the necessary precautions to maintain a safe working environment. This includes taking common sense precautions, such as requiring two engineers to be present when work is being completed while standing on a ladder, as well as implementing the safety precautions necessary to prevent accidents, injuries, or even death. One such safety precaution is a lock-out–tag-out program. A lock-out–tag-out program requires that an engineer shut-off the power to any equipment while work is being completed on the respective equipment; this includes repairs and routine maintenance tasks. For example, if an engineer is working on a refrigeration compressor, the engineer completing the work must shut the power off to the unit at the breaker box that feeds unit. The breaker switch should be tagged, indicating the date and time at which the power was shut-off, and the breaker box locked so that another engineer or associate cannot open the box and restore power to the unit. The breaker box should only be unlocked, the tag removed from the switch, and the power restored to the unit by the engineer that originally tagged the breaker switch as out-of-service.

BOX 10.1: PM BEFORE IT'S TOO LATE!

Darryl Hartley-Leonard, the retired President of *Hyatt Hotels Corporation*, professed that hotel owners and managers have made a multi-million dollar mistake if all they have done is make their guests feel *at home* while visiting their property. Afterall, hotel owners invest millions-of-dollars to design and construct hotels. As a result, the ultimate goal is to create a special place, where guests feel *better* than simply being at home!

© August_0802/Shutterstock.com

Maintaining the hotel's environment is critical to ensuring that a hotel remains a special place long after its initial construction. John Ceriale—a hotel advisor who has enjoyed a long and illustrious career managing and investing in world-class hotels—served as General Manager of a newly opened *Marriott Hotel* early in his career. Within weeks of the hotel's initial opening, John started the hotel's in-house painters on their never-ending mission—to re-paint the hotel's interior from top-to-bottom. As a young manager, fresh out of *Marriott's Individual Development* training program at the time, I questioned why Mr. Ceriale already felt that the hotel required a fresh coat of paint—we had just barely opened our doors! John responded to my curiosity by explaining that it was critically important that the hotel be impeccably maintained; we were just given the keys to a brand-new hotel—it was our responsibility to keep the hotel—and our operating equipment—looking and functioning like new. By the time it looks like a surface requires a fresh coat of paint, it is simply too late—the condition of the hotel has deteriorated to an unacceptable condition.

The critical importance of the POM function was re-confirmed later in my hotel career, while serving as a general manager (GM) of a hotel in suburban Atlanta, Georgia. At the time, hotels in the market were struggling financially due to overbuilding—the supply of hotel rooms in the area had nearly doubled during a 2-year time frame, whereas the increase in demand for accommodations had failed to keep pace. As a result, the hotel was not achieving its financial goals. One way to reduce costs and help maintain forecasted profit margins was to reduce POM costs; however, within weeks, deferred maintenance began to impact the operation, negatively impacting the guest experience, associate productivity, and the hotel's competitive position. After walking through the hotel with the investors' asset manager to assess the impact of our prescribed austerity program, the hotel's POM budget was fully restored. Planned capital expenditure projects, which had been placed on hold, were put back on schedule. As the asset manager stated, jeopardizing the value of a multi-million dollar real estate investment to save tens-of-thousands-of-dollars, by deferring necessary maintenance and reinvestment projects, is *penny-wise and pound-foolish*.

> asset manager:
> a real estate professional that serves as the interface between ownership and management, responsible for representing ownership's interests

This lesson served me well throughout my hotel industry career: always maintain the asset—doing otherwise is simply not an option!
Michael D. Collins, author of *Delivering the Guest Experience*

INFORMATION TECHNOLOGY

facility management
system (FMS):
an IT system used to
track and schedule POM
activities related to the
maintenance and repair of
a real estate asset, including buildings, building
systems, and equipment

Two primary IT systems support the POM or engineering department: a facility management system (FMS) and an energy management system. Many FMSs are cloud-based, providing access to a database that outlines the maintenance requirements of specific building systems and equipment. Engineering management enters a list of all major machinery and equipment within the hotel into the FMS so that an electronic file is created for each piece of equipment, allowing all routine maintenance and repairs performed to be recorded and tracked individually and collectively—including the time invested by engineering associates or outside contractors and any additional costs associated with the maintenance work. The system also assists in the successful management of the PM program, generating a list of specific tasks that must be completed each week to maintain the hotel's major equipment and building systems. Some FMSs include an electronic work order system that receives and tracks maintenance requests sent to the POM department, although a separate electronic system, or a manual system, may be used in some hotel settings. An electronic system may also include a mobile application that allows engineers access to their assigned work orders on their smartphones, as well as electronic dashboards that track employee productivity and costs.

energy management
system (EMS):
an IT system used to mon-
itor and manage a hotel's
energy consumption

The energy management system (EMS) is used to monitor and manage a hotel's energy consumption. Hotels are massive consumers of utility resources, including electricity. The EMS monitors the consumption of electricity throughout the hotel, shutting down systems when appropriate. For example, while the in-room thermostat may control a meeting room's temperature when a meeting is scheduled to be in progress, the system may override the thermostat settings when the room is not scheduled to be in use. A similar phenomenon may take place in the guestrooms, allowing the EMS to automatically reduce or eliminate energy consumption in vacant hotel guestrooms. Energy consumption in public areas of the hotel, including lobbies, pre-function space, and F&B outlets may also be reduced when these areas are not scheduled to be in use. Because electric utility rates vary based upon the peak demand generated by a business, the EMS often has the capability of cycling the hotel's equipment that consumes the largest amounts of electricity on-and-off to minimize the hotel's peak demand for electricity, lowering its utility rates.

maintenance contract:
outlines the terms and
defines the inclusions,
exclusions, and costs
for a vendor to provide
maintenance services for
a specific asset for the
specified time period

OUTSIDE CONTRACTORS

Although a hotel typically performs as many maintenance functions in-house as possible, there are some functions that require the expertise and support of outside contractors. Maintenance contracts are typically in place with outside vendors to maintain the hotel's elevators and escalators. Elevators must be periodically inspect-

© Dmitry Kalinovsky/Shutterstock.com

ed, and the cables replaced on a scheduled basis to ensure their safety. Repairs to these complex mechanical devices are often time consuming and require specific skills that must be performed by trained personnel that are extremely familiar with their mechanical systems and technology. Maintenance of a hotel's exterior signs, lawn and grounds maintenance, snow removal, and pest control are other examples of services typically provided by outside vendors. Periodic parking lot or garage maintenance, including sealing and re-striping, is also contracted out, as needed.

Life safety equipment, such as fire extinguishers, fire axes, fire hoses, defibrillators, and first aid kits, must also be maintained, in addition to the life-safety and fire suppression systems. The presence of fire safety equipment in proper locations throughout the hotel are verified by loss prevention officers when they make their periodic rounds each day, whereas the routine testing of the fire alarm system, pressurized stairwells, fire-door-release systems, and emergency generator is completed and documented on a regularly scheduled basis; however, the maintenance of the life safety system is typically provided by an outside contractor that verifies that the system is in proper working order on a periodic basis, which may reduce the hotel's potential liability. Quite frankly, a hotel cannot afford to risk a system malfunction in an actual emergency.

life safety equipment: equipment used in a medical or emergency situation to include fire extinguishers, fire axes, fire hoses, defibrillators, and first aid kits

Information technology (IT) throughout the hotel must also be maintained. Although in-house POM personnel may support or coordinate hardware maintenance in some hotels, the software maintenance for each management information system (MIS) is typically assigned to a system administrator from among the software application's users (e.g. a sales administrative assistant for the sales management system; accounting personnel for the accounting or EMS; a guest services manager for the PMS; the revenue manager for the revenue management system [RMS]; and an F&B manager for the F&B POS system). Of course, a member of the engineering management team typically serves as the system administrator for the facilities management or energy management system.

system administrator: the in-house associate assigned to serve as the interface between the users of a software application and the software provider

Because many software applications are cloud-based, annual or multi-year licenses are purchased based upon the number of users requiring access to the respective system, which are billed monthly and include ongoing technical support and periodic software updates; many software applications support a range of related services and are priced based upon the specific software functions covered by the hotel's licensing agreement with the vendor. For example, a base fee may be charged for a basic FMS license, with additional add-on functions, such as a work order system, labor-management package, or maintenance cost tracking system available, each at an additional cost. The same type of graduated pricing schedule is typically provided on all categories of business application software—including enterprise management, sales management, revenue management, property management, human resource management, purchasing and receiving, and point-of-sale (POS) software packages.

cloud-based: computer and mobile software applications that run and store data on an off-premise server maintained by the software provider

Finally, many hotels operate a fleet of commercial vehicles—including vans and automobiles—to provide guest transportation, as well as utility vehicles, to support the operation. A resort hotel, particularly if spread over several acres or among multiple buildings, may maintain a fleet of motorized carts to transport guests, personnel, laundry, banquet, and other equipment on the grounds or between buildings. If lawn, landscaping, and snow removal maintenance is provided in-house, the appropriate equipment must be acquired, stored, and maintained. A hotel that maintains just one or two vehicles will typically use a local automotive service facility to maintain the vehicle; however, if the hotel or resort maintains a large fleet of electric carts, a technician qualified to service and repair the vehicles may be included on-staff.

commercial vehicles: automobiles, buses, trucks, vans, and other vehicles used to support the hotel's operation

SUCCESSFUL ENGINEERING MANAGEMENT

Accountability

As is essential to the successful management of any area of the hotel's operation, a system of accountability must be established within the engineering department. As stated in *Chapter 7: Housekeeping and Laundry Operations*, it is important that managers *inspect-what-they-expect*. Consequently, engineering management must walk through the hotel on a daily basis and personally inspect the work that is being completed by engineering associates—including both repair work and PM tasks; weekly walk-throughs with the GM, director of engineering, rooms director, F&B director, and executive housekeeper should include guestrooms, public areas, and heart-of-the-house areas. As the cleanliness of an area is inspected, so should engineering details. Feedback should be provided to engineers regarding the quality of their work and appreciation expressed when a job is well-done.

Guest comments about maintenance-related concerns, posted on review sites, mentioned in comment cards, or reported to hotel associates, must be relayed to the POM department through the submission of work orders, as well as by two-way radio if a concern is urgent. Periodically, the GM and senior managers of the hotel should randomly check to ensure that maintenance concerns reported by guests have been addressed by POM, verifying that an effective guest feedback loop is in place. If a maintenance item within a guestroom will potentially cause a guest inconvenience, the guestroom must be placed out-of-service until the necessary repair is made; however, allowing guestrooms to remain out-of-service overnight must be avoided—maintenance items that impact guestroom availability must be prioritized, particularly on nights that a room can be rented.

feedback loop: a system that seeks continuous input from stakeholders to assess, evaluate, and enhance the effectiveness of systems, processes, procedures, and tactics, thereby ensuring continuous improvement of business outcomes

out-of-service: equipment or guestrooms that cannot be utilized until essential repairs are completed

Recordkeeping

Keeping detailed records, a responsibility often facilitated by the FMS, is critical. Detailed maintenance records allow the director of engineering to track the productivity of engineering associates; the cost of maintaining each building system and piece of major operating equipment; the status of all work in-progress; and all work completed within each guestroom, meeting room, heart-of-the-house, and public area, while keeping PM programs on schedule. At the start of each day, the director of engineering should verify that each team member was productive during the previous day, while confirming that an appropriate workload is assigned to each engineering associate for the current day; tasks should be prioritized so that most important items are completed first, allowing less important items to roll-over to the following day, if necessary. Engineers should be assigned to complete duties individually, unless a specific task requires two or more engineers. Engineers should review their assigned work prior to leaving the maintenance shop so that appropriate tools and equipment can be placed in tool belts or on maintenance carts, eliminating unnecessary trips to-and-from the shop.

© Patiwat Sariya/Shutterstock.com

CAPITAL EXPENDITURES

Most day-to-day expenses incurred by a hotel are operating expenses—basic supplies, materials, and equipment that are consumed by guests or used by associates to deliver the services, products, and experiences offered by the hotel. Examples of operating expenses include cleaning supplies, F&B products, replacement of damaged glassware and linen, guestroom amenities, and the parts necessary to make repairs to equipment, just to list a handful of examples. These expenses are approved by hotel management and recorded each month in the appropriate expense category on the hotel's profit and loss (P&L) statement. Please refer to *Chapter 11: Administration and Control: Human Resources, Accounting, and Loss Prevention* for a more detailed discussion on financial statements.

capital expense:
an expenditure that exceeds a defined minimum value to purchase and place into service an asset that has a useful life of longer than 1 year

A capital expense is an expenditure that exceeds a defined minimum value to purchase and place into service an asset that has a useful life of longer than 1 year; hotel management firms specifically define the minimum value and life-expectancy of a capital asset. For example, a firm may establish a policy that only an aggregate purchase in excess of $2,500 for assets with a useful life of a minimum of 3 years may be capitalized. This policy specifies an aggregate purchase since installation, training, and other costs may be included in the capitalized expense, not just the asset

capital asset:
a depreciable asset with a value and useful life that exceed defined minimums

alone; this ensures that ancillary costs associated with the capital expenditure are not absorbed into the hotel's operating costs. Capital assets are recorded on the hotel's balance sheet as assets and depreciated over their useful life. In other words, the expense does not immediately impact the hotel's P&L statement but increases the value of the hotel's assets listed on its balance sheet, being expensed on the P&L statement over its useful life as a depreciation expense, rather than as a one-time operating expense. Again, please refer to *Chapter 11* for additional information regarding these accounting practices.

In a hotel setting, capital expenditures commonly involve the purchase of furniture, fixtures, and equipment (FF&E) to renovate areas of the hotel, such as the guestrooms, guestroom corridors, meeting spaces, food and beverage outlets, or lobbies and public spaces. The replacement of kitchen equipment, laundry equipment, HVAC units, and the upgrading of life-safety systems or MIS are also examples of common capital expenditures within a hotel setting. In addition to the cost of the physical assets, extra costs often included in a capital expenditure are design costs, purchasing fees, freight, installation, labor costs, and taxes. If, for example, a hotel is renovating its guestrooms, the interior design fees; the cost of the FF&E; any purchasing fees, taxes, and freight costs; payments to contractors; and the housekeeping labor costs to clean the newly renovated guestrooms to initially prepare them for guest occupancy may all be recorded as capital expenses. When installing new computer systems, training associates to use the system may also be included in the capital expense.

furniture, fixtures, and equipment (FF&E): capital assets that enhance the quality of the hotel's servicescape or operating effectiveness/efficiency

Creating a 5-Year Capital Expenditure Plan

A hotel management firm's contract to manage a hotel typically includes a requirement that a specific percentage of each year's revenue—typically, a minimum of 3% to 5% of revenue, depending upon the age of the property—is set aside for capital expenditures; a hotel's franchise agreement typically includes a similar provision. This ensures that hotel management has capital available in a capital reserve fund to replace major equipment and to renovate and maintain the condition of the hotel property, ensuring that it meets guests' expectations and the brand's standards. A portion of the funds may be set aside for emergency or unanticipated capital expenses, such as the failure of a major piece of equipment. When such an unanticipated capital need arises, a net present value (NPV) calculation may determine if the use of capital funds may be warranted. Please refer to *Box 10.2: Repair or Replace? The Dollars and Cents (Sense)* for additional insight.

capital reserve fund: money set aside to be invested in capital assets

net present value (NPV): the current worth of a series of projected future cash-flows, adjusted to allow for the time value of money

5-year capital expenditure plan (CapEx Plan): a planning document that lists the anticipated capital reserve contributions and expenditures for the next 5-years

The 5-year capital expenditure plan (CapEx Plan) is a document that outlines the amount of capital funds that are anticipated to be available for reinvestment back into the hotel over the subsequent 5-year period, based upon anticipated revenues and the contracted capital expenditure reserve. Capital funds are not generally spent in their entirety each year because many major projects—such as guestroom renovations or the renovation of meeting spaces, F&B outlets, or public areas—must be completed every 5 to 7 years, requiring more funds than the hotel will set aside in any single year. Consequently, the 5-year CapEx Plan is a planning document that clearly outlines the capital expenditures anticipated to be made in the upcoming year, while identifying additional expenditures that will need to be made in subsequent years. The document also provides the hotel's ownership with advance notice if the capital reserve fund may be inadequate to support the hotel's capital requirements necessary to maintain its competitive position or brand standards. It is important that hotel management notify the hotel's investors of additional capital needs a minimum of 2 to 3 years in advance.

BOX 10.2: REPAIR OR REPLACE? THE DOLLARS AND CENTS (SENSE)

© Joyseulay/Shutterstock.com

The director of engineering must often decide whether it is the best financial interest of hotel ownership for a repair to be made on a piece of equipment or if the equipment should be replaced. An NPV calculation may be used to identify the prudent financial decision.

As an example, assume that an HVAC unit requires an immediate repair expected to cost $710. The director of engineering has received a quote from an outside contractor to replace the unit for $9,375. If the unit is replaced, routine maintenance on the new unit will cost $25 per quarter whereas the ongoing cost of maintaining the repaired unit is estimated to run at least 20% higher at $30 quarterly. Although the HVAC mechanic has indicated that the current unit can be maintained in acceptable working order for at least 3 more years, the director of engineering wants to evaluate if replacing the unit now is a better business decision because the unit will eventually require replacement.

An NPV calculation can be used to evaluate this decision. To accurately calculate the NPV of a capital project, the director of engineering must know the hotel ownership's cost of capital or discount rate, coupled with the impact of the project on the hotel's cash-flow over the life of the project, using *Formula 10.1: NPV Formula.*

$$NPV = \sum_{t=0}^{n} \left[\frac{R_t}{(1+i)^t} \right]$$

Where: R_t = net cash inflow-outflows during a single period t

i = required return on investment or the discount rate

t = number of time periods

Formula 10.1: NPV Formula

To complete a cost-benefit analysis, the director of engineering must compare the NPV of the cash flows resulting from the immediate replacement of the unit with the cash flows that will result if the unit is replaced 3 years from now. *Table 10.1a: NPV of a Potential HVAC Replacement* estimates these cash flows. The actual cash flows resulting from the immediate replacement of the unit is a total outflow (negative amount) of $9,675 over the next 3 years, which is $9,375 in immediate outflow for the purchase and installation of the replacement unit plus the $25 cost of servicing the new unit each quarter. The hotel's controller has informed the director of engineering that the hotel's ownership expects at least a 10% return on capital expenditure projects. Therefore, using *Formula 10.1*, the director of engineering calculates the NPV of the resulting cash flows will total -$9,631.44 if the unit is replaced immediately. Notice that the initial $9,375 expenditure is not discounted using the NPV formula since this expenditure is made at the start of the 3 year period whereas the initial $25 maintenance cost is discounted since it occurs at the end of the first quarter following replacement.

If the current unit is repaired at a cost of $710, delaying the replacement of the unit for 3 years, the anticipated cash flows for the 3 year period total -$11,284.32, assuming the cost of replacing the unit rises to $10,244.32 using a 3% annual inflation factor; however, using the NPV formula and a 10% discount rate, the NPV of the cash flows resulting from the repair and delayed replacement of the unit is -$8,612.65. Again, the immediate outlay of $710 for the repair is not discounted, although future anticipated cash flows are due to the time value of money.

Therefore, it is in ownership's best financial interest not to replace the unit immediately, which would cost ownership approximately $1,000 more over the 3 year period (-$9,631.44 for immediate replacement versus -$8,612.65 for the repair and delayed replacement). Because a $8,665 difference exists between the cost of immediately replacing the unit for $9,375 and repairing the unit for $710, ownership can invest this difference in an alternative investment and the 10% annual return earned on this capital more than offsets the higher cost of replacing the unit after 3 years, coupled with the 20% increase in quarterly maintenance expense on the repaired unit.

Repair cost $	710.00
Current installed cost of replacement unit $	9,375.00
Replacement cost at end of 3-years (3% inflation) $	10,244.32

| Quarterly maintenance with replacement $ | 25.00 |
| Quarterly maintenance without replacement $ | 30.00 |

Quarter	3-year Total	Year 1				Year 2				Year 3			
		1st	2nd	3rd	4th	1st	2nd	3rd	4th	1st	2nd	3rd	4th
Cash-flow with immediate replacement	(9,675.00)	(9,400.00)	(25.00)	(25.00)	(25.00)	(25.00)	(25.00)	(25.00)	(25.00)	(25.00)	(25.00)	(25.00)	(25.00)
NPV of cash-flows with immediate replacement[1]	$ (9,631.44)	(9,399.39)	(23.80)	(23.21)	(22.65)	(22.10)	(21.56)	(21.03)	(20.52)	(20.02)	(19.53)	(19.05)	(18.59)
Cash-flow with delayed replacement	(11,284.32)	(740.00)	(30.00)	(30.00)	(30.00)	(30.00)	(30.00)	(30.00)	(30.00)	(30.00)	(30.00)	(30.00)	(10,244.32)
NPV of cash-flows with delayed replacement[1]	$ (8,612.65)	(739.27)	(28.55)	(27.86)	(27.18)	(26.52)	(25.87)	(25.24)	(24.62)	(24.02)	(23.44)	(22.86)	(7,617.22)

[1]NPV of the projected cash flows provided using R, from each corresponding quarter; i = 2.5% per quarter or 1/4 of the annual 10% discount rate; and t = 1 through 12 for each of the 12-quarters over the 3 year period.

Table 10.1a: NPV of a potential HVAC replacement

Source: Michael D. Collins

Although the financial implications of the decision are important, there may also be qualitative considerations. For example, if the repairs are inconveniencing guests, because the unit serves the hotel's restaurant or a frequently used meeting room, causing discomfort to guests when it is not working, or if frequent repairs to the unit prevent the hotel's HVAC technician from performing timely preventative maintenance on other HVAC units, then these factors must also be considered. When calculating the return on a potential capital investment, the director of engineering must identify all cash flows impacted by the decision, as opposed to considering strictly the maintenance costs alone, to accurately assess the financial impact of the decision.

Returning to the HVAC replacement example, suppose the director of F&B and the director of catering & convention services express disappointment with the decision not to replace the unit because this specific HVAC unit serves an executive board room popular with the hotel's meeting clientele—it is often used for high-level meetings or as a convention office for in-house conferences. Even though this meeting room is often provided to large groups on a complimentary basis, it is discovered that the invoice of at least one conference is being reduced by $400 to $500 each quarter to compensate group clients for inconveniences caused by the air conditioning not working properly in this boardroom during a portion of their respective conferences. With this added information, the director of engineering may appropriately add $450 in additional cash flow each quarter or $5,400 over the 3 year period to the analysis if the unit is replaced immediately. This, in turn, improves the NPV of the cash flows resulting from the immediate replacement of the unit to a net outflow of $5,844.72 versus an outflow of $8,612.65 over the 3 year period if replacement is delayed, saving hotel ownership $2,767.93. Consequently, replacing the unit is in the best financial interest of hotel ownership with this revised analysis, as outlined in *Table 10.1b: Revised NPV of a Potential HVAC Replacement*.

In summary, an NPV calculation may be used to evaluate the financial feasibility of a capital expenditure; however, it is important that the full economic impact of the investment be used to evaluate capital decisions. Although hotel investors require a financial analysis, qualitative factors must also be considered when assessing the impact of the

		Repair cost $	710.00		Quarterly maintenance with replacement $	25.00							
		Current cost of replacement $	9,375.00		Quarterly maintenance without replacement $	30.00							
		Replacement cost at end of 3-years (5% inflation) $	10,244.32		Quarterly revenue loss due to equipment failure $	450.00							

Quarter	3-year Total	Year 1				Year 2				Year 3			
		1st	2nd	3rd	4th	1st	2nd	3rd	4th	1st	2nd	3rd	4th
Revenue retention due to replacement of unit	$ 5,400.00	450.00	450.00	450.00	450.00	450.00	450.00	450.00	450.00	450.00	450.00	450.00	450.00
Cash-flow with immediate replacement	(4,275.00)	(8,950.00)	425.00	425.00	425.00	425.00	425.00	425.00	425.00	425.00	425.00	425.00	425.00
NPV of cash-flows with immediate replacement[1]	$ (5,844.72)	(9,789.63)	404.52	394.65	385.03	375.64	366.48	357.54	348.82	340.31	332.01	323.91	316.01
Cash-flow with delayed replacement	(11,284.32)	(740.00)	(30.00)	(30.00)	(30.00)	(30.00)	(30.00)	(30.00)	(30.00)	(30.00)	(30.00)	(30.00)	(10,244.32)
NPV of cash-flows with delayed replacement[1]	$ (8,612.65)	(739.27)	(28.55)	(27.86)	(27.18)	(26.52)	(25.87)	(25.24)	(24.62)	(24.02)	(23.44)	(22.86)	(7,617.22)

[1]NPV of the projected cash flows provided using R, from each corresponding quarter; i = 2.5% per quarter or 1/4 of the annual 10% discount rate; and t = 1 through 12 for each of the 12-quarters over the 3 year period.

Source: Michael D. Collins

Table 10.1b: *Revised NPV of a potential HVAC replacement*

expenditure. A wise hotel manager evaluates the impact of a capital expenditure on revenue, labor productivity, and operating costs—as well as upon guests' experiences and the quality of associates' work environment—including an estimate of the financial impact on each within the analysis.

The 5-year CapEx planning process is outlined in *Diagram 10.2: 5-Year CapEx Planning Process.* The capital expenditure planning process is often spearheaded by the hotel's director of engineering, working in partnership with the hotel's controller, although the entire EOC must be involved in the process to ensure that no capital needs are overlooked. The estimated cost of common hotel renovations, by scale-of-hotel,

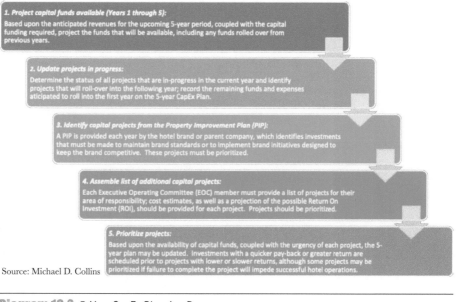

Source: Michael D. Collins

Diagram 10.2: 5-Year CapEx Planning Process

is generated each year by Jonathan Nehmer & Associates and HVS Design, which is an invaluable tool when creating a CapEx Plan; this resource may be found online at: https://www.hvs.com/article/8303-Hotel-Cost-Estimating-Guide (Feldman, 2018). Hotel parent companies also provide renovation cost guidance for their branded hotels. A hotel's ownership is directly involved in the CapEx planning and approval process. Consequently, additional details regarding the capital expenditure planning, review, and approval process are outlined in *Chapter 12: Hotel Investment.*

SUSTAINABILITY

The director of engineering, in partnership with the director of services, executive housekeeper, executive chef, executive steward, and director of loss prevention, is responsible for a hotel's sustainability efforts. Recycling programs, as well as many energy conservation efforts, require the support and participation of all hotel associates. Therefore, the formation of a sustainability committee, chaired by the director or assistant director of engineering, that includes representation from all hotel departments, may help raise awareness of a hotel's green efforts.

Each year, hotels dispose of thousands of tons of food waste, debris, trash, and recyclable items. Many of these items can be recycled or re-used. Food waste can be separated, collected, and re-deployed in animal feeds. Partially used bottles of shampoo, soap, and other guest amenities may be collected and re-processed for use in commercial soaps and detergents. Glass bottles and damaged glassware, as well as cans and metal, can be recycled. The environmental impact of some garbage may be reduced through liquification. Corrugated cardboard may be flattened, bundled, collected, and recycled. A hotel's waste removal costs are substantial and many of these efforts may significantly reduce these costs. Not only do these efforts potentially reduce operating costs, these sustainability programs are simply the right thing to do; however, hotel personnel must embrace greening efforts.

Hotels are also major consumers of water, gas, and electricity; however, the director of engineering, working with the sustainability committee, spearheads a variety of strategies to reduce utility consumption. In addition to the use of an EMS, as previously discussed, hotels also install efficient interior and exterior lighting systems, motion sensors, and high-efficiency heating and cooling systems to minimize energy consumption. Solar panels are often installed on hotel rooftops and porte-cocheres to supplement the hotel's electricity needs. Low-flow plumbing fixtures and water-efficient toilets, using 1.6 gallons of water or less per flush, and faucets with motion sensors are used to reduce water consumption and sewage costs.

Many newly constructed hotels seek LEED certification or, at a minimum, are designed with energy efficiency in mind. Reflective glass and other exterior surfaces may be selected, and live plant materials that do not require irrigation may be placed on the hotel's rooftop, which help maintain a comfortable building temperature while reducing greenhouse gas emissions and stormwater run-off. Not only do green building efforts pay dividends in terms of protecting the environment while reducing utility costs, many communities offer tax incentives and utility rebates for taking specific steps to minimize a hotel's carbon footprint, increasing the ROI associated with specific sustainability design strategies and capital projects, even though the initial costs of construction may be higher.

sustainability committee: a group of associates, including representatives from each department, chaired by the director of engineering, charged with raising awareness and ensuring compliance with a hotel's efforts to operate in an environmentally responsible manner

green efforts: actions taken to operate in an environmentally responsible manner

LEED certification: a building that meets 'Leadership in Energy and Environmental Design' standards

CHAPTER SUMMARY

The POM, or engineering department, is responsible for maintaining the hotel's physical assets, including all building systems and operating equipment. The director of engineering oversees a team of skilled technicians and shift engineers that perform a variety of routine or preventative maintenance tasks, in addition to responding to requests from guests and associates to make specific repairs. The status of all building systems, including electrical, water, HVAC, and life-safety, as well as all major operating equipment, is tracked in a FMS that provides engineering management with guidance regarding the routine maintenance tasks that must be performed each day to properly maintain the hotel and its operating equipment. Ultimately, a hotel is a real estate investment that must be maintained and periodically updated to maintain the value of the asset, while ensuring the hotel's facilities remain competitive in the marketplace. Consequently, the director of engineering spearheads the CapEx planning process, working with hotel ownership to prioritize the reinvestment of the capital expenditure reserve fund to replace capital equipment, as well as to renovate and update hotel facilities. The director also spearheads the hotel's sustainability efforts, working in partnership with managers throughout the hotel, to reduce the hotel's carbon footprint, thereby minimizing utility and waste removal costs.

KEY TERMS AND CONCEPTS

5-year capital expenditure plan (CapEx Plan)
asset manager
assistant director of engineering
boiler mechanic
building systems
capital asset
capital expense
capital reserve fund
carpenter
centralized heating and cooling system
chief engineer
cloud-based
commercial vehicles
decentralized HVAC system
director of engineering
electric distribution system

electrician
emergency generator
energy management system (EMS)
engineers
equipment PM technicians
facility management system (FMS)
feedback loop
fire control panel
fire doors
fire suppression system
furniture, fixtures, and equipment (FF&E)
general mechanic
gray water
green
guestroom PM technician
heating, ventilation, and air conditioning (HVAC) systems

HVAC or refrigeration mechanic
kitchen mechanic
LEED certification
life safety equipment
life safety system
lighting systems
lock-out–tag-out
maintenance contract
maintenance request
mason
natural gas
net present value (NPV)
out-of-service
package unit
painter and wall vinyl technician
Pareto chart
plumber
potable water

pressurized escape stairwells	public area PM technician	sustainability committee
preventative maintenance (PM)	pull-station	system administrator
property operations and maintenance (POM) or engineering department	second effort program	work order system
	shift engineer	
	sprinkler system	

DISCUSSION QUESTIONS

1. Discuss the role and function of the POM or engineering department. Describe the KSAs that associates in the department ideally possess, as a collective team, explaining how each KSA benefits the hotel.

2. Identify a hotel's major building systems and categories of operating equipment. What systems, operating equipment, or areas of the hotel are most likely to be maintained in-house and which by outside contractors, explaining the reasons why?

3. Describe the PM program—in guestrooms, public areas, and for major equipment. What is the potential impact on the hotel if PM activities are not routinely performed?

4. Describe the lock-out–tag-out procedure and explain its importance. Discuss other safety precautions that must be taken in the engineering department.

5. Explain how the FMS and EMS support POM. How are these and other MIS throughout the hotel supported and maintained?

6. Hotel management is debating whether a complete guestroom renovation, at a cost of $31,500 per guestroom, or a more modest replacement of soft goods only, at a cost of $9,500 per key, should be recommended to hotel's ownership on this year's CapEx plan. The complete renovation includes replacement of bathroom tile, vanities, and fixtures, as well as case goods (furniture), in addition to soft-goods and is projected to have a 7-year life. A soft goods renovation includes the replacement of carpet, window treatments, duvet covers, light fixtures and shades, wall vinyl and fresh paint throughout the guestroom and bath, as well as the reupholstery of guestroom lounge chairs/sofas; a soft goods renovation is expected to have a 5-year life, after which additional guestroom upgrades will be needed. The 400-room hotel is operating at 74.8% occupancy, with an average daily rate of $182.12. If no renovation is completed, hotel room revenue is expected to remain static next year and then begin to deteriorate—declining by approximately 1% of total room revenue per year starting 2 years from now. With the soft goods renovation, hotel management projects that the hotel's historical guestroom revenue increase of a modest 2% per year will continue. If the renovation is completed, the hotel will be able to boost its guestroom revenue by a projected 6% in the first year following the renovation, capitalizing on the newly upgraded guestrooms to boost hotel room rates, and will then enjoy room revenue increases of approximately 3% per year in years 2 through 7 following the renovation. Based upon an NPV calculation, which renovation option is in the hotel investor's best financial interest? Identify qualitative factors that should also be considered when contemplating the two options.

7. Identify keys to effective engineering management, explaining the impact of each.
8. Explain strategies that may be employed to minimize the environmental impact of a hotel's operation. What are the financial impacts of greening the operation?

ENDNOTES

Feldman, W.G. (2018). *Hotel Cost Estimating Guide - 2018*; JN&A and HVS Design; Rockville, MD. Accessed online at: https://www.hvs.com/article/8303-Hotel-Cost-Estimating-Guide; 125 pages.

STR (2017). *Host report: Upper-upscale hotels for year-ending 2015*. SHARE Center.

Chapter 11

Administration and Control: Human Resources, Accounting, and Loss Prevention

This chapter outlines strategies to successfully employ and manage a team of hospitality professionals prepared to deliver exceptional guest experiences, while simultaneously driving the profitability of the hotel. The chapter outlines the key human resource strategies and accounting processes necessary to deliver successful business outcomes, while also exploring the role of the loss prevention team.

PURPOSE AND LEARNING OBJECTIVES:

Hotel managers working in a full-service hotel environment, particularly in upper-upscale and luxury hotels, are supported by a team of administrative professionals. This chapter prepares readers to:

- Explain the role of the hotel general manager and the structure of the administrative team.
- Identify human resource strategies employed by hotels to position a hotel management firm or an individual property as an employer of choice.
- Describe an effective hiring process and explain why employee selection is critical to a hotel's success.
- Identify key accounting functions, explaining the importance of each in achieving the hotel's financial goals.
- Explain how guest transactions impact hotel financial statements, including the profit and loss statement and balance sheet.
- Discuss the role of loss prevention officers.
- Identify the purpose of the hotel safety committee, describing the make-up of the committee.

ADMINISTRATIVE AND GENERAL DEPARTMENT

The administrative and general (A&G) team is comprised of the hotel's general manager (GM), executive administrative assistant, controller, director of human resources, director of loss prevention, and loss prevention officers; the salaries and wages of any additional accounting or human resource professionals employed at the property level are also included as part of the hotel's A&G undistributed operating expenses. Traditionally, upper-upscale and luxury hotels have employed a full accounting and human resource staff, as depicted in *Diagram 11.1: Administrative and General Personnel/Functions*; however, in recent years, many administrative functions—particularly accounting and human resource functions—have been centralized within many hotel firms.

© Dima Sidelnikov/Shutterstock.com

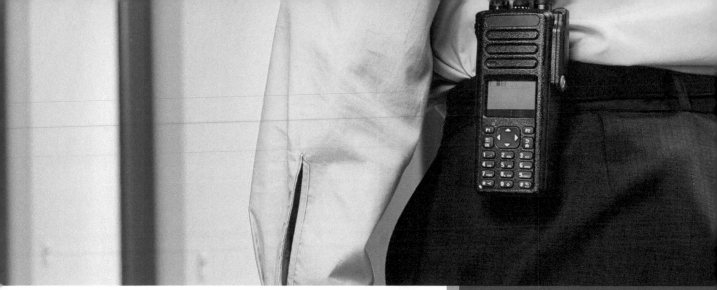

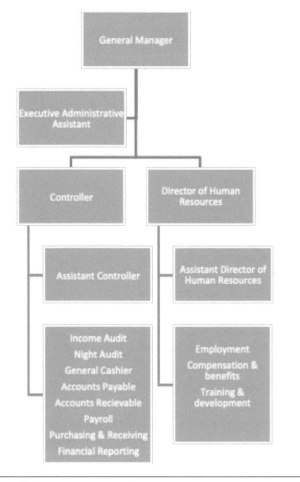

Diagram 11.1: Administrative and General Personnel/Functions

Source: Michael D. Collins

Centralized Functions

Branded management companies and large hotel management firms that operate multiple properties within a single destination or region may employ a team of accounting or human resource professionals to support multiple hotel properties. Information technology (IT) capabilities facilitate the ability of administrative professionals to work remotely and to perform their assigned functions for multiple properties. In addition to centralizing administrative functions, including many accounting and human resource (HR) tasks, it is also increasingly common for multiple hotels, located adjacent or in proximity to one another, to be operated by a single management team; the properties may be overseen by a single GM, sometimes referred to as a cluster manager, and may share other key personnel, such as the director of sales, revenue manager, director of engineering, human resource manager, or controller. The ability for hotels to share personnel, or for management firms to centralize functions in corporate or regional offices, allows the hotels to reduce overhead costs while increasing the productivity of the associates serving in these administrative and executive roles. Regional sales and reservations offices, as well as the use of skilled maintenance technicians to support multiple properties, often prove to be prudent strategies, providing the participating properties with access to a higher degree of expertise and support than the properties could afford independently.

On-Property Administrative Personnel

At a minimum, a hotel property will require leadership from an on-property GM that fulfills the senior leadership role at the hotel, providing direction for the entire management team while serving as the primary interface with the corporate office and hotel ownership. The GM is assisted by an executive administrative assistant, typically assigned the responsibility of tracking and following up on the myriad of tasks, projects, and priorities that the GM is overseeing; the executive assistant also commonly serves as the central clearinghouse for all guest feedback, ensuring appropriate follow-up with guests in response to their concerns, while simultaneously ensuring that the division heads and department manager are notified of guest concerns so that corrective action may be taken. A hotel also employs a controller, assisted by an assistant controller in a larger property, to oversee the accounting functions; at a minimum, an on-property bookkeeper or accounting manager will be employed, if the accounting function is centralized, responsible for relaying accounting information from the property to the central or regional accounting office, as well as back to the property's management team. If HR functions are centralized, the executive administrative assistant or bookkeeper may also serve as the liaison with the corporate or regional HR team.

cluster manager:
a GM that oversees multiple hotel properties located in close proximity

controller:
an exempt manager that oversees the accounting function and serves on the executive operating committee

assistant controller:
an exempt manager that assists in overseeing the accounting function

bookkeeper or accounting manager:
an exempt administrative associate that performs various accounting duties

The size and scope of the hotel operation will determine the number of A&G personnel that are employed at the individual hotel; however, regardless of the number of administrative associates that are employed—or whether the associates are on-property or working remotely—a wide variety of administrative functions must be performed for any hotel of any size.

© Ikonoklast Fotografie/Shutterstock.com

HUMAN RESOURCE FUNCTIONS AND STRATEGIES

As has been emphasized throughout *Delivering the Guest Experience*, the success of a hotel is determined by the quality of the guest experiences delivered by the associates employed by the hotel. Hotel associates must consistently deliver mutually profitable, memorable, and personalized guest experiences. Consequently, the hotel management team must prioritize providing an exceptional workplace environment to the associates that deliver these memorable and personalized experiences or that support those that do.

HR: Every Manager's Responsibility

Although hotel managers are supported by a team of HR professionals, the responsibility of delivering an exceptional workplace environment lies with every member of a hotel's management team. The HR team is responsible for overseeing HR functions; however, hotel managers that work hands-on, side-by-side with hotel associates, have a far greater impact on employees' perceptions of workplace quality. Afterall, department managers and their assistants schedule, train, coach, and interact daily with the hotel's employees. As a result, each manager must understand their role in delivering an exceptional associate experience.

Recall from *Chapter 2: Successful Hotel Management* the satisfaction mirror: employee satisfaction drives guest satisfaction. It is the responsibility of each manager to assume a servant-leadership role, ensuring that the needs of each associate under his/her care receives the support and guidance necessary to be successful. The role of the HR team is to support managers in their performance of HR duties. HR recruits potential employees; however, the department and division heads ultimately interview the candidates and make the hiring decisions. Although HR may provide an orientation program for new hires, training associates on how to properly perform their duties is the responsibility of the department managers and their assistants. HR may remind managers that it is time for associates to receive their annual evaluations; however, the department and division heads ultimately provide the employee feedback and devise a plan for the associate's professional development. In other words, it is ultimately the hotel managers—division heads, department heads, and assistant department managers—that are responsible for ensuring that a hotel becomes an employer of choice. Please refer to *Box 11.1: Becoming an Employer of Choice* for more details.

BOX 11.1: BECOMING AN EMPLOYER OF CHOICE

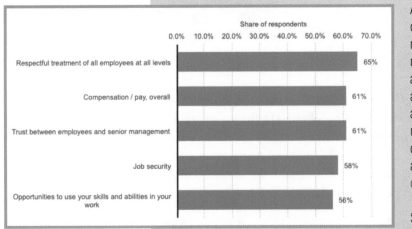

Diagram 11.2: Factors Leading to Employee Satisfaction (*SHRM, 2017*)

employer of choice: the goal of being perceived as a preferred employer by current and potential employees

Attracting a team of highly qualified, capable associates is the number one challenge faced by many hospitality organizations— and competition for the best associates available is fierce. As a result, the most successful hotel management firms and parent companies work diligently to earn a reputation as an employer of choice.

Strategies employed by the industry's best employers, earning them recognition as employers of choice, extend beyond providing competitive compensation (pay) and benefits; an employer of choice also provides quality training, professional development, and growth opportunities, and most importantly, managers throughout the organization treat associates with respect and genuine concern each and every day. *Diagram 11.2* identifies the share of employees in the United States by the contributors that they consider very important to job satisfaction (SHRM, 2017). Although providing competitive pay and benefits (overall compensation) is important, the most important factor is that employees, at all levels of an organization, are treated with respect. It is also important that employees trust management, feel secure in their jobs, and can do what they feel they do best while at work. Employees want to feel competent and appreciated, and that they are making a meaningful contribution to the success of their employer (Collins, 2007).

Compensation

As discussed in *Chapter 6: Guest Services Operations*, all hotel associates are categorized as exempt or non-exempt, as defined by the US Department of Labor. Exempt associates do not receive overtime compensation by virtue of an administrative, executive, professional, computer technology, or sales exemption, and must earn a minimum salary of $913 per week ($47,476 annually); non-exempt associates are paid on an hourly basis and receive overtime pay, 1.5 times their standard pay rate for

© stoatphoto/Shutterstock.com

hours worked in excess of 40 in the 7-day workweek, as defined by the employer. Employers of choice conduct regular wage surveys, at least annually, to ensure that its employees are being compensated at wage rates that are highly competitive within the local market; employees also receive pay increases on a scheduled basis based upon time in position or superior job performance. Management salaries must be competitive nationally, with cost-of-living allowances offered in high-cost areas. Incentive compensation is also offered to reward associates for achieving clearly defined goals.

In addition to a competitive salary or wage, an employer of choice also provides a generous benefit package to include, at a minimum, health, dental, disability, and life insurance; a retirement program; and holiday pay and paid vacation time. Because of the nature of the hotel industry, many hotels provide a variety of perks to its employees including shift meals while on duty; uniform cleaning; and complimentary or deeply discounted hotel services—including hotel accommodations and meals—when traveling. It should be recognized that the lion's share of the cost of many of these benefits is borne by the hotel, although the associate may be required to make a small contribution toward the cost of the benefit. For example, an associate may be required to pay 5% to 15% of the health insurance premium with the employer bearing 85% to 95% of the cost. Many employers also match 50% or more of the employees' contributions to a 401(k) retirement plan, which is up to 6% of the associates' annual compensation. Quality employers often commonly provide their associates with access to an employee assistance program, which provides employees access to a variety of services, including a range of counseling support and legal consultation.

employee assistance program:
provides employees access to a variety of services, including a range of counseling support and legal consultation

In addition to the cost of wages and benefits, a variety of taxes are collected on the wages paid to associates. Federal Insurance Contribution Act (FICA) taxes are assessed at 15.3% of wages and split evenly between the employer and the employee.

The hotel and the associate contribute 6.2% of wages each (12.4% total) to the Social Security Administration and 1.45% each (2.9% total) to provide Medicare coverage, which partially covers health care costs for US citizens and permanent residents after reaching 65-years-of-age or if they become disabled. Federal, state, and local income taxes must also be deducted from the employees' wages, as required. It is important for an HR professional to explain these payroll deductions to associates when they are hired, typically during the new employee orientation process, so that associates fully understand and appreciate each deduction that is included on their paystub. It is also appropriate for the total-cost-of-employment to be explained and calculated during orientation. It is common for the hotel to incur a total employment cost of approximately 35% above-and-beyond the base wage, due to the employer's share of FICA taxes (7.65%), coupled with employee benefit costs; employers are also assessed a state payroll tax to cover unemployment and workers compensation claims. Consequently, a full-time employee earning $15.00 per hour, for example, incurs a total cost-of-employment to the hotel of approximately $20.25 = [$15 + ($15 X 35%)] per hour.

total-cost-of-employment: includes the cost of employer paid payroll taxes and employee benefits (PT&EB) in addition to wages

Unemployment and Workers Compensation

Unemployment and workers compensation claims are covered by state governments. As previously mentioned, a state payroll tax is assessed on wages to generate a fund from which unemployment claims and workers compensation is paid. The amount of the state payroll tax varies based upon an employer's actual claims rate. When employees become unemployed or under-employed, through no fault of their own, or are injured at work, they may seek unemployment or workers compensation through the state's employment security commission. Due to the seasonal nature of the hotel industry, it is not uncommon for associates' work schedules to be reduced during periods of low demand; during these periods, hotel employees may seek partial unemployment. Although an employer of choice does not want to prevent associates from receiving benefits to which they are legally entitled, the HR department is charged with the responsibility of managing claims to ensure that all claims against the employer's account are legitimate. In addition, the HR department works with department managers to minimize claims. This may be accomplished by placing employees that have been injured at work on light duty, which allows an employee to work in an alternative position if they have been injured on the job and are unable to perform their normal duties. The HR department also must review the documentation of any progressive discipline that took place prior to the termination of an associate's employment because an employee terminated for cause may not be eligible to receive unemployment compensation or for any unemployment compensation that is paid to the former associate to be charged against the employer's account.

light duty: allows an employee to work in an alternative position if they have been injured on the job and are unable to perform their normal duties

Legal Compliance

There are a variety of laws and regulations that impact the employer-employee relationship, including the Fair Labor Standards Act (FLSA) of 1938, which established a national minimum wage, rules governing overtime pay, and the assessment of FICA taxes to fund Social Security benefits, while restricting the employment of children; the Equal Pay Act of 1963, intended to address gender disparity in wages; and multiple Civil Rights Acts, including the Civil Rights Act of 1964, which established the Equal Employment Opportunity Commission (EEOC), regulations, and reporting requirements intended to address discrimination in the workplace (Reich, 2016). A detailed discussion of employment laws and regulations is outside the scope of this textbook; however, it is important that HR professionals understand and spearhead compliance with all pertinent employment laws and reporting requirements. As a hotel manager, assigned with the responsibility of creating a quality workplace environment, a detailed knowledge of employment laws and regulations is not necessary—the key is for every hotel manager to treat every associate with genuine concern and respect. In today's business environment, a workplace must be free of any type of discrimination or harassment, which is the joint responsibility of HR and every member of the hotel's management team.

Hiring Associates

An employer of choice creates a hiring process designed to attract highly qualified candidates and to then select the best qualified from among the available candidates. Many hospitality industry employers underestimate the importance of employee selection, assuming any candidate can be taught to perform the required tasks to an acceptable level. The Cycle of Success, illustrated in *Diagram 2.3* within *Chapter 2: Successful Hotel Management*, identifies employee selection as critical to the successful management of a hotel operation. Quite simply, mutually profitable, personalized guest experiences may only be delivered by hotel associates genuinely concerned about the comfort and well-being of hotel guests and this trait is not learned—it is an innate attribute. Its presence must be assessed during the screening and interview process.

© wavebreakmedia/Shutterstock.com

A department manager that requires additional personnel submits an employee requisition to the HR department, which has been approved by the manager's division head and the GM. At a minimum, an employee requisition includes the job title, rate of pay, preferred start date, and the specific qualifications required of candidates including

employee requisition: a form submitted by management to notify the human resources department of a staffing need

job specifications:
a listing of the required education, knowledge, skills, abilities, and behavioral characteristics an associate needs to be successful in a position

job analysis:
the process of identifying the knowledge, skills, abilities, and behavioral characteristics an associate needs to be successful in a position

job description:
outlines the specific responsibilities of a position

employment manager:
an exempt HR professional responsible for recruitment and hiring

education, knowledge, skills, abilities, behavioral characteristics, and experience; the requisition also identifies scheduling requirements or shifts a successful candidate must be able to work. Typically, the job specifications outlined on the requisition are determined through a job analysis that is conducted when a job description for a position is originally created. After receiving an approved employee requisition, the employment manager, or HR professional responsible for recruitment and hiring, creates a job posting to market the position to potential candidates; he/she will also review employment applications on file to identify candidates from the hotel's existing pool of applicants.

An effective hiring process includes the following:
1. Identify reliable sources of applicants.
2. Screen applicants based upon job specifications.
3. Identify any red flag issues with candidates that meet job specifications.
4. Conduct behavioral-based interviews.
5. Assess and rate candidates, involving multiple people.
6. Complete references and background checks.
7. Establish realistic expectations.

In addition to the job boards, particularly those dedicated to the hospitality industry such as Hcareers (www.hcareers.com), reliable sources of applicants include colleges, universities, and trade-schools that prepare students for careers in the hospitality industry; many high schools also offer training for students considering careers in the industry, particularly in the culinary field. Most hospitality education programs require some form of professional industry work experience or internship, which allow students to gain valuable hands-on experience in guest service, entry-level, and front-line supervisory positions. Social and human service agencies, including government, non-profit, and religious-based organizations, are often reliable sources of entry-level employees. And finally, the social networks of associates currently employed by the hotel may also be mined for quality job candidates—chances are, a hotel's best associates have acquaintances and friends that may be highly qualified candidates. Managers should also be encouraged to recruit candidates through their customer service interactions during their day-to-day activities; there is no harm in complimenting someone that provides great service by asking, "Have you ever considered putting your great customer service skills to work in the hotel industry?"

A process must be established to ensure that job candidates experience a positive impression of the hotel, as an employer, during the application process. Quite frankly, pursuing employment is often a frustrating experience. It is common for applicants to never receive a reply from a potential employer after submitting an online application or, if a reply is received, it may be weeks following the submission. Developing a candidate-friendly application process is an effective recruiting tool. A candidate that walks into a hotel in response to an employment posting must not be turned away but welcomed to the hotel and referred to the employment manager or the designated HR/administrative professional. Highly qualified candidates that are visiting a hotel property in search of employment are likely to continue visiting hotels and other potential employers until a position is secured; this may result in the hotel missing out on a highly qualified candidate if the hotel fails to screen and interview a candidate on his/her initial visit to the property. Employers must realize that an interview process is a two-way assessment—the potential employer is assessing the candidate, while the candidate is also assessing the hotel as a potential employer.

Candidates identified are then screened against the job specifications listed in the employee requisition. Meeting the required specifications is a yes or no proposition—the candidate either meets the qualifications specified and can work the required schedule or he/she cannot. If a candidate does not meet the requirements, then the candidate should be promptly notified; if the candidate does meet the required specifications then the next step in the hiring process may be scheduled. Some employers move directly to an initial interview, while others may require candidates to complete a pre-employment assessment.

pre-employment assessment: a psychometrically sound survey tool used to identify whether a job candidate has specific behavioral characteristics, knowledge, or skills

Pre-employment assessments are psychometrically sound survey tools used to identify whether a job candidate has specific behavioral characteristics, knowledge, or skills. They may vary by position; however, assessments, if used, must be completed by every candidate that is considered for a specific position. It is important that the screening and interview process is consistent—the same for every candidate—for two primary reasons: First, multiple candidates cannot be compared, to identify the most qualified candidate for the position, if each candidate completes a different assessment and interview process. In addition, requiring only some candidates to complete a pre-employment assessment may be viewed as discriminatory, opening the hotel up to a possible claim of bias in the hiring process.

Many hotel management firms use pre-employment assessments designed to identify specific behavioral characteristics, including whether a candidate tends to be more socially-oriented or introspective; detailed or big-picture-oriented; whether he/she prefers clear direction or to use his/her own methods when completing tasks; and other characteristics that may determine the candidate's potential job fit. Although an assessment should not be used to eliminate an otherwise qualified candidate from further consideration, it may provide an indication that a candidate is very well-suited for a specific position or identify some concerns that may be further explored during the interview process. Assessments may also be used to verify that a candidate possesses specific knowledge or skills essential to successfully performing in the position.

job fit: an assessment as to how well a candidate's personality and innate behavioral tendencies align with the job requirements

If an interview is extended to an applicant, two types of questions are asked. Red flag questions are unique to each candidate and address any questions or concerns

red flag questions: interview questions, unique to each candidate, that address questions or concerns resulting from a review of the candidate's application materials

that result from a review of the candidate's application materials, such as a gap in employment or frequent changes of employers. If a pre-employment assessment has been completed, red flag questions may also be used to explore any concerns that may have arisen as a result of the assessment results. For example, if the candidate has applied for a guest-contact position that requires a high-degree of guest interaction, and the assessment reveals that the candidate tends to be introspective versus socially-oriented, then the interviewer may want to discuss whether the assessment is accurate and, if so, how a high-level of guest interaction has impacted the candidate in previous employment environments. If the candidate responds in a manner that allays any red flag concerns identified during the screening process, then the interviewer may move on to a series of questions designed to assess specific knowledge, skills, and abilities (KSAs).

Each interview question should be designed to assess a specific KSA that must be asked of each candidate interviewed; this ensures that candidates' responses may be scored, and candidates' overall scores compared to identify the most qualified candidate for the job. It is important to note that managers are not seeking friends or the candidate that they like the most—their goal must be to hire the most highly qualified candidate for the position. Consequently, a hiring process is typically more effective if multiple people are involved in the hiring process; this may be accomplished through panel interviews or by having multiple managers interview candidates, who should be required to rate each candidate's response to each interview question, allowing an overall score to be calculated for each candidate. This process will make the hiring process more objective. An example of a job candidate scorecard is illustrated in *Diagram 11.3* within *Box 11.2: Developing a Job Candidate Scorecard*. It should be noted that it is important that all interview questions are screened by an HR professional that understands questions that can and cannot be legally used during the interview process.

To ensure that interviews are behavioral-based, questions developed to assess KSAs must require that candidates provide specific examples from past experiences to illustrate how they have responded to situations or circumstances that have been previously encountered. For example, to assess how a job candidate responds to a difficult guest service challenge, the interviewer may ask, "Tell me about a time when you had to address a service complaint from an irate customer. What were the specific circumstances and how did you resolve the matter?" When conducting a behavioral-based interview, it is important to require the candidate to provide specific, actual examples and to not allow the candidate to discuss what they *usually do* or *would do* in a specific circumstance. The best indicator of future performance is past performance—the candidate must be strongly encouraged to speak from experience versus hypothetically. If a candidate does not use specific, real-life experiences during his/her response, then the manager must stop the candidate from answering further, give him/her time to think of a specific situation, and be silent until the candidate is able to respond to the question using a specific example.

Additional, non-behavioral-based questions, to better understand the candidate's career goals, for example, may also be asked during the interview process; however, behavioral-based interviews will provide insight into how the candidate is likely to respond to specific situations commonly encountered in the work environment. In the hospitality industry, it is critical that employers hire the candidate with the desired qualities—most skills required for success in the industry can be learned.

References and Background Checks

Following the interview process, it is important to complete references and background checks to verify information contained in the application and obtained through the interview process. It is common in the hospitality industry to conduct pre-employment drug screenings and, for some positions, criminal background checks—particularly for associates that will have access to hotel guestrooms. It is not uncommon for credit checks to be performed prior to hiring management and accounting personnel. Candidates should be notified of any pre-employment drug testing or other requirements prior to the application process; this may deter unqualified candidates from submitting applications. If a hotel's competitors require pre-employment drug screenings, it likely that a hotel that does not do the same may receive more applications from candidates that may present an employment risk. Although many employers receiving a request for a reference on a former employee may be reluctant to voluntarily share information that may dissuade a potential employer from hiring the candidate, most employers will verify information presented by the candidate during the application process, such as dates of employment and position; a former employer will also commonly share whether the former associate is eligible for re-hire. Pre-employment drug testing and background checks are typically completed after the candidate is interviewed and reference checks are completed, and prior to extending an offer, because there is typically a significant cost involved.

Once the preferred candidate has been identified, and all references and required pre-employment assessments and tests are successfully completed, a job offer may be extended. For most line positions, a verbal offer is typically extended whereas with management hires the details of the offer are often provided in writing, particularly if the candidate is leaving a management position with another firm. Although a candidate must often be sold on the benefits of accepting the position, it is important to establish realistic expectations regarding the position offered; a psychological contract is established during the interview process based upon representations made by the managers and HR professionals that screen and interview candidates. Fail-

psychological contract: an unwritten contract or set of expectations established during the interview process as a result of representations made by managers during the screening, interviewing, and hiring process

Job Candidate Scorecard

Candidate's name: Claudia Garcia	Position: Guest Service Agent

Essential items:	Yes	No
Appearance, grooming and professionalism	✓	
Required education for position	✓	
Required training for the position	✓	
Required experience for the position	✓	
Communication skills adequate	✓	
Available to work required work schedule	✓	

Note: **Do not interview candidate if they fail to meet any of the above requirements.**

'Red flag' items:	Yes	No
Prior to you current position, you were employed at a restaurant for less than 3 months. Why the short tenure?	✓	
The assessment you completed indicated that you have a reserved personality. Do you feel this is accurate?	✓	
How have you enjoyed working in a customer service role?	✓	

Note: **Do not interview candidate if they fail to adequately explain all 'red flag' items.**

KSA interview questions:	Response quality:					Points awarded
	Excellent 5	Good 4	Fair 3	Weak 2	Poor 1	
1. Tell me about a time when you encountered a difficult guest situation.		✓				4
2. Tell me about a time when you had to prioritize multiple, important tasks.	✓					5
3. Tell me about a time when you had a conflict or disagreement with a co-worker.				✓		2
4. Tell me what you enjoy the most about your present job? the least?		✓				4
5. Why are you seeking a new position?		✓				4
6. Where do you see yourself professionally one-year from now? Five-years from now?	✓					5
7.						
8.						
					Total Points:	24

Diagram 11.3: Job Candidate Scorecard

An example of a completed *Job Candidate Scorecard* is illustrated in *Diagram 11.3*, which has been completed for a candidate that is applying for a guest service agent's position. Outlined below are the details regarding the evaluation of this job candidate, Claudia Garcia.

Essential items: The items within the initial section of the scorecard verify that the candidate meets the minimum requirements for the position, as specified on the employee requisition, in terms of professional appearance, education, training, experience, communication, and scheduling availability. Out of respect for the candidate's time, as well as the manager's, a candidate is not interviewed if these criteria are not completely met.

"Red flag" items: The next set of questions have been developed based upon a review of the candidate's application materials and pre-employment assessment. In this example, Ms. Garcia had a short job tenure at a restaurant in June through August of the previous year. Claudia indicated that the position was a summer job at a family-owned restaurant, prior to starting college in August of last year, which has satisfied the interviewer's concern with this "red flag" item. In addition, the pre-employment assessment indicates that Ms. Garcia tends to be introspective versus socially-oriented; she prefers to spend time alone or with family and close friends rather than to socialize with acquaintances that she does not know well. While Claudia has confirmed this to be accurate, she has indicated that she has enjoyed the customer service environment in which she is currently employed more than she expected—she particularly enjoys the relationships that she has built with the frequent customers of the business. Again, this response has satisfied the interviewer.

KSA interview questions: The six KSA interview questions asked of each candidate for the specific position are noted on the *Job Candidate Scorecard.* Each question is designed to assess a specific skill or ability that is important to the potential candidate's success in the available guest service agent position. In this example, the first question assesses guest service skills and asks candidates to provide a specific example of a difficult guest encounter that the candidate has had to resolve. The second question assesses the candidate's ability to prioritize multiple tasks. The third assesses whether the candidate has proven to be a team-player in his/her previous work environments. The fourth seeks to identify factors that may lead the candidate to seek an alternative position, assessing his/her level of commitment and loyalty to his/her employer. And finally, the sixth question is designed to ensure that the candidate has reasonable expectations regarding career advancement. Although the primary questions are noted on the scorecard, the interviewer may need to remind the candidate to be as specific and detailed as possible when responding to each question.

Claudia Garcia's response to each question has been evaluated and scored by the interviewer and a total score calculated by adding up the ratings from the individual questions. Note that there is no space on the scorecard for notations to be made, which prevents interviewers from making notes that may be viewed as discriminatory. It is also important to note that the rating is anonymous. Candidates are typically interviewed by multiple managers or HR professionals. By submitting the scorecards anonymously, all managers involved in the process are given equal input, making the process more objective. Scores can then be averaged for each candidate and the average scores of multiple candidates compared. A consistent interview process, using a *Job Candidate Scorecard* such as the one illustrated in *Diagram 11.3*, assists hotel managers in hiring the best qualified candidate for each available position.

ure to fulfill the unwritten commitments that are perceived by the candidate to have been made during the hiring process may result in employee turnover (Collins, 2010). A realistic job preview is an effective tool for establishing clear expectations for job candidates prior to their hire. Candidates not hired—that were interviewed for the position—should be contacted as soon as the position is filled, as a courtesy, because hotel management may want to re-consider a qualified candidate when a future position becomes available.

Recruitment, Hiring, and Affirmative Action

It is important for a hotel or any organization to assemble a leadership and management team that is consistent—in terms of race, ethnicity, gender, and national origin—with the overall employee population. Hotel associates need role models that they feel understand their needs and appreciate their culture and background. Consequently, hotels need to recruit a diverse management team. There is much debate about the effectiveness and even the legality of Affirmative Action (AA) programs. Recent court cases have challenged the use of AA in candidate selection, including its use in college admissions and hiring decisions. Effective strategies that may be used to recruit supervisors and managers from diverse backgrounds include the following:

- Always hire the most qualified candidate for a position; AA forbids establishing quotas. The use of quotas may result in hiring an unqualified candidate, which will backfire if the candidate fails in the position; however, it is appropriate to give preference to a fully-qualified candidate from an under-represented group when selecting from among candidates with similar qualifications.
- When identifying sources for generating applicants, seek sources of quality minority candidates. This may include professional organizations designed to support minorities working or pursuing education in the hospitality industry, such as the *National Society of Minorities in Hospitality*.
- Leaders from under-represented groups should also be developed in-house. Managers should be encouraged to mentor employees that demonstrate leadership potential. Most employers of choice provide some type of educational benefit, such as a tuition reimbursement program. Use these programs to help associates from diverse backgrounds acquire the education and other qualifications necessary to advance their careers within the hotel management firm.

Orientation and Training

Once a candidate has been hired, orientation and training must be provided. A formal orientation program is provided to initiate a new hire's socialization process with the hotel. It is important that orientation occur on the associate's first day of employment. To ensure that this occurs, it is common for many hotels to offer an orientation program on the same day each week and to start any associates hired during the previous week on this regularly scheduled orientation day. Under no circumstances should an associate be permitted to begin their departmental training without first completing the orientation program because an employer only has one opportunity to make a positive first impression.

Orientation should be organized to ensure that clear expectations are established in terms of what the associate may expect from management and what hotel management expects from the associate, without overwhelming the newly hired employee. Basic questions should be answered about workplace logistics—where employees park, enter and exit the building, change into their uniforms, clock-in and out, details regarding breaks and associate meals, pay dates and payroll processes, etc. Typically, an employee name tag will be provided at orientation, as well as an appropriate uniform. In addition, a brief history of the company and general expectations in terms of service standards and the company's culture, including the vision, mission, and values of the firm, are also provided. Associates may also complete new hire paperwork, if it has not already been completed, and are informed about benefits that are available, as well as the waiting periods prior to being given access to specific benefits. Associates are also provided access to an associate website or given an employee handbook in which additional details regarding the employer-employee relationship are explained. Key management personnel, including the hotel's GM and executive operating committee (EOC) members, often stop by orientation to introduce themselves and to extend a warm welcome to the hotel's newest team members.

Although an associate's initial orientation is typically provided by the hotel's HR professionals, training to perform the specific duties of an associate's assigned position is provided by the employee's department manager. Training checklists are created for every position, which lists all KSAs necessary to successfully perform in the position, as well as the anticipated timeline for completing the initial training process. Multiple methodologies must be used during the training process, including computer-aided instruction, demonstration, job shadowing, reading, discussion, and role-playing. The department head should meet with a newly hired associate at least weekly to discuss, assess, and document his/her progress until training is complete.

Once an associate's initial training has been completed, the training and professional development of the associate must continue. Each day, during the daily pre-shift line-up, service standards are discussed and reinforced; policies and procedures that are not being consistently executed are also reviewed. Classroom instruction may be scheduled to introduce new procedures or to enhance associates' KSAs; however, classroom instruction only starts the training process. Effective training changes behavior. To change behavior, a manager must follow-up on-the-job to ensure that new or revised procedures introduced during classroom training are being properly executed in the workplace. Employers of choice realize that training is never complete—the goal is to constantly reinforce procedures so that the proper, most effective and efficient way of doing things becomes a way-of-life.

HR's role in the training process is to ensure that associates receive the training required to be successful. Consequently, HR will follow up with department managers and newly hired associates to monitor their progress. HR may also spearhead the implementation of specific training initiatives that impact multiple departments—such as guest service or associate empowerment training, although it is important that such training is supported by the hotel's department managers when associates are back on-the-job. Professional development programs are also commonly implemented by HR and are designed to help associates realize their full potential, preparing associates and managers for future promotion. By providing associates at all levels of the organization with ongoing training and development opportunities, a hotel may further position itself as an employer of choice while reducing associate turnover.

Coaching, Counseling, and Performance Evaluations

performance evaluation system:
a process during which an employee receives documented, thorough feedback on his/her job performance

Employees need and desire feedback on their job performance; department managers must provide that feedback. Formal feedback processes include the hotel's performance evaluation system; hotel policy dictates when an associate receives a perfor-

© Antonio Guillem/Shutterstock.com

mance evaluation—typically, following the first 90 days or probationary period of employment and then annually, either on the anniversary of each associate's initial hire or during a specified month of the year for all associates. Specific evaluation criteria are established for all line positions, with a separate set of criteria established for management personnel. These criteria will include factors such as *guest service skills*, *dependability*, and *problem-solving skills*. Evaluation ratings typically are provided on a 5-point scale, including *distinguished*, *above standards*, *fully meets standards*, *requires improvement*, or *well below standards* or a similar rating system.

Although a detailed discussion of performance evaluation systems is outside the scope of this text, the following points must be noted regarding performance evaluation processes:

- If a 5-point scale is used, the mid-point on the scale or a "3" rating should be received on most criteria by most associates—after all, the mid-point is "average" and employees should average-out to an "average" rating. Therefore "fully meets standards" is used as the mid-point rating in the rating system suggested above.
- "Fully meets standards" or the mid-point rating should be understood as doing a "good job." Quality organizations employ high-quality associates and standards are set high. So, performing to standards must be interpreted as performing well—to the hotel firm's high standards.
- "Exceeds standards" and "distinguished" ratings must be applied sparingly, and the manager must identify specific examples of exceptional performance to support these ratings.
- If performance "requires improvement" or is "well below standards," again, specific examples of behaviors that led to these ratings must be clearly identified. Quite frankly, it is the responsibility of management to address poor performance when it occurs, which should minimize the need to rate associates lower than "fully meets expectations" on any criterion, particularly if managers' employee counseling sessions and interventions are effective.
- Managers should avoid the halo effect, in which an associate's overall positive job performance is reflected across all criteria, or the devil horns effect, in which overall negative performance impacts all criteria. An associate's performance evaluation must look at each criterion independently of the others.

> **halo effect:**
> an associate's positive overall job performance is reflected across all job performance criteria ratings
>
> **devil horns effect:**
> an associate's negative overall job performance is reflected across all job performance criteria ratings

It is common for managers, particularly inexperienced managers, to overrate employee performance. This occurs for two reasons: First, managers often want to avoid conflict with associates. In addition, the education-system commonly assigns grades on an "A" through "F" basis, in which a "C" or the mid-point grade, is often defined as just barely acceptable and "As" and "Bs" are common. This has led to grade-inflation, including in the workplace.

If employee coaching and counseling are effective, an associate's performance evaluation should not provide any surprises. Department managers, throughout the year, should document and discuss performance outside the norm—whether positive or negative. By documenting and discussing job performance, associates understand how their job performance is perceived by their managers. Although every discussion does not need to be documented, it is better for a manager to err on the side of too much documentation than too little. Positive feedback may be documented when positive comments are posted about an employee's performance on a review site; a manager witnesses an associate providing exceptional guest service; an associate comes into work when contacted because another associate called-off; or when an associate serves as a trainer for a newly hired associate, just to mention a few examples. Attendance problems, negative interactions between an associate and guests or other associates, a lack of professionalism while on-the-job, excessive cash discrepancies, and other behaviors that negatively impact key stakeholders—guests, associates, investors, or the community—must also be documented. Documents generated in appreciation of an associate's good work, as well as to provide guidance when negative behavior must be addressed, may be reviewed when it is time to complete the associate's annual evaluation, which will ensure that the manager has a balanced view of the associate's performance over the past year.

When addressing negative performance, it is important to attack the problem and not the person. Managers must never assume they know the motive behind the behavior or attempt to address an associate's attitude—this will be interpreted as a personal attack, creating a defensive reaction. Instead, the focus must be on the undesired behavior. Clearly identify the behavior and discuss why the behavior is unacceptable, identifying the negative impact of the behavior on the hotel operation. The associate and manager should then identify how the behavior needs to change or be addressed, as well as a timeline for rectifying the situation. The manager must then hold the associate accountable if the error is repeated.

progressive discipline process:
a coaching and counseling process intended to encourage an associate to improve his/her job performance

HR policies typically define a three-step progressive discipline process in which negative employee performance or behavior is first discussed, although this discussion must be documented so that a record of the conversation is maintained; a repeat performance of the same or similar behavior is then documented in the form of a written warning; and finally, if a third offense occurs, typically within a 12-month period, an employee may be suspended from employment pending possible termination. The violation of specific workplace policies identified in the employee handbook/website or extreme behaviors—such as stealing or fighting with co-workers—may result in immediate suspension, pending termination of employment, bypassing the standard three-step progressive discipline process. It is important that disciplinary processes be handled by management discretely with only the impacted associates involved.

In most hotel organizations, only the GM, in consultation with the director of human resources, may terminate an associate's employment. The suspension of an associate is not to be used as a punitive measure. Typically, a suspension is for a 3-day time period, which allows time for an investigation into the matter to be conducted by a neutral HR professional; it also allows a cooling-down period, particularly if the situation is emotionally-charged. Following the suspension, the GM, an HR professional, the department manager, and associate involved meet to bring closure to the matter. It is generally better to rehabilitate an associate rather than to terminate an associate's employment. Consequently, the goal of progressive discipline is to solve problems versus to terminate associates' employment.

Employee Opinion Survey

Employers of choice survey their associates annually to better understand employee perceptions of the workplace. Perceptions of all aspects of the employment relationship are assessed, including quality of supervision; compensation and benefits; incentive and recognition programs; service quality provided to guests; cleanliness and maintenance of facilities; quality and availability of equipment and supplies; social programs; quality of employee meals; style and functionality of uniforms; and more. Employee opinion survey results are compared to comparable hotels and other quality hospitality organizations. After the results of this annual survey are received, hotel management, spearheaded by the GM, director of human resources, and remaining members of the EOC, create an action plan to address associate concerns identified by the survey. It is important that the results of the survey, and the subsequent plan to address the concerns identified, are communicated to all associates within the hotel; this ensures associates that their concerns are being heard and addressed. Typically, the hotel's performance on the employee survey impacts the annual incentive compensation that is earned by the hotel's GM and EOC.

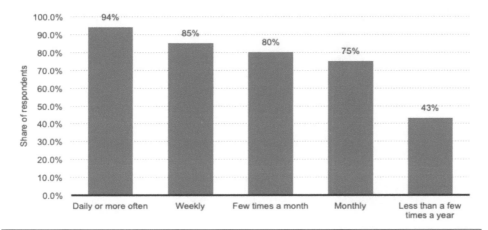

Diagram 11.4: Share of US Employees Satisfied with their Job by Frequency of Supervisors' Positive Recognition (*Bamboo, 2016*)

Employee Recognition and Celebrations

As outlined in the Cycle of Success, employee recognition is essential to associate satisfaction. As outlined in *Diagram 11.4*, expressing daily appreciation to hotel associates in recognition of a job well-done may have a substantial impact on employee satisfaction. A variety of formal and informal recognition programs are supported by an employer of choice, including employee-of-the-month, employee-of-the-year, anniversary luncheons, an annual employee picnic, annual awards celebration, and more. It is also common for a hotel to be aligned with the local chapter of a national charity and to provide volunteer opportunities for associates.

An employee-of-the-month and employee-of-the-year program are supported in many hotels. Two associates, a front-of-the-house and heart-of-the-house employee, may be recognized in a larger hotel. A manager-of-the-quarter may also receive recognition from senior management. These programs formally recognize associates for exceptional dedication to their jobs—including delivering exceptional service quality to guests and their fellow associates. These associates typically are given a small financial incentive and other perks, and honored at a monthly luncheon, but most importantly to the associate, they are publicly recognized among their peers; photographs of employees-of-the-month are typically posted in a conspicuous location. Many hotels select, from among the employees-of-the-month, an employee-of-the-year that is often awarded additional paid vacation time off, including airfare, accommodations, or spending money. Quarterly management appreciation functions are also held, for exempt associates, at which a manager-of-the-quarter is recognized.

BOX 11.3: THE POWER OF APPRECIATION

© Nattakorn_Maneerat/
Shutterstock.com

Although formal recognition programs are important, nothing is more important than a simple "thank you," sincerely delivered by a supervisor or co-worker. Managers are problem-solvers and it is all too common for managers to be problem-focused—constantly identifying and discussing operational challenges to improve operations and enhance the guest experience. As a result, managers often develop a reputation, and deservedly so, of being negative—constantly focused on what is wrong with the operation. A wise manager realizes that a focus on the positive—what associates are doing well—creates a more positive and supportive work environment, ultimately enhancing operations, *esprit de corps*, and the guest experience.

No one in the hotel industry is better at focusing on the positive than Abdul M. Suleman. Mr. Suleman, founder of *Equinox Hospitality*, a hotel development and management firm based in San Francisco, California, previously served in a variety of roles, including Regional Vice President, over a 20-year tenure with *Hyatt Hotels Corporation*. He made it a point to make the rounds every afternoon to personally thank as many associates as possible for their efforts to effectively serve guests on behalf of the company; however, Abdul's *thought-of-the-day* was legendary.

It seemed like a little thing—a simple quote or word-of-advice—that Abdul would share daily with the associates throughout his day. Managers would arrive on property each day and seek out the thought-of-the-day to share with associates during pre-shift line-ups; the thought would also be posted on employee information boards throughout the heart-of-the-house areas. The thought often addressed a topic that was more personal than work-related, but that is exactly why it was effective. It was not the thought *per se*, it was the fact that hotel leadership sincerely cared about the hotel's associates. Abdul cared enough about the personal well-being of the hotel associates to take the time, each-and-every-day, to find a thought or idea that he felt would personally benefit, enlighten, or uplift associates. And this level of caring lifted the spirit of everyone in the hotel!

From my heart, Abdul, I say, "Thank you!" Thanks for being an exceptional role-model, leader, and mentor.

Sincerely,
Michael D. Collins, author of *Delivering the Guest Experience*

ACCOUNTING AND CONTROL FUNCTIONS

In addition to HR support, the A&G department also performs the following accounting functions within a hotel.

Income and Night Audit

Revenue is posted and verified daily. Night auditors work during the overnight shift and are responsible for charging room and tax revenue to each guest's folio or room account prior to rolling the date within the property management system (PMS). Night auditors also confirm that all banquet revenue has been posted to group

night auditor: a non-exempt associate that provides front office coverage during the overnight shift while completing a wide-range of accounting-related responsibilities

master accounts or closed out, as appropriate; although pre-payment is required for most banquet functions, guests accommodated above the guarantee and cash bar balances must be settled via cash or credit card at the conclusion of each function, unless a client has been approved for direct billing. The night audit team also closes out the Food & Beverage (F&B) point-of-sale (POS) system for the day, ensuring that all outlet guest checks have been properly closed. Each morning, the income auditor verifies the accuracy of the night auditors' work and ensures that the previous day's revenue is accurately recorded on the proper revenue ledger prior to generating a daily revenue report or updating financial dashboards.

income auditor:
a non-exempt accounting associate responsible for accurately recording all hotel revenue

General Cashier

general cashier:
a non-exempt accounting associate responsible for preparing daily bank deposits, and maintaining and monitoring all cashiers' banks

The general cashier is responsible for pulling all cash deposits from the drop safe, which is where guest service agents, working the hotel's front desk; food servers and outlet cashiers; banquet managers or captains; and other retail cashiers deposit any cash receipts collected during their respective shifts. The general cashier consolidates all these cash deposits and prepares a bank deposit each business day. The bank deposit must be reconciled against the ledger entry made for cash receipts for the day, less any direct deposits or automated clearing house (ACH) payments. The general cashier also issues banks and change to cashiers, randomly auditing banks to ensure they are being properly maintained by cashiers.

accounts payable clerk:
a non-exempt associate responsible for accurately recording expenses and paying vendors based upon prescribed payment terms

Accounts Payable

The accounts payable clerk, bookkeeper, or accountant is responsible for processing invoices to ensure that expenses are charged to the appropriate department and expense ledger, and that payments are made to vendors based upon the prescribed payment terms; purchases must be properly approved, in advance, through the purchase order (PO) system and the receipt of the goods or services must verified by the appropriate department or division head before an invoice is paid.

purchase order (PO):
a printed or electronic document that authorizes the acquisition of goods, products, or services

Accounts Receivable

accounts receivable clerk:
a non-exempt associate responsible for collecting payments for products and services rendered, including credit card and direct bill accounts

Accounts receivable personnel assemble invoices for the meetings, conventions, and events that take place at the hotel and prepare billing summaries for group clients. In large conference hotels, an invoice for a single conference may be comprised of hundreds of guestroom folios, banquet checks, audio-visual invoices, and other documents that support the charges that have been billed to the group's master account.

Many hotels employ a credit manager that oversees the collection process, approving direct billing privileges for group clients only after he/she can verify that the client has a good payment history by contacting hotels that have hosted previous conferences for the client.

credit manager: an exempt manager responsible for approving billing privileges and overseeing the accounts receivable process

Payroll

Payroll is typically a highly automated process managed by the accounting department; the timekeeping system, in which hotel associates clock-in and out, commonly interfaces with the payroll system, which is often provided by an outside payroll processing vendor, such as ADP (www.adp.com). Employee timekeeping systems often support the employee scheduling process and help hotel managers closely monitor employees' punctuality, overtime, and the gratuities received by associates, which are taxable income.

Purchasing and Receiving

It is important that the purchasing and receiving functions are separated from the accounts payable function; this check-and-balance ensures that payments are not made for goods or services that are not needed or received by the hotel. A large hotel may employ a separate purchasing manager, although in many hotels the department heads, such as the executive steward and director of services, as examples, manage the purchasing function for their respective areas. With the exception of food and beverage products, which must be ordered frequently, managers generate a purchase order that must be approved by the division head, controller, and GM before an order may be placed. The rooms director, director of F&B, director of engineering, or other division head verifies that the proposed expenditure is necessary and that the specifications and cost are appropriate, which is confirmed by the controller prior to final approval by the GM. Multiple bids should be obtained for purchases that are not made from approved vendors. Astute managers often maintain a declining checkbook balance, as described in *Box 11.4: Controlling Expenses: Declining Balance Sheet*, to track purchases against the budget as a cost control measure. Orders must be verified against the PO upon delivery to ensure that the specifications and quantities are correct, and that the purchase was authorized.

purchasing manager: an exempt manager responsible for the acquisition of operating supplies and equipment

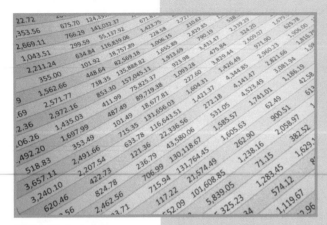

©Aaban/Shutterstock.com

Processes designed to effectively manage payroll costs, as well as food cost and beverage cost of goods sold (COGS), have been discussed extensively throughout various chapters of *Delivering the Guest Experience*, including *Chapter 6: Guest Services Operations*, *Chapter 7: Housekeeping and Laundry Operations*, and *Chapter 8: Food and Beverage Operations*; however, little attention has been given to managing other controllable expenses, including the cost of operating supplies and other expenses. These expenses are often controlled using a declining checkbook balance or declining balance spreadsheet.

declining checkbook balance or declining balance spreadsheet: a method of managing and controlling expenses associated with the purchasing of operating supplies and equipment

accrual basis accounting: an accounting method in which financial statements reflect the revenue for products and services rendered, and the corresponding expenses incurred to support that revenue, during the accounting period

cash basis accounting: an accounting method in which financial statements reflect revenue and expenses based upon the in-flow and out-flow of payments from guests and to vendors during the accounting period

At the start of each month, each divisional director—the director of rooms, director of F&B, director of sales, director of engineering, director of human resources, and controller—creates a spreadsheet, with columns labeled with each controllable expense category within their respective purview. In the first row, the available budget for the month will be recorded as the opening balance; the amount of the opening balance is adjusted based upon forecasted occupancy or revenue for the month. The available budget or opening balance will be calculated based upon the budgeted cost-per-occupied-room (CPOR), cost per cover (CPC), or percentage of revenue, as appropriate; this ensures that budgeted contribution margins are maintained despite fluctuations in revenue. Each time a PO is approved, the PO number, vendor, and the amount of the purchase will be recorded within the appropriate column(s) and deducted from the balance remaining for the corresponding expense account. At month's end, this spreadsheet may be used to verify the accuracy of the financial statement and to explain any variances to budget. It may also be used to identify accruals that need to be made, because an expense may be incurred, and the product or service received, but the invoice may not have been received or processed by accounts payable.

Hotels generally operate using accrual basis accounting as opposed to cash basis accounting. With cash basis accounting, revenue is recorded when payments are received, and expenses recorded when payments are made by the business; this may result in substantial fluctuations in contribution margins, particularly in a large business such as a hotel operation. The goal of accrual basis accounting is to record revenue when products and services are consumed by guests, and to align expenses with the corresponding revenue; this accounting method increases the stability and consistency of financial results.

To illustrate, assume that a hotel anticipates that a hotel's guestroom linen will need to be replaced at a cost of $0.58 per occupied room. Recall from *Box 7.4* in *Chapter 7: Housekeeping and Laundry Operations*, that guestroom linen is inventoried quarterly, every 3 months, at which time an order is placed to bring the hotel back up to a full 3-par of guestroom linen. If 11,412 room nights are occupied during the month of January; 9,947 are consumed in February; and 10,712 room nights sold in March, the hotel will be expected to incur a linen expense of $18,601 or [(11,412 + 9,947 + 10,712) x $0.58] during the first quarter of the year. At the end of the first quarter, on March 31, the big-four inventory reveals that a $17,454 purchase of guestroom linen is required to re-establish a 3-par of guestroom linen.

If a hotel operates using cash basis accounting, no linen expense ($0) will be recorded for January, February, or March; however, a $17,454 expense will be recorded in the month of April when the linen order is placed and received. This results in overstating the hotel's profitability in January, February, and March, as well as understating profitability in the month of April—or even the month of May, if the full order is not received or the invoice is not paid until May.

Using accrual basis accounting, an accrual is made each month, at a rate of $0.58 per occupied room, which provides an allowance for linen replacement. Consequently, in this example, an expense of $6,619 or (11,412 x $0.58), is recorded in January; $5,769 or (9,947 x $0.58) is recorded February; and $6,213 or (10,712 x $0.58) is recorded in March. When the big-four inventory is completed at the end of March, and it is determined that a $17,454 expense is required to re-establish a 3-par of guestroom linen, an adjusting journal entry will be made of -$1,147 to adjust the accrued linen expense to reflect the actual amount of linen expense that was incurred during the first quarter of the year. As a result, the linen expense accrued in April, assuming 9,954 room nights are consumed during the month, will be $4,626 or ([9,954 x $0.58) - $1,1470]. Accrual basis accounting results in more accurate financial statements and aligns expenses with the corresponding revenue.

Returning to the discussion of the declining checkbook balance spreadsheet, assume that no linen purchases are made or received during the first quarter of the year. Therefore, the director of rooms, in this scenario, opens the month of April with an opening balance of $24,374 available for linen purchases; this opening balance represents the $18,601 in linen accruals carried over from the months of January, February, and March, plus the April accrual (9,954 x $0.58). After the big-four inventory is completed on March 31, and a purchase order (PO) is prepared by the director of services or executive housekeeper to make a $17,454 linen purchase to re-establish a 3-par of guestroom linen, the director of rooms will approve the PO with confidence knowing that the purchase can be made, and the hotel's linen expense will be maintained within budgeted guidelines. The opening balance for linen expense carried over on the declining checkbook to May will reflect the $1,147 linen savings realized during the first quarter because the actual linen accrual of $4,426 recorded on April's financial statement is added to May's linen accrual to calculate the amount of funds available for any linen purchases that may be made in May.

accrual:
an accounting entry made to reflect an expense incurred for which an invoice has not been received nor a payment has been made

adjusting journal entry:
an accounting entry made to alter an accrual based upon the amount of the actual expense

© Dima Sidelnikov/Shutterstock.com

Financial Reporting

As with any business, a variety of financial reports are produced by the hotel's accounting team to manage and assess a hotel's financial performance. A financial statement provides a snapshot of the financial standing of a business at a specific point in time. Financial benchmarks are reference points against which a hotel's actual financial performance may be compared. Financial statements typically use last year's values for the equivalent time frame, as well as budgeted values, as benchmarks against which the hotel's current financial performance is assessed. Hotel management firms may operate on a calendar year or fiscal year basis, in which the fiscal year is defined by the business (e.g. July 1 through June 30), and may elect to prepare financial statements monthly or choose, instead, to break the year into thirteen 28-day accounting periods.

Daily reports and financial dashboards are generated each day by the accounting team, which facilitate management's ability to successfully manage the financial performance of the hotel. A daily report provides a breakdown of revenue for the previous day and month-to-date (MTD) or period-to-date (PTD), coupled with key operating statistics including occupancy, average daily rate (ADR), and revenue per available room (RevPAR); the daily report also includes F&B cover counts and aver-

financial statement:
provides a snapshot of the financial standing of a business at a specific point in time

financial benchmark:
a reference point against which a hotel's actual performance may be compared

daily report and financial dashboards:
an estimate of the hotel's financial performance, in terms of revenue, expenses, and operating statistics, for a specific date and the accounting period-to-date

age checks by outlet, as well as for the banquet department, which is typically broken down by meal period. Estimates of payroll expenditures for the previous day and MTD or PTD are also included on the daily report, including productivity statistics such as the payroll cost ratios, hours per occupied room (HPOR) statistics, and F&B revenue-per-labor-hour for the F&B division. Finally, food cost and beverage cost ratios are also estimated based upon food purchases and beverage purchases received MTD or PTD.

Key data and statistics may be communicated to department managers electronically via financial dashboards, which may present key financial data and cost ratios that may be customized based upon a manager's specific responsibilities. As examples, the executive housekeeper may set-up a financial dashboard that reports the daily and MTD or PTD housekeeping payroll ratio, coupled with room attendant HPOR; and the executive chef may establish a dashboard that reports food-revenue-per-culinary-labor-hour and the food cost ratio MTD or PTD. The wide-array of IT systems used throughout hotel operations facilitate the accounting team's ability to provide real-time financial performance data daily, which is essential to the successful management of a hotel's financial results.

The profit-and-loss statement, or P&L, outlines the financial performance of a hotel for a defined time period. A P&L is generated each month or accounting period, providing a summary P&L on the cover page; *Table 11.1* provides a *Hotel P&L template*. The summary P&L includes, in the first section, basic operating statistics—room nights, occupancy, ADR, and RevPAR. Section two provides a break-down of revenue by source—rooms, F&B, other operating income, and total revenue. Section three lists operating expenses for each operating division and the total departmental operating expenses. In Section 4, operating expenses are deducted from the corresponding revenue, which leads to departmental operating profit or the contribution made by the rooms division, F&B division, and other operating departments, respectively, as well as for all operating departments combined. Undistributed operating expenses, which include A&G, sales and marketing, property operations and maintenance (POM), and utility costs are included in Section 5 of the summary P&L; total undistributed operating expenses are subtracted from the hotel's total departmental income to calculate gross operating profit (GOP).

> **profit-and-loss state-ment or P&L:** outlines the financial performance of a hotel for a defined time period
>
> **summary P&L:** provides an overview of the hotel's financial performance, including each of the operating divisions

The summary P&L also includes expense lines for franchise, base, and incentive management fees, which are deducted from GOP leaving income before fixed charges (IBFC). Real estate taxes, property and general liability insurance, and a capital replacement reserve—expenses that the hotel's ownership is contractually obligated to fund—are deducted from IBFC, leaving earnings before interest, taxes, depreciation, and amortization (EBITDA). Some hotels may include a line for capital leases or miscellaneous ownership expenses within the *fixed charges* section of the P&L. EBITDA represents the profit generated by the hotel operation that is available for the hotel's ownership to cover its financial obligations associated with the property, including any debt service, and to provide investors with a return on investment (ROI). Recall that *Table 2.1: Financial Performance of a 'Typical' Upper-Upscale Hotel* provides an example of a summary P&L statement in this format, with sample values, down to IBFC.

Several additional financial statements are provided, as part of the P&L, to support the summary P&L. Separate, detailed departmental P&Ls are provided for each operating department, including the rooms division, F&B division, telecommunications and guestroom entertainment, and any additional operating departments such as retail operations, spa or wellness facilities, and golf operations or other recreational departments; these departmental P&Ls each provide a detailed breakdown of labor expenses by position, COGS, and other controllable expenses by expense category. Miscellaneous operating income, such as interest earned, or rents collected from retail tenants, are also listed by income category. For each undistributed operating department—A&G, sales and marketing, POM, and utilities—a detailed statement is provided, detailing all labor costs by position and expenses incurred by expense category. Payroll taxes and employee benefit (PT&EB) expenses are also detailed, which are distributed to the operating and undistributed departments proportionately based upon each department's labor expense. The cost of operating the in-house laundry, if applicable, is also provided, including payroll, PT&EB, and controllable expenses, in detail, which is typically allocated back as a line-item expense on the rooms and F&B statements respectively. A variety of operating statistics and ratios may also be provided to assist hotel managers in analyzing the financial results for the month or accounting period and year to date.

discrepancy report:
a financial report that explains substantial variances between actual results and financial benchmarks

The P&L typically provides 12 columns of values, including current month, same month (or period) last year, current month's (or period's) budget, year-to-date, previous year-to-date, and year-to-date budgeted, as well as the corresponding ratio (%) for each of these six values. This information allows management to analyze financial results by comparing the hotel's current performance against the relevant financial benchmarks. Typically, corporate management and hotel ownership require hotel management to provide a detailed discrepancy report in which any significant variance to budget or last year are explained. This ensures that management is held accountable for achieving sales goals, while appropriately managing payroll costs, COGS, and operating expenses.

balance sheet:
a financial statement that reflects the assets and liabilities of a business at a specified point in time

assets:
cash, receivables, and items of value held by a business

liabilities:
payables and other financial commitments of a business, including owners' equity

The balance sheet is an additional month-end and year-end financial report that is generated by the hotel accounting department, which supports the P&L. It provides details regarding the hotel's current financial standing in terms of assets—things of value the hotel owns or has purchased—and liabilities—financial commitments or responsibilities of the hotel. A *Template of a Hotel Balance Sheet* is provided in *Table 11.2*.

Hotel Profit and Loss (P&L) Statement		
Month-ending: MM/DD/YYYY		
Operating statistics: Room nights Occupancy Average Daily Rate (ADR) Revenue per Available Room (RevPAR)	#,### ##.#% $ ###.## $ ###.##	
Revenue:	**Value ($)**	**Ratio (%)**
Rooms revenue	a	$=\left(\dfrac{a}{a+b+c}\right)\times100$
Food and Beverage (F&B) revenue	b	$=\left(\dfrac{b}{a+b+c}\right)\times100$
Other operating revenue	c	$=\left(\dfrac{c}{a+b+c}\right)\times100$
Total revenue	$=(a+b+c)$	$=100.0\%$
Department expenses: Room division	d	$=\left(\dfrac{d}{a}\right)\times100$
F&B division	e	$=\left(\dfrac{e}{b}\right)\times100$
Other operating departments	f	$=\left(\dfrac{f}{c}\right)\times100$
Total department expenses	$=(d+e+f)$	$=\left(\dfrac{d+e+f}{a+b+c}\right)\times100$
Department profit: Room division	$=a-d$	$=\left(\dfrac{a-d}{a}\right)\times100$
F&B division	$=b-e$	$=\left(\dfrac{b-e}{b}\right)\times100$
Other operating departments	$=c-f$	$=\left(\dfrac{c-f}{c}\right)\times100$
Total department profit	$=(a-d)+(b-e)+(c-f)$	$=\left[\dfrac{[(a-d)+(b-e)+(c-f)]}{(a+b+c)}\right]\times100$
Undistributed operating expenses: Administrative & General	g	$=\left(\dfrac{g}{a+b+c}\right)\times100$
Sales & Marketing	h	$=\left(\dfrac{h}{a+b+c}\right)\times100$
Property Operations & Maintenance	i	$=\left(\dfrac{i}{a+b+c}\right)\times100$
Utilities	j	$=\left(\dfrac{j}{a+b+c}\right)\times100$
Total undistributed operating expenses	$=g+h+i+j$	$=\left[\dfrac{(g+h+i+j)}{(a+b+c)}\right]\times100$
Gross Operating Profit (GOP)	$=[(a-d)+(b-e)+(c-f)]-(g+h+i+j)$	$=\left[\dfrac{[(a-d)+(b-e)+(c-f)]-(g+h+i+j)}{(a+b+c)}\right]\times100$

Fees:		
Franchise fees[1]	k	$= \left(\dfrac{k}{a+b+c}\right) \times 100$
Base management fees	l	$= \left(\dfrac{l}{a+b+c}\right) \times 100$
Incentive management fees	m	$= \left(\dfrac{m}{a+b+c}\right) \times 100$
Income Before Fixed Charges (IBFC)	$= GOP^2 - (k+l+m)$	$= \left[\dfrac{(GOP^2 - (k+l+m))}{(a+b+c)}\right] \times 100$
Fixed charges:		
Real estate taxes	n	$= \left(\dfrac{n}{a+b+c}\right) \times 100$
Property & general liability insurance	o	$= \left(\dfrac{o}{a+b+c}\right) \times 100$
Reserve for capital replacement	p	$= \left(\dfrac{p}{a+b+c}\right) \times 100$
Earnings Before Interest, Taxes, Depreciation & Amortization (EBITDA)	$= IBFC^3 - (n+o+p)$	$= \left[\dfrac{(IBFC^3 - (n+o+p))}{(a+b+c)}\right] \times 100$

[1]Franchise fee may be included in Undistributed Operating Expenses in some hotels.
[2]GOP represents the GOP value calculated in the cell above.
[3]IBFC represents the IBFC value calculated in the cell above.

Table 11.1: Hotel P&L Template

guest ledger:
the sum of the guest and group account balances due the hotel from hotel guests and groups currently in-house

city ledger:
represents the balances of all accounts that have been direct billed to clients and are awaiting payment

allowance for doubtful accounts:
an estimate of the amount of the outstanding accounts receivable balance that may go uncollected

contra-asset account:
an asset account with a zero or credit balance

On the asset side of the balance sheet, the guest ledger is the sum of the guest and group account balances due the hotel from hotel guests and groups currently in-house. The city ledger represents the balances of all accounts that have been direct billed to clients and are awaiting payment. Any credit card payments being processed are also included in the accounts receivable total, although electronic processing allows credit card receivables to be converted into cash within just one or two business days. Hotels that carry a large balance of accounts receivable may accrue an allowance for doubtful accounts, which is recorded on the balance sheet in a contra-asset account that lowers the outstanding accounts receivable balance. Maintaining an allowance for doubtful accounts minimizes the impact of an account receivable that is deemed uncollectible on the financial statements in a specific accounting period, allowing bad debt expense to be estimated and spread over several months.

On the liability-side of the ledger, accounts payable includes balances due to vendors for services and supplies. Advance deposits, which typically include prepaid hotel reservations and deposits received from banquet clientele, are reflected as a liability because these funds remain unearned; the hotel will charge revenue against the deposits

Balance Sheet	
Month-ending: MM/DD/YYYY	
Item	*Description*
Assets:	
Current assets: Cash Marketable securities Accounts receivable *less provision for doubtful accounts* Inventories Pre-paid expenses	• Current assets may be immediately converted to cash or will benefit the operation within the next 12 months and include: current bank balances (cash), short-term investments (marketable securities), and accounts receivable, which includes the current guest ledger and city ledger, less any allowance for doubtful accounts. • Inventories include food, beverage, and big-4 inventory items (china, glass, service-ware, and linen). • Pre-paid expenses include any expenses, such as insurance, which have been paid up to 12 months in advance.
Non-current assets: Non-current receivables Long-term investments Real assets Furniture, Fixtures and Equipment (FF&E) *less accumulated depreciation* Other assets	• Non-current assets include all assets that are not immediately convertible to cash or anticipated to provide a benefit to the operation within the next 12 months. • Real assets include land and buildings. • FF&E includes the hotel's depreciable operating equipment, such as laundry and kitchen equipment, and all hotel furnishings. • Other assets include intangible assets, including the value of franchise rights, trade-names, pre-opening expenses, and the goodwill of the business.
Total assets:	• The sum of all current and non-current assets.
Liabilities:	
Current liabilities: Accounts payable Notes payable Long-term debt payable Advance deposits Wages payable Taxes payable	• Current liabilities are financial obligations of the hotel that are payable within the next 12 months, including accounts payable to vendors, short-term notes, payments due on long-term debts, deposits paid on unearned revenue. • Salaries and wages earned by associates but not yet paid and taxes collected by the hotel that are payable to government taxing authorities are recorded as current liabilities.
Long-term liabilities: Long-term debt	• Long-term liabilities are financial obligations that are payable beyond 12 months into the future, including long-term debt.
Equity: Ownership equity	• Equity estimates the current value of the investors' investment in the hotel. • This value is calculated by subtracting the total liabilities of the hotel from total assets.
Total liabilities & ownership equity:	• This value must equal total assets.

Table 11.2: Hotel Balance Sheet Template

once the service products have been delivered to the guests. If for any reason the contracted services are not provided, then the hotel must be prepared to refund the client's funds, unless a deposit is forfeited by the terms of the guest's hotel reservation or client's contract. If the end of an accounting period and employee pay period do not coincide, then any salaries and wages due associates of the hotel for hours worked through the end of the accounting period that have not yet been paid are reflected as a liability on the balance sheet. Sales taxes, hotel occupancy taxes, and payroll taxes collected by the hotel, as well as payroll taxes that are the responsibility of the hotel, remaining payable at the end of an accounting period, are also listed as a current liability.

ownership equity:
estimates the current value of the investors' financial interest in the hotel

book value:
represents the amount originally paid to acquire an asset less accumulated depreciation

accumulated depreciation:
the amount of depreciation expensed-to-date against the acquisition cost of an asset

Total assets equal the sum of total liabilities plus ownership's equity; the two sides of the balance sheet must remain in balance. Consequently, ownership equity estimates the current value of the investors' financial interest in the hotel, assuming all hotel assets are liquidated at book value and liabilities of the hotel are satisfied. In layman's terms, it represents the money that would be left if the hotel and all its assets were sold, after paying all outstanding bills and debts of the hotel. Book value represents the amount originally paid to acquire an asset less accumulated depreciation. Recall from the discussion of capital expenditures in *Chapter 10: Maintaining the Hotel Asset and Sustainability* that depreciation is a non-cash expense that is recorded each accounting period over the useful life of an asset to account for its declining value; accumulated depreciation is the total amount of depreciation that has been recorded since acquiring an asset. Once the book value reaches the asset's salvage value, which is the amount for which an unusable asset may be sold, or zero ($0.00), if the asset has no salvage value and accumulated depreciation equals the asset's acquisition cost, the asset is removed from the balance sheet.

Relationship between the P&L and the Balance Sheet

Although a detailed discussion of accounting principles is outside the scope of this textbook, hotel managers must understand the relationship between the P&L and the balance sheet. Every time a business transaction occurs—for example, a guest is charged for overnight accommodations; a banquet is held in the hotel's ballroom, or a department manager purchases operating supplies—both of these financial statements are potentially impacted; a journal entry is made that impacts the P&L statement, with an offsetting entry (or entries) made that impact the balance sheet or, alternatively, offsetting transactions are made on the balance sheet. This principle is the foundation of dual-entry accounting.

journal entry:
the recording of the financial impacts of a business transaction on the appropriate accounting ledgers

To illustrate how the P&L and balance sheet work together to track the financial standing of the hotel, assume a business traveler arrives at a hotel, enjoys a glass of wine in the lobby bar, sleeps overnight, enjoys breakfast in the hotel's dining room, and then checks out, paying with a credit card. Upon registration, the guest establishes a guest ledger account by checking into the hotel; payment on the account is guaranteed with the credit card presented at check-in. The accounting transactions outlined in *Table 11.3a* illustrate how the guest's business transactions impact the P&L and the balance sheet, respectively, over the course of the guest's stay, as well as following the traveler's departure.

| Activity: | Impact upon: | |
	Profit & Loss (P&L)	Balance Sheet
Guest enjoys a glass of wine in the lobby bar for $13.00, including a $2.00 tip and $1.00 in sales tax.	Beverage revenue increases by $10.00.	The guest ledger, a current asset account, increases by $13.00. Wages payable, a current liability, increases by $2.00; taxes payable, also a liability, increases by $1.00. The net impact on the balance sheet is $10.00, which offsets the $10.00 recorded on the P&L as beverage revenue.
Night audit posts a room charge of $149.00, plus $17.88 in hotel occupancy taxes.	Room revenue increases by $149.00.	The guest ledger increases by $166.88; the guest's account, a current asset, now stands at $179.88 owed to the hotel. Hotel taxes of $17.88 are added to taxes payable. The net impact on the balance sheet offsets the $149.00 in room revenue posted on the P&L.
The guest enjoys breakfast in the restaurant for $24.00, including sales tax of $1.80 and a $4.20 tip.	Food revenue increases by $18.00.	Guest ledger increases by $24.00; wages payable increases by $4.20; and taxes payable by $1.80— offsetting the $18.00 increase in food revenue on the P&L. The guest's account balance now stands at $203.88.
The guest checks out of the hotel, settling the $203.88 balance due on her credit card.	No impact on the P&L.	The guest ledger decreases by $203.88 and credit card receivables increases by $203.88. These two offsetting transactions are applied to two current asset accounts.
The credit card transaction is processed electronically, and the credit card payment is deposited directly into the hotel's bank account; the bank deducts a 3.0% credit card transaction fee of $6.12.	Credit card commissions, an A&G expense, increases by $6.12.	Once the payment is received from the credit card company, cash increases by $197.76 and credit card receivables decreases by $203.88. These largely offsetting transactions, within two current asset accounts, have a net impact of decreasing current assets by $6.12, the amount of the increase in credit card commission expense recorded on the P&L.
Payroll is processed and the gratuities of $2.00 and $4.20 are paid out to the Cocktail Server and Food Server, respectively, in their paychecks.	No impact on the P&L.	Cash, an asset account, is decreased by $6.20 and wages payable, a liability account, is also decreased by $6.20.
Sales taxes are paid to the appropriate taxing authorities.	No impact on the P&L.	Cash, an asset, decreases by $20.68 and taxes payable, a liability, decreases by $20.68.

Table 11.3a: Impact of Business Transactions on Financial Statements

Table 11.3a: Impact of Business Transactions of Financial Statements provides insight regarding the role of the hotel accounting team. Every business transaction that occurs within a hotel property must be recorded through a series of accounting entries, referred to as journal entries, ensuring that revenue, expenses, assets, and liabilities are accurately reflected on the hotel's financial statements. Fortunately, the hotel's IT systems assist the accounting team in tracking, summarizing, and recording the journal entries that need to be made.

Table 11.3b: Understanding Common Accounting Transactions, summarizes the possible combinations of offsetting dual entries that must be automated or entered by accounting personnel to record common financial transactions. Notice that entries that impact just the balance sheet must be made to two accounts on the same side of the ledger (both asset accounts or both liability accounts) in opposite directions (an increase with an offsetting decrease) or to two accounts on the opposite side of the ledger (impacting an asset and a liability) in the same direction (both increase or both decrease).

Transaction	Initial journal entry	Typical offsetting entry
Record revenue	Increase revenue ledger	Increase asset account (cash or receivable)
Record expenses[1]	Increase expense ledger	Increase a liability account (payables) or decrease an asset account (cash)
Record payroll expenses	Increase payroll expense ledger	Increase a liability account (wages payable)
Collect guest payment	Decrease an asset account (accounts receivable)	Increase an asset account (cash)
Collect tax from guest	Increase liability account (taxes payable)	Increase asset account (cash or receivable)
Pay a vendor's invoice	Decrease liability account (accounts payable)	Decrease asset account (cash)
Pay employees	Decrease liability account (wages payable)	Decrease asset account (cash)
Pay taxes	Decrease liability account (taxes payable)	Decrease asset account (cash)
[1]Some expenses may require direct payment, such as the purchase of alcoholic beverages in many states, which decreases cash versus increasing payables at the time the expense is recorded because the product is delivered with payment terms of cash (or ACH payment) upon delivery.		

Table 11.3b: Understanding Common Accounting Transactions

The senior accounting executive within a hotel is referred to as the controller, because his/her primary responsibility is to ensure that control systems are in place so that all revenue is accurately recorded and collected; payroll and expenses are properly managed; and hotel assets, including cash and inventories, are adequately protected. However, achieving the hotel's financial goals is a shared responsibility of the entire hotel management team. To do so, all hotel managers and supervisors must understand accounting functions, processes, and controls, collectively executing these systems to achieve financial success.

LOSS PREVENTION

The security team within a hotel, referred to as the loss prevention department, is responsible for protecting a hotel's assets, while minimizing the hotel's liability. This department is headed by a director of loss prevention or loss prevention supervisor supported by a team of loss prevention officers (LPOs). Although an A&G expense area, the director of loss prevention will often report directly to the director of rooms, director of operations, or assistant general manager, depending upon the exact structure of the hotel's executive operating committee.

© Dmitry Kalinovsky/Shutterstock.com

Whereas a small or select-service hotel may contract out the security function, it is typically more cost effective for the hotel to employ the loss prevention associates directly. Most importantly, hotel management maintains control over the specific duties of the LPOs, as well as responsibility for the selection and hiring of the officers, by directly employing the loss prevention team; it is important for the loss prevention team to be fully integrated into the hotel's culture and operation. Quite frankly, LPOs must be more guest-focused than security-focused in a hotel environment. Afterall, the most valuable asset a hotel can lose is a hotel guest. While a LPO must be observant, detail-focused, and able to respond to potentially stressful emergency situations, he/she must always be diplomatic and courteous—yet often firm—when interacting with guests or associates, regardless of the circumstances.

loss prevention department: the security team within a hotel

director of loss prevention or loss prevention supervisor: an exempt manager or non-exempt supervisor that directly oversees the security and loss prevention team

loss prevention officer (LPO): a non-exempt associate responsible for protecting hotel guests, associates, and assets from loss or harm

Role of the Loss Prevention Officers

There are three primary roles served by LPOs. First, LPOs make rounds throughout the hotel, ensuring that doors and storerooms are secure, associates are in the appropriate locations, and that safety hazards are quickly addressed. A hotel is a hazardous environment—wet or slick floors, sharp knives, open flames, and hot surfaces are just some of the hazards that may potentially cause employee or guest injuries. Because LPOs are constantly roving throughout the hotel property, they may serve as the eyes-and-ears of the hotel, quickly bringing any potential concerns to the prompt attention of associates or management. Although it is important that the LPOs be provided clear direction on areas to be inspected and the frequency of those inspections—with an emphasis on particularly vulnerable areas of the property—it is also important that an LPO does not repeatedly follow the same route and time schedule; this allows others to anticipate where the LPO will be at specific times, jeopardizing the effectiveness of his/her patrols. The LPO should maintain a log of his/her activities and make notes of any unusual circumstances encountered, such as an employee found in an area of the hotel where he/she would not normally be found (e.g. a steward on a guestroom floor or a room attendant in the kitchen) or a storeroom door propped open. At the end of each shift, the roving LPO should generate a security report, which summarizes activities and observations made during the LPO's shift and is reviewed by the director of loss prevention, director of rooms, or GM.

security report:
summarizes activities and observations made during the LPO's shift

In addition to making rounds, a second responsibility of loss prevention is to monitor the associate entrance of the hotel—often referred to as back-door security. It is common for monitors to be placed at the back-door security station, if security cameras are used within the hotel; the back-door LPO quickly radios the roving LPO to immediately respond to any suspicious activity observed on the monitors. The back-door LPO also maintains control of hotel keys, except for electronic guestroom master key cards issued to Room Attendants by housekeeping management. Key sets are numbered and specific managers, supervisors, or associates are permitted to sign out key sets that provide access to only the storerooms and areas of the hotel necessary for the respective employee to perform the responsibilities of his/her position. No keys are permitted to leave the hotel grounds and key inventories are completed at the change of each back-door LPO's shift; this ensures that all key sets are either secured in the lockbox or signed out by an authorized associate that is currently working on the property. Key rings are welded shut so that individual keys cannot be removed from a key ring or duplicated. Back-door security also inspects all bags being brought onto the property or being removed from the property by hotel associates; by inspecting every bag, every time, the inspection procedure becomes a way-of-life within the hotel, eliminating potential conflicts between back-door security LPOs and hotel associates. An associate that is given permission to take an item home with them, for any reason, must obtain a red-tag, which is placed on the item and approved by management. Associates are never authorized to remove alcohol from the premises.

back-door security:
a non-exempt associate that monitors the associate entrance and security cameras, inspects packages and bags, controls keys, and performs other essential loss prevention duties

red-tag:
a tag placed on an item by management authorizing an associate to remove the item from the premises

incident report:
a written or electronic record of an extraordinary event, particularly one that involves loss or injury

The third responsibility of loss prevention is to complete an incident report when any security breach or a guest or employee accident occurs within the hotel. The LPO should record the day, date, and time of the incident; the names and contact information of all people involved—guests or associates; the names and contact information of any witnesses to the event; a detailed description of the event that has occurred; and the consequences of the event, including damage to property, loss of assets, or injuries to people. The value of any property lost or damaged should be estimated. Any action taken by hotel personnel in response to the circumstances should also be recorded along with the time that the action was taken. Photographs should be taken, as soon as possible, of the area in which the incident occurred from multiple angles. All statements recorded on the incident should be stated as factually as possible, avoiding the attribution of cause or the statement of an opinion.

For example, it is appropriate to state, "The guest fell to the floor in the lobby of the hotel. The floor appeared to be wet. A "Caution: Wet Floor" sign was posted in the area, per the photograph included with this report." It is not appropriate to state, "A guest slipped on the wet floor in the hotel lobby and fell, even though a "wet floor" sign was posted." It is also appropriate for the LPO to research the incident while the circumstances are fresh in people's minds, collecting statements from the individuals involved and available witnesses. Regarding the wet floor example, the LPO may want to find out when the "wet floor" sign was posted and by whom, providing evidence if possible. "James Jones, the Public Area Houseman on duty this evening, mopped the lobby floor and placed the "Caution: Wet Floor" sign in the lobby at 8:15 p.m.; please refer to attached public area checklist." Finally, LPOs should not accept responsibility on behalf of the hotel, expressing "disappointment" that the incident occurred versus apologizing, which may be interpreted as acceptance of liability. Involvement of the manager-on-duty (MOD), director of rooms, director of loss prevention, or GM should be solicited, particularly when a substantial loss or injury has occurred. Copies of all incident reports completed during a shift should be attached and referenced within the LPO's shift-end security report.

Emergency responders should be contacted immediately for severe medical emergencies; a radio call may be placed to the PBX Operator or at your service (AYS) attendant, who will immediately call 911, freeing the LPO at the scene to attend to the situation. Minor injuries may be treated by first-aid certified hotel personnel and the guest or associate offered additional medical treatment, as appropriate; all LPOs, as well as hotel managers, are required to maintain current first-aid and cardiopulmonary resuscitation (CPR) certification. Employee injuries are covered by workers' compensation and associates should be referred to or transported to the hotel's preferred medical clinic or immediate care facility. Whereas policies may vary by hotel management firm, it is often a good practice for a hotel to pay for the initial emergency treatment of any guest injuries that occur on the premises, as a goodwill gesture. Medical records are legally protected. Consequently, if a guest is injured on property and pays for their own medical treatment, the hotel will not have access to the records; however, the hotel will be provided with details regarding any medical treatment paid for by the hotel. Having access to the initial injury report, and the medical treatment that occurred, may help hotel management, the corporate office risk management team, or the hotel's general liability insurance company determine how to best respond to a liability claim made by a hotel guest.

It is always best to avoid discussions of liability or financial responsibility for incidents that occur. Instead, the focus should be on ensuring that everyone receives any required medical attention and that guests are prepared to accomplish the personal or professional goals that motivated their hotel stay. Hotels and guests typically carry insurance policies that protect both parties from catastrophic loss. Furthermore, innkeeper laws, which vary state-to-state, clearly define and often limit a hotelier's liability. Guests should be encouraged to allow the insurance companies representing each party to determine financial responsibility. As a goodwill gesture, hotel management may offer to make a payment to offset all or a portion of the insurance deductible incurred by the guest when a loss occurs, not because the hotel is accepting liability, but simply to maintain a positive guest relationship.

©Rido/Shutterstock.com

manager-on-duty or MOD:
a manager assigned responsibility for overseeing the entire hotel operation in the absence of the hotel's GM

Manager-on-Duty Program

During the traditional workweek, Monday through Friday, the hotel's GM and many of the hotel's EOC members are working at the hotel throughout each day. Consequently, senior managers are on-property, available to respond to challenging situations, including guest incidents, employee accidents, and emergencies; however, the GM has a responsibility to assign a specific individual to be in-charge of the hotel operation in his/her absence. A manager-on-duty program fulfills this responsibility. A manager-on-duty or MOD is assigned to cover each evening shift during the week, as well as each weekend shift, during the absence of the GM. MOD programs vary. Some GMs will split the weekends into multiple shifts, while others require the MOD to check into the hotel for the entire weekend, allowing the MOD the added benefit of experiencing the hotel from a guest's perspective.

Managers must be trained and qualified to serve as the MOD. The manager must know emergency procedures, be first aid and CPR certified, be trained to properly complete an incident report, and be well-versed in addressing guest service issues. The MOD must also be prepared to address employee or operational challenges that may arise during his/her shift. A well-managed MOD program is an excellent management development tool, providing managers with a broad-range of responsibilities, as well as the opportunity to develop skills outside the scope of the manager's normally assigned duties. MODs should not be expected to perform dual roles—to serve as MOD while also overseeing a shift within an operating department—particularly in a large hotel. The MOD is often provided with a checklist of activities to complete, which ensures that the MOD is out-and-about the hotel, making rounds, and supporting the delivery of exceptional guest experiences. A detailed report should be submitted to the GM at the end of the MOD's shift. A senior night auditor, guest service supervisor, or experienced LPO may serve as MOD on the overnight shift if the hotel does not employ a night manager.

Emergency Procedures

Detailed emergency procedures must be developed and written for emergency situations that are likely to occur within a hotel. The hotel's legal counsel, corporate-level risk management, insurance carrier, and property-level management must all be involved in developing emergency procedures that are appropriate to a specific hotel. Although many aspects of the policy may apply to any hotel, it is important that emergency procedures are customized to each specific property based upon the life-safety systems, staffing, design and construction, and other factors unique to each hotel. Emergency procedures should cover medical emergencies (code blue), fire emergencies (code red), bomb threats (code purple), active shooter situations, and weather emergencies or natural disasters, likely to occur within the destination (e.g. tornado, earthquake, hurricane, tsunami, etc.). Policies should provide step-by-step direction, with each responsibility clearly assigned to a specific job position; alternative assignment of responsibilities should be noted, which are put into effect in the absence of the primary personnel assigned a specific responsibility.

code blue:
medical emergency

code red:
fire emergency

code purple:
bomb threat

Emergency drills should take place at least quarterly to assess the hotel's level of preparation for an actual emergency. The director of loss prevention or director of engineering, if the hotel does not employ a director of loss prevention, is often assigned the primary responsibility of coordinating emergency training and drills, as well as the assessment of management and line employees' performance during scheduled drills. It is not uncommon for a drill to be coordinated with the appropriate first responders' participation. Managers and associates that serve in positions that are assigned specific responsibilities in response to an emergency are referred to as a brigade. Assembling the brigades, such as the fire brigade, medical brigade, etc., to train together on specific emergency procedures is particularly effective. Hotel associates that are not part of a brigade must know where to report and assemble if the hotel must be evacuated; this ensures that the well-being and safety of each associate may be confirmed in an emergency. Hotel personnel must also be assigned the responsibility of directing guests in an evacuation and to assist guests that may require personal assistance.

brigade:
the specific team of managers and associates assigned and trained to respond to a specific emergency situation

A variety of life-safety systems are required in a hotel, including a fire panel and alarm system; fire suppression systems targeting ovens, grills, deep fryers, and other fire-prone appliances, as well as automatic sprinklers in the guestrooms and guestroom corridors; pressurized evacuation stairwells; fire pumps; an emergency generator; and more. These systems must be meticulously maintained and periodically tested, as discussed in *Chapter 10: Maintaining the Hotel Asset and Sustainability*. No responsibility is more important than maintaining a safe and secure hotel environment for hotel guests and associates.

BOX 11.5: ACCESSING EVERY GUESTROOM, EVERY DAY

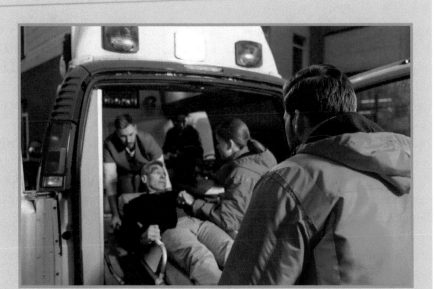

© LightField Studios/Shutterstock.com

On October 1, 2017, the deadliest mass shooting in United States history occurred at the *Route 91 Harvest Festival*—a country music concert in Las Vegas, Nevada. Fifty-eight people were killed—hundreds of others were injured—as Stephen Paddock fired down on a crowd of approximately 22,000 people for 9 to 11 additional minutes after the first 911 call was received by emergency dispatch, according to police; the shots were fired from a hotel suite on the 32nd floor of a hotel located across the street from the outdoor concert venue. Twenty-three weapons were found in Stephen Paddock's hotel room, which he had checked into on September 28, 2017 (CNN, 2017).

Unfortunately, hotels may attract individuals planning to engage in illegal, immoral, or other undesirable behaviors. As a result, it is important for guests to be required to present positive identification upon registration. When a guest registers, a credit card is provided to positively identify the guest and to establish credit; credit cards are verified electronically upon registration, which ensures that the card presented has not been reported lost or stolen, and that the guest has an adequate credit line available to cover his/her anticipated charges. When a guest pays with cash, the guest must be required to present a government-issued form of identification, such as a driver's license, identification card, or passport. The name on the registration must match the name of the guest registered into the guestroom. This ensures that if inappropriate or illegal activities do occur in a guestroom, the hotel is able to positively identify the guest responsible for the behavior. Therefore, guests are discouraged from engaging in inappropriate behaviors if a hotel requires positive identification.

Hotel personnel, particularly guest services, housekeeping, and loss prevention team members must be alert and respond to warning signs that inappropriate behavior may be planned by a hotel guest. These warning signs include:

1. *Large cash payment upon registration:* Often, the first warning sign of a potential problem is a guest that pays for the entire hotel stay in cash, refusing or unable to present a credit card to establish credit with the hotel.
2. *Indefinite plans:* The guest will often not make a room reservation in advance, simply walking into the hotel and requesting a room, with little concern regarding the price charged for the guestroom; the guest may also indicate that he/she is uncertain of when he/she will be departing from the hotel.
3. *Hesitancy to provide positive identification:* The guest may be reluctant to present positive identification upon registration or present false identification.
4. *High guestroom traffic:* The guest may have a high volume of visitors to his/her room, including throughout the late night and early morning hours.
5. *Denying access to guestroom:* The guest may keep the "do not disturb" notice posted on the guestroom door and decline housekeeping service; the guest may specifically request that hotel personnel not visit or enter the guestroom.
6. *Contraband in the guestroom:* Hotel personnel notice large sums of cash, weapons, or what may appear to be drugs or drug paraphernalia lying about the room.

Although a hotel's management and staff have a responsibility to respect the privacy of hotel guests, the safety of hotel guests and associates, as well as the reputation of the hotel, cannot be jeopardized. As a result, hotel personnel concerned about the behavior or circumstances regarding a hotel guest must bring it to the attention of management for follow-up. If hotel management investigates and remains concerned about the potential situation, then law enforcement officials should be notified—it is important that management or LPOs not take matters into their own hands. Law enforcement officers will provide sound guidance to management, often suggesting a range of options to potentially resolve the concern, remaining on-site until the matter is fully resolved.

Although hotel employees in the Las Vegas shooting state that they had been in Stephen Paddock's room before the shooting and did not notice anything amiss, it is difficult to understand how hotel employees failed to notice 23 weapons in the room, including multiple rifles, many with scopes (CNN, 2017). This incident does highlight the following common-sense loss prevention policies that should be in place within a hotel context:

1. *Access every guestroom, every day:* A "do not disturb" sign is a request for privacy; however, hotel management has the right to enter a guestroom even if a request for privacy is posted. If a sign is posted for an entire day—from the morning hours until 4 p.m. or later—then the guest should be contacted by telephone. If the guest fails to answer the telephone, then the room should be entered for the guest's safety—it is possible that a medical emergency occurred after the request for privacy was posted. It is also not uncommon for a hotel guest to inadvertently leave the "do not disturb" sign posted when leaving the guestroom in the morning. This afternoon room check ensures the safety of guests and facilitates housekeeping's ability to adequately service all guestrooms. At a minimum, an effort should be made to exchange the towels in the room if the guest denies housekeeping full access; a towel exchange will facilitate housekeeping's ability to quickly check the room. If access is denied for more than a single day, law enforcement may be contacted, particularly if any of the previous concerns are present.
2. *Firearms are not permitted in guestrooms:* There simply is no reason for firearms, weapons, or fireworks of any type to be permitted in hotel guestrooms or on the guestroom floors. The only exception may be for law enforcement officers. In states that allow concealed weapons to be carried with a permit, a sign may need to be posted at the entrance of the hotel to restrict concealed carry within the hotel—hotel management must verify and fully comply with state and local regulations. Guests traveling with weapons should, preferably, secure them in a location outside of the hotel or be required to place firearms in a safety deposit box in the front office of the hotel, if available.
3. *Every guest requiring independent access must be registered:* Access to hotel rooms may only be provided for the guest(s) officially registered in a guestroom. The number of guests occupying a room should be verified during registration. If more than one guest will be occupying a room, the guest service agent should ask if the additional guest(s) may need independent access to the room. If so, the names of the additional guests should be added to the registration record. Because someone presents an identification (ID) with the same last name of the guest registered—and may even have the same home address listed on their ID—this does not mean that the registered guest wants this person to have access to his/her hotel room.

4. *Contact law enforcement:* If any security concerns arise, contact law enforcement. It is always best to err on the side of caution by discussing concerns with law enforcement prior to the occurrence of an actual security breach.

5. *Notify others in the hotel community:* When a guest is requested to leave a hotel—or if a security breach occurs at a hotel property—notify other hotels within the community. A guest that is asked to leave a property, due to a security concern, is likely to seek accommodations in a nearby hotel. Although management at the receiving hotel must make their own decision regarding the potential accommodation of the guest, communicating concerns regarding the guest—such as when a guest brings firearms into a hotel room, for example—may prevent another member of the hotel community from experiencing a security problem. In addition, crimes perpetrated at one hotel may be replicated at other properties in the local community. Simply notifying other hotels of the crime may raise awareness among others in the hotel community, which may prevent further losses.

Safety Committee

The director of loss prevention chairs the hotel safety committee; a representative from every area of the hotel is selected to serve on the committee, which meets monthly to review incident reports, looking for trends and recurring incidents that require corrective action or follow-up. The committee also develops, communicates, and promotes safety incentive programs within the hotel. Committee members serve as advocates throughout the hotel, ensuring that the maintenance of a safe environment—for associates and guests—is a priority within each department. Not only do employee injuries place a substantial hardship on the associates impacted, workers compensation is also a major expense for many hotels that can best be managed through a reduction in the frequency and severity of workplace accidents.

safety committee: a group of representatives from each department charged with reviewing injury-causing events, as well as developing strategies and implementing activities to reduce injuries

CHAPTER SUMMARY

The A&G department includes the GM, executive administrative assistant, HR management team, accounting team, and loss prevention department. Depending on the size and complexity of a hotel operation, coupled with the structure of the parent or management company operating the hotel, a full staff of A&G personnel may be employed by the hotel or some functions may be supported by a regional or corporate team of administrative professionals. The four primary functions of the A&G department are to provide overall direction and leadership to the hotel's team of operations managers and associates; ensure effective HR practices to support management's effort to be an employer of choice; maintain appropriate accounting controls to deliver and report positive, accurate financial results; and minimize the hotel's liability, protecting guests and associates from injury and hotel assets from loss or damage.

KEY TERMS AND CONCEPTS

accounts payable

accounts receivable

accrual

accrual basis accounting

accumulated depreciation

adjusting journal entry

allowance for doubtful accounts

assets

assistant controller

back-door security

balance sheet

book value

bookkeeper or accounting manager

brigade

cash basis accounting

city ledger

cluster manager

code blue

code purple

code red

contra-asset account

controller

credit manager

daily reports and financial dashboards

declining checkbook balance or declining balance spreadsheet

devil horns effect

director of loss prevention or loss prevention supervisor

discrepancy report

employee assistance program

employee requisition

employee turnover

employer of choice

employment manager

financial benchmark

financial statement

general cashier

guest ledger

halo effect

incident report

income auditor

job analysis

job description

job fit

job specifications

journal entry

liabilities

life-safety systems

light duty

loss prevention department

loss prevention officer (LPO)

manager-on-duty or MOD

night auditor

ownership equity

performance evaluation system

pre-employment assessment

profit-and-loss statement or P&L

progressive discipline process

psychological contract

purchase order (PO)

purchasing manager

realistic job preview

red flag questions

red-tag

safety committee

security report

summary P&L

total-cost-of-employment

DISCUSSION QUESTIONS:

1. Identify the various positions charged as A&G undistributed operating expenses and define the role of each. Discuss the trend of centralizing many A&G functions. What are the benefits and risks of centralizing various administrative roles?

2. Discuss why it is important for a hotel to be regarded as an employer of choice. Outline specific strategies that may be employed for a hotel to earn a positive reputation as an employer of choice. Explain why the operations managers have a far greater influence on associates' levels of job satisfaction than the HR team.

3. Why is recruiting and hiring critically important in a hotel setting? Identify the steps in an effective hiring process; what is the ultimate goal of the process? Discuss how diversity (EEO and AA) may impact hiring decisions.

4. Identify and discuss each accounting function (e.g. accounts payable, accounts receivable, income audit, etc.). How does each function impact the hotel's P&L? How does each function impact the hotel's balance sheet? Discuss the details of the accounting transactions outlined in *Tables 11.3a* and *11.3b*; explain why dual-accounting requires that for every *action* taken by an accountant, there must be a corresponding or offsetting *reaction*.

5. Discuss the role of LPOs. What may be the impact of using an outside security services provider rather than an in-house team of LPOs?

6. Discuss the types of weather events or natural disasters that may occur in the local area. Identify the emergency procedures and strategies that may need to be in place to manage these possible situations. How much advance notice and planning will hotel management have regarding each potential scenario? How does the lead-time available affect emergency plans?

ENDNOTES

Bamboo, H. R. (2016). *Share of U.S. employees who are satisfied with their job by frequency of supervisors' positive recognition*. April 2016; accessed online from the *Statista* database at : https://www-statista-com.ezproxy.fgcu.edu/ through the Florida Gulf Coast University library database.

CNN (2017). *Las Vegas shooting: What we know*; Updated 8:44 AM ET, Tue October 3, 2017. Accessed online on January 1, 2019 at: https://www.cnn.com/2017/10/02/us/las-vegas-shooting-what-we-know/index.html

Collins, M.D. (2007). Understanding the Relationships between Leader-Member-Exchange (LMX), Psychological Empowerment, Job Satisfaction, and Turnover Intent in a Limited-Service Restaurant Environment; doctoral dissertation completed at *The Ohio State University*, Columbus, OH; available online at: https://search-proquest-com.ezproxy.fgcu.edu/central/docview/304833648/C008115E3924362PQ/1?accountid=10919

Collins, M.D. (2010). The effect of psychological contract fulfillment on manager turnover intentions and its role as a mediator in a casual, limited-service restaurant environment. *International Journal of Hospitality Management, 29*(4), 736 – 742.

Reich, A. (2016). *Management of Hospitality Human Resources: Theory and Practice for Maximizing Management and Employee Potential*, 2nd Edition; Kendall Hunt Publishing, Dubuque, IA.

SHRM (2017). *Employee Job Satisfaction and Engagement: The Doors of Opportunity Are Open Executive Summary.* April 2017, p 3; accessed online from the *Statista* database at: https://www-statista-com.ezproxy.fgcu.edu/ through the Florida Gulf Coast University library database.

Chapter 12

Hotel Investment

This chapter takes a deeper look at hotel operations from the perspective of hotel investors, including the assessment of a hotel's performance as a real estate investment.

PURPOSE AND LEARNING OBJECTIVES:

As has been emphasized throughout *Delivering the Guest Experience: Successful Hotel, Lodging, and Resort Management,* delivering exceptional guest experiences is the priority of hotel management because this ultimately facilitates the long-term financial success of the property. Hotel managers responsible for the day-to-day operation of a hotel are typically employed by a hotel management firm, or parent company, that has secured a management contract with the hotel's ownership. Ultimately, the return generated for the hotel's investors is the standard by which the performance of the management firm or parent company is assessed by hotel ownership. This chapter is designed to help current and future hotel managers better understand how investors evaluate a hotel's financial performance. Specifically, readers will be able to do the following after reading this chapter:

- Identify and describe various types of hotel investors.
- Explain factors that motivate hotel investment.
- Identify three factors that make hotel investment a higher risk than investing in alternative types of commercial real estate.
- Calculate the cash-on-cash yield and capitalization or cap rate of a hotel investment.
- Identify the three ways that owners earn a return on a hotel investment.
- Estimate the value of a hotel property.
- Identify factors owners may consider when negotiating a management contract or franchise agreement.
- Explain the role of an asset manager.

CHAPTER OUTLINE:

Like any business, a hotel is built to achieve an economic objective. Thus far, the focus of this textbook, *Delivering the Guest Experience: Successful Hotel, Lodging, and Resort Management,* has been to provide current and prospective hotel managers with the knowledge necessary to consistently deliver exceptional guest experiences, while effectively and proactively managing the business operation; however, ultimately, an effective hotel manager must ensure that the hotel delivers a satisfactory return on the investment made by its owners or investors. Consequently, an understanding of the relationship that must be established and maintained between hotel owners and managers is important.

Although all hotel owners have an economic objective in mind when investing in a hotel, various hotel owners may have additional motivation to invest in a hotel asset specifically. A hotel

© fizkes/Shutterstock.com

is often one component in a larger mixed-use development, which may include office space, retail outlets, entertainment, recreational, or residential units. In this situation, it is anticipated that the synergy among the various real estate assets will enhance the financial performance and value of each individual property. In some cases, a hotel developer may receive financial or tax incentives from a city, county, or development authority to develop a hotel, which may be viewed as an engine for economic growth or re-development in the area. For other hotel owners, a hotel may be a trophy-asset that is not developed for the potential economic benefit alone, but to be used as a place where a high-profile, successful business leader, group of investors, or corporation within the community can meet, accommodate, and entertain clients, employees, and other associates.

mixed-use development:
a commercial real estate asset consisting of a blend of real estate types, such as office, retail, residential, or hotel

trophy-asset:
used as a place where a high-profile, successful business leader, group of investors, or corporation within the community can meet, accommodate, and entertain clients, employees, and other associates

As introduced in *Chapter 1: Introduction to the Hotel Industry*, the successful development and operation of a hotel brings together three complementary, yet distinct, hotel-related business functions—hotel operations, real estate financing and investment, and hotel branding. Because the hotel industry is very capital intensive, hotel owners and investors focus on raising and minimizing the cost of capital necessary to develop, build, and re-invest in hotel properties. The role of a hotel management firm is to tend to the day-to-day operation of hotels, whereas hotel brands focus on developing, supporting, and expanding hotel concepts attractive to specific segments of travelers. Some firms perform all three of these business functions for an individual property; however, most hotel properties enlist the services of multiple organizations, each performing one specific function essential to the successful development, branding, and operation of the hospitality enterprise. The focus of this chapter is the interface between hotel investors and management.

HOTEL INVESTORS

Whether an investor is developing a new hotel or purchasing an existing property, a multi-million dollar investment is required. In the United States, hotels are typically valued at between $100,000 and $500,000 per key or guestroom depending on the hotel's location and service level; this translates into a $40 million to a $200 million investment to acquire a 400-room hotel. Depending upon the lending environment, which fluctuates based upon general economic conditions and the availability of credit, a lender may require that an ownership group make an equity investment in the property of at least 20% to 30%. As a result, an investor group may be required to invest a minimum of $8 million to $60 million in cash to develop or acquire a single 400-room hotel property. With these capital requirements, individual ownership of hotel assets is rare in today's world, particularly of larger upper-upscale or luxury hotels. Even if an individual has the financial resources and credit worthiness to make such an investment independently, few investors are interested in making such a significant investment in a single asset. Consequently, most large, upper-upscale or luxury hotel properties are owned by large institutional investors, partnerships, or real estate investment trusts (REITs).

real estate investment trust (REIT): a legal entity that sells shares to investors, investing the capital raised into income-producing real estate assets, which generate dividends for shareholders

Categories of Investors

institutional investors: investment banks, pension funds, large corporations, and other commercial investors that are typically seeking long-term capital appreciation

Institutional investors include investment banks, pension funds, large corporations, and other commercial investors that are typically seeking long-term capital appreciation. Institutional investors have large sums of capital to invest and aggressively seek investment opportunities that allow them to achieve specific objectives. These investors are financially motivated, and often invest in hotels due to potentially higher returns as compared with other real estate investments. Consequently, their primary concern is that the hotel delivers the targeted return on investment over the long-term.

limited liability partnerships: an ownership entity in which the investors' risk is typically limited to the amount of their investment in the hotel

Limited liability partnerships may be formed specifically to develop a new hotel property or to purchase or re-develop an existing hotel. The general partner recruits a group of limited liability partners that each invests a relatively small portion of the overall investment required to develop or acquire the property. The general partner manages the investment, although the general partner's investment typically does not exceed the combined investment of the limited partners. The partners typically contribute the upfront equity investment necessary to develop or acquire the asset, while debt is used to fund the bulk of the investment, which is secured by the real estate asset. The success of the investment is predicated upon the hotel operation generating adequate cash flow to fully cover the hotel's debt service, which is the principle and interest payments that must be made to the lender. The partners' risk or liability is typically limited to the amount of capital that they invest in the hotel; however, if

debt service: the principle and interest payments that must be made to the lender

cash flow from hotel operations cannot service the debt, the limited partners may elect to invest additional funds to cover short-term debt service payments to protect their long-term interest in the hotel.

Joint venture partnerships are formed through negotiated relationships between partners that have a vested interest in the development of a hotel property. Hotel parent companies and management companies sometimes make a significant, yet relatively small investment in a hotel property to secure a long-term contract to manage or brand the hotel asset; by risking their own capital, the hotel's primary investors are assured that the hotel management firm is more likely to look out for the owners' best interest in their day-to-day operation of the property. Other joint venture partners may include the landowner, property's developer, a major corporation located in proximity to the hotel, institutional investors, and individual investors. Investors share an economic interest in the success of the property but may have other non-financial interests as well. For example, a major corporation located adjacent to the hotel may desire to have an upper-upscale or luxury hotel adjacent to its corporate offices to house the many vendors and other guests that visit its corporate offices, as well as to service many of its corporate meetings and events.

joint venture partnerships: formed through negotiated relationships between partners that have a vested interest in the development of a hotel property

Individual investors often invest in smaller, limited-service and economy hotels due to the large capital investment required to own a hotel—many small, economy hotels continue to operate, whether franchised or independent, as family-owned businesses. These hotel operators often rely upon organizations like the Asian American Hotel Owners Association (AAHOA) and the American Hotel & Lodging Association (AHLA) to advance and support the business interests of individual hotel owners; the AAHOA boasts 18,000 members that collectively own nearly half of the hotel properties in the United States, according to the Association's website (AAHOA, 2019). Although many individually or family-owned properties are smaller economy, midscale, and upper-midscale select-service properties, the effective management of these hotels may eventually lead successful operators to ownership of larger, more upscale hotels.

individual investors: individuals or families that typically invest in smaller, limited-service and economy hotels

Asian American Hotel Owners Association (AAHOA): a trade association that supports hotel owners by improving access to products, services, financing, and education

An individual's investment in a larger upper-upscale or luxury hotel is often motivated by more than economic reasons; the investment is commonly made by a high profile business owner or entrepreneur that seeks access to a hotel facility that can accommodate guests, vendors, and clients of his or her firm as well as business meetings and social functions. In many cases, the individual investor views the hotel investment as a trophy asset that further elevates his/her status as a business leader in the community; in such cases, the financial return generated by the hotel, although important, may not be as highly valued as the ability of the owner to entertain business associates and others at "his/her" hotel.

American Hotel & Lodging Association (AHLA): the trade association that supports and promotes the interests of the hotel and lodging industry within the United States

REITs are investment funds that receive specific tax benefits intended by the US government to encourage commercial real estate investment; the Internal Revenue

Service (IRS) tax code states, "To qualify as a REIT, a domestic corporation must, among other things, annually satisfy the gross income requirements... [with] at least 95 percent of the corporation's gross income derived from certain enumerated sources, including dividends, interest, rents from real property, and gain from the sale or other disposition of stock, securities, and real property; [and] ...at least 75 percent of the corporation's gross income must be derived from a similar but narrower set of enumerated sources, generally focused on income from real estate assets" (IRS, 2018).

REITs pool funds from multiple investors, executing a specific investment strategy to achieve the economic objective of the REIT. Many REITs specialize in a specific segment of real estate investment, including hotels, apartments, retail malls, office buildings, medical facilities, warehouse space, and more. Some REITs take a more balanced approach and diversify their holdings among multiple forms of real estate with the goal of achieving a specific economic objective, such as maximizing long-term capital appreciation or dividend payouts. Shares in a REIT trade at a price that fluctuates, like a stock price, based upon several factors including, the general economic conditions; the financial performance of the real estate assets owned by the REIT; changes in the underlying value of the real estate investments owned by the REIT; as well as the acquisition and disposal of specific real estate assets. Because many REITs are publicly traded, an investment in a REIT may be more liquid than a typical real estate investment, allowing an investor to purchase shares one day and sell them the next.

Some hotel management companies work in partnership with a REIT to provide the capital necessary for the hotel management firm to expand the portfolio of hotels under its control, facilitating the firm's ability to achieve its long-term growth plans. As discussed in *Chapter 1:Introduction to the Hotel Industry*, REITs own thousands of hotels that include hundreds-of-thousands of hotel rooms, many in the upper-upscale and luxury segments. The largest hotel ownership groups, which include several REITs, are listed in *Table 1.3: Global Hotel Ownership Firms*.

Understanding an Investor's Motivation

The first step hotel management must take to develop a positive relationship with hotel ownership is to understand the investor's objectives. A commercial real estate investor invests in a hotel for a reason, and hotel management must understand the factors that motivated the construction or acquisition of the hotel, including the investor's financial goals. As previously outlined, investors' motivations vary widely and often include multiple objectives. Therefore, management must understand the varied needs of ownership, which may be assessed by establishing an ongoing and open dialog. The manager must also understand the investor's cash position or access to capital, which impacts the financial goals and decisions of ownership. For example, a highly-leveraged hotel owner in a poor cash position requires cash flow to service the debt and may be reluctant to make additional capital investments, whereas a well-capitalized, institutional investor seeking long-term capital appreciation, with a large amount of equity in the hotel, may welcome capital investment opportunities, particularly if the investments increase the hotel's valuation.

Owners typically meet with hotel management on a regularly scheduled basis, whether that be quarterly, semi-annually, or annually. These meetings allow hotel management to gain a deeper appreciation for the owners' perspective, while capitalizing on the owners' expertise and experiences as a commercial real estate investor. Quite frankly, meetings with ownership allow hotel managers to look beyond the day-to-day minutia and challenges of running the hotel to contemplate the hotel's potential. Hotel investors typically have more of a long-term perspective and often challenge managers to think more strategically. Owners are more likely to make additional capital investments in a hotel if ownership has confidence in management's ability to deliver exceptional guest experiences while optimizing profitability. Ownership meetings are management's opportunity to earn ownership's confidence and trust.

High-Risk Investment

A hotel is a higher-risk investment when compared with many alternative commercial real estate investments, making it even more important for hotel management to gain ownership's confidence. When general economic conditions are favorable, business and leisure travel is strong, generating high occupancy, enabling hoteliers to increase average daily rates (ADRs), which drives revenue per available room (RevPAR) and operating profits; however, when general economic conditions deteriorate, business and leisure travel contract rapidly. Travel expenditures are discretionary, allowing both businesses and individual households to quickly reduce or eliminate travel expenditures as soon as weaker economic conditions are on the horizon. Ownership must have confidence in management's ability to proactively respond to changing economic conditions.

Secondly, the fundamental nature of a hotel stay exacerbates the risk of a hotel investment. Unlike many real estate-based businesses that use long-term lease arrangements to minimize risk, hotel rooms are rented one night at a time, requiring a hotel operator to secure guests for each day of the year, for each room in the hotel, through the hotel's sales and marketing efforts. Office space, apartments, retail space, warehouses, and other real estate assets are leased for long periods of time—often for terms of 1 to 5 years or even longer. In addition, the tenants are responsible, in many cases, for the build-out and maintenance of the leased space, as well for providing the necessary furniture, fixtures, and equipment associated with operating their business within the space leased, which leads to the third factor that increases the risk of hotel investment.

Hotel investment is capital intensive. Hotel owners not only construct and maintain the building, its infrastructure, and public areas, as do other real estate investors, they also own and maintain the furniture, fixtures, and equipment necessary to operate the business. Each hotel room must include a private bathroom; the room must be furnished; linens, window treatments, televisions with a selection of premium channels, and wireless Internet access must be provided. A commercial kitchen, laundry, and other heart-of-the-house areas must be constructed, which often include hundreds-of-thousands-of-dollars of necessary operating equipment to support the hotel operation. Meeting and conference space, restaurants, and wellness facilities, such as pools, exercise facilities, or spas are also necessary hotel amenities in many categories of hotels and markets. Consequently, the level of initial and ongoing capital investment is much greater with hotel ownership than with other commercial real estate investments, particularly when evaluated on an investment per-square-foot basis.

In summary, three characteristics of a hotel investment—the cyclical nature or economic sensitivity of the industry, the short duration of hotel stays, and the sheer amount and intensity of capital investment required—make a hotel a high-risk real estate investment. These risk factors are moderated, to a certain degree, by high barriers to entry. Because a large amount of capital is required to develop a hotel, it is challenging for new hotels to enter a market unless the fundamentals of the market are strong; in other words, demand for hotel accommodations and the ADR within the market must be able to support the cost of a new hotel's construction. In addition, in many highly developed, urban markets, such as New York City, San Francisco, Paris, and Hong Kong, there is little real estate available to be developed into hotel assets, particularly in premium locations.

The scale of a hotel operation also impacts the level of investment risk. Small, select-service hotels require less capital investment and a larger proportion of the building's total square footage is devoted to profit-producing space—there is a smaller heart-of-the-house and most of the hotel's interior space consists of hotel guestrooms, which generates the largest contribution margin. As hotels grow in size and scale, a larger investment is required in non-revenue producing, heart-of-the-house areas, such as kitchens, storage areas, and offices, as well as less profitable public areas, including meeting rooms and food and beverage outlets; finishes and furnishings also increase in quality and cost, particularly in upper-upscale and luxury hotels, which further increases the risk associated with investments in high-end hotels. When economic conditions change, upper-upscale and luxury hotels are subject to wider variations in financial performance. Consequently, more conservative hotel investors, seeking lower risk, are more likely to invest in select-service hotels, whereas more aggressive investors—with access to substantial amounts of capital—are more likely to invest in upscale, upper-upscale, and luxury hotels.

As with any investment, the higher the risk, the higher the expected return. This rule of investment holds true in the hotel industry. Commercial real estate investors typically require the financial proforma for a potential hotel investment to generate a higher capitalization or cap rate than alternative real estate investments with lower risk. The cap rate is the anticipated total annual return, expressed as a percentage of the total amount of investment required; it is calculated by dividing the anticipated annual net operating income, typically expressed as earnings before interest, taxes, depreciation and amortization (EBITDA), by the cost of developing or acquiring the hotel. So, for example, a hotel that is anticipated to generate $10 million in EBITDA, which can be acquired for $75 million, has a cap rate of 13.3% = ($10 million ÷ $75 million). The cap rate allows investors to assess how quickly they may be able to recover their investment. The higher returns required of hotel investments may be generated by strong anticipated cash flows from the hotel operation alone, or the return may be supplemented through higher returns generated due to the hotel's synergy with simultaneous commercial real estate investments such as retail space, an office building, or condominiums. In recent years, this latter strategy has commonly been used to lower the risk of developing luxury hotels.

financial proforma: a projection of financial results and returns generated by a potential investment opportunity

capitalization or cap rate: the anticipated total annual return, expressed as a percentage of the total amount of investment required

Minimizing Risk Through Mixed-Use Development

Many newly constructed luxury hotels are built as part of mixed-use real estate developments, which may include commercial office space or luxury condominiums. For example, a developer may build a multistory tower in a downtown, urban market that includes a parking garage built below ground, which serves as the foundation for a 12-story hotel constructed at the base of the building, with luxury condominiums developed on the upper-20 floors of the building. A motor and pedestrian lobby, as well as retail space, may be built on the street level; the hotel lobby, restaurant, and bar may be built on the second level; meeting space and wellness facilities are included on floors 3 through 5 of the building, allowing the guestrooms to start several stories above the urban noise experienced on the lowest floors. Luxury condominiums are placed on the highest floors—where the increased light, views, and distance from street-level noise allow the developer to command higher prices for each unit.

Although the luxury condominiums are typically accessed by residents through a separate building entrance and set of elevators, the inclusion of the hotel below the condominiums adds an increased level of service to condominium ownership that would not be available in a strictly residential building. Residents have convenient access to the hotel's restaurant, bar, meeting space, and wellness facilities, which may include a spa and health club, within the building. Residents may also enjoy food and beverage services catered by the hotel to their individual condominium unit for private parties. Even housekeeping, concierge, and business services may be offered to condominium residents through the hotel operation. The availability of these value-added hospitality services creates a higher standard of living for the residents within the condominiums which, when coupled with the building's association with a luxury hotel brand (e.g. *The Residences at the Four Seasons*), allows the developer to command higher prices when initially selling the units. The premium prices received from the sale of the condominiums, in turn, offsets a larger proportion of the total cost of developing the entire building, lowering the amount of profit the hotel must produce to generate a reasonable return to the project's investors.

In a traditional residential development, the cash flow enjoyed by the developer ends once all the condominium units are sold; however, in this scenario, the hotel operation will continue to generate cash flow for the developer indefinitely until the asset is sold or liquidated, allowing the developer to increase their total return on the project. Finally, a portion of the ongoing capital expenditures necessary to maintain common areas, equipment, and building infrastructure may be split between the hotel operation and the condominium owners association, which further minimizes the developer's risk.

Return on Investment

return on investment (ROI):
payments r or savings eceived as a result of an investment, often expressed as a percentage of the amount invested

cash-on-cash yield or the cash return:
the net cash-flow generated by an investment divided by the amount of cash invested

return on equity (ROE):
net income from an investment divided by owners' equity

depreciation:
the decrease in an asset's value over time, which is a non-cash expense

Hotel owners often evaluate their return on investment (ROI) based upon the cash flow generated by hotel operations, less any debt service payments, in relationship to the amount of capital invested to develop or acquire the property. This analysis of return is referred to as cash-on-cash yield or the cash return. Recall that investors may use the capitalization or cap rate to evaluate their return on a hotel investment. The cap rate measures the investors' return based upon the EBITDA, or cash flow from operations, as compared with the total investment made to acquire the hotel. Because a significant portion of the acquisition cost is typically financed using debt, the cash-on-cash yield informs investors of the return received on the cash portion of their investment in the hotel. Please refer to *Formula 12.1: Cash-on-Cash Yield*. This calculation of ROI is commonly used with commercial real estate investments, as an alternative to return on equity (ROE), which is calculated by dividing net income by owners' equity, because real estate investments typically incur a substantial depreciation expense.

$$C\% = \frac{f}{i}$$

Where: $C\%$ = annual cash-on-cash yield

f = annual cash flow

i = cash investment

Formula 12.1: Cash-on-Cash Yield

Recall that depreciation is the portion of the cost of acquiring a capital asset that is charged against the operating profits generated by the asset over its useful life. In other words, hotel investors deduct the cost of acquiring a hotel from the amount of cash earnings generated by the hotel over its lifetime. Depreciation is a non-cash expense; no cash payment is required to cover the expense—the payment for the expense was previously made at the time of purchase by the capital invested and debt assumed by the hotel's ownership. Although the value of the hotel is depreciated on the balance sheet, the actual value of the hotel—what the investors can potentially earn by selling the hotel—typically appreciates over time. Therefore, the depreciation expense recorded on the financial statement for the acquisition cost of the real property is often recaptured in the form of capital gains when the hotel is liquidated or sold at a future date.

Depreciation expense also provides real estate investors with a tax advantage. Because a real estate investment incurs a substantial depreciation expense each year, this non-cash expense lowers the taxable net income earned by the investment without negatively impacting cash flow. Consequently, a portion of the cash earnings received by investors is offset by depreciation expense, providing the investor with a tax shelter. Potential tax benefits include a positive cash flow from hotel operations that is not taxable or only partially taxable, due to an offsetting depreciation expense; a postponement or reduction in tax liability; or both. Because capital gains are typically taxed at a rate lower than the corporate tax rate, the additional capital gains earned when the hotel is sold, due to the accumulated depreciation expense recorded while the hotel was owned by the seller, is taxed at the lower tax rate on capital gains.

capital gains:
the increase in value of an asset over time, calculated by subtracting the acquisition cost from the price at which the asset is sold

tax shelter:
an investment that lowers or minimizes the investor's tax liability

long-term debt:
debt that is to be repaid over a time period of longer than one year

mezzanine financing:
short-term financing that is provided to fill the gap between the amount of capital that the investors' have available to invest in a real estate project and the amount of the long-term financing that investors have been able to secure

Debt

Commercial real estate investors also use debt to optimize their ROI. The amount of capital, or cash, invested into a hotel, as well as the amount and structure of the debt used to acquire the property or make additional capital investments in the property impacts an investor's return. Debt may come in the form of long-term debt, such as a mortgage that may be amortized over 10 to 30 years, or short-term financing, including mezzanine financing. Mezzanine financing is short-term financing that is provided to fill the gap between the amount of capital that the investors' have available to invest in a real estate project and the amount of the long-term financing that

© James R. Martin/Shutterstock.com

investors have been able to secure to accumulate the total funds needed to close the transaction. Although mezzanine financing is secured by the real estate asset, it is in a secondary position, whereas the long-term debt is in the primary position. As a result, the mezzanine financier assumes more risk and charges a higher interest rate than a long-term mortgage lender.

To illustrate the impact of debt and its structure on a hotel investment, assume that a hotel is being purchased for $45 million; the buyer plans to spend $5 million to renovate, re-brand, and re-position the hotel, bringing the total investment to $50 million. The investor anticipates that the newly renovated and re-branded hotel will generate $5 million in EBITDA in its first year. The cap rate on the investment is 10% = $5 million ÷ $50 million. If the investor has the cash available to not assume any debt, then the cash-on-cash yield, using *Formula 12.1*, would be the same as the cap rate, or 10%. Because the investor is not prepared to make a $50 million cash investment, he/she has decided to explore his/her options, which include the following: Invest $25 million (50%) in cash and use long-term financing for the remaining $25 million (50%) needed for the project. Invest $10 million (20%) in cash, financing the remaining 80% of the funds needed through the acquisition of $40.0 million in long-term financing; or, finally, the investor can invest $10 million (20%) in cash, secure the remaining $35 million (70%) in long-term financing needed to purchase the hotel, and then assume an additional $5 million (10%) short-term note to cover the cost of the renovation.

In each case, the long-term debt is borrowed at a 5% interest rate and amortized with monthly payments over 15 years. The short-term debt to finance the $5 million renovation can be obtained at 7.5% interest and amortized over 5 years. *Table 12.1: Impact of Debt Structure on Cash-on-Cash Yield* calculates the first year's cash-on-cash yield for each of these options.

Cash investment & debt structure	Cash invested	Debt-service	EBITDA	Cash flow	Cash yield
Cash investment (no debt)	50,000,000	-	5,000,000	5,000,000	10.0%
50% equity/50% long-term debt[1]	25,000,000	2,372,381	5,000,000	2,627,619	10.5%
20% equity/80% long-term debt[1]	10,000,000	3,795,809	5,000,000	1,204,191	12.0%
20% equity/10% short-term/70% long-term[1,2]	10,000,000	4,523,610	5,000,000	476,390	4.8%

[1]Long-term debt financed at 5.0% interest over 15-years
[2]Short-term debt financed at 7.5% interest over 5-years

Table 12.1: Impact of Debt Structure on Cash-on-Cash Yield

From *Table 12.1*, the option that provides the best cash-on-cash return is to invest $10 million or 20% of the project's total investment in cash and to secure long-term financing for the remaining $40 million, which represents 80% of the investment required. In this case, the investor will enjoy a cash-on-cash yield of 12%, which is calculated using *Formula 12.1* as follows:

$$f = \text{annual cash flow} = \text{EBITDA} - \text{debt service} = \$5,000,000 - \$3,795,809 = \$1,204,191$$
$$i = \text{cash investment} = \$10,000,000$$
$$C\% = \text{cash-on-cash yield} = \$1,204,191/\$10,000,000 = 12\%$$

This example illustrates why cash-on-cash return is a more meaningful measurement of ROI than ROE when evaluating a real estate investment. The actual net operating income is negative—the hotel appears to be operating at a loss—yet the hotel investors actually realize a cash gain of $1,204,191. The cash yield statistic accurately reflects the 12% return that ownership earns during the first year on their $10 million cash investment in the hotel.

Net income in this scenario is calculated as EBITDA minus interest paid on the debt minus depreciation expense, assuming there are no additional fixed expenses incurred by ownership, or:

$$\$<202,340> = \$5,000,000 - \$1,869,007 - \$3,333,333$$

For the purpose of this discussion, the equity the investors have in the hotel investment after the first year may be estimated by the amount of the initial investment plus the amount of principle paid with the first year's debt service payments or:

$$\$15,664,816 = \$10,000,000 + \$5,664,618$$

ROE can be calculated by dividing net operating income by the owner's equity or:

$$ROE = \$<202,340>/\$15,664,816 = -1.3\%$$

A ROE of -1.3% implies that ownership suffered a financial loss during their first year; however, investors actually enjoyed a positive cash flow in excess of $1.2 million, as indicated by the cash-on-cash yield statistic of 12.0%. It should be noted that the first year's depreciation expense is calculated assuming a 25% salvage value and a 30-year useful life, using the double-declining balance depreciation method.

Please note: Owners' equity is impacted by a variety of factors and calculated as noted in *Table 11.2: A Hotel Balance Sheet Template*. A detailed discussion of how depreciation expense and debt service payments are calculated is beyond the scope of this textbook;

however, an *Excel* spreadsheet that accompanies this textbook, available on the companion site, provides detailed calculations. Readers interested in a more detailed discussion of these topics should consult an accounting, finance, or real estate finance textbook.

Structuring the investment in this manner—20% equity with 80% long-term debt—also provides the investors with a tax benefit. The $1,204,191 in positive cash flow received by ownership in year one is sheltered from taxes because the net operating income for the first year is an operating loss of $202,340 (as previously calculated). If the owners do not assume any debt, paying for the entire investment with $50 million in cash, taxes would be assessed on $1,666,667 of the $5 million in positive cash flow earned by ownership, which is the amount by which the $5 million in EBITDA, or positive cash flow from operations, exceeds the $3,333,333 recorded on the financial statement in depreciation expense. At a 20% corporate tax rate, this lowers the investor's return by $333,333 (= $1,666,667 x 0.20) to $4,666,667, further eroding the ownership's cash-on-cash yield to 9.3% in the all-cash, no-debt scenario.

double-declining-balance depreciation: an aggressive method of calculating depreciation expense, using the book value of the asset, allowing a more rapid reduction in the value of the asset

sum-of-the-year's-digits depreciation: a method of calculating depreciation expense that reduces the value of an asset more rapidly during the early years of its useful life

straight-line depreciation: a conservative approach to calculating depreciation expense in which the value of an asset is reduced by the same amount each accounting period over its useful life

Although this discussion is rather tedious, the important takeaway for hotel managers is that maximizing the cash flow generated by hotel operations provides hotel investors with maximum flexibility in structuring the investment to achieve the specific financial objectives that are most important to them, whether that is to generate cash flow, minimize taxes, invest capital for long-term appreciation, or a specific combination of these objectives. There are many strategies employed by commercial real estate investors to manage their return, including the use of interest-only loans, for example, to increase their cash flow, thereby improving their cash return, or by selecting an aggressive, double-declining-balance; moderate, sum-of-the-year's-digits; or conservative, straight-line, depreciation calculation methodology. By managing the many variables associated with the investment—the amount of cash invested; the debt, including the term, structure, and interest rate or cost of capital; the depreciation expense, managed by adjusting the depreciation calculation method, salvage value, and the useful life of the asset—a savvy real estate investor can optimize the return, based upon the specific financial objectives of ownership.

A detailed example regarding a hotel investment is provided in *Box 12.1: Assessing a Hotel's Return on Investment: The Owners' Perspective*, that may help clarify many of these concepts.

© Chanclos/Shutterstock.com

Assume an institutional investor acquires a 400-room upper-upscale hotel for $187,500 per key or $75 million. The investor purchased the hotel, investing $22.5 million of capital while securing long-term debt for the remaining 70%, or $52.5 million of the acquisition cost. The debt is financed over 15 years (180 payments) at a 4.75% interest rate, resulting in a monthly debt service of $408,362 and $4,900,341 annually. During the first year, the hotel enjoys a gross operating profit (GOP) of $11,384,934 and income before fixed charges of $10,469,771 after deducting management and incentive fees, which is retrieved from *Table 2.1: Financial Performance of a "Typical" Upper-Upscale Hotel* (STR, 2017) and transferred to *Table 12.2a: A Hotel Investor's Return on Investment*.

The institutional investor has an annual capital lease expense of $72,318, property taxes of $342,612, and an annual fire, casualty, and general liability insurance premium payment of $293,491, which brings EBITDA to $9,761,350; this value represents the hotel's cash flow before debt service.

An amortization schedule, reflecting the amount of principle and interest paid each month over the course of the 180 scheduled debt service payments, based upon the terms of the loan, indicates that the first year's interest expense totals $2,440,659. The depreciation expense, using the sum-of-the-years-digits depreciation method over a useful life of 20 years with a salvage value of $25 million or one-third (33%) of the hotel's $75 million acquisition cost, has been calculated, which totals $4,761,905 during the first year. These values are also reflected in *Table 12.2a*.

capital lease:
operating assets that are acquired by ownership through a leasing arrangement as opposed to being purchased and added to inventory

amortization schedule:
a break-down of debt service payments over the term of a loan, detailing the amount of principle and interest paid each month

Hotel occupancy & ADR[1]	74.8%	$182.12
Total hotel revenue[1]	**$ 31,446,101**	**100.0%**
Gross Operating Profit (GOP)[1]	**11,384,934**	**36.2%**
Management fees[1]	828,889	2.6%
Incentive fees[1]	86,274	0.3%
Income Before Fixed Charges[1]	**10,469,771**	**33.3%**
Capital leases	72,318	0.2%
Property taxes	342,612	1.1%
Fire, casualty and liability insurance	293,491	0.9%
Earnings Before Interest, Taxes, Depreciation & Amortization (EBITDA)	**9,761,350**	**31.0%**
Interest expense (1st year)[2]	2,440,659	7.8%
Depreciation (1st year)[3]	4,761,905	15.1%
Net income before taxes	2,558,786	8.1%
Taxes[4]	511,757	1.6%
Net income	2,047,029	6.5%
Cash flow analysis:		
Debt payments	4,900,341	15.6%
Cash flow before taxes (EBITDA less debt service)	4,861,009	15.5%
Net Cash flow (after deducting taxes paid)	4,349,252	13.8%
Cash-on-cash yield	19.3%	
Cash flow sheltered from taxes	2,302,223	47.4%
Tax savings at 20%	460,445	

[1]Values from: *Table 2.1: Financial Performance of a 'Typical' Upper-Upscale Hotel.*
[2]Amortization schedule based upon $52.5 million loan with a 4.75% interest rate compounded monthly over 15-years (180 payments).
[3]Sum-of-the-years' digits depreciation method over a 20-year useful life with a 33% salvage value.
[4]Corporate tax rate = 20.0%.

Table 12.2a: A Hotel Investor's Return on Investment

Calculating the First Year ROI

After deducting interest charges of $2,440,659 and depreciation expense of $4,761,905, the net income before taxes is $2,558,786. Taxes are then calculated, assuming a 20% corporate tax rate, which total $511,757 (= $2,558,786 X 0.20), bringing net income after taxes to $2,047,029. Because taxes are paid on the net income before taxes, versus the actual cash flow after debt service of $4,861,009, $2,302,223 (= $4,861,009 − $2,558,786), representing 47.5% of the cash flow, is sheltered from taxes, which lowers the investor's tax liability by $460,445 (= $2,302,223 X 0.20) in the first year.

After deducting the annual debt service payment of $4,900,341 and taxes of $511,757, the investor enjoys a positive net cash flow of $4,349,252 or 13.8% of revenue, and a net income of 6.5%. Therefore, the cash-on-cash yield or cash return may be calculated using *Formula 12.1* as outlined below:

$$C\% = \$4,349,252/\$22,500,000 = 19.3\%$$

This indicates that the hotel generated 19.3% of the initial $22.5 million cash investment, or $4,349,252 in net positive cash flow during its first year, which includes a $460,445 tax benefit. Assuming this return is replicated each year, the payback period is estimated to be 5.17 years (= $22.5 million ÷ $4,349,252), which suggests that the owners may potentially receive their initial investment back in just over 5 years. It is also significant to note that the outstanding principle owed to the lender decreased by $2,459,682 (= $4,900,341 - $2,440,659) during the first year, or the total debt service payment less first year's interest expense, increasing the capital gains the hotel investor will capture when the investment is liquidated.

payback period:
the period of time required for an investor to receive total returns equal to the amount of the initial investment

Return on the Sale of the Hotel

In addition to the annual operating returns, commercial real estate investors may also enjoy additional profits when selling or liquidating an asset. Assume the hotel is sold for $100.0 million after being held for 5 years. The total 5-year return on the investor's original $22.5 million investment is $78,782,816 or 350.1%, based upon the operating results and sales transaction outlined in *Table 12.2b: Hotel Investor's Annual and Total ROI (Over 5 Years)*. In other words, the investor has more than tripled the initial cash investment, earning 3.5 times the original investment.

Year	Revenue	EBITDA	%	Interest expense	Depreciation	Taxes	Net income	%	Cash flow	Cash yield
1	$31,446,101	$9,761,350	31.0%	$2,440,659	$4,761,905	$511,757	$2,047,029	6.5%	$4,349,252	19.3%
2	32,389,484	10,200,611	31.5%	2,321,247	4,523,810	671,111	2,684,444	8.3%	4,629,159	20.6%
3	33,361,169	10,659,638	32.0%	2,196,037	4,285,714	835,577	3,342,309	10.0%	4,923,720	21.9%
4	34,362,004	11,139,322	32.4%	2,064,749	4,047,619	1,005,391	4,021,563	11.7%	5,233,590	23.3%
5	$35,392,864	$11,640,591	32.9%	$1,927,087	3,809,524	1,180,796	4,723,185	13.3%	5,559,454	24.7%
				Accumulated depreciation:	$21,428,571	5-year total:	$16,818,530	10.1%	$24,695,174	109.8%
			Original purchase price:	$75,000,000			Original capital investment:		$22,500,000	
			Sale price:	100,000,000			Capital gains:		46,428,571	
			Total debt payments:	24,501,705			Book value of hotel:		53,571,429	
			Total interest expense:	10,949,778			Capital gains tax (at 15.0%):		6,964,286	
			Reduction in principle:	13,551,927			Net proceeds (after taxes):		54,087,641	
			Long-term debt outstanding:	38,948,073			Total return (year 5):		59,647,095	265.1%
			Owner's proceeds before taxes:	$61,051,927			**Total Return on Investment:**		**$78,782,816**	**350.1%**

Table 12.2b: Hotel Investor's Annual and Total ROI (Over 5 Years)

As anticipated by the estimated payback period of 5.17 years, calculated at the end of the investor's first year of ownership, the institutional investor's original investment of $22.5 million was paid back by the cash flow from operations over the 5-year period; the total cash-on-cash yield averaged 22% per year, producing a 109.8% cash yield or $24,569,174 for the entire 5-year period. The capital gains on the transaction totals $46,428,571, which includes appreciation of $25 million (= $100.0 million - $75.0 million) and the re-capturing of the $21,428,571 in depreciation expense recorded over the 5-year period. The 15% or $6,964,286 in capital gains tax represents a tax savings of $2,321,429 because the capital gains tax is 5 points lower than the corporate tax rate of 20%; tax liabilities were also postponed because corporate income taxes were not assessed on the portion of each year's operating cash flow offset by depreciation expense over the term of the investment. The investor receives $61,051,927 in proceeds from the sale at closing and, after paying capital gains tax of $6,964,286, realizes net proceeds of $54,087,641. The total gain for the fifth year of the investment is $59,647,095, which includes the net proceeds, less capital gains tax, plus the fifth-year cash flow of $5,559,454, representing a 265.1% cash-on-cash yield in year five.

Although this is a simplified example—it is likely that ownership would have made additional capital investments into the hotel over the 5-year window, the debt structure is simple, the owners' tax liabilities may differ based upon specific tax rates and regulations, and there is no accounting for closing costs in the sales transaction—the intent is to illustrate the many ways that a commercial real estate investor potentially generates a financial return from a hotel investment. These include: the cash return from operations; capital gains from the recapture of depreciation expense and the further appreciation of the value of the real property; and tax savings, including the postponement of tax liability.

MARKET PERFORMANCE VERSUS INVESTMENT (FINANCIAL) PERFORMANCE

Recall from *Chapter 5: Optimizing Revenue* that a hotel's room revenue performance—the key driver of a hotel's profitability—is measured through key performance indicators (KPIs), including occupancy percentage, ADR, and RevPAR. The comparison of a hotel's performance against its competitive set can be assessed in terms of RevPAR index, as outlined in *Box 5.5: Benchmarking a Hotel's Performance*; a RevPAR index in excess of 100% provides an indication that the hotel is outperforming its comp set. Although optimizing a hotel's market performance is critical to maximizing

© TZIDO SUN/Shutterstock.com

the return for hotel investors, it does not guarantee that a hotel will achieve its financial goals. Many factors impact the investment performance of a hotel in addition to market performance, including the development or acquisition cost, the amount of debt carried on the property, and the cost of capital, as well as the general economic conditions. A downturn in the economy that lowers demand for hotel accommodations in the market may hurt the hotel's financial performance even if the hotel is still outperforming its competitors in terms of market performance.

Consider the hotel profiled in *Box 12.1: Assessing a Hotel's Return on Investment: The Owners' Perspective.* Suppose the hotel is sold for $100 million, but continues to enjoy similar operating results, with approximately $10 million in EBITDA. The cap rate enjoyed by the new owners is just 10% (or $10 million ÷ $100 million) versus 13.3% for the previous owners, a reduction of over three percentage points or 25%, due to the new owner's higher basis. If the new owners invest $25 million in cash at the time of acquisition, they will increase the debt carried by the hotel to $75 million, and finance that debt at 1.5% higher interest (5.25% versus 4.75%). The cash flow received by the hotel's new ownership decreases 36.4% or $1,584,199 to $2,765,101 from $4,349,299, lowering the cash-on-cash yield to 11.1% versus the 19.3% enjoyed by the previous owner in the first year; this represents a 42.8% decrease in financial

basis:
the total investment made to purchase an asset, which serves as the basis for calculating depreciation expense, ROI, and capital gains

performance. The net operating income now reflects an operating loss of $206,512, after deducting interest and depreciation expenses for the first year, using the same depreciation method and assumptions.

The important point illustrated by this example is that a hotel's financial performance is determined only in part by its market performance. The investor's acquisition cost, the cost of capital, and the hotel's debt burden, as well as the structure of the debt, impact the hotel's performance as a commercial real estate investment. Because hotel management does not typically have control over these factors, management incentives are typically tied to achieving a targeted GOP or EBITDA; however, ownership often structures the management company's incentive fees contingent upon generating operating cash flows (EBITDA) adequate to fulfill the investor's financial objectives. As a result, a change in ownership—particularly when it includes an increase in the hotel's debt service—often requires hotel management to improve operating cash flows, regardless how well the hotel is performing in the market, to meet investors' financial goals.

ESTIMATING A HOTEL'S VALUE

A hotel's value or hotel valuation, like any real estate investment, is determined by the price that a qualified buyer is willing and able to pay to purchase the hotel; that value may be estimated several ways.

> hotel valuation: determined by the price that a qualified buyer is willing and able to pay to purchase the hotel

ADR and Guestroom Count

A quick rule-of-thumb, often used in the hotel industry, is that a hotel's value is equal to $1,000-per-dollar-generated in average rate, multiplied by the hotel's room-count. In other words, a 300-room hotel that generates a $200-per-night ADR is worth approximately $60 million = $1,000 X 200 X 300. Obviously, this calculation, the ADR valuation-method, provides a quick estimate of the value and a more detailed analysis is required to provide a more accurate estimate.

> ADR valuation-method: estimates the value of a hotel by multiplying the hotel's ADR in dollars by 1,000 and then by the number of guestrooms

Targeted Cap Rate

Another efficient method to estimate the hotel valuation is to divide the hotel's EBITDA by the annual cap rate the buyer desires to achieve through the investment. Consequently, a hotel generating $7.5 million in EBITDA is valued at $50 million if the investor expects to earn a 15% cap rate (= $7.5 million ÷ 0.15). Of course, a targeted cap rate valuation is only as accurate as the estimate of EBITDA.

> targeted cap rate valuation: estimates the value of a hotel by dividing the hotel's annual EBITDA or cash-flow by the targeted capitalization rate desired by the investor

Asset-Based Methods

comparables:
similar real estate assets, particularly hotels in the same market, market position, or with a similar ADR and RevPAR

Asset-based methods include using public records of recent real estate transactions to identify the price at which similar hotel properties or comparables have recently sold, although it may be difficult to identify recent hotel transactions in the exact same market; often hotels in markets with similar ADRs, occupancy levels, customer segmentation, or market conditions may be used. Other asset-based methods include replacement or construction cost; price-per-square-foot multiplied by the hotel's total building space; or an alternative use estimate.

replacement or construction cost:
the projected cost to replace or construct a similar hotel

Discounted Cash Flow

price-per-square-foot:
using an average price-per-square-foot paid for similar hotels, in terms of chain-scale or class, to estimate a hotel's value

A more accurate methodology, referred to as the discounted cash flow method, is to calculate the net present value (NPV) of projected future cash flows using the formula introduced in *Chapter 10: Maintaining the Hotel Asset and Sustainability*. This provides an estimate of the business value of the hotel's operation. In other words, it provides an estimate of what the potential buyer may be willing to pay to purchase the future income generated by the hotel, discounted due to the time-value-of-money—a dollar today is worth more than a dollar one, two, or three-or-more years from now. Of course, this leaves two dilemmas: first, this value does not compensate the seller for the value of the assets necessary to generate the cash flows, such as the hotel's real property, including the land and building; the hotel's furniture, fixtures, and equipment (FF&E); and the hotel's operating inventories. Secondly, a hotel can potentially deliver cash flows indefinitely.

alternative use:
estimating a hotel's value based upon the net return that may be gained through redeveloping or converting the hotel into a different category of real estate investment

discounted cash flow method:
estimates the value of a hotel asset based upon its acquisition price, projected cash-flows, and estimated terminal value

To address the first issue, the value of the hotel may be estimated using an alternative method, such as the ADR-method, cap rate method, or an asset-based method. This value may then be adjusted based upon a further analysis of future cash flows and other factors. Because the purchase of a real estate asset requires negotiation, a potential buyer requires a starting point, from which a mutually-acceptable price may be reached through the negotiation process. The discounted cash flow method begins with the preparation of a forecast of operating cash flow, which is typically achieved through the use of market data, such as a STR report; from this, an estimate of the hotel's annual EBITDA for the first year may be calculated and then divided by the investor's cap rate to estimate the hotel's value. The cap rate is the minimum return that the investor will accept on an investment or, to put it another way, the rate of return the investor would expect to receive on an alternative investment. This same cap rate is also typically used to discount future cash flows.

time-value-of-money:
money received today has greater value than money to be received in the future

terminal value:
the projected future value of an asset assuming the asset is liquidated at the end of the forecast period

The second issue is addressed by assigning a timeline for the investment and a terminal value at the conclusion of the investment's timeline. The timeline may represent the duration the buyer is planning to hold the investment, although this timeline may be shortened depending upon the buyer's confidence in being able to accurately forecast future cash flows. Economic conditions may change in the future, affecting cash flow. Consequently, the buyer may feel it is only reasonable to accurately forecast cash flow 3 to 5 years into the future. As a result, the buyer often estimates the terminal value at a specified point in the future even though the investor may plan to hold the investment for a longer or indefinite time frame. The terminal value is the projected future value of the asset assuming the investment is liquidated at the end of the forecast period. A specific example of how the discounted-cash flow method is used to provide a hotel valuation may help clarify this concept.

Table 12.3a: Hotel Valuation (Discounted Cash Flow - 10% Cap Rate) provides details regarding a potential hotel investment. First, a forecast is prepared to estimate 5 years of operating cash flows, labeled as EBITDA, in the first row of the table. Next, the cash flows are discounted using the NPV formula, provided in Chapter 10, and outlined below:

$$NPV = \sum_{t=0}^{n} \left[\frac{R_t}{(1 + i)^t} \right]$$

Where: R_t = net cash inflow-outflows during a single period t
i = required return on investment or the discount rate
t = number of time periods

Formula 10.1: NPV Formula

The cash flows are discounted, assuming a 10% discount rate, in the corresponding columns under "Year 1" through "Year 5" with the total sum of the 5-year discounted cash flow provided in the "Total or Year 0" column in the row labeled "NPV (gross)," indicating that the NPV of the 5 years of projected cash to be received from operations total $23,702,997. This represents the portion of the eventual purchase price of the hotel that is reasonable to pay for the first 5 years of operating cash flow.

Next, the investor needs to establish a reasonable price to use as a starting point for the analysis. Because the discount rate is set at 10%, the NPV of the 1st-year's cash flow, $5,239,469, is divided by 0.10, the cap rate, which establishes an initial evaluation of $52,394,691 recorded in the "Total or Year 0" column toward the bottom of *Table 12a* in the row labeled "valuation." It should be noted that the investor may use a cap rate that is higher than the discount rate if the investor believes the hotel is a higher risk than the alternative investment used to set the discount rate. The investor may now estimate the ROI if the hotel is purchased at this estimated valuation price and determine if the price is acceptable to the potential buyer.

To calculate the return, the investor must establish a terminal value. This is calculated by applying an appreciation rate to the initial valuation over the course of the investment period, which is 5 years in this case. Assume, in this example, the investor has determined that commercial real estate investments are increasing in value at a rate of approximately 5% per year within the local commercial real estate market. Consequently, in the bottom row of *Table 12.3a*, labeled "anticipated appreciation," the initial valuation of $52,239,469 is multiplied by 1.05, with the result being carried into the "Year 1" column; this calculation is repeated using the previous year's appreciated valuation as the basis for years "2" through "5," which brings the estimated value of the hotel at the end of the 5-year investment period to $66,870,378. This is the terminal value.

The initial purchase price and the terminal values can be entered in the gross cash flow as an outflow, when the hotel is purchased, and an in-flow at the end of the 5-year period when the asset is liquidated. These are recorded in the column labeled "purchase & sale of asset," which result in the updated values recorded as "gross cash."

As with most hotel investments, the buyer will acquire debt to fund a substantial portion of the investment. Assume the investor, in this case, has a commitment from a lender to provide an interest-only loan, at 4.75% interest over the 5-year period, provided the buyer invests 25% of the purchase price in cash. These loan terms are entered in the next row, labeled "debt (interest only);" the total debt is 75% of the hotel's valuation at the time of purchase, because the potential buyer is investing 25% equity.

The "gross cash" values may then be adjusted to reflect the initial outlay of cash, for 25% of the valuation, representing the initial cash investment made by the investor, and the interest on the debt that must be paid to the lender, resulting in the "net cash flow" specified in *Table 12. 3a*, for each year of the investment period. In the fifth year, the amount of the loan recorded in "Total or Year 0" column is also deducted from "gross cash," because this debt must be retired when the hotel is liquidated. These cash flows may also be discounted, using the 10% discount rate, to estimate the present value of the cash flows based upon the actual cash invested into the project and the cash received from the investment after paying interest on the debt. The NPV of the investment's net cash flows, including the portion of the appreciation the investor will receive on the value of the hotel over the 5-year investment timeline, total $34,121,178, which is recorded in the "Total or Year 0" column.

The NPV of the net cash flows may be used to calculate the cash-on-cash yield the buyer may anticipate receiving each year over the duration of the investment period as well as the overall cash-yield for the entire 5-year investment period. Finally, the internal rate of return (IRR) may be calculated using the IRR function in *Micro-*

soft Excel. The IRR is a metric used to estimate the profitability of potential investments. Using the NPV formula, the IRR calculates the discount rate that generates an NPV of zero ($0.00) for all cash flows generated by the project. In this example, the hotel, using the 10% cap rate valuation, will generate an annual return of nearly sixteen-percent (15.9%) based upon the total value of the investment and corresponding cash flows not considering debt service (gross cash), with a return of 42.8% on the cash portion of the investment, based upon the anticipated cash flows and the required minimum-level of cash investment required by the lender, which is 25% of the purchase price in this example.

	Total or Year 0	Year 1	Year 2	Year 3	Year 4	Year 5	IRR
EBITDA:		$5,763,416	$6,051,587	$6,233,134	$6,607,122	$6,871,107	
NPV (gross):	**$23,702,997**	5,239,469	5,001,311	4,683,046	4,512,754	4,266,417	
Purchase & sale of asset:	(52,394,691)					66,870,378	
Gross cash:	(52,394,691)	5,763,416	6,051,587	6,233,134	6,607,122	73,741,48	15.9%
Debt (interest only):	39,296,018	(1,768,321)	(1,768,321)	(1,768,321)	(1,768,321)	(1,768,321)	
Net cash flow:	(13,098,673)	3,995,095	4,283,266	4,464,814	4,838,802	32,677,146	42.8%
NPV:	**$34,121,178**	3,631,905	3,539,889	3,354,481	3,304,967	20,289,937	
Cash-on-cash yield:	260.5%	27.7%	27.0%	25.6%	25.2%	154.9%	
Valuation:	**$52,394,691**						
Anticipated appreciation (5%):		$55,014,425	$57,765,147	$60,653,404	$63,686,074	$66,870,378	

Table 12.3a: Hotel Valuation (Discounted Cash Flow - 10% Cap Rate)

	Total or Year 0	Year 1	Year 2	Year 3	Year 4	Year 5	IRR
EBITDA:		$5,763,416	$6,051,587	$6,233,134	$6,607,122	$6,871,107	
NPV (gross):	**$25,348,926**	5,361,317	5,236,635	5,017,427	4,947,417	4,786,129	
Purchase & sale of asset:	(71,484,229)					91,234,004	
Gross cash:	(71,484,229)	5,763,416	6,051,587	6,233,134	6,607,122	98,105,111	13.0%
Debt (interest only):	53,613,172	(2,412,593)	(2,412,593)	(2,412,593)	(2,412,593)	(2,412,593)	
Net cash flow:	(17,871,057)	3,350,823	3,638,994	3,820,542	4,194,530	42,079,346	32.6%
NPV:	**$41,792,968**	3,117,045	3,148,940	3,075,385	3,140,866	29,310,732	
Cash-on-cash yield:	233.9%	17.4%	17.6%	17.2%	17.6%	164.0%	
Valuation:	**$71,484,229**						
Anticipated appreciation (5%):		$75,058,441	$78,811,363	$82,751,931	$86,889,528	$91,234,004	

Table 12.3b: Hotel Valuation (Discounted Cash Flow - 7.5% Cap Rate)

	Total or Year 0	Year 1	Year 2	Year 3	Year 4	Year 5	IRR
EBITDA:		$5,763,416	$6,051,587	$6,233,134	$6,607,122	$6,871,107	
NPV (gross):	**$23,702,997**	5,239,469	5,001,311	4,683,046	4,512,754	4,266,417	
Purchase & sale of asset:	(62,500,000)					79,767,598	
Gross cash:	(62,500,000)	5,763,416	6,051,587	6,233,134	6,607,122	86,638,705	14.1%
Debt (interest only):	46,875,000	(2,109,375)	(2,109,375)	(2,109,375)	(2,109,375)	(2,109,375)	
Net cash flow:	(15,625,000)	3,654,041	3,942,212	4,123,759	4,497,747	37,654,330	36.6%
NPV:	**$36,130,521**	3,321,855	3,258,026	3,098,241	3,072,022	23,380,376	
Cash-on-cash yield:	231.2%	21.3%	20.9%	19.8%	19.7%	149.6%	
Valuation:	**$62,500,000**						
Anticipated appreciation (5%):		$65,625,000	$68,906,250	$72,351,563	$75,969,141	$79,767,598	

Table 12.3c: Hotel Valuation (Discounted Cash Flow - Negotiated Purchase Price; 10% Discount Rate)

A hotel buyer may complete multiple analyses on a potential hotel investment, often identifying a range of reasonable valuations, establishing an upper- and lower-limit that the buyer may consider. The analysis completed in *Table 12.3a* is replicated in *Table 12.3b*; however, the discount rate is set at 7.5%. Although the EBITDA estimates of cash flow are identical, the lower cap rate of 7.5% generates a substantially higher valuation of the property of $71,484,229 and higher NPV values of projected future cash flows, lowering the potential buyer's ROI. The model may also be used to estimate the ROI investors may receive at any price negotiated between the upper and lower limits established, as displayed in *Table 12.3c*, where the valuation is set at $62.5 million, which potentially generates a 36.6% IRR on the buyer's cash investment.

CONTRACTUAL RELATIONSHIPS

The hotel owner or investor assumes the primary financial risk of a hotel investment; the hotel investor must make a substantial upfront capital investment to develop or acquire a hotel, while also being responsible for making any required debt service payments to lenders, whether the hotel generates adequate cash flow to service the debt or not. The hotel operator prioritizes the payment of employees, tax liabilities, vendors and suppliers, franchise fees, and the hotel management company's own fees prior to delivering any cash flow from the hotel's operation to the hotel's ownership. Consequently, hotel ownership must deliberately negotiate the terms of the management contract or hotel management agreement to protect their interests and to minimize misunderstandings once the contract is in place, particularly because management agreements may have terms of 20 years or longer.

Hotel Management Agreement

The management contract or hotel management agreement (HMA) governs the relationship between the hotel owners and hotel management firm. The contract specifies the obligations of hotel management and the hotel's ownership on a wide-variety of issues, many of which are identified in *Table 12.4: Negotiated Provisions within Hotel Management Agreements or Franchise Agreements.* Because the management company has considerable flexibility and autonomy relative to the day-to-day operation of the hotel, the terms of the HMA must typically be approved by the lender and the parent company providing the brand through a separate franchise or licensing agreement. Management fees include a base fee, which is typically a percentage of the hotel's gross revenue, and incentive fees, which are additional fees earned by the management firm if the hotel delivers targeted cash flows to the hotel's investors. Hotel management fees are commonly between 2% and 3% of total hotel revenue; the average upper-upscale hotel generated management fees of 2.3% of total hotel revenue, and incentive fees of 0.3% of revenue in 2015 (STR, 2017). Readers interested in a more detailed discussion regarding a HMA are encouraged to access any number of available resources, including *The HMA & Franchise Agreement Handbook: Hotel Management Agreements & Franchise Agreements for Owners, Developers, Investors, & Lenders* (Butler & Braun, 2014).

Franchise or Licensing Agreement

A closely-related agreement is the franchise or licensing agreement, which outlines the terms of the relationship between the hotel's ownership or hotel management company and the parent company providing the hotel's brand. Recall from *Chapter 1: Introduction to the Hotel Industry* that, in the case of a branded hotel management company, the hotel parent company may provide the hotel's brand and brand-related support services, as well as hotel management services through the parent organization's management services division. In other words, some hotels may be branded and managed by the same firm, in which case the HMA and the licensing agreement are consolidated into a single contract; however, in most cases, the HMA and franchise agreement are separate contracts.

If separate agreements, each party—the hotel management firm and the hotel brand—must be engaged in negotiating the relationship formed with hotel ownership because, ultimately, the management firm is responsible for maintaining brand standards and optimizing the use of brand resources, including the reservation system, sales and marketing support, and the guest loyalty program to maximize the hotel owner's ROI. The investor's lenders may also want a seat at the table during this complex negotiation process because, in the event of default, the lender may be forced into taking an ownership interest in the property.

management contract or hotel management agreement (HMA): outlines the details of the relationship between the hotel owners and the hotel management firm, including but not limited to, the term of the agreement, fee structure, operating performance requirements, budgeting procedures, expenditure limits, decision authority, indemnification, corporate expense allocation, and termination procedures

management fees: fee paid to a hotel management firm by a hotel owner for managing the day-to-day operation of a hotel

base fee: management fee calculated as a percentage of a hotel's gross revenues

incentive fees: additional fees earned by the management firm if the hotel delivers targeted cash flows to the hotel's investors

franchise or licensing agreement: a contract that outlines the terms of the relationship between the hotel's owners and the parent organization or franchisor of the selected brand, granting the owner a license to operate the hotel utilizing a specific trademark

Term	Performance tests
Initial term	RevPAR test
Renewal terms	Budget test
Fees	Owner's return test
Base fee	Single- or two-prong test
Incentive fees	Measuring period
Fee caps	Cures for unsatisfactory performance
Franchise fees, including types and restrictions on use of fees	No-confidence; exploration of alternative operators
Subordination of fees	**Operating standards**
Alignment of interests	Capital investment requirements
Shared investment & joint venture structures	Fiduciary responsibility to maximize net present value (NPV) to owner
Net operating income or GOP guarantees; protection from negative operating cash flow	Property Improvement Plan (PIP)
Credit enhancement	**Budgets**
Impact issues	Content of operating budget
Operator duties	Timing
Detailed listing of operator duties	Approval of operating budget
Limits on operator authority	Capital expenditure plan and budget
Control over reimbursements	Compliance with budget
Termination	**Reports and inspections**
Termination for cause	Frequency of reports and meetings
Termination on sale	Audited financial statements
Termination for failure to meet performance standards	Audit rights of the ownership: financials and operations
Termination of brand: for failure to meet growth plans or critical mass; to provide adequate marketing support; due to the brand's deterioration or public perception; changes in key personnel; or the bankruptcy or insolvency of the brand	Periodic inspection of property by hotel ownership
Management of the transition in the case of a termination of the HMA	Annual franchise inspections
Miscellaneous Issues	
Employment of staff, including union avoidance	Non-compete term, area, brands
Licensing and permits, including liquor license	Indemnification—what exclusions to owner's indemnifications of operator
Subordination, non-disturbance and attornment agreements with lenders now and in the future	Exculpation—limit liability of owner to its interest in the hotel
Limitation on owner contributions to working capital	Sale of the hotel—operators transfer of rights under the hotel management agreement—what restrictions or approvals
Right of first refusal	Arbitration and expert resolution

Table 12.4: Negotiated Provisions within a Hotel Management Agreement or Franchise Agreement (Butler & Braun, 2015)

From *HMA Pro Checklist, in The HMA & Franchise Agreement Handbook,* 3rd edition by Jim Butler & Bob Braun. Published by the Global Hospitality Group® of JMBM Los Angeles, California, April 2014. © 2011, 2012, 2014 JMBM's Global Hospitality Group®. All rights reserved. Used by permission of Jeffer Mangels Butler & Mitchell LLP. Available at www.HotelLawyer.com.

The franchise agreement specifically identifies the brand support provided by the franchisor, which includes defining required core and peripheral services; providing hotel operating standards, design services, and construction support; purchasing services; access to a range of marketing support, including recognized brand and related trademarks; advertising; reservation services, including a central reservations office (CRO) and revenue optimization support; a guest loyalty program; direct sales representation; and technology, including web services, a branded mobile application (app), and often access to cloud-based information technology (IT) solutions to support operations and sales functions. The franchisor also inspects the property, at least annually, creating a property improvement plan (PIP), which is used to help guide capital expenditure investments. Finally, many hotel owners are also concerned with impact or the effect of another hotel of the same brand, or a brand supported by the same hotel parent company, opening within close proximity. Consequently, non-compete clauses or territorial boundaries may be specified in the agreement, although brands typically try to avoid such restrictions on their growth. Again, the provisions outlined in *Table 12.4* identify a range of issues that potentially impact hotel ownership, the management firm, franchisor, and lenders, which must be negotiated between the four parties.

impact:
the effect of another hotel of the same brand, or a brand supported by the same hotel parent company, operating within close proximity

The franchise agreement also defines the fees associated with each of these support services. Franchise fees are typically assessed as a percentage of gross room revenue (GRR), because the marketing focus of hotel brands is to attract overnight hotel guests, coupled with the substantial contribution margin generated by guestroom revenue, although franchise fees for some upscale, upper-upscale, and luxury brands may be based upon total hotel revenue, particularly if the brand is managing the property. The total cost of the most expensive hotel brand franchises may run nearly 14% of GRR, although some hotel brand franchise costs run as low as 5% of guestroom revenue, with the industry median running just shy of twelve percent (11.7%; Russell & Kim, 2016).

Franchise fees include an initial fee to purchase the franchise, which is often assessed as a base fee plus a fee-per-room (e.g. $50,000 plus $350 for each room over 100-guestrooms). Ongoing fees include the royalty fee, marketing or advertising contribution fee, reservation fees, and guest loyalty fees, which support the brand's frequent traveler program. There are also miscellaneous fees, such as purchasing fees, design services, and fees to cover the brand's annual conference, among others. Many of these fees, such as advertising or marketing fees, are spent in their entirety by the parent company for the designated purpose, while others, such as the royalty fee, provide revenue for the franchisor.

Diagram 12.1: Hotel Franchise Fees across Product Type identifies the average ongoing royalty, marketing, and guest loyalty franchise fees assessed by hotel parent organizations for branded hotels by type of hotel operation. Reservation fees are not included, because these typically vary based upon the specific value and number of hotel reservations generated for the property by the brand's CRO, website, and mobile app; royalty, marketing, and guest loyalty fees are included. Reservation and other fees may run an additional 3% to 5% of room revenue, typically bringing the total cost of a hotel franchise to around 12% of GRR.

ASSET MANAGER

Many hotel investors employ an asset manager to serve as their owners' representative. An asset manager typically has extensive hotel management experience but has shifted his/her focus to hotel investment. Commercial real estate investors with multiple hotels within their real estate portfolio may employ an asset manager directly or may contract with an independent hotel asset manager, particularly if the investor has one or few hotel assets. Because of their hotel management experience, typically as a general manager or in the executive suite of a successful hotel management firm, an asset manager is better able to hold hotel management accountable for optimizing the long-term market performance of a hotel—the asset manager understands what it takes to deliver exceptional guest experiences, to optimize revenue, to manage labor productivity, and the like. An asset manager is also better able to evaluate a pro forma financial projection for a potential hotel acquisition; to assess the potential impact of a hotel renovation on the hotel's ADR and EBITDA; or to assess the financial return generated by a potential capital expenditure.

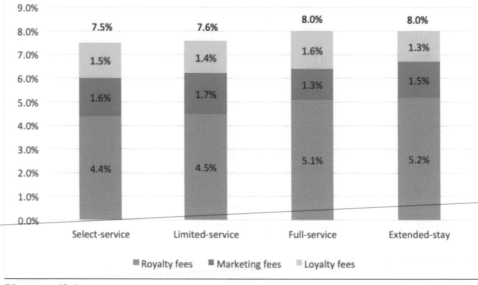

Diagram 12.1: Hotel Franchise Fees across Product Type

From *Marketing and Loyalty Fees Consistent across Product Types, 2015-16 United States Hotel Franchise Fee Guide* by Kasia M. Russell and Bomie Kim, HVS, Mineola, NY. Copyright © 2016 by HVS. Used by permission.

CHAPTER SUMMARY

There are three distinct business functions associated with the hotel industry: hotel management, hotel branding, and hotel ownership. Ultimately, the goal of hotel management is to maximize the financial return generated for hotel investors, which is achieved, in part, by hotel associates' abilities to consistently deliver exceptional guest experiences while optimizing the hotel's market performance; however, the cost of developing or acquiring the hotel; the amount and structure of the hotel's debt; and the cost of capital will also impact the financial performance of the hotel as a commercial real estate investment. Hotels are high-risk commercial real estate investments due to the industry's sensitivity to general economic conditions, the short duration of a hotel stay, and because hotel investments are capital intensive. Consequently, hotel investors expect higher returns—often measured in terms of cap rate and cash-on-cash yield—than in alternative, lower-risk real estate investments.

Hotel owners ideally earn a return from the cash flow generated by hotel operations, after covering payroll and operating expenses, management and franchise fees, taxes, capital reserves, and debt service. Hotel investors can shelter much of the positive cash flow earned from taxes because a hotel incurs a large depreciation expense, which is a non-cash expense, even though the underlying value of hotel real estate typically appreciates over time. The hotel's appreciation allows hotel investors to recapture the depreciation expense as capital gains when the asset is liquidated. The value of a hotel is ultimately determined by the price that a buyer is willing and able to pay for the asset; however, the amount of EBITDA generated by the hotel's operations, divided by a hotel investor's targeted cap rate, provides an accurate estimate of the hotel's value. Another rule-of-thumb often used to estimate the value of the hotel is to multiply the hotel's ADR by $1,000 and then multiply this factor by the total number of hotel guestrooms.

Hotel management must understand the motivations and financial goals of the hotel investor to build a relationship of mutual respect and trust, creating a strategic partnership that facilitates wise capital investment decisions that enhance market performance while maximizing the value of the hotel asset. Hotel management firms create this partnership with the hotel's ownership by securing a HMA to operate the hotel in exchange for a management fee, which typically runs 3% of revenue. Branded hotels are licensed through franchise agreements, which generate royalty, marketing, guest loyalty, reservation, and additional fees for the hotel parent company that commonly total 12% of GRR. It is common for hotel investors to employ asset managers to work with hotel management firms and the hotel brands over the duration of their respective contracts to evaluate operational performance and capital expenditure projects, ensuring hotels are competitively positioned in their respective markets while maximizing the investors' return.

KEY TERMS AND CONCEPTS

ADR valuation-method
alternative use
American Hotel & Lodging
   Association (AHLA)
amortization schedule
Asian American Hotel Owners
   Association (AAHOA)
base fee
basis
capital gains
capital intensive
capital lease
capitalization or cap rate
cash-on-cash yield or the cash
   return
comparables
debt service

depreciation
discounted cash flow
double-declining-balance
   depreciation
financial proforma
franchise or licensing agreement
hotel valuation
impact
incentive fees
individual investors
institutional investors
joint venture partnerships
limited liability partnerships
long-term debt
management contract or hotel
   management agreement (HMA)
management fees

mezzanine financing
mixed-use development
payback period
price-per-square-foot
primary position
real estate investment trusts (REIT)
replacement or construction cost
return on equity (ROE)
return on investment (ROI)
secondary position
straight-line depreciation
sum-of-the-year's-digits depreciation
targeted cap rate valuation
tax shelter
terminal value
time-value-of-money
trophy-asset

DISCUSSION QUESTIONS

1. Discuss the three distinct business functions associated with the hotel industry. Why are these functions typically separated? What steps must management take to establish a positive relationship with hotel ownership?

2. Discuss the various types of hotel investors. Which investors might be the most challenging to work with and why? What are the benefits of working for a well-capitalized institutional investor? What are the challenges of working with such an investor?

3. Explain the reasons a hotel is a high-risk commercial real estate investment. One way risk is reduced by investors is to develop a hotel property as part of a mixed-use development. What creative operational and marketing strategies may hotel managers employ to possibly reduce the owner's risk of investing in a hotel?

4. Identify three ways that investors can earn a ROI from a hotel. Some hotel investors purchase a hotel renovate it and reposition the property within the marketplace, much like a real estate investor, on a smaller scale, "flips" a house. Explain how an investor might approach "flipping" a hotel. How does the investor generate an ROI when repositioning a hotel?

5. Discuss how debt is used to maximize an investor's ROI from a hotel investment. Assume a hotel can be purchased for $40 million dollars and the investor has loan offers from two lenders; one at a 5.25% annual interest rate for 15 years that requires the investors to invest 15% equity and a second that requires the investor to invest 20% equity to receive credit terms of 5% interest amortized over 20 years. Which option provides the best annual cash-on-cash yield? Why?

6. A 400-room upper-upscale hotel has generated approximately $8.5 million in EBITDA last year with an ADR of $174.79 ADR and annual occupancy of 68.4%. Estimate the value of the hotel using the ADR and room-count method. Estimate the value using a cap rate of 12.5%.

7. Explain why it is important for hotel management to understand the reasons why the hotel owners invested specifically in a hotel. How might the reasons that have been identified impact management decision-making? Ultimately, how does management maximize the investors' ROI? Why is it important that hotel ownership have confidence in the management team's ability to maximize the ROI?

8. Identify 10 or more provisions that must be negotiated in a HMA. Explain the difference between an HMA and a franchise or licensing agreement. Compare and contrast the types of fees paid to hotel management firms and to parent companies (franchisors).

9. Identify the types and corresponding amounts of fees typically paid by hotel investors to parent companies to brand a hotel. Despite the high cost of hotel branding, which commonly costs a hotel owner nearly 12% of gross revenue, why are over 70% of hotels in the United States branded? Why might certain provisions within an HMA or licensing agreement require lender approval?

10. Discuss the role of the asset manager. Why may a hotel manager prefer working with a professional asset manager versus the owner or investors directly? As a hotel manager, what are the potential drawbacks of working with an asset manager?

ENDNOTES

AAHOA (2019). *About AAHOA*; from the Asian American Hotel Owners Association website accessed March 15, 2019 at: https://www.aahoa.com/about-aahoa.

Butler, J. & Braun, B. (2014). *The HMA & Franchise Agreement Handbook; Hotel Management Agreements & Franchise Agreements for Owners, Developers, Investors, & Lenders (3rd edition);* Global Hospitality Group of JMBH; Los Angeles, CA; 134 pages.

IRS (2018). *Internal Revenue Bulletin: Part III. Administrative, Procedural, and Miscellaneous; Revised process 2018-48, Section III*; posted October 01, 2018 online at: https://www.irs.gov/irb/2018-40_IRB#RP-2018-48; accessed January 21, 2019.

Russell, K.M. & Kim, B. (2016). *2015–16 United States Hotel Franchise Fee Guide*; HVS, Mineola, NY; available online at www.hvs.com; 24 pages.

STR (2017). *Host report: Upper-upscale hotels for year-ending 2015.* SHARE Center.

HOTEL DEVELOPMENT PROJECT

Assignment 6: Hotel Development Proposal Presentation:

Use content from: Additional information required for this final presentation is supported, primarily, by *Chapter 11: Administration and Control: Human Resources, Accounting, and Loss Prevention* and *Chapter 12: Hotel Investment*, although information from other chapters may be helpful.

This assignment brings together all elements of the Hotel Development Proposal generated in Assignments 1 through 5 and requires students to put together a final presentation that may be presented to their classmates, instructor, and any industry professionals that may be invited to evaluate the proposals.

Prior to assembling the final presentation, the following additional information must be created:
1. Undistributed operating expenses; these expenses may be estimated as a percentage of revenue based upon the hotel's chain-scale, although instructors may require a listing of hotel staff that may be included within the undistributed operating departments (e.g. administrative and general [A&G] personnel; sales personnel, including deployment; and property, operations and maintenance [POM] or engineering personnel).
2. Breakdown of franchise fees; these are typically estimated as a percentage of room revenue or as a flat fee-per-room and include the initial, one-time franchise fee, as well as ongoing royalty, reservation, guest loyalty, and marketing fees. The *HVS Hotel Franchise Fee Guide* (Russell & Kim, 2016) is a reliable source of information to use when estimating these fees.
3. Management fees, which may be estimated as a percentage of total hotel revenue, although there may be an incentive fee for EBITDA generated above a specified dollar amount. The incentive fee may be estimated as a percentage of the incremental cash flow generated above the established base-EBITDA.
4. Capital expenditure reserve contributions, which may also be estimated as a percentage of total hotel revenue.

Once the above costs have been estimated, a final presentation, using presentation software, should be created and presented by students that includes the following:
1. Name, brand, and location of the proposed hotel, including a brief overview of the parent company and explanation of the value the brand selected will bring to the property.
2. A breakdown of the guest segments to be served by the hotel and the resulting occupancy, ADR, and RevPAR by month and for the hotel's first year of operation.
3. A breakdown of franchise fees, including the initial fee, the ongoing royalty, reservation, guest loyalty, marketing, and any other fees associated with the brand.
4. A summary of the proposed F&B operation, including a listing of outlets and meeting space configuration.
5. A review of the hotel's proposed P&L and EBITDA or cash flow generated for the hotel's ownership. This will include a projection of management fees.
6. An estimate of the value of the hotel, based upon these cash flows or EBITDA and a specified capitalization rate (cap rate). This provides an indication regarding the dollar amount that investors may afford to invest in development and construction costs to achieve the targeted ROI.

Appendix

HOTEL DEVELOPMENT PROJECT

Students completing a course in hotel, lodging, or resort management are encouraged to complete a hotel development project over the course of the semester/term, working in small groups of 3 – 5 students. This appendix outlines the project in its entirety.

At the conclusion of select chapters, students will be provided additional instructions to assist them in completing the assignment. Students will be advised which chapters in the textbook are directly related to the assignment. The six individual assignments associated with the project are to be completed sequentially over the course of the semester, which will ensure the timely completion of the project without students being overwhelmed at semester's end. The completion of the individual assignments will also assist students in acquiring the skills, knowledge, and abilities covered within the corresponding chapters of *Delivering the Guest Experience: Successful Hotel, Lodging, and Resort Management.*

Instructors are encouraged to require students to make a brief presentation upon the completion of *Assignment 3: Defining the Hotel: Brand, Guestroom Count, Facilities, and Experiences* to ensure that all teams are on-track with the assignment half-way through the semester. Students often request that they be permitted to develop an independent hotel; however, 70% of hotels are brand-affiliated in the United States, 50% are brand-affiliated outside the United States, and this proportion is rising. Consequently, students should be required to select a brand affiliation for the property; of course, students that would like more flexibility when naming their hotel and defining the guest's experience may select a "soft brand," such as *Marriott's Autograph Collection* or *Curio by Hilton*. The sixth and final assignment is a presentation that summarizes the information required in each of the preceding five assignments; instructors are encouraged to invite local hotel industry executives, managers, or commercial real estate developers to provide feedback on their final proposals.

As a starting point, the instructor of the course must select a specific location for the hotel that will be developed. Because this textbook focuses upon the successful management of a hotel's operation, the project focuses upon identifying the hotel's brand, market position, and guestroom count, as well as the array of services and facilities (including the configuration of any meeting space) the hotel will offer; these decisions are to be based upon the demand generators located in proximity to the site and the competitive set of hotels within the market. In addition, students will project the hotel's revenues, develop a staffing plan, and prepare an annual budget for the hotel, projecting the hotel's profitability down to the earnings before interest taxes, depreciation, and amortization (EBITDA). Consequently, the assignment does not require the projection of construction costs or address permitting issues, equipment specification, etc. because this assignment is intended for an operations-focused versus development-focused hotel management course. Instructors should assume that each group of students will be able to construct any hotel of their choice, in terms of guestroom count and facilities, on the site provided. Additional information on site selection is provided with the support materials for the course. An excel spreadsheet is also provided with the support materials, which may be used to forecast revenues and generate the annual operating budget.

The individual assignments that constitute this hotel development project are as follows:

ASSIGNMENT 1: UNDERSTANDING THE LOCATION AND MARKET

Located at the conclusion of Chapter 1.

Use Content From: Chapter 1: Introduction to the Hotel Industry

The course instructor will provide students with the specific street address at which the proposed hotel will be developed. This address is selected at the discretion of the instructor and may or may not actually be available for development, although instructors may find it beneficial to select an available site. Ideally, this address will be in the same city or town as the college or university at which the course is being delivered (or a nearby city or town) so that students are familiar with the market and can potentially visit the proposed hotel site.

Upon the conclusion of Chapter 1, instructors should provide the following information, which is available from the **STR SHARE** Center:
1. Property census for the market in which the address is located including a "radial" report using the proposed hotel site's address.
2. A hotel pipeline report listing hotels currently under consideration or development in the market (e.g. planning stage, final planning, or under construction).

From these reports, students should identify the following information:

1. The hotel supply in the market in terms of the number of hotels and the number of hotel rooms (from which students may also calculate the average size of the hotel).
2. The distribution of the existing hotel supply by class or chain scale.
3. What parent companies and brands have the largest distribution within the market? Which parent companies and brands have weak distribution or are not represented in the market?
4. How prevalent are independent hotels within the market?
5. Which 10 to 12 hotels are in closest proximity to the proposed site?
6. How many hotels are currently being planned or constructed in the market? What brands are represented in this hotel "pipeline"? How will the possible addition of these hotel properties impact the distribution of supply in terms of chain scale or class?
7. Identify a preliminary comp set for the hotel—the 5 to 6 hotels that the proposed hotel will compete with directly within the market. The course instructor will assist students in ensuring that the comp set established by each group meets STR's sufficiency requirements. In addition, the instructor will obtain from the STR SHARE Center key performance indicators (KPIs) for the preliminary comp set of hotels for the past 3 years, which will be used when completing *Hotel Development Project Assignment 3: Defining the Hotel: Brand, Guestroom Count, Facilities, and Experiences.*

ASSIGNMENT 2: VISION, MISSION, AND VALUES

Located at the conclusion of Chapter 2.

Use Content From: Chapter 2: Successful Hotel Management

Assume the proposed hotel being developed will be managed by a newly established third-party hotel management firm. Based upon the information provided within this chapter, please develop the following for this newly established hospitality management company:

1. An aspirational corporate vision statement.
2. Keeping the "all-square" operating philosophy in mind, create a mission statement.
3. Define the corporate values that will be used to guide the beliefs and behaviors of associates employed by the firm.
4. Describe the corporate culture that the firm will strive to create and preserve.
5. Based upon this vision, mission, and these values, create a name for this hospitality or hotel management firm.

ASSIGNMENT 3: DEFINING THE HOTEL: BRAND, GUESTROOM COUNT, FACILITIES, AND EXPERIENCES

Located at the conclusion of Chapter 5.

Use Content From: Chapter 3: Defining Customer Segments; Chapter 4: Effective Sales and Marketing; and Chapter 5: Optimizing Revenue

Based upon the key demand generators identified within the market, the current mix of hotel accommodations, and hotels in the pipeline, please identify the following information about the proposed hotel for the site:

1. The key guest segments that the hotel will target. Be certain to identify a variety of customer segments that will use the hotel during the week, as well as on weekends and during holiday periods.

2. Based upon the guest segments targeted, describe the guest experience that will be delivered to guests of the hotel, as well as the brand and chain-scale that has been selected for the hotel. Provide an overview of the brand's parent company and its family of brands. Explain how the brand standards of the specific brand selected align with the targeted guest experience for the various customer segments the hotel will serve.

3. Using the STR data provided by the course instructor, which is based upon the property's preliminary comp set identified in *Assignment 1: Understanding the Location and Market*, estimate the hotel's annual occupancy, average daily rate (ADR), and revenue per available room (RevPAR). Identify the number of hotel guestrooms, proposed rate structure, and market mix for the hotel that is designed to generate the targeted occupancy, ADR, and RevPAR (e.g. rack rate or range of "best available rates"; corporate and volume rates; government; leisure and discounted rates; and weekday and weekend group rooms).

4. Modify the comp set, as necessary, based upon the brand and parent company proposed. If the comp set changes, the instructor will acquire modified benchmark data from STR's SHARE Center, which will be used for *Assignment 6: Hotel Development Proposal Presentation*.

ASSIGNMENT 4: ROOMS DIVISION: SERVICE AND STAFFING

Located at the conclusion of Chapter 7.

Use Content From: Chapter 6: Guest Services Operations and Chapter 7: Housekeeping and Laundry Operations

With the hotel room count, brand, and rate structure for the hotel identified, a rooms division profit and loss (P&L) statement may be created. The following information may be presented in an Excel spreadsheet:

1. Occupied room nights, occupancy, ADR, room revenue, and RevPAR by month for the hotel's first 12 months of operation, including annual totals. Room nights, ADR, and revenue should be broken out by guest segment.
2. Rooms division payroll expenses, by position, including hours, wage or salary rates, and total wages, broken out by month. Include an additional 35% for payroll taxes and employee benefits (PT&EB). For each position, identify if staffing is determined based upon a fixed or variable staffing level and include at least one productivity factor used for any positions that are variably staffed. Calculate the number of rooms division associates or full-time equivalents (FTEs) needed to staff the rooms division.
3. Forecast other controllable expenses for the hotel rooms division as a percentage of revenue or on a cost-per-occupied-room (CPOR) basis, based upon the hotel's chain-scale and month-by-month, including an annual total.
4. Rooms division departmental profit or contribution margin is also to be provided, as a dollar amount and as a percentage of hotel revenue, month-by-month and on an annual basis.

ASSIGNMENT 5: DEFINING THE F&B CONCEPT: OUTLETS AND SERVICES

Located at the conclusion of Chapter 8.

Use Content From: Chapter 4: Effective Sales and Marketing; and Chapter 5: Optimizing Revenue; and Chapter 8: Food and Beverage Operations

Based upon the brand and chain-scale of the proposed hotel, define the scope of the food and beverage (F&B) operation; create a departmental P&L statement for the F&B operating division.

The scope of the F&B operation should include the following:

1. A list of each F&B outlet or service that will be available to guests (e.g. breakfast room with buffet-line and seating for 50 guests; a three-meal restaurant; 35-seat lobby lounge; etc.). Students are encouraged to get creative and name or assign themes to the various outlets, as appropriate.

2. The types of items and price range of F&B products made available on the menu of each F&B outlet by meal period.

3. The total square footage of meeting space and the breakdown of this space (e.g. 40,000 square feet (sf) of total meeting and function space, including a 12,000 sf ballroom; 8,000 sf junior ballroom; 10,000 sf of break-out rooms, and 10,000 of pre-function space).

In addition, an F&B P&L should be generated for each of the first 12 months of the hotel's operation, including the annual total, in an Excel format that includes the following:

1. The covers, average check, and revenue for each F&B outlet; use a covers-per-occupied-transient guestroom as the basis for forecasting covers.

2. The banquet revenue per group room (BRGR) and corresponding banquet revenue forecast each month; students are encouraged to use a separate BRGR for weekday and weekend groups.

3. Beverage revenue, broken down between outlet beverage and banquet beverage, for each month and for the year.

4. Food and beverage cost of goods sold (COGS), which will be forecast as a percentage of revenue.

5. F&B division payroll expenses, by position, including hours, wage or salary rates, and total wages. Include an additional 35% for PT&EB. For each position, identify if staffing is determined based upon a fixed or variable staffing level and include at least one productivity factor used for any positions that are variably staffed. Calculate the number of associates or FTEs anticipated to be employed within the F&B division.

6. Other expenses for the F&B division, which may be forecast as a percentage of revenue based upon the scope of the F&B operation and chain-scale of the brand selected.

7. F&B division departmental profit or contribution margin, as a dollar amount and as a percentage of hotel revenue.

ASSIGNMENT 6: HOTEL DEVELOPMENT PROPOSAL PRESENTATION

Located at the conclusion of Chapter 12.

Use Content From: Additional information required for this final presentation is supported, primarily, by Chapter 12: Hotel Investment, although information from other chapters may be helpful.

This assignment brings together all elements of the Hotel Development Proposal generated in Assignments 1 through 5 and requires students to put together a final presentation that may be presented to their classmates, instructor, and any industry professionals that may be invited to evaluate the proposals.

Prior to assembling the final presentation, the following additional information must be created:
1. Undistributed operating expenses; these expenses may be estimated as a percentage of revenue based upon the hotel's chain-scale, although instructors may require a listing of hotel staff that may be included within the undistributed operating departments (e.g. administrative and general [A&G] personnel; sales personnel, including deployment; and property, operations and maintenance [POMS] or engineering personnel).
2. Breakdown of franchise fees; these are typically estimated as a percentage of room revenue or as a flat fee-per-room and include the initial, one-time franchise fee, as well as ongoing royalty, reservation, guest loyalty, and marketing fees. The *HVS Hotel Franchise Fee Guide* (Russell & Kim, 2016) is a reliable source of information to use when estimating these fees.
3. Management fees, which may be estimated as a percentage of total hotel revenue, although there may be an incentive fee for EBITDA generated above a specified dollar-amount. The incentive fee may be estimated as a percentage of the incremental cash-flow generated above the established base-EBITDA.
4. Capital expenditure allowance, which may also be estimated as a percentage of total hotel revenue.

Once the above costs have been estimated, a final presentation, using presentation software, should be created and presented by students that includes the following:
1. Name, brand, and location of the proposed hotel, including a brief overview of the parent company and explanation of the value the brand selected will bring to the property.
2. A breakdown of the guest segments to be served by the hotel and the resulting occupancy, ADR, and RevPAR by month and for the hotel's first year of operation.

3. A breakdown of franchise fees, including the initial fee, the ongoing royalty, reservation, guest loyalty, marketing, and any other fees associated with the brand.
4. A summary of the proposed F&B operation, including a listing of outlets and meeting space configuration.
5. A review of the hotel's proposed P&L and EBITDA or cash-flow generated for the hotel's ownership. This will include a projection of management fees.
6. An estimate of the value of the hotel, based upon these cash flows or EBITDA and a specified capitalization rate (cap rate). This provides an indication regarding the dollar amount that investors may afford to invest in development and construction costs to achieve the targeted return on investment.

ENDNOTE

Russell, K.M. & Kim, B. (2016). *2015-16 United States Hotel Franchise Fee Guide*; HVS, Mineola, NY; available online at www.hvs.com; 24 pages.

Glossary

5-year capital expenditure plan (CapEx Plan): a planning document that lists the anticipated capital reserve contributions and expenditures for the next 5-years

6-week pick-up trends: provides an indication as to how many reservations are being sold during the final 6-week booking window immediately preceding an arrival date

a la carte: the pricing and sale of products and services individually

abandons: when potential guests abandon the reservation process midstream, which are also counted as turn-downs

accessible guestroom: a hotel guestroom designed for guests with mobility and other challenges that complies with the Americans with Disabilities Act (ADA)

accounts payable clerk: a non-exempt associate responsible for accurately recording expenses and paying vendors based upon prescribed payment terms

accounts receivable clerk: a non-exempt associate responsible for collecting payments for products and services rendered, including credit card and direct bill accounts

accrual basis accounting: an accounting method in which financial statements reflect the revenue for products and services rendered, and the corresponding expenses incurred to support that revenue, during the accounting period

accrual: an accounting entry made to reflect an expense incurred for which an invoice has not been received nor a payment has been made

accumulated depreciation: the amount of depreciation expensed-to-date against the acquisition cost of an asset

action-station: a station included on a buffet line at which a culinary associate freshly prepares and serves a food item directly to guests

adjusting journal entry: an accounting entry made to alter an accrual based upon the amount of the actual expense

ADR index: a measure of a hotel's pricing performance, which compares the hotel's ADR with the ADR of hotels within its competitive set

ADR valuation-method: estimates the value of a hotel by multiplying the hotel's ADR in dollars by 1,000 and then by the number of guestrooms

adventure sports: activities that involve some risk and often include interaction with nature

algorithm: sequence of steps or rules to be followed when solving a problem

all-suite hotels: provide exclusively oversized accommodations or suites that may range in size from 350 to over 600 square feet and, in addition to a bedroom and private bathroom, may provide additional functional areas such as separate living/work areas, wet bars, or a small kitchens

allowance for doubtful accounts: an estimate of the amount of the outstanding accounts receivable balance that may go uncollected

alternative use: estimating a hotel's value based upon the net return that may be gained through redeveloping or converting the hotel into a different category of real estate investment

amenity spa: a spa designed to enhance and complement a guest's overall experience at the resort, by delivering highly personalized services

American Hotel & Lodging Association (AHLA): the trade association that supports and promotes the interests of the hotel and lodging industry within the United States

amortization schedule: a break-down of debt service payments over the term of a loan, detailing the amount of principle and interest paid each month

arrival manifest: a listing of each day's anticipated check-ins listed in sequential order based upon the projected arrival times

Asian American Hotel Owners Association (AAHOA): a trade association that supports hotel owners by improving access to products, services, financing, and education

asset light strategy: a business approach through which a firm generates revenue without assuming debt or title to the real assets used to generate the revenue

asset manager: a real estate professional that serves as the interface between ownership and management, responsible for representing ownership's interests

assets: cash, receivables, and items of value held by a business

assistant controller: an exempt manager that assists in overseeing the accounting function

assistant director of engineering: an exempt manager that assists the director of engineering in overseeing the POM department

assistant executive housekeeper: an exempt manager that assists in overseeing the housekeeping operation

assistant food server (busser): a non-exempt associate that assists food servers in providing guest service in a high volume or high service quality F&B outlet

association: an organization of people with a common purpose and a formal structure

attrition clause: a fee that is incurred if a group fails to pick up its contracted guestroom block

average daily rate (ADR): the average price paid by guests for an individual guestroom per night

average price: the arithmetic mean of the amounts paid by customers for a single unit of a service, product, or experience

back nine: holes 10 through 18 on a golf course

back-door security: a non-exempt associate that monitors the associate entrance and security cameras, inspects packages and bags, controls keys, and performs other essential loss prevention duties

baker: a non-exempt culinary associate that prepares breads, pastries, and confections

balance sheet: a financial statement that reflects the assets and liabilities of a business at a specified point in time

banquet captain: a non-exempt supervisor that oversees the delivery of F&B services in the hotel's meeting and event space

banquet cook: a non-exempt culinary associate assigned to prepare food and meals for consumption in the hotel's meeting and event space

banquet event order (BEO) or banquet prospectus (BP): a printed or electronic document that fully details the needs of a client for a meeting, banquet, or event to include the space assigned and set-up required; style-of-service; food menu; beverage requirements; and any additional client needs, including audio-visual

banquet houseman: a non-exempt associate responsible for setting, clearing, and cleaning the hotel's meeting and event space to meet clients' specifications

banquet manager: an exempt associate that oversees the execution of all F&B services within the hotel's conference, meeting and event space

banquet rounds: large, round tables that may seat 8 - 12 guests

banquet server: a non-exempt associate responsible for providing food and beverage products and services in the hotel's meeting and event space

barback: a non-exempt associate that assists the bartender by running ice, glassware, and other supplies to and from the bar

bartender fee: a fee charged to a client that requests alcoholic beverage service

bartender: a non-exempt associate that prepares and responsibly serves alcoholic beverages

base fee: management fee calculated as a percentage of a hotel's gross revenues

basis: the total investment made to purchase an asset, which serves as the basis for calculating depreciation expense, ROI, and capital gains

bell captain: non-exempt supervisor that oversees the bell and transportation staff

bell staff: non-exempt associates, including doorpersons, bellpersons, and transportation drivers, responsible for providing personalized and memorable arrival experiences, as well as luggage and transportation assistance, to hotel guests

benchmark: a meaningful reference point against which current performance may be compared

BEO review meeting: a gathering of the managers and supervisors involved in the execution of meetings, banquets, and events with the catering and conference sales team to review and plan for upcoming functions

best available rate (BAR): non-discounted room rate offered to travelers for their requested dates

beverage cart: a vehicle that circulates on a golf course, providing snacks and refreshments

beverage cost ratio: calculated by dividing the cost of the beverage by its retail price

beverage manager: a non-exempt manager that oversees the receipt, distribution, and sale of alcoholic beverages throughout the hotel operation

big four inventory: the quarterly inventory of 4 operating supplies, including linen, glassware, china, and service-ware, that require periodic replacement

binomial probability distribution function: allows the probability of a given number of successes out of a given number of trials to be calculated based upon the probability of achieving a single successful outcome provided there are only two possible outcomes

body treatment: a treatment to cleanse, detoxify, and hydrate the client's skin

boiler mechanic: a non-exempt associate with the skills to repair and maintain high pressure boilers and heat exchangers

book value: represents the amount originally paid to acquire an asset less accumulated depreciation

book: a term commonly used whenever a hotel room is rented (sold) or group contract is executed

booking pace: a measure of how quickly available guestrooms are being sold (rented) for future dates

bookkeeper or accounting manager: an exempt administrative associate that performs various accounting duties

bottle-for-bottle exchange: a policy that requires an empty beverage bottle be provided by the bartender to acquire a replacement bottle

boutique hotels: typically smaller, historic hotels that have been renewed into stylish, upscale properties providing personalized service, many of which also feature signature restaurants

branded management company: manage the day-to-day operation of a hotel while also including a licensing agreement to provide the hotel's brand name, marketing support, and operating standards

breakage: the difference between the retail price paid by the consumer and the cost of the services

breaking-out-the-house: sub-dividing the guestrooms occupied the previous night into sections for each scheduled room attendant to service

breakout sessions: meetings held at a conference that are attended by subsets of the conference participants

brigade: the specific team of managers and associates assigned and trained to respond to a specific emergency situation

building systems: essential equipment required to make a structure functional and safe, including electrical systems, plumbing, lighting, ventilation, and life safety systems

business model: the economic formula commonly used by firms in a specific industry that allow the needs of the four key stakeholders to be simultaneously fulfilled

call liquor: a beverage served using the brand of liquor requested by the guest and priced accordingly

cancellation fee: fee imposed by a hotel on a client that cancels a group contract

capital asset: a depreciable asset with a value and useful life that exceed defined minimums

capital expenditure assessment: an annual fee charged vacation owners to maintain, update, and renovate the resort as required

capital expense: an expenditure that exceeds a defined minimum value to purchase and place into service an asset that has a useful life of longer than 1 year

capital gains: the increase in value of an asset over time, calculated by subtracting the acquisition cost from the price at which the asset is sold

capital intensive: an investment that requires a larger investment than similar alternative investments

capital lease: operating assets that are acquired by ownership through a leasing arrangement as opposed to being purchased and added to inventory

capital reserve fund: money set aside to be invested in capital assets

capitalization or cap rate: the anticipated total annual return, expressed as a percentage of the total amount of investment required

capture ratios: the percentage of in-house guests that are anticipated to use a specific F&B outlet

carpenter: a non-exempt associate skilled at constructing and repairing shelves, cabinets, walls, doors and door frames, and other structures

cart-and-green fees: a payment made to a golf course that allows access to play the course utilizing a course-provided golf cart

cash basis accounting: an accounting method in which financial statements reflect revenue and expenses based upon the in-flow and out-flow of payments from guests and to vendors during the accounting period

cash-on-cash yield or the cash return: the net cash-flow generated by an investment divided by the amount of cash invested

cashier: a non-exempt associate that collects payments from guests for hotel services, products, and experiences

centralized heating and cooling system: pumps hot or cold fluids through a system of pipes from a central cooling tower, chiller, or boiler to individual air handlers throughout the building

certified hotel industry analyst (CHIA): an industry certification that identifies hotel revenue management professionals capable of accurately assessing a hotel's market performance

channel manager: information technology that monitors a hotel's guestroom availability to optimize room revenue by controlling access and room rates through the various distribution channels

check-in time: a time specified by the hotel after which guests can expect their accommodations to be immediately available following the registration process

chef concierge: a non-exempt supervisor that oversees the concierge and guest activities associates

chef's table: a sales technique and relationship-building event during which clients watch the chef prepare their meal, which is often served at a table set-up in the kitchen

chief engineer: a non-exempt supervisor that assists engineering management in overseeing the POM department

chit: a paper ticket printed by the POS system authorizing the production of a food or beverage product

city ledger: represents the balances of all accounts that have been direct billed to clients and are awaiting payment

citywide conventions: conferences and events that take place in a municipality's convention center and generate room nights for multiple hotels within the destination

classroom configuration: a group seating arrangement with meeting attendees seated at rectangular tables set up in parallel rows

client tasting: a sales technique that allows a potential client to sample various items available on the banquet menu

closing inventory: the total value of all items in the hotel's inventory on the last day of a month, year, or accounting period

cloud-based: computer and mobile software applications that run and store data on an off-premise server maintained by the software provider

cluster manager: a GM that oversees multiple hotel properties located in close proximity

cocktail server: a non-exempt associate that sells and responsibly serves alcoholic beverages and other F&B products to guests

code blue: medical emergency

code purple: bomb threat

code red: fire emergency

commercial vehicles: automobiles, buses, trucks, vans, and other vehicles used to support the hotel's operation

commission model: travel agents or sites that accept a commission from a hotel, allowing the guest to book at the hotel's BAR or non-discounted rate while paying the hotel directly

comparables: similar real estate assets, particularly hotels in the same market, market position, or with a similar ADR and RevPAR

competitive set: a group of hotels against which a hotel competes for guests and market share

concierge: a non-exempt associate that tends to guests' special needs including dining reservations, arranging sightseeing tours, acquiring theater tickets, and other specific requests

condominium hotel: a lodging operation in which the title to each individual hotel room or lodging unit is separately held

contra-asset account: an asset account with a zero or credit balance

contract guests: clients that secure a specific number of rooms over a continuous set of dates of 30-days or longer

contribution margin: revenue minus the variable costs necessary to generate the corresponding revenue

controller: an exempt manager that oversees the accounting function and serves on the executive operating committee

cooperative (co-op) advertisting: marketing communications that promote two or more entities simultaneously, for their mutual benefit, allowing the entities to share the cost of the promotion

core competencies: essential abilities

core service: the primary service product offered to meet customers' needs common to all service providers within a specified industry

core-course design: multiple fairways run parallel to one another and the golf holes are clustered around a clubhouse

corporate citizen: the concept that a firm, like any citizen, is required to meet its economic, ethical, legal, and social responsibilities

corporate or organizational culture: organically developed beliefs and behaviors that determine how employees interact with internal and external stakeholders

corporate rate: a room rate offered to IBTs that do not qualify for a discount

corporate social responsibilities: the requirement that a business enterprise operates as a good citizen within the community

corporate travelers: IBTs that do not qualify for a specific discounted room rate

cost-per-occupied-room (CPOR): a ratio used to measure efficiency, calculated by dividing an expense by the corresponding number of room nights serviced

credit manager: an exempt manager responsible for approving billing privileges and overseeing the accounts receivable process

cut-off date: the date until which a group's room block will be retained

daily discrepancy report: a physical check of all guestrooms for which no room revenue was posted to prevent the loss of revenue

daily line-up: pre-shift meetings that provide updated information to associates while reinforcing corporate values, service standards, and expectations

daily report and financial dashboards: an estimate of the hotel's financial performance, in terms of revenue, expenses, and operating statistics, for a specific date and the accounting period-to-date

daily special: a specific priority item to be covered in each guestroom when it is serviced that specific day

debt service: the principle and interest payments that must be made to the lender

decentralized HVAC system: the use of a network of self-contained, individual air conditioning units to maintain a comfortable air temperature throughout a building

declining checkbook balance or declining balance spreadsheet: a method of managing and controlling expenses associated with the purchasing of operating supplies and equipment

deep-clean: the periodic, systematic, and thorough cleaning of a guestroom, tending to details that cannot be maintained through daily servicing alone

demand generator: an attraction, facility, or event that motivates travelers to journey to a specific destination to visit, conduct business, or attend

demand: a term utilized by STR equivalent to the number of room nights rented (sold) for a specific time period

departure experience: a process that ensures a guest's efficient departure from the hotel, allowing the hotel to express appreciation for the guest's patronage

deposited reservation: a reservation that is guaranteed through the payment of an advanced deposit equivalent to the first night's room and tax charges

depreciation: the decrease in an asset's value over time, which is a non-cash expense

destination marketing organizations (DMO)/convention and visitor bureau (CVB): a government or non-profit entity formed to promote in-bound travel to a community

destination resort hotel: a large property designed to be a self-contained escape from the outside world offering a full-range of services including overnight accommodations, food, beverage, conference, and recreational services

destination spa: a resort focused on wellness and lifestyle change, with extensive spa facilities and services

devil horns effect: an associate's negative overall job performance is reflected across all job performance criteria ratings

direct labor charge: a fee charged to directly offset the cost of providing an F&B associate to perform a service requested by the client

direct sales: one-to-one marketing of products, services, and experiences through the development of trusted relationships between buyers and a representative of the supplier

director of engineering: an exempt manager that oversees the maintenance of the hotel's physical assets, building systems, and equipment, serving as a member of the executive operating committee

director of F&B: an exempt manager that oversees the F&B operating division and serves on the executive operating committee

director of guest services or front office manager: an exempt manager that oversees the entire guest services or front office operation, including front desk, concierge, bell services, transportation, and communications

director of loss prevention or loss prevention supervisor: an exempt manager or non-exempt supervisor that directly oversees the security and loss prevention team

director of outlets: an exempt department head that oversees all F&B outlets, including in-room dining

director of services: an exempt manager that oversees the housekeeping and laundry operation

discounted cash flow method: estimates the value of a hotel asset based upon its acquisition price, projected cash-flows, and estimated terminal value

discrepancy report: a financial report that explains substantial variances between actual results and financial benchmarks

discrepant room: a room recorded as vacant by the front office (night audit) the previous night that is actually occupied or requires servicing

displacement analysis: analysis conducted to determine the MAR that a hotel should accept for a long-term room contract

displacement cost: room revenue lost when a reservation is accepted at a lower room rate than an alternative reservation for specific dates

disruptor: an innovation or new technology that fundamentally changes the status quo in an industry

distribution channel: a chain of intermediaries through which a product or service passes from the provider to the end user

distribution: the degree to which a hotel brand has widespread representation in appropriate markets

division of duties: the requirement that specific duties, including the ordering, receiving, and payment for F&B products, be performed by different hotel associates to prevent theft

doorperson: a non-exempt associate responsible for assisting guests arriving and departing the hotel

double-declining-balance depreciation: an aggressive method of calculating depreciation expense, using the book value of the asset, allowing a more rapid reduction in the value of the asset

double-tee: refers to sending groups off the 1st hole or front nine and the 10th hole or back nine of a golf course simultaneously

dram shop laws: allow employees that serve alcohol, hotel managers, and the ownership of the hotel with an on-premise liquor license to each be held personally liable for the injury or death of any person resulting from the service of alcoholic beverages to persons under the age of 21 years, patrons served to the point of intoxication, or guests that are served alcohol that appear intoxicated at the time of service

dynamic pricing strategy: a pricing approach in which room rates fluctuate based upon anticipated demand

dynamic pricing: takes advantage of the basic economic principle of supply and demand to charge higher prices during periods of higher demand, while leveraging the concept of elasticity of demand by lowering prices during periods of lower demand

economic objective: the requirement for a business to operate profitably

economies-of-scale: cost advantages received when a business enjoys a sufficient volume of business to operate efficiently

economy hotels: very basic hotels that provide overnight accommodations—a bedroom with a private bathroom—and are typically absent of public spaces, other than perhaps a small registration lobby

effectiveness: the degree to which a system or process consistently delivers the targeted outcome or result

efficiency: the degree to which a system or process consistently delivers the targeted outcome at the lowest reasonable cost

electric distribution system: receives power from its source, typically the local electric utility, and distributes it throughout the property

electrician: a non-exempt associate trained and licensed to repair electrical systems and equipment

emergency generator: a diesel engine that generates sufficient electricity to maintain basic lighting, the life safety system, and other essential operating systems in the event of a power outage

empirical rule: if a random sample is selected from a population in which the observations are normally distributed, then 68.2% of observations will be found within one standard deviation of the mean, whereas 95.4% of observations will be within two standard deviations of the mean, and virtually all observations (99.7%) will be within three standard deviation units of the mean

employee assistance program: provides employees access to a variety of services, including a range of counseling support and legal consultation

employee requisition: a form submitted by management to notify the human resources department of a staffing need

employee turnover: the rate at which associates terminate their employment

employer of choice: the goal of being perceived as a preferred employer by current and potential employees

employment manager: an exempt HR professional responsible for recruitment and hiring

energy management system (EMS): an IT system used to monitor and manage a hotel's energy consumption

engineer: a general term that refers to all non-exempt POM personnel

equipment PM technician: a non-exempt POM associate that routinely inspects hotel equipment and building systems, as assigned, completing necessary PM tasks and other repairs as required

estheticians: treatment providers trained and licensed to perform skin care, hair removal, and application of cosmetics

ethical reponsibility: the requirement to do what is morally right

exchange fees: fees assessed to vacation owners when they elect to visit an alternative property rather than their own vacation property

executive chef: an exempt manager responsible for all food production that may serve on the executive operating committee

executive housekeeper: an exempt manager that oversees the housekeeping operation

executive operating committee (EOC): the senior management team responsible for achieving the hotel's strategic objectives

executive sous chef: an exempt manager responsible for overseeing the food production or culinary department

executive steward: an exempt manager that oversees the inventories and cleanliness of all food production areas, equipment, china, glass, and service-ware

exempt or salaried associate: an administrative, management, or sales associate that is not eligible to receive overtime compensation

expense: a cost incurred to provide products, services, or experiences

express checkout: allows guests to depart the hotel without requiring them to complete the transaction at the front desk of the hotel

extrinsic job satisfiers (hygiene factors): essential rewards provided in exchange for an employee's labor, including compensation

F&B minimum: the minimum amount of F&B revenue that must be generated by the group, meeting, or event

facial: a treatment to cleanse and refresh the client's facial skin

facility management system (FMS): an IT system used to track and schedule POM activities related to the maintenance and repair of a real estate asset, including buildings, building systems, and equipment

fair market share: achieved when a hotel's share of occupied room nights is equal to its proportion of available rooms in the comp set, achieving a 100% occupancy index

fair rate share: achieved when a hotel's ADR is in-line with its competitors, achieving a 100% ADR index

fair revenue share: achieved when a hotel's RevPAR is in-line with its competitors, achieving a 100% RevPAR index

fair share: when the proportion of room nights or revenue sold by a hotel is equal to the hotel's proportion of available rooms within its competitive set

feedback loop: a system that seeks continuous input from stakeholders to assess, evaluate, and enhance the effectiveness of systems, processes, procedures, and tactics, thereby ensuring continuous improvement of business outcomes

fiduciary responsibility: a legal and ethical obligation to work in the best interest of the employer

financial benchmark: a reference point against which a hotel's actual performance may be compared

financial proforma: a projection of financial results and returns generated by a potential investment opportunity

financial statement: provides a snapshot of the financial standing of a business at a specific point in time

fire control panel: the central panel to which all fire detection and suppression devices are connected, which displays the location and cause of an alarm

fire doors: doors with a specified burn-through rating that close automatically when fire is detected to minimize the spread of a fire and the smoke produced

fire suppression system: devices including overhead sprinklers and dry chemical systems designed to extinguish a fire automatically upon being detected by the system

folio: an itemized accounting record of a guest's stay at a hotel

food runner: a non-exempt associate that assists in delivering prepared foods to guests in a high volume F&B outlet

food server: a non-exempt associate that sells and serves prepared foods to guests

foursome: a group of golfers playing a course, which is typically comprised of four golfers

franchise or licensing agreement: a contract that outlines the terms of the relationship between the hotel's owners and the parent organization or franchisor of the selected brand, granting the owner a license to operate the hotel utilizing a specific trademark

front nine: holes 1 through 9 on a golf course

full-service hotels: offer, at a minimum, overnight accommodations; F&B services for breakfast, lunch, and dinner; and conference space and meeting services

full-time equivalent (FTE): an associate that works an average of 40 hours per week or approximately 2,000 hours annually

functional organization structure: work groups or teams of associates are supervised based upon the type of work that they do

furniture, fixtures, and equipment (FF&E): capital assets that enhance the quality of the hotel's servicescape or operating effectiveness/efficiency

garde manger: a non-exempt culinary associate specializing in the preparation of cold foods

general cashier: a non-exempt accounting associate responsible for preparing daily bank deposits, and maintaining and monitoring all cashiers' banks

general mechanic: a non-exempt associate qualified to repair and maintain a hotel's mechanical devices, including laundry equipment

global distribution system (GDS): a computer network used to facilitate the electronic distribution of travel services

gratuities: payments made directly to hotel associates by guests in appreciation for services provided

gray water: treated or reusable water used for specific applications

green efforts: actions taken to operate in an environmentally responsible manner

grill cook: a non-exempt culinary associate that specializes in grilling meats and vegetables

group ceiling: the targeted number of group room nights that are to be sold each day, with the remaining inventory set aside for sale to transient guest segments

guarantee: the number of guests a client anticipates will participate in a scheduled banquet, meeting, or event

guaranteed reservation: a hotel reservation for which the hotel is guaranteed the first night's payment if a guest fails to arrive as scheduled

guest experience mapping: the macro-level analysis of the series of processes that collectively comprise the entire guest experience, from initial awareness through post-departure communication

guest ledger: the sum of the guest and group account balances due the hotel from hotel guests and groups currently in-house

guest loyalty loop: post-departure communication and other activities designed to maintain guest engagement, encouraging repeat patronage and loyalty

guest mix: the proportion of total guests that are paying each of the various room rates offered by the hotel, synonymous with market mix

guest relocations (walks): circumstances created by a hotel's inability to honor a guest's reservation, resulting in the transfer of the guest to a nearby, comparable hotel

guest service agent (GSA): a non-exempt associate responsible for registering arriving guests, checking-out departing guests, and providing guests with personalized, memorable experiences

guest service index (GSI): a measure of guests' perceptions of service quality, calculated within many hotel organizations as the percentage of positive responses from guests that complete service quality surveys

guestroom amenities: soaps, shampoo, lotion, and other in-room convenience items

guestroom PM technician: a non-exempt POM associate that routinely inspects guestrooms, completing necessary PM tasks and other repairs as required

halo effect: an associate's positive overall job performance is reflected across all job performance criteria ratings

hard goods: retail items which include golf balls, clubs, and equipment

heating, ventilation, and air conditioning (HVAC) systems: designed to maintain comfortable temperatures in all areas of the hotel

high-handicap golfers: poorly skilled golfers that require many strokes above par to complete their rounds

historical demand: actual room nights sold (rented), by guest segment and in total, for previous dates

host: a non-exempt associate that greets, seats, and performs other guest service functions in an F&B outlet

hotel chain: multiple lodging properties that operate under a common brand name, prominently displayed and promoted by all properties sharing the brand, in compliance with clearly defined brand operating standards

hotel management firm: responsible for the day-to-day operation of the hotel to the established brand standards, if applicable, while maximizing profitability, to achieve the financial objectives targeted by the hotel's ownership

hotel ownership: the investors that hold title to the real property associated with a hotel

hotel parent company: a firm that provides a wide variety of support services to hotels including hotel brands

hotel valuation: determined by the price that a qualified buyer is willing and able to pay to purchase the hotel

hours-per-occupied-room (HPOR): a labor productivity ratio using labor hours as the measure of work time and room nights as the measure of output

house pour wine: the standard wine served when a specific varietal is ordered by a guest

housekeeping supervisors: non-exempt supervisors that directly oversee the work of housekeeping personnel, holding them accountable for maintaining quality standards while achieving labor productivity goals

houseman: a non-exempt associate that assists the room attendants by running linen and supplies, while maintaining guestroom corridors and other assigned areas

HVAC or refrigeration mechanic: a non-exempt associate with the skills and certification to repair and maintain refrigeration and HVAC systems

impact: the effect of another hotel of the same brand, or a brand supported by the same hotel parent company, operating within close proximity

in-process linen: linen currently being processed by the laundry associates

in-service linen: linen currently in the guestrooms for guest use

incentive fees: additional fees earned by the management firm if the hotel delivers targeted cash flows to the hotel's investors

incident report: a written or electronic record of an extraordinary event, particularly one that involves loss or injury

income auditor: a non-exempt accounting associate responsible for accurately recording all hotel revenue

incremental revenue: the room revenue gained when accepting one reservation over an alternative reservation

individual business travelers (IBT): transient guests traveling for work-related purposes

individual investors: individuals or families that typically invest in smaller, limited-service and economy hotels

individual or transient guests: a party of guests requiring fewer than 10 total room nights during a single stay

inquiry: a reservation request where a specific date or dates have been shopped by a potential guest

inspector or inspectress: a non-exempt housekeeping supervisor responsible for maintaining the cleanliness and quality of their assigned guestrooms

institutional investors: investment banks, pension funds, large corporations, and other commercial investors that are typically seeking long-term capital appreciation

interval or vacation ownership (timeshare): a partial- or shared-ownership interest in a resort real estate property, which allows exclusive access for a specified time period

intrinsic job satisfiers (motivators): workplace rewards that add value to an employee's experience, including meaningful work and career growth

job analysis: the process of identifying the knowledge, skills, abilities, and behavioral characteristics an associate needs to be successful in a position

job description: outlines the specific responsibilities of a position

job fit: an assessment as to how well a candidate's personality and innate behavioral tendencies align with the job requirements

job specifications: a listing of the required education, knowledge, skills, abilities, and behavioral characteristics an associate needs to be successful in a position

joint venture partnerships: formed through negotiated relationships between partners that have a vested interest in the development of a hotel property

journal entry: the recording of the financial impacts of a business transaction on the appropriate accounting ledgers

key performance indicators (KPIs): used to assess the performance of the revenue optimization team; include occupancy (%), average daily rate (ADR), and RevPAR

kitchen mechanic: a non-exempt associate qualified to repair and maintain the wide-variety of kitchen equipment found within a hotel

labor offsets: charges added to guest invoices, including gratuities, service charges, set-up fees, and meeting room rental, used to allocate the cost of labor directly to the customer

labor productivity: a measure of the amount of output generated or work completed per unit of an employee's compensated work time

last room availability: provides a client with access to a negotiated or volume discount on dates when discounted room rates are not being offered

laundry attendant: a non-exempt associate that effectively and efficiently processes hotel linens

laundry manager: an exempt manager that oversees the laundry operation

laundry supervisor: a non-exempt housekeeping supervisor responsible for ensuring the quality of linen production and productivity of laundry associates

law of large numbers: the accuracy of an estimate of a value within a population, based upon a sample, improves as the sample size increases

lazy river: allows guests to leisurely float on a tube around the perimeter of the pool area

lead cook: a non-exempt associate that supervises food production personnel

LEED certification: a building that meets 'Leadership in Energy and Environmental Design' standards

legal responsibility: the requirement to comply with laws and regulations

leisure guests: transient travelers traveling for personal reasons

liabilities: payables and other financial commitments of a business, including owners' equity

life safety equipment: equipment used in a medical or emergency situation to include fire extinguishers, fire axes, fire hoses, defibrillators, and first aid kits

life safety system: a network of visual and audible alarms, as well as fire suppression devices, connected at a central control panel designed to protect human life and physical assets

lifestyle hotels: hotels that offer a carefully selected array of services, coupled with unique design elements, aesthetics, service environment, and customer experience intended to appeal to a specific customer niche based upon demographic and psychographic variables

light duty: allows an employee to work in an alternative position if they have been injured on the job and are unable to perform their normal duties

lighting systems : systems that provide ambient light to supplement natural light, basic visual light, and a range of lighting options in the meeting and event space

limited liability partnerships: an ownership entity in which the investors' risk is typically limited to the amount of their investment in the hotel

line cook: a non-exempt associate that prepares food products and meals for guests

line-of-interaction: indicates points at which guests interact with staff to provide input into the service process

line-of-support: identifies the processes that may be fulfilled by support personnel within the organization, by other departments, or by vendors or sub-contractors

line-of-visibility: separates the processes that are executed in view of the customer

line-up: pre-shift meetings that provide updated information to associates while reinforcing corporate values, service standards, and expectations

linear system: thoughtfully designed process or procedure that must be executed in the specified sequence to consistently produce the targeted outcome

linen par: the quantity of each linen item that is required to properly supply each guestroom in the hotel one time

linen room attendant: a non-exempt associate that performs administrative duties for the housekeeping department, including controlling access to housekeeping supply inventories

load-factor: the utilization rate or proportion of airline seats sold on a specific commercial airline flight

lobbying: advocating for an industry or members of an association with government representatives

lock-out–tag-out: requires that an engineer shut-off the power to any equipment while work is being completed on the respective equipment; this includes repairs and routine maintenance tasks

long-term debt: debt that is to be repaid over a time period of longer than one year

loss prevention department: the security team within a hotel

loss prevention officer (LPO): a non-exempt associate responsible for protecting hotel guests, associates, and assets from loss or harm

loss: when expenses exceed revenue

low-handicap golfers: highly skilled golfers that typically require fewer strokes above par to complete their rounds

luxury hotels: offer the highest level of personalized service and a full-range of services designed to satisfy the most demanding guests

maintenance contract: outlines the terms and defines the inclusions, exclusions, and costs for a vendor to provide maintenance services for a specific asset for the specified time period

maintenance request: a work order requesting the POM department to make a repair or to complete a specific task

make-the-turn: refers to a golfer or foursome moving from the 9th hole to the 10th hole on the course

management contract or hotel management agreement (HMA): outlines the details of the relationship between the hotel owners and the hotel management firm, including but not limited to, the term of the agreement, fee structure, operating performance requirements, budgeting procedures, expenditure limits, decision authority, indemnification, corporate expense allocation, and termination procedures

management fees: fee paid to a hotel management firm by a hotel owner for managing the day-to-day operation of a hotel

manager-on-duty or MOD: a manager assigned responsibility for overseeing the entire hotel operation in the absence of the hotel's GM

market equilibrium: when demand for a product or service is equal to supply

market mix: the proportion of total guests that are paying each of the various room rates offered by the hotel, synonymous with guest mix

market or guest segment: a specific group of travelers that may be defined based upon demographic or psychographic variables or by purpose of travel

mason: a non-exempt associate skilled in installing and repairing tile, pavers, and bricks/blocks

massage therapists: treatment providers trained and licensed to provide clients with massage treatments

material safety data sheets (MSDS): provide information regarding the proper use and remedies to address improper exposure to chemicals

meat or valuables locker: a secured area within a food or beverage storage area for high-cost food and beverage products

meeting room rental: a fee charged to a client in exchange for the use of a meeting room or event space

meeting space intensive: groups that require a larger amount of meeting space per group room night relative to alternative groups

membership association: a hotel brand or chain owned by its franchisees

membership fee: payments made at regular intervals that provide access to specific facilities, services, or other specified privileges

menu abstract: provides a detailed listing of the quantities sold of each menu item by date or for a specified time period

menu mix: the quantities of each menu item sold and the proportion of total food revenue generated by each item

merchant model: travel agents or sites that price and market hotel accommodations, collect payment for the accommodations directly from guests, while paying hotels deeply discounted negotiated room rates

metasearch sites: travel sites that allow the side-by-side comparison of prices offered for identical travel services through multiple electronic distribution channels simultaneously

mezzanine financing: short-term financing that is provided to fill the gap between the amount of capital that the investors' have available to invest in a real estate project and the amount of the long-term financing that investors have been able to secure

midscale hotels: select-service properties that provide overnight accommodations and typically some form of a morning breakfast buffet, although the availability of hot breakfast items may be limited

minimum acceptable rate (MAR): a room rate specified for each night below which a hotel will not accept a reservation

minimum-length-of-stay (MLOS): any reservation request for the restricted night must stay the specified number of nights or longer to be accepted by the hotel

mission statement: defines the goals of the organization more specifically, typically in terms of the core products, services, and/or outcomes the organization plans to deliver to each key stakeholder

mixed-use development: a commercial real estate asset consisting of a blend of real estate types, such as office, retail, residential, or hotel

moment of truth: a point of contact between a business and a customer that contributes to the guest's perception of the firm, particularly an interaction between a guest and a front-line employee

mountain resort: a resort that provides guests with access to skiing, snowboarding, snowtubing, and other mountain-based activities

mud months: the spring season at a mountain resort, during which occupancy is typically the lowest

natural gas: a flammable gas that naturally occurs underground, containing a high level of methane, that may be used as fuel

net present value (NPV): the current worth of a series of projected future cash-flows, adjusted to allow for the time value of money

net revenue: the incremental revenue gained less the displacement cost

night auditor: a non-exempt associate that provides front office coverage during the overnight shift while completing a wide-range of accounting-related responsibilities

no-show: a guest that is scheduled to arrive on a specific date and fails to arrive as scheduled

non-exempt or hourly associate: a front-line associate or supervisor that is eligible to receive overtime compensation

non-linear system: a set of guidelines or a procedure that must be continuously supported by all associates to achieve the targeted outcome

occupancy, occupancy rate, or occupancy percentage: the proportion of available hotel rooms sold (rented) during a specified time period

on-tap: refers to beer that is served from a keg using a beer glass or mug

online travel agents (OTAs): intermediaries that market and sell travel products and services Online and through mobile applications

opening inventory: the total value of all items in the hotel's inventory on the first day of a month, year, or accounting period

operable walls or airwalls: mechanical walls that may be used to subdivide a large meeting space into smaller rooms

options: provides a group client that requests dates for which a contract has already been issued the ability to book their guestrooms, meeting, or event over the same dates should the client in the primary position opt to not execute or fulfill the contract that has been issued

out-of-service: equipment or guestrooms that cannot be utilized until essential repairs are completed

outlet or restaurant manager: an exempt manager that oversees the operation of a specific F&B outlet or shift

ownership equity: estimates the current value of the investors' financial interest in the hotel

pace-of-play: the speed at which golfers are able to complete a round of golf

package unit: a self-contained single HVAC unit that can heat and cool the air temperature in a room

packages: service bundles that improve the value proposition by providing discounted access to desired services or activities

painter and wall vinyl technician: a non-exempt associate skilled in painting and wall-vinyl repair and installation

paired-structure: two closely aligned firms, one established to invest in real assets and a second to manage those assets

par-level: the inventory required of each operating supply

Pareto chart: a graph that identifies the number of observations on the primary y-axis and the cumulative proportion of total observations on the secondary y-axis, listing the items observed from most-to-least frequent on the x-axis

partition-pricing: the practice of splitting prices into components

pastry chef: an exempt manager that oversees the production of baked goods, desserts, and confections

payback period: the period of time required for an investor to receive total returns equal to the amount of the initial investment

PBX operator or at-your-service (AYS) agent: a non-exempt associate responsible for providing communications services for hotel guests and staff

peer-to-peer rentals or sharing-economy: the marketing and contracting of short-term, overnight real estate rentals through online services

penetration index (or occupany index): a measure of a hotel's market penetration, which compares the hotel's occupancy with the occupancy of hotels within its competitive set

per diem: the daily reimbursement rate for travel expenses, including hotel accommodations, for government travelers

performance evaluation system: a process during which an employee receives documented, thorough feedback on his/her job performance

peripheral services: ancillary services that are provided to customers to add value to the customer experience

plenary session: a single meeting at a conference expected to be attended by all conference participants

plumber: a non-exempt associate qualified to repair and maintain water and sewage systems

plus-plus (++): refers to the automatic addition of taxes and a service charge to food and beverage revenues

pool gratuities: the distribution of all service charges for the pay period among all banquet service associates based upon the proportion of total hours worked by each banquet associate

pools, splash parks, and waterslides (water features): water-focused amenities are the most common recreational amenities found in a resort property

potable water: water for human consuption

potential or theoretical beverage cost: the cost of ingredients for all alcoholic beverages served assuming all drinks are accurately prepared and precisely measured

potential or theoretical food cost: the expected total cost of the food ingredients necessary to prepare all food items sold during a specified time period

pre-block: the assignment of a specific guestroom prior to the guest's arrival

pre-convention meeting: a meeting held with a client, conference services manager, and key hotel managers to review the client's expectations and prepare for the group's conference

pre-employment assessment: a psychometrically sound survey tool used to identify whether a job candidate has specific behavioral characteristics, knowledge, or skills

pre-function space: consists of lobbies and corridors outside of the meeting space that may be used to hold guests waiting to enter a scheduled meeting or event, for registration tables, and for coffee breaks, receptions, and other group events that do not require an enclosed, private conference room

pre-paid reservation: the hotel receives payment for the estimated room and tax charges for a guest's entire stay at the time of booking

pre-stage: the advanced preparation of a guestroom prior to the guest's arrival, or a sales tour, to ensure the guestroom is welcoming

premium liquor: a beverage served utilizing the hotel's most expensive liquor available for which a higher price is charged

premium pour wine: higher priced wines sold to guests using the vintner's label

pressurized escape stairwells: emergency escape paths that lead guests out of the building while protecting them from smoke inhalation

preventative maintenance (PM): routine tasks that must be completed at scheduled intervals to maintain the hotel, building systems, and equipment

price gouging: taking advantage of strong demand to charge excessive room rates that fail to offer equitable value

price or rate integrity: the practice of maintaining relatively consistent room rates, avoiding wide dispersion in pricing, to manage guests' perceptions of value

price-per-square-foot: using an average price-per-square-foot paid for similar hotels, in terms of chain-scale or class, to estimate a hotel's value

primary cleaning chemicals: chemicals used in a variety of cleaning applications, including glass and all-purpose cleaners, and disinfectants

primary position: a lender or investor with the first lien or financial claim on an asset

prime cost: the cost of labor, coupled with the cost of food

prime selling time: generally the hours between 9:00 a.m. and 4:00 p.m., in the clients' respective time zone, Monday through Friday

private lifestyle community: a resort community that restricts access to the community and its amenities to property owners and their guests

profit-and-loss statement or P&L: outlines the financial performance of a hotel for a defined time period

profit: the amount by which revenue exceeds expenses

progressive discipline process: a coaching and counseling process intended to encourage an associate to improve his/her job performance

property management company: a company employed by a property owner to rent, manage, and maintain a real estate asset

property operations and maintenance (POM) or engineering department: maintains the hotel's physical assets, building systems, and equipment

psychological contract: an unwritten contract or set of expectations established during the interview process as a result of representations made by managers during the screening, interviewing, and hiring process

psychological empowerment: the degree to which an employee is intrinsically motivated to make a difference in the work environment

psychological or just-below pricing strategy: the use of prices that end with a "9" in the singles-digit position

public area attendant: a non-exempt associate that maintains the cleanliness of public areas, including lobbies and restrooms

public area PM technician: a non-exempt POM associate that routinely inspects the hotel's public areas, completing necessary PM tasks and other repairs as required

public area supervisor: a non-exempt housekeeping supervisor responsible for maintaining the cleanliness of the hotel's public areas

published rate: room rate being marketed by the hotel through a specific distribution channel

pull-stations: a device that may be used to manually activate the life-safety alarm system

purchase order (PO): a printed or electronic document that authorizes the acquisition of goods, products, or services

purchasing manager: an exempt manager responsible for the acquisition of operating supplies and equipment

pure measure of productivity: a labor productivity measure expressed as a ratio of labor hours relative to occupied guestrooms

qualified discount: a discount offered to guests that can provide evidence of their eligibility to receive the discount

quiet or adults-only pool: a pool with restricted access, which allows guests a more relaxing, peaceful environment

rack rate: the highest non-discounted room rate offered by a hotel

rate fence: a pricing strategy that prohibits guestrooms from being sold (rented) to guest segments priced below a specific room rate (fence) based upon anticipated demand each day

rate parity: when the price for a hotel room for a specific date does not vary depending upon the distribution channel or the booking site where the reservation is made

real estate investment trust (REIT): a legal entity that sells shares to investors, investing the capital raised into income-producing real estate assets, which generate dividends for shareholders

realistic job preview: a process during which a job candidate shadows an associate or works in a position prior to being hired

recipe card: a detailed record of a menu item that includes a photograph of the prepared food item; a list of all ingredients; the cost of each ingredient; a 5% allowance of the total cost of individual ingredients to cover kitchen costs; and a step-by-step description of the item's preparation method

red flag questions: interview questions, unique to each candidate, that address questions or concerns resulting from a review of the candidate's application materials

red-tag: a tag placed on an item by management authorizing an associate to remove the item from the premises

rental pool: privately owned condominiums, villas, or homes that are made available as vacation rentals by outside residents

replacement or construction cost: the projected cost to replace or construct a similar hotel

representation firm: a sales organization that provides direct sales support to suppliers in exchange for a fee

required pooling: a condominium hotel in which owners are required to give control of their individual units to the management company hired to manage the property

resort community: a collection of private residences and businesses, with a focus on recreational activities, that form a cooperative to support common interests

resort services fee: a flat daily charge added to each guest's room account to cover the cost of providing resort services

return on equity (ROE): net income from an investment divided by owners' equity

return on investment (ROI): payments or savings received as a result of an investment, often expressed as a percentage of the amount invested

revenue manager: an exempt manager responsible for optimizing hotel revenue that directly supervises the reservations sales agents

revenue: payments received in exchange for products, services, or experiences

RevPAR: the amount of room revenue generated per available hotel room for a specified time period

RevPASH: the amount of F&B revenue generated per available seat per hour for a specified time period

room attendant: a non-exempt associate responsible for effectively and efficiently servicing assigned guestrooms each day

room night: a hotel accommodation occupied by a guest or guests for a single night

rooming procedure: the linear-process of assisting a guest to their room, while introducing hotel services and technology, and attending to any initial needs

run-of-the-house: any available overnight accommodation versus a specific room type

safety committee: a group of representatives from each department charged with reviewing injury-causing events, as well as developing strategies and implementing activities to reduce injuries

sales prospecting: the process of identifying potential clients, assessing their needs, and evaluating the fit between these needs and the services, products, and experiences offered by the firm

sales team demployment: the specific guest segments that will be assigned to each sales manager and for which he/she will be held accountable

satisfaction mirror: employee satisfaction drives customer satisfaction and vice versa

saucier: a non-exempt culinary associate that prepares hot food items, particularly dishes including sauces

second effort program: a system to ensure guest satisfaction that requires guest services personnel to verify guest satisfaction following the resolution of a guest request by hotel personnel

secondary position: a lender or investor whose interest is subjugated to another lender or investor

security report: summarizes activities and observations made during the LPO's shift

select-service hotels: offer overnight accommodations and no, or only a limited degree of peripheral services

sell strategy: a combination of BARs, MARs, and stay restrictions put in place by the revenue optimization team to optimize room revenue each night

selling guestrooms: in a housekeeping context, refers to compensating room attendants for servicing additional guestrooms, above the standard allotment, during their scheduled shift

servant leadership: a management philosophy in which a leader recognizes that his/her most important role is to support his/her followers by fulfilling their needs

service blueprint: a detailed, step-by-step illustration of a process or service experience that clearly identifies each step in a process and the sequence in which the steps are to be performed

service bundle: two or more service products that are offered for purchase in combination with one another for a single price

service capacity: the maximum number of customers that may be appropriately served in a specified time period

service charge: a fee charged to offset the cost of labor, typically set at between 18% and 24% of F&B revenue

service standards: succinct, clearly stated rules of behavior to be followed by all associates of the firm

set-up fee: a fee charged to a client to offset the cost of setting up and breaking down a meeting room

set-up manager (convention service manager): an exempt manager that oversees the set-up, clearing, and cleaning of all meeting, conference, and event space to clients' specifications

shift engineers: non-exempt associates that provide basic coverage of the POM department, responding to guest and associate calls for maintenance support

short-order cook: a non-exempt culinary associate that prepares fresh meals, particularly in the hotel's 3-meal restaurant

shot-gun start: foursomes are assigned to each of the 18 holes on the course and play begins at the same time for up to 72 golfers on the course

single-fairway design: a golf course at which fairways are lined with homes, villas, or condominiums versus adjacent fairways

SMERF groups: guests with a social, military, educational, religious or fraternal affiliation generating 10 or more room nights

social responsibility: the requirement to serve as a good corporate citizen

soft brands: each hotel affiliated with a soft brand may maintain its individual name and reputation, while also promoting itself to guests loyal to the parent company's brands—providing these hotels with the ability to maximize revenue and investor return

soft goods: retail items that include clothing, such as logoed golf shirts, caps, and other attire

sous chef: an exempt manager responsible for overseeing food production for a specific outlet or during an assigned shift

spa manager or director: an exempt manager responsible for overseeing the operation of the spa, ensuring its financial success

spa menu: a listing of spa services available with pricing, organized by type of service

spa services: personalized services intended to contribute to a guest's well-being, including massage, facial, body, and beauty treatments

specialty cleaning chemicals: chemicals required for specific cleaning applications

specialty or signature cocktail: a mixed drink that requires more than a standard 1.5-ounce pour of liquor, specialty mixes and garnishes, or is served in specialized or commemorative glassware

sprinkler systems: a network of sprinklers located throughout the public areas and guestrooms designed to extinguish a fire upon detection

staffing guide: a tool that uses measures of labor productivity to manage payroll costs

stakeholder: any individual or group that is impacted by the actions of the organization

stan cap: a protective cover placed on glassware after it has been cleaned and sanitized

standard operating procedures (SOPs): detailed processes designed to ensure that guests consistently receive quality experiences that meet or exceed their expectations, to make certain that appropriate control procedures are in place, and to ensure effective, efficient internal processes to support the operation

stay restriction: reservation controls established to ensure that the sale of available guestroom inventory optimizes revenue

stayover: a registered guest that is not scheduled to depart

steward: a non-exempt associate that maintains the cleanliness of food production areas, equipment, china, glass, and service-ware

STR: the largest supplier of market data to the hotel industry

straight-line depreciation: a conservative approach to calculating depreciation expense in which the value of an asset is reduced by the same amount each accounting period over its useful life

sufficiency requirements: guidelines established by STR that hotels must follow when identifying its competitive set to protect the confidentiality of each property's individual data

sum-of-the-year's-digits depreciation: a method of calculating depreciation expense that reduces the value of an asset more rapidly during the early years of its useful life

summary P&L: provides an overview of the hotel's financial performance, including each of the operating divisions

supply: the number of available hotel rooms for a specified time period; STR's equivalent to hotel service capacity

sustainability committee: a group of associates, including representatives from each department, chaired by the director of engineering, charged with raising awareness and ensuring compliance with a hotel's efforts to operate in an environmentally responsible manner

sustainability: eliminating or minimizing negative environmental impacts, while maintaining a long-term perspective

sustainable competitive advantage: a system, process, or asset that allows a firm to operate more effectively or efficiently than its competitive firms, which may not be quickly replicated by competitors

system administrator: the in-house associate assigned to serve as the interface between the users of a software application and the software provider

systems-thinking: processes and procedures designed to ensure consistent outcomes

targeted cap rate valuation: estimates the value of a hotel by dividing the hotel's annual EBITDA or cash-flow by the targeted capitalization rate desired by the investor

tax shelter: an investment that lowers or minimizes the investor's tax liability

taxonomies: sets of categories used to classify items that are mutually exclusive and collectively exhaustive

technicians: treatment providers trained and licensed to provide hair and beauty-related services

terminal value: the projected future value of an asset assuming the asset is liquidated at the end of the forecast period

theater configuration: the most efficient group seating arrangement with a seat for each meeting attendee arranged in rows

thread-count: a measure of a linen's quality indicating the number of threads per square inch

three-tier inspection program: the systematic inspection of a hotel's accommodations by front-line supervisors, housekeeping management, and senior management to impeccably maintain the cleanliness and quality of the hotel's core service product

time-value-of-money: money received today has greater value than money to be received in the future

total-cost-of-employment: includes the cost of employer paid payroll taxes and employee benefits (PT&EB) in addition to wages

trade-outs, barter, or sponsorship agreements: marketing services or promotion provided in exchange for products or services

traditional hotel: a lodging property of any class or service-level that offers overnight accommodations owned by single ownership group or investor

trail fee: a payment made annually or seasonally to allow a golfer to utilize his/her personal golf cart on a golf course

travel consortium: a group of travel agencies that form a voluntary alliance to leverage their collective purchasing power to obtain more deeply discounted pricing for their clients on travel services

treatment providers: massage therapists; estheticians that perform skin care; and technicians that provide beauty-related services

triple-sheet: the use of three sheets on a bed, including a base sheet and two top sheets placed on each side of the blanket

trophy-asset: used as a place where a high-profile, successful business leader, group of investors, or corporation within the community can meet, accommodate, and entertain clients, employees, and other associates

turn-away (denial): a reservation inquiry for one or more specific dates that is not booked because the guest's request did comply with the stay restrictions in place for the date(s) requested

turn-down: when a guest is offered the opportunity to book accommodations, at a specific rate, but chooses not to make the reservation

turn-the-house: providing housekeeping service to each and every guestroom within the hotel occupied the previous night

turndown attendant: a non-exempt associate that provides evening turndown and other housekeeping services to guests

turndown service: evening housekeeping service during which the room is refreshed and bedding is turned down for the guest

turning meeting, function or banquet space: the clearing, cleaning, and re-setting of a hotel function room

undistributed operating expenses: the costs incurred at a hotel property that support the entire hotel operation and are not directly associated with a single operating division

upper-midscale hotels: typically select-service hotels, although some upper-midscale properties may offer a range of peripheral services and all will include some form of food service, at least for the breakfast meal period

upper-upscale hotels: full-service hotels, offering a full range of personalized services to include food and beverage (F&B) services, featuring at least one three-meal restaurant; meeting and event space; and a full range of guest, meeting, and business services; as well as access to quality exercise facilities or a full-service fitness club

usage factor: the number of a specific guestroom amenity consumed per room night

user-generated content: any form of communication media, including photographs, videos, audio files, descriptions, or reviews, created by the consumers of a product or service

utilization rate: the proportion of service capacity that is consumed during a specified time period

vacation rental: a privately-owned condominium, villa, or home that may be rented by visitors for short-term visits of less than 30-days

value equation: a formula conceptualizing how customers calculate the perceived worth of a product, service, or experience

value statements: moral code or core principles that govern the behavior of all associates of the firm

value: the customer's perception of the benefits received, coupled with the quality of the acquisition process, in relationship to the total cost of purchase

virgin (non-alcoholic) cocktails: specialty beverages designed to mimic alcoholic cocktails that do not include alcohol

virtuous feedback loops: a system that seeks continuous input from stakeholders to assess, evaluate, and enhance the effectiveness of systems, processes, procedures, and tactics, thereby ensuring the continuous improvement of business outcomes

vision statement: an aspirational expression of the impact the firm strives to have on society

volume accounts: organizations that negotiate a discounted room rate in exchange for generating a specified number of room nights annually

wait procedure: a linear-process implemented when a guest's accommodations are not immediately available upon check-in

well liquor: a beverage served using the hotel's least expensive brand of liquor

wholesaler: a travel intermediary that purchases hotel accommodations and other travel services at deep discounts, bundling them into vacation packages sold at a single price

work order system: the IT or manual system used to record and track all maintenance requests

yield index (or RevPAR index): a measure of a hotel's revenue performance, which compares the hotel's RevPAR with the RevPAR of hotels within its competitve set

yield management: the practice of optimizing revenue by carefully selecting the guests to whom available service capacity is sold based upon specific factors

yield: the amount of revenue generated per revenue producing opportunity

Index

high-risk investment, 435–437
mixed-use development, minimizing risk through, 437–438
motivation, understanding of, 434–435
return on investment, 438–439, 443–447

J

Job analysis, 390
Job description, 390
Job fit, 391
Job specifications, 390
Joint venture partnerships, 433
Journal entry, 414
Just-below pricing, 123

K

Key performance indicators (KPIs), 116
Kitchen mechanic, 359
KPIs. *See* Key performance indicators (KPIs)

L

Labor offsets, 292
Labor productivity, 202
    factor, 202
Last room availability, 124
Laundry attendant, 223
Laundry manager, 222
Laundry operations, 254–264. *See also* Housekeeping operations
    allocating laundry expenses, 263–264
    laundry chemicals, 258
    laundry equipment, 259–262
    prioritizing laundry workload, 262–263
    reclaiming linen, 258
    types of linen, 254–258

Laundry supervisor, 223
Law of large numbers, 155
Lazy river, 330
Lead cook, 286
LEED certification, 376
Legal compliance, 389
Legal responsibility, 31
Leisure guests, 60
Liabilities, 410
Licensing agreement, 10, 455–458
Life safety equipment, 367
Life-safety systems, 356, 422
Lifestyle hotels, 22
Lift, 342
Light duty, 388
Lighting systems, 357
Limited liability partnerships, 432
Linear systems, 35
    food and beverage operations and, 309
Line cook, 286
Linen room attendant, 222
Line-of-interaction, 36
Line-of-support, 36
Line-of-visibility, 36
Line-up, 244
Line-ups, 38
Load-factor, 343
Lobbying, 64
Lock-out–tag-out, 364
Lodging, types of, 321–329
    interval or vacation owner-ship, 327–329
    resort communities, 322–323
    traditional hotels *versus* destination resort hotels, 321–322
    vacation rentals and the shar-ing economy, 323–325
Lodging segments, hotel industry, 12–23
    full-service *versus* select-service, 13
    future of independent *versus* branded hotels, 22–23

pricing and service strategies, 20–21
    six categories of hotels, 13–20
    specialty segments, 21–22
Long-term debt, 439
Loss, 114
Loss prevention, 417–425
    emergency procedures, 421–422
    manager-on-duty program, 420–421
    officers role in, 417–420
    safety committee, 425
Loss prevention department, 417
Loss prevention officer (LPO), 417
Loss prevention supervisor, 417
Low-handicap golfers, 334
Loyalty program, 91
LPO. *See* Loss prevention officer (LPO)
Luxury hotels, 14

M

Maintenance contracts, 366
Maintenance requests, 362
Make-the-turn, golf, 333
Management contract or hotel man-agement agreement, 9, 455
Management fees, 455
Manager-on-duty (MOD), 420
MAR. *See* Minimum acceptable rate (MAR)
Market
    equilibrium, 40
    mix, 126
    segment, 6
Marketing partnerships, 98–101
Marketing plan, 101–104
    analyses of changes in reve-nue and the guest segment mix, 103
    food, beverage, and ancillary revenue forecast, 103
    group booking goals, 102